JOHN DANIEL

Scarlet and the Beast

II

TWO FACES OF FREEMASONRY

OMNIA VERITAS.

JOHN DANIEL

Two faces of Freemasonry
A Picture Book Supplement to Volume One of
Scarlet and the Beast

© Omnia Veritas Limited – 2018

�womNIA VERITAS.

www.omnia-veritas.com

MASONIC AUTHOR ARTHUR EDWARD WAITE, P.M., P.Z. (1857-1942) ROYAL ARCH MASON 9

SECTION 1 MASONIC CLUBS & SYMBOLOGY 10

MASONIC OATHS FOR FIRST THREE DEGREES *QUOTED FROM RONAYNE'S HANDBOOK OF FREEMASONRY* 26
CLUBS AND FREEMASONRY 28
1876 FOUNDERS OF THE ANCIENT, ARABIC ORDER OF THE NOBLES OF THE MYSTIC SHRINE 37

SECTION 2 MASONIC PERSONALITIES!!! ARRANGED IN NO PARTICULAR ORDER..86

QUOTES FROM ALBERT PIKE..86

SECTION 3 AMERICAN MASONIC REVOLUTION 164

SECTION 4 ANTI-MASONIC PERIOD 1826 THRU CIVIL WAR 242

SECTION 5 RECONSTRUCTION PERIOD TO WORLD WAR I 338

SECTION 6 FEDERAL RESERVE ACT WAS PASSED BY FREEMASONRY WHILE THE SAME FREEMASONRY WAS PLANNING WORLD WAR ONE !!!..364

SECTION 7 RUSSIAN COMMUNIST REVOLUTION OF 1917 373

SECTION 8 BETWEEN TWO WORLD WARS 394

SECTION 9 FREEMASONRY "TRIGGERS" WORLD WAR TWO TO HALT THE ANTI-MASONIC MOVEMENT IN EUROPE & JAPAN !!!..421

BIRTH AND DEATH OF THE LEAGUE OF NATIONS.............................. 424
THE YALTA CONFERENCE - FEBRUARY 1945...................................... 478
HISTORY'S HARSH LIGHT 481

SECTION 10 POST WORLD WAR II FREEMASONRY, MASONIC SPACE TRAVELERS & MISCELLANEOUS....................................485

MAU MAU REBELLION 488
SCARLET AND THE BEAST VOLUME 3 — CHAP. 8 VIETNAM AND THE DRUG WARS 497
B'NAI B'RITH IS THE MASONIC LODGE FOR JEWS 515

SECTION 11 THE CRUSADES 1099 1314 THE MUSLIM EXCUSE FOR THE "SECRET SOCIETY" BEHIND OSAMA BIN LADEN AND HIS AL-QAEDA 543

FIRST CRUSADE 543
THIRD CRUSADE 546
EUROPEAN FREEMASONRY FOUNDS TERRORIST YOUTH CORPS...................... 550

FREEMASONRY'S YOUNG SOCIETIES VIS-À-VIS MUSLIM BROTHERHOOD'S AL-QAEDA..562

HITLER, MUSLIMS, AND WORLD WAR II'S ANTI-SEMITISM.............................566

OTHER PUBLICATIONS **581**

SCARLET

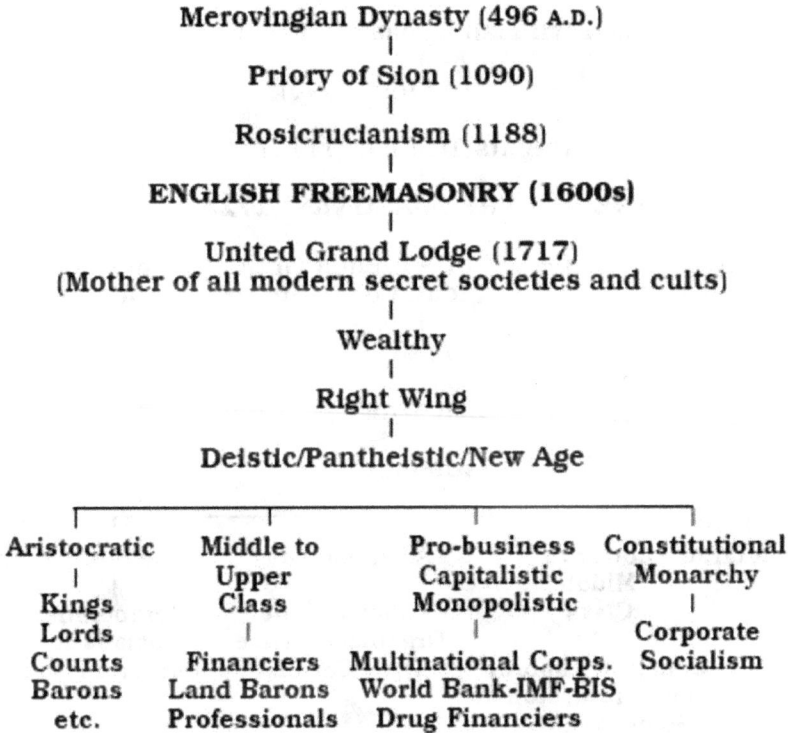

Merovingian Dynasty (496 A.D.)
|
Priory of Sion (1090)
|
Rosicrucianism (1188)
|
ENGLISH FREEMASONRY (1600s)
|
United Grand Lodge (1717)
(Mother of all modern secret societies and cults)
|
Wealthy
|
Right Wing
|
Deistic/Pantheistic/New Age

Aristocratic	Middle to Upper Class	Pro-business Capitalistic Monopolistic	Constitutional Monarchy
Kings Lords Counts Barons etc.	Financiers Land Barons Professionals	Multinational Corps. World Bank-IMF-BIS Drug Financiers	Corporate Socialism

Dominates:
> Great Britain, Canada, Northeast USA (Eastern Establishment), most oriental countries, Hong Kong, Australia, and South Africa.

THE BEAST

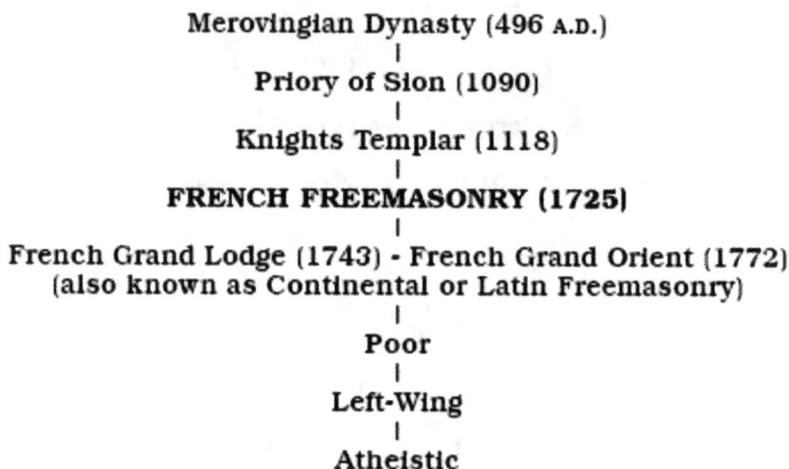

Merovingian Dynasty (496 A.D.)
|
Priory of Sion (1090)
|
Knights Templar (1118)
|
FRENCH FREEMASONRY (1725)
|
French Grand Lodge (1743) - French Grand Orient (1772)
(also known as Continental or Latin Freemasonry)
|
Poor
|
Left-Wing
|
Atheistic

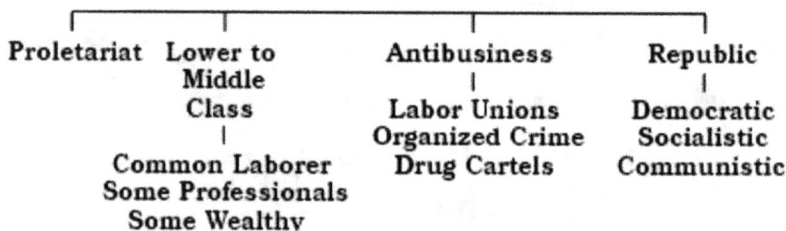

Proletariat	Lower to Middle Class	Antibusiness	Republic
	|	|	|
	Common Laborer Some Professionals Some Wealthy	Labor Unions Organized Crime Drug Cartels	Democratic Socialistic Communistic

Dominates:
Continent of Europe, Southern and Western U.S.A., former U.S.S.R., Communist China, Pacific Islands, Philippines, Latin and South America, Africa (during 1990s has taken over South Africa).

MASONIC AUTHOR ARTHUR EDWARD WAITE, P.M., P.Z. (1857-1942) ROYAL ARCH MASON

A New Encyclopaedia of Freemasonry (two volumes) New York: Weathervane Books, MCMLXX
Reared a Catholic, but later left the Church Waite's Masonic credentials:
Initiated 9/19/1901; Raised 2/10/1902; Exalted 5/1/1902. Past Senior Grand Warden of Iowa; Past Provincial Deputy Grand Director of Ceremonies (Bucks.). Past Grand Inner Guard (English Grand Mark) Past Great Captain of the Guards. Past Grand Historiographer, etc. etc.

A. E. Waite
(1857-1942)

In *A New Encyclopaedia of Freemasonry*, Waite best describes from a Masonic point of view the modern rift between *Scarlet and the Beast.*

"Grand Orient — It remains that in 1877 the Grand Orient, without denying God, proclaimed its atheism, which word is negative like the later denomination agnostic. A theist is one who affirms God and an atheist is one who does not so affirm. Now, in England the charge of Freemasonry to every one of its members is: "Fear God and honour the king." But French [Grand Orient] Freemasonry has neither a king to honour nor a God to fear. There is no ground of union between two institutions so diverse as these are, and any proposition for healing the breach between them by a process of restoring communion — presumably without stipulations — is on the face of it foredoomed to failure, while in the heart of it there is sown already the poisonous seed of insincerity."

In *Scarlet and the Beast*, John Daniel gives overwhelming evidence of this war between English and French Freemasonry.

SECTION 1
MASONIC CLUBS & SYMBOLOGY

Freemasonry is a religion of works. One of its many symbols is the balance. Masons believe they will be judged by their works, based upon the balance of right and wrong in their lives. In this Picture Book you will see the true nature of Freemasonry. In II Cor. 11:13-15 we read of the "works" religions:

> *"For such are false apostles, deceitful workers, transforming themselves into the apostles of Christ. And no marvel; for Satan himself is transformed into an angel of light. Therefore, it is no great thing if his ministers also be transformed as the ministers of righteousness; whose end shall be <u>according to their works</u>."*

Fig.1 — Speculative Masons secretly practicing their art of medical research.

Drawing of "medical practice" on cadaver in England. Notice Masonic skull & crossbones lower left and Masonic cable-tow around the cadaver's neck. This medical practice was taking place in a Rosicrucian Masonic Lodge. Rosicrucians were forced to practice alchemy in secret, inside their Masonic Lodges. Such experiments were considered witchcraft by Crown and Church, hence forbidden. Speculative Masons caught in this act were subject to being put to death. (British Museum). See *Scarlet and the Beast*, Vol. 1, Introduction & Chapters 2 & 7.

The Goose and Gridiron Tavern at London in 1717
The Grand Lodge of England was Organized in this Building

Fig 2 — There appears to be a contra- diction in which tavern Grand Lodge was formed.

This photo is from *Mackey's History of FM* by 33O Robert Ingham Clegg, 1898, 1906, and 1921, published by the Masonic History Company. Yet, in *Mackey's Revised Ency. of FM*, Vol.1, by 33O Albert G. Mackey, enlarged by 33O Robert I. Clegg, 1909, 1912, and 1929, 5th printing 1950, p.91 reads "APPLETREE TAVERN. The place where four Lodges of London met in 1717, and organized Grand Lodge of England. This tavern was situated in Charles Street, Covent Garden." The apparent contra- diction will be explained in *Scarlet and the Beast*, Vol. I.

Fig. 3 — Masons view the Tower of Babel (Gen.11) as a symbol of Masonry's "works religion." The tower below contains 33 steps for Scottish Rite on left, and 13 steps for York Rite on right. Both meet at the top. The three-stepped base represents the three degrees of the Blue Lodge. The arched center contains additional male and female lodges in America.

Masonic appendages: All Masons in America enter Blue Lodge, which contains three degrees, illustrated by the three steps at the base of the pyramid. Most Masons (85%) never progress beyond Blue Degrees. Those who wish to delve deeper into the mysteries choose either the Scottish Rite (also called Jewish Rite) of 30 degrees on the left side of the pyramid, or the York Rite (also called Christian Rite) of 10 degrees on the right side of the pyramid, for a total of 33 and 13 degrees respectively. York Rite is practiced only in the Americas, whereas the Scottish Rite is worldwide. Both are Templar Rites. Many Masons in America join both Rites.

The highest degree a Mason can earn is 32° Scottish Rite or 13° York Rite. Both are equal in prestige. 33° cannot be earned. It is honorary, awarded by the ruling body of Universal Freemasonry — the Supreme Council. At any given time approximately 5,000 33rd degree Masons are in the world — most of whom hold high positions in their governments.

Initially, only 32° Scottish Rite Masons and 13° York Rite Masons could join the Shrine. Shriners, who operate Children's Hospitals, take an oath and pray to Allah, the god of Moslems (see pp. 28-30 this section). However, since 9/11 terrorist attacks on America by Moslems, Shriner membership has been decimated. To keep their Children's Hospitals open, Shriners have opened membership to 3° Master Masons.

Fig. 4 — Masons also view good works as worship. This is similar to Communist dogma
"Labor will make you free!" From *Mackey's Ency.*

3°
Master
Mason

1917
Communist
Masonic
version reads
"Labor will
make you
free."

1°
Entered
Apprentice

2°
Fellow
Craftsman

Labor is Worship

Fig. 5 — Masons view good works as building their eternal mansion on high. In this drawing the Entered Apprentice, Fellow Craftsman, and Master Mason clasp hands on a job well done, as they view their good works. Notice the **"All-Seeing Eye"** of pagan religions atop the pyramid.

Mackey's Ency. of Freemasonry

Onward to the Heights
The Vision of the Craft for Labor, Unity, Brotherhood

Fig. 6 — The "All-Seeing-Eye" in the occult has various forms. In the end it is the "Eye of Lucifer."

See *Scarlet and the Beast*, Vol. 1. chaps. 5, 10 & 30.

Egyptian ANKH.
ANKH means EYE
In Hinduism.

Eye of Osiris ▲

3rd eye in Hinduism

Eye of
Time Warner ▼

Fidelity Investments uses the pyramid and capstone as its logo. "EYE is understood.

The three major news networks use the eye as their emblem. CBS blatantly uses the eye in its program "Eye on America." ABC uses the sundisk, a pagan symbol of the eye. NBC uses the Peacock with its many eyes in its tail feathers.

George Washington's
Masonic Apron with
All-Seeing Eye hovering
above seven stars

Seal of Illuminati,
created May 1, 1776
by Adam Weishaupt. ▼

Clairvoyant
EYE of
Witchcraft ▲

MDCCLXXVI

Fig. 7 — 3° Master Mason below takes Chief Cornerstone position of Jesus Christ. *Lost Keys of Freemasonry* by 33° Manly P. Hall, p.53, 1976. Notice Egyptian ANKH in left hand of Master Mason. ANKH is a phallic symbol. The upright represents the male reproductive organ, whereas the circle represents the female reproductive organ. In the Hindu religion, ANKH also means "eye." This photo is reproduced again in Section 1, Fig. 89, p. 81 to confirm Freemasonry's Luciferian connection.

The Master Mason

"In this picture is concealed the allegory of the Lost Word. The Master Mason, having completed his labors, becomes a worker on a higher plane than the one in which the ordinary builder is permitted to work. The Master Mason becomes the capstone of the Universal Temple." Hall, p.50.

"Eye" or "Eyes" in the capstone

In Rev. 3:14, Jesus Christ, speaking of Himself to the church at Laodicea, says, "These things saith the Amen, the faithful and true witness, the **beginning** of the creation of God..."

In Greek, *beginning* is spelled "arche," meaning chief (in various applications of order, time, place or rank):.. corner... first... magistrate, power, principality, principle, rule." In plain English, Christ is saying of Himself that He is "the Magistrate, the arch, the Chief Cornerstone, the Power which preceded creation, or the One Who rules over creation."

Prophesying of Christ, the penman of Psalms 118:22 writes: "The stone which the builders refused is become the head stone of the corner."

Isaiah 28:16 records God's words to the prophet, "Behold, I lay in Zion for a foundation a stone, a tried stone, a precious corner stone.

In Matt. 21:42, referring to Himself in Old Testament prophecies, "Jesus saith unto them, Did ye never read in the scriptures, The stone which the builder's rejected, the same is become the head of the corner...?"

With this in mind, read again the caption beneath Fig. 7. There the Lodge teaches that Master Masons usurp the capstone position of Jesus Christ.

In Dan. 7:7-8 the prophet writes, "After this I saw in the night visions, and behold a fourth beast, dreadful and terrible, and strong exceedingly; and it had great iron teeth: it devoured and brake in pieces, and stamped the residue with the feet of it: and it was diverse from all the beasts that were before it; and it had ten horns. I considered the horns, and, behold, there came up among them another **little horn**, before whom there were three of the first horns plucked up by the roots: and, behold, in this horn were eyes like the eyes of man, and a mouth speaking great things."

Horn in Aramaic (language in which Daniel 7 was written), has various meanings, "a *peak* (of a mountain), a *ray* (of light); fig. *power*."

Eyes in the horn are indeed plural in the original text, meaning at least "two eyes," but could mean three eyes, as pictured in Fig. 6, p.7, the "3rd eye" in Hinduism. Likewise, in Fig. 7 we see at the feet of the Master Mason a corner view of a 4-sided capstone. On the right side facing out are two weeping eyes of Osiris. On the left side is the Masonic "point within the circle," which has dual meaning. It is a stylized "eye" as well as a phallic symbol, representing the union of male and female reproductive organs. The Hindu ankh in the left hand of the Master Mason carries the same meaning, for ANKH in Hinduism means *eye*.

Daniel saw at least the two eyes of Osiris in the "mountain peak." And as a captive in Babylon, he may have learned that both the ANKH and the Point within the Circle were occult forms of the eye.

Our founding fathers, most of whom were Masons, selected as our national emblem the single eye on the left side of the capstone, but conspicuously rotated both the pyramid and capstone to the right, thus concealing the multiple eyes seen by the prophet (see back of $1 bill, Fig. 8, p. 10). The capstone hovering above the base signifies an unfinished project, just as the pyramid seen by the prophet was unfinished.

Fig. 8 — Great Seal of the United States of America, specifically the All-Seeing Eye atop the pyramid, and 13 stars in the Glory Cloud shaped like the sixpointed star, which is a rendition of the Square & Compass, the blasphemous sex force symbol. See *Scarlet and the Beast*, Vol. 1; 3rd ed.; chaps 5, 15, & 30. Notice the Latin words on the Great Seal on left: "Annuit Coeptis Novus Ordo Seclorum." Translated it means, "Announcing The Birth of a New Secular Order." Secular means "without God." Using our national emblem as a precedence, our Masonic Supreme Court Justices ruled that the intent of our founding fathers was to separate Church from state. You can read the entire horrific story in *Scarlet and the Beast*, Vol 1, 3rd ed., ch. 10.

THE GREAT SEAL OF THE UNITED STATES
(notice 13 stars are positioned so as to shape a 6-pointed star)

THE GLORY CLOUD

Fig. 9 — The pagan All-Seeing Eye on May 1987 cover of *Discover* mag. becomes the All-Creating Eye, thus usurping the position of Jesus Christ as the Creator of the Heavens and the Earth.

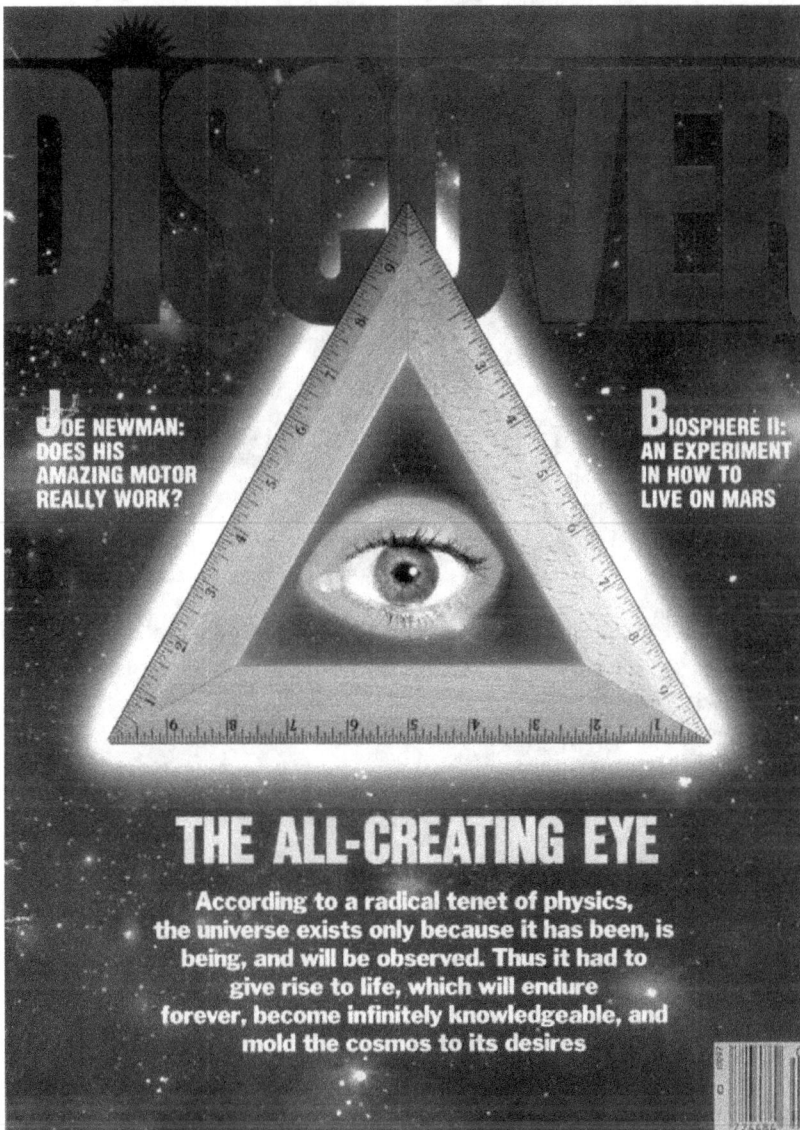

Figure 10 — So called Image of an all-seeing eye sent back from space by NASA's Hubble telescope. *National Geogrophic*, April 1997.

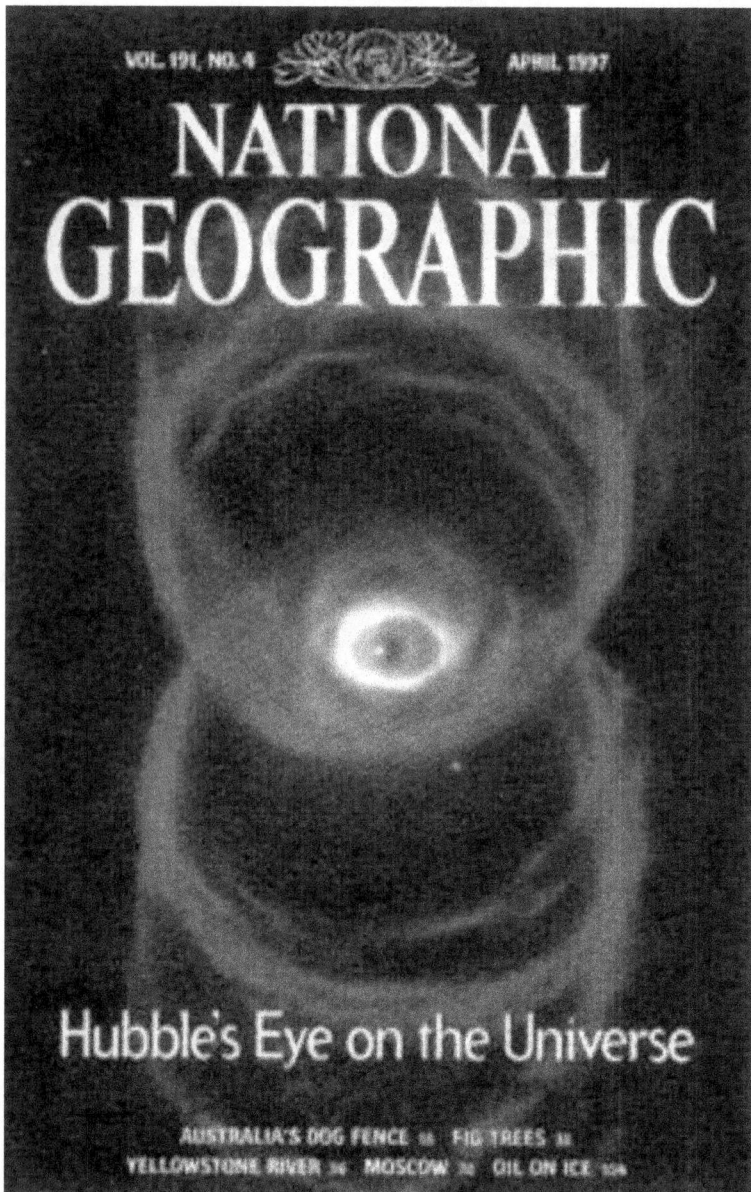

Figure 11 — United Nations Meditation Room. For detailed explanation of religions represented in mural, see *Scarlet and the Beast* Vol.1, chap. 5.

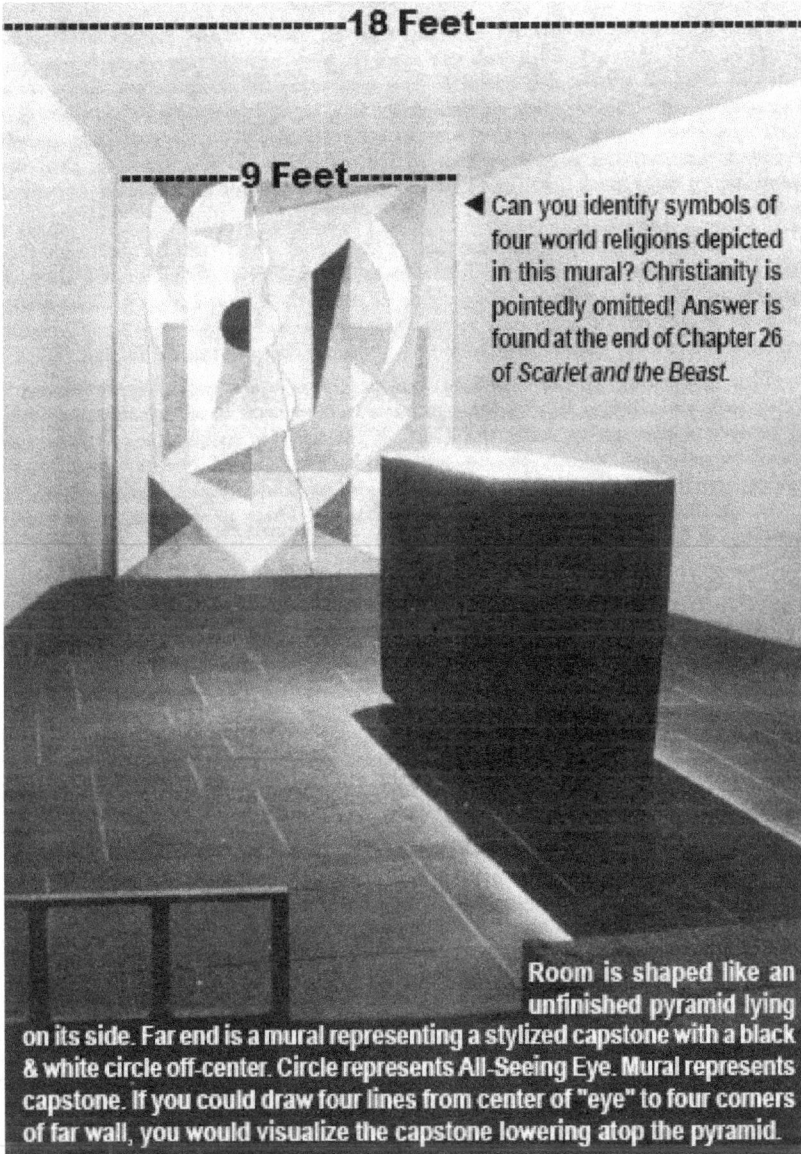

------18 Feet------

------9 Feet------

◀ Can you identify symbols of four world religions depicted in this mural? Christianity is pointedly omitted! Answer is found at the end of Chapter 26 of *Scarlet and the Beast.*

Room is shaped like an unfinished pyramid lying on its side. Far end is a mural representing a stylized capstone with a black & white circle off-center. Circle represents All-Seeing Eye. Mural represents capstone. If you could draw four lines from center of "eye" to four corners of far wall, you would visualize the capstone lowering atop the pyramid.

Fig. 12 — Freemasonry's "olive branch of peace" on earth, overseen by the all-seeing eye of providence. From *Mackey's Ency.*

ENCYCLOPEDIA
FREEMASONRY

Fig. 13 — United Nations' olive branch of "peace on earth." Read in *Scarlet and the Beast*, Vol. 1, of Freemasonry's involvement in founding both the League of Nations and the United Nations for the express purpose of bringing "Peace on Earth" through representative government (democracy).

PEACE
on
EARTH
through
force of
ARMS

Fig. 14 — Job's Daughters install new officers of Bethel Lodge No. 3, St. Paul, MN. Honored Queen leads group in hymn.

Jr. and Sr. Princesses kneel in the form of a pyramid with other new officers.

Former officers stand in background. (Female Masonic Functions cannot meet without male Masons present. Females are not permitted at male Masonic functions).

Masonic appendages — *LIFE mag.* 10-8-56

Fig. 15 — Order of DeMolay (sons of Masons) holds flower talk ceremony in Granite City, IL.

Candidate (center) hears talk on motherhood, given by male Mason. Mothers of candidate, although members of female Masonic auxiliaries, cannot give this "talk"

Fig. 16 — Masonic appendages — Daughters of the Nile in Omaha, NE. Civic Auditorium salute new Supreme Queen (on throne). LIFE mag. 10-8-56.

On stage with queen are past Supreme Queens. Seated in front of stage are 110 Temple Queens wearing gold coronets. They have just received the year's secret password. Man at altar (left center) is drillmaster. Daughters were founded by Shriners' wives in 1913, to acquire philosophy of life.

Fig. 17 — Rainbow Girls install officers of Washington, Idaho, and Alaska Grand Assembly in Pasco, WA high school gym. The new officers stand in semicircle. Masonic appendages — Life magazine, October 8, 1956

Fig. 18 — 3° Master Mason initiation is dramatized by Hartford, CT Masons. Temple workmen are kneeling before King of Tyre, Solomon, and Hiram Abif. (Read S&B, Vol.1, Ch.1 and (PB.S11.F1-10) for history behind this initiation). The intensive interrogation phrase, "He gave me the third degree," originated from this brutal Masonic initiation.

MASONIC OATHS FOR FIRST THREE DEGREES
QUOTED FROM RONAYNE'S HANDBOOK OF FREEMASONRY

First Degree — Entered Apprentice

After the Entered Apprentice agrees to "ever conceal and never reveal any of the secret arts, parts or points of the hidden mysteries of Ancient Freemasonry," he takes the following blood oath:

"All this I most solemnly and sincerely promise and swear, with afirm and steadfast resolution, to keep and perform the same without any equivocation, mental reservation or secret evasion of mind whatever, *binding myself under a no less penalty than that of having my throat cut across, my tongue torn out by its roots and buried in the rough sands of the sea at low water mark, where the tide ebbs and flows twice in twenty-four hours,* should I ever knowingly violate this my solemn obligation of an Entered Apprentice Mason. So help me God, and keep me steadfast in the due performance of the same."

Second Degree — Fellow Craft

After having promised never to reveal Masonic secrets, always ready to obey all Masonic authority above him, and never "cheat, wrong nor defraud a lodge of Fellow Crafts," the initiate takes the following blood oath:

"All this I most solemnly and sincerely promise and swear with a firm and steadfast resolution to keep and perform the same, without any equivocation, mental reservation or secret evasion of mind whatever, *binding myself under a no less penalty than that of having my left breast torn open, my heart plucked out and given as a prey to the beasts of the field and the fowls of the air* should I ever knowingly violate this my solemn obligation of a Fellow Craft Mason, so help me God and keep me steadfast in the due performance of the same."

Third Degree — Master Mason

After promising never to "cheat, wrong nor defraud a Master Mason Lodge," and stating that he "will not have illicit carnal intercourse with a brother Master Mason's wife, his mother, sister or daughter, I knowing them to be such," the Master Mason takes the following blood oath:

"All this I most solemnly and sincerely promise and swear with a firm and steadfast resolution to keep and perform the same without any equivocation, mental reservation, or secret evasion of mind whatever, binding myself under a no less penalty than that of having my body severed in twain, my bowels taken from thence and burned to ashes, and the ashes scattered to the four winds of heaven, that no trace or remembrance may be had of so vile and perjured a wretch as I, should I ever knowingly violate this my solemn obligation as a Master Mason. So help me, God, and keep me steadfast in the due performance of the same."

Fig. 19 — The 3rd degree initiation in Blue Lodge Masonry is a reenactment of the interrogation and execution of Jacques de Molay. It is a brutal initiation, from which comes the common phrase by someone questioned about his dubious activity, "He gave me the 'third degree.'" (PB.S11.F10). Below is another brutal Masonic initiation, not the Master Mason initiation, but one more frightening. It is an initiation into a Masonic auxiliary club, which cost the initiate his life.

3-15-2004

St Louis POST

Masons suspend lodge after shooting

NEW YORK TIMES

NEW YORK — A week after a man was shot dead inside a Masonic lodge on Long Island, N.Y., leaders of the state's Masonic organization made the rare move on Sunday of suspending the lodge while a panel of lawyers investigates the culture and ritual that led to the shooting.

"We at the Grand Lodge were deeply outraged and anguished over this incident," said Carl Fitje, the grand master of the Grand Lodge of New York, which oversees the state's Masonic groups. "This just came out of left field."

William James, a new arrival to the lodge, South Side 493 Masons of Patchogue, was killed last Monday night as he was being initiated into a social club connected to the Masons but not officially part of the organization. Albert Eid, 76, a member of the social club, the Fellow Craft Club, was supposed to fire a gun loaded with blanks but instead reached into the wrong pocket, drew a licensed, loaded handgun and shot James, 47, in the face, police say.

Though Masonic initiations are often darkly theatrical, Fitje and other Masonic experts have said that pulling a gun on someone has never been part of any sanctioned ritual.

Eid pleaded not guilty last week to second-degree manslaughter charges in Suffolk County District Court. His lawyer said Eid held no malice toward James.

See list of Masonic appendages and Masonic social clubs this section, pages 20-22, such as Police Fellowcraft Club, Post Office Fellowcraft Club, Fireman's Fellowcraft Club, etc. These Masonic Clubs are for Masons employed by these public services.

Retiree sentenced in Mason shooting

Jan. 8, 2005

RIVERHEAD, N.Y. — A retiree who accidentally shot a friend to death during an initiation ceremony at a Masonic lodge pleaded guilty Friday to criminally negligent homicide and was sentenced to five years' probation. Albert Eid, 77, past master of the Long Island lodge, appeared tearful as he told a judge he was sorry for shooting William James.

James, 47, was shot in the face last March. During the initiation, he was seated in a chair, and a small platform with cans was placed near his head. Eid was supposed to fire blanks from about 20 feet away. Police said Eid mistakenly pulled a loaded .32-caliber handgun from his left pants pocket instead of a .22-caliber pistol with blanks that was in his right pocket.

CLUBS AND FREEMASONRY

Copied verbatim from *MACKEY'S REVISED ENCYCLOPEDIA OF FREEMASONRY*
Vol. 3, 1946, pp. 1190-1191

"The formation of the first Grand Lodge of Speculative Freemasonry in 1717 coincided with a sudden and almost explosive multiplication of clubs. They broke out like a rash over the whole of England. In every village or town was at least one tavern or inn and one or more clubs were sure to meet in it. There was an amazing number of categories of clubs, from clubs for elderly high churchmen to the most outré extravagances of those eccentrics who in France and Italy won for travelers the soubriquet of "mad Englishmen": political clubs, scientific clubs (the Royal Society was one), betting clubs, bottle clubs, shooting clubs, music clubs, coffee clubs, odd fellows clubs, clubs for fat men, bald men, dwarfs, hen-pecked men, one-eyed men, insurance clubs, burial clubs, clubs male and female, clubs that were a sort of lay church, and clubs for opium smokers, etc., etc..., all founded by Masons.

"When the first of the new Lodges of Speculative Freemasonry began to attract attention the populace took them for a new species of clubs. More than one attempt has been made to turn that popular impression into an argument, more often by social historians than by Masonic writers; it has never succeeded, because while a Lodge may often have been a clubbable society, few things could be less alike in substance or in purpose than a club and a Lodge. The truth of that statement is proved by the fact that even in cities with hundreds of Lodges their members form Masonic clubs on the side.

"**Note**. Side orders and Masonic clubs have the same status in the eyes of Masonic law. When Masonic clubs first began to be formed about the beginning of this [20th] century their officers and members took the ground that since they were not Lodges, were not, properly speaking, Masonic organizations, and acted independently of Lodges and Grand Lodges, neither Masters nor Grand Masters held any authority over them; and in the beginning the majority of Grand Masters agreed with this opinion. But after some twenty years of experience with them, Grand Masters and Grand Lodges began to hold that while a Masonic officer cannot supervise a club as such, a Lodge or a Grand Lodge can discipline club members in their capacity as Masons. A Grand Master of Masons in Iowa notified the members of a Side Order that if they held a street carnival of a kind as planned he would order them tried for un-Masonic conduct; one or two years later a Grand Master of Masons in Michigan followed a similar course with another Side Order because of the indecent posters with which it was advertising an indoor circus. Grand Lodges uphold that reading of the question; if a man is guilty of conduct unbecoming a Mason he is subject to discipline without regard to where he was guilty."

Masonic clubs and appendages founded by Masons for the express purpose of creating a source from which to recruit future Freemasons.

Kiwanis International

Jackson A. Raney (?). President of Kiwanis International in 1955. Member of Versailles Lodge No. 7 (Indiana) and AASR officer.

Lions Club International

32° R. Ray Keaton (?). Director-General of Lions Club International, and editor of *The Lion* since 1950. Member of Phoenix Lodge No. 275, Weatherford, TX, receiving degrees on June 9 and Dec. 23, 1937, and Oct. 27, 1939. Knights Templar and Shriner.

33° Monroe L. Nute (?). President of Lions Club International in 1954. Member of Kennett Lodge No. 475, Kennett Square, PA. 33° AASR (NJ) in Delaware Consistory.

Masonic appendages founded by Freemasons

from *10,000 Famous Freemasons*, Vols. 1-4, by 33° Denslow

American Federation of Labor
American Legion
Boy Scouts of America
B'nai B'rith
Brotherhood of Locomotive
Firemen and Engineers
Brotherhood of Railroad Trainmen
Elk's Lodge
Fireman's Square Club
Foreman's Association of America
Fraternal Order of Police
Kiwanis International
Knights of Labor — forerunner to labor unions
Loyal Order of the Moose & Mooseheart
Noble Order of the Knights of Labor
Order of Railway Conductors and Brakemen
Police Fellowcraft Club Post Office
Fellowcraft Club Rotary International
Schoolboy Patrol
Sanitary Commission — forerunner of the Red Cross
United Brotherhood of Carpenters and Joiners
United Mine Workers of America

Fig. 20 — Masons who either founded or were the leaders of Masonic clubs. From *10,000 Famous Freemasons,* by 33° William R. Denslow.

Freemason
◀ **Rodney H. Brandon**
(1881-?)

Organizer of Loyal Order of the Moose in 1906, and one of its officials until 1929. In 1913, Brandon supervised construction of Mooseheart and established Moosehaven, FL in 1922. He was a Freemason.

▲ **33° James J. Davis** (1873-1947)

Founder of Mooseheart Home and School. Chairman of Mooseheart governors as well as Home for Old Folk, Moosehaven, Florida. Member of Quincy Lodge No. 23, Elwood, Ind. Received 32° in Albert Pike Consistory No. 1, Washington, DC on Dec. 15, 1925. Received 33° on Sept. 19, 1929. Also member of Tall Cedars of Lebanon and Syria Shrine Temple of Pittsburgh, PA.

▲ **Freemason Malcolm R. Giles** (1894-1953)

Supreme Secretary, Loyal Order of Moose, 1925-49. Director General from 1949-1953. Affiliated with Jerusalem Temple Lodge No. 90, Aurora IL.

◀ **13° Robert C. Fletcher** (1869-?)
York Rite Mason

One of the 1905 founders of Rotary International. Member of LaGrange Lodge No. 770 at LaGrange, IL. Recorder of Trinity Commandery No. 80, Knights Templar of LaGrange (York Rite Masonry).

Mason O. Sam Cummings ▶
(1893-?)
Organizer of Kiwanis,
International.

Owner of O. Sam Cummings Ins. Agency, and state agent for Kansas City Life Ins. Co. in Texas. He is recognized internationally for development of Kiwanis organization in the U.S. and Canada. He was first international executive secretary of the Kiwanis Clubs of the U.S. and Canada from 1918-21, and international president in 1928. He was a Mason.

Figure 21 — Catholic fraternities to counter Masonic fraternities.

Knights of Columbus

The Catholic Church has long denounced membership in secret societies. Therefore, to keep its parishioners from being tempted to join Freemasonry, it founded Knights of Columbus in 1882 as it's counter to the Lodge. Source: *Compton's Encyclopedia*, a division of *Ency. Britannica*.

■■■■■■■■■■■■■■■■■■■■■■■■■■■■■■

International Order of the Alhambra

Another Catholic benevolent society, the International Order of the Alhambra, was founded 1904 to counter the Shriners. Source: *Compton's Encyclopedia*, division of *Encyclopaedia Britannica*.

Fig. 22 — There are two jurisdictions of Scottish Rite Freemasonry in America, southern and northern. The Southern Jurisdiction is French and the Northern Jurisdiction is British. In *Scarlet and the Beast*, Vol. 1, 3rd edition (Introduction and Chap. 15), you will learn why the Northern Jurisdiction was founded in secrecy in opposition to the Southern Jurisdiction, and why they remain in opposition to this day. LIFE mag. 10-8-56.

33° George E. Bushnell
(1887-?)

Former Michigan supreme court justice. In 1956 was the reigning 33° Sovereign Grand Commander of the Northern Jurisdiction (NJ) of Scottish Rite Freemasonry.

33° Luther A. Smith
(1887-?)

Began law practice in Hattiesburg, MS. Appointed judge of court of chancery in 1953. Became Sovereign Grand Commander of the Supreme Council, 33° Scottish Rite, Southern Jurisdiction (SJ) from Oct. 21, 1955.

Fig. 23 — Is Freemasonry a Christian institution? LIFE mag. 10-8-56.

Marching to Church

Lexington, KY Masons, all with their aprons, leave their Masonic temple (background, building with belfry). Anually, the Lodge goes to church together.

At the service in the Methodist church, Masons sing hymns. The Minister of the church is studying to be a Mason. Each year the Lodge attends services at a different church.

Figs. 24-25 — Rose Croix table in shape of cross. Masons fight with Pope. LIFE mag.
10-8-56

FEAST OF THE PASCHAL LAMB is celebrated by Brooklyn's Aurora Grata Chapter of Rose Croix, whose members are 18° Scottish Rite Masons. Ritual is observed every year on Maundy Thursday. The 13 Masons wearing dark robes and seated at cross-shaped table represent participants at the Last Supper. The ceremony, combining Jewish Passover and Christian observance, lasts 1-1/2 hours, includes music, prayer, recitations. It ends with candles being put out one by one.

◀ **FIGHT WITH THE CHURCH** is satirized by 1884 cartoon in *Puck* magazine depicting an argument between the Pope (left) and Masons.

Figure 26 — King James Version of Masonic Bible on Altar of Sacrifice. Masons prefer KJV because King James I was a Scottish Templar Mason. LIFE mag. 10-8-56

Crossed swords on a Bible indicate Scottish Rite's Supreme Council is in session.

Freemasonry claims that crossed swords on the Bible represent its protection of God's Holy Word. Yet, we document time and again in *Scarlet and the Beast* that Masonry plans to destroy Christianity. First, by infiltration. If that fails, by separation of church and state. If that fails, by relentless persecution. You will witness all three in *Scarlet and the Beast.*

Fig. 27 — Is Freemasonry a Moslem institution? The Ancient Arabic Order of Nobles of the Mystic Shrine (the Shriners) is the playhouse of Freemasonry. Masons who join the Shrine are required to take their vows on the faith of a Moslem. The incredible truth is that many so-called Christian ministers, who have joined Masonry, have also joined the Shrine and taken the Shriner's oath on the next page.

Masonic appendages LIFE mag. 10-8-56

Shriners — the playhouse of Freemasonry

Shriner's oath to the Muslim god Allah:

> *"...on my voluntary desire, uninfluenced and of free accord do hereby assume, without reserve, the Obligations of the Nobility of the Mystic Shrine, as did the elect of the Temple of Mecca, the Moslem and the Mohammedan. I do hereby, upon the Bible, and on the mysterious legend of the Koran, and its dedication to the Mohammedan faith, promise and swear and vow on the faith and honor of an upright man, come weal or woe, adversity or success, that I will never reveal any secret part or portion whatsoever of the ceremonies I have already received..."*

This is a lengthy oath, which also carries a ghastly penalty:

> *"In wilful violation whereof may I incur the fearful penalty of having my eyeballs pierced to the center with a three-edged blade, my feet flayed and I be forced to walk the hot sands upon the sterile shores of the Red Sea until the flaming sun shall strike me with a livid plague, and may Allah, the god of Arab, Moslem, and Mohammedan, the god of our fathers, support me to the entire fulfillment of the same. Amen. Amen. Amen."*

Writes E.M. Storms, author of *Should a Christian be a Mason?*, (1980), in which is published the above oaths:

> *"Can the Christian glibly state that Mohammed is the 'god of our fathers?' Should he call upon Allah, god of the lost Moslem? "At one time in the history of our nation, May 1833 [during the height of the Anti-Masonic Movement], fourteen hundred citizens petitioned the United States Congress to prohibit, by law, the Masonic oaths. The committee from the House of Representatives recommended that the oaths be legally prohibited on the grounds that they were not lawfully authorized; they bind a person to violate the law; they were subversive and blasphemous; their penalties were forbidden by the U.S. Constitution." (More on Anti-Masonic Movement in Section 4).*

1876 FOUNDERS OF THE ANCIENT, ARABIC ORDER OF THE NOBLES OF THE MYSTIC SHRINE

13° **Walter M. Fleming** (1838-1913) — One of three founders of the Ancient, Arabic Order of the Nobles of the Mystic Shrine (June 6, 1876), and its first imperial potentate, serving for 12 years. Born in Portland, Maine. Occupation: physician. Raised (3°) in Rochester Lodge No. 660 (Feb. 13, 1869), and affiliated with New York Lodge No. 330 (Dec. 3, 1872). Became a member of Columbian York Rite Commandery No. 1, K.T. at New York City (Dec. 2, 1871), and was its commander (1873-77).

33° **William Jermyn Florence** (1831-1891) — Stage name for Bernard Conlin, an American actor who is recognized as one of the three founders of the Ancient and Arabic Order, Nobles of the Mystic Shrine.

Florence excelled in dialect impersonation. During one of his trips abroad in North Africa, he conceived the idea of the Shrine, and on his return conveyed the idea to his friend, Dr. Walter M. Fleming. Together they founded the organization in New York City (June 6, 1876), with Fleming as first potentate of Mecca Temple.

Florence received all three degrees of Blue Lodge by special dispensation in Mt. Moriah Lodge No. 155, Philadelphia, PA (Oct. 12, 1853), and joined the lodge (Nov. 22) that same year. Became a member of Zerubbabel Chapter No. 162, R.A.M. (June 12, 1854), and of Pittsburgh Commandery No. 1, K.T. (June 13, 1854). He was a 33° AASR (NJ). Buried in a Protestant cemetery with Catholic rites, the latter being arranged by his wife.

32° Albert Rawson (1828-1902). Artist, author, scholar and one of the three founders of the Ancient Arabic Order of the Nobles of the Mystic Shrine. Received D.D. and LL.D. at Christ College, Oxford, England. Received M.D. from the Sorbonne, Paris. Studied law under William H. Seward, a Freemason. Studied medicine under Prof. Webster of Massachusetts Medical College, and theology under Elder Graves. He made several visits to the Orient, and on a pilgrimage from Cairo to Mecca with the annual caravan, disguised himself as a Muslim medical student. He was adopted as a "brother" by Adwan Bedouins of Moab. He was initiated by the Druses on Mt. Lebanon. He was one of the three founders of the Shrine, and one of the four founders of the Theosophical Society in the U.S.A. He wrote rituals for many secret societies. Was "General for Life" in the Society of the Rosy Cross. Was a 32° Ancient and Accepted Scottish Rite Mason (AASR); and had received the 95 degrees of the Egyptian Rite of Memphis.

Most Eminent Grand Master of Grand Encampment of Knights Templar

General Grand Master of Royal Arch

Figure 28

1956

York Rite

Grand Masters

LIFE mag. 10-8-56

PARTIAL LIST OF MASONIC APPENDAGES USED BY MASONRY TO BOTH RECRUIT AND MOLD FUTURE MASONS AND PROMOTE ECUMENICALISM

Acacia Fraternity: Cements freindships at college. Only for Protestant men recommended by two Master Masons.

Loyal Orange Institution of the United States of America, Inc.: Upholds Protestantism. Ecumenical, meaning any American Protestant. Anti-Catholic.

Order of DeMolay: Males 14-21 years of age. Develops character, teaches citizenship, and love of parents. Sons of Masons and sons' male friends,

Order of the Amaranth: Promotes Masonic charities. Developes future pool of doners. Female relatives of Master Masons.

Order of the Builders: Ecumenical. Teaches religious and democratic understanding. Males 13-21. Laodicean.

Order of the Constellation of Junior Stars:Teaches inter-denominational religion to children of Masons, who in turn promote same in their churches.

Fig. 29 — Is Masonry a Jewish institution? Ark of Covenant worship. Rev. 2:9
identifies the persecutors of the Church. Christ says, "I know the blasphemy of them
which say they are Jews, and are not, but are the synagogue of Satan. Fear none of those
things which thou shalt suffer."

LIFE mag. 10-8-56

Mackey's Ency. of Freemasonry confirms Rev. 2:9: "Each Lodge is and must
be a symbol of the Jewish Temple: each Master in the chair representing the
Jewish King; and every Freemason a personation of the Jewish Workman."

Dedication of Solomon's Temple is reenacted by Brooklyn Royal Arch Masons
(R.A.M.), Orient Chapter 138. Ritual is part of ceremony awarding Most Excellent Master
degree to prospective Royal Arch Masons. High Priest of Jews (center) kneels before
cherubim-decorated Ark of the Covenant flanked by members of the Jewish tribes. King
Solomon stands before Bible (background) surrounded by princes, workmen and court
attendants. See *Scarlet and the Beast*; Vol. 1, Chaps. 1, 7, 9; & Vol. 2 entire.

Fig. 30 — From *Mackey's Revised Encyclopedia of Freemasonry*, Vol. 2

"... them which say they are Jews, and are not..." Rev. 2:9

Masonic Symbolism, the Private Language of the Craft
Tabernacle in the Wilderness, Ark of the Covenant, and the Cherubims (sic)
Furniture of the Lodge
CAPTION & PICTURES from *Mackey's*, Vol. 2, facing p. 1050.

Fig. 31 — Beginning the first millennium, the Eleusinian Mysteries of Ancient Greece, from which Freemasonry was patterned, initiated their candidates into becoming a Jew. The scenes and characters of the mysterious drama, as found in the Eleusinian Orgies of Greece, are:

Lesser Degrees

1° — Eleusis: The Advent, or coming-in of light
2° — Hierophant: The Expounder of Mysteries
3° — Hupereet: The Minister
4° — Diaconos: The Deacon
5° — Diadochos: The Torch-bearer
6° — Photagogue: The Bringer-in of Light

Six month waiting period

Greater Degrees

7° — Autoptos: Temple-goer 8o — Autopsy: Seer of Light
9° — Hebrew: The Completed One
10° — Teleios: The Adept, or Perfected One 11° — God-seer, purified from all guile
12° — Jew: Candidate becomes his own God

"... them which say they are Jews, and are not..." Rev. 2:9

The above from *Occult Theocrasy* by Edith Starr Miller, first published 1933; second printing 1968; third printing 1976, by The Christian Book Club of America, Hawthorne CA 90250.

Mackey's Encylopedia of Freemasonry states: "The Eleusinian Mysteries exerted a powerful influence on the secret societies of the Middle Ages, such as the Rosicrucians and the Nights Templar orders, from which came modern Freemasonry. Freemasonry makes use of the Eleusinian Mysteries, specifically in the initiation ceremony of the 3° Master Mason."

Fig. 32 — Is Freemasonry a satanist order? Does it display Satanic symbols like this rock band? 1980s rock band Motley Crue promo shot. See *Scarlet and the Beast,* Vol. 1, chap. 6, "Music and Revolution."

Nikki Sixx standing beneath flag, which contains band's logo — circle around an inverted pentagram. This rendition of the upside-down five-pointed star is a symbol of Satan, known as Baphomet, or Goat of Mendes, the god of lust. More specifically, the inverted star represents the male sex force, whereas the circle represents the female sex force.

Fig. 33 — Legacy of the Pentagram continued.

Lt. Col. Michael Aquino & wife, Lilith, posing beneath inverted pentagram.

Aquino is High priest of Set (Satan). To this day, this symbol remains in Wewelsburg castle, placed there by Nazi SS leader Heinrich Himmler.

Anton Szandor LaVey Former head of California based Church of Satan and author of *The Satanic Bible*. LaVey is wearing upside down pentagram necklace with Nazi lightning bolt shaped like "S" in center. A lighting bolt is a symbol of Satan, as is the upside down star, also known as "Baphomet," the "Goat of Mendes." See *Scarlet and Beast*, Vol. 1, 3rd ed., chapters 16 & 25.

In Luke 10:18, Jesus Christ said, "I beheld Satan as lightning fall from heaven."

Fig. 34 Initiation Certificate of Completion into LaVey's Satanism.
From book, *Mormonism's Temple of Doom*

Be It Known

That having committed to memory and provided sufficient evidence of a working knowledge of Satanic Theology, and undefiled wisdom of the Black Arts, *Christopher P. Syn*, on this 21st day of *March* in the 12th year of Our Lord Satan, has been granted the Degree of the 2nd, that which is called by the name of *Warlock*, and is duly licensed to perform and sustain that which falls within the realm of this Degree as in accord with the tenets and philosophies of

The Church of Satan

having passed before the Council of Nine, Order of the Trapezoid, By all the powers of HELL, So it is Done.

Anton Szandor LaVey
High Priest & Magus of the Black Order

Fig. 35 — Anton LaVey is author of The Satanic Bible.

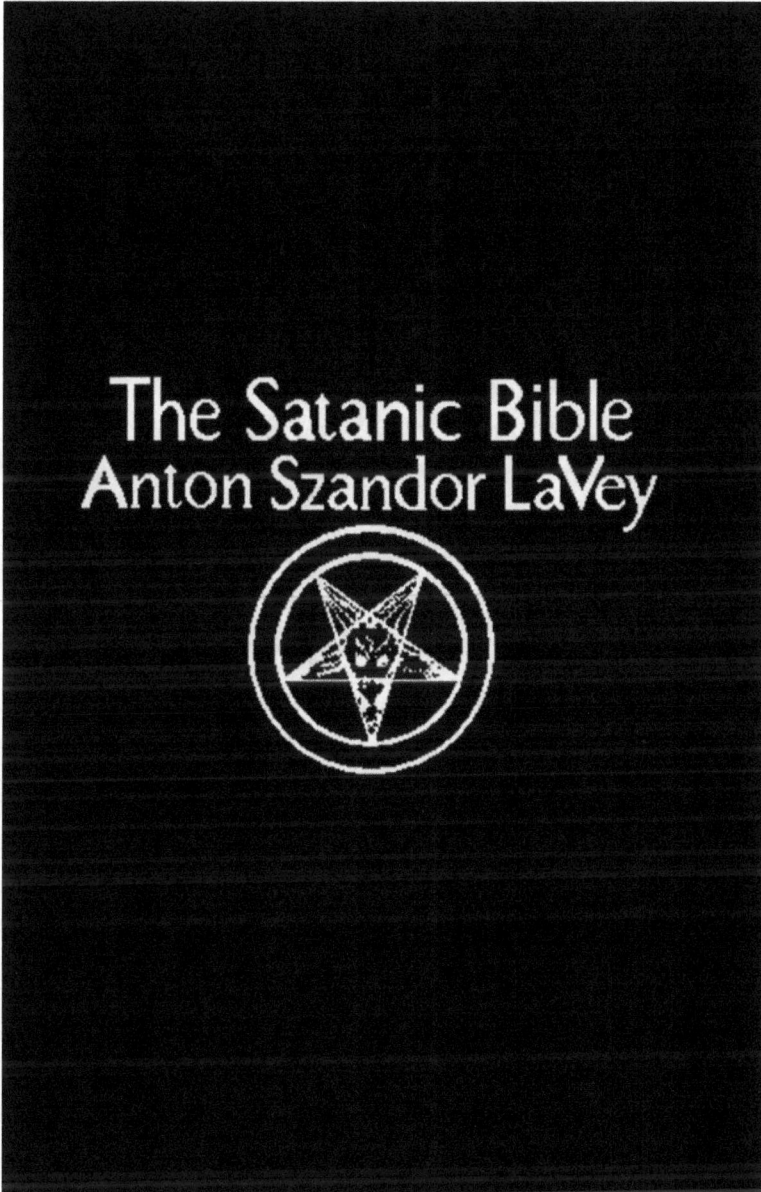

Fig. 36 — An early ritual at the Church of Satan (1966).
See *Scarlet and the Beast,* Vol. 1, 3rd edition, chapters 16&25

The phallic object in the hand of the woman on the right is an aspergillum, or holy water sprinkler. The man holding the skull, Forrest Satterfield, was the first man to be wed by the Church of Satan in 1966 — long before the publicized satanic wedding of Judith Case and John Raymond.

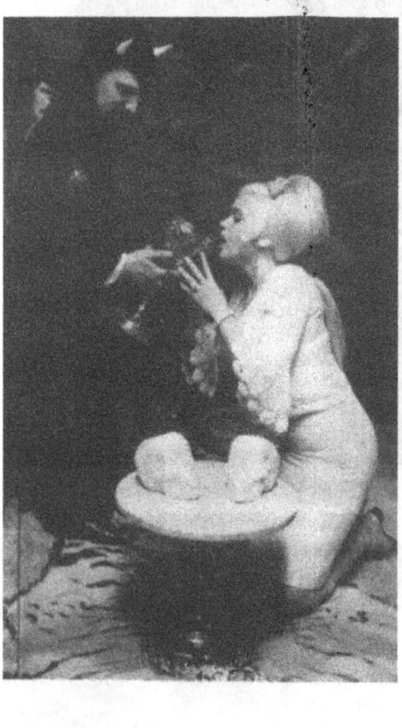

Fig. 37 — Jane Mansfield was a member of the Church of Satan.

Jane Mansfield (1933-1967)

Film actress, born Vera Jayne Palmer in Bryn Mawr, PA. One year before her tragic death in an automobile accident, Mansfield was initiated into the Church of Satan at her Pink Palace home in Hollywood. The skull and chalice above were owned by Jayne and used by her in the Satanic rites she regularly practiced during the year preceding her tragic death.

Fig. 38 — Underground filmmaker, author of Hollywood Babylon, Crowley disciple, and with Anton Szandor LaVey, founding member of the Church of Satan. See *Scarlet and the Beast*, Vol. 3, chapter 7.

Kenneth Anger (?)

During the 1980s, not only were Rock stars fascinated with Masonic symbols on their album covers, Masonic doctrine sung in their lyrics, and Masonic initiation ceremonies staged in their theatrics, many were themselves Freemasons. For example, Jimmy Page, lead guitarist for Led Zeppelin, in the early 1970s was initiated into the English Masonic order called the Hermetic Order of the Golden Dawn by Freemason Kenneth Anger. Anger was Crowley's disciple. Crowley, until his death in 1947, was Grand Master of both the Golden Dawn and the O.T.O.

Fig. 39 — The Church of Satan high priest, Anton LaVey (?) in the company of onetime follower, Sammy Davis, Jr. (1925-1990) See *Scarlet and the Beast*, Vol. 1, chap. 16 and Vol. 3, chap. 7.

Fig. 40 — Martin Lamers (?), High Priest of the Church of Satan in Amsterdam, Netherlands, flashing the satanic "sign of the horns."

Fig. 41 — Robert DeGrimston (?), founder of The Process Church of the Final Judgement. This photo was taken after DeGrimston had decided he was Jesus, as can be seen by the carefully cultivated likeness.
See Process Church in *Scarlet and the Beast*, Vol. 1, 3rd edition, chap. 17.

Fig. 42 — 1988 aray of heavy metal rock albums featuring Satanic themes by MOTLEY CRE. See *Scarlet and the Beast*, Vol. 1, 3rd ed, chaps. 6 & 16.

Fig. 43 — Richard Ramirez (?) "Night Stalker" killer in California. Responsible for 16 ritual murders. Captured Sept. 2, 1985. After his arraignment for murder, as he was led from the court room, he held up his palm to display a satanic pentagram he had drawn, and yelled, "Hail Satan!" (See *Scarlet and the Beast*, Volume 1, 3rd edition, chapter 16).

Fig. 44 — Is Freemasonry a Satanic institution? Masonry displays the same symbols as the Church of Satan. Upside down star is called Baphomet, an occult symbol of Satan. It is also the symbol of the Eastern Star — lodge for wives of Masons. In witchcraft the inverted pentagram has one use only — to call up the power of Satan! See *S&B*, V1, ch. 15&19.

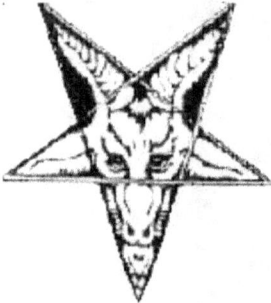

◄ **BAPHOMET** ►
symbol of
Satan

BAPHOMET IS KNOWN
AS HERMAPHRODITIC
GOAT OF MENDES

GOAT OF MENDES IS
THE "GOD OF LUST"

Mark of
BAPHOMET
On cap to left is
upright "mark" of
BAPHOMET

PAST SOVEREIGN GRAND
COMMANDER of FREEMASONRY
and MEMBER of LUCIFER TRUST
33' HENRY C. CLAUSEN
1905-1993

SOVEREIGN PONTIFF
OF UNIVERSAL
FREEMASONRY
33° GEN. ALBERT PIKE
1809-1891

Directly below is symbol of Baphomet on 1991 letterhead of the Sovereign Grand Commander. C. Fred Kleinknecht, head of Freemasonry S.J.

SOVEREIGN
GRAND
COMMANDER
SUPREME
COUNCIL
33°

Fig. 45 — God of the Holy Bible has always protected a righteous nation. When Israel shared her temple with pagan gods, God sent them into captivity.

Zephaniah 3:4-5 — "Her prophets are light and treacherous persons: her priests have polluted the sanctuary, they have done violence to the law. The just Lord is in the midst thereof; he will not do iniquity: every morning doth he bring his judgment to light, he faileth not; but the unjust knoweth no shame." See Appendix 16 in *S&B*, Vol.1, 3rd ed.

Fig. 46 — Obelisk, also called "Ashtoreth Pole" dating beyond 1000 B.C., is the uncircumsized reproductive organ of Baal. Ashtoreth, mistress of Baal, was an ancient Semitic goddess identified with the Phoenician Astarte.

Figs. 47 & 48 — **Point Within the Circle** and the **Washington Monument** are two forms of the ANKH (EYE). Both are phallic symbols. The Point represents the male reproductive organ and the Circle represents the female reproductive organ.

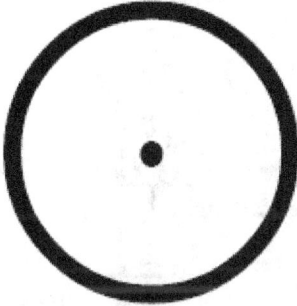

See *S&B*, Vol. 1, chaps. 4, 10, 30.

The Washington Monument is designed to represent the Point within the Circle. At the base of the monument is a circular drive. If it were possible to view the Monument from an airplane directly above, the monument within the circular drive would look identical to the point within the circle. (See figure 49 this section).

Freemason Robert Mills (1781-1855) of South Carolina was the architect called to Washington, DC in 1830 to design several buildings, one of which was the Washington Monument. (*10,000 Famous Freemasons* by 33° William Denslow).

Dr. Cathy Burns, in *Masonic and Occult Symbols Illustrated*, quotes a former witch: "The obelisk is a long pointed four-sided shaft, the uppermost portion of which forms a pyramid. The word 'obelisk' literally means 'Baal's Shaft' or Baal's organ of reproduction."

More specifically, the pyramid atop the shaft represents Baal's *uncircumcised* reproductive organ, as recognized by the pagan Ashtoreth Pole (Figs. 46-47), to which God forbade the Jews bow down and worship.

Fig. 49 — "A curious piece of the Masonic conspiracy puzzle in the founding of America is the actual street layout for our Capital city, Washington, D.C. Actually it's as much the audacity of the thing as the conspiratorial nature of it. You see, the city was laid out in the form of key Masonic Symbols, the Square, the Compass, the Rule and the Pentagram." *Freemasonry: Satan's Door to America?*, by J. Edward Decker. (see PB.S1.F32-45 & 69-78).

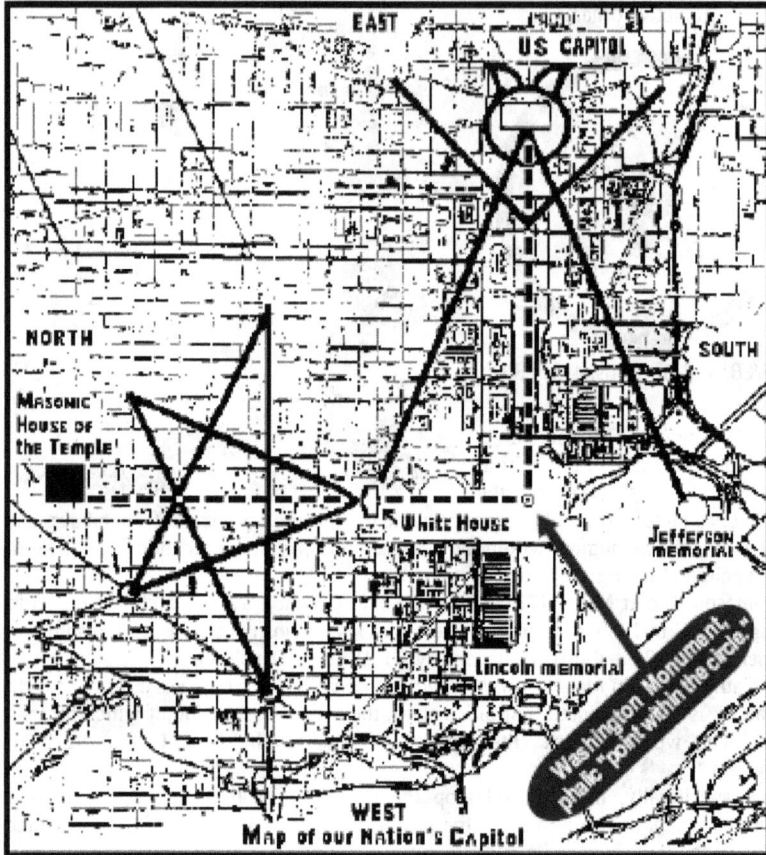

Map of our Nation's Capitol

"Take any good street map of downtown Washington, D.C. and find the Capitol Building. Facing the Capitol from the Mall and using the Capitol as the head or top of the Compass, the left leg is represented by Pennsylvania Ave. and the right leg, Maryland Ave. The Square is found in the usual Masonic position with the intersection of Canal St. and Louisiana Ave. The left leg of the Compass stands on the White House and the right leg stands on the Jefferson Memorial. The circle drive and short streets behind the Capitol form the head and ears of what Satanists call the Goat Of Mendes, or Goat's head.

"On top of the White House is an inverted 5 pointed star, or Pentagram. The point is facing South in true occult fashion. It sits within the intersections of Connecticut and Vermont Avenues north to Dupont and Logan Circles, with Rhode Island and Massachusetts going to Washinton Circle to the West and Mt. Vernon Square on the East.

"The center of the Pentagram is 16th St. where, thirteen blocks due north of the very center of the White House, the Masonic House of the Temple sits at the top of this occult iceberg.

"The Washington Monument stands in perfect line to the intersecting point of the form of the Masonic square, stretching from the House of the Temple to the Capitol building. Within the Hypotenuse of that right traiangle sit many of the headquarter buildings for the most powerful departments of government, such as the Justice Dept. U.S. Senate and the Internal Revenue Service.

"Every key Federal building from the White House to the Capitol Building has had a cornerstone laid in a Masonic ritual and had specific Masonic paraphernalia placed in each one.

"The cornerstones of all these buildings have been laid in Masonic ritual, dedicated to the demonic god of Masonry, Jao-Bul-On. That is the secret name of the Masonic god, the 'Lost Word' in the rite of the Royal Arch degree. 'JAO' is the Greek name for the god of the Gnostics, Laidabaoth or Lao. 'BUL' is a rendering of the name, Ba'al, and 'ON' is the Babylonian name of Osiris.

"The Washington Monument actually represents the Phalic Principle upon which Speculative Masonry is based. From above, the monument and its circular drive form the esoteric 'Masonic Point within a Circle.' The Reflecting Pool bears its shadowed image, with the illusion duplicated in the Lincoln Memorial.

"Strange? Not if you understand the occult principles involved. The respected Masonic author and authority, Albert Mackey states in *Mackey's Masonic Ritualist* (pp. 62-63): 'The point within a circle is an interesting and important symbol in Freemasonry... The symbol is a beautiful but somewhat abstruse allusion to...sun-worship and introduces us for the first time to that modification of it known among the ancients as the Phallus. The Phallus was an imitation of the male generative organ. It was represented usually by a column, which was surrounded by a circle at its base, intended for the cteis, or female generative organ. This union of the Phallus and the cteis, which is well represented by the point within the circle, was intended by the ancients as a type of the prolific powers of nature, which they worshipped under the united form of the active or male principle and the passive or female principle.'"

Fig. 50 — Found in Scotland (upper right) is Knights Templar splayed cross with octagonal pattern surrounding cross. Octagon is a phallic symbol.

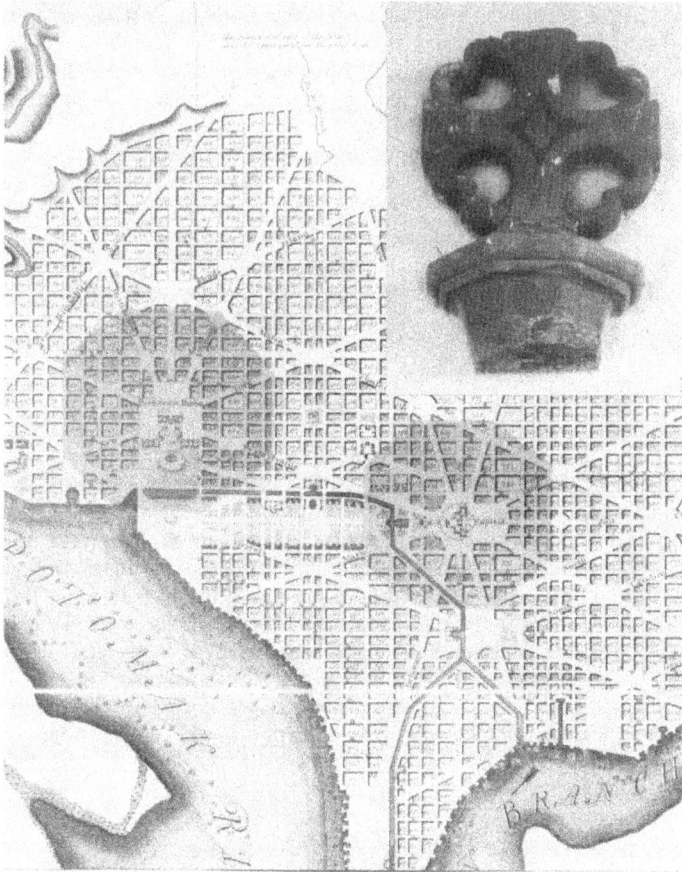

Map of the city of Washington, DC, 1792, incorporating modifications introduced by Washington and Jefferson. Of specific importance are the octagonal patterns of the Knights Templar centered upon the White House and the Capital Building, which carries a prophetic, yet sinister apocalyptic meaning discussed in *Scarlet and the Beast*, Vol. 1, chap. 30. Inset is a Templar cross with an octagon pattern found in Garway, Herefordshire, near the Welsh border. Figure 51 is another rendition of the same.

Fig. 51 — Jewel of 33rd degree. Its meaning is the same as all Eastern Religions. See next 5 pages, Figs. 52-60. Also see *Scarlet and the Beast,* Vol. 1, 3rd edition; chapters 6, 10, 18, 19, 24, 25, 28, 30.

Cross behind the Jewel is another form of the Templar splayed cross. Three interlaced triangles represent three planes of occult creation in all pagan religions — Heaven, Earth and Hell (see Figs. 52-60). Snake biting its own tail is symbolic of the occult god (zero), which is the serpent religion of evolution (reincarnation in Eastern religions). Latin words in the circle translate "Order Out of Chaos," representing the scientific "confusion of tongues" at Babylon by Almighty God, and Freemasonry's plan to resurrect the Babylonian system to "scientific order." Crossed swords also have a dual meaning. First, the extended hand of fellowship at one point represents a peaceful return to the Babylonian religion. The sharp point on the second sword represents the military means by which the Babylonian system will be restored, should the peaceful means fail. The two-headed eagle in the center looking east and west represents the universal Masonic revival in the West of ancient Roman democracy in the East.

Figures 52-60 — Eastern religions, from which Freemasonry is patterned, have 33 degrees or steps to reach heaven. In the doctrine of reincarnation, the individual is stationed somewhere in heaven, earth or hell. When he dies and is reborn (so the doctrine goes), he will either advance in degrees or regress, depending upon his good works.

In the book *Father of Lies*, Warren Weston illustrates how Freemasonry is patterned after the false religions, which religions are condemned by the God of the Bible.

Fig. 52

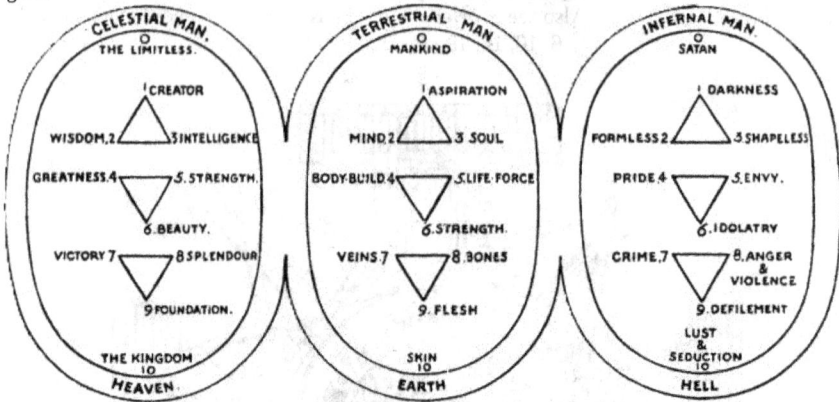

TRIPLE HENDEKAGLYPH

Fig. 53

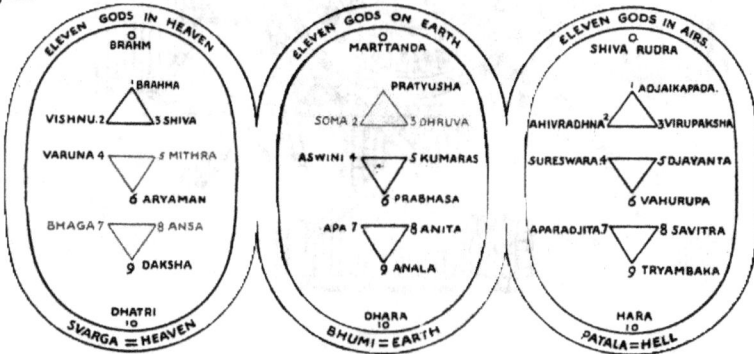

BRAHMINISM (The Three Worlds)

Fig. 54

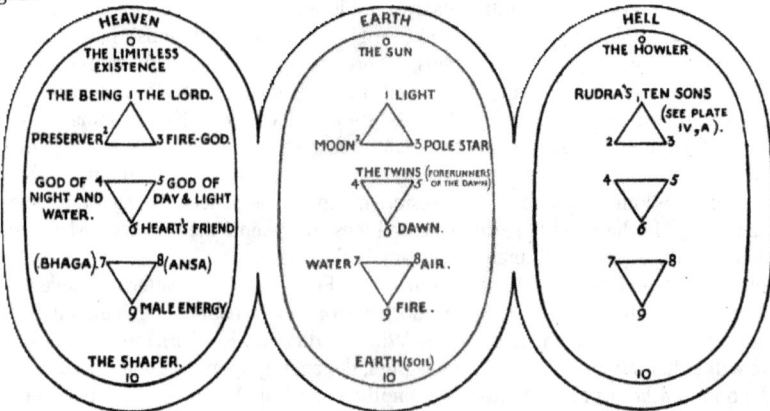

BRAHMINISM (English Terms)

Fig. 55

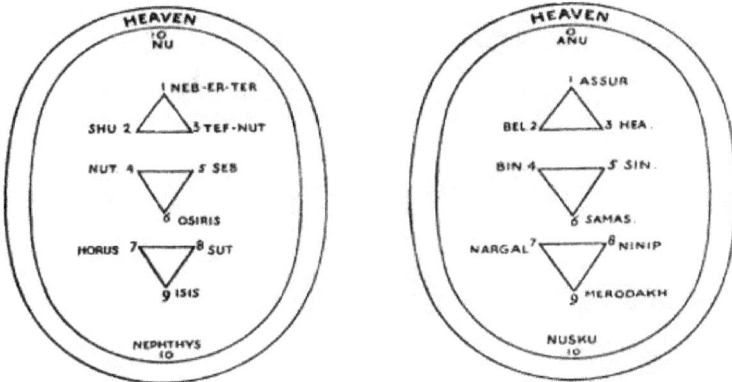

EGYPTIAN THEOGONY ASSYRIAN & BABYLONIAN THEOGONY

Fig. 56

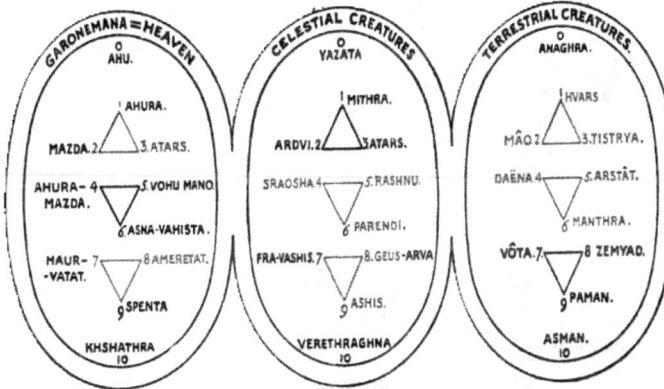

ZOROASTRIANISM

Fig. 57

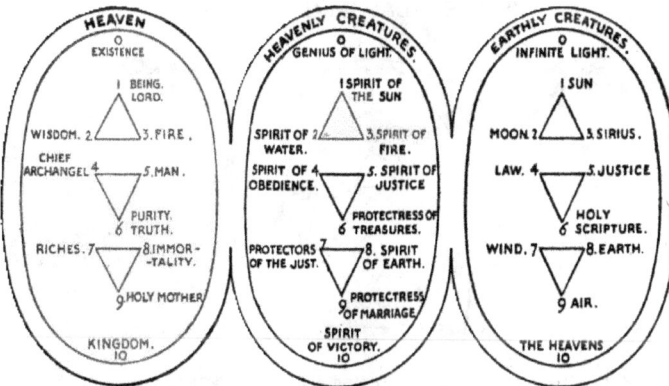

ZOROASTRIANISM (English Terms)

Fig. 58

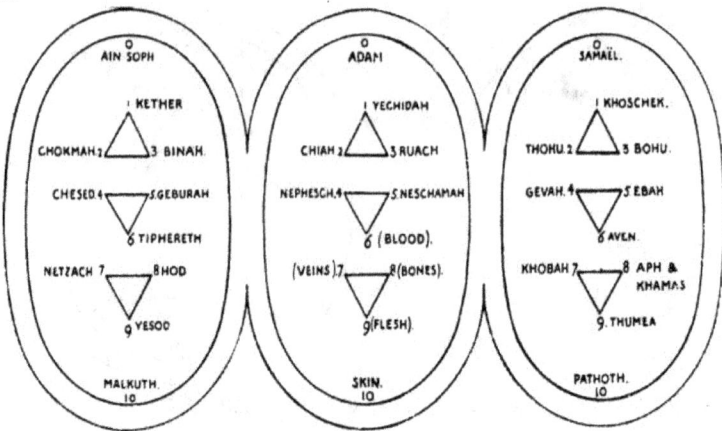

THE KABBALAH Triple Hendhendekaglyph

Fig. 59

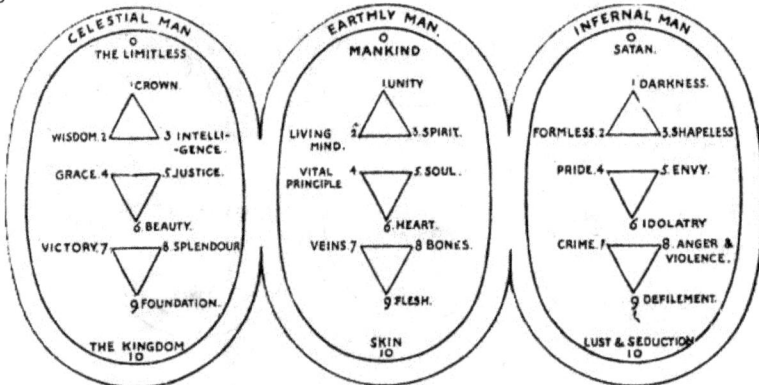

THE KABBALAH (English Terms)

Fig. 60

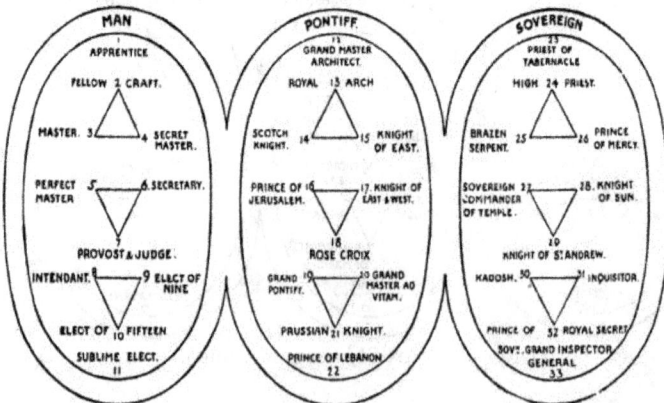

THE SCOTTISH RITE Names of Degrees

Fig. 61. Six-pointed star represents the balance of good and evil. Likewise the Chinese yin and yang and the right and left handed Hindu swastika.
See *hexagram, swastika*, in index of *Scarlet and the Beast, Vol. 1, 3rd ed.*

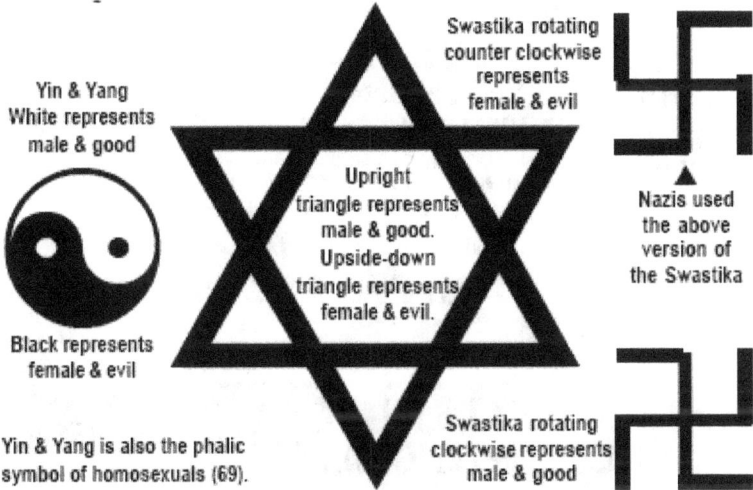

Swastika rotating counter clockwise represents female & evil

Yin & Yang
White represents male & good

Upright triangle represents male & good.
Upside-down triangle represents female & evil.

Nazis used the above version of the Swastika

Black represents female & evil

Yin & Yang is also the phalic symbol of homosexuals (69).

Swastika rotating clockwise represents male & good

Fig. 62 — Tuesday, Dec. 10, 1946

LATE Edition

JERUSALEM
TUESDAY, DEC. 10, 1946

PRICE:
VOL. XXI.

THE PALESTINE POST

HEAD OUT LS

nch-mor-
Govern-
iz stated
strict of
vernment

WEIZMANN OPENS FIRST POST-WAR ZIONIST CONGRESS
NATIONAL HOME MUST BECOME JEWISH STATE
WHITE PAPER DIRECTLY RESPONSIBLE FOR PALESTINE TROUBLES

Wednesday, July 9, 1947

LATE Edition

JERUSALEM
Wednesday, July 9, 1947

PRICE 20 MILS
VOL. XXII. No. 6453

THE PALESTINE POST

DR. WEIZMANN URGES UNSCOP TO PRESS FOR PARTITION

DOCUMENTS

G.O.C.
ACT
SE

Confirm
death se

Monday, Sept. 1, 1947

THE PALESTINE POST

PRICE 30 MILS
VOL. XXII. No. 6439

JERUSALEM
MONDAY, SEPT. 1, 1947

UNSCOP MAJORITY RECOMMENDS ECONOMIC UNION OF ARAB STATE, JEWISH STATE and CITY OF JERUSALEM

INDEPENDENCE IN TWO YEARS; U.N. HELP FOR BRITAIN DURING TRANSITION; 6,250 IMMIGRANTS MONTHLY; EAST GALILEE, COASTAL PLAIN, AND NEGEV FOR JEWS; TWO FREE CORRIDORS

Monday, Sept. 28, 1947

JACOB ROSE
General Agent for
UNITED STATES LINES
Travel and Shipping
Correspondent for
THE AMERICAN EXPRESS
COMPANY INC.

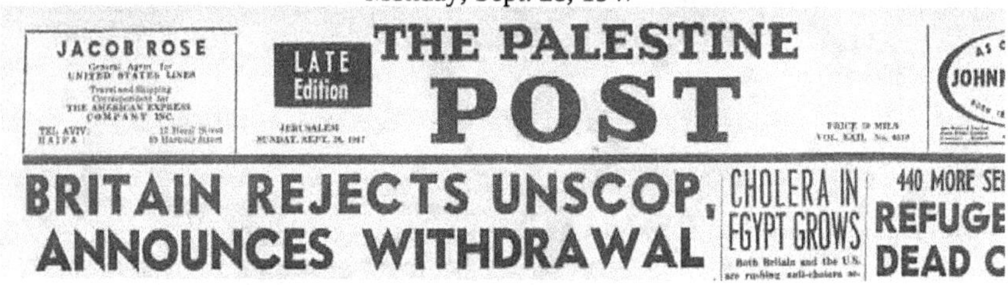

LATE Edition

THE PALESTINE POST

PRICE 30 MILS
VOL. XXII. No. 6459

JERUSALEM
SUNDAY, SEPT. 28, 1947

BRITAIN REJECTS UNSCOP, ANNOUNCES WITHDRAWAL

CHOLERA IN EGYPT GROWS
Both Britain and the U.S. are rushing anti-cholera se-

440 MORE SE
REFUGE
DEAD C

Fig. 63 — Tuesday, Oct. 14, 1947

THE PALESTINE POST

JERUSALEM
TUESDAY, OCT. 14, 1947

PRICE 30 MILS
VOL. XXII. No. 6351

ATID NAVIGATION Co. Ltd.

RUSSIA SUPPORTS JEWISH STATE

LAKE SUCCESS, Monday (Reuter) — The Jews cannot be denied the right to create their own State in Palestine, M. S. K. Tsarapkin, of Russia, told the United Nations Palestine Committee tonight. Russia supported in principle the Majority recommendations of the United Nations Committee on Palestine — that the country should be partitioned between Arabs and Jews.

Another Month to Give Up

Iraq Protests, US Mission Trip Off

BAGHDAD, Monday (Reuter) — The official visit of the U.S. Congressional Committee to Baghdad has been called today because of a protest to the Iraqi Government and people against the American discrimin

Yishuv Prepares For Self-Defence

NO IMMEDIATE ARAB THREAT

BRITAIN'S NOTE TO SYRIAN GOVT

Sunday, Nov. 30, 1947

TEL AVIV
3 PRINCESS
MARY AVE.
JERUSALEM

CARL MARX
Lighting, Heating, Cooking, Refrigeration

THE PALESTINE POST

JERUSALEM
SUNDAY, NOV. 30, 1947

PRICE
VOL. XX

PARTITION APPROVED BY MORE THAN 2/3; 33 TO 13

Friday, March 26, 1948

THE PALESTINE 6 PAGES

POST

JERUSALEM

ELECTRICAL

J. Lifshits

ATTLEE JUSTIFIES COMMUNIST PURGE ON WAR GROUNDS
"Secrets Must Be Preserved"

Promises
No General

Negev Road Scoured

Snow on Their Periscopes?

Communications Maintained

TRUMAN REAFFIRMS TWO STATE PLAN WITH TEMPORARY TRUSTEE

WANTS TRUSTEESHIP TO FILL VACUUM LEFT BY BRITISH WITHDRAWAL

Sunday, May 16, 1948

THE PALESTINE

POST

CARL MARX

STATE OF ISRAEL IS BORN

Fig. 64 — Two Masonic Brothers — one Gentile, one Jewish. Read the part each played in the Masonic conspiracy. *Scarlet and the Beast*, Vol. I, 3rd edition, chapters 22, 24 and 27. See meaning of hexagram, Figs. 65-73. Truman is holding a Torah, a hand-written scroll of the five books of Moses in Hebrew, that Weizmann has given him. Notice the 6-pointed star on cover of the Torah.

Gentile Freemasonry claims to be Jewish. In the Book of Revelation, where the Apostle John is writing to the seven churches, we read Christ's words in chapter 2, verse 9, "I know the blasphemy of them which say they are Jews, and are not, but are the synagogue of Satan." (see Section 1, Fig. 29).

33° Harry Truman
1884-1992

33° Chaim Weizman
1874-1952

Fig. 65 — Six-pointed star is the symbol of Zionism.
See *Scarlet and the Beast*; Vol. 1; 3rd Edition; Chapter 6-7, 25.

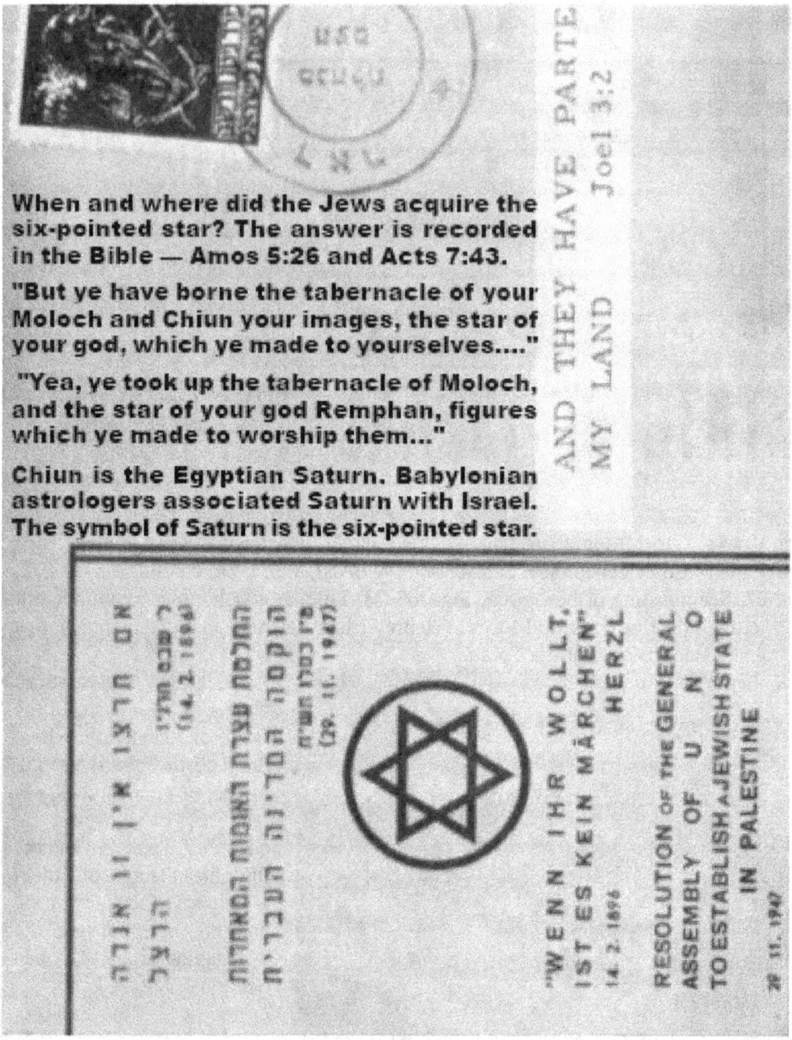
When and where did the Jews acquire the six-pointed star? The answer is recorded in the Bible — Amos 5:26 and Acts 7:43.
"But ye have borne the tabernacle of your Moloch and Chiun your images, the star of your god, which ye made to yourselves...."
"Yea, ye took up the tabernacle of Moloch, and the star of your god Remphan, figures which ye made to worship them..."
Chiun is the Egyptian Saturn. Babylonian astrologers associated Saturn with Israel. The symbol of Saturn is the six-pointed star.
AND THEY HAVE PARTE
MY LAND
Joel 3:2
"WENN IHR WOLLT, IST ES KEIN MÄRCHEN"
HERZL
RESOLUTION OF THE GENERAL ASSEMBLY OF U N O TO ESTABLISH A JEWISH STATE IN PALESTINE

Fig. 66 — When Israel was reborn in 1948 on May 14/15, (date differs depending upon who you read), it had already been prophesied in Isaiah 66:8. "Who hath heard such a thing? who hath seen such things? Shall the earth be made to bring forth in one day? or shall a nation be born at once? for as soon as Zion travailed, she brought forth her children." Ironically, this Scripture uses the name Zion, by which the Diaspora had been known since 1897. Zion travailed during the Nazi holocaust, as prophesied above. See *Scarlet and the Beast*; Vol. 1; 3rd Edition; Chapter 25.

May 14, 1948
Israel was reborn
in one day

Jews were persecuted under the name Zion. After World War II, Jews petitioned the United Nations to permit them to establish a new nation in their ancient homeland and name it Zion. By one vote the name Zion was denied, and as prophesied in Isaiah 66:8, Israel was reborn in one day.

Fig. 67 — Figure of hermit from tarot taken from inside cover of Led Zeppelin album. Notice hexagram (6-pointed star) in lantern. The hexagram comes from tantric Hinduism. "Hex" means "to bewitch." In the occult the 6-pointed star is called LUCIFER. See chap. 6 and Index of *S&B*, V1; 3rd ed.

Figure 68 — Caption on ribbon below reads: "The Grand Conclave of Masonic Knights Templar in England and Wales." Notice the interwoven six-pointed star of the Priory of Sion (hexagram), original founders of the Knights Templar in the year 1018 A.D.

Figure 69 — Mosaic of six-pointed star on Masonic Lodge floor

FLOOR OF THE LODGE

Figure 70 — Evolution of Square and Compass into the six-pointed star.

Square and Compass.

A. Square of ninety degrees.

B. Square progressed to sixty degrees.

C. Third side added making it an equilateral triangle, the symbol of deity.

D. Interlaced six-pointed star, symbol of the perfect union of God and man.

E. Third side added, making it an equilateral triangle (pointing upward), symbol of the perfect man.

F. Compasses.

Figure 71 — Square and Compass with the letter "G." Arm and Hammer shaped like a "G." Hammer and Sickle shaped like an upside down "G." All these symbols of labor represent the "works" religion of Freemasonry as well as the human reproduction action of male and female.

BRITISH ARM & HAMMER
FORM THE LETTER "G"

33RD DEGREE MASON ARMAND
HAMMER OWNED STOCK IN THIS
COMPANY.
See Section 7, Figure 19

FRENCH MASONRY
&
COMMUNISM
Hammer & Cycle form upside
down "G" which represents the
negation of God, or atheism.

AMERICAN "G"
Said to represent God.
Esoterically it represents
GNOSIS (knowledge), knowledge
of good & evil, which Satan first
offered man at the Garden of Eden.

Figures 72-73 — Square & Compass are also sex force symbols, which represent both male & female. See Scarlet and the Beast, Vol. 1, chs. 5-7

Masonic Square and Compass and the Hexagram both represent the "sex force." The square and the black upside down triangle represent the female, whereas the compass and the upright triangle represent the male. Knowing this, how can a Christian join Masonry and wear these symbols?

Figure 74-75 — Below: Masonic Square & Compass sex force in action.

Notice erotic sex positions carved into Hindu Kandariya Mahadev temple at Khujarao, India are identical to the shape of the Masonic Square & Compass, which Freemasonry claims represents male and female intercourse positions. The "god" of pagan religions is the "sex force."
(Photos from Sex in History, Tannahill, 1980).

Figure 76 — Cover of Masonic Bible — King James Version. Notice prominent position of Square & Compass — the blasphemous sex force.

Figure 77 — King James Version of Bible is placed on Masonic altar in all so-called Christian Lodges. Notice sex-force on open Bible.

LET THERE BE LIGHT

Figure 78 — Masonic Bible — Page for posting initiation dates, with sex force radiating above it.

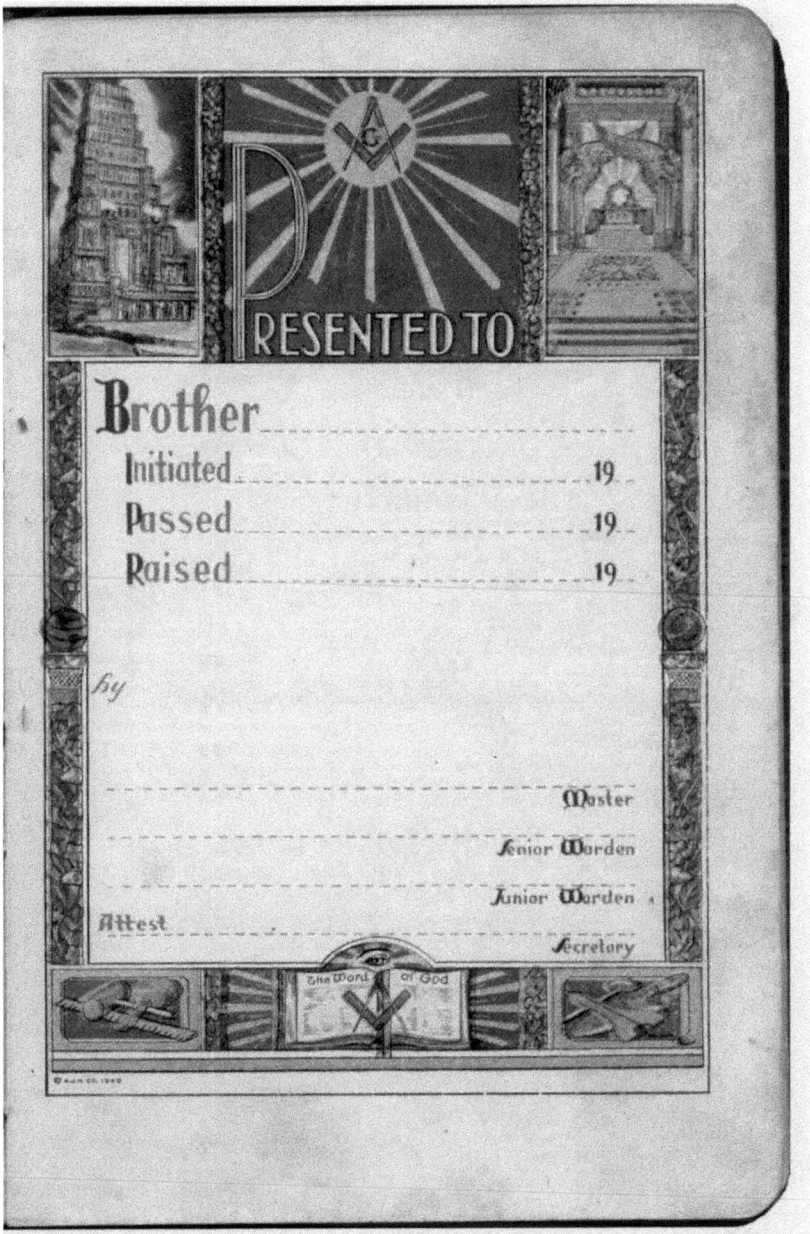

Figure 79 — Masonic Bible — Under "The Masonic Belief" notice lax attitude toward prayer
"Prayer with God is helpful."

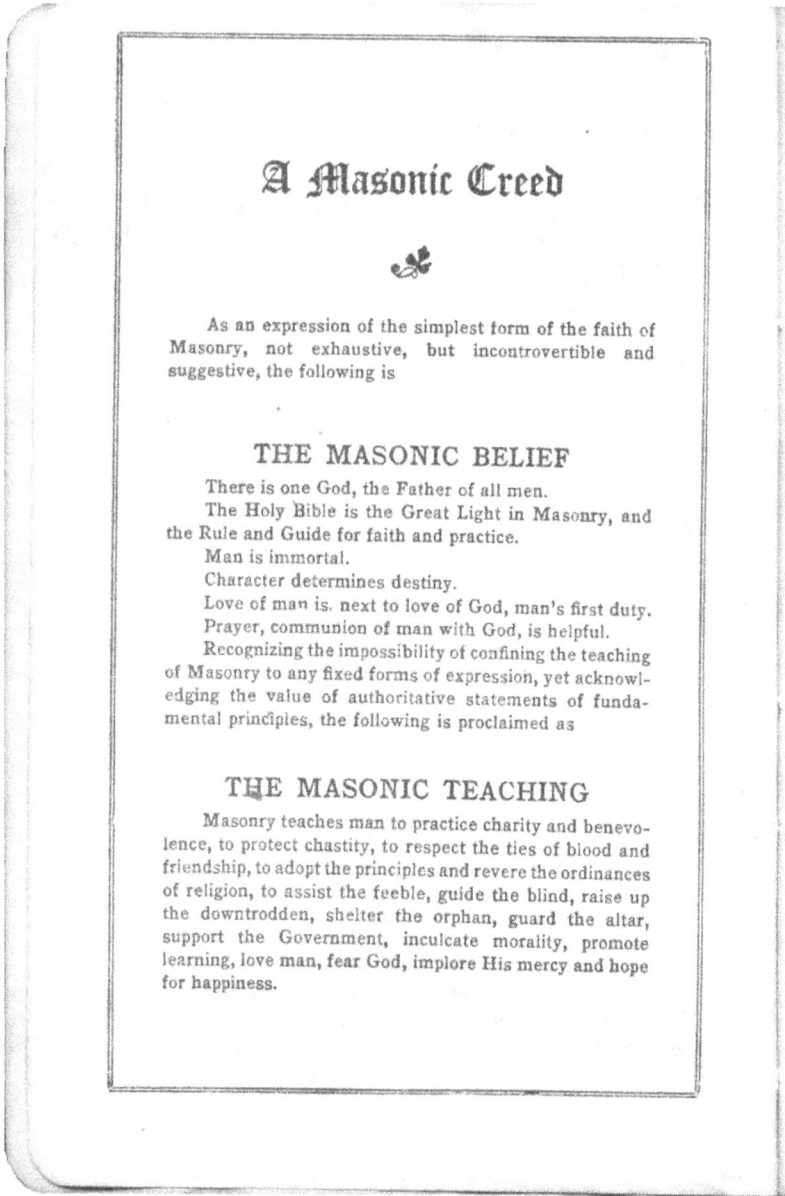

A Masonic Creed

As an expression of the simplest form of the faith of Masonry, not exhaustive, but incontrovertible and suggestive, the following is

THE MASONIC BELIEF

There is one God, the Father of all men.

The Holy Bible is the Great Light in Masonry, and the Rule and Guide for faith and practice.

Man is immortal.

Character determines destiny.

Love of man is, next to love of God, man's first duty.

Prayer, communion of man with God, is helpful.

Recognizing the impossibility of confining the teaching of Masonry to any fixed forms of expression, yet acknowledging the value of authoritative statements of fundamental principles, the following is proclaimed as

THE MASONIC TEACHING

Masonry teaches man to practice charity and benevolence, to protect chastity, to respect the ties of blood and friendship, to adopt the principles and revere the ordinances of religion, to assist the feeble, guide the blind, raise up the downtrodden, shelter the orphan, guard the altar, support the Government, inculcate morality, promote learning, love man, fear God, implore His mercy and hope for happiness.

Figure 80 — Masonic Bible — Freemasonry teaches its initiates that Masons built Solomon's Temple (see bottom of page).

THE BIBLE AND KING SOLOMON'S TEMPLE IN MASONRY

The traditions and romance of King Solomon's Temple are of great interest to everyone who reads the Bible. They are of transcendent importance to Masons. The Temple is the outstanding symbol in Masonry, and the legendary story of the building of the Temple is the fundamental basis of the Masonic rule and guide for conduct in life.

The skill of many artists and architects has gone into Dr. Kelchner's restoration of King Solomon's Temple and Citadel. The cream of Masonic historical and philosophical writing has been drawn upon for his description of the Temple and its relation to Masonic ritual.

ACKNOWLEDGMENT

To the Editor of the Masonic Outlook and to the Librarian of the Board of General Activities we give unstinted praise and thanks for their assistance in setting forth the relation of King Solomon's Temple to Masonry. Their care and thoughtfulness have added immeasurably to the Masonic usefulness of the work.

Here we present to Masons, in a Bible commemorative of their initiation, a printed compendium of their Craft. We lay emphatic stress on the divine principles of the Fraternity, on its religious backgrounds, and on the irrevocable place of the Bible as the foundation of Masonry.

THE PUBLISHER.

HIRAM OF ABIF   KING SOLOMON
HIRAM OF TYRE

THE BUILDERS OF KING SOLOMON'S TEMPLE

For the construction of King Solomon's Temple,
3 Grand Master Masons,
3,600 Master Masons,
80,000 Fellowcraft Masons
and 70,000 Entered Apprentice Masons were employed.

Freemasonry claims that Masons ("carpenters") built Solomon's Temple. See S&B, 3rd ed. chp. 28, p.688

Fig. 81 — Front cover Freemasonry's *New Age Magazine,* April, 1985. Rose entwined around cross is Rosicrucian phallic symbol. Has same phallic meaning as Square & Compass, Figs. 45-49.
See *S&B*, V.1; 3rd ed., ch. 18-19.

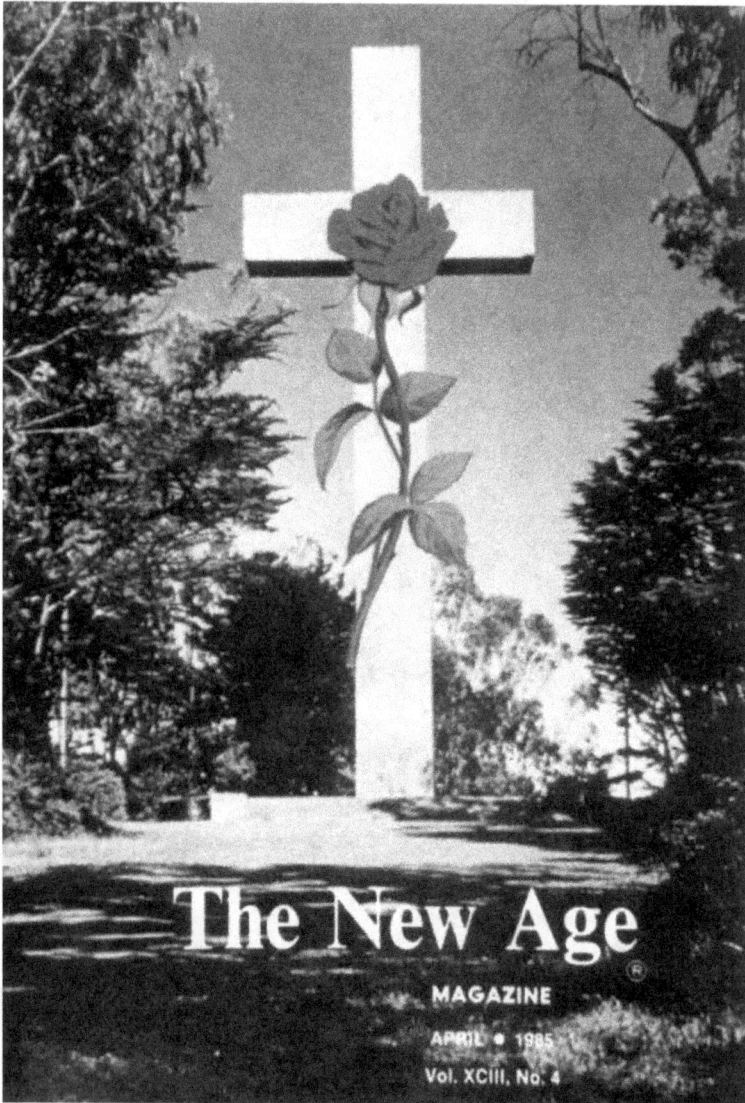

After Paul Fisher exposed the anti-Christian bias of Freemasonry's *New Age Magazine* in his book *Behind the Lodge Door* (1988), the Scottish Rite Southern Jurisdiction changed the name to *Scottish Rite Journal.*

Figure 82 — Front cover of Freemasonry's *Scottish Rite Journal*, March 1991 issue. Name was changed after Paul Fisher exposed Freemasonry as the force behind the New Age Movement.

On next page read Masonic credentials of 33° Dr. Norman Vincent Peale (1898-1993). Also see *Scarlet and the Beast*, Vol. 1, chap. 10.

33° **Dr. Norman Vincent Peale** (1898-1993)

Christian Reformed pastor and writer. Born in Bowersville, OH. Graduate of Ohio Wesleyan U. in 1920; Boston U. in 1924; Syracuse U. in 1931; Duke U. in 1938. Ordained Methodist Episcopal minister in 1922. For next ten years held pastorates at Berkeley RI, Brooklyn NY and Syracuse NY, after which he began his long ministry at Marble Collegiate Reformed Church, NYC, 1932-84. Next door he established a psychiatric clinic called the American Foundation of Religion and Psychiatry. He wrote the best seller, *The Power of Positive Thinking* (1952), and was much in demand as a lecturer. Dr. Peale was president of the National Temperance Society; a lecturer on public affairs and personal effectiveness; and recipient of Freedom Foundation Award. On Feb. 24, 1991, Dr. Peale spoke to the congregation at Robert Schuller's Crystal Cathedral in California. Peale said, "Jesus Christ, Buddha and Krishna are examples of great philosophers who taught how to use mind power."

Dr. Peale had a regular question and answer column in *Look Magazine*. He was editor of *Guidepost,* an inspirational magazine. At a 1980s Christian writer's convention in Dallas TX, Dina Donahue, contributing editor of *Guidepost,* made this comment from the podium: "If you want to write for *Guidepost,* we have certain requirements concerning articles about Jesus Christ. You must never mention Jesus as Mediator between God and man. Nor can Christ be portrayed as the only Truth, as God incarnate, the only means for salvation, or the only way to God the Father. Your article can mention Jesus in His historical position as a prophet and philosopher. Guidepost is an interfaith magazine. Dr. Peale does not want to offend those who are not Christians."

Dr. Peal was a member of Midwood Lodge No. 1062, Brooklyn NY; Grand Chaplain of the Grand Lodge of New York (1949-51); and a 33° AASR Mason (NJ). As member of the Ancient Arabic Order of the Mystic Shrine, he was a life member of Crescent Shrine Temple, Trenton NJ. He was also Past Imperial Grand Chaplain of the Shrine.

The Shrine was founded for the purpose of uniting both the York and Scottish Rites of Freemasonry. The first Shriner Temple in America (1872) was named Gotham. It was changed to Mecca Temple when it was decided that all Shrine Temples should have Arabic or Egyptian titles.

On the altar in every Shrine Temple is the Koran. Every candidate for initiation must kneel before the altar and Koran, taking the same oath that Dr. Norman Vicent Peale took: "...binding myself under a no less penalty than that of having my eyeballs pierced to the center with a sharp, three-edged blade... So help me, Allah, the God of Arab, Moslem and Mohammedan, the God of our fathers." (see Fig. 27-28, this section).

Fig. 83 — Believe it or not, a European Female Mason! See *Scarlet and the Beast,* Vol. 1; 3rd edition; chaps. 16-18, 25, 30. Also Figures 84-88.

Helena Petrovna Blavatsky (1831-1891)

In 1848, Helena P. Hahn of Russia married Blavatsky, a Russian military officer and provincial governor, but left him after several months to begin a series of international travels. For 20 years she visited Istanbul, Cairo, Paris, Rome, New Orleans, Tokyo, and Calcutta. She claimed to have spent seven years in Tibet studying under Hindu Mahatmas. In 1875 she founded the Theosophical Society. In 1877 she wrote the book *Isis Unveiled*, which became the text-book of Theosophists. This expression of fundamental Theosophy strove to fuse Vedantic (Hindu) thought and Egyptian serpent worship, which she attributed to her Tibetan masters. (source: *Ency. Britannica*). In *Freemasonry Universal*, Volume V, part 2, "Autumn Equinox," 1929, we read, "Madame Blavatsky's Masonic [sic] certificate in the Ancient and Primitive Rite of Masonry was issued in the year 1877." Her Masonic credentials are also confirmed in *Mackey's Encyclopedia of Freemasonry*. Before joining Freemasonry, Madam Blavatsky was already a Luciferian. In 1856 she was initiated into Grand Orient Carbonary (Italian Freemasonry) by Giuseppe Mazzini.

Blatvatsky did more than publish her revolutionary ideals; she lived them. In 1866 she joined 33rd degree Grand Orient Freemason General Garibaldi in battle during the Italian revolution at Viterbo and then at Mentana, where she was seriously wounded and left on the field as dead. In 1875 she founded the Theosophical Society in NYC, joined the Egyptian Rite of English Masonry in 1877 (documented above), and settled in London in 1887. In London she published her **Theosophical magazine,** *Lucifer the Light-bringer*, as well as *Secret Doctrine* and *Isis Unveiled*. A follower of Blavatsky was Alice Bailey, a self-proclaimed witch whose husband was a Freemason. Alice Bailey founded **Lucifer Publishing Company** of New York in 1922. To disguise its Luciferian connection in America, the name was changed to *Lucis Trust*. *Lucis* is Latin for Lucifer. See Fig. 88 for 1989 American membership in Lucis Trust.

Fig. 84 — **H. P. Blavatsky** (1831-1891):
Theosophist, born in Yekaterinoslav,
Ukraine.

She had a brief marriage in her teens to a Russian general, but left him and travelled widely in the East. She moved to the USA in 1873, and in 1875, with Henry Steel Olcott, founded the Theosophical Society in New York City, later carrying on her work in India. Her psychic powers were widely acclaimed, but did not survive investigation by the Society for Psychical Research. However, this did not deter her large following, which included Annie Besant (*The Cambridge Biographical Encyclopedia*, 1998). RIGHT PHOTO Blavatsky was so fat she had to be hauled by buggy.

American Biography by Scribners, 1929, wrote about Helena Petrovna Blavatsky in her latter years: "She was enormously fat, slovenly in dress, gorging herself on fat meat, smoking incessantly, and swearing like a trooper... (She was) one of the most evil & immoral women who ever lived...(with) personal duplicity & profound contempt for humanity." She was so fat she had to be hauledby buggy!!!

Theosophist and related movements have stopped using the name LUCIFER because of public outrage, and some years ago had switched to LUCIS TRUST (see Figs. 87 and 88 this section). In 1960 the above pictured volume of LUCIFER was in the library of Lyn Blessing, talented and famous "vibes" player, who was a student of the occult for many years.

This book is a rare bound collected vol. of Blavatsky's Theosophical magzine, LUCIFER — THE LIGHT-BRINGER. It is nearly impossible to find copies of this mag. today.

Fig. 85 — Notice the swastika at the top of the circle. Blavatsky used the swastika as her coat of arms a century before it became a Nazi symbol.

THE SECRET DOCTRINE

THE SYNTHESIS OF SCIENCE, RELIGION AND PHILOSOPHY

by

H P. BLAVATSKY

Volume 4

ANTHROPOGY

PART 2

THE ADYAR EDITION

——— 1938 ———

THE THEOSOPHICAL PUBLISHING HOUSE

Fig. 86 — Lytton's novels greatly influenced Blavatsky.
See Fig. 83 and *Scarlet and the Beast*, Vol. 1, 3rd ed., chapter 25.

Edward George Earl Bulwer-Lytton
(1803-1873)
Rosicrucian Freemason

Born in London, England. Politician, poet, and critic. He is chiefly remembered as a prolific novelist.

Lytton was influenced by the Romanticism of Freemason Goethe. His plots are elaborate and involved, his characterization is exaggerated and unreal, and his style is grandiose and ornate. His books, though dated, remain immensely readable to this day. And his personal experience of society and politics gives his work an unusual historical interest.

Bulwer-Lytton was the youngest son of Gen. William Bulwer and Elizabeth Lytton. After university at Cambridge, he went to France and visited Paris and Versailles. It was in France that he was influenced by the occult, which is revealed in *Zanoni* (1842) and *A Strange Story* (1862). He presented his utopia novel in *Vril: The Power of the Coming Race* (1871), which prior to World War One heavily influenced Adolf Hitler.

Fourteen years after Lytton's death, the first mystic society based on his novel, *Vril: The Power of the Coming Race* was founded at the behest of the Quatuor Coronati Lodge of Masonic Research, known as the Hermetic Order of the Golden Dawn, a Rosicrucian Society. The swastika was a key symbol of the Golden Dawn.

Actually, the Golden Dawn's racist rituals had a second source — heavily derived from Holy Grail mysticism.

Another secret society founded at that time can be traced to Bulwer-Lytton. Before his death Lytton had been intimate with female Freemason Helena Blavatsky, who later became a member of the Golden Dawn. In fact, Lytton had so influenced Blavatsky by the Isis cult that she wrote the book *Isis Unveiled*. In another multi-volume book *Secret Doctrine* (PB.S1.F85), Blavatsky warns her readers against Lytton's *Vril* as "the terrible sidereal [astral] Force, known to, and named by the Atlanteans... and by the Aryan[s].... It is the Vril of Bulwer Lytton's *Coming Race*...it is this Satanic Force that our generations were to be allowed to add to their stock of Anarchist's baby-toys.... It is this destructive agency, which, once in the hands of some modern Attila... would reduce Europe in a few days to its primitive chaotic state with no man left alive to tell the tale." Yet, Blavatsky persistently drew upon Lytton's novels for the Theosophical Society's teachings and rituals. Hitler fulfilled her prophesy.

Figure 88 — Yellow lotus flower is rendition of two 6-pointed stars & one All-Seeing Eye of Lucifer. Ad in *Reader's Digest*, Dec. 1991, facing p. 200.

THE GREAT INVOCATION

From the point of Light within the Mind of God
Let light stream forth into the minds of men.
Let Light descend on Earth.

From the point of Love within the Heart of God
Let love stream forth into the hearts of men.
May Christ return to Earth.

From the centre where the Will of God is known
Let purpose guide the little wills of men—
The purpose which the Masters know and serve.

From the centre which we call the race of men
Let the Plan of Love and Light work out
And may it seal the door where evil dwells.

Let Light and Love and Power restore the Plan on Earth.

The Great Invocation belongs to all humanity. Will you join the millions who daily use this prayer to invoke peace on earth? Become a co-worker in God's Plan, for only through humanity can the Plan work out.

Card Copies (without charge) from:
Lucis Trust, 866 United Nations Plaza, Suite 566l7, New York, NY 10017-1888
Tel. (212) 421-1577

Lucis Trust was originally founded under the name Lucifer Publishing Company. Read its history in *Scarlet and the Beast*, Vol. 1, 3rd ed., Chap. 10, 19, 24, 28, 30.

Figure 88 — Yellow lotus flower is rendition of two 6-pointed stars & one All-Seeing Eye of Lucifer. Ad in Reader's Digest, Dec. 1991, facing p. 200.

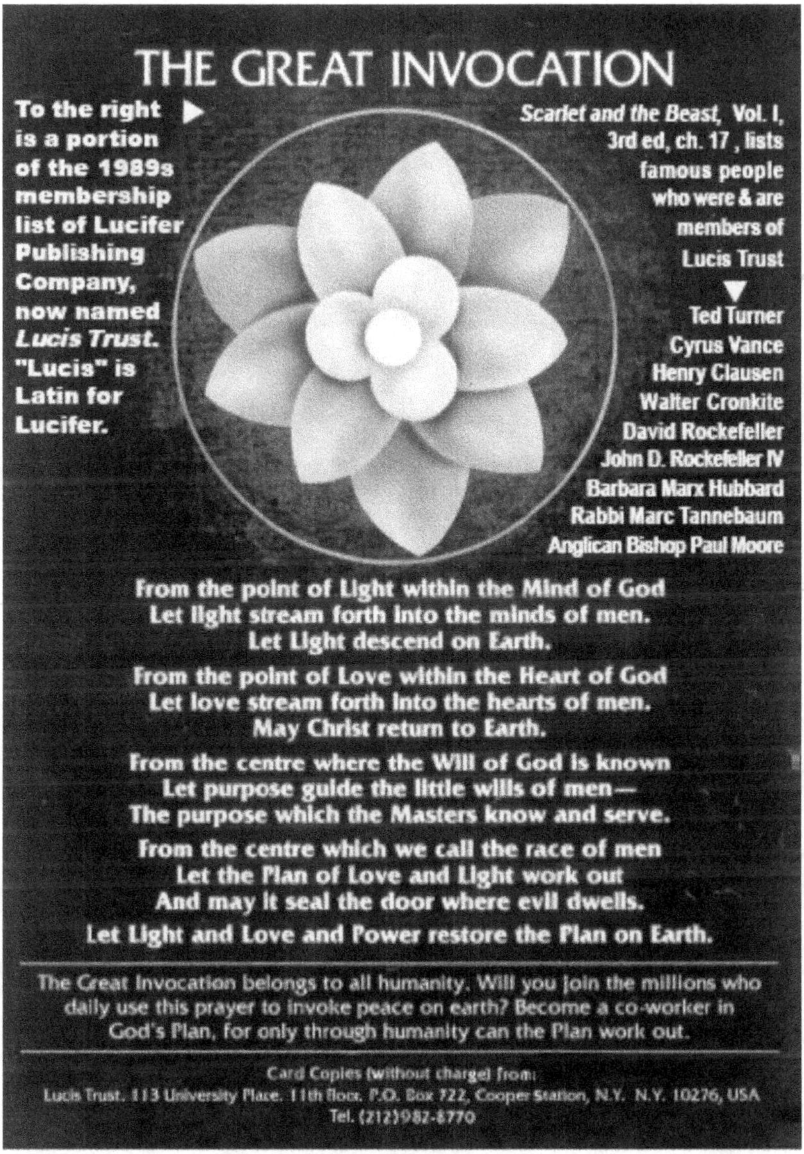

Fig. 89 — This photo is also in Sect. 1, Fig. 7. We have reproduced it here to confirm the Luciferian connection in Freemasonry, as explained by 33° Freemasonry Manly P. Hall, author of *Lost Keys of Freemasonry*, 1976. The original photo below is found opposite p. 52 of Hall's book. On p. 48 Hall confirms, "When the Mason learns that the key to the warrior on the block is the proper application of the dynamo of living power, he has learned the mystery of his Craft. The seething energies of Lucifer are in his hands...."

3° Mason has the "seething energies of Lucifer in his hands"

Read more on the Luciferian connection in Freemasonry by other Masonic authors quoted throughout *Scarlet and the Beast*, Vol. 1, 3rd ed.

Fig. 90 — 70-foot tall pyramid in the Napoleon Courtyard, Paris, France.
33° Freemason, Pres. Francois Mitterrand gave Chinese- American architect I.M. Pei
charge of the project in 1983. "The number of windowpanes in the pyramid is 666. And
the pyramid form itself reflects the president's passion for Masonic symbols." *Insight on
the News*, July 3, 1989, p.58

SECTION 2
MASONIC PERSONALITIES!!!
ARRANGED IN NO PARTICULAR ORDER

Fig. 1 — Hierarchy of Freemasonry. **33° (SJ) Albert Pike** (1809-1891). Masonic philosopher and ritualist. See *Scarlet and Beast,* Vols.1, 2, & 3. Pike, from 1859 until his death in 1891, occupied simultaneously the positions of Grand Master of the Central Directory of Scottish Rite Freemasonry at Washington, D.C., Sovereign Grand Commander of the Supreme Council of Scottish Rite Freemasonry, Southern Jurisdiction (SJ) at Charleston, S.C., and Sovereign Pontiff of Universal Freemasonry.

Albert Pike 33°
Masonic Philosopher and Ritualist

QUOTES FROM ALBERT PIKE

Pike describes the cabalistic view of Satan in his book *Morals and Dogma*:

"The true name of Satan, the Kabalist say, is that of Yahveh reversed; for Satan is not a black god, but the negation of God. The Devil is the personification of Atheism or Idolatry.

"For the Initiates, this is not a Person, but a Force, created for good, but which may serve for evil. It is the instrument of Liberty or Free Will. They represent this Force, which presides over the Physical generation, under the mythologic and horned form of the God Pan; thence came the he-goat of the Sabbat, brother of the Ancient Serpent, and the lightbearer or Phosphor, of which the poets have made the false Lucifer of the Legend." Pike, Albert, *Morals and Dogma* 1871. Richmond VA: L.H. Jenkins, 1942. p.102.

Pike's view of the Catholic Inquisitions: "The dunces who led primitive Christianity astray, by substituting faith for science, reverie for experience, the fantastic for the reality; and the inquisitor who for so many ages waged against Magism a war of extermination, have succeeded in shrouding in darkness the ancient discoveries of the human mind; so that we now grope in the dark to find again the key of the phenomena of nature." Pike, 732.

Pike took fifty years to develop and gradually introduce his Luciferian Rite to a select few within the 33rd Degree Supreme Council at Charleston. He also converted the Masonic hierarchy in London, Berlin, and Rome. During the latter half of his work, however, French atheists began to attack spiritism and symbolism within French Lodges. By 1877 French Freemasonry overtly declared what it had covertly taught from 1840 on; that there is no god but humanity. English Freemasonry, which demands a belief in deity, immediately broke fellowship with the French Grand Orient. Pike, as Sovereign Pontiff of Universal Freemasonry, wanted to heal the rift by presenting his Luciferian Doctrine at the July 15, 1889, Supreme Council convention in Paris, France. Unable to travel due to poor health, he instead explicated the doctrine in a letter to be read on the convention floor. Immediately following the convention the letter was published in French by A.C. De La Rive in *La Femme et L'Enfant dans la Franc-Maconnerie Universelle* (p.588). *The Freemason*, a Masonic periodical in England, noted the reading of the letter in its January 19, 1935, issue. Count Leon de Poncins quotes portions of the letter in *Freemasonry and the Vatican*, (1968). The most comprehensive quote, however, comes to us from Edith Starr Miller in *Occult Theocrasy* (1933). Following is Albert Pike's 1889 concept of how Lucifer should be presented to high degree Masons, while keeping the lower degree initiates and the general public ignorant:

"That which we must say to the crowd is — We worship a God, but it is the God that one adores without superstition.

To you, Sovereign Grand Inspectors General [of the 33rd degree], we say this, that you may repeat it to the Brethren of the 32nd, 31st, and 30th degrees — The Masonic religion should be, by all of us initiates of the high degrees, maintained in the purity of the Luciferian Doctrine.

If Lucifer were not God, would Adonay, the God of the Christians, whose deeds prove his cruelty, perfidy, and hatred of man, barbarism and repulsion for science, would Adonay and his priests, calumniate him?

Yes, Lucifer is God, and, unfortunately, Adonay is also God. For the eternal law is that there is no light without shade, no beauty without ugliness, no white without black, for the absolute can only exist as two Gods: darkness being necessary to light to serve as its foil, as the pedestal is necessary to the statue, and the brake to the locomotive.

In analogical and universal dynamics one can only lean on that which will resist. Thus the universe is balanced by two forces which maintain its equilibrium, the force of attraction and that of repulsion. These two forces exist in physics, philosophy and religion. And the scientific reality of the divine dualism is demonstrated by the phenomena of polarity and by the universal law of sympathies and antipathies. That is why the Gnostics, the Manicheans and the Templars have admitted, as the only logical metaphysical conception, the system of the divine principles fighting eternally, and one cannot believe the one inferior in power to the other.

Thus, the doctrine of Satanism is a heresy; and the true and pure philosophic religion is the belief in Lucifer, the equal of Adonay; but Lucifer, God of Light and God of Good, is struggling for humanity against Adonay, the God of Darkness and Evil."

Following the above convention, many European Masons were converted to Albert Pike's "Luciferian Doctrine." Read more on Luciferian Doctrine of Freemasonry, and names of the European Masons who followed this doctrine. *Scarlet and Beast*, Vol. 1; 3rd ed., chaps. 15 & 21; and Vols. 2 & 3.

Fig. 2 — Hierarchy of Freemasonry. **33° (SJ) Albert G. Mackey**(1808-1881). Masonic historian and jurist. See *Scarlet and Beast*, Vol.1, 3rd ed., ch. 15.

Fig. 3 — Hierarchy of Freemasonry. **33° (NJ) Robert I. Clegg** (1866-1931). Masonic revisor of Mackey's History of Freemasonry, Encyclopedia of Freemasonry, Jurisprudence of Freemasonry, and Symbolism of Freemasonry. See Scarlet and Beast, Volume 1, chapters 5 & 10.

Fig. 4 — **Thomas Smith Webb** (1771-1819). Founder of the American, or York Rite of Freemasonry. In 1797 he published at Albany the first edition of his *Freemasons Monitor* (see copy of origanal release, Figures 5 and 6.

Thomas Smith Webb
Founder of the American Rites

Fig. 5 — Front page of an original first-run printing of Webb's 336-page leather-bound book published in 1797. Signed by the purchaser, it reads "Andrew Finley his book bought 14th June 1818" (see signature and date next page). Book is in the possession of the author of *Scarlet and the Beast*.

Freemason's Monitor

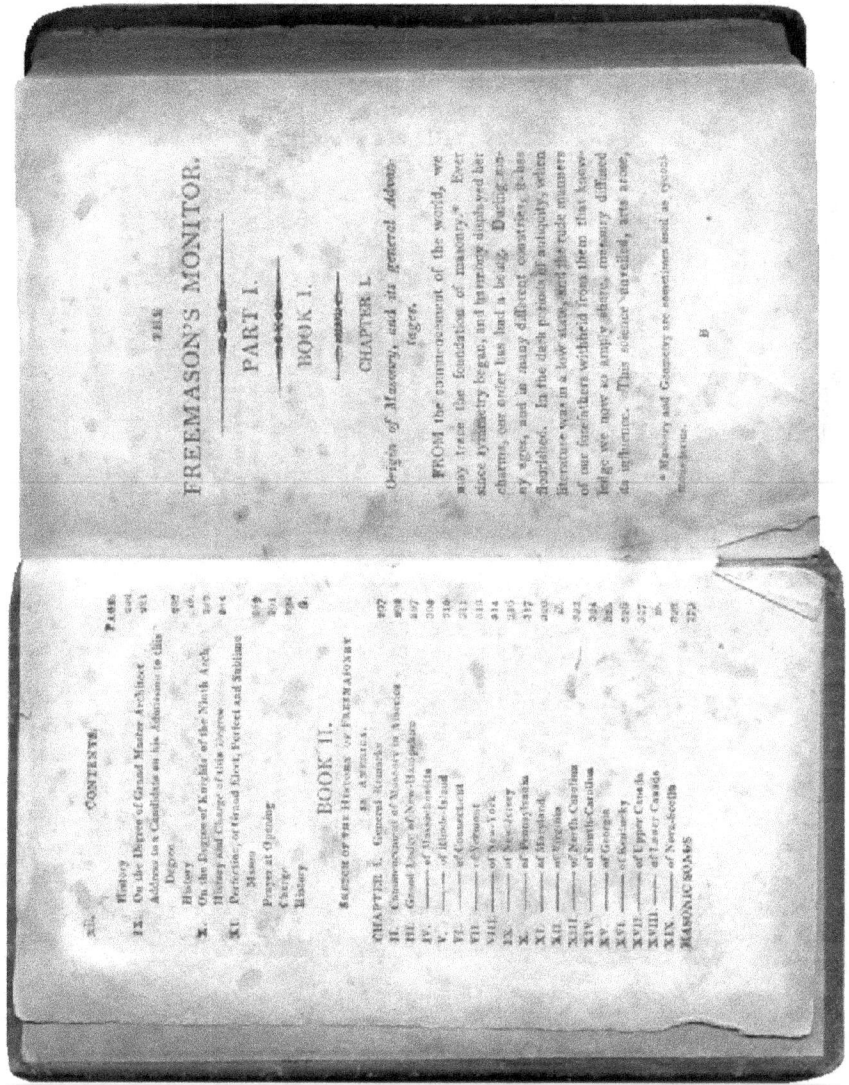

Fig. 6 — Back inside cover of an original first-run printing of this 336-page leather-bound book published by Webb in 1797. Signed by the purchaser twice. Second signature reads, "Andrew Finley landed from England 17th November 1815." Book is in excellent condition with all pages readable.

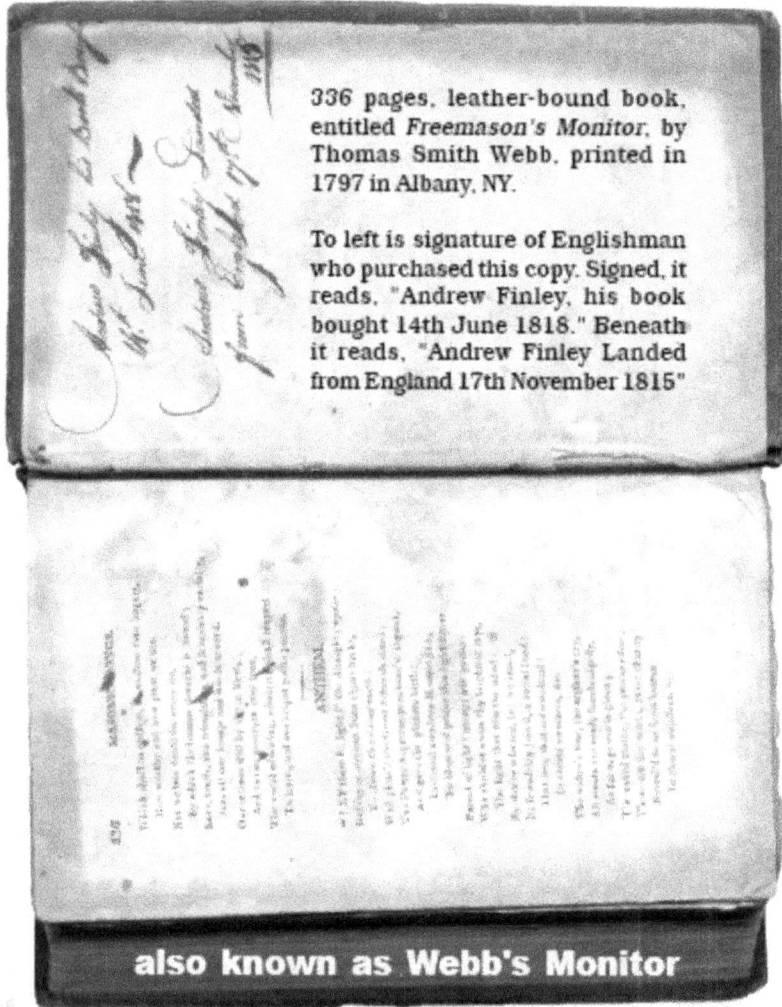

336 pages, leather-bound book, entitled *Freemason's Monitor*, by Thomas Smith Webb, printed in 1797 in Albany, NY.

To left is signature of Englishman who purchased this copy. Signed, it reads, "Andrew Finley, his book bought 14th June 1818." Beneath it reads, "Andrew Finley Landed from England 17th November 1815"

also known as Webb's Monitor

Fig. 7 — Oliver Cromwell. English soldier and statesman of outstanding gifts and a forceful character shaped by a devout Calvinist/Puritan faith. Was Lord Protector of the republican Commonwealth of England Scotland, and Ireland from 1653 to 1658. As were many English Protestants, Cromwell was a Rosicrucian Freemason. See S&B, Vol. 1, 3rd ed., ch. 2 and 7.

Oliver Cromwell (1599-1658)

History and Evolution of Freemasonry, a Masonic publication, affirms Oliver Cromwell's links to Masonry. "Cromwell," it says, "regularly met at the Masonic Lodge in the tavern called Crown." This was a Lodge for the aristocratic Rosicrucian gentry, the new elite who were the newly rich. Cromwell was supposed by many to be a Rosicrucian himself, since he was on the best of terms with them. This view is endorsed by the *Encyclopedia of Freemasonry*. See *S&B*, Vol. 1, 3rd ed., chapter 2.

Fig. 8 — Hierarchy of Freemasonry. **John Theophilus Desaguliers** (16831744). Known as "father of modern speculative Freemasonry." Son of a French Protestant clergyman. Received Master of Arts in 1712 from Christ Church, Oxford. See *Scarlet and Beast*, Volume 1, chapters 2-4.

J. T. Desaguliers, Doctor of Laws, Fellow of the Royal Society of London; Chaplain to the Duke of Chandos, Lecturer in Natural Philosophy.

Fig. 9 — Pike and his Luciferians

33⁰
Giuseppe
(Joseph)
Mazzini
(1805-1872)

33⁰ Albert Pike
(1809-1891)

Albert Pike taught his "Luciferian Doctrine" to many Masons. However, Bismarck and Mazzini were two of his most ardent students who practiced the Luciferian Doctrine at the highest levels of Freemasonry. This trio planned to use Freemasonry to trigger two World Wars, after which "the world would be ready to worship Lucifer as God." (*S&B* Vol. 1; 3rd ed; chap. 12,17.)

33⁰ Otto von Bismarck
(1815-1898)

Count Camillo Benso di Cavour, Grand Master of Italian Grand Lodge, was opposed to Mazzini's Grand Orient republicanism, yet was able to come to terms with him to unite Italy under a Savoy constitutional monarchy. (See *Scarlet and Beast*: Vol. 1; 3rd ed; chaps 17&21).

Count
Cavour
(1810-1861)

Fig. 10 — Infamous British Mason. 33° Mason Aleister Crowley, Satanist & Grand
Master of the Ordo Templi Orentis (O.T.O.). For more information, see *Scarlet and
Beast*, Vol. 1, 3rd ed., chps. 6, 15, 17-19, 25. **33° Aleister Crowley** (1875-1947). Photo
of Crowley taken in 1912, at age 37.
Notice Baphomet symbol of Satan to left of his signature.

Crowley's
mother said
her son was the
incarnation of the
Beast of Revelation.

Crowley's father,
a leader in
Plymouth Brethren,
preached up and
down England, "Get
right with God."

In the occult there is a significant difference between Satan and Lucifer. To the
Luciferian there is no Satan. Satan is atheism, the negation of God. Luciferians worship
Lucifer as the angel of light, who they say is not fallen, but (for now) is simply less
transcendent than the God of the Theologians, Who is evil because He will not permit
advancement in science. Examples: (1) the confusion of tongues at Babylon; and (2) the
Catholic Inquisitions, which were partly directed against scientific achievements. Lucifer
teaches that man can become gods through advancement in science. Eastern religions call
it reincarnation. Our secular schools call it evolution. Satanists, on the other hand, know
their god is totally evil. They worship him because he permits anything and everything.
And their hatred for the God of Theologians causes them to go overboard in their
debauchery.

Crowley was a Satanist. He liked to be known as "the great beast 666" and "the
wickedest man alive." Many who associated with him died tragically. Crowley became
interested in the occult while an undergraduate at Cambridge. He travelled widely,
settling for some years in Sicily with a group of disciples at the Abbey of Thelema, near
Cefalu. He claimed to have sacrificed to Satan 150 young males. Once he forced a male
goat to copulate with his girlfriend. Rumors of drugs, orgies, and magical ceremonies led
to his expulsion from Italy. See next three pages for Crowley's Masonic credentials.

Fig. 11 — Charter issued by 33° John Yarker & others admitting Crowley to the highest grade (33°) of Ancient and Accepted Rite of Masonry, 1910. English Masonry does not recognize Scottish Rite, which was founded by French Masonry, hence the reason for omitting "Scottish" from Certificate.
Notice Baphomet symbol next to the six signatories of the three Masons, who signed twice each.

Fig. 12 — Certificate of appointment of Aleister "St" Edward Crowley as national Grand Master of the O.T.O. for Great Britain and Ireland, signed by **33rd degree Grand Orient Freemason Theodore Reuss** (see bottom/ center). Notice sign of the Baphomet in front of the signature of Reuss. Both Reuss and Crowley were 33, 90°, and 96° Masons.

INSTRUCTION FOR HUMAN SACRIFICE IN THE MASONIC O.T.O. LODGES

"Do what thou wilt shall be the whole of the Law."

"The Supreme and Most Holy King is appointed by the O.T.O. His is the ultimate responsibility for all within his holy kingdom. Succession to the high office of O.T.O. is decided in a manner not here to be declared; but this you may learn, O Brother Magician, that he may be chosen even from the grade of a Minerval. And herein lieth a most sacred Mystery."

Aleister Crowley claims to have performed 150 human sacrifices, killing the victims with a silver knife. He wrote instruction for O.T.O. human sacrifices in his book *Magick*, published 1930, p. 93:

"The blood is the life. This simple statement is explained by the Hindus by saying that the blood is the principal vehicle of vital Prana. There is some ground for the belief that there is a definite substance, not isolated as yet, whose presence makes all the difference between live and dead matter.

"It would be unwise to condemn as irrational the practice of those savages who tear the heart and liver from an adversary, and devour them while yet warm. In any case it was the theory of the ancient Magicians, that any living being is a storehouse of energy varying in quantity according to the size and health of the animal, and in quality according to its mental and moral character. At the death of the animal this energy is liberated suddenly.

"The animal should therefore be killed within the Circle, or the Triangle, as the case may be, so that its energy cannot escape. An animal should be selected whose nature accords with that of the ceremony, thus, by sacrificing a female lamb one would not obtain any appreciable quantity of the fierce energy useful to a Magician who was invoking Mars. In such a case a ram would be more suitable. And this ram should be virgin — the whole potential of its original total energy should not have been diminished in any way. For the highest spiritual working one must accordingly choose that victim which contains the greatest and purest force. A male child of perfect innocence and high intelligence is the most satisfactory and suitable victim.

"For evocations it would be more convenient to place the blood of the victim in the Triangle, the idea being that the spirit might obtain from the blood this subtle but physical substance which was the quintessence of its life in such a manner as to enable it to take on a visible and tangible shape." Those magicians who object to the use of blood have endeavoured to replace it with incense. For such a purpose the incense of Abramelin may be burnt in large quantities.

"But the bloody sacrifice, though more dangerous, is more efficacious; and for nearly all purposes human sacrifice is the best. (O.T.O. Law quoted from the O.T.O. *Book of Equinox*, page 241).

Figure 13 — O.T.O. haunted house in Nyack, New York.
Read *Scarlet and the Beast,* Vol. 1, 3rd edition; chaps. 17 & 27.

House is haunted, appeals court says

NEW YORK (AP) — A big Victorian house on the Hudson, where the ghosts leave gifts and where The Amazing Kreskin wanted to hold a seance, has been declared haunted — "as a matter of law" — by an appeals court.

That was good news for Jeffrey and Patrice Stambovsky, who had decided in 1989 to buy the old 18-room mansion in Nyack for $650,000 — but changed their mind after a local architect told them, "Oh, you're buying the haunted house."

It seems they hadn't been told before they put down a $32,500 binder that the owner, Helen Ackley, had claimed for years that she'd been seeing poltergeists. In a 1977 article in Reader's Digest, she said one of the men was a "cheerful apple-cheeked man" who looked like Santa Claus.

In a local newspaper in 1982, she

described the spirits as "dressed in Revolutionary period clothing, perhaps frozen in a time warp, waiting for someone or some reason to move on."

In a 1989 article about a house sour in suburban Nyack, the house was described as "riverfront Victorian — with ghost."

Ackley, who now lives in Orlando, Fla., said she and her family had been seeing ghosts in the house since her family moved in 24 years ago. She said her husband, George, died 12 years ago.

"I feel they are very good friends," she said last year. Occasionally they would leave little gifts. "It's very comforting to have them around when you are by yourself."

The gifts included a small ring left on the stairs leading up to the second floor and a small knickknack box.

An appeals court has ruled that this riverfront house in Nyack, N.Y. is indeed haunted and a prospective buyer can sue to get his deposit back.

Stambovsky, a 38-year-old bond trader, said he didn't believe is such things. He said his wife, who was pregnant at the time, was bothered by the idea.

"Would you want to bump into George Washington in the middle of the night?" William Stein, Stambovsky's lawyer, asked in a New York Newsday article last year.

During WWI, Aleister Crowley established four O.T.O. centers in the USA (ND,TX,CA,NY). When lines are drawn on a map from their geographic centers north to south & east to west, they blasphemously form a cross. At the end of WWII, the center in Nyack NY closed. In 1952 the abandoned headquarters of New York O.T.O. sold to the CMA, Christian and Missionary Alliance Church, which then moved its college onto the former O.T.O. campgrounds, which became Nyack College. Initially, the CMA Conference was unaware of the former O.T.O operation. When demonic activity manifested itself on campus, the CMA investigated its history, then performed exorcisms throughout campus. Author John Daniel received from the College its occult history, which you can read in Scarlet and the Beast, ch. 17 & 27, 3rd ed. This 1992 news clipping of a haunted house, not on campus, but within the city of Nyack, confirms demonic activity caused by the O.T.O. continues to manifest itself in Nyack to this day.

Fig. 14 — Freemason William (Wild Bill) Donovan was a member of O.T.O.

O.T.O & 33° William (Joseph) Donovan nicknamed
"Wild Bill" Donovan (1883-1959)

Mason, US Soldier and public official, born in Buffalo NY. A much-decorated World War I veteran. Was an assistant to the US attorney general (1925-29). Served as an unofficial observer for the US government in Italy, Spain, and the Balkans (1935-41). Assigned by Roosevelt to head the US Office of Strategic Services (OSS, 1942-45). In this capacity, Donovan had responsibility for undercover operations during WW2. Was later appointed ambassador to Thailand (1953-54).

Donovan was a 33° Mason, a member of Aleister Crowley's OTO, and frequent guest at the OTO campgrounds at Nyack NY. In this latter position he was privileged to know all occult figures in Europe who attended the campgrounds. Pres. Roosevelt wanted to capitalize on Donovan's contacts. See *S&B*, Vol.1, 3rd ed., ch. 27.

Near the end of World War Two, Pres. Roosevelt started the process by which the Nazi SS would be protected. Even before America entered the Second World War, Roosevelt wanted to know what Hitler had at his disposal that enabled him to gain power so rapidly, solidify control so completely, and destroy Continental Freemasonry so resolutely. To find out he sent "Wild Bill" Donovan to Europe on a fact-finding mission.

32° Roosevelt could not have picked a more able man than Donovan, a student of eastern mysticism and Masonry. In Europe, Donovan discovered that Interpol (International Police), founded at Vienna in 1923, had been taken over by the Nazis after their invasion of Austria in 1938. By 1940 the Nazis had transferred the entire Interpol apparatus to Wannsee near Berlin. Under the direction of Nazi intelligence chief Reinhard Heydrick, Interpol became the world's most advanced international intelligence force. Donovan returned to Washington and recommended to the President the founding of a central intelligence agency on the scale of Heydrick's Interpol. In 1941 Donovan was made head of the new Office of Coordinator of Information (OCI), later to be renamed Office of Strategic Services (OSS).

You can read the story in *Scarlet and the Beast*, Vol. 1, 3rd ed., chp. 27. On "War Stories," Apr. 30, 2006, it was confirmed that the C.I.A. contracted 33° Bill Donovan to kill Gen. Patton. The reason? "Patton wanted to fight the Russians, which would have triggered World War III. The OSS staged Patton's auto accident. All facts about Patton's death have been expunged from history."

Fig. 15 — Freemason L. Ron Hubbard was a
member of Crowley's O.T.O.
See *Scarlet and the Beast*, Vol. 1, 3rd edition,
Introduction & chap. 17.

O.T.O. Freemason L. Ron Hubbard (1911-1986)
Writer and founder of the Church of Scientology. Born in Tilden, NE. He wrote science-fiction stories before his most famous work, *Dianetics: the Modern Science of Mental Health* (1950), which became an instant best seller. Dianetics became the basic text of the Scientology movement. While writing *Dianetics*, Hubbard claimed to have visited heaven twice. Aleister Crowley initiated L. Ron Hubbard into the O.T.O. in 1944. In 1964, Charles Manson was recruited by Scientology before he himself was initiated into the O.T.O. In 1967, the O.T.O. in England founded the Process Church of the final Judgement soon after the rise of The Beatles rock group. In the late 60s and early 70s, the Process set up cells in a number of U.S. cities.

After Crowley's death, the O.T.O. was headquartered for a time in Hubbard's Church of Scientology. In 1992, *The Auditor*, the journal of Scientology, reported that there were 146 Scientology centers worldwide, with 54 in the United States and Canada. *Time* magazine, May 6, 1991, reports "700 centers in 65 countries." This greater number includes Scientology affiliates, many of which are front organizations for recruiting unsuspecting clientele.

In 1968, amid public concern over his aims and methods in Great Britain, he was banned from reentering that nation. In 1984 he was accused of embezzlement. His Church's tax-exempt status was revoked by the US government. As a result he withdrew into seclusion.

Fig. 16 — After founding the Illuminati on **May 1, 1776**, **May 1st became May Day**, and has since been celebrated by workers' unions worldwide. Following the Bolshivic Revoluion, May 1st became the national holiday of all Communist countries. See *Scarlet and the Beast*, Vol.1 entire.

Adam Weishaupt (1748-1830)
Founder of the Order of Illuminati
Born in Ingoldstadt, Germany. Educated by the Jesuits. In 1772 he was named "professor of law extraordinaire." In 1775 he was professor of both natural law and canon law.

Weishaupt's views were cosmopolitan and liberal. He condemned the bigotry and superstitions of the established church and gained a following of young students who would meet in his private apartment to discuss philosophic subjects. This was the beginning of the Order of the Illuminati, or "Enlightened Ones." At first it was not connected to

Freemasonry, for Weishaupt was not initiated into the Craft until 1777, when he received the degrees in the Lodge Theodore of Good Counsel at Munich. He then sought to incorporate the Illuminati into Freemasonry by infiltration. Eventually the organization became a corrupt political instrument, and fell into disfavor. In 1784 all secret associations were prohibited by French royal decree. The following year Weishaupt was deprived of his professorship and banished from the country.

All the above comes directly from *10,000 Famous Freemasons*. The following comes from *Mackey's Encyclopedia of Freemasonry*, Vol. 3, published in 1946 after two World Wars revealed the long-lasting effect of the Illuminati.

"The Order of Illuminati was the greatest single misfortune ever to befall European Freemasonry because it became at once the pattern and the point of departure for a succession of secret, underground, political conspiracies which...divided Masonry and brought disgrace upon its name."

Fig. 17 — The Illuminati's founding on May 1st is called May Day, and has from that time been a holiday in all Communist countries. It is still observed by workers' unions today.
AP newsclipping dated **May 1, 1985**.

Workers worldwide march to mark May Day holiday

By The Associated Press

Millions of workers marched in officially sanctioned and anti-government demonstrations worldwide to mark the May Day labor holiday. Two people were killed in a bombing in Belgium linked to the observance.

Polish Solidarity leader Lech Walesa was turned back by riot police as he attempted to join an official parade in his hometown of Gdansk, but several hundred other Solidarity activists stormed the procession and were scattered by police.

In Moscow, Soviet Communist Party leader Mikhail S. Gorbachev presided over a carefully controlled parade of thousands of workers carrying paper flowers, balloons and placards. President Reagan's son Ronald was among the spectators.

Leftist terrorists in Brussels, Belgium, claimed responsibility for a bombing that killed two firemen and wounded 12 people, saying the attack was in "solidarity with workers on Labor Day." The firemen responded to a report of a burning van, and the van exploded as they approached, police said.

Walesa, attempting to walk with supporters from his apartment to the parade in Gdansk, back by hundreds of riot police about the parade route.

"In spite of the clearly peaceful charac were prevented by force from reaching t this year's parade of the working peo said.

Other Solidarity supporters forced th the parade twice, the second time forcing Both times they were scattered by helm lice wielding truncheons. Several arre ported.

In Warsaw, an estimated 15,000 attended a Roman Catholic Mass at the slain pro-Solidarity priest, the Rev. Jerz ko. An estimated 7,000 to 10,000 then marx a steel mill north of the church and aw official parade.

The chanting Solidarity supporters w by helmeted police and forced down a where they were eventually dispersed.

Fig. 18 — Creator of the forms of initiation into the Order of the Illuminati.
See *Scarlet and the Beast*, Vol. 1 entire.

Adolf Franz Freiderich Ludwig "Baron von Knigge" (1752-1796)

German author born at Brendenbeck, near Hanover. He wrote novels and translated Mozart's *Figaro* (1791). His most popular non-Masonic work was *On Conversations With Men*. Although he was one of the most prominent Freemasons of his time, his association with Masonry was to benefit him alone, or he made trouble for the fraternity, such as publishing the names of the membership of the Illuminati. He was initiated into Freemasonry on Jan. 20, 1772 at Cassel, Germany in the Lodge of Stricte Observance, but was not impressed with the institution. He expressed his disillusion by letter to Prince Charles of Hesse (a Freemason), that its ceremonies were "absurd, juggling tricks."

In 1780 he entered the Order of the Illuminati, which had been set up by Adam Weishaupt (a fellow Freemason) as a grandiose new society of his own, with vague but vast aims. Among the Illuminati Knigge was known as *Philo*. When he appealed to Weishaupt for more light, the latter confessed that the higher degrees did not exist except in his own brain, and challenged Knigge to expand the system to the highest degrees, promising him full authority. Knigge secured the aid of Bode, another Freemason, and was quite successful in propagating the rite. When Weishaupt interfered, Knigge became disgusted and withdrew from the order, and soon after, from Freemasonry itself. *Editor's note* : This withdrawal was a ruse, for we confirm in *Scarlet and the Beast* that the above was published to make it look as if the Order died. From *Mackey's Encyclopedia of Freemasonry*, Vol. 3, 1946, we read: "The Order of Illuminati was the greatest single misfortune ever to befall European Freemasonry because it became at once the pattern and the point of departure for a succession of secret, underground, political conspiracies which...divided Masonry and brought disgrace upon its name."

Illuminati Oath

"I, protest before you, the worthy Plenipotentiary of the venerable Order into which I wish to be admitted, that I acknowledge my natural weakness and inability, and that I, with all my possessions, rank, honors, and titles which I hold in political society, am, at bottom, only a man; I can enjoy these things only through my fellowmen, and through them also I may lose them. The approbation and consideration of my fellowmen are indispensably necessary, and I must try to maintain them by all my talents. These I will never use to the prejudice of universal good, but will oppose, with all my might, the enemies of the human race, and of political society. I will embrace every opportunity of saving mankind, by improving my understanding and my affections, and by imparting all important knowledge, as the good and statutes of this Order require of me. I bind myself to perpetual silence and unshaken loyalty and submission to the Order, in the persons of my Superiors; here making a faithful and complete surrender of my private judgement, my own will, and every narrow-minded employment of my power and influence. I pledge myself to account the good of the Order as my own, and am ready to serve it with my fortune, my honor, and my blood. Should I, through omission, neglect, passion, or wickedness, behave contrary to this good of the Order, I subject myself to what reproof or punishment my Superiors shall enjoin. The friends and enemies of the Order shall be my friends and enemies; and with respect to both I will conduct myself as directed by the Order, and am ready, in every lawful way, to devote myself to its increase and promotion, and therein to employ all my ability. All this I promise, and protest, without secret reservation, according to the intention of the Society which requires from me this engagement. This I do as I am, and as I hope to continue, a Man of Honor."

Quoted from John Robison's 1798 *Proofs of a Conspiracy*, p.71.

Fig. 19 — "On July 14, 1789, a Grand Orient led mob stormed the Bastille in Paris, officially triggering the bloodbath known as the French Revolution." *Spotlight Magazine* — Feb. 3, 1992, p.13

Fig. 20 — Robespierre, See *Scarlet and the Beast,* Vol. 1, chaps. 7 & 10.

Maximilien-Francois   Robespierre (1758-1794)

By 1794 there were 6,800 Jacobin Clubs, 500,000 strong. All were Grand Orient Masons. Although this dominant force propelled the revolution, it began to falter. In seeking to bolster their power, the Jacobin/Templars turned on Royalist and began to slay them. The bloodbath was so intense that the Beast began to slay its own.

When the three Masonic architects of the Terror (Marat, Danton, & Robespierre) were themselves assassinated or beheaded, Paris slowly returned to normal.

The word "terrorism" was coined in France in 1795 to describe the 1793 "Reign of Terror" during which time two million French, both men and women, were beheaded in nine months. Another six million were drowned, dashed to pieces when thrown over cliffs, or starved to death.

During the Reign of Terror, all houses of worship were closed in accordance with Jacobin antireligious policy. Churches & synagogues were reopened after Robespierre was guillotined July 28, 1794, signalling the end of terror & the Jacobin power base.

REIGN OF TERROR

Revolutionary France became the first terrorist state. From the ninemonth Reign of Terror eight million Frenchmen were killed! The word "terrorism" was coined in 1795 to describe this catastrophe.

Right : Beheading of Freemason Robespierre

Figure 21 — Famous French and Prussian Mason.

30.

Voltaire (1694-1778)

Full name, Francois Marie Arouet de Voltaire. French writer and Philosopher. Gained fame as defender of victims of religious intolerance. Educated by Jesuits. Began writing at an early age.

In 1750 he accepted an invitation to visit Frederick the Great, a Freemason, and King of Prussia. While there he produced his greatest historical work. He was initiated into Freemasonry on April 7, 1778, less than two months before his death. The event took place at Paris in the lodge of *Les Neuf Soeurs*. The ceremony was conducted by the celebrated French astronomer, Joseph Lalande. He entered the lodge escorted by Benjamin Franklin, the American ambassador. It is recorded that the scene was one of unusual brilliance. Voltaire was a Diest rather than an Athiest. (Read more in *Scarlet and Beast*, Vol. 1, Chaps. 3-5, 8-10, 12,

32° Frederick the Great (1712-1786)

King of Prussia (1740-1786). A patron of literature, he invited Voltaire to live at his court (175053). He was greatly interested in the American Revolution and an admirer of George Washington.

He was initiated into Freemasonry on the night of Aug. 1415, 1738 in a special lodge called at Brunswick, receiving all 32 degrees, and became head of the Scottish Rite of Freemasonry. (Read more in Scarlet and the Beast, Volume 1, 3rd edition, chapters 3-4 and 7-10.)

Figure 22 — Famous French Masons.

Louis Philippe Joseph, Duke of Orleans Philippe Egalite (1747-1793)

One of Weishaupt's first initiates was Louis Philippe Joseph, Duke of Orleans, cousin to the Bourbon king of France, and traitor to his own royal house. The Duke had already been initiated into French Grand Lodge Freemasonry, and according to *Mackey's Encyclopedia of Freemasonry*, "was elected Grand Master in the year 1771, upon the death of the Count de'Clermont."

On returning from a mission to England in July 1790, Orleans took a seat in the National Assembly. He was admitted to the politically radical Jacobin club in 1791. After the fall of the monarchy in august 1792, he renounced his title of nobility and accepted from the Paris Commune the name Philippe Egalite.

His treason occurred when he broke from the Masonic turmoil in France, which revolved around British obedience in the French Grand Lodge. He founded the clandestine French Grand Orient Lodge in 1772. The traitor Duke, according to Mackey, held the position of Grand Master in this opposition lodge.

Egalite voted for the execution of Louis, but he fell under suspicion when his son Louis-Philippe, duc de Chartres, defected to the Austrians. Accused of being an accomplice, Egalite was arrested on April 6, 1793, and was sent to the guillotine in November.

Figure 23 — Famous French Masons.

Napoleon I (1769-1821)

Napoleon I was initiated in an Army Philadelphé Lodge between 1795-98. In 1801 the official report of a Masonic festival at Dijon of that year described Masonic honors paid to Bonaparte. Napoleon's four brothers were also Freemasons, as were his stepson, brotherin-law, Murat, and nephew, Jerome, most of whom held high Masonic rank. Those who were chosen by Napoleon for high honor and office in the state were usually Freemasons. Of the nine lesser imperial officers of state, six at least were active Masons. Of the marshals of France who served under Napoleon, at least 22 of the first 30 were Masons, many of them grand officers of the Grand Orient. See *Scarlet and Beast*, Vol. I, chps. 10-11.

Talleyrand (1754-1838)

In one 45-year period France had six Masonic revolutionary changes of government. Talleyrand had a major role in them all. He influenced French history from the start of the French Revolution (1789) until 1834. He was often out of favor because of his intrigues and graft. His abilities, however, made the rulers call him back again and again to advise them. He was an ordained priest in the Catholic Church, yet he fought against the Church during his administrations. During the Reign of Terror, Talleyrand was out of favor in France. When Napoleon came to power, Talleyrand again became foreign minister. He was an Illuminati/Freemason. Read of his Masonic intrigues and political adroitness in *Scarlet and the Beast*, Vol. I, chapters 7 & 11.

Figure 24 — Famous British Mason — Arthur, Duke of Wellington, defeated Napoleon I at Watterloo.

Duke of Wellington (1769-1852)

British general and statesman known as "The Iron Duke, "defeated Napoleon at Waterloo.

Wellington entered the army in 1787. He was an Irish member of Parliament from 1790-95.

After commanding a division in the war with Tipu in 1799, he returned to England as Irish Secretary for three years. In 1808 he was Lieutenant General during the Peninsular War. He defeated the forces of Joseph (Bonaparte) at Talavers; forced the French to retreat under Massena and defeated them at Salamanaca.

Given supreme command of Spain, he drove the French across the Pyrenees in 1814 and was created 1st Duke of Wellington that year. With the Prussian Blucher, he crushed Napoleon at Waterloo in 1815.

Wellington was active in politics the remainder of his life, becoming Prime Minister of England in 1828-30, and Commander in Chief of the armed forces 1827-28 and 1842-52.

Wellington's father, Gafrett, Earl of Mornington, was Grand Master of the Grand Lodge of Ireland in 1776, and his brother Richard, 1st Marquess of Wellesley and 2nd Earl of Mornington, was Grand Master of Ireland in 1782. "The Iron Duke" himself was initiated on Dec. 7, 1790 in the family Lodge No. 494 at Trim. His father was Master of the lodge at this time and his brother was also present in the lodge. Wellington continued as a subscribing member until 1795.

It is curious, however, that towards the end of his life, when pestered by an importunate correspondent, the Duke denied "any recollection of having been admitted a Freemason." See *S&B*, Vol. I, chaps. 10-11.

Figure 25 — Architect of the Peace of Europe after Napoleon.

Prince K.W.N. Lothar Metternich (1773-1859)

Austrian Minister of Foreign Affairs

Napoleon no longer wanted to be Emperor. He wanted to be King. In 1809 he divorced Josephine of the House of Bourbon. Prince Metternich, Austrian minister of foreign affairs, responded in an effort to bring peace to Europe, and arranged for Napoleon to marry a Merovingian princess, Archduchess Marie Louise of the House of Habsburg.

Freemasonry feared that the Emperor's power might be perpetuated with this alliance, the consequence of which would be an heir to his throne. A second Napoleon would cause danger to the universal republic Freemasonry could otherwise inaugurate at the death of the first Napoleon. Msgr. Dillon writes that Freemasonry observed as the Emperor "began to show a coldness for the sect, and sought means to prevent it from the propagandism of its diabolical aims. Then Freemasonry became his enemy, and his end was not far off."

In 1810 Napoleon became the first excommunicate of Freemasonry. Msgr. Dillon writes that in 1812, "Members of the sect urged on his mad expedition to Moscow. His resources were paralyzed; and he was, in one word, sold by secret, invisible foes into the hands of his enemies." Read in *Scarlet and the Beast*, Vol. 1, 3rd edition, chps. 11 & 22 how the ouster of Napoleon by the "Big Four" (Russia, Prussia, Austria, and Great Britain), was the brilliant plan of Metternich, at the Congress of Vienna (Sept. 1814 to June 1815).

Figure 26 — Famous French Masons.

33° Adolphe Crémieux (1796-1880)
French lawyer and political figure
Crémieux was an active leader in the French Communist Revolution in 1848, when all Europe was in political turmoil. He was also a member of the Paris Commune (1870-71).

After a distinguished legal career in Nimes, he was appointed advocate of the Cour d'Appel (Court of Appeals) in Paris (1830), where he gained renown for his legal skill and oratory.

In 1842 Crémieux was elected to the Chamber of Deputies from the Indre-et-Loire department and quickly emerged as a leading member of the radical left. He played a prominent role in the Masonic revolutionary movements of 1848 and served as minister of Justice in the provisional government of 1848-49. He voted for the presidential candidacy of Louis-Napoleon (Napoleon III), but when he withdrew his support, Napoleon had him imprisoned. After his release, he returned to the bar and left-wing politics. He returned to the Chamber in 1869, representing a Parisian district, and when the Second Empire collapsed he joined the Government of National Defense (1870-71) as minister of Justice. Subsequently, he served as deputy from Algiers (1871-75) and then Senator (1875-80). Crémieux was an important leader of the French Jewish community.

He lent his prestige and political influence to numerous campaigns for the normalization of Jewish life in France and Algeria, backing the enfranchisement of North African Jews. In 1858 he founded the influential Alliance Israelite Universelle and was its first president.

Crémieux's real name was Isaac Moise. He was a member of the French Masonic Lodge — Alsace Lorraine. He was also a 33° ruling chief, sitting on the Supreme Council of the Ancient and Primitive Rite of Mizraim Freemasonry in Paris. The original copy of documents, later to known as the *Protocols of the Learned Elders of Sion*, were stolen from this lodge. Read in *Scarlet and the Beast*, Vol. 1, 3rd edition, chapter 12 & 17, of Crémieux's involvement with Maurice Joly in writing the *Dialogues of Geneva*, from which the original version of the *Protocols of the Learned Elders of Sion* allegedly were plagiarized (in French). Also read of his involvement with Victor Hugo, Grand Master of the Priory of Sion.

Two-page excerpt of Crémieux's Masonic activity
from *Scarlet and the Beast*, Vol. I, chap. 12

The French Communist Revolution of 1848

1848. Another year of disturbance. In a trance-like state occultist Sobrier touches off demonstrations which lead to the fall of the Orleans monarchy in France; Louis Philippe dethroned and Second Republic begins; Louis Napoleon elected president of the assembly. Republic established in Rome. Abdication of Ferdinand I of Austria. Freedom briefly declared in Hungary under Louis Kossuth. Revolts in Denmark, Ireland, Lombardy, Schleswig-Holstein and Venice. Germany briefly united in a parliament at Frankfort; unity destroyed by the King of Prussia.

Each of the revolutionary leaders operating throughout Europe were known Masons — Masons who had communicated in their lodge meetings the timing of each eruption. France was in the forefront. When the Orleans monarchy was toppled on March 6, 1848, the new provisional government was made up of eleven members, nine of whom were Grand Orient Masons. The first order of business was to receive an official delegation from the lodges — a Masonic parade with all the finery of their regalia.

According to Miller, this delegation consisted of 300 Freemasons: "with their banners flying over the brethren of every rite representing French Freemasonry [they] marched to the Hotel de Ville, and there offered their banners to the Provisional Government of the Republic, proclaiming aloud the part they had just taken in the glorious Revolution."

On March 7, 1848, the Paris newspaper, *Le Moniteur,* reported on this so-called "worker's communist revolution." De Poncins quotes:

They saluted the triumph of their principles and congratulated themselves for being able to say that the whole country has received masonic [sic] consecration through the members of the government. Forty thousands masons [sic], distributed in more than five hundred workshops, forming between them but a single heart and mind, were promising their support to achieve the work already begun.

Two weeks later a new delegation from the Grand Orient, arrayed in their Masonic scarfs and jewels, marched to the Hotel de Ville. Waiting to receive them was Adolphe Crémieux and Gamier Pages, both attended by their political staffs, who also wore their Masonic emblems. Miller quotes a portion of the speech given by the representative of the Grand Master:

French Freemasonry cannot contain her universal burst of sympathy with the great social and national movement which has just been effected. The Freemasons hail with joy the triumph of their principles, and boast of being able to say that the whole country has received through you a Masonic consecration. Forty thousand Freemasons in 500 lodges, forming but one heart and one soul, assure you here of their support happily to lead to the end the work of regeneration so gloriously begun.

Adolphe Isaac Crémieux (1796-1880), a Jewish Mason, and member of the Provisional Government, replied:

Citizens and brothers of the Grand Orient, the Provisional Government accepts with pleasure your useful and complete adhesion. The Republic exists in Freemasonry. If the Republic does as the Freemasons have done, it will become the glowing pledge of union with all men, in all parts of the globe, and on all sides of our triangle.

When the National Assembly was formed, Freemasonry was back in control of France and the Second Republic began. Elected as a deputy for Paris was Victor Hugo, Grand Master of the Priory of Sion (GM 18441885). Freemason Louis Napoleon, nephew of Napoleon Bonaparte, was elected president of the Assembly. At first Hugo backed Napoleon, but the more the President embraced an authoritarianism of the right, the more Hugo moved toward the Assembly's left.

Since Freemasonry held a majority in the Assembly, the lodge suggested the Assembly follow its dictates. To guarantee Masonic control of the new Republic, Freemasonry proposed to outlaw all competing secret societies, which Communist dictatorships are prone to do. Consequently, a debate arose in the Assembly concerning this question. Non-Masons wanted all secret societies, including Freemasonry, outlawed. A few Masons agreed, stating that Freemasonry was no longer needed, now that the Republic was a reality. Other Masons, however, feared a return of royalty, who might use a competing lodge to subvert the Republic....

Concerning the French government, de Poncins informs us that despite the fact that the government was essentially Masonic, the elected National Assembly was patriotic, refusing to obey the guidelines set down by Freemasonry. The Grand Orient, without hesitation, then turned to a man whom it knew to be its own, and in December 1851 assisted Louis Napoleon in a coup d'etat. Victor Hugo made one attempt to resist and then fled to Brussels.

Figure 27 — Famous French Masons.

Napoleon III (1808-1873)

Napoleon III was son of Louis Bonaparte and nephew of Napoleon I. He became head of the family when Napoleon II died in 1832. After the Revolution of 1848 he was welcomed to Paris, elected to the national assembly, and became president of the Republic, Dec. 10, 1848. In 1852 he defied Freemasonry and proclaimed himself Emperor Napoleon III. After a new constitution was decreed, he instituted a dictatorial regime sanctioned by periodic plebiscites. Napoleon became an enemy of the same Grand Orient that raised him to power. He was a member of the Ancient and Accepted Scottish Rite of France. See *Scarlet and Beast,* Vol. I, chps. 10, 12.

Victor Hugo (1802-1885)

Grand Master of the Priory of Sion (1844-1885)

Following the communist uprisings of 1848 in France, Hugo coined the phrase, the "United States of Europe" at the Masonic Peace Conference in 1849. In 1851, when Napoleon III perfected his coup d'etat, Hugo made one attempt to resist and then fled to Brussels. While in exile he wrote satirical poems, which presented Napoleon as a thief and a killer. These works ultimately toppled Napoleon. **See *Scarlet and the Beast*, Vol. 1, 3rd edition, chaps. 12 & 17.**

Figure 28 — Famous British Masons

18° Sir Thomas Stamford Raffles (1781-1826)

English Administrator; founder of the city of Singapore and of the London Zoo.

He joined the East India Co. as a clerk at age 13 and became a brilliant administrator, scholar, traveler, and naturalist.

In 1805 he was sent to Penang as assistant secretary to the first governor. He persuaded Lord Minto of the necessity of taking Java from the French, and accompanied the expedition. He was lieutenant governor of Java from 1811-1816 and introduced a new system of land tenure, removing fetters imposed on trade.

He was appalled at the selfish and cruel trade monopolies, forced labor, slavery, piracy, and general lawlessness, and hoped to end this by spreading British protection over the area.

Cheated of his ambitions for the whole Eastern Archipelago, he did, however, obtain the pirate island of Singapore from the rulers of Johore. He justly referred to "my city of Singapore," saying "I have declared that the port of Singapore is a free port and the trade thereof open to ships and vessels of every nation."

Sir Thomas was initiated in Lodge *Vertutis et Artis Aminci*, established on the Pondoz-Gedeh coffee estate near Buitenzorg, Java, only two months after his conquest of the Dutch. The Master was a former Governor of Java, and a second candidate was a member of the Dutch council. Both these brethren were markedly hostile to the British in public life, but such was the character of Raffles that he was welcomed into their midst. He was passed (2o) in this lodge, but raised (3°) on July 5, 1813 in the Lodge of Friendship at Surabaja, Java, and subsequently made Past Master by his Dutch brethren. He received the 18° in the Rose Croix chapter, *La Vertueuse* in Batavia.

Figure 29 — Famous British Masons

3° Sir Walter Scott a great storyteller (1771-1832)

Scottish poet, novelist historian and biographer. He was called to the bar in 1792, and was sheriff of Selkirk in 1799. Became a principal clerk to court of session, but withdrew from the bar to devote himself to writing and publishing.

He was initiated, passed, and raised at an emergency meeting of Lodge Saint David No. 36 of Edinburgh on Monday, March 2, 1801. His father had been initiated in the same lodge in Jan. 1754, and his elder brother was also a member. Later his son was initiated in Lodge Canongate Kilwinning No. 2, on Nov. 19, 1826.

On June 4, 1816, he laid the foundation stone of a new lodge room at Selkirk in the presence of the Provincial Grand Master, the Marquis of Lothian, and was elected an honorary member of that lodge on the occasion. He was created a Baronet in grandmastership of the Royal Grand Conclave of Knights Templar of Scotland, but declined because of "age and health not permitting me to undertake the duties."

He attended lodge frequently, as was attested by the secretary in 1841, when proposing that the name of Saint David Lodge be altered to "Sir Walter Scott's Lodge." The proposal, however, was defeated.

St. David Lodge subscribed to the monument to Sir Walter in Princess St., Edinburgh, and attended the laying of the cornerstone with Masonic honors by the Grand Master in 1840.

Figure 30 — Famous British Masons.

Robert Falcon Scott (1868-1912)

On March 29, 1912, three dying men lay in a little tent on the frozen Antarctic continent — three heroic men who had made their painful way to the South Pole. On their way back they had been caught by a terrible blizzard within 11 miles of a depot where they had left food and fuel. While the gale beat and howled outside the flimsy shelter, their commander feebly wrote these words: "We shall stick it out to the end, but we are getting weaker of course and the end cannot be far. It seems a pity but I cannot write any more. — R. Scott.

So ended the two-year British Antarctic expedition. His records and diaries were found by a search party in Nov., 1912. Robert Scott was a member of Drury Land Lodge No. 2127, London, in 1901. He was also a member of St. Alban's Lodge No. 2597, Christ Church, New Zealand, and Navy Lodge No. 2613, of England.

Viscount Horatio Nelson (1758-1805)
British Naval hero. Saw first service in the West Indies in 1780. Served under Hood in taking Bastia and Calvi, losing his right eye in last engagement. He completed the reduction of Corsica in 1794. He gained victory over French and Spanish fleets off Cape St. Vincent in 1797 and named Rear Admiral. Was shot through right elbow in attempting to take Santa Cruz de Tenerife in 1797, and lost his arm by amputation. Captured or sank all but two frigates of the French fleet in Battle of the Nile, 1798. Won the Battle of Trafalgar with the French fleet in 1805, but was struck by a sharpshooter's musket ball that broke his spine. He died as victory was completed. In *Freemasons' Quarterly Review*, 1839, Nelson is claimed as a Mason. In *History of Freemasonry in Norfolk* it is written, "In Memory of Bro. V. Nelson of the Nile, who lost his life in battle." At his funeral was carried a framed reading by York Lodge No. 256, "We rejoice with our Country but mourn our Brother."

Figure 31 — Famous British Masons.
See *Scarlet and the Beast*, Vol.1, 3rd ed., chap. 2-4; 23-24; Vol. 2, ch. 1.

King Edward VII (1841-1910)
Grand Master of all England (1874-1897)

Dr. Erasmus Darwin (1731-1802) Was made a Mason in the famous Canongate Kilwinning Lodge No.2 of Edinburgh, Scotland. Was a physician.

Charles Darwin (1809-1882) born in Shrewsbury, Shropshire England Charles Darwin's grandfather, Dr. Erasmus Darwin (above), was a Mason. Charles' brothers were Masons. Some suggest Charles, an atheist, may have been a Grand Orient Mason, but there are no records.

3° Cecil J. Rhodes (1853-1902) Famed for Rhodes Scholarship. Was member of Prince Rose Croix No. 30, AASR at Oxford. *Scarlet and Beast,* vol.1, 3rd ed., chap.24.

Figure 32

Thomas H. Huxley (1825-1895)
son
Leonard Huxley (1860-1933)
Grandson
Julian Huxley (1887-1975)
The British Masonic Royal Society promoted the theory of Charles Darwin through Freemason, Dr. Thomas H. Huxley. In 1850, T.H. Huxley, with no obvious accomplishments to his name, was made a Fellow of the Royal Society at the relatively young age of twentysix. As the major protagonist for the theory of evolution, Huxley encouraged Darwin, a timid man, to put his evolutionary thoughts on paper. Dr. Huxley, therefore, became the official spokesman for the recluse Darwin. The 33rd degree Supreme Council of Mizraim Freemasonry at Paris, reveals in its minutes its promotion of evolution as science, while they themselves scoffed at the theory: "It is

with this object in view [scientific theory of evolution] that we are constantly, by means of our press, arousing a blind confidence in these theories. The intellectuals...will puff themselves up with their knowledge and without any logical verification of them will put into effect all the information available from science, which our agentur specialists have cunningly pieced together for the purpose of educating their minds in the direction we want. Do not suppose for a moment that these statements are empty words: think carefully of the successes we arranged for Darwinism...."

Freemasonry in America has picked up the mantle of Mizraim. In it's March, 1922, *New Age* magazine, it states: "the Craft believes the kingdom of God is to be established among men by the evolution and development of man himself..."

Julian Huxley (above) and his brother, Aldous Huxley (1894-1963), had both been under the Masonic tutelage of 33° Freemason H.G. Wells (18661946). In the 1920s, Wells directed the brothers to 33° Freemason Aleister Crowley for further training. Crowley inducted them into the Golden Dawn drug-using cult where they were trained on how to subvert a nation through drug addiction. Read more in *Scarlet and the Beast*, Volume 2, chapter 1 and Volume 3, chapter 7.

Figure 33 — British Masonic Royalty.

Queen Alexandria Victoria (1819-1901)

Royal Patroness of Freemason in the British Empire

Queen of England, 1837-1901. She was the only child of George III's fourth son, Edward, Duke of Kent (a Freemason). Her father was the last Grand Master of the "Ancients" in England (1813). Her son, Edward VII, became Grand Master of the United Grand Lodge of England in 1875.

At the death of her father, she announced that as a monument to his memory, she would appoint herself as Royal Patroness of the Masonic Fraternity in the British Empire.

She also became Patroness of the Royal Masonic Institution for Boys in 1852, and Chief Patroness of the Royal Masonic Institution for Girls in 1882.

At a great assembly of Freemasons at the Royal Albert Hall under the presidency of the Prince of Wales, an address was voted to Her Majesty on her Jubilee. She then received a deputation from the Grand Lodge on Aug. 2, 1887, when the address was presented. The same occurred in 1897 on her Diamond Jubilee.

Figure 34 — British Masonic Royalty.

33° Edward VII (1841-1910)

Eldest son of Queen Victoria of the house of Saxe-Coburg. Studied at Edinburgh, Oxford, and Cambridge. Was created Prince of Wales in 1841. Served as a Colonel in the Army in 1858. In 1863 he took a seat in the house of lords as Duke of Cornwall. Queen Victoria, however, would not allow him to take part in foreign negotiations until Gladstone's last ministry in 1892-94.

As King of England (1901-10), he promoted international amity by visits to European capitals. He brought the crown into active participation in public life and with all sections of the empire.

Called "The Peacemaker, "he was the first British royal prince to visit a colony — visiting Canada in 1860. While there he laid the cornerstone of the Canadian Parliament building at Ottawa. It is interesting to note that the Canadian government would not allow the Freemasons to take part in the ceremonies, but did welcome them to appear in their regalia. Edward VII was initiated into Freemasonry in 1868 at Stockholm, Sweden by King Adolphus Frederick, who was Grand Master of Sweden. Five years later Edward was made Master of Apollo University Lodge at Oxford; in 1875 he received all 33 degrees of the AASR; on April 28, 1875 he was elected Grand Master of the Grand Lodge of England and installed that date in a ceremony at Albert Hall conducted by the Earl of Carnarvon in the presence of 10,000 Masons; he served as Grand Master until 1901, when he ascended the throne and took the title — "Protector of the Craft." Queen Alexandria Lodge No. 2932 of London was named for his queen with her permission and good wishes.

Edward VII was Master of Prince of Wales Lodge No. 250, London; Master of Royal Alpha Lodge, London. Patron of the Grand Lodge of Scotland and Ireland; honorary member of Edinburgh Lodge No. 1; and patron of the Supreme Council of the 33° of England.

Figure 35 — Famous British Masons. Bertie, Prince of Wales, a Mason, a womanizer, and the cause behind the so-called Jack-the-Ripper murders.

Albert Victor Christian Edward "Bertie"
Prince of Wales (1864-1892)

It was customary for the Prince of Wales to join English Freemasonry. On April 28, 1875, Prince Albert Edward (Bertie) was installed as Grand Master. He did not, however, uphold the royal virtues demanded of him by society, and this reflected negatively on Freemasonry. He was an embarrassment both to the Brotherhood and to the Crown. His sole purpose in life appeared to be pleasure seeking.

Bertie was a womanizer. One of the women, a commoner, was carrying his child. She, with several other women of the street, planned to blackmail the monarchy. As a result, in 1881 Prince Edward received an anonymous letter from the British Grand Lodge, chastising him for his debauchery, and warning him of the consequence to Great Britain should he not repent. Bertie, however, did not heed the warning of his Masonic brothers, and continued his debauchery.

To save the reputation of the monarchy and Freemasonry, the Lodge decided to take action. The result was the Masonic ritual murder of the women who were blackmailing the monarchy. The murders followed precisely the mimed bloody murders during the initiation of the first three degrees of Freemasonry. Afterwards, Scotland Yard took pictures of the bodies and created Jack the Ripper. You can read the details in *Scarlet and the Beast,* Vol. 1, 3rd edition, chapters 6 and 23.

Fig. 36 — British Masonic Royalty.

33° Edward VIII (1894-1972)
King of England Jan. thru Dec. 1936

Edward VIII was the eldest son of King Edward VII, and brother of King George V, whose wife was Queen Mary. Edward's full name : Edward Albert Christian George Andrew Patrick David.

When Edward succeeded his father on Jan. 20, 1936 as Edward VIII, he was crowned both king and Grand Master of English Freemasonry simultaneously.

He was the first bachelor king in 176 years. When he proposed to marry Mrs. Wallis Simpson, an American divorced commoner, and elevate her to queen, it raised a storm of protests, resulting in his abdication eleven months later. Before ascending the throne, Edward was Prince of Wales. After abdication he became Duke of Windsor.

Edward was initiated into Freemasonry on May 2, 1919 in the Household Brigade Lodge (No. 2614) by H.R.H. Arthur, Duke of Connaught and Strathearn. He was appointed Senior Warden of the lodge in 1920 and elected Deputy Master in 1921. On Oct. 25, 1922 he was installed as Senior Grand Warden of the Grand Lodge of England in Royal Albert Hall in the presence of nearly 9,000 brethren. He was named Provincial Grand Master for Surrey on July 22, 1924, and Grand Master of the Grand Lodge of England in 1936. Served as Grand Superintendent of Royal Arch Masonry for Surrey. Was an honorary 33° of the Supreme Council Scottish Rite of England.

During World War II, Edward VIII not only supported Hitler, he did so loudly. Speaking in Masonic terms, the King expressed his views concerning Hitler: "Whatever happens, whatever the outcome, a New Order is going to come into the world..." (see *Scarlet and the Beast*, Vol. 1, 3rd ed., chapter 25; also see PB.S9.F27).

Figure 37— British Masonic Royalty.

lizabeth II (1926-) Queen of the United Kingdom since 1952, and head of the Commonwealth. Born in London, England, the daughter of George VI. Formerly Princess Elizabeth Alexandra Mary, she was proclaimed queen on 6 February 1952, and crowned on 2 June 1953. Her husband was created Duke of Edinburgh on the eve of their wedding (20 Nov. 1947), and styled Prince Philip in 1957. They have three sons, Charles Philip Arthur George (b. 1948); Andrew Albert Christian Edward (b. 1960); Edward Anthony Richard Louis (b. 1964); and one daughter, Anne Elizabeth Alice Louise (b. 1950).

Queen Elizabeth is Grand Patroness of each ofthethreeRoyalMasonic Benevolent Institutions conducted by the Grand Lodge of England; one for old people and one each for boys and girls. When she married Lord Mounbatten, now Philip, Duke of Edinburgh, the United Grand Lodge of Eng. presented her with a $2,500 gift in appreciation of the services her father, King George VI, rendered to the Craft.

Fig. 38 — Masonic speech given by His Royal Highness, Philip, Duke of Kent, Grand Master of English Freemasonry. Philip was initiated in Navy Lodge No. 2612 of London on Dec. 5, 1952. Present at his initiation was 33° Mason Geoffrey Francis Fisher,Archbishop of Canterbury.
See Fisher's Masonic credentials on next page. Prince Charles, son of Elizabeth and Philip, has steadfastly refused to join the Masons. From King James I, all British kings have been Freemasons. Look for Prince William, son of Charles, to join the Lodge and be next King of England — if Prince Charles holds out.

Duke orders new image for Masons

NOT SO long ago my tongue would be "cut out by the root and buried in the sand below low-water mark" for saying a word out of turn about the Freemasons. But now the Duke of Kent, Grand Master of the United Grand Lodge of England and the nation's leading Freemason, is determined to roll up the proverbial trouser leg and expose Masonic rites to public scrutiny.

He has ordered all Masonic branches to launch publicity drives, and a video is now on sale singing the praises of the funny handshake.

It is a revolution for this most secret of secret societies whose reputation has

RITES: Duke of Kent

been truly blackened in recent years.

The Church of England's General Synod has expressed doubts about the compatibility of Freemasonry and Christianity. Its influence is said to

have corrupted our police force and provided a cover for the Mafia. And when in 1982 'God's Banker' Roberto Calvi was found hanging from Blackfriars Bridge not 100 yards from where I sit, a sinister Masonic lodge was implicated.

Now the Duke — his brother, Prince Michael of Kent is also a member as is Prince Philip — has declared that it is time for Masonic glasnost.

"He made his wishes quite clear that immediate steps are to be taken to give assurance to those who were not Masons that the fraternity was very proud of its heritage and achievements, and that every effort is to be made to make Masonry and its ideals known," says my man in the Masonic apron.

The Duke is determined to restore the society's good name. I can only hope his open policy pays off by next year, when the Masons plan to celebrate their 275th anniversary at the most Christian St. Paul's cathedral where Prince Charles, who has steadfastly refused to join the Masons, was married.

Figure 39 — Masonic speech given by His Royal Highness, Duke of Kent, Grand Master of English Freemasonry. Speech printed in *The Northern Light*, Aug. 1997, AASR, Northern Jurisdiction (NJ) of Freemasonry, U.S.A.

HIGHLIGHTS OF GRAND MASTER'S ADDRESS
at the 275th anniversary ceremony

I believe that there cannot now be many who doubt the wisdom of our decision in 1984 to leave behind a Dark Age, when our habit of responding to any criticism or indeed comment, however inaccurate, with a wall of silence seemed to confirm people's worst fears about Freemasonry.

As our policy on public relations has changed, so the craft has, I believe, become more lively. In preparing to explain ourselves, we have had to take a close look at what we are and what we do, and the exercise has done us no end of good.

It can do no harm occasionally, though not too often, to go back to first principles and so try to make certain we are navigating by the right stars. This anniversary offers a good occasion to ask such questions.

What, then, is Freemasonry? Clearly it must be more than what the Archbishop of York called a "fairly harmless eccentricity" in 1987. If that was all that Freemasonry was about, it would not have flourished as it has for over three hundred years, attracting and retaining the interest of millions of men today all over the world.

Freemasonry brings people together from vastly different backgrounds. With its sensible rule prohibiting discussion of religion or politics within its lodges, it removes two likely causes of dissension, and allows Freemasons to concentrate instead on what they have in common — and that, in this world, cannot be bad.

On the contrary, with its encouragement of good fellowship and of consideration for one's fellow men, and its insistence on a belief in God, Freemasonry can reasonably be held to be a force for good in society. It is up to all Masons to ensure that that enviable position is only enhanced.

—*HRH The Duke of Kent*

AASR, Northern Jurisdiction

Figure 40 — British Masonic Royalty. Prince Charles will not become King of England until he joins Freemasonry. If and when he becomes King of England, you can rest assured that he did indeed join the British Brotherhood.

Prince Charles (1948)

Prince of Wales. Eldest son of Queen Elizabeth II and Prince Philip, Duke of Edinburgh, and heir apparent to the throne. Born in Buckingham Palace, London, England, UK. As the eldest son of the monarch, he was given the title of Prince of Wales in 1958. He studied at Cheam and Gordonstoun, and entered Trinity College, Cambridge in 1967. He served in the RAF and Royal Navy, 1971-76. In 1981 married Lady Diana Frances, younger daughter of the 8th Earl of Spencer. They had two sons: Prince William, born in 1982, and Prince Charles Albert. The couple separated in 1992, and divorced in 1996.

Prince Charles refuses to join Freemasonry, which means he will not ascend the throne following the reign of Queen Elizabeth II. However, the British tabloids depict Charles, who has shown an interest in the occult, participating in primitive rituals, dancing beneath the stars with dusky African beauties, and summoning up the spirits of the dead.

To Charles, his life is consistent with the teachings of the occultist he admires, the 20th century Swiss psychiatrist Carl Jung. To endow his predestined life with meaning, Charles has become a disciple of Jung, who believed, among other things, in the "collective unconscious," the premise that diverse cultures share basic myths and symbols.

One day Charles is making solemn speeches about the realities of British trade, the next he is reportedly trying to contact his late mentor, Lord Montbatten, via a spiritual medium. (Life *Magazine,* Sept. 1987, pgs. 32-37). When Charles joins Freemasonry, he will be crowned King.

Figure 41 — Famous British Masons.
See *Scarlet and the Beast*, Volume 1, 3rd edition, chapters. 10 & 18-19.

3° Sir Walter Besant (1836-1901)

English novelist. Educated in King's College, London and Christ's College, Cambridge. Was co-author with James Rice of a series of novels including *Ready-Money Mortiboy* (1872) and *The Seamy Side* (1881). Sole author of *All Sorts and Conditions of Men* (1882) and *Children of Gibeon* (1886).

Besant was raised (3°) in Mauritius Lodge in 1862 and became Master of Marquis of Dalhousie Lodge No. 1159, London, in 1873. He conceived the idea of establishing a lodge of research and as a result became one of the founders of the famous Quatuor Coronati Lodge No. 2076 of London, serving as its treasurer at one time.

His sister-in-law, Annie Besant, a hefty woman, was more famous than he in the occult world. In fact, she spoke at many Masonic functions. Annie was a female Mason, drug-pusher, and promoter of free sex. Albert Pike was one of Annie's many lovers.

Annie was a member of the population control Malthusian League. In reality, birth control was promoted to offset the obvious results of Annie Besants promotion of women's sexual liberation. (See more on Walter and Annie in *Scarlet and the Beast*, Volume 1, 3rd edition, chaps. 10,18-20, 22).

Benjamin Disraeli (1804-1881)

Prime Minister of England under Queen Victoria. Was titled the 1st Earl of Beaconsfield. Some authors have reported him as a Mason, because Beaconsfield Lodge No. 1662 of London was named for him and consecrated Feb. 24, 1877 with his permission to use his title as Earl of Beaconsfield and his armorial bearings. *10,000 Famous Freemasons* informs us he was not a Mason. He was of Jewish descent. His father, Isaac Disraeli had his children baptized into the Anglican Church. See *Scarlet and the Beast*, Vol. 1, 3rd ed., chaps. 12, 20, and 25.

Figure 42 — Rothschild family — famous Masons & financiers. See *Scarlet and the Beast*, Vol. 1, 3rd edition, chaps. 7, 11, 12, 21, 24, 26.

◀ **3° Baron Nathan Rothschild**
(1777-1836)

Third son of Meyer Amachel Rothschild (1743-1812), German/Jewish founder of the family banking empire, which became one of the richest and most affluent of all time. Nathan was London representative of banking family, & family's first baron; established London branch. Member Lodge Emulation, London, Oct. 4, 1802.

▲
33° James Meyer Rothschild
(1792-1868)

Financier. Bro. of Nathan. James established branch at Paris. Was 33° AASR of French Supreme Council. See *Scarlet & Beast*, V. 3, Ch. 4, for his involvement in triggering our Civil War.

Sons & descendants were all Masons:
Amschel 1773-1885
Solomon Meyer 1774-1855
Nathan Meyer (standing)
Carl 1788-1855
James Meyer (to right)
Lionel 1808-1879
33° Edmond de 20th C.
James de 20th C.
Lord Nathan Meyer 20th C.

Father of clan, Meyer Rothschild (1743-1812) not a Mason.

Figure 43 — Famous German Masons.

Admiral von Tirpitz (1849-1930)

German naval commander who is credited with the creation of the modern German Navy. He advocated unrestricted submarine warfare in WWI. This led to the entry of the U.S. in the war. At the fall of the German empire, he took refuge in Switzerland where he published his memoirs. Shortly after 1924 he returned to Germany and became a member of the Nazi Reichstag. He Masonic affiliation was in the lodge called *Zum Aufrichtigen Herzen* at FrankfurtOrder.

Johann Gottfried von Herder (1744-1803)

German philosopher and man of letters. Among his works are *Kritische Walder* (1769); *Abhandlung uber den Ursprung der Sprache* (1772); and various editions of German folksongs. He was made a Mason at Riga in the lodge *Zum Schwert* in 1766.

Figure 44 — Famous German Masons.

William I (1797-1888)

King of Prussia, 1861-88. Emperor of Germany, 1871-88. Full name was Wilhelm Friedrich Ludwig.

Fought against Napoleon in 1814-15. Became Prince of Prussia in 1840 when his brother Frederick William IV became emperor. Was unpopular because of his absolutist ideas and suppression of insurrections. He fled to England in 1848, the year all Europe was in political chaos — chaos created by Freemasonry (see Masonic slogan, Sect. 1, Fig. 51, "Order out of Chaos"). On becoming King of Prussia in 1861, he proclaimed he "ruled by the favor of God and of no one else." He had continuous struggles with liberals.

In the war with Austria in 1866 he personally commanded at Sadowa and led the German armies in the Franco-Prussian War of 1870-71.

Again he personally commanded at Gravelotte and Sedan, and was proclaimed emperor of Germany at Versailles on Jan. 18, 1871. He strengthened Bismarck and his generals in exercising Prussian control of Germany.

William was initiated in a special lodge of the *Grosse Landesloge* at Berlin on May 22, 1840, at which time the three Grand Masters of the Berlin Grand Lodges participated. He was honorary member of the Grand Lodge of Scotland and protector of Freemasonry in Germany.

The proceedings of the Grand Lodge of New York in 1888 stated: "It would be superfluous now to mention his wonderful career. Despite the cares of state, he had upon frequent occasions manifested his attachment to our Fraternity, of which for many years he had been a member. He held the office, unknown among us, of Protector of the eight German Grand Lodges comprising the Grand Lodge League within his dominion."

Fig. 45 — Famous German Masons. See *S&B*, Vol. 1, chaps, 6, 7, 8.

Johann Wolfgang von Goethe (1749-1832). German poet and intellectual. He made an extended trip with the Duke of Weimar in 1799 and found evidence of the advantages of Masonic member-ship. He received the higher Templar degrees of the Rite of Strict Observance. His writings contain numerous Masonic allu-sions and references. ▼

Johann C.F. von Schiller ▲ (1759-1805). German poet and Playwright. Regarded as 2nd only to Goethe in the field of German literature. He was a member of Rudolstadt Lodge of Berlin.

◄ **Gotthold E. Lessing** (1729-1781). German dramatist & critic. Two of his writings are Masonic; *Nathan the Wise* is a dramatic poem on religious toler-ation, preaching universal brother-hood. It was put on stage by Schiller and Goethe. *Ernst and Falk* is a defense of Masonry. In 1771 he was initiated in the lodge *Zu den drei Goldenen Rosen* at Hamburg.

Moses Mendelssohn (1729-1796)

German Jewish philosopher, called "The German Socrates." He was the grandfather of Felix Mendelssohn, the composer. He formed a close friendship with Lessing in 1754, which inspired the latter to write *Nathan der Weise* (*Nathan the Wise*), a dramatic poem on toleration. He was also a friend of Nicolia, Lavater, and Kant, contributing to several of their works as a critic. He wrote *Phandon* in support of the immortality of the soul and his *Jerusalem oder uber Religiose Macht und Judentum* was a plea for religious tolerance.

The bulletin of the International Masonic Congress of 1917 lists him as a Freemason, and Beswick, in his *Swedenborg Rite*, states Mendelssohn was a Scottish Rite Mason.

Mendelssohn was also a member of the Illuminati. His closest friend and fellow Illuminatus was Gotthold Lessing, a rebel son of the head Lutheran pastor in Kamenz, Germany. Lessing hated Jesus Christ and all things Christian, writing diatribes against the Church. Lessing defended Mendelssohn's work for the greater Illuminati cause — the total destruction of both Christianity and Judaism.

Orthodox Rabbi Marvin S. Antelman writes in *To Eliminate The Opiate*, "Moses Mendelssohn is regarded by many as the father of the Haskala movement." Haskala is the name given those early Jewish liberals who were known as "enlighteners" and later called Jewish Reform Movement. In America they founded the American Civil Liberties Union (ACLU) to destroy Christianity there. Haskala were followers of a false Messiah, Shabbetai Zevi (1626-1676), known as Frankists in Mendelssohn's day, named after Jacob Frank (1726-1791), the Jew who resurrected the Sabbatai movement for the express purpose of destroying Orthodox Judaism.

Prior to the founding of the Illuminati in 1776, Mendelssohn, a Scottish Rite Mason, was known as the leader of the Haskala. Freemasonry, however was his vehicle to prominence. In *Scarlet and the Beast* you can also read about his involvement with a chain of whore houses (named Union of Virtue), in which many Masonic plots were hatched.

Fig. 47 — Famous magician Mason. See *S&B*, Vol. 1, chap. 7.

Daniel Wolf (?) alias The Comte de Saint-Germain

Another member of the Illuminati sect was Daniel Wolf, mentor of Cagliostro (1743-95), Daniel Wolf (alias Saint-Germain), son of a Jewish doctor from Strasburg. He delighted the King of France and Madame de Pompadour with his magic.

Saint-Germain made many false and outrageous claims. He declared he was Grand Master of Continental Freemasonry at a time when that position was held by Frederick the Great, King of Prussia. He also claimed he had discovered the secret of retaining his youth, displaying himself as an example. When he was only fifty he said he was seventy-four. Dr. Mackey confirms that St. Germain "laid claim to the highest rank of Freemasonry, the Order being at that time strong in France, claiming also that he was over five hundred years of age, had been born in Chaldaea, [and] possessed the secrets of the Egyptian sages...."[7] At his death he had increased his age to 1,500 years, maintaining he had gone through several incarnations. Although he died in 1784, his admirers upheld that he was in some remote corner of Europe.

Fig. 48 — Famous Austrian Mason. See *S&B*, Vol. 1, 3rd ed., ch, 6, 18, 19.

Wolfgang Amadeus Mozart (1756-1791)

Austrian composer who created more than 600 works during his short life, covering almost every known field of music. Son of Leopold, also a composer and a Freemason.

Wolfgang wrote *Fellow Craft's Journey* to honor his father's initiation into the 2o of Freemasonry.

As a child prodigy, Mozart toured with his father and sister, composing his first published works at the age of seven. He was brought to London at the age of eight, playing before the royal family. In 1768, at age 12, he received an imperial commission to compose and conduct an opera, and was made concertmaster to the archbishop of Salzburg in 1769. That same year he was made a chevalier of the Golden Spur by the pope. Returning to Salzburg, he broke with the new archbishop, Hieronymus, who had attempted to hold him in ecclesiastical bondage.

In 1782 he settled in Vienna as a teacher and composer. In spite of his position as royal chamber composer to Emperor Joseph II (also a Freemason), he lived in poverty.

On December 5, 1784, Mozart was proposed for membership in the Masonic Lodge Zur Wohltatigkeit and was initiated on December 14, becoming the 20th person initiated in that lodge. Ten days later he attended lodge *Zur wahren Eintracht* and on Jan. 7, 1785, and received the second degree in the latter lodge at the request of his mother lodge. On December 1, 1785, his own lodge, *Zur Wohltatigkeit*, united with the lodges *Zu den drei Feuern* and *Zum heiligen neugekroentin Hoffnung*. This was by decree of Emperor Joseph II. For the occasion, Mozart wrote *Opening Ode* (Op. K483). The text includes: "Oh sing today beloved brothers... Your song of jubilation... For Joseph's benevolence... has crowned anew our hope... For in our hearts a threefold flame now gleams."

His best music was composed after his initiation, of which a great amount had Masonic connections. His greatest work is perhaps *The Magic Flute*, his last opera. Mozart felt that Freemasonry was being persecuted and this opera was intended to vindicate the aims of the institution. The overture contains three chords, played thrice to the rhythm of the three raps in the third degree of Freemasonry. The second act is laid in the temple of Isis and Osiris and the Masonic allusion is very striking. At that time it was thought that the Craft was of Egyptian origin. Here the high priest puts three questions: "Is he virtuous? Is he charitable? Can he be silent?, and three cords are heard once again.

In 1785 he wrote *Die Gessellenreise* (Journey of the Fellowcrafts, the 2nd degree of Freemasonry), as Masonic song (Opus 468). On April 20, 1785 he wrote *Maurerfreude* (Opus 471), a short cantata which was performed on April 24 in a special lodge held that day to celebrate Von Born's discovery of the method of working ores by amalgamation.

Mozart's last Masonic work was written for the dedication of a Masonic temple in Vienna on Nov. 15, 1791. The words were by Schikaneder, a member of the lodge, who

also wrote the libretto for *The Magic Flute* (Opus 623), written for two tenors and a bass with orchestral accompaniment. It was the last finished composition of which Mozart conducted the performance. It contains an appendix and a hymn for closing of the lodge, which was probably Mozart's farewell to the Craft.

The words to the hymn, in part, are: "Today we consecrate this habitation for our temple, for the first time we within this new seat of knowledge and of virtue, and look, the consecration is completed. Oh! that the work were finished also that consecrates our hearts."

Mozart was present when his good friend and fellow composer Granz Joseph Hayden, was initiated in *Lodge Zur Wahrn Eintracht* of Vienna on February 4, 1785.

Mozart's death came under unusual circumstances while on a trip to Berlin, and it is thought he was poisoned by a man named Salieri. He was buried in an unknown grave.

A lodge of mourning was held for him and the oration delivered there was published in 1792, and sold for the benefit of his family. The oration: "It has pleased the everlasting Master Builder to tear our beloved Brother from the chain of our brotherhood. Who did not know him? Who did not value him? Who did not love him, our worthy Brother, Mozart? Only a few weeks ago he stood in our midst, and with the magic tones added such beauty to the dedication of our Masonic Temple. Mozart's death brings irreparable loss to his art; his talents which were apparent in his earliest youth have made him even then the greatest marvel of his time. Half Europe valued him. The great called him their favorite..., and we called him Brother... He was a most enthusiastic follower of our Order...," etc., etc. Read of Mozart's revolutionary activity in *Scarlet and the Beast*, Vol. 1, 3rd edition, chaps. 6, 18, 19.

Fig. 49 — Front cover of Mosart Jubilee Edition 1956 album.

Below is top portion of back cover. Not listed in this photo are the Masonic pieces. On bottom of back cover is a Masonic tribute to Mozart (see below).

"That the Masonic order knew whom it had lost in Mozart when he died on December 5, 1791, less than 36 years old, is shown in this brief excerpt from the long oration read at the Lodge shortly thereafter: 'It has pleased the Almighty to take from among us our best-beloved and most estimable member." etc., etc.

Fig. 50 — Famous Austrian Mason. See *Scarlet and the Beast*, Vol. 1, chapter 6.

Franz Joseph Haydn (1732-1809)
Austrian composer, regarded as the first great master of the symphony and the quartet. He was known by the nickname Papa Haydn. The name shows the deep affection in which he was held. He acted like a father to his associates and to struggling young men of talent. Haydn's father, a man of refined tastes and fond of music, was a mechanic in the town of Rohrau, in lower Austria. In his childhood, Haydn Jr. spent the evenings listening to his father play the harp, while his mother sang the folk songs of Hungary. The themes of these songs later found their way into some of the finest compositions of the master.

Haydn sang in the cathedral choir of St. Stephen's at Vienna from 1740-49. From 1760-90 he was *kapellmeister* in the service of the Esterhazy family, and it was during this period that he wrote some of his greatest music, operas, Masses, piano sonatas, symphonies and overtures.

Haydn had a long friendship with Mozart, beginning in 1781. Mozart's influence aided him in developing a fuller mastery of orchestral effects in his later symphonies. While in England from 1791-92, he wrote and conducted six symphonies, and again in 1794-95, wrote another six symphonies while in that country. He was a resident of the Vienna suburbs from 1795, where he wrote his last eight Masses, his finest chamber music, the Austrian national anthem, and the two great oratorios, *The Creation*, and *The Seasons*.

It is probable that his association with Mozart led him to petition Freemasonry. He joined the lodge three years after their close association started. Haydn received his Entered Apprentice degree on Feb. 4, 1785 in the lodge Zur Wahrn Eintracht at Vienna. Mozart was present on that occasion.

Figure 51 — Famous German Masons. See *Scarlet and the Beast*, Vol. 1, chapter 6 — "Music and Revolution."

Lugvig von Beethoven (1770-1827)

Maynard Solomon's book, *Late Beethoven*, subtitled: *Music, Thought, Imagination*, deals with the composer's music from 1812 until his death in 1827.

Several of the dozen essays in this book originally were written for academic publications and conferences, so the reader must contend with more than 60 musical examples. There is much lofty theorizing, too, much of it provocative (the significance of immobility in his late music), and some of it faintly silly phallic overtones in writings by Beethoven and his circle about the beauty of trees.

Despite that, Solomon has made news with this book. His research indicates that Beethoven was a practicing Freemason well into his late years.

No records survive to show that Beethoven was a member of any lodge, but Solomon's examination of the "Tagebuch," or diary, Beethoven kept from 1812 to 1818 shows that many of the passages from obscure literature the composer copied into the book can be explained only by reference to Masonic sources, and that keeping the diary itself was part of the self-education process required of would-be initiates.

Of course, many public figures of the late 18th century were Masons; the secret society's focus on universal brotherhood went hand in hand with the Enlightenment. In addition to composers like Haydn and Mozart ("The Magic Flute" is a Masonic opera) Gothe, George Washington and Ben Franklin also knew the secret handshake.

Solomon's focus on Masonic influence on Beethoven, however, enables us to see many of his last works in a very different light, most notably the "Ninth Symphony." The Choral finalé of that work sets to music the "Ode to Joy" of Friedrich Schiller, a poem recognized in its day as Masonic.

Fig. 52 — Founder of "Mesmerism," precursor to "hypnotism." See *Scarlet and the Beast*, Vol. 1, chaps. 6, 9, and 10 to learn how he used Mesmerism in mind control leading up to the French Revolution.

Frederic Antoine Mesmer (1733-1815)

Physician, born near Constance, Austria. He studied and practised medicine at Vienna, and in 1772 took up the idea that there exists a power which he called "animal magnetism." This led to the founding of *mesmerism*, precursor of hypnotism in modern psychotherapy. In 1778 he went to Paris, where he created a sensation curing diseases at seances. In 1785, when a learned commission denounced him as an imposter, he retired to Switzerland.

Nesta Webster describes how Mesmer used a form of music to mesmerize: "Mesmer himself — stirring the fluid in his magic bucket, around which his disciples wept, slept, fell into trances or convulsions, raved or prophesied.... Freemasonry, eager to discover the secret of the magic bucket, hastened to enroll him in their Order, and Mesmer was received into the Primitive Rite of Free and Accepted Masons in 1785.

While in France he became a member of Philadelphia Lodge at Norbonne. Later he founded his own society in France called *Order of Universal Harmony*. and became involved with the famous charlatan, Cagliostro (real name Joseph Balsamo). Cagliostro used Mesmer's "Animal Magnetism" in his Masonic initiations.

Fig. 53 — Famous German Masons. See *Scarlet and the Beast*, Vol. 1, 3rd ed., chaps, 19 and 25.

Richard Wagner (1813-1883)

German composer. Some say Wagner was a Mason, because Masonry played a large part in much of his music. Freemasonry says he was not a Mason, but wanted to be.

Wagner had many Masonic influences in his life, including his family and friends. His brother-in-law, Prof. Oswald Marbach, was one of the most important personalities in Freemasonry during Wagner's time, and in view of the Masonic aspect of his *Parsifal*, it is speculated that he learned much of Masonic ritual and ideas from Marbach, who held the chair of the chapter *Balduin, Zur Lindi* of Leipzig for more than 30 years, and was an honorary member of more than 50 lodges.

Another great friend of Wagner was the banker, Feustel in Bayreuth, who from 1863-69 was master of the lodge *Zur Sonne* in Bayreuth. In 1847 Feustel proposed that the lodge abolish the restrictions on nonChristians becoming members, apparently at the request of Wagner, since Wagner informed Feustel of his desire to become a member of the lodge *Eleusis zur Verschuregenheit* in Bayreuth. But, Feustel was advised not to submit a formal petition, since there were members who reproached Wagner for his personal life.

Wagner was selfish and vain. He was unkind to his friends and made those near him unhappy. For example, when Wagner's first wife died in 1866, he married his best friend's wife in 1870, after she had deserted her husband for Wagner.

Wagner took part in the German political revolt in 1848-49, when all Europe exploded with Masonic revolutions. He was forced to flee to Switzerland, where he stayed for the next ten years.

Wagner's opera "Rienzi" was successfully produced at Dresden in 1842 and resulted in his appointment as musical director of the Saxon court. Seventy years later this work would influence a man named Adolph Hitler, who considered himself a reincarnation of Rienzi, destined to throw off the yoke of the Judao/Masonic conspiracy.

Fig. 54 — Mary Magdalene arriving pregnant on the shores of southern France, supposedly carrying the male child of Jesus Christ. This child's ancestry is supposed to have founded the Merovingian dynasty, which is credited with birthing most of Europe's royalty. This family also was the catalyst behind founding both the Priory of Sion and the Knight's Templar, which respectively founded the English and French branches of Freemasonry. Author John Daniel, with Holy Scripture as his guide, tells the true story behind this heresy in *Scarlet and the Beast*, Vol. 1.

Painting by Andrew Jones, 2001

Fig. 55 — **Grand Masters of the Priory of Sion** — From latest to earliest dates.
Priory of Sion founded Rosecrucian Freemasonry, which today is English Freemasonry.
See *Scarlet and the Beast*, Vol. 1, 3rd ed., entire.

Jean Cocteau (1897-1967)
Grand Master — 1918-1963

Claude Debussy (1862-1918)
Grand Master —1885-1918

Victor Hugo (1802-1885)
Grand Master — 1844-1885

Sir Isaac Newton (1642-1727)
Grand Master —1691-1727

Fig. 56 — **Grand Masters of Priory of Sion.** From latest to earliest dates.

Robert Boyle (1627-1691)
Grand Master — 1654-1691

Robert Fludd (1574-1637)
Grand Master — 1695-1637

Remaining Grand Masters
(from earliest to latest)

Jean de Gisors	1188-1220
Marie de St-Clair	1220-1266
Guillaume de Gisors	1266-1307
Edouard de Bar	1307-1336
Jeanne De Bar	1336-1351
Jean de St-Clair	1351-1366
Blanche d'Evreux	1366-1398
Nicolas Flamel	1398-1418
René d'Anjou	1418-1480
Iolande de Bar	1480-1483
Sandro Filipepi	1483-1510
Connétable de Bourbon	1519-1527
Ferdinand de Gonzague	1527-1575
Louis de Nevers	1575-1595
J. Valentin Andrea	1637-1654
Charles Radclyffe	1727-1746
Charles de Lorraine	1746-1780
Maximilian de Lorraine	1780-1801
Charles Nodier	1801-1844

Leonardo da Vinci (1452-1519)
Grand Master — 1510-1519

Fig. 57 **Read Sion's story in** *Scarlet and Beast* **Vol. 1 chaps. 1-3**
Godfroi de Bouillon (1060-1100) King of Jerusalem

Godfroi de Bouillon (1060-1100) wearing crown of thorns to symbolize his so-called blood kinship to Jesus Christ. Painted for Claude de Lorraine. Both Claude and his brother, Charles, duke of Guise, were tutored by Robert Fludd, Grand Master of the Priory of Sion.

Fig. 58 — Still in search of the Grail — May 12, 2004.

In Focus

A SLICE OF LIFE FROM NEAR OR FAR

Oliver and Sheila Lawn, World War II British code-breakers who worked at the intelligence center Bletchley Park, study an inscription on one of eight garden monuments Tuesday at Shugborough Hall in Staffordshire, England.

David Jones
AP Photo

MYSTERY IN MARBLE

Britain's WWII code-breakers tackle 18th-century etching

By JILL LAWLESS
Associated Press

LONDON — The experts who cracked Nazi Germany's secret codes are tackling a 10-letter enigma that has stumped fine minds for more than 250 years — D.O.U.O.S.V.A.V.V.M.

Former code-breakers from Britain's World War II intelligence center at Bletchley Park set out this week to decipher a cryptic inscription on an 18th-century monument at an English country estate.

Legend says it reveals the location of the Holy Grail. Some believe it is a private message to a deceased beloved. No one knows for sure.

"The inscription is obviously a classical reference. It's either Latin or Greek and based on some historical happening," said mathematician Oliver Lawn, 85, a Bletchley Park veteran who is leading the quest along with his linguist wife, Sheila.

The mystery is carved on a marble monument tucked away in the gardens of Shugborough House in central England, the ancestral home of photographer Lord Lichfield.

Based on a painting by French artist Nicholas Poussin, but carved in reverse, the etching depicts three shepherds pointing at an inscription on a tomb that reads "Et in arca-

dia ego" ("And I am in Arcadia, too"), Below the image is a line of letters — O.U.O.S.V. A. V. V. — and beneath that on either end, the letters D and M.

Lawn, who was recruited to Bletchley Park in 1940 while studying mathematics at Cambridge University, proclaimed himself puzzled.

Some believe the monument holds the key to finding the Holy Grail, the cup Jesus Christ drank from at the Last Supper. The Anson family, who built the Shugborough estate in the 17th century, had a long-standing interest in the Knights Templar, a secretive medieval order who claimed to be guardians of the grail.

Shugborough spokesman Russel Gethings said the carving made significant changes to Poussin's painting that could contain clues to the code.

"They changed what one of the shepherds is pointing to," he said. "He's pointing to a completely different letter than in the painting. And they've added a second sarcophagus to the picture."

Christine Large, director of the Bletchley Park museum, said the monument's code was different from the mathematical ciphers used by the Nazis.

"We have to keep an open mind about what kind of solution we're seeking here," Large said. "I think it's likely to be something more prosaic than the Holy Grail, but then most things are."

Fig. 59 — **Nostradamus** (1503-1566). Astrologer and physician. Born in St. Remy, France. Became doctor of medicine in 1529. Practised in Agen, Lyon, and other places. He set himself up as a prophet in 1547. King Charles IX of Valois, following the death Henry de Valois (Henry II), ascended the throne and appointed Nostradamus physician. *Scarlet and the Beast* Vol. 1, chap. 3

Read Nostradamus' so-called prophecies that the Valois dynasty would be destroyed.

Holy Blood, Holy Grail concludes: "Many of Nostradamus' prophecies, in short, may not have been prophecies at all. They may have been crypticmessages,ciphers, schedules, timetables, instructions, blueprints for action."

Fig. 60 — Cardinal Richelieu of France — by Champaigne. See *Scarlet and the Beast*, Vol. 1, chapter 3.

Cardinal Armand-Jean Richelieu (1585-1643)

From 1610 to 1643 the throne of France was occupied by Louis XIII, who was married to Anne of Austria. Louis paid little attention to his queen, who was lonely and desirous of male companionship.

The real power behind the throne was Cardinal Richelieu, the king's prime minister. Richelieu, if not a member of the Priory of Sion, was definitely a hireling. While the rest of Europe flamed in the throes of the Thirty Years War, Richelieu established an unprecedented stability in France — until 1633. Prior to 1633, the Protestants in Germany were being financed by Sionist Rosicrucians from England and the Continent. Richelieu continued a precedent set by Sion during the Religious Wars of France: in 1633 he began financing the German Protestants.

Holy Blood explains this apparently bizarre policy: "In 1633 Cardinal Richelieu embarked on an audacious and seemingly incredible policy. He brought France into the Thirty Years War — but not on the side one would expect.... A Catholic cardinal, presiding over a Catholic country, dispatch[ing] Catholic troops to fight on the Protestant side — against other Catholics.... No historian has ever suggested that Richelieu was a Rosicrucian. But he could not possibly have done anything more in keeping with Rosicrucian attitudes, or more likely to win him Rosicrucian favor."

Fig. 61 — Mazarin, portrait by Philippe de Champaigne, Chantilly, France.

Cardinal Jules Mazarin (1602-1661)

Louis XIII of France (r. 1610-1643) and Anne remained childless. Suddenly, in 1638, after twenty-three years of sterile marriage, Anne produced a child. Few people at the time believed he was legitimate. Gossip had the child's father Cardinal Richelieu, or perhaps a surrogate employed by Richelieu, maybe Cardinal Mazarin, Richelieu's protégé and successor. Both Louis XIII and Richelieu died in 1642. Some historians claim that Cardinal Mazarin afterwards secretly married the Queen Mother Anne.

After the death of Louis XIII, the boy king ascended the throne in 1643. Louis XIV was age five. The queen mother took the regency for her son. Cardinal Mazarin was prime minister of France, an office that the regent, Anne of Austria, entrusted to his experience and his ability in the name of the child Louis XVI.

The Priory of Sion dedicated itself to deposing both Mazarin and the boy king. Read the story in *Scarlet and the Beast*, Vol. 1, Chapter 3.

Fig. 62 — Prince Charles Stuart, exiled to France, attempted to regain the British throne. However, the next Grand Master of the Priory of Sion, Charles Radclyffe, was given the task of making sure the Bonnie Prince did not succeed in his bid to regain the British throne.

Read the Masonic intrigue in *Scarlet and the Beast*, Vol. 1, 3rd editions, chap. 4.

Prince Charles Edward Stuart - Bonnie Prince Charlie - The Young Pretender (1720-1788)

On Jan. 4, 1717, English Masonry sent the Scottish Stuarts to France in permanent exile. With them went Jacobite (Templar) Freemasonry, and closet G.M. of the Priory of Sion — Charles Radclyffe. Radclyffe's assignment? Make sure the Templar Stuarts never returned to England.

The first French Templar Lodge was founded in 1725 by this contingent of exiled Stuart sympathizers. In 1745 Prince Charles Edward Stuart, the Young Pretender, attempted to regain his Scottish throne and was soundly defeated in less than a year. His defeat was engineered by Radclyffe, who gave his own life in the process.

Upon returning to France, the Scottish Templars founded the Ancient and Accepted Scottish Rite of Freemasonry, quickly developing it to 32 degrees by 1755. In 1801 all French lodges accepted the Templar Scottish Rite degrees. That same year the Scottish Rite of Charleston, SC, created the 33rd and final degree in Templar Freemasonry.

Figure 63 — Albert Schweitzer, not a Mason, but honored by Masons.

Albert Schweitzer (1875-1965)

One of the outstanding personalities of the 20th century. Medical missionary, theologian, musician, and philosopher, born in Kaysersberg, Germany. He studied at Strasbourg, Paris, and Berlin. In 1896 made his famous decision that he would live for science and art until he was 30, then devote his life to serving humanity.

He became a curate at Strasbourg (1899), taught at the university (1902), and was appointed principal of the theological college (1903). His religious writings include Von Reimarus zu Wrede (1906). Translated, it means, "The Quest of the Historical Jesus."

He labored for many years as a missionary in French Equatorial Africa. His outstanding medical work in the back country brought him fame and the love of the natives, who he considered as his children.

Peter Leppich, a Catholic priest, by way of defamation, called him "a Protestant Freemason and Socialist." Dr. Schweitzer has never been a member of the Craft, but in 1960, on his 85th birthday, he was honored by the United Grand Lodge of Germany by being presented with the Mathias Claudius Medal — the first time this was given to a non-Mason.

Fig. 64 — Medical discoveries by famous British and French Masons.

30° Sir Alexander Fleming (1881-1955)

Graduate of St. Mary's Hospital Medical School. Professor of bacteriology at Royal Coll. of Surgeons. Discovered penicillin in 1928 for which he was awarded Nobel Prize in 1945. Discovered lysozyme in 1929. Was knighted by George VI in 1944. Was awarded distinguished service citation of Grand Lodge of New York in 1953. Fleming was a member of several English Lodges.

Master of Santa Maria Lodge No. 2682 in 1925, then secretary; Master of Misericordia Lodge No. 3286 in 1935, then treasurer; Senior Grand Deacon of the United Grand Lodge of England in 1942 and promoted to Past Grand Warden in 1948. Served as High Priest of Aesculapius Chapter and was Past Grand Sojourner of the Supreme Grand Chapter, R.A.M. of England. Later was named Past Grand Scribe.

In the Scottish Rite he was 30° and was sovereign of Victory Chapter of Rose Croix. He was also a member of the London Scottish Rifles Lodge No. 2310 and took special pride in the fact that he served as a private in the Scottish Rifles Regiment of London for 14 years.

33° Pierre G. Vassal (1769-1840)

French physician introduced use of small doses of the leaves of Foxglove plant (*Digitalis purpurea*), as treatment for heart disease. Prior to his discovery, heavy doses of Digitalis were used as poison to eliminate enemies.

Shortly after Vassal began ecclesiastical studies, he left for the army for 18 months during the French Revolution. Afterwards he studied medicine and gained a wide reputation as a physician. In 1811 he joined Grand Orient Freemasonry. Soon he was presiding over the Areopagus chapter of the Scottish Rite. In 1819 he was elected secretary-general. In 1827 (as a 33° AASR Mason) he became president of the College of Rites.

Vassal's principal Masonic works are: Historical Essay on the Institution of the Scottish Rite (1827), and General History of Initiation Since Its Origin Up to Its Institution in France (1832).

Fig. 65 Right: Foxglove plant Digitalis purpurea

Fig. 66 — Pope Paul I (1912-1978) had a heart problem for which Digitalis was prescribed.

Albino Lucianni reigned only 33 days as Pope John Paul I

The Masonic murder of Pope John Paul I is documented by David Yallop in his book, *In God's Name* (1984). Subtitled *An Investigation into the Assassination of Pope John Paul I*, Yallop reveals startling information that incriminates Freemasonry in the death of the first John Paul. He notes the mysterious correlation between the 33rd degree of Masonry and the time of the new pope's death: "Sometime during the late evening of September 28, 1978, and the early morning of September 29, 1978, thirty-three days after his election, Albino Luciani [Pope John Paul I] died." Yallop confirms that all the Cardinals and Bishops in the Vatican who were physically proximate to the Pope that night were Grand Orient Masons. He lists some of the lodges in which they were initiated and gives their Masonic code names. He also notes that Italian Grand Orient Freemasonry founded a lodge called Propaganda Two (P-2), the membership of which was, and still is, primarily Mafia.

What would bring the violent hand of Masonry upon such a popular and untested pontiff? According to Yallop, Pope John Paul I's transgression was that he discovered some priests in the Vatican had joined the Masonic Lodge and were at that moment laundering illegal drug money and conducting illegal banking practices through the Vatican Bank in behalf of the P-2 Masonic Lodge. Word leaked that on September 29 the new pope would replace some 20 of the Bishops and Cardinals he knew were involved. During the night of September 28, the Pope was poisoned with an overdose of his own heart medicine — Digitalis. Yallop also suggests that killing the Pope on his thirty-third day in office was a Masonic signature. Read the entire story in *Scarlet and the Beast*, Vol. 1, ch. 8; Vol. 3 ch.1, 6, 7.

Fig. 67 — At the close of World War II, Italian P-2 Freemasonry assisted ex-Nazi SS to escape Europe to South America, where their descendants today are the drug cartels south of our border. Founder of P-2 was Licio Gelli. Read the entire story in *Scarlet and the Beast*, V1, ch. 27; V3, ch. 6.

Licio Gelli (?)

Ency. Britannica (1989-90) reports: "Supremely diabolic Italian who created the maverick Masonic lodge, called the P2 (Propaganda 2, patterned after P1 Lodge founded in 1830 by Italian Mason and MAFIA founder Joseph Mazzini), solely to manipulate politicians, bankers, generals and admirals, and ultimately the entire country... When the Italian public first heard of the nefarious P2 lodge, Gelli was already out of the country, probably in South America."

Bishop Paul Casimir Marcinkus (?-2006)
Head of Vatican Bank

Marcinkus had joined P2 Freemasonry. As a member of P2, and as head of the Vatican Bank, he was in the unique position to increase revenues for the Spouse of Christ by laundering MAFIA drug money through the bank.

Pope John Paul I, on his 33rd day in office, had planned to remove Marcinkus from his banking position, but the Pope died of an overdose of Digitalis in the early morning hours.

Fig. 69 — When Pope John Paul II became the Vicar of Christ, he permitted P2 Freemason Bishop Paul Marcinkus to stay in his position. Read why in excerpt below taken from *Scarlet and the Beast*, Vol. 3, Chap. 1 & 6. Pope Paul (1920-2006)

P-2 Freemasonry Controls Vatican Bank

In May 1981 there was an attempt on John Paul II's life. Several investigators suspect Freemasonry. France, dominated by Grand Orient Freemasonry, tried to shift blame for the attempted assassination to communist Bulgaria. The leading Paris daily, *Le Monde*, reported on Dec. 3, 1982 that, "Soviet factional opponents of former KGB head Yuri Andropov were suspected to be behind revelations of a Bulgarian connection to the May 13, 1981 attempt to assassinate Pope John Paul II."

Based upon subsequent evidence, however, the *Le Monde* article was apparently Masonic disinformation. The Bulgarian government launched its own investigation to clear its name and discovered that the controllers of Mehmet Ali Agca, the would-be assassin, were Turkish Mafia figure Bekir Celenk and two Italian spies held in Bulgaria. In direct response to the international spotlight on the Celenk case, the Bulgarian government announced on December 22, 1982, that it was placing the two accused Italian spies, Paolo Farsetti and his girlfriend Gabriella Trevisini, on trial. Charge? The pair were agents of a Grand Orient Scottish Rite Free Masonic Lodge called Propaganda Two, the same Lodge accused of assassinating Pope John Paul I!

Oddly enough, the attempt on the Pope's life caused John Paul II to change direction and modify his opposition to Freemasonry. On January 12, 1983, the Pope issued a revised code of canon law. George W. Cornell, the Associated Press religion writer, claimed that the revised code "moves ahead in legislating reforms and principles approved by the Second Vatican Council of 1962-1965.... The code implements other changes in church rules, such as permitting Catholics to become Masons."

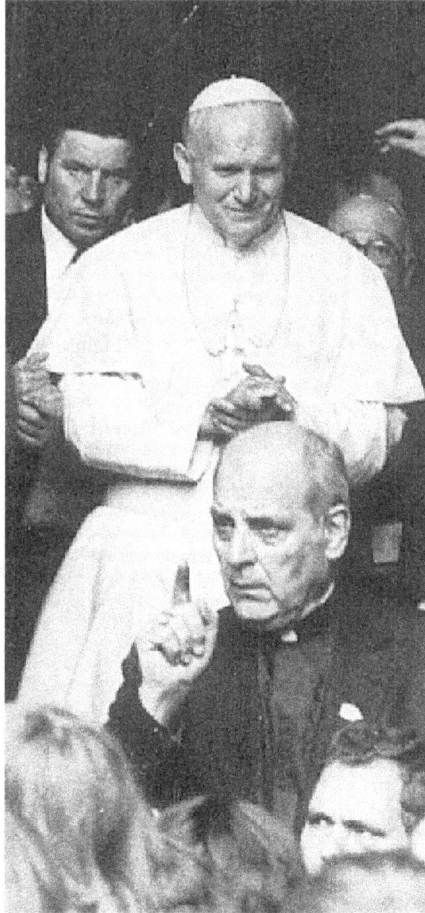

Fig. 70 — Feb. 26, 1987 newspaper clipping below from N.Y. Times News Service stating that a warrant is out for the arrest Archbishop Paul C. Marcinkus, the American prelate who runs the Vatican bank.

American accused in bank failure

N.Y. Times News Service

ROME — Milan magistrates investigating the 1982 collapse of the Banco Ambrosiano were reported Wednesday to have issued arrest orders for Archbishop Paul C. Marcinkus, the American prelate who runs the Vatican bank, and at least two other bank officials.

A Naples newspaper, Il Mattino, said Milan prosecutors intended to issue warrants for the arrest of Marcinkus, a native of Cicero, Ill., and 23 other people in connection with the bank's failure, Italy's largest, and the mysterious death of Roberto Calvi, the bank's managing director and a close associate of Marcinkus. Calvi was found hanged under Blackfriars Bridge in London in 1982.

The Associated Press quoted an unidentified judge in Milan as saying that the warrants had already been issued and that they charged Marcinkus as "an accessory to fraudulent bankruptcy."

Publicly, however, the Milan magistrates handling the case, Antonio Pizzi and Renato Bricchetti, refused to comment. Vatican officials who are in daily contact with Marcinkus said he was not aware of new developments in the case.

In a report from Milan, the Italian news agency ANSA reported that "restrictive provisions" had been taken in the case. But it remained unclear whether the reference was to arrest warrants.

The involvement of its bank in the failure of Banco Ambrosiano was among the most serious scandals to shake the Vatican in recent memory, and it led to cautious change in the way the church bureaucracy manages its financial affairs.

Vatican officials have acknowledged that publicity surrounding the affair led to a falloff in donations by Roman Catholics, whose contributions help support the Vatican.

An arrest order for Marcinkus and other senior Vatican bank officials would confront the Vatican with awkward decisions, including whether to allow church officials to cooperate with the Italian investigators.

The intricacy of the issue was illustrated by reports that investigators would evidently be unable to deliver an arrest order unless the 65-year-old archbishop left Vatican City, which has the status of an independent state.

The report in Il Mattino said the archbishop, who has always denied any wrongdoing, was being charged together with the two other senior Vatican bank officials.

Fig. 71 — Masonic ritual murder of Italian Freemason and Mafioso Roberto Calvi (1920-1982). Calvi was hung from Blackfriar's Bridge in London. Logo of Italian Freemasonry is the Blackfriar.

chunks of Masonry were in his pockets

Masonic Cabletow around his neck.

Above photograph reveals a Masonic ritual murder. Victim? Robert Calvi, an Italian banker and Grand Orient Mason, who was hung from Blackfriar's Bridge in London. Calvi was using the Vatican Bank to launder Mafia drug money. When Pope Paul I learned of the plot, and discovered that several of his Vatican priests were accomplices in the scheme, the Pope planned to fire them all the next day, but was himself killed the evening before with an overdose of Digitilas, prescribed for his heart condition (see Figs. 65-66).

Stephen Knight writes in *The Brotherhood*: "There were many rumours [about Calvi's death]: the Mafia, with whom Calvi had connections, had murdered him; frightened and despairing, he had committed suicide; he had been ritually done to death by Freemasons, a masonic "cabletow" around his neck and his pockets filled symbolically with chunks of masonry, the location of the murder being chosen for its name — in Italy, the logo of the Brotherhood is the figure of a Blackfriar."

At Masonic ritual murders, Masonic symbols are left at the scene for several reasons: (1) to show Masons that this was a Masonic murder; (2) to warn Masons to follow the Masonic code, or suffer like fate; and (3) to prove to Masonic paymasters that the "hit" was accomplished.

What had Calvi done to bring such a gruesome end upon himself? He had committed an unpardonable sin. Calvi stole approximately 1.3 billion dollars from several British Masonic bankers. You can read the story in *Scarlet and the Beast*, Vol. 1, 3rd edition, chapter 23.

Fig. 72 — La Quardia Airport named after him.

3° Fiorello H. LaGuardia (1882-1947)
New York City LaGuardia Airport named after him.

US politician and lawyer. Born in New York City. He became deputy attorney general (1915-17), sat in Congress as a Republican (1917-21 and 1923-33). Held three terms of office as Mayor of NYC (1933-45). Fiorello took a down-at-the-heel city and gave it desperately needed equipment, scores of new school buildings, sewage plants, incinerators, more than double the number of playgrounds and dental clinics for children.

LaGuardia was with the American consulate in Budapest, Hungary and Trieste, Austria, 1901-04, and at Fiume, Hungary, 1904-06. From 190710, he was an interpreter at Ellis Island, NY. He was a graduate of New York University in 1910 and began law practice the same year.

In World War One he was in the U.S. Air Service, achieving the rank of major. He commanded the 8th Centre Aviation School and was attached to night and day bombing squadrons on the Italian front.

In 1946 he was special US ambassador to Brazil, and that same year, director general of the UNRRA.

LaGuardia was raised (3°) in Garibaldi Lodge No. 542, NYC in 1913.

He received life membership in that lodge on Oct. 17, 1933.

Fig. 73 — Baruch, Herter, and Goldwater.
See *Scarlet and the Beast*, Vol. 1, 3rd edition, chaps. 11, 24 and 26; and Vol. 3, chap. 3.

**33°
Bernard
Baruch
(1870-1965)**

Eisenhower
was not a
Freemason,
but held the
fraternity in
high regard.

Bernard Mannes Baruch — Jewish financier and US statesman. Born in Camden, SC. Educated in NYC. Began work as an office boy. Made a fortune in speculating in stocks. Became a powerful political influence and adviser to presidents. Advised Winston Churchill during World War Two.

33° Christian Herter
(1895-1966)

33° Barry Goldwater
(1909-1998)

Secretary of State

Senator for Arizona

Fig. 74 — Famous Rosicrucian Mason and psychologist Carl Jung.

Carl Gustave Jung (1875-1961)

Read Carl Jung's Masonic credentials in the "Introduction" of *Scarlet and the Beast*, Vol. 1, 3rd edition. Also in footnote No. 55 of the "Introduction," read *A Brief Account Of The Similarities Between Jungian Psychology And Freemasonry* by psychologist Alan Hamilton, a 32° Freemason.

Fig. 75

Mary Baker Eddy (1821-1910)
Founder of Christian Science
See *Scarlet and the Beast*, Vol. 1 Chap. 10.

Born in Bow, NH. First married name **Glover**. Founder of the Christian Science Church. Brought up as a Congregationalist. Because of ill health she had little formal education. In 1866 she received severe injuries after a fall, but read about the palsied man in Matthew's Gospel, and claimed to have risen from her bed similarly healed. Thereafter she devoted herself to developing her spiritual discovery. She set out her beliefs in *Science and Health with Key to the Scriptures* (1875), founded the Christian Science Association in 1876, organized the Church of Christ, Scientist, at Boston in 1879, and founded the *Christian Science Monitor* in 1908, quoted as being the "favorite newspaper of politicians."

Her first of three husbands, George Washington Glover, was a Freemason, as well as a member of the Oddfellows. Early in their marriage (1843), Glover moved Mary to the Masonic headquarters at Charleston, SC. Six months later he died. In 1853 Mary married Daniel Patterson, a medical practitioner, from whom she was later separated. She received her "science" from Phineas Parkhurst Quimby, a healer who used the occult art of Animal Magnetism discovered by Freemason Mesmer. The Masonic monthly, *New Age Magazine,* July 1938, notes that her magazine "devotes considerable space to Masonic activities throughout the world. See Masonic editors of *Christian Science Monitor* next page.

Masonic Editors of the *Christian Science Monitor* in alphabetic order by last name.

The Church of Christ, Scientist is nothing more than an arm of Freemasonry!

3° Erwin D. Canham (1904 ?). Began with *Christian Science Monitor* in 1925 as editor. In 1936 received B.A. and M.A. as Rhodes Scholar. Was head of the Washington Bureau from 1932-39. 3° Mason.

32° George Channing (1888-?). Editor of *Christian Science Monitor, Sentinel* and *Herald* since 1949. First reader at mother church in Boston MA, 1941-42. 32° Mason AASR (NJ).

32° Paul S. Deland (?). Has been with *Christian Science Monitor* since 1908. First reader of the mother church, Boston MA 1941-42. From 1945-49 was managing editor and member of editorial council of *C.S.M., Sentinel* and *Herald*. 32° AASR Mason (NJ).

3° Arnold H. Exo (?). Became a Christian Science practitioner in 1942 and later a reader. Was first reader of the First Church of Christ Scientist in Boston beginning in 1956. 3° Mason.

3° Albert F. Gilmore (?-1943). Was first reader of First Church of Christ Scientist at Brooklyn NY from 1914-17. Editor of *Christian Science* weekly and monthly since 1922-29. President of Mother Church, 1922-23. 3° Mason.

32° Charles E. Heitman (1874-1948). Manager of Christian Science Publishing Society, director of Mother Church, 1st Church of Christ, Scientist, Boston. First reader of 2nd Church of Christ, Scientist, at New York 1918-21. President of Mother Church 1923-24. Associate editor of *Christian Science Monitor* 1926-27. Member of Marble Masonic Lodge No. 792 at Tuckahoe NY, and 32° AASR Mason (NJ).

3° R. H. Markham (1887-?). From 1912-18 was a missionary to Bulgaria for American Mission Board of Boston. In 1918 was Y.M.C.A. secretary in Archangel, Russia, returning to Bulgaria with the Mission Board 1920-26. From 1926-39 was the European correspondent with the *Christian Science Monitor* in the Balkans. Returned to the U.S.A. 1939-42. Was author of many Christian Science books. 3° Mason.

3° Archibald McLellan (1857-1917). Beginning in 1880, director of First Church of Christ Scientist, Boston. Editor of the *Christian Science Journal* and *Christian Science Sentinel* from 1902. Editor-in-chief of *Christian Science Monitor*, 1908-14. Initiated in Manhattan Lodge No. 62, N.Y.C. on Nov. 16, 1880. Affiliated with Columbian Lodge, Boston on May 9, 1907. Affiliated with Beth-horon Masonic Lodge, Brookline MA, 1915. 3° Mason.

32° Frederic E. Morgan (?). Rancher in Oregon until 1915 when converted to Christian Science. Graduate of Harvard in 1933. President of Principia, Elsah, IL, a school for sons and daughters of Christian Scientist (from kindergarten through four years of liberal arts college). President of school 1938-54. Chairman of school board since 1942. 32° AASR Mason (NJ).

Both the World Council of Churches and the National Council of Churches are nothing more than an arm of Freemasonry!

First President of the World Council of Churches.

33° G. Bromley Oxnam (1891-?). Methodist Bishop and former president of World Council of Churches. Ordained in Methodist Episcopal ministry, 1916. Professor of U. of Southern CA, and Boston U. School of Theology. President of DePauw W. at Greencastle IN. Elected bishop and served as resident bishop of Omaha area, 193639; Boston area, 1939-44; New York area, 1944-52; and Washington DC area since 1952. Was president of American Federal Council of Churches, 1944-46. In 1948-1954 he became the first American president of the World Council of Churches. Was one of the presiding officers at the organization of the National Council of Churches of Christ in U.S.A. at Cleveland

OH in 1950. Was the author of 16 books, the latest (1954) entitled *I Protest*. He was raised (3°) in Temple Lodge no. 47, Greencastle IN on Nov. 22, 1929; exalted (R.A.M.) in Greencastle Chapter No. 22 on Feb. 2, 1931; knighted in Greencastle Commandery No. 11, K.T. June 2, 1931; received the 32° AASR on Dec. 5, 1929 and honorary 33° (NJ) on Sept. 28, 1949 (See *Scarlet and Beast*, Vol.1, ch.9).

Time **magazine, June 30, 2003**, Freemason Charles Kimball, Baptist minister and past director of the National Council of Churches, says of missionaries in Muslim lands, "Sincerity isn't the issue, or commitment to one's faith. It is...arguably not the time for [missionary] groups coming in, like someone with a lighted match into a room full of explosives, wearing Jesus on their sleeves."

See more on "Masonic Control of the Media" in *Scarlet and the Beast*, Vol. I, chap. 10

Fig. 76 — Famous American founder of Negro Freemasonry. **See *Scarlet and Beast*,** Vol. 1, Intro. and Picture Book, Sect. 5; Fig. 21-22

3° **Prince Hall** (1748-1807)

First Negro Freemason in the United States, and one for whom the Negro Prince Hall Grand Lodges are named. Born in Bridgetown, Barbados, British West Indies, the son of Thomas Prince Hall, an Englishman, whose wife was a free Negro of French descent. "Prince" is not a title, but his first name. In 1765 he arrived in Boston, and through eight years of frugal living, saved enough money to become a freeholder and voter. In 1774 he was converted to Christianity under the preaching of two pioneer Methodists, Richard Bondman and Joseph Gilmore. Using his evenings for study, Hall became an ordained Methodist preacher in Cambridge, MA, and a leader of his race in New England.

On March 6, 1775, he was made a Master Mason, together with 14 other free Negroes of Boston, in a British army lodge of Irish registry that was attached to one of General Gage's regiments. The lodge gave them the privilege of meeting, marching in procession, and burying their dead, but not to confer degrees.

In the Revolutionary War, he espoused the cause of the Colonies and as the spokesman for the Negroes, he won George Washington's approval of the services of free Negroes in the Continental Army. Five thousand responded.

In March 1784, Hall petitioned the Grand Lodge of England for a charter which was issued Sept. 29, 1784, but not delivered until April 29, 1787. On May 6, 1787, African Lodge No. 459 was established. Four years later, on June 24, 1791, the African Grand Lodge was formed with Prince Hall as Grand Master.

The original charter of African Lodge No. 459 is still preserved. It was issued by the authority of the Duke of Cumberland, and attested to by William White, Grand Secretary of the Grand Lodge of England. Today there are Prince Hall Grand Lodges throughout the U.S.A., Canada, and Africa. All claim descent from the original Massachusetts Grand Lodge. Prince Hall led the movement to secure educational facilities for Negro children and was a passionate advocate of equality before the law. He is described as an eloquent,

persuasive speaker, and ardent patriot and a devoted Freemason. Unquestionably, he is the "father of Negro Freemasonry" in the United States of America.

"NEGRO LODGES"
copied verbatim from MACKEY'S REVISED ENCYCLOPEDIA OF FREEMASONRY Vol. 2, p. 702, 1946

The subject of Lodges of colored persons, commonly called *Negro Lodges*, was for many years a source of agitation in the United States, not on account, generally, of the color of the members of these Lodges, but on account of the supposed illegality of their Charters. The history of their organization was thoroughly investigated, many years ago, by Brother Philip S. Tucker, of Vermont, and Brother Charles W. Moore, of Massachusetts, and the result is here given, with the addition of certain facts derived from a statement made by the officers of the Lodge in 1827. Prince Hall and thirteen other Negroes were made Freemasons in a Military Lodge in the British Army then at Boston, on March 6, 1775. When the Army was withdrawn these Negroes applied to the Grand Lodge of England for a Charter and on the 20th of September, 1784, a Charter for a Master's Lodge was granted, although not received until 1787, to Prince Hall and others, all colored men, under the authority of the Grand Lodge of England. The Lodge bore the name of *African Lodge, No. 429*, and was situated in the City of Boston. This Lodge ceased its connection with the Grand Lodge of England for many years, and about the beginning of the nineteenth century its registration was stricken from the rolls of the United Grand Lodge of England, when new lists were made, as were many other Lodges in distant parts of the world, its legal existence, in the meantime, never having been recognized by the Grand Lodge of Massachusetts, to which body it had always refused to acknowledge allegiance.

After the death of Hall and his colleagues, to whom the Charter had been granted, the Lodge, for want of some one to conduct its affairs, fell into abeyance, or, to use the technical phrase, became dormant. After some years it was revived, but by whom, or under what process of Masonic law, is not stated, and information of the revival given to the Grand Lodge of England, but no reply or recognition was received from that Body. After some hesitation as to what would be the proper course to pursue, they came to the conclusion, as they have themselves stated, "that, with what knowledge they possessed of Masonry, and as people of color by themselves, they were, and ought by rights to be, free and independent of other Lodges." Accordingly, on June 18, 1827, they issued a protocol, in which they said: "We publicly declare ourselves free and independent of any Lodge from this day, and we will not be tributary or governed by any Lodge but that of our own."

They soon after assumed the name of the *Prince Hall Grand Lodge*, and issued Charters for the constitution of subordinates, and from it have proceeded Lodges of colored persons now existing in the United States.

Admitting even the legality of the English Charter of 1784 — it will be seen that there was already a Masonic authority in Massachusetts upon whose prerogatives of jurisdiction such Charter was an invasion — it cannot be denied that the unrecognized self-revival of 1827, and the subsequent assumption of Grand Lodge powers, were illegal, and rendered both the Prince Hall Grand Lodge and all the Lodges which emanate from it, clandestine. This has been the general opinion of Masonic jurists in America. However, the movement has spread among the negroes until now they have Lodges and Grand Lodges in the several States and in Canada and Liberia. As they wear emblems of other Bodies it is presumable they claim them as well.

Fig. 77

33° Thurgood Marshall (1908-1993)
Supreme Court Justice (1967-1991)

Negro lawyer and Prince Hall Freemason. Born in Baltimore MD. Graduate of Lincoln U. 1930 and 1947. Admitted to bar in 1933 and practiced at Baltimore, 1933-37, and afterwards in New York City. In 1938 he was special counsel for the National Association for Advancement of Colored People. He won a number of important decisions before the U.S. Supreme Court. In 1951 he visited Korea to make investigation on court martial cases involving Negro soldiers. He won an historic victory in the case of *Brown Vs. Board of Education of Topeka* (1954) which declared that racial segregation in public schools was unconstitutional. He was director and counselor of the Prince Hall Grand Master's Conference. He was 33° AASR Prince Hall Mason. He was nominated to the US Court of Appeals (1961), named solicitor general (1965), and became the first African-American member of the Supreme court (1967-91). Source: *10,000 Famous Freemasons* and *The Cambridge Biographical Ency.*

Fig. 78 — Founder of N.A.A.C.P.
Read the purpose of the N.A.A.C.P. in *Scarlet and the Beast*, Vol. 1, Introduction and Chap. 9.

W. E. B. Du Bois (1868-1963)

It should be pointed out that the Enlightenment spirit went only so far. In spite of its idealism, American Masonry was neither colorblind nor sexually enlightened. Just as blacks and women were kept out of the Constitution, they were barred from Masonry's chummy club as well. For example, when Prince Hall, a free Negro, wanted to open a Masonic Lodge for blacks, American Masonryrefusedhim. SotheBritishgranted him a charter.

Du Bois, historian, writer, and one of the founders of the NAACP (1909), was a member of Prince Hall Freemasonry. *Don't Know Much About History*, Kenneth C. Davis, 2002, p. 124.

As editor of the *Crisis*, W.E.B. Du Bois publicized black achievements and introduced black writers and artists.

Fig. 79 — Negro educator and leader, who was a Prince Hall Freemason.

Booker T. Washington (1859-1915)

Negro educator and leader, who was a Prince Hall Freemason. Born near Hale's Ford, VA. Graduate of Hampton Institute of VA in 1875 and honorary degrees from Harvard and Dartmouth. In 1881 he was appointed principal of the newly opened Tuskegee Institute, AL, and built it up into a major center of black education. He was the foremost black leader in late 19th century in the USA, winning white support by his acceptance of the separation of blacks and whites. He was strongly criticized by Du Bois, and his policies were repudiated by the 20th century civil rights movement. A writer and speaker on racial and educational subjects, he was the author of many books including *Sowing and Reaping; Up From Slavery; Future of the American Negro; Character Building; Working With Hands; The Negro in Business; The Story of the Negro; My Larger Education,* etc. He was made a Mason "at sight" by the Grand Master of the Prince Hall Grand Lodge of Massachusetts.

This caused some difficulty, as he was then a resident of Alabama and this jurisdictional question may have prevented him from affiliating with a lodge in his jurisdiction. *10,000 Famous FM* and *Cambridge Biographical Ency.*

SECTION 3
AMERICAN MASONIC REVOLUTION

Figure 1

James Otis (1725-1783)
American Revolutionary statesman, known for the phrase, "taxation without representation is tyranny." He joined Minute Men at Bunker Hill. Made a Mason in St. John's Lodge, March 11, 1752. Killed by lightning.

Figure 2: "Common Sense." See *Scarlet and the Beast*, Vol. 1., 3rd edition, chapter 30.

Thomas Paine (1737-1809)

Revolutionary philosopher and writer. Born of Quaker parents in Thetford, Norfolk, England, UK. Tried various occupations — a corsetmaker from the age of 13, a sailor, a schoolmaster, and an exciseman, then bankruptcy.

Paine was in London in 1773, when the Boston Tea Party ignited the American Revolution. In 1774, at the suggestion of Benjamin Franklin, who was in England at the time, Paine sailed for Philadelphia and became the editor of *Pennsylvania Magazine*. He served for a time in the Continental Army as an aide to General Nathanael Greene, and was made secretary to the Committee of Foreign Affairs. In 1776 he wrote the 47-page pamphlet *Common Sense*, which argued for complete independence from England. In 1787 he returned to England, where he wrote *The Rights of Man* (1791-2) in support of the French Revolution, urging the British to overthrow their monarchy. Arraigned for treason, he fled to Paris, where he was elected a Deputy to the National Convention. There he offended the party in power (the Grand Orient Masonic Jacobins), for his proposal to offer the king asylum in the USA. For this he was imprisoned.

While in prison he wrote *The Age of Reason*, in favor of deism. Released in 1796, he joined French Grand Orient Freemasonry and became an atheist. It is also claimed that before he returned to America, he went to England and founded several Grand Orient lodges in that island nation. Returning to America in 1802, he became involved in political controversies and lived his last years in ostracism and relative poverty.

Fig. 3: Boston Tea Party. See *Scarlet and Beast*, Vol. 1, 3rd ed, ch. 30.

King George of England levied a tax on tea shipped to the American colonies by the British East India Company. The BEIC was given permission to collect the tax. Meanwhile, in Boston, a group of citizens disguised as Indians tossed the offensive tea into the harbor. This eventually triggered our Revolutionary War. This story is given more detail in Masonic publications.

From the five-volume work *Little Masonic Library*, a chapter entitled "The Customs of Colonial Freemasonry," we read the true story of the "tea party," which action took place in the year 1773.

Colonial lodges were accustomed to meeting at the tavern of a brother Mason. Usually, the tavern-keeper was made a Mason to insure his loyalty and fidelity to the Craft. And so it was at Boston Harbor. The "Tea Party," according to the tradition of St. Andrew's Masonic Lodge, originated within its walls and was carried out under its leadership. The party of 90 Masons then proceeded to the Green Dragon Tavern, where they dressed as Indians. From the Tavern the Masons made their way to the wharf where the tea ships were anchored, broke open the chests and emptied their contents into the harbor.

Figure 4-5: Ben Franklin — diplomat and Freemason.
See *S&B*, V.1, 3rd ed., chs. 5, 8, 30; & V. 3 Epilogue.

3° **Benjamin Franklin** (1706-1790)

American statesman, scientist, philosopher, author. Gained wide recognition with his *Poor Richard's Almanac*. In 1727 he organized the "Leathern Apron Club" as a secret society in Philadelphia (non-Masonic); and on Dec. 8, 1730 printed an article in his paper pretending to reveal Masonic mysteries. Two months later (Feb. 1731) he joined Freemasonry and received his degrees in St. John's Lodge of Philadelphia and became active in its work from the very beginning. He was Secretary of the Lodge from 1735-38; elected Junior Grand Warden of the Grand Lodge of Penn. on June 24, 1732 and Grand Master on June 24, 1734. He was appointed Provincial Grand Master of Boston on June 10, 1749.

In 1760 he was named Provincial Grand Master of Philadelphia. On April 7, 1778 he assisted at the initiation of Voltaire in the Lodge of the Nine Sisters in Paris, France. Further honors are too numerous to mention.

One of Franklin's 1st successful acts as representative of America abroad was to plead the case of the colonies before the British House of Commons to repeal the 1765 Stamp Act.

Figure 6: Was Thomas Jefferson a Mason? See *S&B*, V.1, 3rd ed., ch. 5, 30; Vol. 3, Epilogue.

Thomas Jefferson (1743-1826)

Third President of the United States. Graduate of William and Mary in 1762. Admitted to the bar in 1767. As a member of the Continental Congress, he was chairman of the committee that wrote and presented the Declaration of Independence to that body. He was governor of Virginia from 1779-81, and again member of Continental Congress from 1783-85. From 1785-89 he was U.S. Minister to France, and Secretary of State, 1790-93. He was Vice President of the U.S. from 1798-1801, and President, 1801-09, being elected by the House of Representatives after a tie vote with Aaron Burr. Masonic speakers and periodicals, both Masonic and Anti-Masonic, of the mid-1800's claimed Jefferson was a Freemason. His closest associates were Freemasons. His writings and actions contain Masonic philosophy. It is claimed that the French Dr. Guillotin recorded in his diary that he "attended Lodge in company with Mr. Jefferson and Mr. Paine from the American States." There has been an attempt to link his membership with Door of Virtue Lodge No. 44, Albemarle Co., VA, because his son-in-law, Gov. Thomas M. Randolph, and favorite grandson, Thomas Jefferson Randolph, were members of that lodge, as well as nephews Peter and Samuel Carr. He was identified as marching in procession with Widow's Son Lodge No. 60, and Charlottesville Lodge No. 90, Oct. 6, 1817, at the laying of the cornerstone of Central College (now University of Virginia). On August 21, 1801 a dispensation was ordered for a lodge at Surry Court House, VA to be named Jefferson Lodge No. 65. Some have claimed that he was a member of the Lodge of Nine Muses, Paris. In July, 1826, both the Grand Lodges of Louisiana and Georgia held funeral orations for Jefferson, and on Aug. 2, 1826, the Grand Lodge of S.C. held a funeral procession for him. A letter from Moses Holbrook, 33° Grand Commander of the Supreme Council, (SJ) to Dr. J.M. Allen, Skaneateles, N.Y. dated Aug. 2, at Charleston, SC said: "I have nothing new to write, except tomorrow we have a funeral procession for Thomas Jefferson, and all the societies are invited. I never knew that he was a Freemason."

Kenneth C. Davis, in *Don't Know Much About History*, 2002, HarperCollins Publishers Inc., writes, "Jefferson had...once produced an edited version of the Gospels (still available in book form as *The Jefferson Bible*) in which he highlighted the moral and ethical teachings of Jesus while editing out any reference to his divinity or miracles. He once wrote that it made no difference to him whether his neighbor affirmed one god or twenty, since 'it neither picks my pocket nor breaks my leg.'"

Fig. 7: Continental Congress ready to adopt Declaration of Independence. Thomas Jefferson presents document to John Hancock (seated), Pres. of the Congress. Masonic Bible states, "Of the 55 signers of the document, 53 were Masons." Below are six Masonic credentials. First five are the draftees.
See *Scarlet and the Beast*, Vol. 1, chaps. 5 & 30.

John Adams (1735-1826): Founded Masonic Lodges in New England states.

Roger Sherman (1721-1793): Masonic apron in historical collection at Yale.

Robert R. Livingston (1746-1813): On May 22, 1771, he constituted Solomon's Lodge No. 1, Poughkeepsie, N.Y. Also a Member of St. John's Lodge. He administered oath of office to George Washington upon his inauguration as first president of U.S.A., using the altar Bible of St. John's Lodge. He served as Master of Union Lodge, N.Y.C. In 1784 was elected first Grand Master of the Grand Lodge of New York. Served until 1801.

Thomas Jefferson (1743-1826): Attended lodges in France. Joined Lodge of Nine Muses in Paris. Was member of Illuminati Lodge in Virginia.

Benjamin Franklin (1706-1790): In 1727 organized "Leather Apron Club" as secret society in Philadelphia. Received degrees in St. John's Lodge.

John Hancock — (1737-1793): First signer of Declaration of Independence, with largest signature. When asked why he wrote so boldly, he replied, "So that George III may read it without putting on his glasses." While on a mission to Quebec in 1772, Hancock was made a Mason in Merchants Lodge No. 277. Hancock was also affiliated with St. Andrew's Lodge at Boston.

Figure 8: Patrick Henry fearlessly opposed George III's tax law.
He is famous for saying, "Give me liberty or give me death."

Patrick Henry (1736-1799) — Many references to his being a Freemason, particularly by Grand Lodge orators in the 1800's, but no satisfactory evidence of his membership. It is believed he was a member of Old Tappahannock Lodge of Va. whose records are lost. See *S&B*, Vol.1, 3rd ed., chap. 30.

Figure 9: The Midnight Ride of Paul Revere — a Royal Arch Mason.
See *Scarlet and Beast*, V1, 3rd ed., ch. 30.

3°
Paul
Revere

(R.A.M.): Metalsmith Revolutionary Patriot. (1735-1818)

Son of a French Huguenot refugee and silversmith. Paul served in the French and Indian Wars as a Lieutenant of Artillery. He took part in the famous Boston Tea Party of 1773. April 18, 1775 he made his famous ride from Boston to Lexington, to warn the country side that the British were on the march.

Raised to 3o in St. Andrews Lodge, Boston, Sept. 24, 1760. Became Master of lodge in 1770. Served as Master again from 1777-79 and from 1780-82. This lodge met at the "Green Dragon Tavern" where plans for the famous tea party were hatched. In 1783 Revere was a founding member of Rising States Lodge, and was its first Master. He was Grand Master of the Grand Lodge of Mass. from 1794-97.

Fig. 10 — Famous American Masons during our Revolutionary War.
See *Scarlet and Beast,* V1, chap. 5&29-30.

3° George Washington (1732-1799)

First President of U.S.A. He was Initiated Nov. 4, 1752 in Fredericksburg VA. A praying man who ended all his prayers in the name of the Grand Architect of the Universe.

Concerning Washington's consistent church activity, Kenneth C. Davis, in *Don't Know Much About History,* published 2003, writes: "Washington usually left [the church service] before the communion service, pointedly if silently stating his disbelief in this central ceremony of the Christian faith."

Washington was initiated (1°) in 1752 in the lodge at Fredericksburg, VA. On March 3. 1773 he received the Fellow Craft degree (2o), and the same year was raised to Master Mason (3°).

It is possible that Washington received the Mark Master degree during the French and Indian War. It is also speculated that he received the Royal Arch degree in Fredericksburg Lodge. This claim is made stronger with the fact that Washington's Masonic apron, which was embroidered by Madame Lafayette, contained emblems of the Royal Arch with the letters H.T.W.S.S.T.K.S. in a circle and a beehive within the circle to indicate that it was the weavers' mark. Washington was also a member of several other lodges. Washington wrote to the Grand Lodge of South Carolina in 1791, "I recognize with pleasure my relation to the Brethren of your society...I shall be happy, on every occasion, to evince my regard for the Fraternity.

Fig. 11

Charles Willson Peale (1741-1827)
Early American portrait painter

George Washington gave Peale 14 sittings. Many of the portraits in this first section bear his name. Peale was a member of Williamsburg, VA lodge.

Fig. 12 — Famous American Masons during our Revolutionary War.
See *Scarlet and Beast,* V1, chap. 5&30.

33° Marquis de Lafayette (1757-1834)

Hero of American Revolution. Received Scottish Rite degrees in Cerneau Supreme Council of NY and was made 33° and honorary Grand Commander of that body. He presented to George Washington the Masonic apron made by Madame Lafayette worn by our first President (see Fig. 19).

His father, a soldier, had died at the Battle of Minden a few weeks before his birth, and his mother died in 1770, leaving him a vast estate. He refused a prominent position in the French court to become a soldier in 7771. He withdrew from the service in 1776, outfitted his own ship, *Victoire,* and sailed with 15 other young adventurers, Baron de Kalb, also a Freemason, to fight with the American colonists against England. At first their services were refused by the American Congress, but noting Lafayette's full pocketbook, connections at the French court, and his offer to serve without pay, he was commissioned Major General in the Continental Army on July 31, 1777.

Lafayette became an intimate associate of Washington. He was wounded at Brandywine while rallying the American troops from a retreat. He was then appointed to lead an expedition to invade Canada, but for lack of funds the plan was never carried out.

Lafayette was with Washington at Valley Forge; served on the court martial that tried Major Andre; stationed at Tappan, NY; served in Virginia; and was at bother the Battle of Yorktown and the and the surrender of Cornwallis.

In 1778-1780 he was on furlough in France to assist Franklin in obtaining financial aid from France for the colonists.

In December, 1781, after the American Revolution, Lafayette returned to France — a hero in both nations. He became a member of the French national assembly in 1789, where he showed his liberal sympathies.

Lafayette returned to America in 1784 and stayed five month. He again returned in 1824-25, at the invitation of a grateful Congress, which voted him $200,000. On this visit he toured all 25 states, receiving more Masonic honors than any Freemason before or since. Lodges in all states vied with each other in conferring honorary degrees citations, and membership.

Lafayette named his son George Washington Lafayette.

Fig. 13 — Washington laying the Masonic Corner Stone of United States Capitol Bldg. See *Scarlet and the Beast*, Vol. 1, chapter 30.

"George Washington prayed regularly and fervently...often resorted to calls to 'Providence'... The father of the country regularly attended the Episcopal church... But as Thomas Fleming noted in *Duel*, 'Washington usually left before the communion service, pointedly if silently stating his disbelief in this central ceremony of the Christian faith.'

"Perhaps more significantly, the nominally Episcopalian Washington was also a Freemason, along with numerous other Founders, including John Hancock, Paul Revere, and Franklin... When Washington laid the Cornerstone of the Capitol in 1793, the local Masonic lodge organized the ceremony, and Washington wore a Masonic apron made for him by the wife of the Marquis de Lafayette, who belonged to the Masons as well.

Washington took his oath of office as president with a Masonic Bible." *Don't Know Much About History* by Kenneth C. Davis, HarperCollins Publishers, 2003.

George Washington laying the Cornerstone of the United States Capitol, Sept. 18, 1793

Figure 14: First American Presidential Cabinet was wholly Masonic.
See *Scarlet and the Beast,* Vol.1, 3rd edition, chaps. 29-30.

FIRST AMERICAN PRESIDENTIAL CABINET: From left Henry Knox (1750-1806) Sec. of War. Member of St. John's Regimental Lodge at Morristown; **Thomas Jefferson** (1743-1826) Sec. of State. Member of Illuminati Lodge in Virginia. **Edmund Randolph** (1753-1813) Attorney General. Member of Williamsburg Lodge No. 6. Master of Jerusalem Lodge No. 54. Grand Master of Grand Lodge Virginia in 1786. **Alexander Hamilton** (1757-1804) Sec. of Treasury. Was a Mason in attendance at American Union Military Lodge when Washington raised (3°) General Lafayette to Master on Dec. 27, 1779. **President George Washington**. See *Scarlet and Beast,* V1, ch. 5, 29 & 30.

Figure 15

3° Sir William Johnson (1715-1774)

English Baronet, born in Smithtown, County of Meath, Ireland. He came to America in 1783 to manage his uncle Admiral Sir Peter Warren's property, located 24 miles west of Schenectady. He became a colorful and most powerful figure in pre-revolutionary America, trading with Indians, who he treated with honesty and justice. His manner was always dignified and affable, cultivating their friendship by learning their language, assuming many of their manners, and even their dress. His influence with them was greater than any white man had then possessed.

He was raised (3°) Apr. 4, 1766 in Union Lodge No. 1 (now Mt. Vernon No. 3) of Albany NY. May 23 a charter was issued to St. Patrick's Lodge No. 8 to constitute a regular lodge to be held at Johnson Hall in Albany Co. and the province of New York. First meeting was held Aug. 23, 1776. Johnson was charter Master. His nephew, Guy Johnson, was senior warden. His son-in-law, Daniel Claus, was junior warden. John Butler, of Revolutionary fame, was Secretary.

Today Johnson Hall is amuseum with some of the original lodge furniture still intact.

Figure 16: More on Capt. John Paul Jones.

John Paul Jones (1747-1792)

Father of the American Navy. Born in Kirkbean, Scotland. Went to sea at age 12. At 19 was first mate of a slaver, and captain of a merchantman three years later. Ill fortune struck when a man was killed aboard ship. Hostile witnesses at the inquiry made it rough on Jones, so he fled to Fredricksburg, Va.

He had been a member of St. Bernard's Lodge No. 122 of Kirkcudbright, Scotland, Nov. 27, 1770.

At the outbreak of the American Revolution he obtained a commission in the Continental Navy as a Lieutenant. It is said that fraternal connections obtained it for him. He soon became a Captain, and acted as Commodore of a fleet of privateers through which he established a reputation. Taking the war into European waters, he went to France, and through Franklin's influence, obtained a vessel named the *Bonhomme Richard* which first flew the new American ensign in foreign waters. Two days after a fight with the British *Serapis* (where he is supposed to have uttered the words "I've just begun to fight!"), his ship sank and he made his way back to Paris.

While in Paris he became associated with the famous Lodge of the Nine Sisters, and there are several references to his membership in the Lodge records. This lodge had a bust of Jones made by Houdon. Jones was also a visitor to St. Thomas Lodge in Paris.

Returning to Philadelphia in 1781, he was named to command the *America*, a man-of-war ship under construction. Because of defects discovered before the ship sailed, he was not allowed to take the vessel to sea. He again returned to Paris. In 1787, the American Congress voted him a medal — the only one awarded a naval hero in the Revolution.

After declining service with Denmark, he accepted an appointment as Rear Admiral in the Navy of Empress Catherine of Russia, then at war with the Turks. He was victor in the engagements on the Black Sea, but lost battles in the palace corridors. He returned to Paris in 1790 and died of dropsy. He was buried in the Protestant cemetery of Paris and his grave site was forgotten until 1905, when it was rediscovered. His remains were borne in solemn procession through the streets of Paris prior to shipment to America. They were later interred at Annapolis MD.

Figure 17 — Famous American sea captains who were Masons.

3° Stephen Decatur, Sr. (1751-1808)

Naval officer during American Revolution. Was Captain of a merchantman at an early age, and during the Revolution commanded the privateers, *Royal Louis* and *Fair American*. He was appointed PostCaptain in the Navy in 1798 at the beginning of hostilities with France and commanding the *Delaware*, a 21-gun sloop of war, he captured several French vessels off the coast of New England and in the West Indies. He commanded a squadron of 13 vessels on the Guadeloupe station in 1800. He retired from the sea in 1801 and engaged in business in Philadelphia.

He was a member of Lodge No.16 in Baltimore, MD, being initiated in Aug. 1777. He received his Master's (3°) degree in lodge no. 3 of Pennsylvania charter on April 18, 1780, paying a large fee of $100.00.

Stephen Decatur, Jr. (1779-1820)

Stephen Jr., son of Stephen Sr., made a voyage with his father when he was 8-years-old. In 1803 he commanded the schooner *Enterprise* in Tripolitan waters. In 1804 he performed the daring exploit of burning a frigate captured and held by the Tripolitans. For this he was promoted to Captain and commanded a division of gunboats in attacks on Tripoli. In the "War of 1812" he commanded the *United States* in victory over the British ship *Macedonian*. In 1815 he commanded the *President* in victory over the *Endymion*.

In a banquet he gave the famous toast: "Our Country! In her intercourse with foreign nations may she always be in the right; but our country, right or wrong!"

Steven Jr. was initiated at St. John's Lodge on Oct. 12, 1799.

Figure 18 — Famous American Masons during our Revolutionary War

James Lawrence (1781-1813)

U.S. Naval Captain, famous for his dying words, "Don't Give Up the Ship!" Although it is known that Lawrence was indeed a Mason, his lodge membership remains a mystery. The Grand Lodge of New York passed the following resolution: "Resolved that it be referred to the grand officers, that in case there should be a public funeral of our deceased brother, the late gallant Captain Lawrence, to take measure to assemble the lodges in this city (NYC) to join in the procession." He was buried with military and Masonic honors.

1° John Starke (1728-1822). Major General of American Revolution and last surviving general officer of that war. Born in Londonderry, N.H. While hunting and trapping in his early years, he was captured by the Indians, but ransomed for $103, remarking that he thought he was worth more than that. Joined the famous Rogers' Rangers as a Lieutenant, and served through all the campaigns around Lake George and Lake Champlain. At the close of the French and Indian War, he retired to his farm until the news of the Battle of Lexington reached him. He led several hundred neighbors to join the army at Cambridge. He was famous for his saying "Look yon, men! There are the red coats! Before the night they're ours or Molly Stark's a widow." He is also noted at the Battle of Bunker Hill as saying, "Boys aim at their waistbands."

He became a member of Masters Lodge No. 2 at Albany, N.Y., Jan. 9, 1778. The minutes read, "The petition of Brigadier General John Starke being presented to the body, he was balloted for, met with the unanimous consent of the members present, and was initiated accordingly. Brig. Gen. John Starke paid 5 pounds for his initiation fee, 8 shillings to the Tyler, and 4 shillings for extra lodging."

Figure 19 — Famous American Masons during our Revolutionary War.
See *Scarlet and the Beast*, Vol. 1, 3rd ed.; chap.30.

3° **Horatio Gates** (1728-1806)
Major General of Continental Army in American Revolution.

Born in Maldon, England. He entered the British army and served with Braddock's army in Virginia in 1755. Was wounded at Monogahela. In 1760 he was a brigade-major under Moncton at Fort Pitt, and was his aide in 1762 at the capture of Martinique. In 1772, at the invitation of Washington, he took up land in Virginia and settled down to develop it.

When the Revolution broke out, he sided with the colonies and in 1775 was appointed adjutant-general with the rank of brigadier. The next year he was made Major General of the Continental Army and placed in command of the northern army that had been commanded by Arnold, Wooster, Montgomery, and Sullivan.

Gates was at Fort Ticonderoga for the next two years and received credit for the success in repulsing Burgoyne's army from the north, although Schuyler and Benedict Arnold were responsible for the defense, Arnold was later charged with cowardice at this action.

After this battle his friends formed the noted Conway Cabal to place Gates as commander-in-chief instead of Washington. It failed, and in 1780 he lost the disastrous battle of Camden, SC, for which he was relieved of his command.

He returned to his plantation, where he asked for an official inquire into his conduct at the battle of Camden. In 1782, Congress finally acquitted him, after which he served loyally under Washington for the remainder of the war. During his military absence he remained on his plantation, where his wealthy wife, who spent most of her fortune on the cause of the colonies, nursed wounded patriot Thaddeusz Kosciusko. Gates was a member of a regimental Masonic lodge at Annapolis Royal, Nova Scotia, Canada, which was active between 1738 and 1755. Practically all the officers of the regiment were members.

On Dec. 18, 1778 the minutes of St. John's Grand Lodge of Massachusetts report inviting "The Honorable General Gates, with his male family who were Masons, to dine at the Feast of St. John's Day."

Figure 20 — Famous American Masons during our Revolutionary War.
See *Scarlet and the Beast*, Vol. 1, 3rd ed; chapter 30.

While colonial officers watch, Von Steuben drills Continental soldiers in the maintenance of continuous fire in battle, one rank loading while the other kneels to fire. He did much to turn Washington's unskilled force into an efficient army.

Freemason Baron von Steuben (1730-1794)

Full name — Frederick William Augustus Henry Ferdinand von Steuben. He desired a field command, but did not receive it until late in the war, when he commanded in the Virginia campaign. It was more important that he train the American troops. At Washington's inauguration he had a seat on the platform with the favored few, and soon after became the beneficiary of liberal retirement pay from the new congress. He made frequent trips to New York City where he mingled with his brethren of the Masonic fraternity. It is not known where he received the degrees and earned the title "past master," but it is presumed to have been in Europe. E.A. Sherman states he received his degrees in the "Military Lodge of the Blazing Star" at Berlin. He was a member of Trinity Lodge No. 10 (now 12) of New York City and an honorary member of Holland Lodge No. 8, N.Y.C. On St. John's Day, 1788, he dined with Holland Lodge, and in French addressed the "Veterans of the Royal Art." In the minutes of Feb. 6, 1789, "Bro. Past Master von Steuben" was appointed a member of the committee to inform Washington of his election as an honorary member of the lodge.

Figure 21 — Famous American Masons during our Revolutionary War.
See *Scarlet and the Beast*, Vol. 1, 3rd ed; chapter 30.

Freemason   Benedict   Arnold
(1741-1801)

Born in Norwich, CT. Patriot Officer who loyally served the cause of the American Revolution until 1779, when he shifted his allegiance to the British. Thereafter his name in America became an epithet for "traitor."

As relations between the Colonies and England deteriorated during the 1770s, Arnold (then a prosperous businessman in New Haven, CT) was elected a captain in his state militia. Upon learning of the outbreak of hostilities at Lexington, Mass. (April 1775), he immediately volunteered for service, and the following month participated with Col. Ethan Allen in the successful colonial attack on British-held Ft. Ticonderoga, NY. That autumn, Arnold was appointed by Gen. George Washington to command an expedition to capture Quebec. His march with 700 men by way of the Maine wilderness was a remarkable feat of woodsmanship and endurance, but he awaited reinforcements from Gen. Richard Montgomery before attacking the well-fortified city. The combined assault in a snowstorm (Dec. 31, 1775) failed, Montgomery was killed, and Arnold was severely wounded.

Congress promoted Arnold to brigadier general, and shortly thereafter he constructed a flotilla on Lake Champlain and inflicted severe losses on a greatly superior enemy fleet near Valcour Island, New York (Oct. 11, 1776). He returned a hero, but his rash courage and impatient energy had aroused the enmity of several other officers. In Feb. 1777, when Congress created five new major generalships, Arnold was passed over in favor of his juniors — ostensibly because of the political need to apportion the major generals among the states. Arnold resented this affront, and only Washington's personal persuasion kept him from resigning.

Two months later he repelled a British attack on Danbury, CT, forcing Congress to make him a major general, but his seniority was not restored and Arnold felt his honor impugned. Again he tried to resign, but in July he accepted a government order to help stem the British advance into upper New York. He won a victory at Ft. Stanwix (now Rome) in August 1777 and commanded advance battalions at the Battle of Saratoga in September and October, fighting brilliantly and decisively until seriously wounded. For his services he received a new commission restoring him to his proper relative rank.

Since Arnold's wounds had left him crippled, Washington placed him in command of Philadelphia (June 1778), where he enjoyed the city's social life, moved among families of Loyalist sympathies, and lived extravagantly. To raise money, he violated several state and military regulations, arousing the suspicions and, finally, the denunciations of Pennsylvania's supreme executive council. These charges were then referred to Congress; some were thrown out, but Arnold asked for an immediate court-martial to clear himself of the remaining four.

Meanwhile, in April 1779, Arnold (four years a widower) married Margaret Shippen, a young woman of Loyalist sympathies. Early in May he made secret overtures to British headquarters. He was asked to remain on the American side and send information until he obtained an important post or field command that he could betray.

The following May, he informed the British of a proposed American invasion of Canada and later revealed that he himself expected to obtain the command of West Point, NY. He asked the British for 20,000 British pounds for betraying this post and half that sum if he failed. When the British contact, Maj. John André, was captured by the Americans, Arnold managed to escape on a British ship, leaving André to be hanged as a spy. The sacrifice of André made Arnold odious to Loyalists, and his reputation was further tarnished among his former neighbors when he led a raid on New London, CT in September 1781.

Arnold went to England at the end of 1781 and remained there for the rest of his life. Although he and his wife received small pensions for their wartime services, he never felt adequately compensated by the British government. Inactive, ostracized, and ailing he died in England. There is no question that Arnold was a Freemason. Wallace, in his *Traitorous Hero* says he was admitted a member "in the West Indies" which may well be true, since he was there in his early days before the Revolution. The first record in Book II of Hiram Lodge No. 1, New Haven, CT (April 10, 1765) reads "Brother Benedict Arnold is by R.W. (Nathan Whiting) proposed to be made a member of the R.W. Lodge, and is accordingly made a member in this Lodge." This was ten years before his first action in the Revolution. His name appears frequently on the records of Hiram lodge until about 1772. After his defection the lodge erased his name from membership and he was abandoned as a Mason. On June 12, 1771 he visited Solomons Lodge No. 1 at Poughkeepsie NY, and on May 16, 1781 the lodge, by vote "ordered that the name of Benedict Arnold be considered as obliterated from the minutes of this Lodge, a Traitor, with a figure of a hand pointing to "traitor."

Figure 22 — Famous American Masons during our Revolutionary War.
See *Scarlet and the Beast*, Vol. 1, 3rd ed; chapters 5, 30.

3° Henry Dearborn (1751-1829)
Major General U.S. Army. Sec. of War (1801-09) under Jefferson. Fought in Revolutionary War and War of 1812. Practicing physician in Nottingham, NH. Initiated and Passed in St. John's Lodge No. 1, Portsmouth, NH, March3, 1774. Raised (3°) April 18, 1777. Recorded as visitortoAmericanUnionLodgeofCt.onApr.7, 1779. He had three wives; several sons were named for his brother Masons who were his comrades in the army. Fort Dearborn, presentsiteofChicago,wasnamedforhim.

Nathanael Greene (1742-1786)

Continental Army General under the command of George Washington in the Continental American during the American Revolution. Member of a Rhode Island Lodge and a military lodge. Wore a Masonic medal presented to him by Lafayette. This medal is in the possession of the Grand Lodge of Rhode Island. In 1937 his Masonic apron was presented to Lakewood Lodge No. 601, Lakewood, Ohio. Greene retired from public life to a plantation in Savannah, Georgia.

Alexander Hamilton (1757-1804)

American Statesman and first U.S. Secretary of the Treasury. In 1800 Hamilton ran for the presidency and defeated Aaron Burr. On July 11, 1804, in a duel with Burr, Hamilton was wounded and died the next day. Some say Hamilton was a Mason. They base their claims principally on the fact that he was recorded among the visitors of American Union Lodge (military) at Morristown, N.J. on Dec. 27, 1779, at which time Washington raised General Lafayette to the third degree. A non-Mason is prohibited from attending such initiations.

Fig. 23 — Famous American Masons during our Revolutionary War.

3° John Sevier (1745-1815)

Sevierville, Town named after him. Pioneer, frontiersman, Revolutionary soldier, Indian fighter, first Governor of Tennessee, and first and only Governor of the briefly historic "State of Franklin." Born in Rockingham Co., VA. Educated at the Fredericksburg, VA Academy. Founded village of Newmarket, VA in the Shenandoah Valley. Here he became a celebrated Indian fighter.

He organized every able bodied man from 16-50 years in the militia and became their Colonel. They fought many successful conflicts with border Indians.

Sevier was commissioned Brigadier General in 1789, and the following year elected to Congress as the first Representative from the Valley of the Mississippi. He continued his campaigns against the Creeks and Cherokees, and broke their will to fight in the Etowah campaign of 1793. When Tennessee was admitted to the Union in 1796, Sevier became the first Governor, serving until 1801, and again from 1803 to 1809. He was elected to Congress in 1811 and again in 1815, but died before he took his seat.

Sevier's original lodge in not known, but he was first Master of Tenn. Lodge No. 41. This lodge later became Tenn. Lodge No. 2, under the Grand Lodge of Tenn. The charter was arrested in Oct. 1827. In 1805 his name also appears as a member of Greenville Lodge No. 3.

Count Casimir Pulaski (1748-1779).
Polish nobleman involved in Polish rebellion in 1768, and elected commander-in-chief of Polish forces. Ben Franklin persuaded Pulaski to aid the Colonies in their bid for freedom.

Pulaski was affiliated with the Army Lodge in the Maryland Line. Casimir Pulaski Lodge No. 1167, meeting in Logan Square Masonic Temple, Chicago, is named in his honor. Pulaski, VA is named after him.

Figure 24 — Famous British Masons during our Revolutionary War. See *Scarlet and the Beast*, Vol. 1, 3rd edition; chapters 30.

Lord Charles Cornwallis (1738-1805)
British General of American Revolution, who surrendered to George Washington at Yorktown, thus ending the war.

Born in Suffolk, England, he was 2nd Earl and first Marquis of Cornwallis. At the beginning of the American Revolution he was a Major General. He was created full General in 1793. He defeated Greene at Gilford Court House in 1781.

He performed the grand honors of Masonry at the funeral of Major General DeKalb, who was wounded and taken prisoner on August 17, 1780 at the Battle of Camden.

John Dickinson (1732-1808)
Known as the "Penman of the Revolution." He was president of both Delaware and Pennsylvania and was a signer of the Constitution.

He studied law in Philadelphia and later in England. Returning to America, he practiced law in Philadelphia. He was a member of the Pennsylvania assembly in 1764, and of the Colonial Congress (convened in New York to oppose the Stamp Act in 1765.

He was a member of the first Continental Congress. In 1776 he opposed the adoption of the Declaration of Independence and refused to sign, deeming it premature. During the Revolution he served as a private until 1777 when he was commissioned Brigadier General of Delaware

militia. On Nov. 13, 1781 he became the fifth President of Delaware. On Nov. 4, 1782 he resigned to accept the presidency of Pennsylvania, serving until 1785.

He was raided (3°) Jan. 11, 1780 in Lodge No. 18, Dover, Delaware (under Pennsylvania charter).

Fig. 25 — Famous American Masons during our Revolutionary War.
See *Scarlet and the Beast,* Vol. 1, 3rd edition, chapter 30.

3° Robert R. Livingston (1746-1813)

U.S. Minister to France who negotiated the Louisiana Purchase for the United States.

Graduate of Kings College in N.Y.C. Admitted to the bar in 1773 and for a short time was in partnership with John Jay. In 1775 he was elected to the provincial assembly of N.Y. from Dutchess Co.

In 1775 he was sent by New York provincial assembly as delegate to the Continental Congress. He was one of the Committee of Five that drew up the Declaration of Independence.

On April 30, 1789 Livingston administered the oath of office to George Washington upon his inauguration as the first President of the United States of America, using the altar Bible of St. John's Lodge No. 1 for the ceremony.

Livingston held the office of Secretary of Foreign Affairs for the U.S.A. in 1781-83. He refused the post of Minister to France in 1794, but accepted that post in 1801. He was a close friend of Napoleon Bonaparte. The U.S. acquisition of the Louisiana Territory (Louisiana Purchase) was due in part to Livingston's friendship with Napoleon.

While in France he met Robert Fulton and became interested in steam navigation. When both men returned to America, they secured the exclusive right to navigate the waterways of New York, provided they could build a boat that would make four miles an hour. The first boat of 30 tons sailed at 3 mph. But, in 1807 the *Clermont* made 5 mph.

Livingston was a member of Union Lodge, N.Y.C. and in 1784 served as First Grand Master of the Grand Lodge of New York. In that position, on May 22, 1791, he constituted Solomon's Lodge No. 1 at Poughkeepsi. When the Grand Lodge of New York presented him with a jewel on his retirement, he responded, "I shall wear, with pride and pleasure, the jewel with which the Fraternity has honored me, and consider it as a memorial of the pleasing connection which binds us to each other when the duties I owe the public shall have separated them from me..."

383 Masonic military officers during Revolutionary War and/or War of 1812
in alphabetical order by last name from *10,000 Famous Freemasons,* by 33° William R. Denslow

John Adams (?). Naval officer of *Raleigh* in American Revolution. Member of St. John's Lodge No. 1, Portsmouth, NH.

Richard Adams (?). Privateer and Captain during American Revolution. Member of St. Peter's Lodge, Newburtyport, MA.

Nathaniel Alexander (1756-1808). Surgeon in Revolutionary War. Officer of Grand Lodge in NC. Senior Grand Deacon at his death.

Ethan Allen ((1738-1789). Major General Revolutionary War, commanding "Green Mountain Boys." Received first degree at Windsor, Vt. on July 7, 1777.

Joseph I. Anderson (1757-1837). Captain and Major during Revolutionary War. Member of Military Lodge No. 19 of Pennsylvania, and New Jersey Lodge No. 36 in the New Jersey Brigade. After war, became 1st senior warden of Princeton Lodge No. 38.

Richard C. Anderson (1750-1826). Captain in 5th Virginia Continentals, American Revolution. Close friend of Gen. Washington. First master of Lexington Lodge No. 25 (now No. 1 of Kentucky). After war obtained charter for Louisville (KY) Lodge from Grand Lodge of VA.

Robert Andrews (?). Revolutionary War chaplain of 2nd Virginia regiment in Continental Army. Grand Master of Virginia. Past Grand Master of Williamsburg Lodge, Oct. 13, 1778.

John Armstrong (1758-1843). Deputy Adjutant General in American Revolution. General in War of 1812. Raised (3°) in Army Lodge No. 19. Member of Grand Lodge Pennsylvania; Old Cone Lodge No. 9, Salisbury, NC; and Hibernia Lodge No. 339, NY.

William Bainbridge (1774-1833). Commodore, U.S. Navy, War of 1812. Assumed command of squadron during War of 1812, consisting of flag ship *Constitution*, with *Essex* and *Hornet*. Captured British frigate *Jave* off coast of Brazil, Dec. 1812, and received gold medal. Initiated (1°) in Lodge No. 51, Philadelphia, PA, June 14, 1810.

Isaac D. Barnard (1791-1834). Served as Captain, then Major in 14th Infantry during War of 1812. A Mason.

Joshua Barney (1759-1818). Commodore American Navy during Revolutionary War and War of 1812. Buried at Pittsburgh, PA with military and Masonic honors. Freemason in Lodge of Nine Sisters, Paris, France in 1799.

John Barry (1745-1803). Commodore, U.S. Navy in American Revolution. Initiated in Lodge No. 2, Philadelphia, PA on Oct. 12, 1795.

William Barton (1748-1831). Colonel during American Revolution. Member of St. John's Lodge, Providence, RI, 1779.

Timothy Bedel (1740-1787). Colonel in American Revolution. In command of forces at Battle of the Cedars near Montreal. Member of Union Lodge No. 1, NY.

John Beatty (?). Commissioner General of prisoners (with rank of Colonel) in Revolutionary War. Raised (3°) in Trenton Lodge No. 5, Trenton, NJ. Past Grand Master of Grand Lodge, New Jersey.

Gunning Bedford, Jr. (1742-1812). Colonel and aide to General Washington in Revolution. Raised (3°) Sept. 11, 1782 in Washington Lodge No. 14 of Pennsylvania.

Thomas Benbury (?). Brigadier General of Militia in American Revolution. Served as Master of Unanimity Lodge No. 7, Edenton, NC.

Caleb P. Bennett (1758-1836). During Revolution, entered Delaware regiment as a private. Rose to 1st lieutenant, serving in Battle of Brandywine. In War of 1812 was Major of Delaware State Militia. His Grandmother was Mary Boone, daughter of the famous Daniel Boone. Raised (3°) in Lodge No. 14 at Christina Ferry, Del., Jan. 16, 1781.

William Benton (17501831). Colonel in American Revolution. Set up capture of British General Prescott, for which Congress voted him a sword and a grant of land in Vermont. Member of St. John's Lodge No. 1, Providence, RI in 1779.

Theodoric Bland (1742-1790). Revolutionary War soldier, doctor and member of Continental Congress. Captain of first group of Virginia cavalry, and later Colonel. Although his lodge not known, he was present at Williamsburg Lodge No. 6 on July 7, 1778.

Henry Bloom (?). General in War of 1812. His grave has a Masonic headstone.

Joseph Bloomfield (1753-1823). At beginning of Revolutionary War he was Captain in Dayton's regiment of the 3rd New Jersey in 1776. By end of war, attained rank of Major. During War of 1812 was Brigadier General. Raised (3°) in Bristol Lodge No. 25, Bristol, PA. Served as Master in 1782. Was affiliated with Trenton Lodge No. 5, Trenton, NJ in 1790 and 1799. Grand Master of Grand Lodge of New Jersey.

Oliver Bowen (?-1800). Commodore of American Navy in Revolutionary War. Member of Solomon's Lodge No. 1, Savannah, GA.

Thomas Boyd (?-1779). Lieutenant in American Revolution. After capture by British troops, Boyd's life was spared by Indian Chief Joseph Brant when Boyd gave the Masonic sign of distress. Chief Brant, who was the first Indian Freemason of which there is record, turned Boyd over to Colonel John Butler, who was in the British service during the Revolution. Butler allowed the Seneca Indians to torture Boyd to death when Boyd refused to give troop movements of General Sullivan's army. Boyd was member of Military Lodge No. 19 under warrant from Grand Lodge of Pennsylvania. Boyd was given a Masonic burial by this lodge.

Thomas Bradford (1745-1838). Captain of a military company in Philadelphia, 1775. Later was commissary-general of the Pennsylvania division of Continental Army. Member of Lodge No. 2, Philadelphia.

William Bradford, Jr. (1755-1795). Brother of Thomas Bradford. Served in Revolutionary War as Lieut. Colonel. Member of Lodge No. 2, Philadelphia.

Hugh Brady (1768-1851). Major General in War of 1812. Led 22nd Infantry in Battle of Chippewa. Distinguished himself in battles of Lundy's Lane & Niagara. Initiated (1°) June 9, 1797 in Lodge No. 22, Sunbury, PA.

John Brant (1794-1832). Indian chief of Mohawks and son of the more famous Joseph Brant. Served British with distinction in War of 1812. Member of Union Lodge No. 24.

Joseph Brant (1742-1807). Mohawk Indian chief. First Indian Mason. Most famous Indian of Revolutionary period. Father of John Brant. Fought with English Freemason Sir William Johnson against Americans in Battle of Lake George (1755). Sent to England early in 1776 where he became a Freemason in Hiram's Cliftonian Lodge No. 417, London. Returned to America where he was commissioned Colonel in 1778. Participated in the 1778 Cherry Valley massacre of Americans. During that battle Brant was credited with saving the lives of several American Masons who gave him the Masonic sign of distress. They were Col. John McKinstry (May 30, 1778); Lt. Johnathan Maynard (May 30, 1778); Major John Wood (July 19, 1779); and Lt. Thomas Boyd (Sept. 13, 1779).

David Brearley (1745-1790). Military officer during Revolutionary War. First Grand Master of New Jersey Lodges from 1786 to his death.

Marquis de Britigney (?). Served as Colonel in American Revolution. Member of St. John's Lodge No. 3, New Bern, North Carolina.

Daniel Broadhead (1736-1809). Revolutionary War soldier. Raised a company of riflemen who served in Battle of Long Island, 1775. Colonel of 8th Pennsylvania regiment. Brigadier General after the war. Member of Lodge No. 3, Philadelphia, PA.

Laurens Brooke (?). Surgeon and medical officer to John Paul Jones, father of American Navy. Served on Jones' ships, *Ranger* and *Bon Homme Richard*. Member of Lodge No. 4, Fredericksburg, VA.

Robert Brooke (?). Medical student at University of Edinburgh, England at outbreak of Revolutionary War. Returned to America to serve as 1st Lieutenant of cavalry. Past Master of Lodge No. 4, Fredericksburg, VA. Grand Master of Virginia, Nov. 23, 1795.

John Brooks (1752-1825). Drilled a company of minutemen, who participated in the Battle of Lexington, the Ft. Stanwix expedition, and the Battle of Saratoga. Promoted to Colonel, 1778. Worked with Baron von Steuben in training Continental Army. Became Major General of Militia after the War. Received Entered Apprentice degree (1°) in American Union (Military) Lodge on Aug. 28, 1779. Member of Washington Military Lodge No. 10, under Grand Lodge of Massachusetts.

Jacob Brown (1775-1828). Major General, War of 1812. While in command of 200 mile section along Canadian border, he repulsed several attacks from superior British forces. Commissioned Brigadier General, 1813; Major General, 1814. Initiated (1°) in Ontario

Lodge at Sackets Harbor, NY on Jan. 2, 1806. Raised (3°) at same lodge. Member of Watertown Lodge No. 49, Watertown, NY.

Nathan Brownson (1742-1796). Studied medicine at Yale. Graduated 1761. Practiced in Liberty Co., GA. Member of Provincial Congress of 1775. Delegate to Continental Congresses of 1776 and 1778. Revolutionary War surgeon. Member of North Star Lodge of Manchester, VT.

James Bruff (?). Commandant of Upper Louisiana Territory shortly after U.S. took over Louisiana Purchase. 1st Lieut. with 7th Maryland regiment in Revolutionary War. Original lodge unknown. On record as visitor to several lodges. Recorded as member of Lodge No. 7, Chestertown, MD.

Nathaniel Brush (?). Revolutionary War Colonel, who headed Bennington, VT militia at Battle of Bennington, Aug. 1777. This battle proved to be turning point in the Revolution. He was charter member and first master of North Star Lodge, Manchester, VT., formed in 1775.

William B. Bulloch (1776-1852). Served in War of 1812 in Savannah heavy artillery. Member of Solomon's Lodge, No.1, Savannah, GA.

Edward Buncombe (?-1777). Colonel in American Revolution. Taken prisoner at Germantown. Died of wounds at Philadelphia. Member of Unanimity Lodge No. 7 at Edenton, NC. Received blue degrees May 16 and 25, June 3, 1776.

Henry Burbeck (1754-1848). Founder of West Point. Lieutenant of artillery (May 1775) in American Revolution. Was in battles of Long Island, Brandywine and Germantown. Wintered at Valley Forge. His Revolutionary War credentials are too numerous to mention here. In War of 1812, he commanded harbor defenses at New York, New London and Newport. Retired as Brigadier General, 1815. Was Senior Grand Warden of St. John's Provincial Grand Lodge in Boston.

Johathan Burrall (1753-1834). Revolutionary War soldier. Joined Northern Army under Schuyler, 1776. Became assistant paymaster. At close of war was on the commission to settle accounts of the commissary and quartermaster departments. Admitted to Masters' Lodge No. 2 at Albany, NY, 1778.

Robert Burton (1747-1825). Quartermaster General of militia in American Revolution. Member of Continental Congresses from North Carolina. In 1801 was member of commission to fix boundary between the Carolinas and Georgia. Member of Hiram Lodge No. 24 of Williamsborough, NC.

John Butler (1728-1794). Colonel in British service during American Revolution. Recruited a force of Indians and rangers, known as "Butler's Rangers." Many atrocities have been attributed to him. One example: when Lieut. Thomas Boyd had given a Masonic sign of distress, Butler turned him over to the Indians, who tortured and killed him. Butler was Raised (3°) in Union Lodge No. 1, Albany, NY.

Richard Butler (1743-1791). Lieut. Colonel in Pennsylvania line at beginning of the Revolution. Promoted to Colonel in 9th Pennsylvania regiment at close of war. Promoted to Major General after the war. Initiated (1°) in Lodge No. 2, Philadelphia on April 14, 1779, passed (2o) April 20, and raised (3°) April 27.

Robert Butler (?). General in War of 1812. During war he learned the importance of becoming a Mason, but did not join until after the war. Joined Grand Lodge of Alabama when it was organized on June 3, 1825.

John Cadwalader (1742-1786). Brigadier General in American Revolution. Master of Military Lodge No. 55. Member of Lodge No.8 in PA.

Thomas Cadwalader (1707-1779). During Revolutionary War was medical director of Army hospital at Philadelphia. Senior Grand Warden of the first St. John's Lodge of Philadelphia in 1738.

Thomas Cadwalader (1778-1841). Entered War of 1812 as a private. Advanced to Lieutenant Colonel of cavalry and subsequently Major General of First Division, Pennsylvania Militia. Member of Lodge No. 51, Philadelphia, Oct. 27, 1808.

Newton Cannon (1781-1842). In 1813 served as Colonel in Tennessee Mounted Rifles. Commanded left column in Battle of Tallushatchee. Member of Cumberland Lodge No. 8, Nashville, TN.

Joseph P. E. Capelle (1757-1796). Surgeon during American Revolution. Raised (3°) in Lodge No. 14 at Wilmington on Aug. 21, 1783. Served as Master in 1786 and 1792. On Aug. 6, 1789, received R.A.M. Degree.

Lewis Cass (1782-1866). Brigadier General in War of 1812. On Dec. 5, 1803 he was initiated (1°) in old American Union Lodge No. 1 at Marietta, OH; passed (2o) April 2, 1804; and raised (3°) May 7, 1804. Later he became a R.A.M. (Royal Arch Mason — York Rite).

Stephen Cassin (1783-1857). U.S. Naval officer. Served in War of 1812. Victoriously commanded the *Ticonderoga* in war with Tripoli (modern Libya). For this he was awarded a gold medal by Congress. Member of Holland Lodge No. 8, NYC.

Richard Caswell (1729-1789). General in American Revolution. At battle of Moore's Creek he defeated a large body of Loyalists. Original lodge not known, but was a member of St. John's Lodge No. 3, New Bern, NC. Elected Deputy Grand Master of North Carolina, Dec. 11, 1787, and Grand Master, Nov. 18, 1788.

John Catron (1778-1865). Served in New Orleans campaign in War of 1812. Chosen one of the judges of state of Louisiana, 1824. Member of Cumberland Lodge No. 8, Nashville, TN.

Henry Champion (1751-1824). Company and battalion Commander in Continental Army during Revolutionary War, fighting at Bunker Hill, Long Island, West Plains,

Germantown and Stony Point. Led battalion of selected Connecticut troops in audacious assault of Stony Point on July 15-16, 1779. Initiated in American Union Lodge at Redding in 1779. Served in several positions as an officer of the lodge. Past High Priest of VandenBroek Chapter, York Rite (R.A.M.) Member of Washington Commandery, Knights Templar. Personal friend of Thomas Smith Webb.

John Chandler (1760-1841). Brigadier General, War of 1812. Lodge not known, but attended a session of the Grand Lodge of Maine in 1820.

Isaac Chauncey (1772-1840). American naval hero of War of 1812. When war broke out he was in command of Navy yard at New York, as well as all the Great Lakes except Champlain. Member of Independent Royal Arch Lodge No. 2, NYC., 1796.

John Chipman (1744-1829). Revolutionary War Captain, participating in battles of Hubbardton, Bennington and Saratoga. Raised in Union Lodge, Albany, NY prior to Oct., 1779. After war was Grand Master of Grand Lodge of Vermont, 1797-1814, and Grand High Priest of the Grand Chapter, R.A.M. of Vermont, 1813-15.

Nathaniel Chipman (1752-1843). Served as Lieutenant in Revolutionary War. At Valley Forge in winter of 1777. Present at battles of Monmouth and White Plains. Raised (3°) in a military lodge. In 1795 was a member of Center Lodge No. 6, Rutland, VT, and its first Master.

Joseph Cilley (1735-1799). Revolutionary War soldier. Major General of New Hampshire militia. Immediately after Battle of Lexington, he raised a company of volunteers and led them into Boston. He served at Ticonderoga, and other battles. Raised (3°) in St. John's Lodge No. 1, Portsmouth, NH, June 15, 1775. Fees were waived due to service to his country.

Joseph Cilley (1791-1887). Grandson of Joseph Cilley above. Lieutenant in Infantry during War of 1812. Participated in battles of Chippewa, Lundy's Lane, and Chrysler's Field. Member of Sullivan Lodge No. 19, Lee, NH. Deputy Grand Master of Grand Lodge New Hampshire, 1848-49.

George Rogers Clark (1752-1818). Older brother of explorer and Freemason, William Clark. George was a Brigadier General in American Revolution. Fought the British and Indians in the Illinois and Kentucky regions, saving the two regions for the colonies. His lodge is unknown, but he was buried Masonicly by Abraham Lodge No. 8, Louisville, KY.

Joel Clark (1730-1776). Colonel in Revolutionary War. Served in siege of Boston and defense of New York. Founder of famous American Union Military Lodge, which traveled with Continental Army throughout war.

Green Clay (1757-1826). General in War of 1812. When General Harrison was besieged by British at Fort Meigs in 1813, he came to Clay's relief with 3,000 volunteers, forcing enemy to withdraw. Member of Lexington Lodge No. 1, Lexington, KY.

Moses Cleaveland (1754-1806). Founded Cleveland, Ohio in 1796. Was at Yale when Revolution broke out. Commissioned in Col. Blatchley Webb's Continentals, 1777. While stationed in Hudson Highlands was made a Mason in American Union Lodge (military), Sept. 1779.

John P. Clement (?-1845). British officer, serving as Captain during War of 1812. During a skirmish on July 5, 1814 he saw an Indian in the act of preparing to kill an American prisoner. The prisoner had just given the Masonic Sign of Distress. Clement rescued the brother and took him to a farm house, where he was cared for until he was well enough to go home. Some months later Clement himself was taken prisoner. His jailor was the same man he had rescued earlier. The jailer informed Clement that he would be returned to Canada the next morning. Member of Niagara Lodge No. 2 of Ontario.

James Clinton (1733-1812). Brother of George Clinton and father of Dewitt Clinton. Captain in French and Indian Wars. Revolutionary War Colonel of 3rd New York Continentals in Canadian expedition of 1775. Promoted Brigadier General next year. Wounded at Ft. Montgomery, 1777. Was on Sullivan's expedition at Yorktown, where his Brigade received surrendered British colors. Member of Warren Lodge at Little Britain.

George Clinton (1739-1812). Member of Continental Congress (177576). Brigadier General in American Revolution. Member of Warren Lodge No. 17, NYC, serving as Master in 1800. Represented Warren lodge at Grand Steward's Lodge on May 28, 1800. His nephew was DeWitt Clinton. Lodges in New York named "Clinton" were named for George, not DeWitt.

Sir George Cockburn (1772-1853). British Naval Admiral in War of 1812, who took out his revenge against America on public property. In August 1814 he entered Washington DC with 200 men and burned public buildings, including the White House. Member of Inverness Lodge No. 4, London.

John Cocke (1772-1854). In War of 1812 was Major General of East Tennessee Volunteers in Creek War. Served under Jackson at New Orleans in 1814. Member of Rising Star Lodge No. 44, Rutledge, TN.

John H. Cocke (1780-1866). Brigadier General in War of 1812. Received Entered Apprentice degree in Jefferson Lodge No. 65 at Surry Court House, VA. Became member of Philanthropic Lodge No. 127, from which he was suspended May 18, 1827 for "gross unmasonic conduct," referring to his anti-Masonry following Masonic murder of Capt. William Morgan.

Jacob Collamer (1791-1865). Served in militia in frontier campaign of War of 1812. Member of Rising Sun Lodge No. 7, Royalton, VT.

Lord Charles Cornwallis (1738-1805). British General during American Revolution, who surrendered to Washington at Yorktown, thus ending the Revolutionary War. Cornwallis performed the grand honors of Masonry at the funeral of Major General DeKalb.

Capt. John Cotton (?). Naval Officer of Revolutionary War. By resolution of Congress, it was directed that two frigates of 36 and 28 guns be built in Connecticut. One vessel was "to be built under the supervision of Capt. John Cotton of Middletown." Member of Lodge in Middletown, CT.

Isaac Craig (?). Revolutionary War Naval officer who served as captain under John Paul Jones. Member of Military Lodge No. 19 (now Montgomery No. 19 of Philadelphia, PA). Master of the lodge.

Dr. James Craik (1731-1814). Physician of George Washington, accompanying him in the expedition against French and Indians in 1754. Promoted to Surgeon General of Continental Army during Revolutionary War. First U.S. Surgeon General. One of three physicians who attended Washington during his last illness. Member of Alexandria Lodge No. 22, Alexandria, VA.

John Crane (?) Member of Boston Tea Party. Served as General in Revolutionary War. Made a Mason in American Union Lodge (Military) while encamped at West Point in 1781.

Benjamin W. Crowninshield (1772-1851). Secretary of Navy under Madison and Monroe. During War of 1812 he commanded several ships. Member of Essex Lodge, Salem, MA.

William Cunningham (?-1791). English Captain and Provost Marshal of American Revolution, who was notorious for his treatment of American prisoners. Over 250 were hanged without trial. 2,000 starved to death. His only virtue was in the recovery of stolen jewels, books and records of Lodges No. 2 and 3 in Philadelphia. His own lodge is not known, but he was visitor to Lodge No. 3, Philadelphia on Oct. 10, 1777. After the war he returned to England, where he became a vagabond. He received his comeuppance when he was executed on Aug. 10, 1791 for forging a draft.

Nathanial Cushing (1753-1814). Major in American Revolution. Fought with Massachusetts troops from 1775-1782. At close of war moved to Belpre, OH. Was first Master of Farmers Lodge No. 20, Belpre.

William R. Davie (1756-1820). Member of Constitutional Convention. Revolutionary War officer. Entered War after graduating from Princeton in 1776. Became Major General of militia. Raised (3°) in Occasional Lodge No. 1791. Served as Grand Master of North Carolina (1792-98).

Joseph H. Daviess (1744-1811). Joined army of Gen. William H. Harrison as Major, 1811. In Battle of Tippecanoe, seeing that an exposed angle of the line was likely to give way, led a cavalry charge at that angle and was killed. Grand Master of KY.

Thomas Davis (?). Chaplain of 1st Continental Dragoons during Revolutionary War. Rev. Davis was a member of Alexandria Lodge No. 22, Alexandria, VA, and officiated at the burial of George Washington.

Charles Dayan (1792-1827). Lieutenant Colonel in War of 1812. Was last Master of Jefferson Lodge No. 164, when due to the Anti-Masonic Movement, caused by the 1826 Masonic murder of Captain William Morgan in Batavia, New York, Dayan's lodge was forced to discontinue meetings. In 1848, immediately after the published deathbed confession of one of the murderers of Morgan, Dayan once again joined Freemasonry, and became First Master of Lowville Lodge No. 134, Lowville, NY.

Elias Dayton (1737-1807). Brigadier General of American Revolution. Took prominent part in battles of Springfield, Monmouth, Brandywine and Yorktown. Member of Military Lodge No. 19 of Pennsylvania registry; recorded as a visitor to American Union Lodge.

Jonathan Dayton (1760-1824). Officer in American Revolution. Participated in many battles, including Yorktown. Had a command under Lafayette. Member of Temple Lodge No. 1 at Elizabethtown.

Henry Dearborn (1751-1829). Major General U.S. Army. Secretary of War under Jefferson. Fought in both the Revolutionary War and War of 1812. Initiated (1°) and passed (2o) in St. John's Lodge No. 1, Portsmouth, NH, March 3, 1774. Raised (3°) April 18, 1777.

Baron Johann de Kalb (1721-1780). Major General in Continental Army during Revolutionary War. Served with valor in cause of colonies. De Kalb's statue at Annapolis, MD was unveiled by Grand Lodge of Maryland.

Henry Dodge (1782-1876). Officer in War of 1812. Initiated (1°) Dec. 6, 1806 in Western Star Lodge No. 107, Kaskaskia, IL (Indian Territory). Later affiliated with Louisiana Lodge No. 109 at St. Genevieve, MO. Served as Master for three years. Fort Dodge was named after him.

John Downes (1786-1855). Commodore, U.S. Navy, War of 1812. Commanded captured ship *Essex Junior*. Initiated (1°) in Rising Star Lodge, Stoughton, MA, Oct. 23; passed (2o) Nov. 20; raised (3°) Dec. 4, 1806.

Sir John Doyle (1756-1834). British General who served in American Revolution. His brigade captured Charleston. As a Major, was initiated (1°) May 2, 1792 in Prince of Wales Lodge No. 259 in England. Was later appointed by H.R.H. the Duke of Sussex to the position of Deputy Grand Master of the United Grand Lodge.

Peter Stephen (Etienne) Du Ponceau (1760-1844). In 1777 he accompanied Freemason Baron von Steuben to America as his secretary.

Served in the American Revolutions as aide-de-camp to von Steuben. Became a naturalized citizen in 1781. On Feb. 14, 1782, he petitioned Lodge No. 2, Philadelphia to become a Mason. Received the first two degrees on August 14, 1782. No reference of Master Mason degree.

Victor Marie DuPont (1767-1827). Aide-de-camp to Lafayette. Petitioned to organize Lafayette Lodge No. 14, Wilmington, with charter granted Jan. 17, 1825. Member of

Washington Lodge No. 1 of Delaware on April 1, 1813. Member of Temple Lodge No. 11 on Feb. 11, 1819. Same year was Grand Marshal of Grand Lodge of Delaware. Grand Treasurer, 1825.

John P. Duval (1790-1855). Served as Captain in War of 1812. Member of Jackson Lodge No. 1 at Tallahassee FL. First Grand Master of the Grand Lodge of Florida, 1830.

William P. Duval (1784-1854). Served in War of 1812 against the Indians. Elected to U.S. Congress from Kentucky, 1813-15. Member of Jackson Lodge No.1, Tallahassee, 1829. Assisted in the formation of Grand Lodge of Florida, 1830. Was also a Royal Arch Mason (K.T.) Knights Templar.

William Eaton (1764-1811). Entered Revolutionary army at age 16 and served 19 years. Member of North Star Lodge, Manchester, VT in 1792. Wrote eulogy to George Washington. Last verse concludes: "Approving Heaven, with fostering hand, Gave Masons triumph through this land; And firmly to secure our Craft, From bigot rage and envy's shaft, Sent a Grand Master, Freedom's son, The Godlike patriot, Washington!"

Henry Eckford (1775-1832). In War of 1812 was employed by U.S. Government to build ships. His vessels were superior in strength and speed to all others. Was a member of Fortitude Lodge No. 48 (now No. 19) of Brooklyn, NY, and first Junior Warden of the lodge.

Pierpont Edwards (1750-1826). Served in Revolutionary Army. Initiated (1°) in Hiram Lodge No. 1, New Haven, Dec. 28, 1775. Served as Master of the Lodge (3°) in 1777-78. Was First Grand Master of the Grand Lodge of Connecticut, 1789-90.

Samuel Elbert (1743-1788). Last Grand Master of Georgia to be appointed by United Grand Lodge of England. Brigadier General during Revolutionary War. At Brier Creek, where he commanded 60 continentals and 160 militia, he was surrounded on three sides and made a valiant stand, but was wounded and captured. He was rescued by a British officer who drew him out of line of fire when he had given a Masonic sign. Member of Solomon Lodge No. 1, Savannah, GA. Elbert County named after him.

Nehemiah Emerson (?). Captain in Revolutionary War. Was one of the guards at execution of Major Andre. Received Masonic degrees in Washington Military Lodge No. 10. Member Merrimack Lodge, Haverhill, MA.

Robert Erskine (1735-1795). Surveyor General and Geographer to the Army of the United States during Revolutionary War. At outbreak of the Revolution, he espoused colonial cause and turned his iron production over to the American army. On record as one of the visitors to American Union Lodge at Morristown (Dec. 27, 1779) when the famous military traveling lodge entertained a distinguished assemblage, headed by Gen. Washington. Erskine was made a Mason in either Edinburgh or London.

William Eustis (1753-1825). Entered Revolutionary Army as a regimental surgeon, serving throughout the war. Became Secretary of War, 1807-13. Raised (3°) in St. Andrew's Lodge of Boston on Feb. 6, 1795.

Samuel Fessenden (1784-1869). Served 14 years as Major General of the 12th Massachusetts militia. Raised (3°) Sept. 25, 1805 in Pythagorean Lodge No. 11, Fryeburg.

Joshua Fisher (1748-1833). Graduated from Harvard in 1776. Surgeon on privateer during Revolutionary War. After the war he settled in Beverly, MA. He bequeathed $20,000 to found a Harvard professorship in natural history. Was member of Unity Lodge at Ipswich, MA. Served as secretary of the Lodge.

John Fitzgerald (?). Aide-de-Camp to General Washington (Nov. 1776 to July 1778) in Revolutionary War. Major in the 9th Virginia Regiment. Member of Williamsburg Lodge No. 6.

Jellis A. Fonda (?). Revolutionary War Major in Col. Willett's New York Regiment. Initiated (1°) in St. Patrick's Lodge No. 8 at Johnstown. Member of St. George's Lodge No.1, Schenectady. Master of lodge (3°), 1797-1805.

Robert Foster (?). Captain of Minute Men in Revolutionary War. Master of Essex Lodge, Salem, MA.

John Frost (1738-1810). Brigadier General in American Revolution. Member of St. Andrews Lodge of Boston MA.

Joseph Frye (1711-1794). General in the Revolutionary War. Member of a lodge in Massachusetts.

James Gadsden (1788-1858). Appointed Lieutenant Colonel of engineers, serving with distinction in War of 1812. Served as aide-de-camp to General Jackson in campaign against Seminole Indians, 1818. Went with Jackson to Pensacola when the latter took possession of Florida. Was active in settling dispute between Jackson and the Spanish governor. Member of Jackson Lodge No. 23, Tallahassee, FL.

Edmund P. Gaines (1777-1849). Major General in War of 1812. Was instrumental in arresting Aaron Burr.

Horatio Gates (1728-1806). Major General of Continental Army in American Revolution. Member of a regimental lodge at Annapolis Royal, Nova Scotia, Canada. Dec. 18, 1778 the Grand Lodge of Massachusetts invited "The Hon'bl General Gates...to dine at the Feast of St. John's Day. The minutes of the lodge confirm his attendance.

John Gibson (1740-1822). Commanded a regiment at beginning of American Revolution. Served in New York and in the Jersey retreat. Commanded the western military department from 1781 until peace was established. Received his first two degrees in Lancaster PA, and his 3rd degree in Vincennes Lodge, Indiana on March 14, 1809.

Thomas Gibson (1750-1814). Revolutionary War soldier, who served with distinction. Member of Nova Caesarea Lodge No. 10, Cincinnati OH. First Master of Scioto Lodge No. 2, Chillicothe, OH, 1805-07. Exalted in Cincinnati Chapter No. 2, Royal Arch Mason, Dec. 11, 1799.

Joshua R. Giddings (1795-1864). In War of 1812. Became U.S. Congressman from Ohio. Raised (3°) in Jerusalem Lodge No.19, Hartford, OH.

Nicholas Gilman (1755-1814). Signer of Federal Constitution of 1787. Fought in Revolutionary War. Accounted for the prisoners surrendered by English Freemason Cornwallis at Yorktown. Member St. John's Lodge No. 1, Portsmouth, NH.

George Gilpin (?). Colonel in American Revolution. Pallbearer at George Washington's funeral. Member of Alexandria Lodge No. 22, Alexandria, VA.

Mordecai Gist (1743-1792). Brigadier General during American Revolution. Member of Lodge No. 16, Baltimore MD. First Master of Army Lodge No. 27 of the Maryland Line, chartered by Grand Lodge of Pennsylvania, April 1780.

John Glover (1732-1797). Brigadier General in American Revolution. Commanded the "amphibious regiment." Member of Philanthropic Lodge of Marblehead, Mass. Recorded as visiting St. John's Lodge in Providence, RI while stationed there.

George Gorham (?). Captain during American Revolution. Helped stretch cable across Hudson river to obstruct British in their attempt to sail ships on the river. Member of King Hiram Lodge No. 12, Derby, Conn.

Charles Gratiot (1788-1855). Brigadier General in War of 1812. Was senior warden of Comfort Lodge No. 143 at Old Point Comfort, VA.

John Greaton (1741-1783). Brigadier General in Revolutionary War. While stationed at West Point in 1777, he became a member of Masters' Lodge of Albany, NY. Was J.W. of Washington Lodge No. 10 (Military Lodge) in the Mass. Brigade, when it organized at West Point in 1779.

Christopher Greene (1737-1781). Colonel during American Revolution. Known as the "hero of Red Bank." Killed in battle on May 13, 1781 when his headquarters on the Croton River was surrounded by loyalists. Initiated (1°) March 3, 1779 in St. John's Lodge, Providence, RI.

Nathanael Greene (1742-1786). General during American Revolution. He, with four others, were the only generals who served throughout the war. Member of a Rhode Island Lodge — a military lodge.

Richard Gridley (1711-1796). Major General in American Revolution. Earned the reputation as an artillerist. Commissioned Major General in command of Continental artillery. Entered Masonry in St. John's Lodge of Boston, MA. Was Grand Master of Grand Lodge of Massachusetts.

Thomas Grosvenor (1744-1825). Revolutionary War patriot. Lieutenant under Putnam in 1775, and later a Colonel. Entered Masonry in American Union Lodge, Redding, CT. Served as secretary and Senior Deacon.

Isaac Guion (1755-1823). Revolutionary War soldier commissioned Ensign in Lamb's Artillery at outbreak of hostilities. Discharged in 1783 as Captain. Member of St. John's Lodge No. 3, New Bern, NC.

James Gunn (1739-1801). General in American Revolution. Member of Solomon's Lodge No. 1 of Savannah.

John Habersham (1754-1799). Major in 1st Georgia Continental Regiment, American Revolution. Member Solomon's Lodge No. 1, Savannah, GA.

Joseph Habersham (1751-1815). Brother of John Habersham. As a Major of 1st Georgia Battalion, he defended Savannah from a British naval attack in March, 1776. He also participated in the disastrous attack on Savannah in 1779. Advanced to Lieutenant Colonel at close of war. Member of Solomon's Lodge No. 1, Savannah.

Nathan Hale (1755-1776). In response to a call from General Washington, he volunteered for hazardous spy duty behind British lines on Long Island. Was caught and ordered executed by Sir William Howe. Before he was hanged, his last words were: "I only regret that I have but one life to lose for my country." He was ordered executed by Sir William Howe. Hale's Masonic credentials are questionable. He is sometimes referred to as a member of St. John's Regimental Lodge of New York City.

David Hall (1752-1817). Captain in Haslet's Delaware regiment, 1776. Following year was made Colonel of Delaware regiment. Raised (3°) May 18, 1776 in Lodge No. 18 at Dover, DE. Master of Hiram's Delaware Regimental Lodge No. 30. Charter master of Lodge No. 63, Lewes, DE.

Elijah Hall (?). Naval Captain during Revolutionary War. Raised (3°) in St. John's Lodge No. 1, Portsmouth NH, June 26, 1777.

William Hall (1774-1856). Major General of Tennessee state militia. He commanded a regiment of Tennessee riflemen under General Jackson in War of 1812. Member of King Solomon Lodge No. 6, Gallatin TN.

Alexander Hamilton (1757-1804). In Revolutionary War served in 1789 as Inspector General of the Army, with rank of Major General. Killed in dual with Arron Burr. Was recorded among visitors of American Union Lodge (military) at Morristown NJ, on Dec. 27, 1779, at which time Washington raised General Lafayette to the "third degree" of Freemasonry.

Paul Hamilton (1762-1816). As Secretary of Navy under James Madison, Hamilton's policy was to keep our frigates in port to prevent their capture in War of 1812. Past Master of Lodge No. 8, Charleston SC. In 1806 was Grand Master of Grand Lodge of South Carolina.

Benjamin Hammond (?). Commander of privateer schooner *Greyhound* in Revolutionary War. Member of Essex Lodge, Salem, MA.

John Francis Hamtramck (1756-1803). Colonel in American Revolution. Joined General Montgomery's army, Sept. 1775 as it was marching on Montreal. In 1776, commissioned Lieutenant, then Captain of 5th New York Continentals. Advanced to Major, Jan. 1, 1781. Lt. Colonel in command of the first sub-legion under General Anthony Wayne, Feb. 18, 1793. Assumed command of Detroit, July 13 same year. Member Union Lodge No. 1, Albany, NY (now Mt. Vernon No.3).

Edward Hand (1744-1802). Brigadier General and Adjutant General of Continental Army. At start of Revolution he joined Thompson's brigade as Lieutenant Colonel, serving at siege of Boston and battles of Long Island and Trenton. Was a member of Pennsylvania Military Lodge.

George Handley (1752-1793). During the Revolution (1776) he joined Georgia continental battery as Captain, rising to Lieutenant Colonel. Was captured at Augusta, GA. and sent to Charleston as a prisoner of war. Member of Solomon Lodge No. 1 of Savannah.

Martin D. Hardin (1780-1823). During War of 1812 he joined the army and served under General Harrison as Major of the Kentucky Volunteers. Member of Washington Chapter No. 11, R.A.M. (Royal Arch Mason).

Josiah Harmar (1753-1813). Brigadier General and General-in-Chief of Army in 1789. Initiated (1°) July 2, 1778 in Lodge No. 3 of Philadelphia. Member of Pennsylvania Union Lodge No. 29, and Nova Caesarea Lodge No. 10, (now Harmony Lodge No. 2 of Cincinnati).

John Haywood (1753-1826). Officer in American Revolution. Member of St. Andrews Lodge No. 57, Louisburg, NC.

Jonathan Heart (1744-1791). Officer during American Revolution. Member of the famous military lodge — American Union Lodge. First secretary and third and last master of that lodge.

William Henry (1761-1824). Foot soldier of Revolution and War of 1812. Commissioned Major General of Kentucky volunteers in Aug. 1813. In the year 1803 was both raised (1°) in Union Lodge No. 43 of Pennsylvania and admitted to Lexington Lodge No. 1 of Lexington, KY.

Nicholas Herkimer (1715-1777). Brigadier General of American Revolution in 1776. Fatally wounded in the Battle of Oriskany. Initiated (1°) on April 7, 1768 in St. Patrick's Lodge No. 8 of Johnstown, NY.

Samuel Herrick (?). Brigadier General in War of 1812. Affiliated with Amity Lodge No. 5 of Zanesville, OH (1813).

Joseph Hiester (1752-1832). At beginning of the Revolution he raised and equipped Reading, PA with a company which took part in the battles of Long Island and Germantown. In 1807 he was appointed one of the two Major Generals to command the quota of Pennsylvania military militia called for by the President. Member of Lodge No. 62, Reading, PA.

James Hogun (?-1781). Brigadier General in American Revolution. Member of Lodge No. 3, Philadelphia. Received blue degrees on April 13, 15, and 17, 1779.

Robert L. Hooper, Jr. (1709-1785). Deputy Quartermaster General in American Revolution (1778). Initiated in Lodge No. 2, Phil. Affiliated with Trenton Lodge No. 5. First Deputy Grand Master of Grand Lodge, NY.

Samuel Hopkins (1750-1819). General in Continental Army during the American Revolution and War of 1812. Member of Jerusalem Lodge No. 9 of Henderson, KY.

Timothy Hosmer (1745-1815). Officer in Continental Army during Revolutionary War. Surgeon on General Washington's staff. Attended and certified execution of British spy Major John Andre. Member of both Frederick Lodge, Farmington, CT, and American Union military lodge No. 1, Aug. 20, 1779, signing bylaws on that date. Became charter Master of Ontario Lodge No. 23, Canandaigua, NY, 1792.

Benjamin Chew Howard (1791-1872). Officer in War of 1812. In 1814 he assisted in organizing troops for the defense of Baltimore. April of 1813 became member of Cassia Lodge No. 45, Baltimore.

John E. Howard (1752-1827). Colonel in Revolution. In anticipation of war with France in 1798, Washington made him one of his Major Generals. Member of Army Lodge No. 27 of the Maryland Line.

Robert Howe (1732-1785). Commissioned Major General of American Revolution and led an expedition against Florida, which ended in disaster. Returned to Savannah, GA, but lost that city to the British. For this loss he was court-martialed and acquitted. Was in command at West Point in 1780. Member of Hanover Lodge of Masonborough, NC.

Richard Howell (1753-1802). Commissioned Captain in 2nd N.J. Regiment. Promoted to Major in 1776 when the Revolution began. Member of Trenton Lodge No. 5, Trenton, NJ. Past Master of same.

William Hull (1753-1825). Lt. Colonel in 1779 under Baron Von Steuben. After war was promoted to Major General, then to Brigadier General in War of 1812. Commanded northwestern army. Court-martialed for failing to defend Detroit and sentenced to be shot. The power of Freemasonry is recorded in the fact that after sentence was pronounced, he was told to go home and await his execution, which never came. Hull was a member of Washington Lodge No. 10, a traveling lodge located at West Point. Became first Master of Meridian Lodge, Natick, MA in 1797.

Ebenezer Huntington (1754-1834). Revolutionary War soldier. In 1792 commissioned General in Connecticut state militia. In 1799 promoted to Brigadier General by Washington. Member of Somerset Lodge No. 34 of Norwich, CT. Also a York Rite, Royal Arch Mason.

James Hutchison (1752-1793). Surgeon General of Pennsylvania during the Revolution. Member of Lodge No. 2, Philadelphia.

James Iredell, Jr. (1788-1853). Served in War of 1812. In 1808 he was raised (3°) in Unanimity Lodge No. 54 at Edenton.

Andrew Jackson (1767-1845). Major General of U.S. Army assigned to defend New Orleans in the War of 1812. Seventh President of the U.S.A. Initiated (1°) in Philanthropic Lodge No. 12 at Clover Bottom, TN. Member of Greeneville Lodge No. 3 of TN (formerly No 43 of NC.)

James Jackson (1757-1806). Commissioned Brigadier General in 1788. Took part in defense of Savannah. Saw action at Blackstocks, Augusta, Cowpens, and Long Cane. Initiated (1°) in Solomon's Lodge No. 1, Savannah in 1782. Served as Master (3°) of the Lodge in 1786.

Thomas S. Jessup (1788-1860). Commissioned Lieutenant of Infantry in 1808. Beginning War of 1812 was adjutant-general to Gen. Wm. Hull. Member of Harmony Lodge No. 2, Cincinnati, OH.

George Jones (1766-1838). Fought in Revolutionary War. Imprisoned in 1780-81 on an English ship. Served in War of 1812 as Captain of Savannah reserves. Member of Solomon's Lodge No. 1, Savannah, GA.

Jacob Jones (1768-1850). Commodore, U.S. Navy. Commissioned Commander, 1810. In 1811 was assigned to the ship *Wasp*. In the first naval battle of the War of 1812 the *Wasp* was overpowered by the 74gun British ship *Poietiers*. Member of Holland Lodge No. 8, NYC.

William Jones (?). Lieutenant American Revolution. Killed by Indians at Wyoming, PA. Received a Masonic burial from Military Lodge No. 19, Pennsylvania Artillery.

Lawrence Kearny (1789-1868). Commodore, U.S. Navy. In War of 1812 was assigned to coastal defense of South Carolina and adjacent states. Was raised (3°) in Colombian Lodge, Boston, MA.

John Kendrick (1745-1800). Revolutionary War captain of a privateer. Initiated (1°) a Mason Dec. 10, 1778 in St. Andrew's Lodge, Boston, MA.

Joshua King (?). Lieutenant in Continental Army to whom Major Andre, the British spy, first revealed his identity. Member of Union Lodge No. 40, Danbury, CT.; member of St. Johns Lodge, Norwalk; first treasurer of Jerusalem Lodge No. 49, Ridgefield.

William King (1768-1852). Served in War of 1812 as Colonel. Initiated (1°) in Massachusetts Lodge at Boston on Feb. 3, 1800. Became first Master of Solar Lodge No. 14, Bath, ME on Sept. 10, 1804.

Ephraim Kirby (1757-1804). Enlisted in the volunteer cavalry at age 19. Took part in Battle of Bunker Hill. Fought at Brandywine, Monmouth, Elk River, and Germantown. Left on field as dead at Elk River. Was in 17 battles, receiving 13 wounds. Was discharged an ensign, Aug. 23, 1782. Later he rejoined as a Colonel in the 17th regiment of the Connecticut militia. In 1881 he became a member of St. Paul's Lodge No. 11, Litchfield, CT. He presented his sword to this lodge.

Samuel Kirkland (1741-1808). Revolutionary patriot and clergyman missionary to the Indians. He became a brigade chaplain to General John Sulivan and chaplain to the Continental forces at Fort Schuyler and at Stockbridge, MA. Kirkland was initiated in St. Patrick's Lodge No. 8, Johnstown, NY on Feb. 7, 1767.

Robert Kirkwood (1730-1791). American Revolutionary War hero. Entered the Army as a Lieutenant. In early 1777 was commissioned Captain. He commanded at Cowpens, Guilford, and Eutaw, after which he was breveted a Major. Kirkwood was raised (3°) in Lodge No. 18, Dover, DE.

Henry Knox (1750-1806). Major General in American Revolution. One of George Washington's most trusted advisors and close personal friend. Joined American forces at outbreak of war, first fighting at Bunker Hill. Promoted Brigadier General and Chief of Artillery in Continental Army. After surrender of Cornwallis was promoted to Major General (1781). Commanded West Point in 1782. Secretary of War, 1785-94, first to hold that office in the Federal government. Member of St. John's Regimental Lodge at Morristown, NJ. In 1779 helped constitute Washington Lodge at West Point. Recorded as visiting many other lodges.

33° Marquis de Lafayette (1757-1834). Hero of American Revolution. His father, a French soldier, was killed in battle a few weeks before his birth. His mother died in 1770, leaving him a vast estate. He refused a prominent position in the French court to become a soldier in the French Army in 1771. He withdrew from service in 1776, outfitted his own ship, Victoire, and sailed with 15 other young adventurers to fight with the American colonists against England. His Masonic credentials are too numerous to print here. But, suffice it to say, he was a 33° Scottish Rite Mason.

James Lawrence (1781-1813). Naval Captain. In War of 1812 he cruised the coast of Brazil, blockading the British *Bonne Citoyenne* in the port of Salvador, and sank the *Peacock*. Later, off the shore of Boston about 30 miles, he met the British frigate, *Shannon*, but was out gunned and his ship captured with 47 killed and 99 wounded. Lawrence himself was mortally wounded. *Field Book of the War of 1812* reported that Lawrence was buried with military and Masonic honors.

Sheppard C. Leakin (?). General in War of 1812. Initiated (1°) Mason in Washington Lodge No. 3, Baltimore, MD, Feb. 4, 1812. After the war served as Master (3°) of the lodge for several terms.

Henry Lee (1756-1818). Father of Robert E. Lee. Known as "Light Horse Harry" for his brilliant cavalry operations during Revolutionary War. He joined Washington's army in Penn. as Captain of a Virginia cavalry company. At close of War he was a Colonel. Member of Hiram Lodge No. 59, Westmoreland Co., VA.

William Lenoir (1751-1839). Captain in American Revolution, and Major General of militia following the War. Wounded at the Battle of King's Mountain. Received all three degrees of Blue Lodge on Dec. 30, 1793. In 1804 was Master of Liberty Lodge No. 45, Wilkesboro, NC.

Uriah P. Levy (1795-1862). Joined U.S. Navy as a flag officer at beginning of War of 1812. His ship took the battle to the shores of England, and destroyed 21 vessels in the English Channel. Initiated (1°) Nov. 19, 1812 in Columbia Lodge No. 91, Philadelphia, PA.

Fielding Lewis (1726-1781). Patriot of American Revolution. Married George Washington's sister, Elizabeth. Manufactured guns. Member of Fredericksburg Lodge No. 4, Virginia. Attended Grand Lodge of Virginia.

Morgan Lewis (1754-1844). Colonel of American Revolution and Major General in War of 1812. Served on the Niagara frontier, captured Fort George, and commanded at Sackett's Harbor and French Creek. Initiated (1°) in Union Lodge No. 2 of Albany. Following year admitted to Master's Lodge No. 2. Was unanimously elected Grand Master of Grand Lodge of New York on June 3, 1830, reigning in that position until his death. **Benjamin Lincoln** (1733-1810). Secretary of War and Major General of militia in American Revolution, 1781-84. Active in organizing and training the Continental troops. On Dec. 25, 1780, he received his blue degrees in St. Andrew's Lodge of Boston.

George Little (1754-1809). Revolutionary War naval captain in command of U.S. frigate, *Boston*. Cruised with his ship until end of war. Member of Old Colony Lodge of Hingham, MA — 1792.

Peter Little (1775-1830). Colonel in War of 1812. Served as a mechanic. Member of Concordia Lodge No. 13, Baltimore, MD, 1797. In 1798 he became Grand Secretary of the Grand Lodge of Maryland, and Grand Master of the same in 1818. Member of Chapter No. 2, Royal Arch Mason.

Henry Beekman Livingston (1750-1831). Brother of Robert Livingston. Brigadier General during American Revolution. August, 1775, he raised a company of soldiers and accompanied his brother-in-law, General Richard Montgomery, on his expedition to Canada. In 1776 he became aide-de-camp to Gen. Philip Schuyler. In November he was promoted to Colonel of the 4th battalion of New York volunteers. At close of the war he was promoted to Brigadier General. In 1777 he became a member of Masters Lodge No. 2 of Albany.

James Livingston (1747-1832). Revolutionary War soldier. Given command of a regiment of Canadian auxiliaries at start of hostilities. With General Richard Montgomery at capture of Fort Chambly. Continued with American army as Colonel until close of war. Present at Battle of Stillwater and surrender of Burgoyne, 1777. Command of Stony Point at the time of Benedict Arnold's treason in 1780. Master of Solomon's Lodge No. 1, Poughkeepsie, NY, 1777.

Edward Lloyd (1779-1834). Served in War of 1812 as Lieutenant Colonel in 9th Maryland regiment. Member of Coates Lodge No. 76, Easton, MD.

Robert Lucas (1781-1853). Moved to Ohio in 1800, joined the militia, and was promoted to Major General. In War of 1812 was commissioned Captain in 19th U.S. Infantry. Initiated (1°) in Scioto Lodge No. 6 of Chillicothe, OH.

Augustus Ludlow (?-1813) Lieutenant, U.S. Navy. Killed with Capt. James Lawrence in naval battle between American frigate Chesapeake and British ship Shannon during War of 1812. Buried with Masonic honors by Grand Lodge of Delaware.

Thomas Macdonough (1783-1825). Fought in Revolutionary War. When War of 1812 broke out, he returned to active duty and commanded naval base at Portland, MN. Shortly after taking command (Sept. 12, 1812), he was ordered to assume command of fleet on Lake Champlain. He became a hero in "Battle of Lake Champlain." Outgunned and outmanned by the British, he fought an underdog battle that destroyed or captured every vessel of the British fleet, and compelled the enemy ground troops (14,000 against his 1500) to withdraw. This was the turning point in War of 1812. In thanks, Congress voted him land grants in New York and Vermont. Initiated a Mason in an English Lodge on Island of Malta during a previous Mediterranean tour. Member of a New York Lodge (unknown). Buried with Masonic honors by St. John's Lodge No. 2, Middletown, CT.

Thomas Machin (1744-1816). Member of Boston Tea Party and Captain in Revolutionary War. Fought at Bunker Hill and wounded in the arm. Placed chains across the Hudson River at the Highland to stop British ships. Was again wounded at Fort Montgomery, Oct. 1777. Member of Union Schoharie Lodge and Machin Lodge of New York. Master of latter. York Rite Royal Arch Mason in Ames Mark Lodge, Schoharie, NY.

Alexander Macomb (1782-1841). Major General in War of 1812. As Colonel of 2nd Regiment, fought at Niagara and Fort George. Promoted to Brigadier General (1814) and placed in command of northern frontier, bordering Lake Champlain. For his defense of Plattsburg on Sept. 11, 1814, and in face of superior British forces, he was made Major General, after which he received a gold medal from Congress. After the war he became General-in-Chief of all U.S. Forces. Was Master of Zion Lodge No. 1, Detroit, MI. On his tombstone in the Congressional Cemetery at Washington, DC are displayed several Masonic emblems.

William Malcolm (?). Brigadier General in American Revolution. Member of St. John's Lodge No. 1, NYC., and at one time Deputy Grand Master of the Grand Lodge of New York.

James Mann (1759-1832). Studied medicine at Harvard, graduating in 1776. Surgeon for three years in American Revolutionary Army. Practiced medicine in New York until the War of 1812, when he joined the U.S. Army as a hospital surgeon. He was a member of the secret Society of the Cincinnati. He was a member of Montgomery Lodge, Milford, MA.

Francis Marion (1732-1795). Revolutionary War General, known as "Swamp Fox." Served throughout the Revolution in command of Militia troops in South Carolina. He would harass British Forces by raids and fade into the swamps and forests. Mason.

Meredith Miles Marmaduke (1791-1864). Served as Colonel in War of 1812. At close of war was appointed U.S. Marshal for eastern Virginia. Fifty years later, during the Civil War, he was a staunch Unionist, although his two sons joined the Confederate forces. Marmaduke, Sr. was a member of Arrow Rock Lodge No. 55, Arrow Rock, MO. Saline County history states that Marmaduke was buried "according to the rites of Freemasonry, he having been a Mason for a number of years."

Daniel Marsh (?). Assistant Quartermaster General of American Revolution. Unknown with what lodge in New Jersey he affiliated, but was member of convention at New Brunswick for the formation of a Grand Lodge. Member of St. John's Lodge No. 2 of New York City.

John Marshall (1755-1835). Son of Thomas Marshall. Both father and son served in American Revolution. Fought at Brandywine, Germantown, Monmouth, Stony Point and Yorktown. His father Thomas was a Major in same regiment in which son John was a Lieutenant. Wintered with Washington at Valley Forge, where John became a Mason. Member of Richmond Lodge No. 13 of Richmond, VA, and York Rite Richmond Chapter No. 2, R.A.M. Grand Master of Grand Lodge of Virginia, 1793-95.

Alexander Martin (1740-1807). Member of convention that framed the Constitution. Served in Revolution as a Colonel of 2nd North Carolina regiment at Germantown and Brandywine. Raised (3°) at a communication of Grand Lodge North Carolina held in Fayetteville on Nov. 21, 1788. Was Grand Pursuivant of same in 1805-06, and Junior Grand Warden, 1807. **John Martin** (1730-?). Beginning of Revolutionary War he joined the Continental Army and commissioned Captain, then Lieutenant Colonel (1781). Was member of Solomon's Lodge No. 1, Savannah, GA, and in 1786 Grand Steward of Grand Lodge of Georgia.

Armistead T. Mason (1787-1819). Served as volunteer in War of 1812, first as Colonel and later as Brigadier General of Virginia Militia. Member of Olive Branch Lodge No. 114, Leesburg, VA.

Jonathan Mason, Jr. (?). Privateer in American Revolution. Member of Essex Lodge, Salem, MA.

Nathaniel Massie (1763-1813). Entered Revolutionary Army at age 17. Major General of Militia for several years. Member of Ohio Constitutional Convention of 1802. Member of Scioto Lodge No. 2.

Thomas Matthews (?). Officer in American Revolution. Member of Williamsburg Lodge No. 6, 1778. Grand Master of Grand Lodge of Virginia.

Ebenezer Mattoon (1755-1843). Officer in American Revolution. Major General of 4th Division in War of 1812. Received Masonic degrees in Pacific Lodge, Amherst, MA, 1802. Served as Master of Lodge 1818-19.

Israel D. Maulsby (?). General in War of 1812. Member Mt. Ararat Lodge No. 44, Slate Ridge, MD. Sr. Grand Warden of Grand Lodge of Maryland, 1836-37.

William Maxwell (?-1798). Entered Colonial Service, 1758, serving in French and Indian War until American Revolution. Became Colonel of 2nd New Jersey Battalion. With Canadian expedition of 1776, which ended in disaster. With Schuyler at Lake Champlain. Commissioned Brigadier General, 1776. Harassed enemy till end of War. Member of Pennsylvania Military Lodge No. 19. Recorded as visitor to American Union Lodge. Past Master in Northern Jurisdiction (NJ) proceedings of 1786.

Jonathan Maynard (?). Lieutenant during American Revolution. His life was spared by Indian chief, Joseph Brant, when the latter found him to be a Freemason. The story: "As he was about to be put to death by torture, Brant, who was present, discovered symbols of Masonry marked in ink upon prisoner's arms. Brant, being a Freemason himself, intervened, saving Maynard's life, and saw to it that he was sent as a prisoner to Canada. Several months later he was exchanged and sent home."

Duncan McArthur (1772-1839). Brigadier General during War of 1812. Became Major General of territorial militia in 1808. Commissioned Colonel of 1st Ohio Volunteers in 1812. Commissioned Brigadier General on March 12, 1813. He succeeded General Harrison in command of the Western Army in 1814. Invaded Canada with a force in 1814. Member of Scioto Lodge No. 2 (now No. 6) of Chillicothe, OH.

Andrew McCleary (?). Major in the American Revolution. Killed at the Battle of Bunker Hill. Said to have been the first killed in the War. Member of St. Johns Lodge No. 1, Portsmouth, NH.

John McKinstry (?). American Colonel in Revolutionary War. At Battle of The Cedars (Canada, May 20, 1776) he was taken prisoner. When about to be killed, gave Masonic grand hailing sign of distress, and was saved by Indian Chief, Joseph Brant, who also was a Mason. "McKinstry had already been fastened to the fatal tree, and the preparations for the human sacrifice were rapidly proceeding, when, in the agony of despair, and scarcely conscious of a hope, the captive made the great mystic appeal to a Mason in the hour of danger. It was seen and understood by the Chieftain Brant, who was present on the occasion. Brant at once interfered in his behalf, and succeeded, by the influence of his position, in rescuing his American brother from his impending fate. Having freed him from his bonds, he conducted and guarded him in safety to Quebec, where he placed him in the hands of the English, by whom he was permitted to return to his home on parole. It is said that Brant's friendship with McKinstry continued throughout their lives, and that Brant visited him at his home in Greendale, NY. In 1805 they together attended Hudson Lodge No. 7 in Hudson, NY.

Allan McLane (1746-1829). Revolutionary soldier and jurist. He took an early part in American Revolution. In 1775 was a volunteer in Great Bridge fight near Norfolk, VA, where Virginia militia repelled an assault of 600 British with a loss of 55 enemy and one patriot wounded. Later he joined Rodney's Delaware regiment as a Lieutenant, fought gallantly at battles of Long Island, White Plains, Princeton, Monmouth, and Yorktown, retiring from Army as Colonel at close of War. Member of Lodge No. 2, Philadelphia.

Louis McLane (1786-1857). Officer of American Revolution. Entered Navy as midshipman at age 12. Cruised one year on *Philadelphia* under Freemason Stephen Decatur. In War of 1812 he served as a Volunteer in Freemason Caesar A. Rodney's company at defense of Baltimore in 1814. Raised (3°) in Lafayette Lodge No. 14, Wilmington, DE.

Alexander McNair (1775-1826). Lieutenant in command of a company during whiskey rebellion, 1794. Colonel of Missouri militia, War of 1812. Member of St. Louis Lodge No. 111, chartered by Pennsylvania. Buried in old military cemetery by Missouri Lodge No. 1.

Return Jonathan Meigs, Sr. (1740-1823). Father of Return J. Meigs Jr. Colonel in American Revolution. Origin of his name is as unusual as the name itself. He was in love with a young Quakeress, who repeatedly rejected his suit saying, "Nay, Jonathan, I respect thee much; but I cannot marry thee." On his final rejection, he slowly mounted his horse to leave when the relenting lady said, "Return, Jonathan! Return, Jonathan!" These happy words, which were tacked on to his name by friends, were also given his firstborn in commemoration of the event. During American Revolution, Meigs, Sr. answered the Lexington alarm as Captain of a contingent from Middletown, CT., serving at Bunker Hill and (under Benedict Arnold) in Quebec Expedition. May 23, 1777, with 170 men, he raided Sag Harber, Long Island in Whale boats, taking 90 prisoners, burning 12 vessels, and returning without the loss of a single man. On June 24, 1791 he was raised (3°) a Master Mason.

Thomas Melville (?). Member of "Boston Tea Party" and Major in the American Revolution. Initiated (1°) in Mass. Lodge of Boston, Feb. 3, 1772.

Hugh Mercer (1720-1777). Brigadier General, American Revolution. Arrived in Philadelphia from Scotland in 1746, where he practiced medicine. At outbreak of Revolution he was Colonel of 3rd Virginia Regiment. At Washington's request, was promoted to Brigadier General. At Battle of Princeton he was wounded, then surrounded by enemy. Yet, he fought gallantly, suffering seven bayonet wounds in hand-tohand combat. Left on battlefield as dead. He died nine days later at a farmhouse. In 1761 he became a Mason in Fredericksburg Lodge No. 4.

James Mercer (1736-1793). He first served in French and Indian War, then an American Revolutionary leader. Member of Continental Congress, 1779-80. Educated at William and Mary. Second Grand Master of Freemasonry in Virginia. Member of Fredericksburg Lodge No. 4. Became second Grand Master of Grand Lodge of Virginia, 1774-1786.

Thomas Metcalfe (1780-1855). Captain in War of 1812, commanding a company at Battle of Fort Meigs. Member and onetime secretary of Nicholas Lodge No. 65, Carlisle, KY.

James Miller (1776-1851). Brigadier General in War of 1812. Entered Army as Major of 4th Infantry, and Lieutenant Colonel, 1810. Commanded at Battle of Brownstown, 1812. For his gallantry was promoted to Colonel. Fought at Fort George, Chippewa, and Lundy's Lane. This last battle "won the day" for American forces and he was promoted to Major General. Made an honorary member of St. John's Lodge, Boston, Dec. 6, 1814.

John A. Minor (?). American General in War of 1812. Member of Fredericksburg Lodge No. 4, Fredericksburg, VA.

Richard Montgomery (1736-1775). Delegate to the 1st Provincial Congress in NYC, 1775. Same year was Brigadier General in Continental Army of American Revolution. Captured St. John's, Chambly, and Montreal, Canada, and promoted to Major General. Attached his 300 men to Benedict Arnold's 600 men for a joint assault on Quebec in Dec. 1775. Was killed with first volley of British guns. Carleton, the British Commander, himself a Freemason, gave Montgomery burial within the city. As an early American martyr of the Revolution, he was toasted at Masonic meetings as "one of the three eminent Masons who fell in liberty's cause — Montgomery, Warren and Wooster." This toast was given in American Union Lodge on June 24, 1779, Connecticut Military Lodge. Montgomery was member of Mount Vernon Lodge No. 3, Albany, NY.

Benjamin Mooers (1758-1838). Entered Revolutionary Army as an Ensign, serving as Lieutenant until end of Hostilities. During War of 1812 he was Major General of a command at Battle of Plattsburg on Sept. 11, 1814. His Lodge is not known, but he is listed in 1901 Masonic records as among brethren who served in Revolution and War of 1812.

Andrew Moore (1752-1821). As Lieutenant under General Gates, served in Revolution at Battle of Saratoga. Resigned as Captain in 1779. In 1808 was commissioned Brigadier General of Virginia Militia. That same year was promoted to Major General. Member of Bath Union Lodge No. 42, Warm Springs, VA.

Robert Moore (?). Privateer in American Revolution. Member of Ionic Lodge, Steuben, ME.

Daniel Morgan (1736-1802). Brigadier General in American Revolution. Fought numerous battles throughout Revolution. In 1781 was in command of all light troops and cavalry in Lafayette's army. Commanded large army of Western, PA in 1795. In one of the most brilliant military actions of any war, he defeated Tarleton in Battle of Cowpens with only 900 men. Because of rheumatism he thrice retired. He finally resigned his commission in 1799 in general resentment against congressional promotions. Member of Williamsburg Lodge No. 6, Virginia.

32° James Morrison (1755-1823). Revolutionary Soldier and Quartermaster General of Army in War of 1812. Member of Lexington Lodge No. 1, Lexington, KY. Grand Master of Grand Lodge Kentucky in 1801-02.

Jacob Morton (1756-?). Officer of American Revolution. For 30 years was Major General of 1st Division, NY Militia. Master of St. Johns Lodge No. 1, NYC. Grand Master of Grand Lodge of New York until 1805.

Perez Morton (1751-1837). Patriot of American Revolution. Active in administration of public affairs during Revolution. Became a Freemason in Massachusetts Lodge of Boston on Dec. 21, 1778.

Samuel Mott (1736-1813). Militia General in French and Indian Wars and American Revolution. Was engineer in Northern department during Revolution, building coastal defenses in CT. Initiated (1°) in Military Lodge No. 7, 1761 in the 55th Foot Regiment at Crown Point. Charter member and Master of St. James Lodge No. 23, Norwich, CT.

John Peter Gabriel Muhlenberg (1746-1807). Lutheran minister. Son of Henry M. Muhlenberg, founder of Lutheran Church in America. Major General in Revolutionary War. From pulpit to battlefield began in a dramatic and eloquent sermon to his congregation. He ended by saying: "There is a time for all things — a time to preach and a time to pray; but there is also a time to fight, and that time has now come." Pronouncing the benediction, he went to the door of his church, ordered the drums beat for recruits, and 300 of his congregation responded. They became the 8th Virginia Regiment — also called the "German Regiment," and fought with honor. At close of war he was promoted to Major General. His statue is in U.S. Capitol, Washington, DC. Was a member of Lodge No. 3, Philadelphia, PA. Received blue degrees, April 12, 15, and 17, 1779.

Hardy Murfree (1752-1809). Revolutionary soldier appointed Captain. In first part of the war Murfree served under George Washington. At capture of Stony Point, Murfree commanded the North Carolina battalion of picked men that took position immediately in front of the fort, then opened fire to distract attention as a sidewinder flank moved in for the kill. Three quarters of the officers in this light infantry flank were Masons, and often were seen in American Union Lodge at West Point. Murfree's first visit to this Lodge was on June 24, 1779.

Arnold Naudain (1790-1872). Graduate of Princeton, 1806. Graduate of med-school at U. of Pennsylvania, 1810. Began medical practice at Dover. Surgeon General of Delaware Militia during War of 1912. Member of Union Lodge No. 7, Dover, serving as Master in 1817. Grand Master of Grand Lodge Delaware in 1826.

Roger Nelson (1735-1815). Brigadier General in American Revolution. Severely wounded in battle of Camden and left on field for dead. Member of Hiram Lodge No. 28, Frederick, MD.

Thomas Nelson, Jr. (1738-1789). Signer of the Declaration of Independence. Elected to Continental Congress in 1775, serving until 1777. At siege of Yorktown, he commanded Virginia militia, and ordered artillery turned on his own house, which was supposed to be headquarters for Cornwallis. After the siege of Yorktown he visited Lodge No. 9 at Yorktown, along with Washington and LaFayette. Master of Army Lodge No. 9 at Yorktown.

Robert Newman (?). American Revolutionary patriot who hung the lanterns in the church steeple that started Paul Revere on his ride. Member of St. Johns Lodge, Boston, MA.

Samuel Nicholas (1744-1790). In earlier years at sea he served in Royal Navy as a Marine. In 1775 he was named Captain of the Marines. When he jumped ship to side with the Americans, he was given the duty to recruit and train the first corps. During winter of 1776-77, when vessels of the Navy were immobile, his Marines reinforced Washington's little army, helping "man the boats" that crossed the Delaware at Trenton. A week later his Marines fought in Battle of Princeton. Nicholas was member of Lodge No. 13, Phila. Recorded as Junior Warden, Jan. 24, 1783.

Wilson C. Nicholas (1757-1820). Revolutionary War officer. Commanded Washington's lifeguard until it was disbanded in 1783. Member of the convention that ratified the

Constitution of the United States of America. Was appointed first Master of Warren Lodge No. 33, Warren, VA.

Francis Nichols (1737-1812). Officer in American Revolution. Came to America in 1769. Enlisted in Patriot Army in Cumberland Co., PA in 1775. Rose in commission to Brigadier General. Member of Lodge No. 2, Phil. Recorded as visiting Lodge No. 8, Chester Co., PA during Revolution.

James Nicholson (1737-1804). Commander-in-Chief of American Navy during Revolutionary War. Entered Navy in 1775 on Maryland ship *Defense*. With this ship he recaptured several Continental vessels from the British. In June 1776 he was given command of the 28-gun *Virginia*. In Jan. 1777 he succeeded Commodore Esek Hopkins as commanderin-chief of Navy. Held that post until it was dissolved. His military exploits are too numerous to mention. Initiated (1°) in Lodge No. 7, Kent Co., MD. Was admitted to Lodge No. 16, Baltimore, MD on June 19, 1778.

Samuel Nicholson (1743-1813). During Revolutionary War, Nicholson was in the 1773 sea battle between the *Bon Homme Richard* and the *Serapis*. Commissioned Captain, Sept. 17, 1779, and early in 1782 commanded the frigate *Deane*, with 32 guns. He took many prizes with this ship, including three sloops of war. Was first commander of the famous frigate *Constitution*, which was constructed under his supervision. At his death he was Commander-in-Chief of the U.S. Navy.

John Nixon (1733-1808). Revolutionary War leader. In French War he was Lieutenant of company with which his father had been Captain. May 1776 he was in charge of defenses of the Delaware at Fort Island. July 8, 1776, from State House in Philadelphia, he publicly read to the people the Declaration of Independence for the first time. As Colonel of 3rd battalion of "The Associators" (also known as "silk stockings"), he marched his battalion to Trenton, NJ. Remained there with Washington's army until late January, taking part in Battle of Princeton, while staying with troops at Valley Forge. His lodge in not known, but he is recorded as having been a visitor to American Union Lodge, June 24, 1779.

Caleb North (1753-1840). Revolutionary War soldier. From merchant to Captain in 4th Pennsylvania Battalion, he served in Canada campaign. On return was promoted Major of 10th regiment. After Battle of Germantown, promoted to Lieutenant Colonel of the 11th Penn. regiment, then participated in Battle of Monmouth. After surrender of Cornwallis, he had charge of British prisoners. From 1828 until his death, was president of Society of Cincinnati. Member of Pennsylvania-Union Lodge No. 29, and recorded as having visited Lodge No. 8, Chester Co. Pennsylvania.

Jeremiah O'Brien (1744-1818). Naval Captain in American Revolution. Engineered first Naval engagement of Revolution. When English ship *Margaretta* sailed into Machias Harbor with two lumber sloops, O'Brien commandeered one sloop, and with 60 volunteers, captured the *Margaretta*. Raised (3°) March 26, 1778 in St. Andrew's Lodge, Boston.

Joseph O'Brien (?). Revolutionary War patriot and brother of Jeremiah O'Brien. Assisted in capture of British vessels at Machias, ME. Later served as a private in Revolutionary Army. Member of Warren Lodge No. 2, East Machias, ME.

Aaron Ogden (1756-1839). Revolutionary War officer. Entered war as Lieutenant. Advanced to Brigade Major. In War of 1812 he declined an appointment by President Madison to be Major General. Member of Lodge No. 19, a military lodge of the Pennsylvania Artillery, 1779. Charter member and first Junior Warden of Military Lodge No. 36 of Pennsylvania registry, whose warrant was dated May 25, 1782 and signed by officers of the New Jersey Brigade. Signer of the petition for warrant of Washington Lodge No. 41 (now No. 33) of Elizabeth, NJ, Dec. 28, 1818.

Francis B. Ogden (1783-1857). Nephew of Aaron Ogden. Francis served in War of 1812. Was an aide-de-camp to General Andrew Jackson at the Battle of New Orleans, Jan. 8, 1815. At Liverpool, Ogden built the first propeller boat to be used in the U.S.A. Ogden was U.S. Consul at Liverpool from 1829-40. Member of Holland Lodge No. 8, NYC.

Matthias Ogden (1754-1791). Colonel and Brigadier General of American Revolution. Father of Frances B. Ogden and brother of Aaron Ogden. Joined Army under George Washington at Cambridge. Accompanied Benedict Arnold in his march through Kennebunk Woods in winter of 1775. Participated in attack on Quebec, where he was wounded. Promoted to Lieutenant Colonel of 1st Battalion in 1776, and Colonel of 1st Regiment of N.J. Continental line, which he commanded until end of war. His brother Aaron served under him in this regiment. Both were members of Lodge No. 36 of Pennsylvania registry, which was established in the J.J. Brigade, May 25, 1782.

Eleazer Oswald (1755-1795). Revolutionary War soldier. Lieutenant Colonel of Artillery. Highly regarded as an artillery officer, distinguishing himself at Compo and Monmouth. Member of Lodge No. 2, Philadelphia.

James Otis (1725-1783). American Revolutionary statesman, known for phrase, "taxation without representation is tyranny." Graduate of Harvard, 1743. Studied law under Freemasons Jeremiah Gridley. Began law practice at Plymouth. Moved to Boston, 1750. When he heard rumor of Battle of Bunker Hill, he borrowed a musket and joined the minute men, who were marching to aid troops in the battle. After the war he was killed by lightning while standing in the front doorway of his home. Made a Mason on March 11, 1752 in St. John's Lodge, Boston, MA.

Abraham Owen (1769-1811). During Revolutionary War he became Colonel of first militia regiment raised in Kentucky. Was first to join Gen. William H. Harrison, and was his aide-de-camp. Killed at Battle of Tippecanoe. Past Master of Shelbyville Lodge No. 5, Shelbyville, KY.

John Page (1744-1808). With George Washington on western expedition against French and Indians. During Revolutionary War he raised a regiment of militia to repel a British invasion, after which he was made Colonel in the Continental Army. Member of Botetourt Lodge No. 7, Gloucester, VA.

Gamaliel Painter (1743-1819). Revolutionary War Captain and Quartermaster. Member of Union Lodge No. 5, Middlebury, VT.

William Palfrey (1741-1780). Paymaster General in American Revolution. Active in movement that preceded Revolution. Was aid to Washington from March/April 1776, after which he was appointed paymaster-general, with commission of Lieutenant Colonel. On Jan. 26, 1761 he was initiated into membership at St. Andrews Lodge, Boston, MA. He was charter secretary of Massachusetts Lodge. From 1769-71 he was Grand Secretary of Grand Lodge of Massachusetts.

John Park (1754-1789). Lieutenant Colonel in American Revolution. Entered Continental Army, serving in quartermaster's department. Was with Washington's army until close of hostilities, attaining position of Lieut. Colonel. Original member of American Union Lodge in April, 1776, and Past Master of same. Also was member of Lodge No. 2, Philadelphia.

Samuel H. Parsons (1737-1789). Major General by end of American Revolution. Aug. 1776, joined Ethan Allan at Ticonderoga, participated in Battle of Long Island, and commissioned Brigadier General all in one month. Served at Harlem Heights and White Plains. Stationed at Peekskill, NY to protect the posts on North River. Reinforced Washington in New Jersey. Built fortifications at West Point. Commissioned Major General, 1780. Succeeded General Israel Putnam in command of Connecticut line, serving there until the close of war. His Masonic credentials are to numerous to mention here. Suffice it to say, he belonged to nearly ever Masonic body in the Northeast, receiving his 1st degree on May 18, 1763 in St. John's Lodge No. 2, Middletown, CT. On Oct. 23, 1765 he became a member of Hiram Lodge No. 1, New Haven, Ct. Somewhere he received his Master degree (3°) because he was titular Master of American Union Lodge. He also became Master in 1782 of his original Lodge. Finally, he was an early member of St. John's Mark Lodge of Middletown, his "mark" being the twin stars of a Major General.

John Paterson (1744-1808). Major General in American Revolution. After arrival of news of the Battle of Lexington, he raised a regiment of 600 minutemen and marched for 18 hours to Boston. In November 1776, with only 200 men remaining of the original 600, he joined Washington's forces at Newtown, PA, and participated in battles of Trenton and Princeton. Was promoted to Brigadier General, Feb. 21, 1777, and attached to the Northern department. Fought at Battle of Stillwater, and took part in defeat of General Burgoyne. Promoted to Major General, Sept. 1773. Paterson was first Master of Washington Lodge No. 10, a traveling military lodge under Mass. charter, which later was located at West Point.

John Paulding (1758-1818). Major during American Revolution. With two other soldiers, Paulding captured Major André. (André was the British Major hanged as a spy by the Americans for plotting with Benedict Arnold the betrayal of West Point.) Paulding was a member of Cortland Lodge No. 34, Cortland, NY.

Cromwell Pearce (1772-1852). General of War of 1812. Was Captain of militia, 1793-98. Became First Lieutenant in First U.S. Infantry, 1799. Returning to civilian life in 1800, became first postmaster of West Chester, PA. and Major General of the Militia, 1801. At beginning of War of 1812 he reentered the service as Colonel of the 6th U.S.

Infantry and led his regiment at the capture of Fort George. Before end of war he was promoted to General. Member of Lodge No. 50, Penn.

Edmund Pendleton (1721-1803). Revolutionary War patriot and statesman. Member of First Continental Congress. Member of Fairfax Lodge No. 43, Culpepper, VA.

Nathaniel Pendleton (1756-1821). Revolutionary War soldier. Entered Army at age 19 and received a commission of Major on the staff of Gen. Nathaniel Greene. Member of Solomon's Lodge No. 1, Savannah, GA.

John Percival (1779-1862). Naval officer of War of 1812. Left merchant marines in 1809 and entered U.S. Navy as sailing-master. During war he displayed great courage in capture of British ship, *Eagle*. His rough and eccentric manner won him the nickname "Mad Jack." Member of Holland Lodge No. 8, NYC.

Matthew C. Perry (1794-1858). By end of his career (well beyond the War of 1812) Perry was Commodore of U.S. Navy, and known as "father of the steam Navy." He entered the Navy in 1809 as midshipman on the schooner *Revenge* under his brother Oliver who, in the War of 1812, was a Naval hero. From 1810-13, Matthew was on the flagship *President*, training under John Rogers. In his diary, Perry gives an account of Rogers' chase of the British ship *Belvidera*. "When Rodgers fired on the *Belvidera*, it was the first hostile shot afloat in the War of 1812." Perry transferred to the ship *President*, which sailed to the seas of northern Europe, destroying British commerce, while 20 British ships were in search of the vessel." Matthew Perry was a member of Holland Lodge No. 8, NYC.

William Pierce (1740-1806). Revolutionary War soldier and delegate to the Continental Congress in 1786-87. Entered the Army at start of the Revolution, and was aide-de-camp to General Nathanael Green. Member of Solomon's Lodge No. 1, Savannah, GA.

Henry Piercy (?). Officer in American Revolution and aide-de-camp to George Washington. With Washington at every battle except Yorktown, where, after being wounded the previous day, was carried off the battle field. Member of Alexandria Lodge No. 22, Alexandria, VA.

Zebulon Pike (1779-1813). Brigadier General in War of 1812. His father by the same name (1751-1834) was Captain in the Revolutionary Army, and a member of Lodge No. 3, Philadelphia. Pike, Jr. was the discoverer of Pike's Peak in Colorado. In March, 1799, Pike, Jr. was appointed Ensign in his father's regiment, and was killed in action on April 27, 1813 during the attack on York in Canada. There is no record that Pike Jr. was a Mason, although recorded as such when confused by his father's Masonic credential.

William Polk (1758-1834). Colonel in American Revolution and Brigadier General in War of 1812. Joined Washington as Major with 9th North Carolina Regiment, 1776. Participated in battles of Brandywine and Germantown. While on staff of General Caswell, Polk was present at Battle of Camden. Promoted to Lieut. Colonel of 4th So. Carolina Cavalry. Twice wounded. Member of Hiram Lodge No. 40, Raleigh, NC. Grand Master of Grand Lodge of North Carolina from 1799-1801.

Thomas Posey (1750-1818). Officer in Indian War, Revolutionary War, and War of 1812. In 1774 was quartermaster of a division under Lord Dumore. Took part in battle with the Indians at Point Pleasant. Commissioned Captain in 7th Virginia Regiment. In battles of Bemis Heights and Stillwater. When his men assaulted Stony Point, he was first to enter fortress. Was present for surrender at Yorktown. After promoted to Lieut. Colonel, he served in Georgia. At war's end he settled in Spottsylvania Co., VA. Was Colonel of Militia and Brigadier general in 1793. When war was again threatening in 1809, was commissioned Major General and given charge of organizing Kentucky forces. Moved to Louisiana, after which War of 1812 began. He raised a company of infantry in Baton Rouge and was made Captain. Member of Fredericksburg, Va. Lodge No. 4. His name appeared in proceedings of the lodge from 1800 through 1804.

Jonathan Potts (1745-1781). Leading Revolutionary War surgeon. Studied medicine at Edinburgh, Scotland, with medical training under Dr. Benjamin Rush. When he returned to America he was awarded one of the first medical degrees given in this country. In 1776 General Putnam issued a general order that all officers in charge of any sick soldiers should "make return to Dr. Johathan Potts, at Mr. John Biddle's in Market St." In 1777 Dr. Potts was admitted to Masters' Lodge at Albany. He became first Master of Lodge No. 24 at Reading, PA.

Edward Preble (1761-1807). Commodore, U.S. Navy. One of first five commissioned lieutenants in U.S. Navy. Was on *Protector* in Revolutionary War when it captured the British privateer *Admiral Duff*. He himself was captured while on the *Protector* and imprisoned on the *Jersey* in New York. After release he was on the *Winthrop*. While blockading Tripoli with the *Philadelphia*, he ran aground and was captured and later released. A treaty with Tripoli concluded his marine actions. In 1806, Thomas Jefferson offered him a seat in the cabinet as head of the Navy, but ill health prevented his acceptance. He received his Masonic degrees in St. Andrews Lodge, Boston, MA on May 8, 1783. On Jan. 3, 1786 was elected to membership in Portland Lodge No. 1, Portland, ME. In 1806 he became charter member of Ancient Landmark Lodge No. 17, Portland, ME.

Francis Preston (1765-1835). Major General of Militia in War of 1812. Beginning of war he enlisted with appointment of Colonel of Volunteers, soon advancing to Major General. Member of Abingdon Lodge No. 48, Abingdon, VA.

Count Casimir [or Kazimierz] Pulaski (1748-1779). Polish soldier who rendered valuable aid to the cause of the American colonies. In 1775, Pulaski met Ben Franklin in France and became interested in the American struggle for independence. He came to America in March, 1777 with a recommendation from Franklin, and was immediately attached to the staff at Washington. He organized a corps of lancers in which even deserters and prisoners of war could enlist. It became known as "Pulaski's Legion." He was commissioned Brigadier General and placed in charge of the cavalry. He fought at Brandywine and Haddonfield, NJ, and took part in the Battle of Germantown. He died in battle. Pulaski was raised to the sublime degree of Master Mason (3°) in Gould Lodge of Georgia on June 19, 1779. Was buried with Masonic honors.

Israel Putnam (1718-1790), Major General, Continental Army during Revolutionary War. Was one of the four original Major Generals of the Continentals, and the only one to serve the entire length of the war. His exploits are legendary: single handed he encountered a wolf; he ran the gantlet successfully through a double rank of Mohawk Indians; he put out a fire at Fort Edward powder house; he was spared at the last minute from being burned at the stake; he sat out a powder keg duel until his opponent squirmed and ran away; he immobilized the French vessels on the St. Lawrence by driving wedges in their rudders, and much more. On many occasions he visited Hiram Lodge, journeying about 40 miles to attend. He was also a frequent visitor to the Lodge at Hartford, CT. Many lodges throughout the United States have been named in his honor.

Rufus Putnam (1738-1824). Brigadier General, American Revolution. Cousin of Israel Putnam. After service in the Indian Wars of 1757-60, he settled down to farming in New Braintree, MA. Fifteen years later, during the Revolutionary War he proved to be a resourceful engineer, constructing the siege works at Boston, Newport, New York City, and rebuilding the defenses at West Point. He received his blue degrees (1-3) in American Union Lodge at West Point, NY on July 26, Aug. 26, and Sept. 6, 1879. During a visit to Philadelphia in 1792, he was made a Royal Arch Mason, and from 1797-99 was high priest of American Union Chapter. In 1808 he was unanimously elected as the first Grand Master of the Grand Lodge of Ohio, but declined the honor due to his advanced age.

Dennis Ramsay (?). Colonel during American Revolution. Served as Captain through Colonel in Virginia Line. In 1783 he joined Alexandria Lodge No. 22, Alexandria, VA. Became Junior Warden, 1789-91.

Edmund Randolph (1753-1813). Aide-de-Camp to Washington, 1775-76. Member of Continental Congress, 1779-82. Delegate to Constitutional Convention, 1787. Member of Williamsburg, VA Lodge No. 6. Received blue degrees, Mar. 29, Apr. 2, and May 28, 1774 (original minutes in Library of Congress). Withdrew June 24, 1777 to become charter Master of Jerusalem Lodge No. 54. Deputy Grand Master of Grand Lodge Virginia (1784). Grand Master from Oct. 27, 1786 to Oct. 28, 1788.

Thomas Mann Randolph (1768-1828). Married Thomas Jefferson's daughter, Martha. Served in War of 1812 as Captain in the 20th Infantry. Member of Door to Virtue Lodge No. 44 in Albemarle Co., VA.

Joseph Reed (1741-1785). Revolutionary War patriot. Member of Committee of Correspondence and President of 2nd Provincial Congress, 1774. Commissioned Lt. Colonel of Pennsylvania troops after Battle of Lexington and Adjutant General of American Army, 1776; Brig. General in command of American cavalry, 1777. Served at battles of Brandywine, Germantown and Monmouth. Member of Lodge No. 2, Phila.

Philip Reed (1760-1829). Officer in American Revolution and War of 1812. Served as Captain in Revolution. As Colonel of Militia (Aug. 30, 1814), he defeated the British at Moorefields, MD. Member of Lodge No. 2, Chestertown, MD. At one time served as Junior Warden.

Baron Friedrich Adolph von Riedesel (1738-1800). German army officer, who was Major General in British Army during American Revolution. Commanded Brunswick mercenary contingent under Burgoyne. Captured at Saratoga, 1777. Exchanged in prisoner swap, 1779. Commanded Long Island, 1779-80. Several Masonic Lodges were in the above German regiments, to which he belonged. While in Quebec, Canada he was awarded the honorary Masonic title "Deputy Provincial Grand Master."

Samuel Ringgold (1770-1829). Brigadier General of Maryland militia in War of 1812. Past Master of Mt. Moriah Lodge No. 33, Hagerstown, MD. Junior Grand Warden of Grand Lodge Maryland, 1811.

Daniel Roberdeau (1727-1795). Member of Continental Congress. Was closely associated with Ben Franklin and Alexander Hamilton. First Brigadier General of Pennsylvania troops in Revolutionary War, elected to that position, July 4, 1776. Member of first lodge in Philadelphia. Recorded as a onetime visitor to Lodge No. 3 of Philadelphia. Also recorded as a contributor to the Masonic Hall erected there.

James Robertson (1742-1814). American pioneer and Brigadier General in American Revolution. First settler of Nashville. For many years this small group fought the Indians for that land. In 1776 both Robertson and John Sevier built a fort at Watauga. Upon completion they withstood a siege of 20 days with 40 men. In 1779 he and a band emigrated to the Cumberland region, leaving Sevier in charge at Watauga. Here they had a long conflict with the Cherokees, who outnumbered them 100-1. Through his diplomacy he made friends with both the Choctaws and Chickasaws, who severed their alliance with Great Britain. By the close of the Revolutionary War, he had brought 500 trained Indian fighters into the field. In 1790, George Washington appointed him Brigadier General and Indian Commissioner for the area. Robertson was a member of Harmony Lodge No. 1 of Tennessee. Buried Masonically.

George W. Rodgers (1787-1832). Commodore, U.S. Navy. Entered Navy as midshipman, 1804. Commissioned Lieutenant, 1810. Served on sloop *Wasp* in capture of *Frolic*, 1812. For this action he received commendation of Congress. Married sister of Commodore Perry. Member of Union Lodge No. 31, New London, CT.

Caesar A. Rodney (1772-1824). Commanded rifle corps during War of 1812. Raised (3°) July 10, 1800 in Lodge No. 14, Wilmington, DE. (under Grand Lodge of Pennsylvania). Elected Senior Grand Warden of Grand Lodge of Delaware, 1812. Recorded as having delivered a Masonic oration before that lodge, June 24, 1803. Was on Grand Lodge committee in 1809. Records of 1812 proceedings record him as Past Master of Washington Lodge No. 1, Delaware.

Robert Rogers (1731-1800). During French and Indian Wars, he raised a company of rangers, called "Rogers' Rangers." They saw action in the region of Lake George. In 1758 he was promoted to Major, after which his Rangers became famous for their raids. At start of American Revolution he conspired with the British, and was imprisoned by Gen. Washington on suspicion of espionage. Given another chance, he was paroled by Congress to New Hampshire. While there he again conspired with the British, who offered him a Colonel's commission in the British Army. He accepted and organized "Queen's Rangers." He was banished from America in 1778, and sailed to England. Member of St. Johns Lodge No. 1, Portsmouth, NH, receiving his degrees on April 1756.

William Rogers (1751-1824). Served as chaplain to Col. Samuel Miles' Pennsylvania rifle regiment, 1776-1778. Promoted to Brigade Chaplain in Continental Army. Initiated

(1°) in Proctor's Military Lodge No. 19. Member of Lodge No. 3, Philadelphia, Oct. 17, 1786. Visitor to American Union Lodge. Grand Chaplain of Penn. Grand Lodge, 1803-1824.

John Ross (1726-1800). Revolutionary War patriot and purchasing agent for Continental Army. Appointed Muster-Master of Pennsylvania Navy, 1775. Member of Tun Tavern Lodge of Philadelphia.

Benjamin Russell (1761-1845). Early American journalist and apprentice printer. Commissioned in the Revolutionary Army. Contributed war news to *Spy* magazine, owned by Freemason Isaiah Thomas. This paper was noted for collecting foreign intelligence. To gather breaking news for *Spy* , Russell visited all ships that came into Boston Harbor. Member of Rising States Lodge and St. John's Lodge, both of Boston. Grand Master of Grand Lodge of Massachusetts, 1814-16.

Buel Sackett (?). Revolutionary War soldier. One of the guards at the Oct. 2, 1780 execution of Major André. Raised (3°) in Unity Lodge No. 17, New York in 1796.

Lord George Sackville (1716-1785). Lieutenant General in British Army. As Secretary of State for the colonies in 1775-82, he virtually directed the British efforts in the American Revolution. In 1751 he was Grand Master of the Grand Lodge of Ireland.

Comfort Sage (1731-1799). Brigadier General of Connecticut Militia during Revolution. Participated in battles at Long Island, New York, Harlem Heights, White Plains, Ft. Washington, Danbury, New Haven, etc. Gave asylum to children of Benedict Arnold. Joined masonry on June 12, 1754 in St. John's Lodge. Served as Master, 1768-83. Exalted Oct. 8, 1783. His "mark" was the Bible. High priest of chapter from 1785-95.

Nathan Sage (1752-1833). Privateer Commander in Revolutionary War. Brought in many prizes during war, including an English vessel loaded with gunpowder, which was sorely needed by the Americans. For this he was publicly honored by Congress. Initiated (1°) in St. John's Lodge No. 2, Middletown, CT, Jan. 16, 1786. Royal Arch Mason soon after, in what is now Washington Chapter No. 6. His mark was a "ship."

Arthur St. Clair (1734-1818). Major General in American Revolution. Born in Scotland, in the St. Clair of Roslyn family, a prominent Masonic family of Scotland. Resigned his British commission on April 16, 1762, and settled in Ligonier Valley, PA. Involved in all political and cultural affairs, building a residence and erecting mills. Commissioned Brigadier General on Aug. 9, 1776. Organized New Jersey militia. Participated in battles at Trenton and Princeton. Was appointed Major General, Feb. 19, 1777. Succeeded Horatio Gates in command at Ticonderoga, where he was overwhelmed by the superior forces of Burgoyne. Was delegate to Continental Congress from Pennsylvania, 1785-87. His original Lodge not known, but presumed to be a British military lodge. On Sept. 8, 1791, he was one of those signing a request to the Grand Lodge of New Jersey for a lodge at Cincinnati (Nova Caesarea Harmony Lodge No. 2).

Joseph Remi Valliere de St. Real (1787-1847). British officer in War of 1812. Received Masonic degrees in Les Freres du Canada Lodge under warrant from Provincial Grand

Lodge of Lower Canada (Ancients). In 1820 was Junior Grand Warden of District Grand Lodge of Quebec. In 1821 was Senior Grand Warden of Grand Lodge of Three Rivers.

Haym Salomon (1740-1785). American merchant and financier of the Revolution. In 1776 and 1778 he was imprisoned in New York by the British, who accused him of being a spy. After his second arrest he was condemned to death, but escaped to American lines. In Philadelphia he opened a brokerage business. After accumulating a large fortune, devoted it to the use of the American government during the war. Gave financial aid to many patriot leaders, including Jefferson, Madison, and Randolph. Received first two blue degrees in Lodge No. 1, Philadelphia, June 21 and 23, 1764. Twenty years later, Aug. 9, 1784, he was raised (3°).

Winthrop Sargent (1753-1820). In 1775 he entered the Revolutionary Army and became naval agent at Gloucester. Was commissioned Captain in regiment of artillery, commanded by General Henry Knox. Took part in battles of Long Island, White Plains, Trenton, Brandywine, Germantown, and Monmouth. Major by end of war. Was one of the original members of the Society of the Cincinnati. In Freemasonry he was raised (3°) in the famous American Union Lodge (a military lodge) in 1776.

Alexander Scammell (1747-1781). General in American Revolution. With Sullivan he captured William and Mary Fort at Newcastle in 1775, one of the first overt acts of the Revolution. In 1777 he served under Gen. Gates in Northern Army. Wounded at Saratoga, 1778. Had custody of the spy, André, during his trial and execution. Was given command of a regiment of light infantry in 1781 and was captured and shot at the siege of Yorktown. George Washington obtained permission from British Gen. Cornwallis to evacuate him. He was taken to Williamsburg, where he died. Became a Mason on March 6, 1777 in St. John's Lodge No. 1, Portsmouth, NH, and was a frequent visitor to American Union Lodge.

Jacob J. Seaman (?). General in War of 1812. Charter member of Morton Lodge No. 63, Hempstead, NY.

Isaac Sears (1729-1786). Revolutionary War patriot. Became active member of Sons of Liberty, harassing the British in NYC. Leading a troop on horses in Nov. 1775, he raided the shop of James Rivington, the Royal printer, destroyed his presses and carried away his type to be made into bullets. After 1777 Sears made Boston his base of operation for privateering and trading in captured merchandise. Spent all his fortune in the war. Member of Hiram Lodge No. 1, New Haven, CT., Dec. 1775.

John Shaw (1773-1823). American naval office who commanded the *Enterprise* in hostilities with France. Fought in War of 1812. Son of a British military officer. Came to America in 1790, settling in Philadelphia. Sailor in merchant marine. In 1798, when hostilities with France began, he entered U.S. Navy as Lieutenant. Given command of the *Enterprise* in Dec. 1799 — a 165 ton ship with 12 light guns, especially built for chasing small, fast privateers. In an 8-month cruise he captured eight French privateers and recovered eleven American ships. In his action against the *Flambeau*, he killed half her crew of 100, forcing her to strike her colors in one hour. In 1814 he commanded the squadron in the Thames River that was blockaded by the British. Member of Independent Royal Arch Lodge No. 2, NYC.

Daniel Shays (1747-1825). Officer during American Revolution and insurgent leader of "Shays' Rebellion," 1786-87. Served as Ensign at Battle of Bunker Hill. Promoted to Captain in Continental Army, fighting at Ticonderoga, Saratoga, and Stony Point. Shays signed bylaws of Masters' Lodge in Albany, NY in 1778. Was present at St. John's Day observance of American Union Lodge at West Point, June 24, 1779.

William Shepard (1737-1817). Member of "Committee of Correspondence" for Westfield, 1774. Commissioned Lieutenant Colonel of Minutemen, April 1775. Joined Continental Army, May 1775. Colonel of 4th Mass. Regiment, 1776, serving in that position throughout Revolutionary War. Member of Washington Military Lodge No. 10 at West Point, NY, 1780. His Masonic apron was presented to Mount Moriah Lodge, Westfield, MA, May 21, 1907.

John Simpson (?). Brigadier General of Militia in American Revolution. Member of the first lodge in Pitt County, North Carolina.

John Small (?). British officer of American Revolution, who is said to have been acquainted with General Putnam from the French and Indian Wars. Both Small and Putnam were Freemasons. There is a tradition that when Small was once a close target for an American marksmen, General Putnam grabbed the rifle barrel and shouted, "Spare that officer, for he is as dear to me as a brother."

William Smallwood (1732-1792). Major General of American Revolution. Commissioned Colonel of Maryland battalion, Jan, 2, 1776. July 10 joined Washington in New York. Took active part in Battle of Brooklyn Heights, and bore brunt of fight at White Plains. For this he was appointed Brigadier General, Oct. 23, 1776. Fought at fort Washington, and saved the day at Germantown, Oct. 1777. Appointed Major General, Sept. 1780. Member of Military Lodge No. 27 of Maryland line.

Benjamin Smith (1750-1829). Aide-de-camp to General Washington. Was with Washington in the retreat from Long Island. Participated in defense of Fort Moultrie and served during British invasion of South Carolina. From 1794-1810, served as Major General of militia. Was member of St. John's Lodge No. 1 of Wilmington, NC. Was elected Grand Master of the Grand Lodge of North Carolina in 1809-11.

James Smith (1720-1806). Signer of Declaration of Independence. Possessed considerable property at start of Revolution, but lost it all. Raised a military company of fighting men, 1774. Appointed Brigadier General of Penn. militia, 1782. His Masonic membership is not verified. He is one of two James Smiths. There was a James Smith initiated in Lodge No. 2, Philadelphia on Sept. 11, 1754, and another who received the degrees in Lodge No. 3, Philadelphia in 1851. He is one of the two.

John Speed Smith (1792-1854). In War of 1812 he enlisted as a private and was promoted to Colonel. Was aide-de-camp to General Harrison. Member of Richmond Lodge No. 25 as early as 1813, and served as its Master. Member of Danville Chapter No. 4, Royal Arch Mason, Danville, KY in 1825. Was also a York Rite Knights Templar.

Jonathan Bayard Smith (1742-1812). Member of Continental Congress. Commissioned Lieut. Colonel of battalion of "associators" under his brother-in-law, Col. John Bayard.

Was both a Scottish Rite and York Rite Mason. Raised (3°) in Lodge No. 3, Philadelphia, Dec. 18, 1783. Master, 1785. Grand Master of Grand Lodge of Penn., 1789-94. Exalted in York Rite in Jerusalem Chapter No. 3, Royal Arch Masonry (R.A.M.) of Philadelphia. Grand High Priest of Grand Chapter of Pennsylvania, 1798.

Samuel Smith (1752-1839). Lt. Colonel, American Revolution. Commissioned Major General in War of 1812. Commanded state troops in defense of Baltimore. Severely wounded in one battle. Under President Jefferson (1801), when our nation was short of finances, he served without compensation. His battles in both wars are too numerous to mention here, but he received thanks from Congress for his gallantry. Member of Concordia Lodge No. 13, Baltimore MD.

Simon Spalding (1742-1814). Revolutionary War soldier, who was later promoted to General of Pennsylvania militia. Was a Lieutenant, then a Captain. Fought at Bound Brook, NJ, April 13, 1777. Due to his personal efforts in this battle, the Americans were able to escape with little loss. Member of Rural Amith Lodge No. 70, Athens, PA.

Ebenezer Sproat (1752-1805). Revolutionary War soldier. Entered Provincial Army as Captain early 1775. Promoted to Lieut. Colonel and given command of 2nd Massachusetts Regiment. In battles of Trenton, Princeton, and Monmouth. Appointed Brigade Inspector by Baron Steuben. Sproat was tall and commanding in person; known among the Indians as "The Big Buckeye," from which Ohio derived its nickname, "The Buckeye State." Raised (3°) in American Union Lodge No. 1, Marietta, OH, Dec. 8, 1790.

John Steele (1758-1827). Revolutionary War officer and Brigadier General of Pennsylvania militia. Commanded a company in March, 1779. Seriously wounded at Battle of Brandywine. Retired from service in Jan. 1783. Member of Lodge No. 61, Wilkes-Barre, PA.

Edward Stevens (1745-1820). Brigadier General in American Revolution. Commanded battalion of militia at Battle of Great Bridge, Dec. 1775. Promoted to Colonel, 1776. Joined Washington's Army in New Jersey, 1777. Checked the attack of General Howe's forces at Battle of Brandywine. Served at Germantown, and there promoted to Brigadier General. Joined army of General Horatio Gates with 700 Virginia militia, fighting in Battle of Camden and severely wounded at Guilford Courthouse, Aug. 1780. In his will he left one acre of land near his own family grave yard in Culpeper to be used as a cemetery for the members of his lodge — Fairfax No. 43.

Walter Steward (1756-1796). Early in war he raised a company for the 3rd Pennsylvania Battalion and was commissioned Captain, Jan. 1776. Appointed Aide-de-camp to General Gates, May 1776, serving in that capacity until June, 1777. Led a regiment of Pennsylvania Militia at Brandywine and Germantown. Said to have been the most handsome man in the American Army — known as the "Irish Dandy." Member of Pennsylvania Union Lodge No. 29, A.Y.M.

John Stockton (?). Brigadier General of state militia in War of 1812. Coroner of New Castle Co., DE, 1783. Sheriff, 1788-91. State Senator in 1795. Member of Lodge No. 33, New Castle, DE, March 1, 1790.

Amos Stoddard (1762-1813). Served as a soldier in American Revolution from 1779 until the close of the War. Was appointed Captain of artillery on June 1, 1798; Major on June 30, 1807, and Deputy Quartermaster on July 16, 1812. At the siege of Ft. Meigs, he received a wound that resulted in his death. Member of Kennebec Lodge No. 5, Hallowell, ME.

Joseph Story (1779-1845). Revolutionary War surgeon. Member of Philanthropic Lodge at Marblehead, MA.

Joseph Remi Valliere de St. Real (1787-1847). British officer in the War of 1812. Received Masonic degrees in Les Freres du Canada, under warrant from the provincial Grand Lodge of Lower Canada (Ancients).

Samuel Stringer (1734-1817). Revolutionary War physician who accompanied troops during invasion of Canada. Was dismissed by Congress on Jan. 9, 1777, following an inquiry concerning medicines he had purchased. He then practiced in Albany, achieving a good reputation. Was senior warden of Masters' Lodge No. 2, Albany, 1768. Member of the Ineffable Lodge of Perfection, Scottish Rite at Albany.

Samuel Strong (1762-1832). General in War of 1812. During war he raised a body of soldiers to relieve a garrison under siege at Plattsburg, NY. Member of Dorchester Lodge No. 1, Vergennes.

Jeremiah Sullivan (1794-1870). Major of Volunteers in the War of 1812. Member of Union Lodge No. 2, Madison, IN.

John Sullivan (1740-1795). Major General in American Revolution. Was first commissioned Major of Militia, 1772. Colonel, 1773. Recognized by Congress in June, 1775 as one of the eight original Continental Brigadier Generals. Promoted to Major General, August 1776. Received Entered Apprentice (1°) in St. John's Lodge No. 1, Portsmouth, NH, March 19, 1767; Fellowcraft (2o) Dec. 28, 1768. Grand Master of New Hampshire, 1789. Seated in the Grand East on April 8, 1790.

Jethro Sumner (1730-1790). Brigadier General in American Revolution. Appointed Colonel of 3rd North Carolina Regiment by the 1776 provincial congress, and served under Washington in the north. Commissioned Brigadier General by Continental Congress (1779) and joined General Gates in the south. Was at Battle of Camden, serving under Gen. Nathanael Greene. Member of Royal White Hart Lodge No. 2, Halifax, NC.

Benjamin Tappan (1773-1857). Served in War of 1812 as an aide to General William Wadsworth. Member of Steubenville Lodge No. 45, Steubenville, OH.

Waller Taylor (1786-1826). Served as aide-de-camp to General William H. Harrison in the War of 1812. Promoted to Adjutant General in 1814. Member of Vincennes Lodge No. 1, Vincennes, IN.

Tecumseh (1768-1813). American Indian who threw his lot with the British in the War of 1812. Many have claimed that he was made a Mason while in Philadelphia on a visit. Tecumseh Lodge of New York was named for him.

Simeon Thayer (1737-1800). Soldier in Rogers' Rangers and Major in American Revolution. Appointed Captain by Rhode Island Assembly, and accompanied Benedict Arnold's expedition against Quebec, where he was captured in May of 1775, and later released. On Jan. 1, 1777 he was promoted Major and served with great bravery in defense of Red Bank and Fort Mifflin. Wounded in Battle of Monmouth. Retired from service on Jan. 1, 1781. Member of St. John's Lodge No. 1, Providence, RI.

William Thompson (1736-1781). Commissioned Brigadier General in American Revolution, March 1, 1776 and relieved General Charles Lee of the command of New York Forces. In April of 1776 was ordered to Canada to reinforce General John Thomas. On his way he met a remnant of the Northern Army on its retreat from Quebec, and assumed command, then yielded command to General John Sullivan. Sullivan then ordered the disastrous attack on Three Rivers on June 6, where Thompson was taken prisoner. In August Thompson was released and returned to Philadelphia on parole. While in Philadelphia he received his Masonic degrees on April 13, 15, 17, 1779 in Lodge No. 3, together with two other Generals.

Isaac Tichenor (1754-1838). In 1777, one year into the Revolutionary War, Tichenor was appointed Assistant Commissary General. At that time he had joined York Rite Masonry, Jerusalem Chapter No. 2, Vergennes, Vt. In 1809 he was Grand High Priest of the Grand Chapter (York), as well as deputy Grand Master of the Grand Lodge (Scottish).

Tench Tilghman (1744-1786). Military aide and secretary to George Washington during Revolution. Began as Lieutenant in a company from Philadelphia, known as the Ladies Light Infantry. Promoted to Lieut. Colonel, April 1, 1777. Upon surrender of Cornwallis, Gen. Washington selected Tilghman to take with all speed his dispatch of the surrender to Congress. Member of St. Thomas Lodge No. 37, Baltimore, MD.

James Tilton (1745-1822). Surgeon General of U.S. Army during War of 1812. Was Regimental Surgeon in a Delaware regiment in charge of hospitals, 1776-77. During winter of 1779-80, it was through his efforts that typhus fever was stamped out at camp near Morristown, NJ. In 1814 he issued *Regulations for the Medical Department*, defining clearly for the first time the duties of medical officers and the sanitary staff. He was raised (3°), July 9, 1776 in Lodge No. 18, Dover, DE, a military lodge under Pennsylvania registry. In the same decade he also affiliated with Lodge No. 14, Wilmington, DE.

John Tipton (1786-1839). Brig. Gen. of Militia in War of 1812. Member of Pisgah Lodge No. 32, Corydon, IN. Was Grand Master of the Grand Lodge of Indiana. High Priest of Logan Chap. No. 2, R.A.M., Logansport, IN.

George Tod (1773-1841). Lieutenant Colonel in the War of 1812. Served with honor at the defense of Ft. Meigs in May, 1813. Member of Erie Lodge No. 47, Warren, OH.

Nathan Towson (1748-1854). Major General of U.S. Army. At the beginning the War of 1812, he was appointed Captain in 2nd U.S. Artillery. On Oct. 8, 1812, he captured the brig *Caledonia* from under the guns of Fort Erie. Two years later (July 5, 1814) he served with distinction in the Battle of Chippewa. His lodge is not known, but in the year 1837 he was present at lodge proceedings of the District of Columbia during the installation of the Grand Lodge officers on St. John's Day.

John Trevett (1747-1823). Naval Captain in Revolutionary War. He enlisted in the Continental Navy on Nov. 1775 as a midshipman aboard the *Columbus*. He was soon promoted to Lieutenant, serving under Commander Esek Hopkins. In 1776 he was attached to the *Andrea Doria*, and then the *Providence*, commanding the marines on board. In 1780 he lost his right eye in combat aboard the frigate *Trumbull*. Member and Past Master of Philanthropic Lodge, Marblehead, MA.

William A. Trimble (1786-1821). Major and Lieutenant Colonel of Ohio Volunteers in War of 1812. Member of Scioto Lodge No. 6, Chillicothe, OH.

Samuel Tucker (1747-1833). American Naval Commodore in Revolutionary War. Ran away from home at age 11 and stowed away on English sloop *Royal George*. Before American Revolution he had many voyages to his credit, even commanding a merchantman as Captain. He was in London when the war began and took ship for America. George Washington commissioned him Captain in the Navy on Jan. 20, 1776, commanding the schooner *Franklin*. Tucker transferred to the *Hancock* that same year. With these two ships he captured more than 30 vessels. After commanding several other ships, his total booty was 62 vessels, 600 cannons, and 3,000 prisoners. Initiated (1°) at St. Johns Lodge of Boston on Jan. 30, 1779. His Masonic apron and diploma dated 1779 is in safe keeping at the Bristol Lodge, Bristol Mills, ME.

St. George Tucker (1752-1828). Revolutionary War soldier. Served as Lieutenant Colonel at siege of Yorktown, Jan. 1777. Became second Grand Master of Grand Lodge Missouri. Signed bylaws of Williamsburg Lodge No. 6, Williamsburg, VA, July 6, 1773. Received 3° Dec. 10, 1773. Original minutes of the above are in the Library of Congress.

Benjamin Tupper (1738-1792). General in Revolutionary War. Soldier in French War of 1756-63. Soon after Battle of Lexington was commissioned Major at Boston. Promoted to Lieut. Colonel, Nov. 4, 1775, and Colonel early 1776. In August he commanded gunboats on the North River. Served under Gen. Horatio Gates at Saratoga; promoted to General before close of war. Was first Senior Warden of Washington Lodge No. 10, a traveling lodge located at West Point, NY. Master of Hampshire Lodge, Northampton, MA, 1785.

Daniel Turner (1794-1850). Commodore , U.S. Navy in War of 1812. At age 14 entered Navy as midshipman, 1808. Served with Commodore Perry on Great Lakes. On Lake Erie, Sept. 10, 1813, he commanded the brig *Caledonia* in victory, for which he received a silver medal from Congress. Following year he served on Lakes Huron and Superior, where he commanded a fleet of boats and captured two forts and several prized vessels. He was captured on Sept. 5, 1814, while in command of the Schooner *Scorpion* on Lake Huron. Three years before his death he was in charge of Portsmouth Navy Yard. Member of St. John's Lodge No. 1, NYC.

Philip Turner (1740-1815). Revolutionary War surgeon. In 1759 was appointed assistant surgeon to a provincial regiment that served under General Amherst at Ft. Ticonderoga. In 1775 he was first surgeon of the Connecticut troops stationed at Boston. In 1776 he accompanied the Continental Army to New York during battles of Long Island and White Plains. In 1777 he was appointed Surgeon General of the Eastern Department, holding that post until the close of war. Member of three Connecticut lodges: Norwich; Columbia, with Turner as Master; and Somerset No. 34.

Joseph R. Underwood (1791-1876). Served in War of 1812 as Lieutenant in 13th Kentucky Infantry. Member of following lodges: Allen Lodge No. 24, Glasgow, KY serving as Senior Warden; Clay Mark Lodge No. 7 of Glasgow; Bowling Green Chapter No. 38, R.A.M. Buried Masonically.

Peter Van Cortlandt (1749-1831). Revolutionary War officer. Commissioned Lt. Colonel of 4th battalion, New York Infantry, June 1775. Promoted Colonel by Gen. Washington and placed in 2nd New York Regiment, Nov. 1776. At war's end was breveted Brigadier General by Congress. Military activity: served with General Sullivan on Western New York expedition; present at surrender of Burgoyne; took part in Virginia campaign; witnessed the surrender of Cornwallis at Yorktown. Treasurer of Society of the Cincinnati for New York. Member of Solomon's Lodge No. 1, NYC, Aug. 8, 1777.

Henry Killian Van Rensselaer (1744-1816). Militia General in Revolutionary War. Commanded New York regiment during Revolution. Wounded at capture of Gen. Burgoyne. Carried the ball in his body for 35 years. Member of Masters' Lodge No. 2, Albany, NY; and Albany Lodge of Perfection, AASR.

Jeremiah Van Rensselaer (1741-1810). Actively supported Revolution. Ensign and Army Paymaster. Member of Masters' Lodge No. 2, Albany, NY.

Nicholas Van Rensselaer (1754-1848). Colonel of American Revolution. Served with gallantry on heights of Stillwater. After surrender of Gen. Burgoyne, Rensselaer was sent by General Gates to announce the news in Albany. Member of Masters' Lodge No. 2, Albany, NY.

Stephen Van Rensselaer (1764-1839). Major General New York Militia, 1801. Fought with his Militia in War of 1812 and suffered serious defeat, forcing him to resign his commission. Became Grand Master of Grand Lodge of New York from 1826-29. [He accepted this position as Grand Master at the very beginning of the Anti-Masonic Period, following the 1826 Masonic murder of Captain William Morgan at Batavia, NY, after which 45,000 of the 50,000 Masons in America at that time had quit the Lodge in protest of the murder]. When Gov. DeWitt Clinton (also a Freemason) concluded the ceremony of installing Rensselaer in office, Rensselaer replied, "I accept the distinguished honor conferred on me by the Grand Lodge of this state..." He ended by saying, "No exertions shall be wanting to reunite the brotherhood into one bond of union..."

James M. Varnum (1748-1789). Brigadier General in American Revolution. At start of Revolution, was commissioned Colonel of the 1st Rhode Island Infantry, May 8, 1775. Was present at shelling of Roxbury, MA; siege of Boston; Harlem Heights; and Battle of White Plains. Appointed Brigadier General of troops in Rhode Island, Dec. 12, 1776, and maintained same commission in Continental Army two months later. Commanded American troops on Jersey side of Delaware at Battle of Red Bank. Was at Valley Forge in winter of 1778, when Washington called him "the light of the camp." Was an original member of the Society of the Cincinnati, and member of St. John's Lodge No. 1, Providence, RI.

Peleg Wadsworth (1748-1829). Brigadier General of Militia in Revolutionary War. First served as aide to Gen. Artemas Ward; engineer under Gen. Thomas; Brigadier General of Militia in 1777; and Adjutant General of Massachusetts in 1778. Member of St. John's Lodge of Boston.

George Walton (1750-1835). Revolutionary War officer. As Colonel of First Georgia Brigade, was wounded and captured at Savannah. Member of Solomon's Lodge No. 1, Savannah. As result of war, these lodge records were lost. After war, when Solomon's Lodge was reconstituted in 1785, Walton took his degrees over again.

Reuben H. Walworth (1788-1867). Served in War of 1812 as aide-de-camp to General Benjamin Mooers. Was division Judge Advocate with rank of Colonel. Member of Rising Sun Lodge No. 103, Saratoga Springs, NY. Forty years later became Grand Master of Grand Lodge of New York, 1853.

Samuel Ward (1756-1832). Officer in Revolutionary War. Raised a company and marched to siege of Boston in 1775. Joined Benedict Arnold's forces on Canadian expedition; taken prisoner at Quebec. As a Major he saw action at Red Bank, writing official report of the battle. Was with army at Valley Forge. Retired as Lieutenant Colonel on Jan. 1 1781. Initiated in St. John's Lodge at Providence, RI, Feb. 17, 1779.

John Warren (1753-1815). Physician in American Revolution and brother of Joseph Warren. Attended wounded at Battle of Bunker Hill (where his brother was killed). While attempting to pass a sentry in order to see his brother, received a bayonet wound. Appointed hospital surgeon in 1776, accompanying the Army to New York and New Jersey. Also practiced at Trenton and Princeton. From 1777 until close of war was superintending surgeon of military hospitals in Boston. Initiated (1°) a Mason in St. Andrews Lodge, Boston on April 18, 1777. On June 24, 1783 became Grand Master of Grand Lodge, Massachusetts.

Joseph Warren (1741-1775). American physician and Major General in American Revolution. Brother of Dr. John Warren. It was Joseph Warren who sent both Paul Revere and William Dawes to Lexington on April 17, 1775 to warn Hancock and Adams of their danger. Joe was commissioned Major General of Massachusetts forces, June 14, 1775. Three days later was killed at Battle of Bunker Hill. Warren received blue degrees in St. Andrew Lodge, Boston, 1761. Elected Master of lodge, Nov. 30, 1768.

John R. Watrous (1754-1842). Surgeon in American Revolution. Initiated in American Union Lodge on Feb. 17, 1779. Became secretary on Dec. 15, 1779. Senior Deacon in 1782. Deputy Grand Master, Grand High Priest of the grand Chapter, R.A.M., and first Grand Commander of the Grand Commandery, K.T. of Connecticut.

Anthony Wayne (1745-1796). General in American Revolution. Recruited and led a regiment as Brigadier General, 1777. Appointed Major General by Washington in command of regular army, 1792. Member of Winchester Lodge No. 12. Gave a grand entertainment and banquet to members of the Masonic fraternity, June, 1778. Grand Lodge of New York dedicated a monument to his memory at Stony Point, NY — July 16, 1857.

George Weedon (1730-1790). Brigadier General in American Revolution. Began as Lieutenant Colonel of 3rd Virginia Regiment, Feb. 1776. Commissioned Brigadier General, Feb. 1777, and participated in the battles of Brandywine and Germantown. Retired from Army in dispute with Gen. William Woodford as to supremacy of rank. In 1780 he resumed his command of a brigade and during siege of Yorktown in Oct. 1781, was in charge of Virginia militia at Gloucester. Was made a Mason in Kilwinning Cross Lodge No. 2, Port Royal, VA , May 3, 1757.

Abraham Whipple (1733-1819). Commodore in American Revolution. June 9, 1772, he led volunteers that captured and burned British schooner *Gaspe* in Narragansett Bay, which was first American attack against a British armed vessel. June, 1885, Rhode Island fitted out two armed vessels, placing Whipple in command as Commodore. With them he captured British sloop *Rose*. He later commanded *Columbus* and then *Providence*. While commanding the *Providence* and two other ships in July, 1779, he attacked a fleet of English merchantmen under convoy, capturing eight of them, a prize in excess of one million dollars. In 1780 he went to Charleston, SC to protect the city, but was captured by the British and held prisoner until war's end. Initiated (1°) and passed (2o) in St. Johns Lodge No. 1, Providence, RI, June 4, 1761. His brother, William Whipple, was signer of the Declaration of Independence.

William Whipple (1730-1785). One of the signers of the Declaration of Independence and Brigadier General in American Revolution. Commanded a ship before he was 21 and engaged in European trade. Was elected a delegate to the Continental Congress from New Hampshire in 1775 and served until 1778, declining his reelection. Was commissioned Brigadier General in 1777 and commanded a brigade of state troops at the battles of Saratoga and Stillwater. After Burgoyne's surrender, Whipple signed the articles of capitulation on behalf of General Gates. Member of St. John's Lodge No. 1, Portsmouth, NH on Jan. 2, 1752 at the age of 21.

John Whistler (1756-1829). U.S. Army Captain in American Revolution. First commandant of Ft. Dearborn. Ran away from home at young age and enlisted in British Army, serving under General Burgoyne during American Revolution. After the war he enlisted in U.S. Army. Was promoted to Captain, July 1, 1797. By 1915 he was Major in U.S. Army. Member of Nova Caesarea Lodge No. 10 (now Harmony No. 2) of Cincinnati.

Edward Wigglesworth (1742-1826). Colonel in American Revolution. Third in command in operations of American fleet on Lake Champlain under Benedict Arnold and Horatio Gates. Spent his entire fortune on his service to America. Member of Lodge of St. Andrew, Boston, 1781.

James Wilkinson (1757-1825). American Army officer, Mason, and adventurer, who continually got himself into a peck of trouble, yet in every instance was acquitted. Completed medical studies and entered Continental Army as Captain, 1776. With

Benedict Arnold in retreat from Montreal to Albany, 1776. Promoted to Lieutenant Colonel, then Brigadier General, 1777. Secretary of board of war, 1778, but when involved in Conway Cabal forced to resign his commission. In 1781 engaged in trade in Mississippi Valley region. Conspired with Spanish governor of Louisiana to gain trade monopolies for himself. Charged with attempting to separate Kentucky from the U.S. and turn it over to Spain — acquitted. Again entered the military as Lieutenant Colonel and fought against the Indians. Became Brigadier General, 1792. Took Detroit from the British, 1796, after which he became ranking officer in U.S. Army. Implicated in Aaron Burr's conspiracy, but after witnessing against Burr, was himself acquitted by courtmartial, 1811. Commissioned Major General, 1813. Commanded American forces on Canadian frontier. Acquitted before a board of inquiry for another infraction, 1815. Honorably discharged. Occasional visitor to lodges in the Ohio and Mississippi Valleys, including Harmony No. 7 at Natchez.

Benjamin Williams (1754-1814). Entered Revolutionary Army as Captain. Saw service at Guilford, for which he was promoted to Colonel. Congressman, 1793-95; Governor of North Carolina, 1799-1802 & 1807-08. Received degrees, Dec. 9 & 19, 1795 in St. John's Lodge No. 3, New Bern, NC.

David R. Williams (1776-1830). Brigadier General of Regular U.S. Army in War of 1812. Grand Master of Grand Lodge of South Carolina at same time he was governor of that state.

John Williams (1778-1837). Fought in War of 1812 as Captain and Colonel. Participated in decisive Battle of Horse Shoe Bend in 1813. Initiated in Johnston-Caswell Lodge No. 10, Warrenton, NC. Member of Tennessee Lodge No. 2, Knoxville.

Jonathan Williams (1750-1815). First superintendent of West Point and "father of the corps of engineers." Entered regular army 1801 as Major of Artillery. On Dec. 4, 1801 was made Inspector of Fortifications. Took command of post at West Point, NY. Became superintendent of U.S. Military Academy upon its founding at West Point. At start of War of 1812 asked for command of fort named in his honor, and when refused, he resigned. Member of Massachusetts Lodge, Boston, on Dec. 23, 1771.

Otho H. Williams (1749-1794). Brigadier General of American Revolution. Lieutenant of Maryland troops at siege of Boston, 1775. Wounded and taken prisoner at Ft. Washington. Promoted to Colonel at Battle of Monmouth. Adjutant General under Generals Gates and Greene in southern campaigns. Made Brigadier General by Congress, 1782. Early initiate of American Union Lodge during Siege of Boston, when it was meeting at Roxbury. Initiated (1°) Feb. 26, passed (2o) March 11, and raised (3°) March 13, 1776.

Levin Winder (1756-1819). Lieutenant Colonel before close of Revolutionary War. Later commissioned Brigadier General in Maryland Militia. In 1782 was first Master of Lodge No. 37 in Princess Anne, MD under Pennsylvania charter. Was Grand Master of Grand Lodge of Maryland.

William H. Winder (1775-1824). Brigadier General in War of 1812. Lieutenant Colonel of 14th U.S. Infantry, March 1812. Command of regiment in July. After successful expedition to Canada, promoted Brigadier General, March 1813. Member of Cassia Lodge No. 45, Baltimore at its formation in 1811. Master in 1816. Grand Master of the Grand Lodge of Maryland, 1822-24. Member of York Rite, Phoenix Chapter No. 7, R.A.M., Baltimore.

Henry A. Wise (1806-1876). Governor of Virginia by opposing the "KnowNothings, 1855-59. Brigadier General in Confederate Army. Member of Northampton Lodge No. 11, Eastville, Northampton Co., VA.

James Wood (1750-1813). Served in Virginia line as Colonel in Revolutionary War. Brigadier General of State Troops. Superintendent of all prisoners of war in Virginia. V.P. of Society of Cincinnati in Virginia, 1784. President, 1789, serving in that position till death. "Visiting brother" to Williamsburg Lodge No. 6, Williamsburg, Apr. 5, May 30, June 30, 1774.

William Woodford (1735-1780). Brigadier General in American Revolution. Colonel of 2nd Virginia Regiment. Sank five enemy ships at Hampton Roads. Appointed Brigadier General, Feb. 21, 1777 and given command of 1st Virginia Brigade. Wounded at Battle of Brandywine. Ordered to relieve Charleston, he marched his troops 500 miles in 28 days. Taken prisoner at Charleston, May 12, 1780, and sent to NYC, where he died a prisoner. Member of Fredericksburg Lodge No. 4, Fredericksburg, VA.

David Wooster (1710-1777). Gave up British commission and took half pay to become Major General of Connecticut troops in the American Revolution. Advanced to Brigadier General by end of war. Was in a military traveling lodge at Louisbourg. Secured charter for the first lodge in the state; Hiram No. 1 at New Haven, dated Nov. 12, 1750. Wooster was its first Master, consequently was the "Father of Freemasonry in Connecticut."

William J. Worth (1794-1849). Major General in War of 1812. Commissioned 1st Lieutenant of 23rd Infantry, March, 1813. Fought valiantly at the Battle of Niagara, after which he was promoted to Major General. Mason.

Robert Wright (1752-1826). Served in Revolutionary war as a private and became Captain. Member of Lodge No. 17, Queenstown, MD and member and Past Master of Lodge No. 7, Maryland.

Christopher Yates (1737-1785). Colonel in American Revolution. Initiated in St. Patrick's Lodge No. 4, Johnstown, NY, Sept.. 9, 1769. Charter member and first Master of St. George's Lodge No. 6, Schenectady, NY, Sept. 14, 1774, serving until his death.

Figure 26 — Famous fur trader and opium dealer during the birth of our nation. See *Scarlet and Beast*, Vol. 1, 3rd ed. ch. 25; and Vol.3, ch.2&4.

3° **John Jacob Astor** (1763-1848)

German--American financier and czar of the fur and opium trade. He incorporated the American Fur Co. in 1808 and the Pacific Fur Co. in 1810. He founded the city of Astoria at the mouth of the Columbia River as a trading post but lost it to the British in 1813.

During the War of 1812 he made large and profitable loans to the government. Astor also invested heavily in New York real estate. By 1817 he had monopolized the Mississippi valley fur trade, and from 1822-34 the upper Missouri fur trade.

Astor was one of the first members of Holland Lodge No. 8, NYC, and served as Master in 1788. He was Grand Treasurer of the G.L. of New York from 1798-1801. Was Junior Grand Warden pro tem on two occasions, 1798 & 1801. For a time he was secretary of a commandery that met in Holland Lodge, 66 Liberty St., NYC.

Memorial to Astor's Fur Trade

The Astoria Column in the far northwest overlooks the city Astoria and its scenic surroundings. Astoria is named for John Jacob Astor, whose Pacific Fur Company established the first settlements in Oregon. The British granted Astor the privilege of becoming a BEIC stockholder. This enabled him to pioneer the opium trade from China. The BEIC shipped the drugs to Astoria. Astor transported the drugs east by concealing them in the bundles of fur.

Figure 27 — Famous philanthropist during the birth of our nation.

3° **Stephen Girard** (1750-1831)

Philanthropist. Born in Bordeaux, France. As son of a sea captain, he sailed to the West Indies as a cabin-boy at an early age, and thence to New York. He became a mate, captain, and part owner of a ship. In 1769 he settled in Philadelphia to establish his trade. He was alternately a shipmaster and a merchant. In 1812 he founded the Bank of Stephen Girard to take over the business of the Bank of the United States. During the War of 1812, he financed 95 percent of the war's cost by making five million dollars available to the U.S. government. He aided in establishing the Second Bank of the United States in 1816, of which he was a director, and largely influenced its policy. He amassed a fortune of nine million dollars by the time of his death, which was more than any other American.

Personally, he was an enigma He pinched pennies; gave his help no more than their just wages; was parsimonious and lived a frugal life.

On the other hand, he gave his entire fortune to charity and public improvement, including $20,000 for Masonic charity, which to this day is still administered by the Grand Lodge of Pennsylvania.

The most famous of his bequests was to Girard College of Philadelphia, a home for "poor, white male orphans." One clause in his will regarding the college specified: "I enjoin and require that no ecclesiastic, missionary or minister of any sect whatsoever, shall ever hold or exercise any duty whatsoever in the said college; nor shall any such person ever be admitted for any purpose, or as a visitor, within the premises appropriated to the purposes of the said college... I desire to keep the tender minds of orphans...free from the excitements which clashing doctrines and sectarian controversy are so apt to produce." This would, he explained, "leave them free in future life to choose such active religious tenets as their matured reason may enable them to prefer."

His Masonic affiliations are as follows: The records of Royal Arch Lodge No. 3 of Philadelphia show that on Sept. 7, 1778: "Capt. Stephen Girard was duly balloted for, unanimously approved of, initiated and accordingly paid his dues, $20, into the hands of the treasurer. He was also made a Mason "at sight" in Union Blue Lodge No. 8, Charleston, SC, on Jan. 28, 1788 when he was entered, passed, and raised on that date.

Fig. 28 — Lewis and Clark Expedition (1804-1806).

3° R.A.M. Meriwether Lewis (1774-1809)
Member of Stanton Lodge No. 13, Stanton, VA. It was here that he received the Royal Arch Degree. He withdrew from this lodge in 1800. In 1808 he applied for application to the Grand Lodge of Pennsylvania. Became Past Master of that lodge. Also listed as master of first lodge in St. Louis.

Lewis and Clark crossed Montana on the way to the Pacific. On their return in 1806 they built a fort and spent the winter among Indians in what is now North Dakota.

3° William Clark (1770-1838)
Member of St. Louis Lodge No. 111 (under Pennsylvania charter). He was buried in Bellefontaine Cemetery, St. Louis, with Masonic honors. A large monument with the square and compass is over his grave.

Fig. 29 — "A Memorandum of Articles in Readiness for the Voyage," in William Clark's own hand. Among the hundreds of items that had to be carefully packed and stowed for the journey were 50 kegs of salt pork, 30 half-barrels of flour, 21 bales of gifts for Indians, 7 barrels of fat, 14 bags of parchment, 2 boxes of candles, and a bag of wicks.

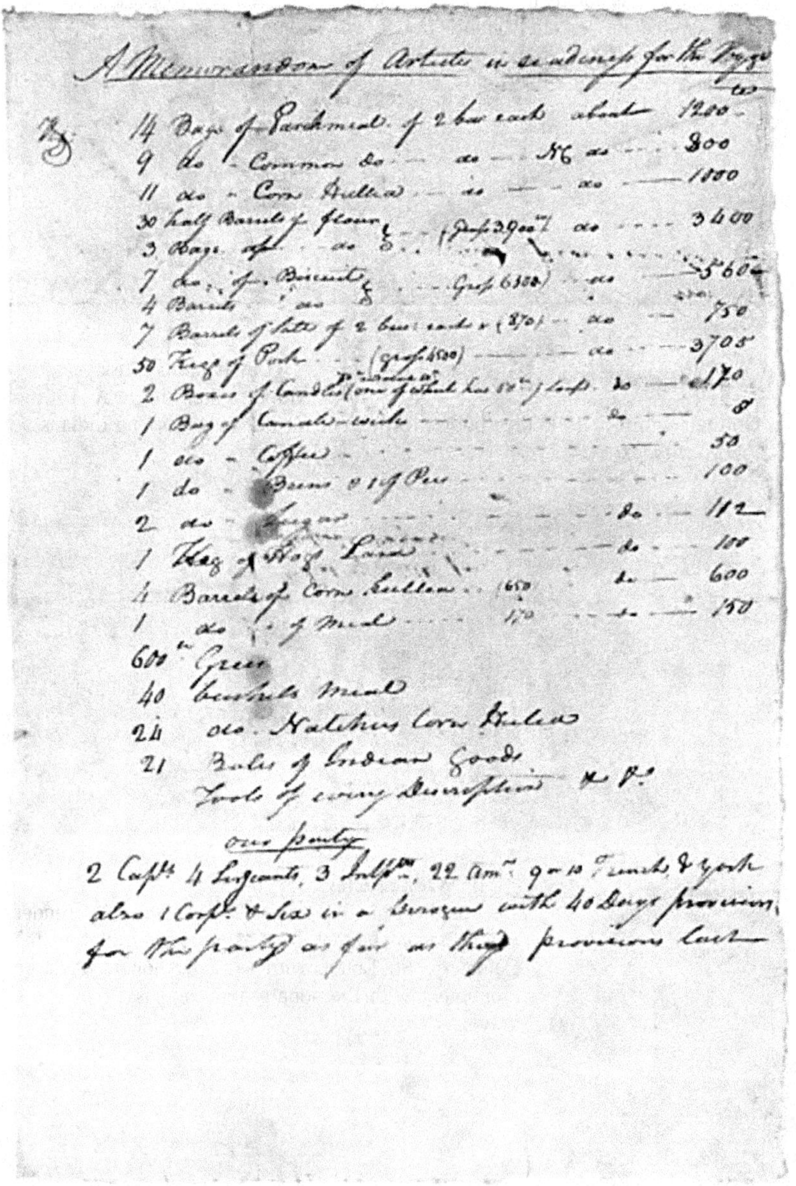

A Memorandum of Articles in readiness for the Voyage

14 Bags of Parchmeal of 2 bus each about 1200
9 do Common do — do — N6 do — 800
11 do Corn Hulled do — do — 1000
30 half Barrels of flour (Gross 3900) do — 3400
3 Bags of do do
7 do of Biscuit (Gross 6300) do — 5600
4 Barrels do
7 Barrels of Salt of 2 bus each (870) do — 750
50 Kegs of Pork (gross 4500) do — 3705
2 Boxes of Candles (one of which has 50 lb of soap) do — 170
1 Bag of Candle-wicks do — 8
1 do Coffee — 50
1 do Beans & 1 of Pees — 100
2 do Sugar do — 112
1 Keg of Hogs Lard do — 100
4 Barrels of Corn hulled 650 do — 600
1 do of Meal 170 do — 150
600 lb Grease
40 bushels Meal
24 do Natchies Corn Hulled
21 Bales of Indian Goods
Tools of every Description &c &c

our party

2 Captns 4 Sergeants, 3 Intrptrs, 22 Amn 9 or 10 French & York
also 1 Corpl & Six in a perogue with 40 Days provision
for the party as far as their provisions last

Fig. 30 — Excerpt from *Scarlet and the Beast*, Vol. 1, 3rd edition, Chapter 30, "Our negotiations with France in 1803 for the Louisiana Purchase involved four Masons: Thomas Jefferson, Robert Livingston, James Monroe, and Napoleon Bonaparte. America took advantage of Napoleon, who was in desperate need of the minuscule amount asked for the Louisiana Territory." A treaty was signed with France in 1803. The amount of $15,000,000 was paid to France for the land extending from the Mississippi River to the Rocky Mountains and from Canada to the Gulf of Mexico. The Louisiana Purchase, now central third of the U.S.A, the conquering of English territory through our Revolutionary War, now the eastern third of the U.S.A., and the conquering of the Spanish territory during the Spanish and American War, are all prophesied in the Bible. You can read about it in *Scarlet and the Beast*, Vol. 1, 3rd ed., chap. 30.

Fig. 31 — The Louisiana Purchase (1803). "Our negotiations with France in 1803 for the Louisiana Purchase involved four Masons: Thomas Jefferson, Robert Livingston, James Monroe, and Napoleon Bonaparte." Read of the account in *Scarlet and the Beast*, Vol. 1, 3rd ed., chap. 30.

USA TODAY — 11/6/03 "WASHINGTON—Coin collectors, get ready for more change. Drawing on the enormous popularity of the state quarter program, the U.S. Mint unveiled two new nickels (which) mark the 200th anniversaries of the Louisiana Purchase & the Lewis & Clark expedition."

Thomas Jefferson
(1769-1821)

James Monroe
(1758-1831)

Nickel on the right represents Masonic players in the Louisiana Purchase

Nickel on the left represents the Masonic backing of the Lewis & Clark Expedition

Explanation of handshake above center

Freemason Mackey writes, "There is [a] Masonic symbol called 'clasped hands.' The right hand has in all ages been an emblem of fidelity and our ancient brethren worshiped Deity under the name of FIDES, represented by two right hands joined." Handshake above center from *Handbook of Freemasonry*.

Robert R. Livingston
(1746-1813)

Napoleon Bonaparte
(1769-1821)

Fig. 32 — Famous American Masons following our Revolutionary War.

3° James H. Carleton (1814-1873)

Major General in U.S. Army. Fought in Aroostook war of 1839 as a lieutenant of the Maine volunteers on the N.E. boundary of the U.S. In the Mexican War he was made captain and then major, serving with General Wool in Mexico. After the Mexican war he engaged in exploration and expeditions against hostile Indians. In one expedition against the Utes and Apaches, **Kit Carson** was his guide. Both Carson and Carleton were Freemasons.

Newsweek 10/09/06
"Though able to 'read' almost any landscapt in which he found himself, Carson was illiterate."

3° Kit Carson (1809-1868), Master Mason.

Kit Carson guides John C. Fremont's second expedition over the high and rugged Sierra Nevada in midwinter. Fremont, known as "the pathfinder," is often referred to as a Freemason, but no proof of membership can be found.

Fig. 33 — Famous American Masons following our Revolutionary War.

Gen. Winfield Scott (1786-1866)

"Old Fuss and Feathers" was the nickname the soldiers gave him because of his fondness for formalities in military dress and behavior. He was the foremost military man in the United States in the half century before the Civil War.

Admitted to the bar in 1806, he entered the Army in 1808 as a captain of light artillery, and the following year at Baton Rouge, La. was courtmartialed for remarks concerning the conduct of his superior, Gen. Wilkinson.

Back in the Army, he fought gallantly in the War of 1812 at Queenstown Heights, Chippewa, and Lundy's Lane. Received promotion to Brigadier General in March, 1814 and Breveted Major General same year. After the war he was on duty in South Carolina and on the Canadian border. He made General-in-Chief of U.S. Army in 1841, and commanded in the Mexican War. He captured Vera Cruz, defeated Mexicans at Cerro Gordo, Contreras, Cerubusco, Molino del Rey, and Chapaultepec, occupying Mexico City on Sept. 24, 1847. He was promoted to Lieutenant General in 1852. That same year he was defeated by Franklin Pierce as the Whig candidate for presidency. He retired in 1861.

Winfield Scott was made a Mason in 1805 in Dinwiddie Union Lodge No. 23, Dinwiddie Court House, Va. (now extinct). In 1825 he is recorded as a visitor to the Grand Lodge of Kentucky. When he died, he was buried at West Point.

Fig. 34 — Famous Mexican Mason following our War of Independence. There are several versions to this story. Here we give the Masonic version. See *Scarlet and the Beast*, Vol. 1, Appendix 1.

Antonio Lopez de Santa Anna (1795-1867)

Mexican general, revolutionist, president and dictator. Unreliable to his word and to his Masonic oath. He led revolts against Iturbide in 1822; Guerreo in 1828; and Bustamante in 1832.

He attempted to crush the Texas revolution; seized the Alamo in 1836, but was defeated and captured by Sam Houston at San Jacinto, April 21, 1836. Forced to sign articles of independence for Texas, he was released in 8 months. Santa Anna was in control of Mexico from 1839-42, and made dictator in 1844.

He commanded the Mexican Army against the U.S. in 1846-47, but was defeated at Vuena Vista, Cerro Gordo, Puebla, and Mexico City by General Scott (Old Fuss and Feathers). Exiled again in 1848, but recalled and made President in 1853-55. Again exiled in 1855. He returned to Mexico City in 1874, where he died June 20, 1876 in poverty and neglect.

Politics in Mexico was a battle between the Scottish Rite and the York Rite. In a political fight, Santa Anna most often favored the Scottish Rite faction over the York Rite. However, he played each against the other. For example, when the Scottish Rite demanded the recall of U.S. Ambassador and Freemason Poinsett, Santa Anna sided with the Yorkist.

Andrew Jackson once wrote Sam Houston that "He (Santa Anna) is the pride of the Mexican soldiers and the favorite of the priesthood."

At age 80, writing his memoirs, Santa Anna stated, "I wish to record also that I defended the Apostolic Roman Catholic religion, the only one in which I believe and in which I must die."

Santa Anna owed his life at San Jacinto to the giving of a Masonic distress signal, first to James A. Sylvester, one of his captors; second, to Sam Houston; and third, to a group of Texas soldiers, among whom were John A. Wharton, George W. Hockley, Richard Bache, Dr. J.E. Phelps and others. These Masons worked together to save the Mexican general's life. After his slaughter of all the American Masons at the Alamo, it was still Freemasonry that ultimately protected him.

Fig. 35 — Famous American Masons following our War of Independence. There are several versions to this story. Here we give the Masonic version. See Scarlet and the Beast, Vol. 1, Appendix 1.

David (Davy) Crockett (1786-1836) American frontiersman born at Limestone, Tenn. He distinguished himself against the Creek Indians in Andrew Jackson's campaign of 1814. His ability to tell humorous stories and shoot a rifle enabled him to be elected to the Tennessee state legislature (1821) and to the U.S. Congress (1826).

When Crockett fell from popular favor, he joined the Texans in their struggle for Independence. His life ended at the Alamo, where as one of the six survivors of the band of 140 Texans (or 189, depending upon which version), all of whom were Freemasons, he surrendered to Santa Anna, only to be shot by order of the General on March 6, 1836.

On April 21, 1836 the Grand Lodge of Texas dedicated a Masonic memorial on the San Jacinto battlefield. The plaque on the monument carried a list of 48 names, including that of Crockett, stating, "A tribute to the fidelity of pioneer Masons under whose outstanding leadership was laid the cornerstone of the Republic of Texas."

Fig. 36 — Famous American Masons following our War of Independence.
See *Scarlet and Beast*, Vol. 1, Appendix 1 and Vol. 3, ch. 4.

R.A.M. Sam Houston (1793-1863)
American patriot and political leader. Governor of Tennessee (1827-29). President of Republic of Texas (1861).

In 1818 Houston began studying law in Nashville, Tenn. He was elected to Congress in 1823 and 1825. In 1827 he was elected Governor of Tenn.

He left Tenn. in disfavor and lived with his former Cherokee family. In 1832 he went to Texas where he was a member of the first convention. April 1, 1833, he was elected General of the militia. On March 2, 1836 he was a member of the convention that declared absolute independence from Mexico and was named Commander-in-Chief of the Armed Forces of Texas. Following the slaughters at the Alamo and Goliad, Houston defeated the Mexicans at Santa Jacinto, took Santa Anna prisoner, and stood him before a firing squad. **When Santa Anna gave the Masonic grand hailing sign of distress, Houston halted the execution and exiled Santa Anna to Cuba.** Houston was elected the first President of the Republic of Texas. He labored for the admission of Texas to the Union, which was accomplished Dec. 29, 1845. On March 1846 he was elected to the U.S. Senate, serving until 1859. He was Governor of Texas from 1859-1861.

Sam Houston received his first three Masonic degrees in Cumberland Lodge No. 8, Nashville, TN on April 19-22, 1817. He demitted (quit) from Cumberland Lodge, Nov. 20, 1817, and re-affiliated June 21, 1821. In another document he is recorded as demitting from Cumberland Lodge, 1831. However, he is listed in the proceedings of 1828 as suspended for unmasonic conduct during the Morgan Affair! He affiliated with Holland Lodge No. 36 of LA in 1837. On Dec. 20, 1837 he presided over the meeting which established the Grand Lodge of Texas. He demitted from Holland Lodge. Next reported as a member of Forest Lodge No. 19, Huntsville, TX in 1851. He is recorded as a visitor to the Grand Lodge of KY in 1825 and the Grand Lodge of AL., 1849. He was present at the dedication of Washington-Centennial Lodge No.14, Washington DC on Jan. 13, 1853. He was a Royal Arch Mason.

Texas Revolution heroes had their own war by Van Craddock
Longview New-Journal — March 13, 2004
(and 10,000 Famous Freemasons)

The Alamo had fallen only a week earlier. Now Santa Anna's Mexican Army was marching east toward the Sabine River, burning every Texas cabin and village it came across.

But this week in March 1836, the biggest fight in Texas likely was between Sam Houston and David Burnet [both of whom were Masons]. On March 2 (it was Houston's birthday), 59 Texans at Washingtonon-the-Brazos had formally declared their independence from Mexico.

Now they were busy drawing up a constitution for what they hoped would be the new Republic of Texas.

The Republic needed a provisional president, and the delegates selected David Burnet for the Temporary post. They also appointed Sam Houston as commander-in-chief of the tiny Texan Army.

The two men picked to lead the government and military hated each other's guts.

Burnet and Houston were as opposite as night and day. Burnet, a New Jersey accountant who often quoted Scripture, neither cursed nor allowed liquor to touch his lips.

On the other hand, Houston could out-cuss the devil and never met a bottle he didn't like (baptized in a creek late in life, Sam remarked, "Lord, help the fish down below").

During the convention at Washington-on-the-Brazos, the humorless Burnet found it impossible to sleep because of the nightly story-tellingand-drinking sessions led by the rough-and-tumble Houston.

Burnet let his displeasure be known to Houston, who responded by calling Burnet a "hog thief."

Several delegates at the convention later said Burnet clearly was jealous of Houston's popularity.

After the convention adjourned on March 17, Houston set about training his little army while President Burnet criticized Sam for not seeking out Santa Anna's troops and avenging the Alamo.

"The enemy are laughing you to scorn. You must fight them," Burnet wrote Houston. "The country expects you to fight."

However, Houston knew his undisciplined army wasn't ready to take on the battle-hardened Mexican soldiers. He knew he couldn't risk a battle yet, and he decided to retreat toward East Texas.

While Burnet burned over Houston's inaction, there was method to Houston's madness. Sam was luring Santa Anna away from his supplies and hoping to divide the Mexican troops.

The plan worked. On April 21, 1836, Houston and his men attacked the Mexicans at San Jacinto. The Battle was decided in less than 20 minutes, but the slaughter continued for hours. More than 600 Mexican soldiers died, and Santa Anna was captured. The Texans lost eight men.

During the fight, Houston's leg was shattered, and his horse was shot out from under him.

In his brief report to the government telling of the decisive victory, Houston described the battle and then closed by saying, "Tell them (Texas residents) to come on and let the people plant corn."

But President Burnet's dislike of Houston wouldn't let him give the general credit.

"Sam Houston has been generally proclaimed the hero of San Jacinto," Burnet wrote. "No fiction of the novelist is farther from the truth. Houston was the only man on the battlefield who deserved censure... the citizens were disgusted at his miserable imbecility."

Burnet even refused to authorize a Texas naval ship to take the wounded Houston to New Orleans for surgery on his shattered leg (Houston had to hire a private schooner).

By the summer of 1836, Texas was stable enough for President Burnet to schedule an election to select permanent officers for the republic. And guess who Texas voters picked as president? Sam Houston.

This really ticked off Burnet, who served as Texas vice president in 1838-40 and then ran against Houston in 1841 for president. Houston won re-election, garnering 7,915 (votes) to Burnet's 3,616.

Houston went on to become a U.S. senator and governor. He opposed Texas' secession in the Civil War and refused to take an oath of loyalty to the Confederate States of America.

For that, he was removed from office and died in 1863, broken-hearted that his beloved state had left the Union.

Burnet outlived Houston by seven years. He died in 1870, a bitter man who still had nothing nice to say about Sam Houston.

MASONIC CREDENTIALS OF DAVID G. BURNET (1788-1870)

In 1826, Burnet migrated from Ohio to Texas, via Louisiana. When Texas declared her independence from Mexico on March 2, 1836, Burnet was chosen as the first President of the Republic, serving until the adoption of a constitution, which took place on Oct. 22, 1836. It was not until three years later (1839) that he became a Mason. He received his Blue Degrees in Holland Lodge No. 1 of Houston on Jan. 18 and 24, and May 21, 1839. In 1841, when defeated by Sam Houston for the presidency of Texas, he retired to his farm. He demitted from the lodge on April 13, 1842. There is no further Masonic record of him.

Fig. 37 — Famous American Masons following our War of Independence. See *Scarlet and the Beast*, Vol. 1, App.1, "Texas Revolution against Mexico."

Royal Arch Mason Joel R. Poinset (1779-1851) U.S. Secretary of War, and Minister to Mexico. Our traditional Christmas flower, the "poinsettia," is named in his honor. His wealthy parents gave him an excellent education in private schools in the U.S., and in medicine at Edinburgh U., Scotland. He traveled widely in Europe and Russia. The Czar of Russia offered him a commission in the Russian Army.

President Madison sent him to South America to inquire into the conditions and the prospects of their success in the struggle with Spain for independence. While Poinset was in Chile, the Spanish captured several American vessels. Poinsett took immediate action, and with a force given him by the Chilean government, retook the vessels.

Back in South Carolina, he served in the state legislature and was elected to U.S. Congress in 1821-25. There he advocated the cause of independence for the South American republics and for Greece.

In 1822, during the reign of Freemason Iturbide, Poinset was sent on a special mission to Mexico. In 1825, during the administration of President J.Q. Adams, Poinset returned to Mexico and served as U.S. Minister until 1829. While there he negotiated a treaty of commerce. The Catholic Church, however, complained that he was interfering. After his return to America, he justified his course of action in written communique. At the request of Freemasons in Mexico, he sent charters granted by the Grand Lodge of New York for five new lodges in Mexico, which subsequently established the Grand Lodge of Mexico. Poinset also introduced Royal Arch Masonry to Mexico.

Poinset is recorded as being a Past Master of both Recovery Lodge No. 31, Greenville, SC; and of Solomon's Lodge No. 1, Charleston, SC. In 1821 he was elected

Deputy Grand Master of the Grand Lodge of South Carolina. That same year he was elected Grand High Priest of the Grand Chapter of S.C., holding office until 1841. He was elected Deputy General Grand High Priest in 1829, 1832, and 1835. Upon the revival of Greenville Lodge No. 5, Greenville, SC in 1849, he became its Master despite his old age.

SECTION 4
ANTI-MASONIC PERIOD 1826 THRU CIVIL WAR

Fig. 1 — The 9/11/1826 abduction and murder of Royal Arch Mason William Morgan triggered the Anti-Masonic Movement. Complete story is in two new chapters in the 3rd edition of *Scarlet and Beast*, Vol. 1, chps. 13-14; *The Morgan Affair Triggers the Anti-Masonic Movement* and the *American Masonic Civil War*.

13° Royal Arch Mason (renounced) CAPTAIN WILLIAM MORGAN
Murdered by Freemasons in 1826 for Revealing the Secrets of Freemasonry.
10,000 Famous Freemasons, by 33° William R. Denslow, reports, "His disappearance gave rise to the Anti-Masonic party, 141 Anti-Masonic newspapers in the U.S.A., and almost killed Freemasonry in America."

Figure 2 — This book contains court transcripts of testimonies given by named witnesses to the abduction & murder of William Morgan.

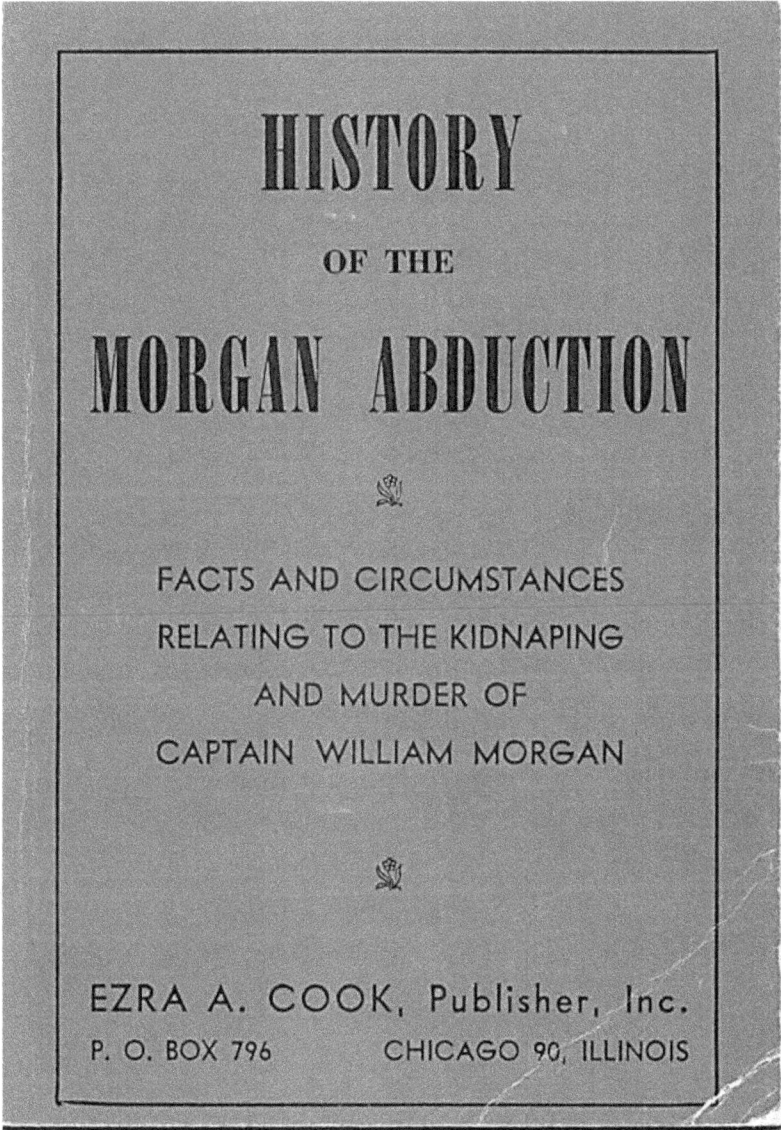

First published in 1965 and reprinted in 1974. It is now out of print. It contains the court records, transcripts, and testimonies of witnesses to the abduction and Masonic murder of William Morgan. You can read the entire story in Scarlet and the Beast, Vol. 1, 3rd edition, chapter 13.

Fig. 3 — Aug. 9, 1826 an advertisement was inserted in a paper printed in Canandaigua. Copy below. The message is only for Masons to understand.
Read the decoded message in *Scarlet and the Beast*, Vol. 1, 3rd ed., ch. 13.

"NOTICE AND CAUTION.

"If a man calling himself William Morgan should intrude himself on the community, they should be on their guard, particularly the MASONIC FRATERNITY. Morgan was in this village in May last, and his conduct while here and elsewhere, calls forth this notice. Any information in relation to Morgan can be obtained by calling at the MASONIC HALL in this village. *Brethren and Companions* are particularly requested to *observe, mark* and *govern* themselves accordingly.

☞ Morgan is considered a swindler and dangerous man.

☞ There are people in this village who would be happy to see this Capt. Morgan.

Figure 4 — Abduction of Captain William Morgan by Masons

Great Kidnapping Furor took place in 1826 over the disappearance of William Morgan, a renegade Mason who was supposedly abducted and then killed by Masons. *Harpers Magazine* drawing shows Masons forcing Morgan into coach.

In the summer of 1848, the deathbed confession of one of the Masonic assassins, Henry L. Valance, was taken down by his doctor, John L. Emery of Racine County Wisconsin. One year following the death of Valance, Dr. Emery published and made public the confession. This confession was also printed in Charles G. Finney's 1869 book entitled *Character, Claims, and Practical Workings of Freemasonry*, which can be purchased on our website at www.scarletandthebeast.com.

1848 deathbed confession of Freemason Henry L. Valance concerning his part in the murder of CAPTAIN WILLIAM MORGAN

"My last hour is approaching; and as the things of this world fade from mental sight, I feel the necessity of making, as far as in my power lies, that atonement which every violator of the great law of right owes to his fellow man. I allude to the abduction and murder of the ill-fated William Morgan. After committing that horrid deed I was an unhappy man by day and by night. I was much like Cain, a fugitive and a vagabond. Go where I would, or do what I would, it was impossible for me to throw off the consciousness of my crime. If the mark of Cain was not upon me, the curse of the first murderer was — the bloodstain was upon my hands and could not be washed out.

"I was one of eight Masons who planned the murder of Morgan. Many plans were proposed and discussed, and rejected. At length being driven to the necessity of doing something immediately for fear of being exposed, it was resolved...that Morgan must be consigned to a confinement from which there is no possibility of escape — the grave.

"Eight pieces of paper were procured, five of which were to remain blank, while the letter 'D' was written on the others. These pieces of paper were placed in a large box, from which each man was to draw one at the same moment. After drawing we were all to separate, without looking at the paper that each held in his hand. So soon as we had arrived at certain distances from the place of rendezvous, the tickets were to be examined, and those who held blanks were to return instantly to their homes; and those who should hold marked tickets were to proceed to the fort at midnight, and there put Morgan to death, in such a manner as should seem...most fitting. "I was one of the three who drew the ballots on which was the signal letter. I returned to the fort, where I was joined by my two companions, who had (also) drawn the death tickets. Arrangements were made immediately for executing the Masonic sentence passed upon our prisoner, which was to sink him in the river with weights; in hopes that he and our crime alike would thus be buried beneath the waves.

"My part was to proceed to the magazine at Ft. Niagara where Morgan was confined, and announce to him his fate — theirs was to procure a boat and weights with which to sink him. On being informed of our proceedings against him, Morgan demanded by what authority we had condemned him, and who were his judges. He commenced wringing his hands, and talking of his wife and children, the recollections of whom, in that awful hour, terribly affected him. His wife, he said, was young and inexperienced, and his children were but infants; what would become of them were he cut off, and they even ignorant of his fate?

"My comrades returned, and informed me that they had procured the boat and weights, and that all things were in readiness on their part. We told Morgan that all his remonstrances were idle, that die he must, and that soon, even before the morning light... We gave him one-half hour to prepare for his inevitable fate. How Morgan passed that time, I cannot tell, but everything was quiet as the tomb within. At the expiration of the allotted time, we entered the magazine, laid hold of our victim, bound his hands behind him, and placed a gag in his mouth. A short time brought us to the boat. I placed Morgan in the bow with myself along side of him. My comrades took the oars, and the boat was rapidly forced out into the river. The night was pitch dark, we could scarcely see a yard before us, and therefore was the time admirably adapted to our hellish purpose.

"Having reached a proper distance from the shore, the oarsmen ceased their labors. The weights were all secured together by a strong cord, and another cord of equal strength, and of several yards in length, proceeded from that. This cord I took in my hand and fastened it around the body of Morgan, just above his hips, using all my skill to make it fast, so that it would hold. Then, in a whisper, I bade the unhappy man to stand up, and after a momentary hesitation he complied with my order. He stood close to the head of the boat, and there was just length enough of rope from his person to the weights to prevent any strain while he was standing. I then requested one of my associates to assist me in lifting the weights from the bottom to the side of the boat, while the other steadied her from the stern. This was done, and as Morgan was standing with his back toward me, I approached him, and gave him a strong push with both my hands, which were placed on the middle of his back. He fell forward, carrying the weights with him, and the waters closed over the mass. We remained quiet for two or three minutes, when my companions, without saying a word, resumed their places, and rowed the boat to the place from which they had taken it."

In Kenneth C. Davis' book, *Don't Know Much About History*, 2003, published by HarperCollins, we read, "An anti-Mason movement took hold in the nineteenth century... Twenty-six Masons were indicted on murder and six came to trial, with four of them convicted on lesser charges."

You can read the entire story in *Scarlet and the Beast*, Volume 1, 3rd edition, chapter 13.

Figure 5 — Monument to anti-Mason, Capt. William Morgan is located at the southwest corner of Batavia Cemetery — New York.

Monument to Morgan erected by donations collected from Anti-Masons

Fig. 6 — Governor DeWitt Clinton, as top Mason in New York State at that time, had the final say in authorizing the capture and murder of Capt. William Morgan. Clinton died the same year Morgan was murdered.

DeWitt Clinton (1769-1828) Illuminatus, Grand Master of New York Lodges (1806-1820)

Royal Arch Mason & Father of the Public School System

Read of Clinton's membership in the American Illuminati in *Scarlet and the Beast,* Vol. 1, chps. 5 and 13.

Governor of New York, U.S. Senator from New York, Mayor of New York City. As mayor he promoted the establishment of public schools, which became the basis for our free school system today (1st thru 12th grade). To fund the schools, Masons collected donations at street corners. (For more on Clinton and schools, see *Scarlet and the Beast,* Vol.I, chap.9) Clinton was elected three terms as governor. He was in his third term when the "Morgan Affair" took place. You can read about his involvement in *Scarlet and the Beast,* Vol. 1, 3rd edition, chapter 9.

Clinton was raised (3°) in Holland Lodge No. 16, Sept. 3, 1790, serving as the Master in 1793 and Grand Master of the Grand Lodge of New York from 1806-1819. He was Grand High Priest of the Grand Chapter, R.A.M. of New York in 1798 and General Grand High Priest of the General Grand Chapter of the U.S. from 1816-1826. He was knighted in Holland Lodge on May 17, 1792, served as Grand Commander of the Grand Commandery,

K.T. of New York from 1814-1828 and was Grand Master of the Grand Encampment of the U.S. from 1818 to his death in 1828.

Figure 7 — Anti-Mason John Quincy Adams was the 6th President of the United States of America (1825-1829) during the height of the Anti-Masonic Movement. See *Scarlet and the Beast*, Vol. 1, chapter 13.

John Quincy Adams (1767-1848)
President of U.S.A. (1825-1829)
Anti-Mason

John Q. Adams studied at Harvard, and was admitted to the bar in 1790. As secretary of state under President Monroe, he negotiated with Spain the treaty for the acquisition of Florida, and was alleged to be the real author of the Monroe Doctrine.

John Q. Adams, son of President John Adams, was the 6th President of the United States (1825-1829) during the height of the Anti-Masonic Movement. He wrote a 30-page pamphlet entitled "Letters on the Masonic Institution," first published at Boston in 1847. Today this pamphlet can be acquired from Acacia Press, PO Box 656, Amherst, MA 01004.

J.Q. Adams was elected to the House of Representatives, where he became a noted promoter of anti-slavery views. Freemasonry dubs Adams "One of the most rabid Anti-Masons of his time."

The following is J.Q. Adams' address to the people of Massachusetts: "I believed, therefore, that the aid of legislative prohibitions, with penalties, would be indispensable for abating the moral nuisance in the community, and I recommend that the Masonic oaths should be prohibited by law upon penalties of fine and imprisonment adequate to deter from the administration of them in the future.

"It is my deliberate opinion that the anti-masonic party ought not to subside or to suspend its exertions till Freemasonry shall have ceased to exist in this country." — *Danger Signals*, edited and supplied by the New England Christian Association (Boston: James H. Earle, Publisher, 1896), p. 11.

Figure 8 — Masonic Lodge at Batavia NY. Contruction on this Masonic Lodge began exactly 84 years following the 9/11/26 abduction and subsequent murder of Royal Arch Mason Capt. William Morgan.

Batavia Masonic Temple building
Above is a circa 1920 postcard showing the Masonic Temple building on Main Street in Batavia. The building was constructed from 1908-10 and the Masons formally dedicated their new temple on June 24, 1911, according to Ruth McEvoy's *History of the City of Batavia.*

In 1833, Congress was petitioned to make Masonic oaths unconstitutional

Rev. John R. Rice, in his book, *Lodges Examined by the Bible,* informs us that following the Morgan Affair a petition was presented to Congress to outlaw Masonic oaths: "At one time in the history of our nation, May 1833 [during the height of the Anti-Masonic Movement], fourteen hundred citizens petitioned the U.S. Congress to prohibit, by law, the Masonic oaths. The committee from the House of Representatives recommended that the oaths be legally prohibited on the grounds that they were not lawfully authorized; they bind a person to violate the law; they were subversive and blasphemous; their penalties were forbidden by the U.S. Constitution." See *S&B*, Vol. 1, 3rd ed., Chap. 13 for the outcome of this petition.

Figure 9 — Freemason Andrew Jackson was 7th President of the United States of America during the height of the Anti-Masonic Movement.

3°Andrew Jackson "Old Hickory" (1767-1845)

Two-term President of the United States (1829-1837)

Seventh President of the United States. Took office as President three years after Morgan was murdered by Masons. His tenure as President was at the height of the Anti-Masonic Movement.

Jackson was admitted to the bar in Salisbury, NC in 1787. A year later he moved to Nashville, TN, where he became a US Congressman (179697); US Senator (1797-98); Judge of the Tennessee Supreme Court (17981804); and Major General of Tennessee militia (1802). He was made Major General of the U.S. Army and assigned to defend New Orleans in the War of 1812. His defense of that city made him a national hero. He conducted many winning battles against the Indians. He was Governor of Florida Territory in 1821 and U.S. Senator in 1823-25. His first presidential race in 1824 was unsuccessful, but successful in 1828, and reelected in 1832. Under his administration the national debt was paid off — the only time in our national history that this was accomplished. As a result, the Britishcontrolled United States Bank was overthrown.

Jackson's Masonic credentials are as follows: Received his degrees at Greeneville Lodge No. 3 of Tenn. Was a member of Harmony Lodge No. 1, Nashville, 1800. Proceedings of 1822 credit him with being a Past Master. Was elected Grand Master of the Grand Lodge of Tennessee in 1822 and 1823. Held positions in many other lodges.

Jackson introduced Lafayette to the Grand Lodge of Tennessee in 1825. Lafayette assisted Jackson in laying the Masonic cornerstone of Jackson City, Tennessee. See *Scarlet and the Beast*, Vol. 1, chap. 13.

Fig. 10 — Famous American Mason turned Anti-Masons and evangelist. In 1826 there was a total of 50,000 Masons in the U.S.A. After the 1826 Morgan Affair, when Finney preached salvation, he included in his altar call the renunciation of Masonic oaths. By 1830, 45,000 Masons had quit the Lodge, resulting in the near destruction of the Fraternity in America.

Former 3° Mason Charles G. Finney (1792-1875)
(See *S&B*, VI, ch. 13)

What Freemasonry writes about Charles Finney:

Anti-Mason, clergyman, abolitionist and president of Oberlin College (Ohio) from 1851-65. He received his Masonic degrees in Meridian Sun Lodge No. 32, Warren, Conn. in 1816. In June of 1818 he made his first visit to Rising Sun Lodge No. 125 at Adams, N.Y. Although not a member of the latter lodge at the time, he was voted to serve as secretary pro tem at a meeting on Feb. 24, 1820. On Dec. 14, 1820 he was admitted a member of the lodge and named secretary at the same meeting. On May 6, 1824, he was discharged by his own request. It was in this year that he was licensed as a minister by the St. Lawrence Presbytery, and two years later he began conducting religious revivals throughout the Middle and Eastern states. He wrote and preached antiMasonry wherever he was, and with former Freemason Jonathan Blanchard, a Presbyterian minister and president of Wheaton College, published an anti-Masonic newspaper called *The Christian Cynosure*. He was active with Blanchard and Bishop David Edwards in the formation of the National Christian Association in 1868, whose purpose was to oppose all secret societies. This grew into the American Party in 1872, and this short-lived organization ran candidates in the 1876 and 1880 elections. Eventually dissension and petty jealousies in the anti-Masonic ranks caused the movement to die. As one biographer stated: "Were he alive today, how surprised he would be to learn that there are more Masons among the undergraduates and graduates of Oberlin College than existed during the Morgan affair in the entire state of New York." You can order Charles G Finney's 1869 book, *The Character, Claims and Practical Workings of Freemasonry* at www.scarletandthebeast.com.

Fig. 11 — 1830s Methodist evangelistic camp meeting

From the "Introduction" of Finney's book, we read, "Before these Masonic outrages, Almighty God had once again set up His standard in America to put the Masonic enemy to flight, and bring revival to our land. At the turn of the 19th century, men such as Francis Asbury, the first bishop of the Methodist Church in America, and Peter Cartwright, Timothy Dwight, and Lyman Beecher, led the way to the Second Great Awakening. The most eminent figure and symbol of the revival was former Mason Charles G. Finney, who, after becoming a Christian in 1824, renounced Freemasonry and two years later began preaching, bringing great revival to the Eastern States. After Morgan's murder, Finney included repentance from Masonry wherever he went, and thousands of Masons renounced their oaths and received Christ as Savior."

1830s lithograph (New York Historical Society Bridgeman Art Library).

Figure 12 — A fickle Anti-Mason.

Edward Everett (1794-1865)

Anti-Mason. Born in Dorchester, MA. U.S. Congressman, 1825-35. Governor of Massachusetts, 1836-40; U.S. Minister to Great Britain, 184145; President of Harvard, 1846-49; U.S. Secretary of State, 1852.

Everett was a part-time Unitarian clergyman and orator of great ability. He took sides in the politics maintained by the anti-Masonic friends of John Quincy Adams, another anti-Mason.

He wrote a letter to the secretary of the Anti-Masonic Committee of Middlesex Co., MA on June 29, 1833, stating among other things "The supremacy of the laws is the fundamental principle of civil society. The allegiance due to the country is the highest human obligation of all men who enter into civil society; and I perceive the institution of Freemasonry to be at war with both these principles."

Ironically, in 1860 he ran on the Constitutional-Union ticket for vicepresident with John Bell, a Tennessee Mason running for president. They received 39 electoral votes.

In his famous orations on Washington and General Warren, he failed to mention either of their Masonic connections.

Figure 13 — Anti-Masonic Movement literally affected the whole world. See *Scarlet and the Beast*, Vol. 1, 3rd ed., Appendix 1.

32° Simon Bolivar (1783-1830)

Born in Caracas, Venezuela. The "George Washington" of South America, who in 20 years of warfare liberated from Spanish tyranny the area which is now Venezuela, Colombia, Ecuador, Peru and Bolivia.

He joined Freemasonry in Cadiz, Spain and received the Scottish Rite degrees in Paris and was knighted in a Commandery of Knights Templar in France in 1807.

While on a diplomatic mission to London in 1810 he was active in Freemasonry in that country. He founded and served as Master of Protectora de las Vertudes Lodge No. 1 in Venezuela and in 1824 founded the Lodge Order and Liberty No. 2 in Peru.

In 1828, when the anti-Masonic wave was sweeping over the world, Bolivar forbade meetings of Masons in Venezuela for their own protection.

His Scottish Rite collar and apron are on exhibit in the New York Grand Lodge museum. Catholic born, he broke away from the church when, in his liberation movement, he found that the clerics who ruled with an iron hand under the Spanish administration were among his chief opponents. On his death bed in 1830, he returned to Catholicism for spiritual aid. Nevertheless it was as a Freemason that he performed the deeds which established him as one of the greatest liberators of the world.

Fig. 14 — Famous Spanish Anti-Mason. The Anti-Masonic Movement had worldwide impact, especially in 1848, when all Europe was in Revolution.

Ferdinand VII (1784-1833)

Anti-Mason. King of Spain, 1814-20 and 1823-33.

Son of Charles IV.

Ferdinand VII was proclaimed king after the forced abdication of his father in 1808. However, Napoleon captured him on a ruse and held him prisoner until 1814, when Napoleon reinstated him to his throne. His reign, therefore, actually began in 1814.

Ferdinand VII had no sooner ascended the throne that he reestablished the Inquisition against the Masons, which had been abolished by his father. He ordered the closing of all lodges under the heaviest penalties.

The following September, twenty-five persons, some of whom were distinguished noblemen, were arrested as "suspected of Freemasonry."

On March 30, 1818, a still more rigorous edict was issued, by which those convicted of being Freemasons were subjected to severe punishment, exile or death.

Ferdinand's rule was cruel and tyrannical. He was overthrown in 1820. But the Holy Alliance, with French troops, restored him in 1823. This final ten-year reign lost Spain all its colonies in North and South America, thus relegating Spain to a second rate European power. (See *S&B*, V1, Appen. 1)

Figure 15 — Famous American Anti-Masons. See *S&B*, Vol. 1, chap. 13.

Charles Dickens (1812-1870)

English novelist and anti-Mason. His childhood was filled with poverty and hardship. Yet, one of the greatest writers of all time. Among his novels are *Oliver Twist, A Christmas Carol, David Copperfield, A Tale of Two Cities, Pickwick Papers* and *Old Curiosity Shop*.

Far from being a Mason, his writings ridicule the ceremonies of the fraternity and he pictures the work in a satyric manner, even to the extent of writing "Freemasonry" with a small "f."

William Henry Harrison (1773-1841)
Anti-Mason
9th President of the U.S.A. Read about his
mysterious death in *Scarlet and the Beast*, V3, ch. 4.

Daniel Webster (1782-1852)
American statesman, US Congressman,
senator and twice secretary of state. With his
friend Isaiah Thompson, he took part in the
Masonic cornerstone laying of the Bunker
Hill Monument on June 17, 1825. In 1826,
following the Masonic murder of William
Morgan, he became an Anti-Mason.

Figure 16 — Famous American Anti-Masons

William H. Seward (1801-1872)
Anti-Mason. Admitted to the bar at Utica
NY in 1822, settling in Auburn in 1823. In
1830 he was named as the Anti-Masonic
candidate for the state senate. Governor of New
York 1839-43. U.S. Senator from New York
1849-61. U.S. Secretary of State 1861-69. In
1857 the Russian minister to the United States
suggested that Alaska might be for sale. The
U.S. Civil War prevented any transaction from
taking place immediately.

Finally, in 1867, a treaty was negotiated by
Secretary of State, Seward by which the United
States purchased Alaska for $7,200,000. This
became known at **Seward's Folly**. See *Scarlet
and the Beast*, V1, ch. 14; V3, ch. 4.

The following statement made by Seward
needs careful consideration by every freedom-
loving person and certainly by every Christian
who enjoys freedom in Christ. Mr. Seward
forcefully asserted:

"Before I would place my hand between the hands of other men in a secret lodge,
order, class or council, and bending on my knees before them, enter into combinations
with them for any object, personal or political, good or bad, I would pray to God that that
hand and that knee might be paralyzed, and that I might become an object of pity and
even the mockery of my fellow men.

"Swear, sir! I, a man, an American citizen, a Christian, swear to submit myself to the guidance and direction of other men, surrendering my own judgment to their judgments, and my own conscience to their keeping! No, No, Sir. I know quite well the fallibility of my own judgment, and my liability to fall into error and temptation. But my life has been spent in breaking the bonds of the slavery of men. I, therefore, know too well the danger of confiding power to irresponsible hands, to make myself a willing slave." — *Danger Signals*, edited and supplied by the New England Christian Association (Boston: James H. Earl, Publisher, 1896, p. 24).

Fig. 17 — Famous American Anti-Masons. *S&B*, V1, ch.5,9,13; V3, ch. 4.

Millard Fillmore (1800-1874)

Fillmore was V.P. to Zachary Taylor, becoming 13th president (1850-53) on Taylor's mysterious death. As an AntiMason at the beginning of the Anti-Masonic period, he was one of the most bitter critics of Freemasonry, which he characterized as "organized treason." Later in life his views seemed to mellow. For example, on July 4, 1851, as President he attended the Masonic cornerstone laying of the extension of the Capitol in Washington and took part in the exercises. This infuriated the Anti-Masons. Consequently, in 1852 the Whigs refused to nominate him for a second term.

Fillmore gave his full support to the Compromise of 1850 because he felt that this was the only way to preserve the Union.

Horace Greeley (1811-1872)

American journalist, political leader, a Mason and member of the Illuminati. Upon the murder of William Morgan, Greeley demitted from both, and in 1831 moved to New York at the height of the Anti-Masonic Movement. With Jonas Winchester, he founded in 1834 the *New Yorker*, a weekly journal. In 1841 he founded the *New York Tribune* and merged the two papers. He supported the Free Soil Movement, encouraged anti-slavery sentiment, and supported the administration in the Civil War. After the war, he was an advocate of universal amnesty and suffrage, believing that the long imprisonment of Jefferson Davis without trial was a violation of Davis' constitutional rights. He accepted the nomination for the presidency by a body of liberal Republicans and was endorsed by the Democrats, but badly beaten in the election of 1872. His biographer, Patton, thus refers to his attitude on Freemasonry: "Our apprentice (Greeley) embraced the anti-Masonic side of this controversy, and embraced it warmly. It was natural that he should. And for the next two or three years he expended more breath in denouncing the Order of Freemasons, than upon any other subject — perhaps than on all other subjects put together. To this day secret societies are his special aversion."

Figure 18 — Famous Morman/Mason during Anti-Masonic Movement.

3° Joseph Smith (1805-1844)

Founder of the Mormon Church (The Church of Jesus Christ of Latter Day Saints). Born in a poor family that migrated to Palmyra NY in 1815.

The angel Moroni is said to have revealed the Book of Mormon to Smith, written on golden plates, which he was able to transcribe by the use of "Urim and Thummim," instruments of magical power.

His critics say that the *Book of Mormon* is based on an imaginative tale written in Biblical style by a former Presbyterian minister, Samuel Spaulding, but never published. The manuscript was delivered to Smith by Sidney Rigdon, who helped revise it. Shortly afterwards Rigdon became one of the presidents of the church.

Book of Mormon was printed in Palmyra, NY in 1830, during the height of the Anti-Masonic Movement. The church was founded on April 6 of that year at the home of Peter Whitmer in Fayette, NY. Smith's first wife was the widow of former Freemason Capt. William Morgan, who was murdered by three Masons four years earlier. In 1831, Smith, with his new wife and band of Mormons, moved to Kirtland, OH, then to Missouri in 1838.

The Mormons ran into trouble at Independence and Far West, MO, and were removed from the state by the militia and settled at Commerce, IL. Smith, Rigdon, and others were arrested for "murder, treason, burglary, arson and larceny," but allowed to escape and join the others at Commerce. Commerce was renamed Nauvoo by the Mormons. Here Smith governed despotically with the aid of a small group of advisors.

In Commerce was a Masonic Lodge to which the leaders of the Mormons attached themselves. When the Mormons renamed the city Nauvoo, so too was the Lodge renamed. In Smith's journal, March 15, 1842, he wrote: "I officiated as Grand Chaplain at the installation of the Nauvoo Lodge of Freemasons at the Grove near the Temple. Grand Master Jonas, of Columbus, being present, a large number of people assembled for the occasion. The day was exceedingly fine; all things were done in order. In the evening I received the first degree in Freemasonry in Nauvoo Lodge." The following day Smith added, "I was with the Masonic Lodge and rose to the sublime degree." At the same time Sidney Rigdon received his degrees "at sight" with Smith.

Over the next five months, the Nauvoo Lodge initiated (1°) 256 candidates and raised (3°) 243. Consequently, Bodley Lodge No. 1 of Illinois preferred charges against Nauvoo Lodge on July 15, 1842, asking the Grand Lodge of Illinois to "make inquiry into the manner the officers of Nauvoo Lodge were installed by the Grand Master of this State, and by what authority the Grand Master initiated (1°), passed (2o) and raised (3°) Smith and Rigdon to the first three degrees of Freemasonry all at once. A special Masonic committee visited Nauvoo, inspected the records and work and recommended that the lodge be permitted to resume labor. After this inspection by Grand Lodge, the Mormons did so much Masonic work that two more lodges were established; Rising Sun Lodge at Montrose, IA, and a dispensation requested at Keokuk, IA. Again the Grand Lodge ordered an investigation, and this time the Mormons refused the committee access to the

minutes. The Grand Lodge then struck all the Mormon Lodges from its rolls. However, Mormon Lodges refused to recognize this, and continued their Masonic work. On Friday, April 5, 1844 the Mormons dedicated the Masonic Hall at Nauvoo.

In the *History of the Church,* Smith wrote that he attended the ceremonies; that about 550 Masons from various parts of the world were present and took part in a procession that was formed, accompanied by the Nauvoo brass band; that the ceremonies were in charge of Hyrum Smith, Worshipful Master; that the principal address of the occasion was delivered by Apostle Erastus Snow; and that he, Joseph Smith and Dr. Goforth also addressed the assembly; and that all visiting Masons were given dinner in the Masonic Hall at the expense of Nauvoo Lodge.

If the above dedication is the same ceremony and date as the cornerstone laying, there is a discrepancy. In 1954 the Mormon Church purchased the old hall for restoration as an historic shrine. The cornerstone box was removed and sent to Salt Lake City, where in the presence of President David O. McKay and the twelve apostles, it was opened; the original documents were retained in Utah, and photostatic copies returned, to be redeposited in two new boxes in the cornerstone at Nauvoo. This ceremony took place June 24, 1954, being reported in the newspapers as "exactly 111 years after the first ceremony."

Inside the cornerstone a document states that Smith was not present in the procession or ceremony, as he was then being sought on an extradition warrant issued by Governor Ford of Missouri. (Missouri never had a man named Ford as governor; Gov. Reynolds had recently died and Lt. Gov. Marmaduke had taken his place.) Although Smith's signature is among the 50 or more names of the prominent Mormons on the document, it was noted therein that it was added later.

When Smith claimed the revelation of Polygamy in 1843, the church split. On June 27, 1844, Smith and his brother Hyrum were both arrested and jailed at Carthage IL. Before nightfall, both men were shot and killed by a mob. Smith must have recognized the mob as Masons, for he gave the Masonic grand hailing sign of distress just before he was shot.

Many of the symbols and ceremonies used by the Mormon Church today are of Masonic origin. For example, carved in the stone walls of the Mormon Temple in Utah is the Masonic Square & Compass and all-seeing eye. On the building which houses the Mormon Tabernacle Choir is the Masonic 6-pointed star. See *S&B*, Vol. 1, 3rd ed, Introduction and Appendix 18.

Fig. 19 — Joseph Smith was arrested & taken to the Carthage, Ill. jail. He felt he was going to his death. Tension grew, both inside & outside the jail. A mob finally broke into the jail, threw Smith out the 2nd floor window, then shot and killed him.

Figure 20 — Masonic Lodge in Nauvoo, Illionis after it was converted into the first Mormon Temple.

Figure 21 — Mormon polygamy

Polygamy introduced to Mormons 1843

When Freemason/Mormon Joseph Smith claimed the revelation of Polygamy in 1843, the church split. After Smith's death, however, polygamy did not die. Brigham Young, who took the Mormons to Utah, continued the practice of polygamy. Above is a Mormon family group in the 1880s, with husband, four wives, and seven children.

"Although the sexual proclivities of Joseph Smith, founder of Church of Latter-Day Saints (the Mormons), appear to have been less than puritan, by the time the Mormons came under the aegis of Freemason Brigham Young, their polygamy, like their whole way of life, had strong Old Testament overtones. Piety, sobriety, industry, frugality, fidelity, and asceticism were the rule, which certainly contributed to long life for those who could bear a long life on such terms." *Sex in History*, 1980, Reay Tannahill.

Figure 22 — After Joseph Smith's death, enter Brigham Young.
For more details see *Scarlet and the Beast*, Vol.1, "Introduction."

Brigham Young (1801-1877)

American Mormon leader who directed the settlement in Nauvoo IL in 1838. Young succeeded Smith as head of the Mormon Church in 1847 and superintended the mass migration of the Mormons to the Great Salt Lake Valley in Utah.

Young was converted to Mormonism in 1831 by Samuel H. Smith, the Prophet's brother. Young was the first governor of the Territory of Utah (1849-57).

Although his Masonic membership has been disavowed by the Mormon Church, there are historic facts that suggest he belonged to the Craft. All the leaders, as well as large numbers of the rank and file of the Mormon Church in the Nauvoo period were members of Nauvoo Lodges. For example, when the cornerstone of the Masonic Temple at Nauvoo was opened on June 24, 1954 by officials of the Mormon Church from Salt Lake City, a list of 50 Mormon-Masons who had signed a document as being present on the historic occasion in 1843, included the name of Brigham Young.

In a publication entitled *The City of the Saints in Picture and Story*, printed by *Desert News* in 1906, is a picture of Young as Governor of Utah. On his shirt is the conventional Masonic emblem — the Square and Compass. (Editor's note: we have taken liberty to place the pin in the approximate spot above where *Desert News* stated it was worn). Moreover, in the *History of Utah*, written by Apostle Orson F. Whitney, it is stated, "A Masonic Temple was likewise projected at Nauvoo, and Joseph and Hyrum Smith, Brigham Young, and other leading Mormons became Freemasons." Some have claimed that Young was a member of Milnor Lodge No. 303, Victor, NY, but this lodge, which was warranted in 1818, sent membership returns regularly to the Grand Lodge until 1830, and Young was not listed.

Fig. 23 — Brigham Young (1801-1877) with Margaret Pierce, one of five women he married in 1846 and the eleventh to bear him a child. Notice the pin centered on Brigham Young's shirt. *Desert News* claims it is the Square & Compass. You decide! We have enlarged it 600 times below/right.

Is there a Square & Compass on center of Brigham Young's shirt — just below his tie? Lower right is cutout of pin on shirt enlarged 600X
10,000 Famous Freemasons lists Young as a Mason

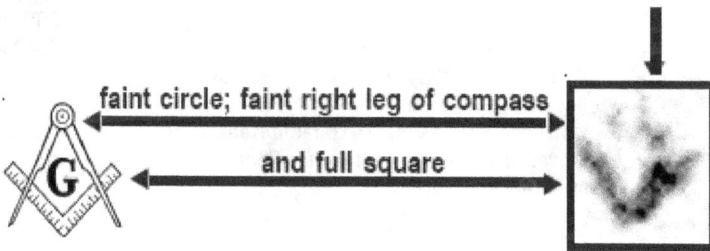

faint circle; faint right leg of compass
and full square

3° **Hyrum Smith** (? 1844)

Brother of Joseph Smith, the founder of Mormonism. Killed with his brother by a mob in the jail at Carthage IL on June 27, 1844. He was first Senior Warden of the Nauvoo Lodge at Nauvoo IL. After the Grand Lodge had ordered the dispensation for this lodge returned, it continued work clandestinely, with Hyrum as Master. In this capacity he officiated at the dedication ceremonies of the Masonic Hall at Nauvoo on April 5, 1844, and his signature is one of those in the cornerstone documents. It has been claimed that both Hyrum and Heber C. Kimball were Masons in Ontario Co. NY, before becoming Mormons.

The Reorganized Church of Jesus Christ of Latter Day Saints in Missouri is simply an arm of Freemasonry.

32° **Frederick M. Smith** (1874-1946)
Scottish Rite Mason — York Rite Mason — Shriner

Frederick was president of the Reorganized Church of Jesus Christ of Latter Day Saints (1915-1946). He was son of Joseph Smith, first president of the reorganized branch, who was the namesake and grandson of Prophet Joseph Smith, founder of Mormonism.

Frederick's father established the reorganized branch of the church in opposition to the Brigham Young group in Utah. Frederick was a graduate of Graceland College in 1898 and 1923; at U. of Missouri, 1908-09; A.M. from U. of Kansas in 1911; and Ph.D. from Clark U. in 1916. He was first counselor of the church, 1902-15, and on the death of his father in 1914, succeeded him as the second president. Frederick was associate editor of *The Saints' Herald*, 1900-04, and editor after 1917.

Frederick became a Mason in 1917. On March 16 of that year, he was raised (3°) in Carbondale Lodge No. 70, Carbondale KN. He was affiliated with Orient Lodge No. 546, Kansas City, MO on April 28, 1928, and was Master of the Lodge in 1934; Grand Orator of the Grand Lodge of Missouri in 1929-30; and Grand Chaplain, Grand Lodge of Missouri, 1940-41.

Frederick was Exalted in Orient Chapter No. 102, R.A.M., Kansas City, June 26, 1928; Greeted in Shekinah Council No. 24, R. & S.M., Kansas City on Sept. 12, 1928; Knighted in Oriental Commandery No. 35, K.T., Kansas City, Dec. 21, 1928; and affiliated with Palestine Commandery No. 17, K.T., of Independence, MO, June 2, 1938. Received 32° AASR (SJ) at Fort Scott KN on April 26, 1927 and affiliated with Western Missouri Consistory in Kansas City, Jan. 25, 1933. He received Shrine in Mirza Temple, Pittsburg KN, May 25, 1927 and affiliated with Ararat in Kansas City, Oct. 8, 1929, and was Potentate in 1941. Served on the board of directors of Shrine Hospital, St. Louis. Was Member of Missouri Lodge of Research.

Fig. 24 — Freemason Sen. Henry Clay introducing *Compromise of 1850*.

Jan. 1850, Sen. Henry Clay of Kentucky introduces to the Senate the *Compromise of 1850*. V.P. Fillmore, top right, is presiding. The *Compromise*, which postponed the Civil War by ten years, was entered six months before the death of Pres. Taylor, whereupon Fillmore became President.

3° Henry Clay (1777-1852). U.S. Senator, Congressman, and Secretary of State. Born in Hanover Co., VA. Self educated. Studied law under Freemason Robert Brooke of Virginia. He moved to Lexington, KY in 1797, where he practiced law. He once defended Freemason Aaron Burr.

Clay was U.S. senator from KY from 1806-07, 1831-42, 1849-52. He served in U.S. Congress from 1811-21 and 1823-25. He was Speaker of the House. From 1825-29 he was Secretary of State.

Masonic credentials: He was raised (3°) in Lexington Lodge No. 1, Lexington, KY, sometime between 1798 and 1801. He served as Master of this lodge. In 1820 he was Grand Master of Kentucky.

Clay was one of the proponents for creating a general Grand Lodge for the U.S.A. In fact, he offered a resolution to that effect on Mar. 9, 1822 at a Masonic conference held in U.S. Senate chambers in Washington, DC. His resolution required a unanimous vote of each state representative. When Massachusetts voted against it, defeating the proposal, he demitted from his lodge. However, he was reinstated at the Grand Lodge session in 1829. Clay was an honorary member of St. John's Lodge No. 1, N.Y.C. During the anti-Masonic period he flirted politically with members of that party. However, when questioned as to his views on Masonry, he answered, "But it must not be said that I concur in the denunciation of Masonry. Nor must it be expected that I will make any formal renunciation of it. I believe it does more good than harm, although it does not practically effect all that it theoretically promises. I would not denounce and formally renounce it to be made President of the United States." Clay was Grand Orator of Grand Lodge of KY in 1806, 1807, and 1809. He was buried with Masonic honors and his monument was Masonically dedicated on July 4, 1858.

Figure 25 — European Masons helped trigger our Civil War thru Young Societies. See *Scarlet and the Beast*, Vol.1, 3rd edition, chaps. 10, 12, 15, 22, 24; Vol.3, chs. 4&7.

33° Giuseppe (Joseph) Mazzini (1805-1872)
founder of Young Societies & MAFIA
Italian patriot and liberator. Practiced law in Genoa. Became associated with democratic movement in Italy. Joined Carbonari (Italian Masonry) in 1830. For this activity he was imprisoned for six months, and released only after he pledged to leave Italy. He made his home in Marseilles, France, and because of a letter he wrote to Charles Albert of Sardinia, a decree of perpetual banishment from Italy was made against him.

In 1832 he organized the revolutionary secret society *Young Italy*, a masonic youth organization of males, ages 16-20. Later, the "liberator," 33° Freemason Garibaldi, joined *Young Italy*.

To fund their revolution, Young Italy robbed banks, assassinated for pay, kidnapped for ransom, and demanded "protection money" from businesses as insurance against being bombed out or burnt down. This rabble became known as "**M**azzini's **A**ssociation **F**or **I**nsurrection & **A**ssassination. Shortened to the acronym M.A.F.I.A., organized crime was born. The purpose of all international *Young Societies* that followed was to throw off the yoke of Crown and Church (or national religion of any land), and unify those nations under a secular and republican form of government. During the 1849 Italian Revolution, Mazzini returned to Italy to form the triumvirate with Freemasons Saffi and Armellini, but went into exile again when the papal control of Rome was reestablished.

Mazzini instigated the rebel youth uprisings in Mantua in 1852; Milan in 1853; America in 1855 (John Brown); Genoa in 1857, and aided in organizing Garibaldi's expeditions in 1860, 1862, and 1867. Mazzini became Past Grand Master of Grand Orient Freemasonry in Italy.

June, 1949 (100 years after the Italian Revolution), the Italian government invited members of Grand Orient Italy to participate in a parade and dedication of the statue of Mazzini in Rome. Three thousand Italian Masons were present. The belated statue was first designed by Ettore Ferrari, former Grand Master of Italy, but the pre-World War II anti-Masonic Mussolini period intervened, and the statue was not erected until after World War II.

Figure 26 — The Anti-Masonic movement not only affected America by triggering our Civil War, it likewise put all Europe into Revolution, giving 32° Grand Orient Mason Karl Marx a platform to sell his book — *Communist Manifesto*.

1848

Marx wrote: "Modern industry has established the world market. All old-established national industries have been destroyed. They are dislodged by new industries whose products are consumed in every corner of the globe. In place of the old wants, we find new wants, requiring for their satisfaction the products of distant lands and climes... All fixed, fast-frozen relations are swept away; all new-formed ones become antiquated before they can ossify. All that is solid melts into air."

"Those sentiments of Karl Marx and Friedrich Engels formed part of the Communist Manifesto, first published in February 1848, a few weeks before revolutions swept through Europe."

Michael Elliott (*Global Agenda*): (TIME, 7/23/01, p.39)

Read about the 1848 European Masonic revolutions in *Scarlet and the Beast*, Vol. 1, 3rd edition, chapters 9 & 12.

Figure 27 — European Masons triggered our Civil War thru Young Societies.
See *S&B*, V1, 3rd ed.; ch. 12, 15, 18, 19, 20; V2, ch. 2-3; V3, ch. 4, 6, 7.

33° Giuseppe (Joseph) Garibaldi (1807-1882)

Italian liberator — the "George Washington" of Italy. There was no Italy when Garibaldi was born, only a group of small backward states. In 1833 he became associated with Freemason and liberator, Giuseppe Mazzini. He joined Mazzini's secret revolutionary society, *Young Italy*, at age 26.

After an ill-timed plot in 1834, a death penalty was leveled at the Liberator, which sent him into self-imposed exile to France. From France he fled to South America in 1836, where he was again engaged in revolution in Brazil. After capture, prison and torture, he was released and went to Uruguay. He raised a small army of his own, and won them their freedom.

In 1848, word from Europe that the Continent was on the threshold of revolution caused Garibaldi to sail for Italy with a picked company of South Americans. He landed at Nice in June 1848, joined the army of the Roman Republic, and with his band of rebels, amazed Europe with his 9-week stubborn defense of Rome. When he lost the battle, he fled to the United States, where he became a naturalized citizen.

When his presence in Italy was no longer feared, he returned to Genoa in May, 1854. On May 5, 1860 he left Genoa with 1,000 handpicked men, known as "red-shirts" and captured Sicily, after which he sailed to the mainland of Italy, expelled the anti-Mason, Francis II, thus defeating the so-called Kingdom of the Two Sicilies.

Only Rome, in French hands, and Venetia, held by Austria, stood in his way for complete independence for Italy.

Masonic Credentials: Garibaldi joined Lodge Les Amis de Patrie of Montevideo, Uruguay in 1844. In U.S.A. (1850s) he affiliated with Tompkins Lodge No. 471, Stapleton, NY. In 1860 he became Grand Master of Grand Lodge at Palermo, Italy. In 1863 was elected Grand Commander of the Supreme Council, 33° AASR, in Italy and became Grand Master of Italian Freemasonry. In 1867 he called a convention to unite all Masonic bodies in Italy, but was unsuccessful. He was honorary member of Egyptian Rite of Memphis. In NYC, Garibaldi Lodge No. 542 was named in his honor.

Figure 28 — Famous American Masons during our Civil War.
See *Scarlet and Beast*, Vol. 1, ch. 12 and 14.

3° Carl Schurz (1829-1906)

Born in Cologne, Germany. He took part in the Masonic revolutions that swept Europe in 1848, when all Europe was in Masonic revolution (see *Scarlet and the Beast*, Vol. 1, chapter 12). He was compelled to flee from Germany to Paris, where he became a newspaper correspondent. Later he taught school in London. In 1850 he returned secretly to Germany to help liberate his friend and teacher, Paul Kinkel, from prison at Spandau. He immigrated to the USA in 1852 and settled in Philadelphia. In 1855 he moved to Watertown, WI, where he studied law and was admitted to the bar, practicing in Milwaukee. He was appointed U.S. Minister to Spain in 1861 but resigned soon after to become a Brigadier General of Volunteers in the Union Army. After the war he engaged in newspaper work at St. Louis and served as Republican U.S. Senator from Missouri, 1869-74. He became Secretary of the Interior, 1877-81, and editor of the *New York Evening Post*, 1881-84. He was also contributor to *Harper's Weekly*, 1892-98. He was president of the National Civil Service Reform League, 1892-1901.

Carl Schurz was a member of Herman Lodge No. 125 at Philadelphia. He received all three blue lodge degrees by special dispensation on Feb. 23, 1855 and elected a member of the lodge on March 23, 1855. He was suspended from the lodge Nov. 23, 1860 (no explanation given).

3° Caleb Cushing (1800-1879)

Brigadier General in Mexican War. Attorney

General of U.S. (1853-57). Harvard graduate. Practiced law at Newburyport, MA. Served in the House and Senate four terms. In 1853 Pres. Pierce appointed him U.S. Attorney General. He was a member of St. John's Lodge, Newburyport, MA.

English Freemasonry needed American Masons who were willing to betray their nation. Caleb Cushing and Albert Pike were chosen. See *S&B*, Vol. 1, ch. 14; Vol.3. ch. 4.

Fig. 29 — European Masons trigger our Civil War thru Young Societies.
See *Scarlet and Beast,* Vol. I, 3rd ed., chps. 12, 16; Vol. 3, chp. 4.

3° R.A.M. Lajos (Louis) Kossuth (1802-1894)

Hungarian patriot and statesman. Imprisoned (1837-40) by Austrian government on political charges, during which time he taught himself English. In 1841 he became editor of the *Pesti Hirlap,* a prominent Hungarian daily, and through it presented his liberal views. Liberal Party seated him as Finance Minister in the government of 1848. He persuaded Hungarian National Assembly to declare independence from Austria (184849), after which he was appointed governor of Hungary with dictatorial powers. When the insurrection was crushed (8/11/1849), Kossuth fled to Turkey. He was imprisoned (1849-51), and finally released by the intervention of the U.S.A., which sent the *U.S. Mississippi* to bring him to London. Later he came to the U.S.A., accompanied by 33° Italian Freemason Adriano Lemmi (18221896). Lemmi was on assignment by Mazzini to set the stage for Civil War in America. He was to establish Young America lodges to indoctrinate youth to agitate against slavery. (See *Scarlet and the Beast,* Vol.1, 3rd ed., chap.14). On Feb. 18, 1852, Cincinnati Lodge No. 133 received an extraordinary letter — a hand written petition from Kossuth, asking permission to be initiated into American Masonry. His petition was given emergency status. On Feb. 19 he was initiated (1°). The next day passed (2o) and raised (3°). Kossuth's staff likewise became members of Cincinnati Chapter No. 2, R.A.M. On Feb. 28, 1852 Kossuth attended a meeting at Center Lodge No. 23, Indianapolis, addressed the lodge, then visited St. John's Lodge No. 1 of Newark, N.J. He also addressed Grand Lodge Massachusetts on May 10, 1852. The content of his address prepared American Masons for Civil War. Lemmi, Kossuth's sidekick, was to prepare Franklin Pierce to be the next President of the United States. Pierce, not a Mason himself, favored Masons. Lemmi sent Pierce a list of "suggested" presidential appointments. His help would assure his presidency. Pierce was aware Lemmi's list were Masons. He was not aware they were prepared to split America north and south. In his quest for the presidency, Pierce obediently appointed Lemmi's list. Mazzini confirmed in his diary that "Almost all Pierce's nominations are such as we desired." The Italian Masonic newspaper, *Rivista della Massoneria Italiana,* said of these men, "Mazzini, Garibaldi and Kossuth shine with unsurpassed glory which make crowned heads turn pale."

Fig. 30 — Franklin Pierce, not a Mason, but favorable to the Craft. To become President, he permitted himself to be used by European Masonry to trigger our Civil War.
See *S&B*, Vol.1, 3rd ed., ch. 14, Vol. 3, ch. 4.

Franklin Pierce (1804-1869)

US Statesman and 14th President of the U.S.A. (1853-57). Born in Hillsborough, NH. Admitted to the bar in 1827. Was elected to Congress as a Jacksonian Democrat, and in 1837 to the US Senate. He advocated the annexation of Texas with or without slavery, and was made Brigadier General in the Mexican War.

Elected US President in 1853, Pierce defended slavery and the fugitive slave law. Among the events of his administration were the repeal of the Missouri Compromise and the passing of the Kansas-Nebraska Act, which division of land kindled a flame that ultimately led to Civil War. The unpopularity of this Act led to Pierce's 1857 forced retirement from politics. President Pierce's first appointment was Freemason Caleb Cushing to the post of U.S. Attorney General. Cushing was a prolific writer against slavery. As U.S. Attorney General he became the master-architect of the Civil War. Cushing's first Masonic assignment was to transfer money from British Masonic banker George Peabody to the Young America abolitionists, who after the elections were calling for the dissolution of the Union.

The handler of the Peabody funds in London was George Sanders, Pierce's appointee to the U.S. Consulate. Sanders, not a Mason, but an enthusiast of Masonic revolutions, opened his London home to every debased revolutionary in Europe. In one gathering alone (Feb. 21, 1854), Sanders hosted the following famous Masons; Giuseppe Mazzini, General Giuseppe Garibaldi; Louis Kossuth; Arnold Ruge, who with Karl Marx was the editor of a revolutionary magazine for Young Germany; Felice Orsine, one of Mazzini's contract terrorists and assassins; and Alexander Herzen of Russia, the man who initiated Freemason Mikhail Bakunin into Mazzini's Young Russia. Also present at that meeting was President Pierce's U.S. Ambassador to England, Freemason James Buchanan, destined to be the next president of the United States.

Five of the eight men present at this fateful meeting were directly involved in creating the Southern Rebellion in America. With help from these men, Caleb Cushing was able to finance Young America abolitionists to instigate a Civil War. Sanders himself operated a cross-border spy ring for the Confederacy during the Civil War. After the war, Sanders and his Canadian spies were indicted for allegedly helping to plan the assassination of Abraham Lincoln. Although charges were later dropped, Sanders' wanderings as a fugitive made him appear suspect.

Figure 31 — John Brown, with funds and backing from European Freemasonry, helped trigger our Civil War. See *Scarlet and the Beast*, Vol. 1, 3rd edition, ch. 14; Vol. 3, ch. 4.

3° John Brown (1800-1859)

Freemason turned anti-Mason; became an Abolitionist, killing proslavery adherents. Executed Dec 2, 1859. Brown's cause was glorified by the famous marching song, *John Brown's Body*.

Brown was a member of Young America, founded in America in 1852 by Hungarian Freemason Louis Kossuth. From 1856 to his death, Brown was obsessed with the idea of abolishing slavery by force. Following a pro-slavery massacre at Lawrence, Kansas, Brown, in retaliation, killed five slavery adherents.

He next made a heroic stand at Osawatomie, KN against a raid by pro-slavery forces from Missouri. He conceived a plan of establishing a new state as a refuge for Negroes. In 1859, with help from Massachusetts abolitionists, he seized the government arsenal at Harpers Ferry, VA, intending the action to signal general insurrection of slaves. Overpowered, then convicted of treason, he was hanged Dec. 2, 1859.

Brown was raised (3°) in Hudson Lodge No. 68, Hudson, Ohio, on May 11, 1824, serving as Junior Deacon in 1825-26. His uncle was the First Master of the Lodge. After William Morgan was murdered by Masons in 1826, Brown renounced Freemasonry and became an adherent to the Anti-Masonic Movement and moved to Pennsylvania. There he verbally denounced Freemasonry and continued to do so on every possible occasion. His son, John Brown, Jr., later became a Freemason and was buried with Masonic honors. His daughter, Sarah, once told a biographer that Brown, Sr. had stated that "the forms of the initiatory ceremonies of the Masons struck him as silly," and in a Negro newspaper Brown wrote, "another of the few errors of my life is that I have joined the Freemasons, Oddfellows, Sons of Temperance, and a score of other secret societies instead of seeking the company of intelligent, wise and good men."

John Brown, however, was not through with Secret Societies. His antislavery actions recorded above were not his own. Through his membership in Young America, he was financed and backed by European Freemasonry for the express purpose of triggering our Civil War. You can read the story in *Scarlet and the Beast*, Vol. 1, 3rd ed., ch. 14; Vol. 3, ch. 4.

Figure 32A — **Abe Lincoln** (1809--1865). 16th President. Read of Lincoln's battle with international bankers, who tried to force on the U.S.A. a central bank and fiat money. Lincoln responded, "I can print my own Greenbacks," and he did! See *S&B*, Vol. 1, 3rd edition, chap. 14; and Vol. 3, chap. 4, 5, 7.

Abe Lincoln (1809--1865)

Mackey's Encyclopedia of Freemasonry reports that the Past Grand Master of Switzerland writes in Swiss Grand Lodge Alpina's publication *Annuaire* (p.44, 1913 and p.59, 1923), that the International Masonic Association listed Lincoln among Illustrious Freemasons.

The P.M.G. continued, "I will further state that Mr. J.H. Brooks, who was Mr. Lincoln's messenger, informed me that Mr. Lincoln was a Mason. The degrees were conferred in an Army Lodge attached to Gen. Grant's army in front of Richmond."

William H. Grimshaw of the Library of Congress likewise confirms, "In *History of Freemasonry*, 1903 (p. 365), Lincoln is listed as a Mason. In fact, in the 1866 memorial volume published by the Government at Washington, there are found the tributes of forty-four foreign Masonic Bodies, most of these plainly referring to Lincoln as a 'Brother.'"

Freemason B.B. French from the Washington office of the Grand Master, Knights Templar, April 21, 1865, answers a letter, "President Lincoln was not a Mason. He once told me in the presence of Most Worshipful Brother J.W. Simons that he had at one time made up his mind to apply for admission to our Fraternity but that he feared he was too lazy to attend to his duty as a Mason...."

In *10,000 Famous Freemasons* we read, "In Oct. of 1860 Robert Morris of Kentucky, called on Lincoln in Springfield, Ill., and in the course of conversation Morris referred to the fact that all Lincoln's presidential opponents were Freemasons. Lincoln replied, 'I am not a Freemason, Dr. Morris, though I have a great respect for the institution.'"

Fig. 32B — A Thanksgiving Day Proclamation in the 17th Century

A New England town of the 17th century shows the town crier reading the governor's Thanksgiving Day proclamation before an inn, while patrons and passersby listen attentively. From the time of the gathering of the first harvest at Plymouth in 1621, it was common for the colonial authorities to appoint a day of thanksgiving to God in the Fall when the harvests were in. There was no uniform date for this annual festival, however, until 1863, when President Abraham Lincoln proclaimed a national Thanksgiving.

Thanksgiving Proclamation made in 1863 by Abraham Lincoln

It is the duty of nations as well as of men to own their dependence upon the overruling power of God; to confess their sins and transgressions in humble sorrow, yet with assured hope that genuine repentance will lead to mercy and pardon; and to recognize the sublime truth, announced in the Holy Scriptures and proven by all history, that those nations are blessed whose God is the Lord.

We know that by His divine law, nations, like individuals, are subjected to punishments and chastisements in this world. May we not justly fear that the awful calamity of civil war which now desolates the land may be a punishment inflicted upon us for our presumptuous sins, to the needful end of our national reformation as a whole people?

We have been recipients of the choicest bounties of heaven; we have been preserved these many years in peace and prosperity; we have grown in numbers, wealth and power as no other nation has ever grown.

But we have forgotten God. We have forgotten the gracious hand which preserved us in peace and multiplied and enriched and strengthened us, and we have vainly imagined, in the deceitfulness of our hearts, that all these blessings were produced by some superior wisdom and virtue of our own. Intoxicated with unbroken success, we have become too self-sufficient to feel the necessity of redeeming and preserving grace, too proud to pray to the God what made us.

It has seemed to me fit and proper that God should be solemnly, reverently, and gratefully acknowledged, as with one heart and one voice, by the whole American people. I do therefore invite my fellow citizens in every part of the United States, and also those who are at sea and those who are sojourning in foreign lands, to set apart and observe the last Thursday of November as a day of Thanksgiving and praise to our beneficent Father so dwelleth in the heavens. *Longview News-Journal* 11-22-06.

Sixteen Masons appointed by Lincoln during his administration

Edward Bates (1793-1869). Appointed Attorney General of United States in Lincoln's cabinet. Member of Missouri Lodge No. 12. Served four terms as Grand Master, 1825-27 and 1831.

Anson Burlingame (1820-1870). President Lincoln appointed him as minister to Austria. Was made a Mason in Amicable Lodge, Cambridge, MA. on Jan. 5, 1854.

3° Simon Cameron (1799-1889). Secretary of War in Lincoln's first cabinet. Lincoln also appointed him U.S. Minister to Russia. Served as Master of Perseverance Lodge No. 21 at Harrisburg, PA in 1833. Member of Perseverance Chapter No. 21, Royal Arch Mason at Harrisburg and St. John's Commandery No. 4, Knights Templar at Philadelphia.

William B. Campbell (1807-1867). In 1862, Lincoln appointed him Brigadier General in the Federal Army, but he was forced to retire in 1863 due to ill health. Member of Lebanon Lodge No. 98, Lebanon, TN.

Edward R. S. Canby (1819-1873). When Civil War broke out, Canby was on an expedition against the Navajos in the Southwest. He was called to Washington by Pres. Lincoln, who appointed him to assist Secretary of War, Edwin M. Stanton. Canby was burried with Masonic honors.

Thomas Corwin (1794-1865). Lincoln appointed him Minister to Mexico. In 1819, became member of Lebanon Lodge No. 26, Lebanon, OH. Served as Master of same. Served as Grand Master of the Grand Lodge of Ohio in 1828. Also was a member of Lebanon Chapter No. 5, Royal Arch Mason. Knighted in Mt. Vernon Commandery, Knights Templar.

John Evans (1814-1897). Lincoln named him territorial governor of Colorado in order to save that territory for the Union cause. When he arrived in Colorado, he discovered that many of the Freemasons in Denver Lodge No. 5 were outspoken against the Union, so Evans organized Union Lodge no. 7 in 1863. In 1844 he was raised (3°) in Attica Lodge No. 18, Attica, IN. In 1846 he also became a Royal Arch York Rite Mason in Indianapolis Chapter No. 5. He was a charter member of Colorado Commandery No. 1, Knights Templar.

Stephen J. Field (1816-1899). He was the last justice appointed by Lincoln. Member Corinthian Lodge No. 9 at Marysville, CA.

Aaron Goodrich (1807-?). In 1861, Lincoln appointed him Secretary of the U.S. Legation at Brussels, Belgium. He served in that capacity for eight years. He was a member of Dover Lodge No. 39, Dover, TN, and later St. Pauls Lodge No. 3, St. Paul, MN. He was Deputy Grand Master of the Grand Lodge of Minnesota at his death.

John S. Phelps (1814-1886). In 1862, Lincoln appointed him military governor of Arkansas. He was recorded in 1857 as a member of United Lodge No. 5, a Scottish Rite lodge in Springfield, MO. On Aug. 15, 1850 he was also affiliated with York Rite Masonry Chapter No. 15, R.A.M, and with its 1867 reorganization following the Civil War. At this latter event he was recommended as High Priest.

Edwin M. Stanton (1814-1869). Lincoln appointed him to Secretary of War, in which position he "masterminded" the Union forces, retiring General McClellan, and placing General Grant as commander-in-chief of the three armies. Grand guided the War Dept. throughout the Civil War. Stanton was a member of Steubenville Lodge No. 45, Steubenville, OH. He was also a member of Washington Lodge No. 253 of Pittsburgh.

William H. Upham (1841-1924). Lincoln appointed him to the U.S. Military Academy. Graduated at close of War. Was a Mason.

Gideon Welles (1802-1878). Secretary of the Navy, 1861-69 in both Lincoln and Johnson's cabinets. Member of St. John's Lodge No. 4 and Pythagoras Chapter No. 17, R.A.M., both of Hartford.

Elisha Whittlesey (1783-1863). Appointed Comptroller of the Treasury by Lincoln. Raised (3°) in Old Erie Lodge No. 3, Warren, OH, 1810. Member of many lodges. Deputy Grand Master of Grand Lodge Ohio, 1820-21.

David Wilmot (1814-1868). Appointed by Lincoln in 1863 to U.S. Court of Claims and served until his death. Member of Lodge No. 108, Towanda, PA, and Harmony Chapter No. 52, R.A.M. of Philadelphia, PA.

Isaac J. Wistar (1827-1905). Brigadier General of Volunteers in Civil War. Mason.

Source: *10,000 Famous Freemasons*, by 33° William R. Denslow

Fig. 33 — Assassination of President Abraham Lincoln.

Why was Lincoln assassinated? The answer is not found in general history. It's behind the closed doors of Lodges, and inside international bank vaults. See *S&B*, Vol. 1, 3rd ed., ch. 14 & Vol. 3, chs. 4 and 5.

33° John Wilkes Booth (1838-1865?)

Generally accepted story of President Abraham Lincoln's assassin John and Edwin Booth were members of one of America's most distinguished acting families of the 19th century. Although not as famous as his brother, John was popular in the South because he was a strong supporter of the Southern cause. In 1865 he, with two accomplices, planned to avenge the defeat of the Confederates. John shot President Lincoln at Ford's Theatre in D.C.

FACTS not in our history books! In 1854 International Freemasonry founded the Knights of the Golden Circle, which absorbed European Freemasonry's Young America. Together the Knights and Young America split the U.S.A. north and south.

John Wilkes Booth, who did the bidding of International Freemasonry and Banking, was outspoken in his advocacy of slavery and his hatred for Presidentelect Lincoln. Playing the "double," he became a member of Mazzini's Carbonari of Italy and joined the Masonic abolitionist youth order Young America. He again switched sides and became a Volunteer in the Richmond, VA militia that hanged Abolitionist John Brown in 1859.

As did many key Masons during the anti-Masonic period, Booth rose rapidly to become a 33° Mason in the Southern Jurisdiction of Freemasonry. When America was reunited after the war, the Golden Circle plotted Lincoln's assassination. Booth volunteered to be the gunman. As a renowned actor, he would not be suspect entering Ford Theater where Lincoln would be seated. After the assassination, Booth fled. The conspirators arranged for a drunk to be found burned in a barn, claiming him to be the charred remains of Booth. The real Booth escaped, living in disguise and dying of old age. Meanwhile, the Knights of the Golden Circle became the Knights of the Ku Klux Klan.

Fig. 34 — Reward poster for the capture of John Wilkes Booth.

SURRAT. BOOTH. HAROLD.

War Department, Washington, April 20, 1865,

$100,000 REWARD!

THE MURDERER

Of our late beloved President, Abraham Lincoln,

IS STILL AT LARGE.

$50,000 REWARD

Will be paid by this Department for his apprehension, in addition to any reward offered by Municipal Authorities or State Executives.

$25,000 REWARD

Will be paid for the apprehension of JOHN H. SURRATT, one of Booth's Accomplices.

$25,000 REWARD

Will be paid for the apprehension of David C. Harold, another of Booth's accomplices.

LIBERAL REWARDS will be paid for any information that shall conduce to the arrest of either of the above-named criminals, or their accomplices.

All persons harboring or secreting the said persons, or either of them, or aiding or assisting their concealment or escape, will be treated as accomplices in the murder of the President and the attempted assassination of the Secretary of State, and shall be subject to trial before a Military Commission and the punishment of DEATH.

Let the stain of innocent blood be removed from the land by the arrest and punishment of the murderers.

All good citizens are exhorted to aid public justice on this occasion. Every man should consider his own conscience charged with this solemn duty, and rest neither night nor day until it be accomplished.

EDWIN M. STANTON, Secretary of War.

DESCRIPTIONS.—BOOTH is Five Feet 7 or 8 inches high, slender build, high forehead, black hair, black eyes, and wears a heavy black moustache.

JOHN H. SURRAT is about 5 feet, 9 inches. Hair rather thin and dark; eyes rather light; no beard. Would weigh 145 or 150 pounds. Complexion rather pale and clear, with color in his cheeks. Wore light clothes of fine quality. Shoulders square; cheek bones rather prominent; chin narrow; ears projecting at the top; forehead rather low and square, but broad. Parts his hair on the right side; neck rather long. His lips are firmly set. A slim man.

DAVID C. HAROLD is five feet six inches high, hair dark, eyes dark, eyebrows rather heavy, full face, nose short, hand short and fleshy, feet small, instep high, round bodied, naturally quick and active, slightly closes his eyes when looking at a person.

NOTICE.—In addition to the above, State and other authorities have offered rewards amounting to almost one hundred thousand dollars, making an aggregate of about TWO HUNDRED THOUSAND DOLLARS.

Fig. 35 — Famous American Masons during our Civil War.

3° R.A.M. Stephen Arnold Douglas (1813-1861)

U.S. Senator and Congressman from Illinois who gained fame by his debates with Abraham Lincoln. Nominated for president by Democratic party in 1860. He was defeated by Lincoln. He loyally supported Lincoln's administration.

A member of Springfield Lodge No. 4. He was initiated June 11, 1840; passed June 24 and raised June 26, 1840. In Oct. he was elected Grand Orator of the Grand Lodge of Illinois. He was exalted in Quincy Chapter No. 3, R.A.M. He had previously received the Mark Master. Upon death he was buried Masonically. A Masonic monument was dedicated to him at Chicago on Sept. 6, 1866 and Freemason President Andrew Johnson attended.

James Warren Nye (1815-1876)

First U.S. Senator from Nevada, 1864-73. Studied law at Troy, N.Y. Admitted to the bar in Madison Co., N.Y. Practiced law in N.Y. Was first president of Metropolitan Board of Police, NYC 1857-60. In 1861 President Lincoln appointed him governor of Washoe (Nevada) Territory. He served in that capacity until elected Senator when Nevada gained statehood in 1864. Member of Hamilton Lodge No. 120, Hamilton, N.Y.

Figure 36 — Southern Rebels and Union officers.
See *Scarlet and the Beast*, Vol. 1, 3rd edition, chapter 14; and Vol. 3, chapters 2-4.

Jefferson Davis (1808-1889)
President of the Confederate States of America. He was not a Mason, although his father, Samuel and brother, Joseph E., were members of the craft. He was, however, friendly to the fraternity.

Following the War the statement below was made in amagazine article against Davis: "Jefferson Davis, a Free and Accepted Mason, headed the great rebellion, and the fact did not even taint his Masonic standing, but did have much to do in receiving his pardon." In answering this to an inquirer, Davis wrote, in part: "I regard the fraternity with respect and have never felt any disapproval of it other than that which pertains to every secret society. Viewing Freemasonry from a distance, and judging the tree by its fruits, I have believed it to be in itself good."

Ulysses S. Grant (1822-1885)
Led Union forces to victory. 18th Pres. of USA. Not a Mason, but had close associations with Masons.

Eleven southern states seceded from the Union, yet the Confederate flag had 13 stars. Read why in *Scarlet & the Beast*, Volume one, chap. 14.

Robert E. Lee (1807-1870)
Commander-in Chief of Confederate Armies Sometimes referred to as a Mason, but was not.

Figure 37 — Famous sculptor Mason.

Edward V. Valentine (1838-1930)
American sculptor from Richmond, VA. Studied art in Europe in 1859. He returned to Richmond and opened a studio. Among his notable works are the recumbent figure of Robert E. Lee for the Lee Mausoleum at Washington and Lee University. Other works: bronze statue of Lee in Statuary Hall, Washington, DC; statue of Jefferson Davis in Richmond, VA; statue of Stonewall Jackson in Lexington, VA; and statue of John J. Audubon in New Orleans.

Member of Dove Lodge No. 21, Richmond, VA.

Figure 38 — Famous American Masons during our Civil War. See *Scarlet and the Beast*, Vol. 1, 3rd edition, chapter 14S.

Senator Thomas Hart Benton (1782-1858)
U.S. Senator from Missouri, 1821-51. Often called "Old Bullion" because he was defender of sound money. He supported Freemason President Jackson in his campaign against the national bank. In the slavery issue he opposed secession, which resulted in his defeat for another senate term in 1850. He did return to Washington from 1853-55 as Congressman. Senator Benton was a charter member of Missouri Lodge No. 1 at St. Louis until the anti-Masonic days of 1831, when he withdrew for political reasons.

3° General Thomas Hart Benton (1816-1879)
Civil War General. Born in Williamson Co. Tenn. Nephew of Missouri Senator above of same name. Raised (3°) July 16, 1849 in Iowa City Lodge No. 4. Later a member of Bluff City Lodge No. 71. Served as Grand Master of Iowa from 1860-62.

As a Union General he saved the valuable Masonic library of Confederate General Albert Pike, by placing a guard of Federal troops around Pike's Little Rock, Ark. home.

13° R.A.M. Major William McKinley (1843-1901)

Destined to be the 25th President of the U.S.A. from 1896-1901. (See Sect. 5, Fig, 25). Although a Union Army major during our Civil War, he received his Masonic degrees in a southern lodge during the war. While protecting and managing the army hospital at Winchester, VA., he was struck by the ties which he saw existing between the Union surgeons and Confederate prisoners. When he learned the reason for such a brotherly spirit in spite of war and hatred, he asked to be admitted to the Craft.

Figure 39 — Postcard at Gettysburg, PA depicting the brotherly love between wounded northern and southern Masons during our Civil War.

Gettysburg

FRIEND TO FRIEND

A Brotherhood Undivided

The monument shows Union General Winfield Scott Hancock tending to Confederate General Lewis Addison Armistead

See next page for more examples of brotherly love between Union & Confederate Masons.

See next page for more examples of brotherly love between Union & Confederate Masons.

HOUSE UNDIVIDED:, for their own protection, The Story of Freemasonry and the Civil War by 32° Allen E. Roberts

In 1856, four years before the Civil War began, Grand Master Love S. Cornwell, during his annual address to the Grand Lodge of Missouri, spoke concerning the universal problems caused by the Anti-Masonic Movement. "This is a year of universal political excitement. Our whole country seems to be convulsed to its very center. Questions of policy are agitated that seem to tend directly and speedily to a dissolution of the union of these States... Parties are being formed of every political nature. (Anti-masonic) demagogues, through religious fanaticism, are endeavoring to elevate themselves to honor and distinction, by the agitation of questions (about Freemasonry) that should rarely ever be discussed, expecting to ride upon the whirlwind, and guide the storm that will place them in a position they are frequently poorly qualified to fill. The great trouble will be that the storm may not only carry them, but also the innocent, into civil war, anarchy and confusion."

When civil war broke out, members of the Craft were among the highest in command of both armies. Nearly 400 military officers in both the Union and Confederate armies were Masons. Read their names and commissions on pp. 311-374. Some may be your own relatives. Other Masons held top political posts, or were at the head of humanitarian agencies.

It was not uncommon to see brethren arrayed against each other, with weapons in their hands, "meeting on the level and parting on the square... In the midst of the war, Masons wearing blue joined hands in peace and harmony with those clad in gray. The sounds of war were stilled while Southern Masons buried their brothers from the North."

J.M. Pelot, M.D., told of his experience in the war. "I saw a poor fellow brought into camp as a spy. He protested his innocence, and pled to be allowed to return to his unprotected wife and children, who were suffering in his absence. But all in vain. Finally he resorted to a mystic (Masonic) sign, when the commander saw the force of his arguments and turned him loose." Where it was in their power to do so, Masons and Masonic property were protected, and in some instances defended by order of leading generals

(see Fig. 37 this section — Gen. Thomas Hart Benton).

At West Point the victory was complete, although heroically defended. More complete, however, was the place won in the memory and affections of a grateful people for the humane and generous treatment meted out to them by their conquerors. Masonic symbols on buildings were sufficient passports to the affections of those who had bowed at the altar of our sublime institution.

When the war was over it was Freemasonry that helped to heal the wounds of ill-will and aided in bringing the North and the South together.

Fig. 40 — **Our Masonic Civil War.** In *Scarlet and the Beast*, Vol.1, chap. 14 we document that our Civil War was triggered by Freemasonry for the express purpose of increasing membership so devastated by the Masonic murder of Capt. William Morgan and the Anti-Masonic Movement that followed. Not only did Masonic Lodges throughout the North and South open their doors to military recruitment, the recruits were also offered initiation into Freemasonry for protection throughout the duration of the War. Likewise military posts, both north and south, displayed Masonic symbols for protection.
Photo below copied from a 1901 Civil War album.

Civil War headquarters of Gen. J.H. Hobart Ward (1823-1903). Notice Masonic square & compass in shape of 6-pointed star. The 6-pointed star did not become a symbol of Zionism until 1897, 30+ yrs after our Civil War. It was first and foremost a symbol of Freemasonry.

J.H.H. Ward (standing above pointer) was a Union Brigadier General of Volunteers in our Civil War. Before that he served as a Sergeant Major in the 7th U.S. Inf. during the Mexican War. He was Commissary General of New York State, 1850-59. As a Colonel at the start of the Civil War, he raised the 38th N.Y. Rgt. of Volunteers and assisted in organizing the Scott Life Guards — both regiments in the Army of Virginia. He commanded the 1st Division and 4th Corps at Gettysburg, Manassas Gap and Kelly's Ford. Ward was made a Mason in Metropolitan Lodge No. 273, NYC in 1855. He was a member of Master Scott Life Guard Lodge, a military lodge in the 38th N.Y. Rgt. He was also a member of the Metropolitan Chapter No. 140, R.A.M., 1856; Palestine Commandery, K.T.; Mecca Shrine Temple, all of N.Y.C. On Sept. 22, 1897, he was made an active 33° AASR (NJ).

Fig. 41 — **Our Masonic Civil War** displayed Masonic symbols for protection.

Notice hanging between the two smokestacks of the *Merrimack* the Masonic Square & Compass with the letter "G" in center.

Copied from a 1901 Civil War album in the possession of John Daniel's in-laws

Photo copied from a 1901 Civil War album. *Merrimack*, first iron clad Gunboat built in America for Quartermaster's Department, armed, supplied, officered and manned jointly by the Union Army and Navy. Confederates acquired it and renamed it *Virginia*. Used against the Union *Monitor* in 1862, next page. Photo given by Gen. M.C. Meigs, a Freemason.

Fig. 42 — Hampton Roads battle (1862) revolutionized naval warfare. Confederate ironclad *Virginia* (formerly *Merrimack*) began destroying wooden Union fleet until driven off by low-lying ironclad *Monitor*.

Fig. 43 — John L. Worden was the U.S. Naval officer who commanded the Union *Monitor* against the Confederate *Merrimac* in the first battle between ironclads (March 9, 1862) in the U.S. Civil War.

John L. Worden (1818-1878)

Rear Admiral U.S. Navy

Commander of the *Monitor* in its famous battle with the *Merrimac* during the Civil War

Worden entered the Navy in 1835 as midshipman. He served on various vessels, receiving his early naval training with the Brazilian Squadron (1835-38). He served on the Pacific Coast during the Mexican War (1846-48) and afterward in both the Mediterranean and the home fleets at the Naval Observatory, until Civil War broke out.

He was a prisoner of war for seven months, and after an exchange of prisoners, was ordered to superintend the completion of the *Monitor*. On Jan. 16, 1862 the ship was deemed seaworthy, and Worden took command. In March he took the cumbersome "cheese box on a raft" down the Atlantic Coast in perilous, stormy weather.

His famous battle with the Confederate *Merrimac* (see Figs. 40-41) occurred two months later, on March 9, 1862. Worden, stationed in the pilothouse, was observing through the slit, when at 11:30 a.m. a shell exploded on the pilothouse of the *Monitor*, temporarily rendering him blind and helpless. He later recovered from the injury to his eyes. The three-hour battle ended when both withdrew from the conflict.

For the rest of the war, Worden commanded monitors stationed with the South Atlantic blockading squadron. Afterward he was promoted to Rear Admiral (1872), and commanded the European squadron from 1875 to 1877. He was retired by Congress in 1886 at full pay for life.

Worden was a member of Lexington Lodge No. 310, Brooklyn, NY. He received his blue lodge degrees on May 25, June 15 and 29, 1857.

Fig. 44 — **Our Masonic Civil War** and its Masonic soldiers.

John M. Chivington (?-1895)
Minister, missionary, soldier

The Confederate conquest of the Southwest seemed to be moving forward. Sibley took Albuquerque and plundered Santa Fe. All that now stood between him and the Colorado goldfields was Fort Union. He sent an advance force to the mouth of Apache Canyon to hold it until his whole army was in place and they could pour through together to crush federal resistance forever. But he had not reckoned on the lastminute arrival of the 1st Colorado Volunteers, mostly miners from the goldfields, hastily trained and hard drinking but itching for a fight. They had marched forty miles a day to get there, through ice and snow and freezing winds. Now, four hundred of them started through the narrow canyon toward the waiting Texans.

In the lead was Colonel John M. Chivington, a big, bearish Methodist parson, the presiding elder of the Rocky Mountain District of his church and as famous for his flamboyance as for his fiery sermons. He sometimes preached with a revolver resting on the pulpit and had refused to serve as regimental chaplain, demanding a "fighting commission" instead, because he thought it would serve better to boost the career in politics he now wished to pursue.

Now, he would get his chance to show what he could do. The Confederates opened fire as soon as they saw Chivington's men, and the Union volunteers fell back for a moment. But then they regrouped and Chivington sent some of his men scurrying up the canyon sides so that they could fire down on the enemy. "They were up on the walls on both sides of us," one Texan remembered, "shooting us down like sheep." Then Chivington, waving two revolvers, ordered in his cavalry. He "chawed his lips with only less energy than he gave his orders," one of his men recalled. "He seemed burdened with a new responsibility, the extent of which he had never before realized, and to have no thought of danger. Of commanding presence, dressed in full regimentals, he was a conspicuous mark for the Texan sharp sharpshooter...As if possessed of a charmed life, he galloped unhurt through the storm of bullets..." *The West, An Illustrated History*, by Geoffrey C. Ward, The West Book Project, Inc., 1996.

John M. Chivington was, paradoxically, both a Methodist missionary to the Indians and an Indian fighter. Born in Ohio, he came to Kansas City, Kansas in 1854 as a missionary to the Indians. While there he became the first Master of the first Lodge in Kansas, the Wyandotte Lodge No. 3, established Aug. 11, 1854.

From Kansas he went to Omaha, NE, and served as grand chaplain of the Grand Lodge of Nebraska. In 1860 he accepted the assignment as presiding elder of the Methodist Church in the new gold mining district of Colorado. In 1861 he became the first Grand Master of the Grand Lodge of Colorado. Later Chivington Lodge No. 6 (now extinct) was named for him. The old Bible from Lodge No. 6 is now at the Lodge at Central City. When the 1st Colorado Cavalry was organized in 1862, Chivington resigned as presiding elder of the church and was commissioned Major in the regiment. He distinguished himself in the Apache Canyon fight, known as the Battle of Glorieta, when he led 500 men in a rear attack on the Confederate troops who were attempting to invade Colorado from New Mexico. His attack saved Colorado and her gold deposits for the Union. For this he was made Colonel.

Indian massacres were troubling Colorado, so Governor John Evans called for volunteers who, under Chivington, engaged the Indians at Sand Creek near Ft. Lyon on Nov. 29, 1864, and killed several hundred of them, including women and children. For this he was defrocked by the Methodist church.

This action, including attacks by the Eastern Press forced him to leave Colorado for several years. Potentially a national hero, he fell into disgrace. He moved to Oregon where he lived for many years, returning to Denver where he was once more identified with the Church and the Masonic Fraternity.

Upon his death more than 500 masons attended his funeral.

Fig. 45 — **Our Masonic Civil War** and its Masonic soldiers.

George E. Pickett (18251875). Confederate Major General of Civil War, famous for his charge at Gettysburg. Born in Richmond, VA. Graduate of U.S. Military Academy, 1846. Served in Mexican war. Following Mexican war, he served in Texas, and on frontier duty in Northwest Territory. On June, 1861 he travel to Virginia, where he was made Colonel in the state forces. A year later he was commissioned Brigadier General in Longstreet's Army of Northern Virginia.

Pickett was severely wounded at the Battle of Gaines's Mills on June 27, 1862. At the Battle of Fredericksburg, his division held the center of Lee's line. At Gettysburg, July 3, 1863, he made his famous charge with 4,500 troops against the Union positions across half a mile of broken ground on Cemetery Ridge, only to be repulsed with the loss of 75% of his division. Pickett was a member of Dove Lodge No. 51, Richmond, VA. During the war he was a member of a military lodge in his division, known as Old Guard Lodge No. 211. He was also a member of St. Alban's Chapter and Richmond Commandery No. 2, Knights Templar. His funeral was attended by Masons.

Fig. 46 — **Our Masonic Civil War** and its Masonic soldiers.

13° Pierre G.T. Beauregard (1818-1893)

Confederate General, Civil War. Graduate of West Point, 1838 and served through Mexican War.

Superintendent of West Point at outbreak of Civil War, but resigned to enter Confederate Army. As a Brigadier General, he was in command of the bombardment of Fort Sumter, serving through the Civil War at Bull Run, Shiloh and Corinth.

After the war he was manager of the Louisiana lottery, 1880-88. At the same time he was commissioner of public works in New Orleans.

He authored Principles and Maxims of the Art of War (1863) and A Commentary on the Campaign and Battle of Manassas (1891).

He was a Scottish Rite Mason and a York Rite Knights Templar.

Fig. 47 — **Our Masonic Civil War** and its Masonic Generals.

Thomas J. "Stonewall" Jackson (1824-1863)

Confederate Major General of Civil War who was nicknamed "Stonewall" because of his stand at Bull Run.

Born in Clarksburg, WV. Graduated from U.S. Military Academy in 1846. Served in Mexican War, but resigned from Army in 1852.

Joined Confederate service at the outbreak of the Civil War, and was made Brigadier General in 1861, then Major General the same year.

In 1862 he led the Confederates in the brilliant Shenandoah Valley campaign. Was mortally wounded by accidental fire from his own troops after routing the Federal right wing at Chancellorsville. Died May, 10, 1863.

There is no record as to his Masonic membership, but many details of his life strongly suggest lodge affiliation. His father and other near relatives were all active members and officers of the Clarksburg, WV Lodge. His father is thought to have been Past Master. At the elder Jackson's death, when young Stonewall was only age 2, his family was left in poor circumstances, so the Lodge contributed to their relief by providing a 3room house at Clarksburg. Stonewall thus had Masonic antecedents, and became beneficiary of the Craft at a young age.

When Stonewall was a faculty member at the Virginia Military Institute at Lexington, VA, he wrote his sister, Laura Jackson Arnold, in 1853 and 1854 concerning a Masonic dependent for whom he hoped to secure aid from the lodge at Staunton. When the local lodge could not help, he wrote his sister that he would be in Richmond "this winter and bring her case before the Grand Lodge of the state."

In Simon Wolf's *Presidents I Have Known*, the author tells of seeing Jackson secure food for General Pope's prisoners. Upon their meeting, Pope gave Jackson the sing of distress, which Jackson answered, and saw that he was safely across Union lines.

If he was a genuine Mason, he was probably a member of a traveling military lodge while in the Mexican War.

Fig. 48A — **Our Masonic Civil War** and its Masonic sea captains.

David G. Farragut (1801-1870)

First Admiral of the U.S. Navy. Son of George Farragut, naval and army officer of the American Revolution. David Farragut was a midshipman at 9 years old. He was placed in command of a prize ship when only 12. From 1810-47 he was on routine naval duty, and commanded the ship Saratoga during the Mexican War. He was on duty on the ship that carried Ambassador (and Freemason) Joel Poinsette to Mexico. He was in the convoy of ships that escorted Lafayette back to France in 1825. He was detailed to establish the Mare Island Naval Base in San Francisco Bay.

Farragut was the outstanding naval office of the Civil War, in command of the West Gulf blockading squadron with orders to take New Orleans, which he did in 1862 without bloodshed. To accomplish this remarkable task, he bombarded Fort Jackson, sailed his ships past the fort, as well as Fort St. Philip.

In 1863 he sailed his flagship, *Hartford*, and one other vessel past Port Hudson, thereby controlling the Mississippi between Port Hudson and Vicksburg. In the Gulf, he silenced Fort Morgan, ran a blockade of mines, dispersed the Confederate fleet and captured Forts Morgan and Gaines.

In December of 1864, Congress created the commission of Vice Admiral for him. In 1866 Congress created the commission of Admiral.

David G. Farragut's lodge is not known, but he is thought to have been made a Mason on the island of Malta in 1818, when he was age 17, serving in the Mediterranean under Bainbridge.

Admiral George W. Baird (a Freemason) wrote the following of him: "While Farragut's Masonic connection is beyond doubt, the writer has been unable to identify his lodge. Naval Lodge No. 87 was instituted at Vallejo, opposite the Navy Yard at Mare Island, and there are members of that lodge still living (1920) who greeted the admiral when he visited there. Surgeon General John Mills Brown of the Navy, who was Grand Master of California, as well as Master of Naval Lodge and an active 33°, was intimate with the admiral in California and remembered him as a Mason and a promoter of Masonry. He did not, however, remember the name of his lodge."

Fig. 48B — Battlefield wounded — Bodies of the dead, perhaps 10,000 in all, lay where they fell. Stench of death extended well beyond the littered battlefield.

U.S. News & World Report — 12-04-06

Fig. 48C — Union cavalry before the action: The two armies, expecting a battle elsewhere, removed most of their medical staffs from Gettysburg.

362 Masonic military officers during the American Civil War. In alphabetical order by last name

Robert Anderson (1805-1871). Union Major General in command of Fort Sumter at time of Confederate Attack. Known as "hero of Fort Sumter." 1825 graduate of West Point. Raised (3°) May 27, 1858 in Mercer Lodge No. 50, Trenton, NJ. Received Knight Templar orders in Columbian Commandery No. 2, NYC, Dec. 1862 and Jan. 1863.

Russell A. Alger (1836-1907). Union Major General. Member of Corinthian Lodge No. 241 of Detroit. Raised (3°) Dec. 9, 1895.

James M. Allen (?). General in Civil War. Mason.

William B. Allison (1829-1908). Raised troops for Civil War. Charter member of Mosaic Lodge No. 125, Dubuque, IA. Honorary Senior Grand Warden of Grand Lodge of Iowa.

George T. Anderson (?). General in Confederate Army. Mason.

13° Robert Anderson (1805-1871). Graduate of West Point in 1825. Hero of Fort Sumter. Major General U.S. Army at Fort Sumter at time of Confederate attack. Raised (3°) in Mercer Lodge No. 50, Trenton, NJ, May 27, 1858. Honorary member of Pacific Lodge No. 233 NYC. Senior Warden of Mercer Lodge, 1859. Received Knight Templar orders in Columbian Commandery No. 1 of NYC, Dec. 1862 and Jan. 1863.

33° Thomas McArthur Anderson (1836-1917). Practiced law until 1861, when he volunteered as a private with 6th Ohio Infantry. Later became Union commissioned officer. Twice wounded. Raised (3°) April 24, 1864 in St. John's Lodge No. 11, Washington. Received 32° AASR at Portland, OR, March 31, 1896; and 33°, Oct. 20, 1899.

Robert H. Anderson (?). Brig. Gen. in Confederate Army. Served in 1886-87 as Commander of Palestine Commandery, K.T. No. 7 at Savannah, GA.

P. C. Archer (?). General in Confederate Army. Member of Paris Commandery, K.T. No. 9 of Texas.

Lewis A. Armistead (1817-1863). Confederate Army officer (1861-63). Commissioned Brigadier General in 1862. Member Alexandria Lodge No. 22, Alexandria, VA. Charter member of Union Lodge No. 7, Ft. Riley, KN.

Turner Ashby (1824-1862). Confederate Brigadier General. Member Equality Lodge No. 44, Martinsburg, WV. Buried Masonically.

Smith D. Atkins (1836-1913). Union Brigadier General of 92nd Illinois Volunteers. Mason and Knight Templar at Galena, IL. Member of Excelsior Lodge No. 97, Freeport, IL..

Joseph E. Bailey (?). Union General. Member of Columbia Lodge No. 124, Wisconsin Dells, WI.

Theodorus Bailey (1805-1877). Rear Admiral, Union Navy. At start of Civil War commanded frigate *Colorado* off Pensacola. Second in command of Farragut's squadron at New Orleans. Led attack in gunboat *Cayuga*. Raised (3°) in Washington Lodge No. 21, NYC on Mar. 3, 1829.

George W. Balloch (?). Union General in Civil War. Member of Stansbury Lodge No. 24, Washington, DC.

32° John Hollis Bankhead (1842-1920). Captain in 16th Alabama Confederate Volunteers of Civil War. Grand Master of Grand Lodge of Alabama in 1883-84.

Nathaniel P. Banks (1816-1894). Served through War as Major General of Union. Member of Monitor Lodge, Waltham, MA.

Henry A. Barnum (1833-?). Union Major General. Member of Syracuse Lodge No. 102, Syracuse Chapter No. 70, R.A.M., of NY.

John L. Barstow (1832-1913). Served as Major in Union Army from 1861-64. Brigadier General of State Troops at time of St. Albans raid. Mason.

William B. Bate (1826-1905). Confederate private who advanced to Major General. Wounded three times. Member King Solomon Lodge No. 94.

George L. Beal (?). Union Brigadier General. Member of Oxford Lodge No. 18, Norway, ME.

Bernard B. Bee, Jr. (?). Confederate General. Graduate of West Point. Bee named General T. J. Jackson "Stonewall" in first battle of Bull Run, where Bee was killed. York Rite Knight Templar, Texas.

Hamilton P. Bee (?). Confederate General. Member of Austin Lodge No. 12, Texas.

Thomas Hart Benton (1782-1858). Union General. Known as Old Bullion because of his opposition to paper currency. He also opposed to slavery. Became senator for Missouri (1820-51). Grand Master of Iowa. Was charter member of Missouri Lodge No. 1 at St. Louis until anti-Masonic days of 1831, when he withdrew for political reasons.

Thomas Hart Benton (1816-1879). Union General. Nephew of Missouri general of same name. Raised (3°) 1949 in Iowa City Lodge No. 4. Grand Master of Iowa 1860-62). Saved valuable Masonic library of Confederate General Albert Pike by placing guard of Federal troops around Pike's Little Rock, AR home.

William P. Benton (1828-1867). Union Brigadier General in Civil War. Raised and trained First Company from Wayne Co., Indiana. Member of Webb Lodge No. 24 at Richmond, IN; and King Solomon Chap. No. 4.

Hiram G. Berry (1824-1863). Union Major General in Civil War. At beginning of war, entered as Colonel of 4th Maine Infantry and took part in battles of Bull Run, Yorktown, Williamsburg, Fair Oaks, 2nd Bull Run and Chantilly. Promoted to Major General shortly before he was killed at battle of Chancellorsville on May 2, 1863. Berry was Junior Deacon of Aurora Lodge No. 50, Rockland, Maine.

Robert Bingham (1838-1927). Captain in 44th North Carolina troop's army of Northern Virginia, Confederate States Army (C.S.A.) Surrendered with General Lee. Grand Master of North Carolina.

David B. Birney (1825-1864). Union Major General of Civil War. Entered army as Lieutenant Colonel. In 1861 made Colonel of 23rd Pennsylvania Volunteers, which he raised at his own expense. Initiated in Franklin Lodge No. 134 of Philadelphia, Oct. 31, 1850.

John C. Black (1839-1915). Union Brigadier General in Civil War. Awarded medal of honor for Battle of Prairie Grove, Ark., in which he was severely wounded. Member of Olive Branch Lodge No. 38, Danville, IL. Was Grand Orator of the Grand Lodge of IL. (1894-95).

Solon Borland (?-1864). Confederate Brigadier General. Entered Civil War early and rose in rank quickly. Mason.

Thomas E. Bramlette (1817-1875). Union Colonel. In 1861 raised 3rd Kentucky Infantry. Was past master of Albany Lodge No. 260, Albany, KY. York Rite Knights Templar Mason.

Mason Brayman (1813-?). Union Major General. Joined volunteer army, 1861. Commissioned Major in 29th Illinois regiment. By end of war was Major General. Member of Springfield, IL Lodge No. 4.

33° John Cabell Breckinridge (1821-1875). 14th V.P. of US, Senator, and Confederate Major General. Beginning of War defended South in Senate. When he entered Confederate service, was expelled from Senate on Dec. 4, 1861. Nine months later promoted to Major General. Next two years fought valiantly in many battles. Member of Temple Chapter No. 19, R.A.M., Webb Commandery No. 2, Knights Templar (both of Lexington). Received 33° AASR (SJ) on Mar. 28, 1860. Upon death, was buried with Knight Templar services.

William C. P. Breckinridge (1837-1904). Entered Union as Captain, 1861. Became Colonel of 9th Kentucky cavalry and commanded brigade when it surrendered. Member of Lexington Lodge No. 1, KY.

13° John J. Brooke (1838-1926). Union Major General in Montgomery Co., PA. Enlisted in 4th Pennsylvania Infantry in 1861. Participated in battles at Cold Harbor, Gettysburg, Spottsylvania Courthouse, and Tolopotomy. Promoted to Brigadier General for gallantry. Member of Columbia Chapter No. 21, R.A.M. (Royal Arch Mason).

Albert G. Brown (1813-1880). U.S. Senator from 1854-58. Reelected in 1859 for six years, but resigned in 1861 to join Confederate Army with his colleague in the Senate, Jefferson Davis. Commissioned Brigadier General in Mississippi State Militia. Member of Gallatin Lodge No. 25, Gallatin, MS (later to become Silas Brown Lodge).

Egbert B. Brown (1816-?). Union Brigadier General. Served in Missouri, Arkansas, and Texas. Saved city of St. Louis from southern rebels at start of Civil War. Severely wounded at Battle of Springfield (1863). Member of Toledo Lodge No. 144, Toledo, OH.

John C. Brown (1827-1889). Joined Confederate Army at start of War. Rose to rank of Major General. Member of Pulaski (Tenn.) Lodge No. 101. Served three years as Master. Was Grand Master of Grand Lodge of Tennessee in 1869.

John H. Brown (1820-1895). Moved to Texas in 1840 with uncle. Attended "Secession Convention" of 1861 and served in Confederate Army until 1862, when he was named Adjutant General. Was raised (3°) in Clarksville Lodge No. 17, Clarksville, MO, March 1, 1845. Later became charter member of Victoria Lodge No. 40, Victoria TX.

33° John M. Browne (1831-1894). Graduate Harvard Medical School, 1852. During Civil War saw service in Atlantic Ocean as surgeon on the *U.S.S. Kearsarge* in its 1864 engagement with *Alabama*. Files in Naval Lodge state he also was surgeon in battle between the ironclads, *Merrimac* and *Monitor*. (see ironclad in Fig. 40-41 this sect.). At 21 Browne was initiated in Philesian Lodge No. 40, Winchester, NH, receiving all three degrees June 3, 1852 by special dispensation. In 1866, on returning to California after Civil War, he had affiliation with many lodges, rising to the highest degree in the Supreme Council of the Scottish Rite (SJ).

Simon Bolivar Buckner (1823-1914). Union Inspector General. Promoted to Brigadier General, then Major General. Prisoner of war two months, 1862. Listed as Freemason in Grand Lodge of KY.

George W. Brush (1842-1927). Physician. Served as Captain with Union Volunteers, 1861-65. Received Congressional Medal of Honor. Mason.

33° Asa S. Bushnell (1834-1904). Served as Union Company Commander in 152nd Ohio volunteer infantry. Was made a Mason "at sight" and received the 33° AASR (NJ).

33° Benjamin F. Butler (1818-93). Entered war in 1861 as Union Brigadier General of Militia. Promoted to Major General same year. In North Carolina he issued General Order No. 38, which was to protect Confederate Masonic property at New Bern. For this deed he was honored after the War with the 33° AASR (NJ), March 16, 1864. On the shady side of Butler (nicknamed "spoons") he is pictured as a hyena, shouldering silver spoons he had stolen from homes of wealthy New Orleanians. He was prominent in the impeachment of President Andrew Johnson.

Daniel Butterfield (1831-1901). Union Major General. Entered war as Colonel of 12th New York militia, taking regiment to front in 1861. Commissioned Major General of volunteers, Nov. 1862. Commanded division of 20th Corps at Atlanta. Received U.S. Congressional Medal of Honor for action at Gaines' Mill. Member Metropolitan Lodge No. 273, New York City.

Robert P. Caldwell (1821-1885). During Civil war he was a Major in the 12th Regiment, Tennessee Infantry of the Confederate Army. Member of Trenton Lodge No. 86 and Trenton Chapter No. 31, R.A.M., both of Trenton, TN.

13° Alexander W. Campbell (1828-?). Brigadier General, Confederate Army in Civil War. Raised (3°) in Jackson, TN on June 1858. Royal Arch Mason in same year. Knighted in Jackson Commandery, K.T. on April 3, 1874.

Jacob M. Campbell (?). Union General in Civil War. Member of Cambria Lodge No. 278 at Johnstown, PA. on Oct. 26, 1858. Demitted April 13, 1875 to become charter member of Johnstown Lodge No. 538, serving as first Senior Warden.

John Campbell (?). Union Civil War General, commanding 3rd Brig., 4th Div., Ohio Militia. Member of Unity Lodge No. 12, Ravenna, OH.

Edward R. S. Canby (1819-1873). When Civil War broke out, Colonel Canby was on an expedition against Navajos in Southwest. There he commanded New Mexico forces that repelled a Confederate thrust into that area. Promoted to Brigadier General and called to Washington to assist Secretary of War Stanton. Canby was member of unnamed lodge in eastern United States. Upon death his body was escorted by the Craft to Masonic Temple at Yreka, where he was buried with Masonic honors.

James Cantey (?). Confederate Brigadier General. Member of Kershaw Lodge No. 29, Camden, SC.

James H. Carleton (1814-1873). Major General in U.S. Army during Civil War. Led "California Column" across Yuma and Gila deserts to Mesilla on the Rio Grande. April 1862 was ordered to relieve General Canby as Commander of department of New Mexico. Advanced to Brigadier General in 1865 and Major General in U.S. forces. Raised (3°) in Montezuma Lodge No. 109 in New Mexico, chartered by Grand Lodge of Missouri. He also belonged to San Diego Lodge No. 35, San Diego, CA.

Frank Chamberlain (1826-1910). Brigadier General of U.S. Forces. During Civil War was Union Commissary General. Mason.

Joshua L. Chamberlain (1828-1914). Union Major General. Awarded Congressional Medal of Honor for "daring heroism." Member of United Lodge No. 8, Brunswick, ME.

Augustus L. Chetlain (1824-?). Major General, Union Army. Commanded post at Memphis and Talladega, AL. His lodge is not known, but he was exalted in Washington Chapter No. 43, R.A.M.

Morgan H. Chrisler (?). Union Brigadier General. Member of St. John's Lodge No. 22, New York. Master of lodge in Greenfield Center, NY, 1861.

Morgan H. Chrysler (1826-?). Union Major General. Enlisted as a private in 1861 and was promoted to Major General in 1865. Commanded all the troops in northern Alabama. Member of St. John's Lodge No. 22, Greenfield Center, NY. Served as Master of the Lodge.

Cassius M. Clay (1810-1903). Son of Green Clay. Abolitionist. In 1845 issued an anti-slavery paper called *The True American.* Was nearly lynched because of it. During Civil War was Union Major General of volunteers in 1862. Member of Davies Lodge No. 22, KY.

Patrick R. Cleburne (1828-1864). Confederate Major General. Commanded 2nd brigade in 3rd corps at Shiloh. Member of Lafayette Lodge No. 16, Helena, AR.

James H. Coates (?). Union Brigadier General. Served with 11th Illinois Infantry. Member (1864) of Acacia Lodge No. 67, LaDalle, IL.

33° Howell Cobb (1815-1868). Brigadier General and later Major General in Confederate Army. Was member of Mt. Vernon Lodge No. 22, Athens, GA, serving as Master in 1843. Was acting Grand Junior Warden of the Grand Lodge of Georgia on Nov. 13, 1843. Became active member of Southern Supreme Council AASR on March 31, 1860.

Richard Coke (1829-?). U.S. Senator & Texas Governor. Served in Confederate Army as Captain. Member of Waco Lodge No. 92, Waco, TX.

Henry S. Commager (1825-1867). Union Brigadier General. Member of Northern Light Lodge No. 40, Toledo, OH.

Edwin H. Conger (1843-1907). Served in Civil War. Breveted Major. Mason.

James Conner (1829-1883). Confederate General. Entered war in 1861 as Captain. Served in many campaigns. Past Master of Landmark Lodge No. 76, Charleston, SC. In 1868 served as Grand Master of Grand Lodge.

James A. Connolly (1843-1914). Served from Private to Lieutenant Colonel in Union Army in 123 Illinois Volunteer Regiment. Member of Elwood Commandery No. 6, Knights Templar of Springfield.

William R. Cox (1832-1919). Union Brigadier General. Wounded eleven times. Served as Grand Master of Grand Lodge of North Carolina for four years. Member of William G. Hill Lodge No. 218.

Samuel J. Crawford (1835-1913). Captain in 1861 in 2nd Kansas Cavalry. Colonel of 83rd U.S.C.T. in 1863. Brigadier General of volunteers in 1865 for "meritorious services." Member of Orient Lodge No. 51, Topeka, KN.

Thomas L. Crittenden (?). Union General. Member of Ward Lodge, and Army Lodge during the war.

Marcellus M. Crocker (1830-1865). Union Brigadier General. Suffered from consumption (tuberculosis) during whole of his military duty. Member of Pioneer Lodge No. 22, Des Moines, IA.

Edward E. Cross (1832-1863). Lieutenant Colonel in Mexican Army in 1860. When news of attack on Fort Sumter reached him, he resigned and hastened to Concord, NH, where he recruited a regiment and was commissioned Colonel. Known as "Fighting Fifth," regiment distinguished itself in many battles. Mortally wounded at battle of Gettysburg, July 2, 1863. Member of North Star Lodge No. 8, Lancaster, NH.

John T. Croxton (1837-1874). Union Major General. In 1861 he began raising troops. He participated in battles of Sherman's army. At close of war he was put in command of military district of southwest Georgia. Given a Masonic burial at his death.

13° Charles Cruft (?-1883). Union Major General. Served with distinction in battles fought near Richmond, KY on Aug. 29-30, 1862. Member of Terre Haute, IN Lodge No. 19; Chapter, R.A.M. No. 11; Council R.&S.M. No. 8; and Commandery No. 16, K.T.; Grand Commander of the Grand Comandery, Knights Templar of Indiana, 1873.

Newton M. Curtis (1835-?). Union Major General. Received Masonic degrees in Ogdensburg, NY. Received chapter degrees on St. John's Day, Dec., 1858. Became member of DeMolay Commandery No. 4, Lynchburg, VA.

Samuel R. Curtis (1807-1866). Union Major General. Gained a decisive victory at Pea Ridge, AR against Generals Price and McCulloch. Commanded Fort Leavenworth and defeated General Price's army. Buried as a Knights Templar Mason.

John A. Dahlgren (1809-1870). Union Rear Admiral. During war he secured Potomac River; commanded Southern Atlantic blockade squadron; attacked Charleston; silenced Fort Sumter. Finally, he led a force up St. John's River. With Sherman, captured Savannah. Mason.

John W. Daniel (1842-1910). Fought with Confederate Army. Wounded four times. Became Adjutant General on General Early's staff. Member of Marshall Lodge No. 39, Lynchburg, VA.

Xavier B. DeBray (?). Confederate General. Member of Austin, Texas Lodge No. 12. Served as secretary of the lodge from 1859-61. Became a member of Holland Lodge No. 1, Texas in 1866.

William DeLacy (?). Union General. Member of Independent Royal Arch Lodge No. 2, New York City.

Henry C. Deming (1815-1872). Reluctant to support Union cause. Finally entered army and became a Colonel. Was at the capture of New Orleans. Became acting mayor of that city. Was a member of St. John's Lodge No. 4, Hartford and a Knights Templar.

Wilmot G. Desaussure (1822-1886). Mason when he entered Civil War as Confederate Lieutenant Colonel. April, 1861, commanded artillery on Morris Island during bombardment of Fort Sumter. Brigadier General by end of War. Grand Master of Grand Council, R.&S.M. in 1873-78; Grand Master of Grand Lodge of S.C. in 1875-77; Grand High Priest of Grand Chapter, R.A.M. of S.C. in 1878-77; Grand Master of Oddfellows.

Francis M. Drake (1830-1903). Served in Union as a Private. Moved up grades to Brigadier General. Member of Unionville Lodge No. 119, Unionville, IA, where (in the early 1860s) his name appears as secretary and Junior Warden. March 30, 1866, admitted a member of Jackson Lodge No. 42, Centerville, IA.

William F. Draper (1842-1910). Union Brigadier General. Enlisted in the 25th Mass. in 1861 and served throughout the war. Member of Montgomery Lodge at Milford, MA.

Richard C. Drum (1825-?). Union Brigadier General. Member of Oriental Lodge No. 144, San Francisco, CA.

Arthur C. Ducat (?). Union Brigadier General. Served in 12th Illinois Infantry. Member of Blaney Lodge No. 271, Chicago, IL, 1864.

Daniel Dustin (?). Union Brigadier General of Volunteers. Commanded 105th Illinois. Member of Sycamore Lodge No. 134, Sycamore, IL..

33° Elisha Dyer (1839-1906). Served in Marine Corps during Civil War. Member of St. John's Lodge No. 1 of Providence. Member of Providence Chapter No. 1, Royal Arch Mason, St. John's Commandery (Knights Templar). Member of Aleppo Shrine Temple, and 33° AASR (NJ).

Alonzo Jay Edgerton (1827-1894), Confederate Brigadier General. Made Mason in 1851 in Grenada Lodge No. 31 of Mississippi. Later became a member of Mantorville Lodge No. 11, Mantorville, Minn., then Grand Scribe of Grand Chapter, R.A.M. of Minn.

William H. Egle (1830-1901). In 1859 graduated in medicine from U. of Penn. During Civil War served as Chief Medical Officer of General Birney's division. Was a member of Perseverance Lodge No. 21 of Harrisburg, PA. Received his first two degrees on Oct. 9 and Nov. 9, 1854. Served as Master of the Lodge in 1866.

Stephen B. Elkins (1841-1911). Served as Captain of 77th Missouri regiment during Civil War. Member of Montezuma Lodge No. 109, NM.

I. H. Elliott (?). Union Brigadier General. Commissioned March 13, 1865 in Volunteers. Member of Bureau Lodge No. 112, Princeton, IL.

John Evans (1814-1897). After Civil War broke out, President Lincoln named him territorial governor of Colorado in order to save that territory for the Union. When Evans arrived in Colorado, he found that many of the Freemasons in Denver Lodge No. 5 were outspoken against the Union. So, he and others organized Union Lodge No. 7 in 1863. When he died in 1897, he was buried by that lodge and Colorado Commandery No. 1, Knights Templar. Was raised (3°) in Attica Lodge No. 18, Attica, IN on July 6, 1844; First Master of Marion Lodge No. 35 at Indianapolis. He became a Royal Arch Mason in Indianapolis Chapter No. 5 in 1846.

David G. Farragut (1801-1870). First Admiral of the U.S. Navy. Son of George Farragut, who was naval and army officer of the American Revolution. Farragut Jr. was an outstanding Union naval officer. Was in command of West Gulf blockading squadron with orders to take New Orleans, which he accomplished without bloodshed in 1862. In 1863 he piloted his flagship, *Hartford*, and one other vessel, past Port Hudson, controlling the Mississippi between Port Hudson and Vicksburg. He also captured Forts Morgan and Gaines. December of 1864 he was promoted to Vice Admiral, and in 1866, full Admiral. His Lodge is not known, but believed to have been made a Mason in 1818, at age 17, on the island of Malta. At his funeral on Aug. 14, 1870, he was buried with Masonic honors by the Grand Master of New Hamphire and St. Johns Lodge No. 1 of Portsmouth.

Charles J. Faulkner, Jr. (1847-1929). Confederate Army. Born in Martinsburg, WV. Entered Virginia Military Institute in 1862. Served with cadets at battle of New Market. Later was aide to Confederate Generals Breckinridge and Wise. Was 8th Grand Master of Grand Lodge of West Virginia, serving in 1880. Was member of Equality Lodge No. 136 (VA charter), now No. 44 of West Virginia charter. Received his blue degrees on Dec. 12 & 26, and Jan. 9, 1869. Served as Master (1876-78).

Charles J. Faulkner, Sr. (1806-1884). U.S. Minister to France in period preceding Civil War. As member of Virginia lower house, he introduced bill for gradual abolition of slavery in Virginia. Was Minister to France in 1859. While there, he encouraged Louis Napoleon to sympathize with southern cause, resulting in his "recall" by President Lincoln. When he returned to America, he was arrested and confined in Fort Warren as a disloyal citizen, but released on a prisoner exchange. He was disbarred from citizenship until 1872. Faulkner, Sr. received his degrees in old Equality Lodge No. 136 (VA charter) in 1867.

33° John Quincy Adams Fellows (1825-1897). Louisiana Freemason who headed all York Rite bodies of that state. Was able to keep passions of Civil War outside lodge doors. Both the Blue and Gray met in Louisiana lodges and forgot for the moment that they were sworn enemies. Fellows also facilitated the passage of many Union prisoners out of Confederate prison camps when they gave him the Masonic grand hailing sign of distress. Fellows was both a York Rite and a Scottish Rite Mason.

33° A. L. Fitzgerald (1840-1921). Serving in the Confederate Army, he saw action in the battles of the Wilderness, Petersburg, and the siege of Richmond. Raised (3°) in Rockwell Lodge No. 600, Ruffin, NC. Received chapter and commandery degrees in Petersburg, VA in 1863. After the war he moved west and in 1884 became Grand Master of the Grand

Lodge of Nevada. He received his Scottish Rite degrees in California in 1870, and became 33° Sovereign Grand Inspector General for Nevada.

Charles Fitzsimmons (1835-1905). Entered Union Army 1861 as Captain 3rd New York Cavalry. Wounded 1863. Returned to service in October as Lieutenant Colonel. Wounded again in 1864 at Ashley's Gap. Transferred to western plains. Served as Brigadier General until mustered out in 1866. Member of Yonnondio Lodge No. 163 of Rochester, NY.

Thomas C. Fletcher (1827-1899). In April, 1861 he volunteered in the Union Army. In 1862 he recruited 31st Missouri Infantry and was commissioned Colonel. In 1864 he organized state troops to resist invasion of General Price. Was brevetted Brigadier General by President Lincoln for his successful defense of Pilot Knob under General Ewing. Was a member of Joachim Lodge No. 164, Hillsboro, MO (of which his father was also a member). Was a member of Jefferson City Chapter No. 34, R.A.M., receiving Mark and Past Master degrees on Dec. 29, 1868, and Royal Arch on Jan. 23, 1871. Was knighted in Ivanhoe Commandery No. 8, K.T., St. Louis on May 25, 1871 and served as commander in 1874.

John B. Floyd (1807-1863). Governor of Virginia, 1850-53; Secretary of War, 1857-60; Brigadier General in Confederate Army. In 1861 he was indicted in Washington for giving aid to secession leaders while he was Secretary of War. He demanded an immediate trial. In Jan. 1861, a committee from the House of Representatives exonerated him. He was a member of St. Johns Lodge No. 36, Richmond, VA. He delivered the oration at the cornerstone laying of the Washington monument.

James M. Forsyth (1842-1915). Rear Admiral, Union Navy. In 1858, age 16, he went to sea. Served throughout Civil War in many engagements. Was with Farragut on the Mississippi, Forts Sumter and Moultrie. Was not commissioned until 1868. Retired in 1901 as Rear Admiral. Was made a Mason in Peru and later affiliated with Union Lodge No. 121 in Philadelphia. Member of Shamokin Chapter No. 264 and Shamokin Commandery No. 77, Knights Templar of Shamokin, PA. On Nov. 5, 1909 he addressed Shamokin Lodge No. 255 on "Freemasonry Abroad."

Greenbury L. Fort (1825-1883). Served in Union with 11th Regiment, Illinois Infantry as First Lieutenant, then Lieutenant Colonel. Knighted in York Rite in Peoria Commandery No. 3, Knights Templar, Peoria, IL.

John Gray Foster (1823-1874). Major General in Union Army. As a Lieutenant he was an assistant professor of engineering at West Point (1855-57). In 1861 he rapidly rose in grades; Brigadier General, Lieutenant General, and Major General. His submarine engineering operations in Boston and Portsmouth harbors were extremely successful. In 1869 he published "Submarine Blasting in Boston Harbor." According to *Freemason's Monthly Magazine* (Boston), he was a Freemason.

Wilbur F. Foster (1834-1922). Engineer. One of the organizers of the Masonic Veterans' Association of Civil War. Raised (3°) March 26, 1857. Past Master of Cumberland Lodge No. 8, Nashville, TN. Past High Priest of Cumberland Chapter No. 1, Nashville. Was Grand Master of Grand Lodge of Tenn. and Grand High Priest of Grand Chapter of Tennessee.

Edward B. Fowler (?-1896). Union Brigadier General. Served with 84th infantry (NY) as Lieutenant Colonel. Promoted to Colonel on Dec. 9, 1862; Brigadier General, March 13, 1865. Member Lexington Lodge No. 310, Brooklyn, NY. Received blue degrees Oct. 23, 30, and Nov. 20, 1865.

33° John Frizzell (1829-1894). Served with the Confederate Army. Member of Cumberland Lodge No. 8; Cumberland Chapter No. 1, Royal Arch Mason; and Nashville Commandery No. 1, Knights Templar. Receive 32° at the hand of Albert Pike, and honorary 33° in 1886.

Robert W. Furnas (1824-1905). Union Colonel in 2nd Nebraska cavalry. Member of Capitol Lodge No. 3 at Omaha, and later served as Master of Nemaha Lodge No. 4, Brownville NE. Was Grand Secretary of Grand Lodge Nebraska, 1858-62, and Grand Master, 1865-66.

Hamilton R. Gamble (1798-1864). Civil War Governor of Missouri credited with saving the state for the Union. Member of Franklin Union Lodge No. 7, where he received his first three (blue) degrees.

Franklin F. Gary (1829-1897). Surgeon in Confederate Army. Grand High Priest of the Grand Chapter, R.A.M. of South Carolina, 1880.

John W. Geary (1819-1873). Union Major General. Beginning of war he raised the 28th Pennsylvania Volunteers; 1862 commissioned Brigadier General; 1865 promoted to Major General. Received first three (blue) degrees of Masonry "at sight" on Jan. 4, 1847 in St. John's Lodge No. 219, Pittsburgh, PA. June 11, 1855 became member of Philanthropy Lodge No. 225, Greensburg, PA.

33° John P. S. Gobin (1837-1910). Union Brigadier General. Made a Mason at Sunbury Lodge No. 22 on Jan. 9, 1860, just before entering the war. Received the 33° AASR (NJ) on May 9, 1906.

George H. Gordon (1825-1886). Union Major General. Member of Bunker Hill Army Lodge No. 5 of Massachusetts.

John B. Gordon (1832-1904). Lieutenant General in Confederate Army. Shot eight times. Survived. Was a Masons, but Lodge not known. Thought to be in Atlanta. Visitor twice to Cherokee Lodge No. 66, Rome GA.

William A. Gorman (1814-1876). Union Brigadier General. Member of Federal Lodge No. 1, Washington DC on July 2, 1850.

Adolphus W. Greely (1844-1935). Union Major General. Wounded three times. Member of St. Mark's Lodge of Newburyport, MA. Honorary member of Kane Lodge No. 454, explorer's lodge of NYC.

Thomas Green (1816-1864). Confederate Major General. Member of Austin Lodge No. 12 (Texas).

John Gregg (1828-1864). Confederate General. Last to command famous Texas Brigade in Lee's Army. Killed in action. Member of Fairfield Lodge No. 103, Fairfield, TX. Received blue degrees May, Aug., Oct., 1855. Member of York Rite Palestine Commandery No. 3, Knights Templar.

William Gurney (1821-1879). Union Brigadier General. After war went to Charleston, SC and established a business. Member of Continental Lodge No. 287, New York. Served as its Master.

Henry H. Hadley (1841-1903). Served in Union Army with Ohio volunteer infantry. Promoted from private to Lieutenant Colonel by 1866. Raised (3°) in Progressive Lodge No. 354, Brooklyn, NY.

John A. Halderman (1833-?). Union Major General. Named in official orders for conspicuous gallantry in action. One of the leaders in Kansas to abolish slavery. Received blue degrees in Leavenworth Lodge No. 2, Leavenworth, KN on Oct. 6, 1855, and Feb. 6 and 23, 1856.

Charles B. Hall (1844-1914). Union 2nd Lieutenant in 25th Maine Volunteer Infantry in 1862. Twice cited for gallantry. Served as Master of Hancock Lodge No. 311, Ft. Leavenworth, KN.

Cyrus Hall (?). Union Brigadier General. Served with 14th Illinois Infantry. Member (1864) Jackson Lodge No. 53, Shelbyville, IL..

James F. Hall (1822-1884). Union Brigadier General, 1865. In 1861, assisted state of New York in equipping 28 regiments, then equipped one for himself, which he led as Colonel. Fought at Port Royal, Tybee Island, Ft. Pulaski, GA., Pocotaligo and Olustee, FL. Commanded with Sherman against Savannah and Charleston.

Robert H. Hall (1837-1914). Union Brig. General. Served throughout war. Cited for bravery in battles of Lookout Mountain and Weldon, VA. Mason.

Charles G. Halpine (1829-1868). Union Major with 69th New York Infantry. Member of Holland Lodge No. 8, NYC.

Joseph E. Hamblin (1828-1870). Union Major General. Member 7th New York regiment prior to war. At outbreak of hostilities, participated in Grant's campaign of 1864, then went to Shenandoah Valley to resist Confederate pressure on Washington, DC and Maryland. Severely wounded at Cedar Creek, after which was promoted to Brigadier General and placed in command of a brigade. Participated with the surrender at Appomattox. Mustered out Jan. 1866 as Major General.

Winfield S. Hancock (1824-1886). Union Major General of Volunteers. Stationed in California when war broke out. Requested to be sent to zone of operations. Aided in organization of Army of the Potomac. Received blue degrees by special dispensation in Charity Lodge No. 190 of Norristown, PA, Oct. 31, 1860.

William Hanna (1833-1907). Union Brigadier General. Assisted in raising troops. Was commissioned Captain of 15th Regiment, Illinois Volunteers. Promoted to Major, Lt. Colonel, Colonel, Brigadier General. Raised (3°) in Justice Military Lodge U.D. (Illinois) in 1862. Exalted R.A.M. in Quincy York Rite lodge, Chapter No. 5. Knighted in Delta Commandery No. 48, Knights Templar of Clayton, serving as Commander.

Roger W. Hanson (1827-1663). Union Brigadier General. Mortally wounded at the Battle of Murfreesboro, TN on Jan 2, 1863. Member of Good Samaritan Lodge No. 174, Lexington KY.

John M. Harlan (1833-1911). Union Colonel in 10th Kentucky Infantry. Member of Hiram Lodge No. 4, Frankfort, KY.

William W. Harllee (?). Confederate General. Member of Clinton Lodge No. 60, Marion, SC.

Walter Harriman (1817-1884). Union Brigadier General. Member of St. Peters Lodge No. 31, Bradford, NH.

George P. Harrison (?). Confederate General. Was Deputy Grand Master of Grand Lodge of Alabama.

John E. Hart (1825-1863). Union Lieutenant Commander of a small side-wheel gunboat *Albatross*. In 1857 was made a Mason in St. George's Lodge No. 6, Schnectady, NY.

John F. Hartranft (1830-?). Union Major General. Member of Charity Lodge No. 190 at Norristown, PA.

Joseph R. Hawley (1826-1905). Union Brigadier General (1864). Major General (1865). Referred to as a Mason, but no records.

Isaac I. Hayes (1832-1881). During war (1862) was commissioned Lieutenant Colonel in Union Army. Served as surgeon of volunteers. Initiated in Lodge No. 51, Philadelphia on Feb. 24, 1859. Before the war was an Arctic explorer. After the war (1875) was made honorary member of explorer's lodge, Kane Lodge No. 454.

Harry T. Hays (?-1876). Confederate Brigadier General. Received all three degrees in New Orleans, Louisiana Lodge No. 102, 1860.

33° Natt Head (1828-1883). Union Adjutant General. Received degrees in 1857 in Washington Lodge No. 61, Manchester, NH. Was both a Knights Templar and 33° AASR (NJ).

Adolphus Heiman (?-1863). Confederate Brigadier General. Member of Cumberland Lodge No. 8, Nashville, TN. Knights Templar.

David B. Henderson (1840-1906). Entered Civil War as a private. Was wounded and discharged. Reentered army in 1864 as a Union Colonel. Made a Mason in Mosaic Lodge No. 125 of Dubuque, IA.

Howard A. M. Henderson (1836-1912). Entered Confederate Army as Captain of Company E, 28th Alabama. In 1864 was assistant Adjutant General. First appeared as a Mason in records of Hiram Lodge No. 4.

William P. Hepburn (1833-1916). Union Lieutenant Colonel, 2nd Iowa Cavalry (1861-65). Member of Nodaway Lodge No. 140 at Clarinda, IA.

Paul O. Herbert (1818-1880). Confederate Brigadier General. Member of Iberville Lodge No. 81, Plaquemine, LA.

32° Francis J. Herron (1837-1902). Union Major General. Saw action in Missouri, Arkansas, and Indian Territory. Wounded at Battle of Pea Ridge. Negotiated and received surrender of Confederate forces west of Mississippi. Charter member of Mosaic Lodge No. 125, Dubuque, IA. 32° AASR.

Henry Heth (1825-1899). Confederate Major General in Virginia. Received Masonic burial by Richmond Lodge No. 10, Richmond, VA.

Thomas Hinkle (?). Confederate Colonel under General Sterling Price. Member of Lexington Lodge No. 32. Received blue degrees in 1841. After war was Wagon boss for pioneer firm of Russell, Majors and Waddell, the great freighting firm of the prairies, which started the Pony Express. Its owners and employees were predominantly Freemasons.

Henry C. Hodges (1831-1917). Confederate chief quartermaster of Army at Cumberland. Was on staff of Gen. Rosecrans during Tennessee Campaign. Member of Willamette Lodge No. 2, Portland OR. Received first two blue degrees on Dec. 9, 1853. Received 3° following night.

John William Hofmann (1824-?). Union General. Recruited 23rd Regiment of Pennsylvania Volunteers. Lieutenant Colonel of 56th regiment. As Colonel, gave orders to open fire at Battle of Gettysburg (July 1, 1863). Member of Lodge No. 51, Philadelphia. Received degrees Feb. 24, March 24, and May 26, 1853.

Henry M. Hoyte (1830-1890). In Union Army helped raise 52nd Penn. regiment, entering as Lieutenant Colonel. Mustered out as Brigadier General. Member of Lodge No. 61 of Wilkes-Barre PA, Dec. 17, 1854. Master of lodge, 1862. Member Red Wing Lodge No. 8, La Grange Chapter No. 4, R.A.M. and Red Wing Commandery No. 10, Knights Templar.

Lucius F. Hubbard (1836-1913). In 1861, enlisted as a private in Union Army, 5th Minnesota Infantry. Commissioned Brigadier General in 1864, for "gallant and distinguished services in actions before Nashville." Member of Red Wing Lodge No. 8,

LaGrange Chapter No. 4, R.A.M. and Red Wing Commandery No. 10, K.T., all of Red Wing, MN.

Aaron K. Hughes (1822-1906). From midshipman in 1838 to Lieutenant in U.S. Army before Civil War began. During the Civil War he served in Union Army in South Atlantic and Gulf Squadrons. Promoted to Rear Admiral after war. Member of Union Lodge No. 95, Elmira NY.

Lyman U. Humphrey (1844-1915). Served in Union Army with the 76th Ohio Infantry. Member of Fortitude Lodge no. 107, Independence, KN.

Stephen A. Hurlbut (1815-1882). Union Major General under Grant. Member of Belvidere Lodge No. 60, Belvidere, IL. Grand Orator of the Grand Lodge of Illinois in 1865.

Rufus Ingalls (1820-?). Union Major General. After war was Quartermaster General of the Army. Initiated (1°) July 22, 1852 in Willamette Lodge No. 2, Portland OR.

Robert G. Ingersoll (1833-1899). Union Colonel of the 11th Illinois Cavalry. Received blue degrees in Peoria IL.

John Ireland (1827-1896). Served in Confederate Army, rising to Lieutenant Colonel of Infantry in 1862. Member of Guadalupe Lodge No. 109, Guadalupe, TX.

Alfred Iverson (1798-1873). Confederate Brigadier General, Nov. 1862. Member of Colombian Lodge No. 8, Columbus, GA.

Conrad F. Jackson (1813-1862). Union Brigadier General. Commanded battle of Dranesville, VA. Fought at South Mountain. Killed at Fredericksburg while commanding the 3rd brigade of McCall's division. Member of Lodge No. 45, Pittsburgh, PA.

James S. Jackson (1823-1862). Union Brigadier General. Killed in the Battle of Perryville while commanding division of McCook's corps. Member of Hopkinsville Lodge No. 37, Hopkinsville, KY.

Albert S. Johnston (1803-1862). Confederate General in command of Confederate forces west of Atlantic states and North of Gulf states. Mason.

Daniel W. Jones (1839-1918). Entered Confederate Army in 1861. Became Colonel of 20th Arkansas Infantry, 1862. Member of Mount Horeb Lodge No. 4, Washington AR.

Edward F. Jones (1828-1913). Union Brigadier General. Mason.

Thomas Jefferson Jordan (?). Union Major General. 1856 Master of Perseverance Lodge No. 21, Harrisburg, PA.

Henry M. Judah (1821-1866). Union Brigadier General. Member of North Star Lodge No. 91, Ft. Jones, CA.

M. F. Kanan (?). Union Captain. First commander of first G.A.R. post established April 6, 1866 at Decatur, IL. Member of Macon Lodge No. 8, Decatur, IL.

Benjamin Kavanaugh (1805-1888). Missionary to Indians. Resident of Texas. Served as chaplain and surgeon with Confederate Army. Became Mason in 1840. After war first Grand Master of Grand Lodge of Wisconsin.

James L. Kemper (1823-?). Confederate Brigadier General. Severely wounded and captured at Gettysburg. Mason. His signature is recorded as attending Grand Lodge Virginia in 1867.

John R. Kenly (1822-?). Union Major General. Credited with saving forces of General Banks from capture at Front Royal. Was wounded and taken prisoner, but shortly freed in an exchange of Masonic prisoners. Member of Maryland York Rite Commandery No. 1, Baltimore MD.

John D. Kennedy (1840-1896). Confederate General. Member of Kershaw Lodge No. 29, Camden, SC. After war, Grand Master of Grand Lodge, SC.

Joseph B. Kershaw (1822-1894). Confederate Major General. Commanded division of Lee's army in final campaigns. Member of Kershaw Lodge No. 29 at Camden, SC.

Nathan Kimball (1822-1898). Union Major General. At Antietam his brigade held its ground but lost nearly 600 men. Member of Mt. Pleasant Lodge No. 168, Mt. Pleasant, IN.

Lewis A. Kimberly (1830-1902). Union Commander of a Civil War ship in 1866 and ended his Navy career as a Rear Admiral. From 1861-62 he served on the frigate *Potomac*. Was executive officer of the *Hartford*. Participated in actions at Port Hudson, Grand Gulf, Warrington, and Mobile Bay. Joined Masonry at St. John Lodge, Boston, MA, Mar. 2, 1857.

Horatio C. King (1837-1918). Union Army Captain, 1862. Received Congressional Medal of Honor for "distinguished bravery." Initiated in a Confederate Lodge in 1864 at Winchester, VA.

Joseph F. Knipe (1823-1901). In 1862, Union Brigadier General. Wounded five times. Mustered out of service, Sept. 1865. Member of Perseverance Lodge No. 21, Harrisburg, PA.

32° Noble D. Larner (1830-1903). Served in Union Army in defense of Washington, DC. His Masonic credentials are too numerous to mention. Mason before the war. Received 32° in 1878 by Albert Pike himself.

33° Samuel C. Lawrence (1832-1911). Union Brigadier General of Mass. Militia (1862-64). Wounded at Battle of Bull Run. Initiated in Hiram Lodge Oct. 26, 1854. Received Scottish Rite degrees in 1862; 33° in 1864; served as Grand Commander of the Northern Jurisdiction, 1867-1910.

Henry W. Lawton (?-1899). Joined Union Army as a sergeant of Company E, 9th Indiana volunteers, 1861. Rose to Captain. Member of Summit City Lodge No. 170, Ft. Wayne, IN.

James G. C. Lee (1836-1916). Union Brigadier General. Served in quartermaster department in control of several supply depots in Virginia. Mason.

Mortimer D. Leggett (1831-?). Union Major General. He raised the 78th Ohio Infantry at beginning of war. Captured Jackson, TN and defended Olivia, TN. Wounded twice. Member Amity Lodge No. 5, Zanesville, OH. Member of Cyprus Commandery No. 10, Knights Templar.

Joseph Leidy (1823-1891). Served as contract surgeon in Satterlee General Hospital at Philadelphia during Civil War. Member of Lodge No. 51, Philadelphia, PA, Feb. 24, 1859.

William Lindsay (1835-1909). Union Captain, 1861-65. Member and Past Master of Hickman Lodge No. 131, Clinton, KY.

Joseph Little (1841-1913). Served with Federal troops as a 1st Liuetenant in Union Army from 1862-64. Member of Kane Lodge No. 454, NYC, receiving degrees on Dec. 2, 1879, Jan. 20 and Feb. 3, 1880. Exalted 1891 in Jerusalem Chapter No. 8 Royal Arch Mason and Knights Templar.

32° John A. Logan (1826-1886). Rose from Brigadier General of volunteers in Union Army to Major General in one year. He fought at Fort Henry, Fort Donelson, Corinth, Jackson, Port Gibson, Raymond Champion Hills, and the siege of Vicksburg, after which he was appointed military governor of Vicksburg. Finally he joined Sherman at Savannah in 1864. He held membership in a number of lodges, both Scottish Rite and York Rite. He was a 32° AASR (NJ) Mason, and was elected to receive the 33° on Sept. 15, 1886, but died before it was conferred.

Phineas C. Lounsbury (1841-1925). Served as Corporal in Union Army, 1862. Member of Jerusalem Lodge No. 49, Ridgefield, CT. Knights Templar.

Mansfield Lovell (1822-1884). Commissioned Brigadier General and Major General in Confederate Army. Was in command of New Orleans. After its capture, he joined Beauregard in northern Mississippi. Member of Holland Lodge No. 8, NYC.

Robert Lowry (1830-1910). Served with Confederate forces as private in Company B of 6th Miss. Regiment. Later was promoted to Brigadier General. Was at Shiloh, and all battles in Georgia Campaign. Wounded twice. Raised (3°) in Brandon Lodge No. 29.

Francis R. Lubbock (1815-1905). Lubbock, Texas was named after him. Lieutenant Governor of Texas, 1857. Refused renomination. Joined Confederate staff of Jefferson Davis, 1863. Captured with Davis and confined in Fort Delaware until Dec., 1865. Moved to Galveston 1867. Member of Holland Lodge No. 1, Houston, TX.

Arthur MacArthur, Jr. (1845-1912). Father of Gen. Douglas MacArthur. Mac, Jr. was Lieutenant General in Union Army. During Civil War he received Congressional Medal of Honor for "seizing colors of regiment at critical moment and planting them on captured works on crest of Missionary Ridge, Nov. 25, 1863." Received Masonic degrees in Magnolia Lodge No. 60, Little Rock, AR.

John B. Magruder (1810-1871). Confederate Army officer. After winning Battle of Big Bethel, made Brigadier General and placed in command of forces on peninsula, with headquarters at Yorktown. There he was promoted to Major General, and in 1862 placed in command of Department of Texas. In 1863 he recovered Galveston from the Nationals, and captured the steamer *Harriet Lane*. Remained in Texas until end of War. Before entering Confederate Army, he received Entered Apprentice degree in San Diego Lodge No. 35, San Diego, CA. Was stopped from further advancement for engaging in a duel with George Tibbetts, treasurer of the Lodge.

Garrick Mallery (1831-1894). Practiced law in Philadelphia until Civil War, when on April 15, 1861 he volunteered as a First Lieutenant with the Pennsylvania troops. Promoted to Colonel. Severely wounded twice. Imprisoned at Libby. After war was promoted to Captain. Member of Columbia Lodge No. 91, Philadelphia. Received blue degrees, Sept. 26, Nov. 28, and Dec. 26, 1853. Master of same in 1855. Also member of Columbia York Rite of Philadelphia, Chapter No. 91, Royal Arch Mason.

Charles F. Manderson (1837-1911). Enlisted in Union Army in 1861 as a Private. Rose to Brigadier General by 1865. Saw service in most midwestern battles. Was severely wounded at Lovejoy's Station, GA. His original Masonic membership was in Ohio. Was affiliated with Nebraska Lodge No. 1, Omaha.

32° Mahlon D. Manson (1820-1895). Union Brigadier General. At beginning of War he enlisted as a Private, and was immediately made Colonel of the 10th Indiana Regiment, which he commanded at the Battle of Rich Mountain, WV, July 1861. Appointed Brigadier General the following March. August 1862, was wounded and taken prisoner at Richmond, KY. Exchanged in December. Commanded many other battles, and again wounded. Made a Mason in Ohio, 1844. Charter member of Montgomery Lodge No. 50, Crawfordsville, IN. Master of same, 1845. In 1859 was deputy Grand Master of Grand Lodge of Indiana. Member of Crawfordsville Chapter No. 40, York Rite Royal Arch Mason and past High Priest and Knights Templar. Was also a 32° AASR (NJ).

John Sappington Marmaduke (1833-1887). Served two years in Utah (1858-59) with expedition sent to quell Mormon revolt. While there he joined Rocky Mountain Lodge No. 205, Camp Floyd, Utah Territory. At outbreak of Civil War, he resigned his commission and joined Confederate forces, much to his father's dismay, who was a staunch Unionist. Was commissioned Lieutenant Colonel and given command of 3rd Infantry. After fighting and wounded at Shiloh, was promoted to Brigadier General and transferred to Mississippi. With 4,000 men he made frequent raids west of Mississippi, after which he was promoted to Major General. Affiliated with Anchor Lodge No. 443 of St. Louis, MO.

Humphrey Marshall (1812-1872). Recruited large force of volunteers for Army and was made Brigadier General. Defeated General Cox at Princeton, VA, and won control of Lynchburg and Knoxville Railroad. When in command of Army of Eastern Kentucky (1862), he fought Battle of Middle Creek with General Garfield. Resigned his commission before war end, and served in Confederate Congress. Buried Masonically.

John A. Martin (1839-1889). Union Brigadier General. Took part in the engagements of the Army of the Cumberland, commanding a brigade at Chickamauga. Member of Washington Lodge No. 5, Atchison, KN.

Thomas S. Martin (1847-1919). Saw military service in Confederate Army with battalion of cadets from Virginia Military Institute. Member of Scottsville Lodge No. 4, Scottsville, VA.

William T. Martin (?). Confederate General. His face represents Mississippi on Stone Mountain carving. Member of Harmony Lodge No. 1, Natchez in 1849).

Stanley Matthews (1824-1889). Union Lieutenant Colonel, 23rd Ohio Regiment, 1861. Participated in battles at Rich Mountain, Carnifex Ferry, Dobb's Ferry, Murfreesborough, Chickamauga, and Lookout Mountain. Colonel when he resigned from Army, 1863. Member of Cincinnati Lodge No. 133, Cincinnati, OH. Received blue degrees Jan. 28, March 11, 1847.

Samuel B. Maxey (1825-1895). Confederate Major General. Raised 9th Texas Infantry, of which he was Colonel. Promoted to Brigadier General, 1862, and Major General, 1864. Commanded Indian Territory military district from 1863-65. Member of Paris Lodge No. 27, and Paris Commandery No. 9, Knights Templar, both of Paris, Texas.

John McArthur (1826-1906). Union Major General. Entered Army as Colonel of 12th Illinois Vol. Made Brigadier General, 1862. Major General following Battle of Nashville. Wounded at Shiloh. Fought in Vicksburg. Receive blue degrees in Cleveland Lodge No. 211, Chicago in 1857.

Daniel C. McCallum (1815-1878). Union Major General. In 1862 was made Colonel and appointed director of all military railroads in U.S. Advanced to Brigadier General, then Major General for meritorious service. Member of Valley Lodge No. 109, Rochester, NY.

George B. McClellan (1826-1885). Union Major General of Ohio Volunteers. Placed in command of Department of Ohio, which included Indiana, Illinois, and portions of Virginia and Pennsyl-vania. Influential in keeping Kentucky in the Union by occupying parts of state. Received all three blue degrees of Freemasonry on Dec. 9, 1853, in Willamette Lodge No. 2, Portland, Oregon by special dispensation of Grand Master.

John A. McClernand (1812-1900). Union Major General. Resigned from Congress to raise the "McClernand Brigade" for war, and was Brigadier General of these volunteers. Made Major General in 1862. Battles fought are too numerous for mention. He was a Mason.

Alexander McDowell McCook (1831-1903). Union General. At battle of Bull Run; capture of Nashville, Shiloh and Perryville, KY. Member Lancaster Lodge No. 106, Timber Post Office, Peoria County, IL.

Edwin S. McCook (1837-1873). Union Major General. At outbreak of War, he raised a company for 31st Illinois Regiment and served with same at Fort Henry and Fort Donelson, where he was severely wounded. Fought three more major battles in South under Sherman in march to the sea. Severely wounded three more times. After the war, while presiding over a public meeting as acting Governor of Dakota, he was shot and killed by a man in the audience. Member of Naval Lodge No. 69, NYC.

James B McCreary (1838-1918). Entered Confederate Army in 1862 as Private and ultimately attained rank of Lieutenant Colonel. Member of Richmond Lodge No. 25 and Richmond York Rite Commandery No. 19, Knights Templar, both of Richmond, KY.

Robert McCulloch (1841-1914). Attended Virginia Military Institute, then served in Confederate Army. Was wounded in Battle of Manassas, and at Gettysburg was left lying on field, listed as dead. After recovery he served as Captain under Col. Robert Withers in 18th Virginia Regiment. Col. Withers presented McCulloch's petition to enter Freemasonry to Natural Bridge Lodge No. 64 in Virginia. McCulloch later served as secretary and Master of this lodge. McCulloch also joined York Rite Freemasonry, later serving as Commander then Grand Commander of the Grand Commandery of Missouri. Was a member of the Scottish Rite and a Shriner — both in St. Louis.

William McKinley (1843-1901). From prospective of Civil War, he was destined to become a future President of the U.S.A. Although a Union Army Major, he received his degrees in a southern lodge during the war. He was protecting and managing the army hospital at Winchester, VA, and was struck by the ties which he saw existing between Union surgeons and Confederate prisoners. When he learned the reason for such a brotherly spirit, in spite of war and hatred, he asked to be admitted to the Craft. His petition was presented to Hiram Lodge No. 21 of Winchester. He was initiated (1°), passed (2o) and raised (3°) May 1, 2, & 3, 1865.

Hugh McLeod (1814-1862). Brigadier General, Republic of Texas, 1841. Joined Confederate Army in 1861 and directed the forces against the Union on the Rio Grande. Member of Holland Lodge No. 1, Houston TX.

Solomon Meredith (1810-1875). Union Major General. At first he was a Colonel of the 10th Indiana Regiment, July 1861. Wounded at Gainesville when his regiment lost half its men. Promoted in 1862 to Brigadier General of Volunteers. His company was known as the "Iron Brigade." It forced a crossing of the Rappahannock, April 1863, took part in Battle of Chancellorsville, and opened Battle of Gettysburg, where Meredith was again wounded. Member of Cambridge Lodge No. l05, Cambridge City, IN.

32° Nelson A. Miles (1839-1925). At start of Civil War, he entered military service as First Lieutenant in the 22nd Massachusetts Infantry. At young age of 25 he was commanding an Army Corps of 26,000 men. Promoted to Brigadier General, then Major General of Volunteers by 1864. Was raised (3°) in Southern California Lodge No. 278, Los Angeles. Received Scottish Rite degrees in Albert Pike Consistory, Washington, DC.

Stephen Miller (1816-1881). Union Brigadier General. Enlisted as private, 1861. Advanced to Brigadier General of volunteers, serving with 1st & 7th Minnesota regiments. Member North Star Lodge No. 23, St. Cloud, MN.

Warner Miller (1838-1918). Served in Union Army with New York volunteer cavalry, advancing from Private to Lieutenant. Taken prisoner in Battle of Winchester. Member of Herkimer Lodge No. 423, Herkimer, NY.

Robert Q. Mills (1832-1911). Enlisted in Confederate Army and served throughout the war, attaining rank of Colonel of 12th Texas Infantry. Wounded at both Missionary Ridge and Atlanta. Member of Corsicana Lodge No. 174, Corsicana, TX.

Robert H. Milroy (1816-?). Union Army Captain of the 9th Indiana volunteers. Commissioned Brigadier General in 1862 and Major General in 1863. Affiliated with Prairie Lodge No. 125, Rensselaer, IN, 1863.

John I. Mitchell (1838-1907). Served in Union Army with the 136th Regiment of Penn. Volunteers as Lieutenant and Captain. Member of Ossea Lodge No. 317, Wellsboro, PA.

Jesse H. Moore (1817-1883). Licensed Methodist minister in 1846. Resigned pastorate at Decatur, IL in 1862 to raise the 115th Regiment of Illinois Volunteers, which he commanded at Chickamauga. Union Brigadier General of Volunteers in 1865. Returned to the pulpit in 1866. Member of Macon Lodge No. 8, Decatur, IL.

Albert P. Morehouse (1835-1891). When Civil War broke out he was commissioned First Lieutenant in Kimball's regiment of enrolled Missouri militia. Member of Maryville Lodge No. 165, Owens Chapter No. 96, Royal Arch Mason, and Maryville Commandery No. 40, Knights Templar.

John Hunt Morgan (1826-1864). Confederate Major General noted for daring raids. Destroyed many millions worth of military stores, captured and burned railroad cars of supplies, tore up tracks, burned bridges, forcing the Union to garrison almost every town of importance in Kentucky, Ohio, and Indiana. Finally captured and sent to Federal prison at Columbus, OH, only to escape, Nov. 1863, with six Confederate captains. Finally killed Sept. 4, 1864 while conducting raid near Greenville, TN. Member of Davies Lodge No. 22, Lexington, KY. Buried with Masonic honors.

John Morrill (?). Union Brigadier General. In 1854 became a member of Occidental Lodge No. 40, Ottawa, IL.

Thaddeus P. Mott (?). Before sailing for America, served as officer in Italian Army. During Civil War, fought on side of Union. Member of Holland Lodge No. 8 and Jerusalem Chapter No. 8, Royal Arch Mason, both of NYC.

John K. Murphy (?). Union Brigadier General. Member of Montgomery Lodge No. 19, and Columbia chapter No. 91, R.A.M.

James S. Negley (1826-1901). Union Major General. Served through war, taking part in many major battles, including Stone River and Chickamauga. Member of Lodge No. 45, Pittsburgh, PA.

Walter C. Newberry (1835-1912). Union Brigadier General. Decorated for "gallant service" at Dinwiddie Court House, where he was severely wounded. Member of Sanger Lodge No. 129, Waterville, NY.

Bradford Nichol (1841-1913). Served in Confederate Army as Lieutenant on staff of General Bate. Raised (3°) in Cumberland Lodge No. 8; exalted in Cumberland Chapter No. 1, K.T., all of Nashville. Twenty years after the war he became Grand Master of Grand Council.

33° Harper M. Orahood (1841-1914). Served in Civil War with Colorado Volunteer Cavalry. Member of Chivington Lodge No. 6, and later Black Hawk Lodge No. 11. 33° AASR (SJ). Grand Master of Grand Lodge of Colorado and Grand Commander of Knights Templar of Colorado.

Albert Ordway (?). Confederate Brigadier General. Member of Lafayette Lodge Chapter No. 43, Richmond, VA.

Ebenezer J. Ormsbee (1834-1924). Union Lieutenant and Captain in 1st and 12th Vermont Volunteer Infantry, 1861-63. Member of St. Paul's Lodge No. 25, Brandon, VT.

33° James L. Orr (1822-1873). Opposed to secession and spoke strongly against it. But at Secession Convention, when his state voted to withdraw, he cast his lot with the South. After Convention he organized a rifle regiment, which he led in the field until elected to the Confederate Senate in 1862. Member of Hiram Lodge No. 68, and Burning Bush Chapter No. 7, Royal Arch Mason, both of Anderson, SC. Was Grand Master of South Carolina from 1865-68.

Godlove S. Orth (1817-1882). Member of Indiana state Senate, 1842-48, and President of same in his last year. In 1862, two years into Civil War, when a call for men to defend Indiana from threatened invasion was issued, he organized a company in two hours and was made its Captain. He received his Masonic degrees in 1861-62 in Perry Lodge No. 37, Lafayette, IN.

Thomas W. Osborn (1836-1898). Born in New Jersey. Moved with his parents to New York in 1842. Graduate of Madison University in 1860 and admitted to the bar in 1861. During Civil War served in Union Army with ranks of Lieutenant and Colonel. Mason.

Joshua T. Owens (1821-1887). Union Brigadier General. Entered forces as a private in 1861. After three months was placed in command of the 69th Pennsylvania Regiment. Participated in every battle fought by Army of the Potomac, from Fair Oakes to Cold Harbor. Was promoted Brigadier General of Volunteers for meritorious conduct at Battle of Glendale on Nov. 29, 1862. Mustered out of service in 1864. Was first Master of William B. Schnider Lodge No. 419 Philadelphia.

Eleazar A. Paine (1815-1882). Union Brigadier General of Volunteers. In 1861 entered war as Colonel of 9th Illinois Volunteers. Promoted to Brigadier General in September of same year. In 1862 led brigade at Paducah, KY and Cairo, IL. Same year was under Gen. John Pope in Army of Mississippi; participated in Battle of New Madrid, MO; in command of Galatin, TN; and commanded Western Kentucky District at end of war. Member of Monmouth Lodge No. 37, Monmouth, IL.

George W. Palmer (1835-1887). Union Brigadier General. Served in Quartermaster General's office. Commissioned Captain and Provost Marshal of 31st district of NY. Became military secretary to Gov. Reuben E. Fenton in 1864, and later commissary-general of ordnance of New York State, with commission of Brigadier General. Commissioned Quartermaster General, 1868. Member of Bunting Lodge No. 655, NYC.

Henry E. Palmer (1841-1911). Enlisted in Union Army in 1861 and rose in commission to Captain. Was Chief of Staff on Gen. P. E. Connor's command in the Powder River Indian expedition of 1865. Affiliated with Macoy Lodge No. 22; demitted to Covert Lodge No. 11, Omaha.

John M. Palmer (1817-1900). Union Major General. In 1861 was commissioned Colonel of 14th Illinois Infantry. Two years later (1863) was commanding 14th Army Corp. as Major General. Raised (3°) Sept. 24, 1849 at first meeting of Mt. Nebo Lodge U.D. at Carlinville, and held every office in lodge, except Master. Also served as Grand Orator of the Grand Lodge of Illinois.

Joseph B. Palmer (1825-1890). Confederate Brigadier General. Member of Mt. Moriah Lodge No. 18, Nashville, TN, July, 1847. Served as Master. Exalted in Pythagoras Chapter No. 23, R.A.M. Became high priest. Knighted in Nashville Commandery No. 1 in 1850. Became charter member of Murfreesboro Commandery No. 10, then commander. Nothing is mentioned of his military prowess, but his Masonic credentials made him well equipped to survive the War.

Ely S. Parker (1828-1895). American Indian and Union Brigadier General. Became Grant's secretary (1863). Was present at surrender of General Lee, writing official document of surrender. Raised (3°) in Batavia Lodge No. 88, Batavia, NY, where the Anti-Masonic Movement began in 1827 following the Masonic murder of Capt. William Morgan. His Masonic credentials are too long for this space. Suffice it to say, he belonged to nearly every type of Masonic order in the land.

33° Robert E. Patterson (1877-1950). Union Brigadier General. As a York Rite Mason, he was Past Commander of Kadosh Commandery No. 29, Knights Templar, Philadelphia. As a Scottish Rite Mason, he was a 33° AASR (NJ) and member of the Masonic Veterans Association.

Theodore S. Peck (1843-1918). From Private to Captain. Recipient of Congressional Medal of Honor in Civil War. Was preparing for college when he enlisted in the Union Forces. Served in 1st Vermont Cavalry and 9th Vermont Infantry. Was on staff of Army of Potomac nearly four years. Received Congressional Medal of Honor "for distinguished gallantry in action at Newport Barracks, NC, Feb. 2, 1864." As a Mason, he was Grand Marshal of the Grand Lodge of Vermont for 10 years.

William A. Peffer (1831-1912). Enlisted in the Union Army as a Private in 83rd Illinois Volunteer Infantry, and later became an officer. Received Masonic degrees in Keystone Lodge No. 102, Coffeyville, KN.

Edward A. Perry (1833-?). Confederate Brigadier General. At start of war, Captain Perry became Colonel of a regiment, which he commanded at the Battle of Seven Pines, then other battles around Richmond. Was wounded at Fraser's Farm, and again at second Battle of the Wilderness. Made Brigadier General. In 1861 the Grand Lodge of Florida lists him as Junior Warden of Escambia Lodge No. 15, Pensacola. It also lists him in 1864 as Master of Dawkins Military Lodge, FL.

John S. Phelps (1814-1886). Union Brigadier General of volunteers. In 1862, President Lincoln appointed him military governor of Arkansas. He distinguished himself at the Battle of Pea Ridge, AR. He was recorded in 1857 as a member of United Lodge No. 5, a Scottish Rite lodge in Springfield, MO. On Aug. 15, 1850 he was also affiliated with York Rite Masonry Chapter No. 15, R.A.M, and with its 1867 reorganization following the Civil War. At this latter event he was recommended as High Priest.

John W. Philip (1840-1900). Comodore, U.S. Navy (Union Navy blockade service). While executive officer of Pawnee, was wounded in leg during Stone River Battle. Member of Catskill Lodge No. 468, Catskill, NY.

George E. Pickett (1825-1875). Confederate Major General, famous for charge at Gettysburg. Commissioned Brigadier General (Feb. 1862) in Longstreet's Army of Potomac, which became Army of Northern Virginia. Severely wounded at Battle of Gaines's Mills, June 27, 1862. At Battle of Fredericksburg, his division held center of Lee's line. At Gettysburg, July 3, 1863, with 4,500 men spread across half a mile of broken ground, he made his famous charge against Union positions on Cemetery Ridge, only to be repulsed with loss of three-fourths of his division. Before war Pickett was member of Dove Lodge No. 51, Richmond, VA. During war he was affiliated with two lodges. First, the military Scottish Rite lodge in his division, known as Old Guard Lodge No. 211. Second, a York Rite Lodge — St. Alban's Chapter and Richmond Commandery No. 2, Knights Templar. His funeral was attended by the Masonic Fraternity.

33° Albert Pike (1809-1891). 8th Grand Commander of the Southern Supreme Council of Ancient and Accepted Scottish Rite of Freemasonry (AASR), and Sovereign Pontiff of Universal Freemasonry. When Civil War broke out in 1861, he cast his lot with the Confederacy and was named Indian agent and Brigadier General of the area, which included Indian Territory. In one battle with the Indians against the Union forces, he was accused and convicted of permitting his Indian troops to scalp 400 Union soldiers while they were yet alive. For this he was convicted as a war criminal, but pardoned by 32° President Andrew Johnson. In reaction to Pike's pardon, Congress impeached the President, but fell short one vote for conviction. Pike is buried in the House of the Temple,

Washington, DC. To commemorate Pike's Civil War service, Freemasonry erected his statue in Washington, DC. Pike's rapid rise in Freemasonry is unprecedented to this day. He received his first three degrees of Freemasonry, Aug. 1850. March 20, 1853, he received all the Scottish Rite degrees (4°-32°) from Albert G. Mackey in Charleston, SC. In 1857 he received the 33° in New Orleans. Following year (1858) Pike was elected 8th Grand Commander of the Southern Supreme Council of the Ancient and Accepted Scottish Rite of Freemasonry (AASR). Shortly before his death in 1890, Pike was recognized as Sovereign Pontiff of Universal Freemasonry.

32° Joseph C. Pinckney (1821-1881). Union Brigadier General. Member of Eureka Lodge No. 243, Metropolitan Chapter No. 40, R.A.M., Morton Commandery No. 4, Knights Templar, and 32° AASR (NJ). A member of the Elks Lodge, an appendage founded by Freemasonry.

Alfred Pleasonton (1824-1897). Entered Union Army as Major of 2nd Cavalry. At end of Virginia peninsular campaign became Brigadier General of Volunteers. Fought at Boonesborough, Stone Mountain, Antietam, Fredericksburg, and Chancellorsville. Breveted Lt. Colonel for action at Antietam. Major General of Volunteers in June 1863. Commander-inChief of Cavalry in Battle of Gettysburg. Transferred to Missouri in 1864 and drove forces of General Sterling Price out of State. Member of Franklin Lodge No. 134, Philadelphia on Jan. 31, 1853.

Preston B. Plumb (1837-1891). Entered Union Army in 1862 as Lt. Colonel. Received Masonic degrees at Emporia, Kansas Lodge No. 12, June 12, 1859. Member of Emporia Commandery No. 8, Knights Templar.

William D. Porter (1809-1864). Commodore, U.S. Navy. At start of Civil War was on the sloop, *St. Mary's*, in the Pacific, after which he went east to command the Union ship *Essex*. He fought with the *Essex* at Fort Henry and Fort Donelson, then ran her through the batteries on the Mississippi to join fleet at Vicksburg, bombarding Vicksburg, Natchez, and Port Hudson. Promoted to Commodore on July 16, 1862. Member of St. John Lodge No. 1, Washington, DC. Raised (3°) on May 11, 1846.

Parke Postles (1840-1908). Awarded Congressional Medal of Honor in Civil War for gallantry at Battle of Gettysburg. Entered Union Army in 1861 as a private in Company A of First Delaware Regt. of Volunteers. For his gallantry at Battle of Antietam he was promoted to Captain. In Feb. 1863 was appointed to staff of Gen. William Hughes, participating in battles of Fredericksburg, Chancellorsville, and Gettysburg. Was raised (3°) in Eureka Lodge No. 23, Delaware.

Samuel Woodson Price (1828-1918). Union Brigadier General. Was first a Colonel of 21st Kentucky Volunteers. Participated in battles of Stone River, Resaca, and Kennesaw Mountain, where he was seriously wounded above the heart. Promoted to Brigadier General of Volunteers on March 13, 1865. Served as Military Commandant of Lexington, KY in 1865. Member of Good Samaritan Lodge No. 174 of Lexington, 1850-52. Member of Lexington Lodge No. 1, Lexington KY, 1867-74.

William A. Quarles (1820-?). Brigadier General in Confederate Army. Member of Clarksville Lodge No. 89, Clarksville Chapter No. 3, R.A.M., and Clarksville Commandery No. 8, K.T., Clarksville, TN.

Matthew S. Quay (1833-1904). Served in Union Army with Pennsylvania Volunteers as Major and Lieutenant Colonel in commissary and transportation departments. Member of St. James Lodge No. 457, Beaver, PA.

Samuel J. Randall (1828-1890). Union officer. Served in 1861 with First Troop of Philadelphia. Promoted to Captain in 1863. Raised (3°) in Montgomery Lodge No. 19, Philadelphia, PA, Dec. 1, 1864.

Matthew W. Ransom (1826-1904). Entered Confederate Army as a private in 1861. Served throughout war, attaining commission of Major General. Received first two blue degrees in Johnson-Caswell Lodge No. 10, Warrenton, NC, 1850. Lodge ceased operations (1858). but resuscitated in 1902. Was raised to 3° two years before he died.

Thomas E. G. Ransom (1834-1864). Union Major General. Entered service as Lieutenant Colonel of 11th Illinois Infantry. Wounded Aug. 1861 while leading charge at Charleston, MO. Participated in assault on Fort Henry, then led regiment in assault on Fort Donelson, where he was severely wounded. Promoted to Colonel for bravery. At Shiloh was again wounded. Promoted to Brigadier General in 1863. Commanded 17th corps at Atlanta, and was breveted Major General in 1864. Was in Battle of Vicksburg. In his final Battle of Sabine Cross-Roads he received another wound from which he never recovered. Member of St. John's Lodge No. 13, Peru, IL. Knighted in Ottawa Commandery No. 10 Ottawa, IL on July 23, 1864 in Ottawa Commandery No. 10, Ottawa, IL.

John A. Rawlins (1831-1869). Union Major General. It was after listening to a speech by Rawlins that Ulysses S. Grant offered his services to the country. When Grant was given command of a brigade (Aug. 7, 1861), he offered post of aide-de-camp to Rawlins. From then until end of War, Rawlins was constantly at Grant's side. Rawlins became a top-ranking military expert, and closest confidant of Grant. Member of Miners Lodge No. 273, Galena, IL. Grant himself was not a Mason, but surrounded himself with Masons, who became his closest associates and advisors.

33° John Meredith Read, Jr. (1837-1896). Both his father and grandfather were Freemasons. His grandfather, George Read, was a signer of the Declaration of Independence and the Constitution. His father (of the same name) was Chief Justice of the Supreme Court of Pennsylvania. Read, Jr. graduated from Brown U., Albany Law School, and studied international law in Europe. From 1860-66 Read, Jr. was Union Adjutant General of the State of New York. He had great ability in organizing, equipping and forwarding troops for the Civil War. Member of St. John's Lodge No. 1, Providence, RI. Received Blue degrees on May 5, 12, and June 21, 1858. After the War he received the 33° AASR in Greece, 1878.

Hiram R. Revels (1827-1901). Ordained minister of AME (African Methodist Episcopal) Church at Baltimore, MD. At outbreak of Civil War, assisted the Union Army in organization of first two Negro regiments in Maryland. Served in Civil War as chaplain of a Negro regiment. After War (1866) settled in Natchez, MS. He was a Prince Hall Freemason, serving as Grand Chaplain of the Prince Hall Grand Lodge of Ohio.

Joseph Warren Revere (1812-1880). Grandson of Paul Revere and professional soldier. U.S. Navy Midshipman, April 1828. Commissioned Lieutenant, 1841. Resigned from American military service in 1850 to enter Mexican Army. For saving lives of several Spaniards, was knighted by Queen Isabella of Spain. Fought many battles from Texas to California, until Civil War began. Moved east to join Union Army. In 1861 was Colonel of 7th regiment of New Jersey Volunteers. Promoted Brigadier General of U.S. Volunteers, 1862. Led brigade at Fredericksburg, after which he was reprimanded for withdrawal without orders. Tried by courtmartial (May 1863) and dismissed from service. He earnestly defended his conduct, appealing to Pres. Lincoln, who revoked his sentence and accepted his resignation from the service. Member of St. John's Lodge, Boston.

George D. Reynolds (1841-1921). As a private, served in Civil War with 2nd Illinois Light Artillery and rose in commission to Lieutenant Colonel. Original Lodge not known, but affiliated with Potosi Lodge No. 131 and Tuscan Lodge no. 360 of St. Louis, MO.

William Reynolds (1815-1879). Rear Admiral, U.S. Navy. Began naval career as midshipman, 1831; Lieutenant, 1841; retired 1851. During Civil War he returned to active duty in the Confederacy. Was made Commander in 1862 in charge of naval forces at Port Royal, SC. Became Captain in 1866; Commodore in 1870. In 1873 served as Chief of Bureau, acting Secretary of the Navy, and promoted to Rear Admiral. Retired in 1877 due to poor health. Was a member of Lodge No. 325, Gibraltar. Was buried Nov. 8, 1879 by Lodge No. 43, Lancaster, PA.

Benjamin F. Rice (1828-1905). Moved from Kentucky to Minnesota in 1860. Served in Civil War as Captain in Union Army. Moved to Little Rock, AR in 1864. Practiced Law. Active in organizing the Republican Party. Upon readmission of Arkansas to representation in Washington, DC, he was elected to U.S. Senate. After term in the Senate, he returned to law practice in Arkansas. Member of Hyperian Lodge No. 48, Long View, AR.

Robert M. Richardson (?). Union General. Member of Central City Lodge No. 305, Syracuse, NY.

33° Charles N. Rix (1843-1927). Served until 1867 in Union Army as paymaster officer. Received Masonic degrees in 1866 at Dowagiac Lodge No. 10, Dowagiac, MI. Became member and Past Master of Hot Springs Lodge No. 62, Arkansas. Served as Grand High Priest, Grand Master of the Grand Council, and Grand Commander of Arkansas.

John S. Roane (1817-1867). Brigadier General in the provisional Confederate Army, commanding district of Little Rock. From 1855-65 was on the board of visitors from the Grand Lodge of Arkansas to St. Johns Masonic College.

Oran M. Roberts (1815-1898). Confederate Army Colonel from 1862-64. Raised (3°) in McFarland Lodge No. 3, San Augustine, TX on Feb. 4, 1846. Demitted to Clinton Lodge No. 23, Henderson, TX; then back to McFarland Lodge; finally to St. John Lodge No. 53, Tyler, TX.

Edward D. Robie (1831-1911). Rear Admiral, U.S. Navy. His career in Navy began in 1852 as assistant engineer. Circumnavigated the globe in the *U.S.S. Mississippi* in Perry's Japan expedition of 1852-55. On May 29, 1906 Congress commissioned him Rear Admiral for his Civil War service. Was a member of Binghamton Lodge No. 177, Binghamton, NY.

Charles Robinson (1818-1894). June, 1854, went to Kansas as agent of New England emigrants' aid society. Settled in Lawrence, became the leader of the Free State Party, and commander-in-chief of the Kansas volunteers. Member of Topeka convention that adopted a free-state constitution in 1855. Elected governor of free state of Kansas in 1856, resulting in his indictment for treason and usurpation of office, but acquitted by jury. Was again elected by the Free-State Party in 1858, and again in 1859. Organized most of Kansas regiments for Civil War. Member of Lawrence Lodge No. 6. Raised (3°) July 21, 1859.

John C. Robinson (1817-1897). Major General, Union Army. Beginning Civil War he was in command of Fort McHenry, Baltimore. Commissioned Brigadier General of Volunteers in 1862 and commanded a brigade at Newport News. Transferred to Army of Potomac, took part in the Seven Days' battles before Richmond, and commanded division at Fredericksburg, Chancellorsville, and Gettysburg. Was at Mine Run, Wilderness, and Spotsylvania Court House. Wounded in latter battle, losing his left leg. Breveted Major General, U.S. Army, March, 1865. Member of Binghamton Lodge No. 177, Binghamton, NY. First Master of Rocky Mountain Lodge No. 205, Camp Floyd, Utah Territory. Knighted on Feb. 4, 1851 in Monroe Commandery No. 12, Rochester, NY. Recorded as visitor to Otseningo Lodge No. 435, Binghamton, NY, Jan. 5, 1860.

Francis A. Roe (1823-1901). Graduate of U.S. Naval Academy in 1847. Executive officer of the *Pensacola* in 1861 when it passed down the Potomac through nine miles of Confederate batteries. Was in Farragut's first fleet in many Civil War naval battles, 1862-63. He suppressed two insurrections on the Great Lakes during the Civil War. Commanded the *U.S.S. Saxcacus* on May 5, 1864, in action against the rebel ram, *Albemarle*, off the North Carolina coast, defeating it. Retired as Rear Admiral, U.S. Navy. Member of Union Lodge No. 95, Elmira, NY.

Francis A. Roe (1823-1901). Rear Admiral, Union Navy. Suppressed two insurrections on Great Lakes. Executive officer of *Pensacola* (1861) when it sailed down the Potomac through nine miles of Confederate batteries. In Farragut's first fleet, 1862-63. Commanded *U.S.S. Saxcacus* in action with rebel ram, *Albemarle*, defeating it on May 5, 1864 off coast of North Carolina. Member of Union Lodge No. 95, Elmira, NY.

Horatio Rogers (1836-1904). Union Brigadier General. Mason.

33° Charles Roome (1812-1890). Union Brigadier General. Raised and commanded the 37th New York Regiment in Civil War. Made a Mason in Kane Lodge No. 454, NYC in Jan, 1866, and beginning in 1868 served as Master of the Lodge, which was his first of four terms. That same year he also joined York Rite Freemasonry. Was Exalted in Jerusalem Chapter No. 8, R.A.M., and subsequently knighted in Coeur De Lion Commandery No. 23, K.T., serving as Commander for three years. Received 32° AASR (NJ) in 1866, and 33° in 1872.

Edmund G. Ross (1826-1907). Served in Union Army from private to Major. U.S. Senator from Kansas, 1866-71. To protect his Masonic brother in the impeachment of President Johnson he voted "not guilty," although he knew it meant political suicide. Member of Topeka Lodge No. 17, Topeka, KN.

Lawrence S. Ross (1838-1898). Commissioned Brigadier General in Confederate Army on Dec. 21, 1863. Led a Brigade in Wheeler's Cavalry Corps of the Army of Tennessee. Member of Waco Lodge No. 92, Waco, Texas. Received all three blue degrees, March 23, May 11 & June 6, 1861.

Leonard F. Ross (1823-?). Union Brigadier General of Volunteers. Began as Colonel of 17th Illinois Regiment, which he raised and commended in Missouri and Kentucky. Commissioned Brigadier General in April, 1862. Later commanded a division at Bolivar, TN. Member of Lewistown Lodge No. 104, Lewistown, IL.

Lovell H. Rousseau (1818-1869). Union Major General. In 1861 commissioned Colonel of 5th Kentucky Volunteers. Oct. of same year commissioned Brigadier General of Volunteers. Took part in Battle of Shiloh, Stone River, Tullahoma Campaign, and Battle of Chickamauga. Made raids into Alabama, destroying railway lines. Was in command of middle Tennessee district. His Lodge not known, but referred to as a "brother" on one occasion when he accompanied Andrew Johnson. Was present at dedication of Masonic Temple in Boston, June 24, 1867. Was buried Masonically by Past Grand Master Samual A. Todd of Louisiana.

Stephen C. Rowan (1808-1890). Union Vice Admiral, U. S. Navy. Commanded *Pawnee* at Acquia Creek in first naval engagement of Civil War by attacking Confederate batteries. Destroyed Ft. Ocracoke. Captured forts at Roanoke Island, New Berne, and Beaufort, NC. Commanded *New Ironside*, 1862. Promoted to Rear Admiral, 1866; Vice Admiral, 1870. Initiated (1°) on May 4, 1865 in Montgomery Lodge No. 19, Philadelphia.

Thomas A. Rowley (1808-?). Union Brigadier General. At beginning of Civil War was Captain in 13th Pennsylvania Volunteers. Promoted Colonel of 102nd Volunteers. Brigadier General at Fredericksburg, VA. Received blue degrees on April 20, June 13, and Aug, 29, 1845.

13° William R. Rowley (1824-1886). Union Brigadier General. Entered war as 1st Lieutenant in 45th Illinois Regiment. After capture of Ft. Donelson, was promoted Captain, then appointed aide-de-camp to General Grant. Rode into the thickest battle at Shiloh with orders for Gen. Lew Wallace to bring his troops to the field. For this he was promoted to Major. On March 13, 1865 was promoted to Brigadier General. Raised (3°) May 15, 1858 in Miners Lodge No. 273, Galena, IL; exalted in Jo Daviess Chapter No. 51, Galena, June 11, 1859; greeted in Ely S. Parker Council, Galena, July 9, 1873; knighted (13o) York Rite in Galena Commandery No. 40, Sept. 29, 1871.

Daniel Ruggles (1810-?). Confederate Major General. Graduate of U.S. Military Academy in 1833. Fought frontier battles until he entered the Mexican War. Resigned to join the Confederate Army. Commissioned Brigadier General. Served at New Orleans. Led a division at Shiloh and Baton Rouge. Promoted to Major General (1863) in command of Department of Mississippi. Repelled raids on Northern and Southern borders of Mississippi. Member of Fredericksburg Lodge No. 4, Fredericksburg, VA.

Jeremiah M. Rusk (1830-1893). Union Major in 25th Wisconsin Regiment, 1862. Served under Gen. Sherman from siege of Vicksburg til close of war. For meritorious service at Battle of Salkehatchie (1865), promoted Brigadier General of Volunteers. Member Frontier Lodge No. 45, La Crosse, WI, 1855. Member of Scottish Rite, York Rite & Shrine.

Ceran St. Vrain (1797-1870). When Civil War broke out, he organized the First New Mexico Cavalry and became its Colonel, with Kit Carson as Lieutenant Colonel. Following war he moved to Mora near Ft. Union, which was then principal military base in Southwest. This location was more convenient for him to conduct his business of furnishing supplies to Union troops. His upright dealing, fairness and courteous treatment of all with whom he came in contact, won him a host of friends. Jan. 25, 1855 was raised (3°) in Montezuma Lodge No. 109 (now No.1) of Missouri.

George A. H. Sala (1828-1895). During Civil War he was American correspondent of the *London Daily Telegraph*. He wrote several books, two of which were *America in the Midst of War* and *America Revisited*. He was a member of Drury Land Lodge No. 2127, London.

William J. Samford (1844-1901). In 1862 he enlisted as a Private in the Confederate Army. By close of war he had advanced to Captain in command of a company. Member of Auburn Lodge No. 76, Auburn, AL.

Rufus Saxton (1824-1908). General in Union Army. Graduate of U.S. Military Academy in 1849. Advanced to Brigadier General of Volunteers in 1862. Awarded Congressional Medal of Honor for distinguished gallantry in defense of Harper's Ferry, VA (May 1862). Breveted Major General of Volunteers, 1865. Member of Washington York Rite Masonry, Chapter No. 2, (R.A.M.) of Washington, DC. Member of St. John's Lodge No. 11, Scottish Rite Masonry, Washington, DC.

Joseph D. Sayers (1841-1929). Moved to Bastrop, TX in 1851. Educated in Bastrop Military Institute. Served as an officer in the Confederate Army from 1861-65. Member of Gamble Lodge No. 244, Bastrop. Grand Master of Grand Lodge of Texas.

William R. Shafter (1835-1906). Union Brigadier General. Won Congressional Medal of Honor for action at Battle of Fair Oaks. Commissioned as 1st Lieut. of 7th Michigan Infantry. Mustered out as Brigadier General, 1865. Member of Masonic Veterans Association of Illinois.

Oliver L. Shepherd (1815-1894). Union Brigadier General. At start of Civil War commanded battalion of 3rd Infantry in defense of Washington, DC. Served in Tennessee and Mississippi campaigns. Commissioned Colonel for siege of Corinth, 1862; Brigadier General for service at Stone River, 1865. Retired 1870. Received blue degrees on July 22, 26; Aug, 19, 1850 in Clinton Lodge No. 140, Waterford, NY. Note on Lodge return reads: "Major Shepherd did not join the lodge, but for protection Grand Lodge gave him Grand Lodge Certificate before he traveled to the South."

33° Buren R. Sherman (1836-1904). Entered Union Army in 1861 as 2nd Lieutenant in Company E, 14th Iowa Volunteer Infantry. Was severely wounded at Shiloh, April 6, 1862; three weeks later promoted to Captain and because of wounds resigned same day. Member of Vinton Lodge No. 62, Vinton, IA. Coronated 33° AASR (SJ) in 1883.

James Shields (1806-1879). Breveted Major General for gallantry at Cerro Cordo in Mexican War. At outbreak of Civil War was commissioned Brigadier General, and fought in the Shenandoah Valley campaign. Resigned his commission in 1863 and moved to Carrollton, MO. His Masonic credentials are too lengthy to mention them all. Was raised (3°) Jan. 4, 1841 in Springfield Lodge No. 4, serving as Junior Warden same year. Exalted in Springfield Chapter No. 1, Royal Arch Masonry (R.A.M.), 1841. When he moved to Washington, DC as Land Commissioner, he became charter Master of National Lodge No. 12, Oct. 27, 1846.

George L. Shoup (1836-1904). He engaged in mining and mercantile pursuits until the Civil War. As a Union Lieutenant, he did scouting duty on the Canadian, Pecos, and Red Rivers until the end of the War. He was raised (3°) July 13, 1864 in Denver Lodge No. 5, Denver, CO. Member of several other lodges. Served as Grand Master of Grand Lodge of Idaho. Became member of Almas Shrine, Temple, Washington, DC.

Horatio G. Sickel (1817-1890). Union Major General. Entered Federal Service, June 1861, as Colonel of 3rd Regiment of Pennsylvania Reserves. Commanded brigade in Kanawha Valley expedition of 1864. Participated in principal battles of Army of the Potomac, losing his left elbow joint. Commissioned Brigadier General, Oct. 1864; Major General, March 1865. Member and Past Master of St. John's Lodge No. 115, Philadelphia. During war was member of Lodge of Potomac, U.D., of the 3rd Regiment.

Michael P. Small (1831-1892). Union Brigadier General. Served as Chief Commissary of 13th Army Corps. Was Supervising Commissary officer of Illinois and Indiana, 1863-64. Chief Commissary of department of Virginia and N. Carolina at Fort Monroe. Promoted to Colonel in 1865; Brigadier General same year. Member of York Lodge No. 266, York, PA.

Robert Smalls (1839-1915). Negro Naval Captain in Union. Appointed pilot in U.S. Navy and served in that capacity on the *Keokuk* in the attack on Fort Sumter. Promoted in 1863 to Captain for gallant and meritorious conduct. Placed in command of *Planter*, and served until that vessel was decommissioned in 1866. Prince Hall Freemason.

Charles E. Smith (1842-1908). Engaged in raising and organizing Union regiments in Civil War. Made a Mason "at sight" by Judge Michael Arnold, Grand Master of the Grand Lodge of Pennsylvania.

Green Clay Smith (1826-1895). Major General of Union volunteers. Commissioned Colonel of 4th Regt., Kentucky Volunteer Cavalry, 1862; July of same year made Brigadier General of volunteers; March 13, 1865, commissioned Major General of Volunteers. Member of Richmond Lodge No. 25, Richmond, KY; Grand Orator of Grand Lodge of Kentucky.

Gustavus W. Smith (1822-1896). Confederate Major General. Entered Confederate service, Sept. 1861, as Major General. Succeeded Gen. Joseph E. Johnston in Temporary command of Army of Northern Virginia and subsequently Richmond, May 1862. In charge of forces of Georgia, 1864-65. Taken prisoner at Macon, April 20, 1865. Member of Keystone Lodge No. 235, NYC.

32° John Corson Smith (1832-1910). Union Brigadier General. Enlisted as a private in the 74th Illinois Volunteers in 1862. Same year he raised Company One of the 96th Illinois Infantry and was made Major on Sept. 6. Breveted Brigadier General of volunteers "for meritorious services," June 20, 1865. Participated in many more battles, the last in which he was severely wounded. He Masonic credentials are too lengthy to mention. But condensed they read: member of Miners' Lodge No. 273 of Galena, IL; raised (3°) May 21, 1859; Master, 1870-74; Grand Master of Illinois Grand Lodge 1887-88. Grand Master of the Oddfellows. York Rite Royal Arch Mason. Received 32° AASR (NJ) May 28, 1873 at Freeport.

John Eugene Smith (1816-1897). Major General in both the volunteers and Union Army. Entered service April 15,1861. Military credentials and his battle activity are too numerous to mention here. In short, he fought at Fort Henry, Fort Donelson, Shiloh, Corinth, Vicksburg, Missionary Ridge, Atlanta, and Carolina campaigns. His Lodge memberships and affiliations are as numerous as his battles. Suffice it to say that he entered Freemasonry on Dec. 27, 1838 and remained an active member his whole life, serving as Master in the Scottish Rite, exalted in the York Rite, and member of the Masonic Veteran Association.

Joseph B. Smith (?-1862). Union naval officer. Was killed on board Union ship *Congress* when it was attacked by the *Merrimac* on March 8, 1862. His father by same name, who fought in Revolutionary War, when informed that the *Congress* had surrendered, said, "Then Joe is dead." Smith the younger was raised (3°) Jan. 24, 1852 in National Lodge No. 12. Knighted in Washington DC Commandery No. 1, Knights Templar of York Rite Masonry on Mar. 5, 1853.

Robert W. Smith (?). Union Brigadier General. Past Master of Oriental Lodge No. 33, Chicago. Member of Illinois Masonic Veterans Association. Delegate to the 1860 convention that nominated Lincoln for presidency.

Thomas A. Smyth (1832-1865). Union Brigadier General. Beginning of Civil War, raised a company of fighting men, called Delaware Regiment. Earned reputation for bravery in following battles: Antietam, Fredericksburg, Chancellorsville, Gettysburg, Bristow Station, Warrenton, Centreville, Culpepper, Wilderness, Spottsylvania, Petersburg, and Hatcher's Run. Last Union General to be killed in war. Died two days after felled by sniper's bullet — same day of Lee's surrender. Freemason for only 28 days. Received degrees in Washington Lodge No. 1, Wilmington, DE, on March 6, 1865, by special dispensation of Grand Master A.V. Lesley. Masonic funeral held April 17, 1865, Brandywine Cemetery, Wilmington.

Oliver L. Spaulding (1833-1922). Union Brigadier General. Entered war in 1862 as Captain of Company A, 23rd Michigan Infantry. Promoted to Brigadier General of Volunteers, June 25, 1865. Initiated (1°) July 15, 1861 in St. Johns Lodge No. 105, St. Johns, MI., and raised (3°) Aug. 2, 1861. Elected Senior Deacon same year. His Masonic activity after the war is too numerous to mention here. Suffice it to say, he was a member of both the Scottish Rite and York Rite.

Edwin M. Stanton (1814-1869). Secretary of War, 1862-68, guiding war department through Civil War. Was "mastermind" behind winning war, retiring General McClellan, and placing General Grant as commander in chief of the three armies. After Lincoln's death, Stanton (remaining Secretary of War) opposed Pres. Johnson, conspiring with congressional groups against him. Johnson suspended Stanton Aug. 1867. But the U.S. Senate restored him in Jan. 1868. On Feb. 21 Johnson once again dismissed Stanton, but Stanton refused to leave office. Again, the Senate supported Stanton. This last action by Pres. Johnson led in part to impeachment charges against him. When impeachment failed by one vote, Johnson stayed in power and Stanton resigned his post. Stanton was a member of Steubenville Lodge No. 45, Steubenville, OH. When he moved to Pittsburgh, PA. he became charter member of Washington Lodge No. 253 of Pittsburgh, March 25, 1851.

James B. Steedman (1818-1883). Union Major General. When Civil War began he was Colonel of 4th Ohio Regiment. Promoted to Brigadier General, July 1862. While stationed at Perryville he commanded 1st division of reserve corps of Cumberland Army and reinforced General H. Thomas at Battle of Chickmauga. Promoted to Major General in April 1864. Relieved garrison at Dalton, and defeated General Wheeler's cavalry, June 1864. Resigned in July, 1866. Received blue degrees in Northern Light Lodge No. 40 (Scottish Rite), Waynesfield, OH in summer of 1851. Was also a Knights Templar Royal Arch Mason (York Rite).

Atherton H. Stevens, Jr. (?). Union Major who, during the Civil War, gave protection to the Masonic Hall at Richmond, VA. He was a member of Putnam Lodge, East Cambridge, MA.

Walter H. Stevens (1827-1867). Confederate Brigadier General and Chief engineer of Lee's Army. May 1861, he accompanied General Beauregard to Virginia as chief engineer. Remained chief engineer of Northern Virginia Army until 1862, when placed in charge of fortifications at Richmond. Became chief engineer of Lee's army, and continued in that position until close of war. Member of Richmond Lodge No. 10, Richmond, VA. Receive Masonic burial by same lodge.

Carter L. Stevenson (?). Confederate Major General. Was first Junior Warden of Rocky Mountain Lodge No. 205, Camp Floyd, UT military lodge.

John M. Stone (1830-1900. Served in Confederate Army from Captain to Colonel of the 2nd Mississippi Volunteers. Member of Iuka Lodge No. 94, Iuka, MS. Senior Warden in 1860. Master in 1875. Grand Master of Grand Lodge of Mississippi in 1898.

William A. Stone (1846-1920). Served in Union Army as Second Lieutenant in Co. A, 187th Pennsylvania Volunteers. Member of Allegheny Lodge No. 223, Allegheny City, PA. Made a Mason "at sight."

William M. Stone (1827-1893). Entered Civil War as a private and assisted in organizing Company B of the 3rd Iowa Infantry. He participated in battles of Fort Gibson, Champion

Hills, Black River and Vicksburg. Became Captain, Major and Brigadier General in 1864. Wounded in Battle of Blue Mills, MO. Taken prisoner at Shiloh. In 1865 was at Ford's Theatre when Lincoln was assassinated and was with the President until his death. Later he accompanied Lincoln's remains to Springfield, IL. Received degrees in Coshocton Lodge No. 96, Coshocton, OH on Nov. 19, Dec. 1 and 4, 1852. In Iowa he was petitioner for the dispensation for Oriental Lodge No. 61, Knoxville, and was Charter Senior Warden in 1855. Member of Tadmor Chapter No. 18, R.A.M. of Knoxville and Captain of the host in 1861. Was knighted in Depayens Commandery No. 6, Oskaloosa in 1874.

George Stoneman (1822-1894). Union Major General. In 1862 appointed Brigadier General and Chief of Cavalry in the Army of Potomac. His battles are too numerous to mention. Suffice it to say, he fought 14 battles from Texas to Ohio to Georgia. Member of Benicia Lodge No. 5, Benicia, CA and Temple Lodge No. 14, Sonoma, CA. Member of Benicia Chapter No. 7, R.A.M.

Silas A. Strickland (?). Civil War General. Member Capitol Lodge No. 3, Omaha, NE.

33° Willim B. Taliaferro (1822-1898). Confederate Major General in Civil War. Born in Belleville, VA. Educated at Harvard and William and Mary Coll. Member of board of visitors of V.M.I. and William and Mary. Received Masonic degrees in one day in Williamsburg Lodge No. 6. Became first senior warden of Botetourt Lodge No. 7, Cloucester Court House, VA. Grand Master (1876-77) of Grand Lodge of Virginia.

James W. Taylor (1833-1925). Served as Captain of Confederate First Georgia Cavalry, 1861-62. Raised (3°) in Haralson Lodge No. 142, Nov. 25, 1854. Never missed a roll call of Grand Lodge Georgia from 18591925. To accomplish this, he obtained furloughs during Civil War to attend Masonic meetings. His Masonic credentials are too lengthy to mention here. He was a member of both the Scottish and the York Rite.

William M. Taylor (1817-1871). Confederate Brigadier General who recruited a brigade for service, but never saw action. After the war was a delegate to the reconstruction convention of 1866. His Masonic credentials are too lengthy to mention here. Suffice it to say that before the Civil War (beginning in 1845 through 1857) he was a member of both the Scottish Rite and the York Rite, holding high positions in both.

John M. Thayer (1820-1906). Major General in Civil War. Was Brigadier General and Major General in the territorial forces operating against the Pawnee Indians (1855-61). In the Civil War (July 21, 1861) he was Commissioned Colonel of the 1st Nebraska Volunteers. Promoted to Brigadier General in 1863 and Major General on March 13, 1865. Original lodge not known, but was admitted before the war as a charter member of Capitol Lodge No. 101, Omaha, NE.

Bryan M. Thomas (1836-1905). Civil War Brigadier General. Graduate of U.S. Military Academy in 1858, then sent on frontier duty at Camp Floyd, Utah as a Lieutenant. While there his troops suppressed the Mormons, and he became a member of Rocky Mountain Lodge No. 203. After that assignment he spent four years in the Confederate Army during the Civil War, advancing from First Lieutenant to Brigadier General.

George H. Thomas (1816-1870). Graduate of U.S. Military Academy in 1840. Commissioned Brigadier General of Volunteers in Union Army in Aug. 1861. Promoted to Major General, April 1862. When he fought at Perryville, he gained fame as "the Rock of Chickamauga" by holding his defensive position at the Battle of Chickamauga, Sept. 1863. Fought and won many more battles. On record as visiting Ward Lodge, and Army Lodge in Ohio during the war.

John R. Thomas (1846-1914). Union Army, rising from Private to Captain in Company D, 120th Indiana Volunteers. Received degrees in Metropolis Lodge No. 91, Metropolis, IL.

Lorenzo Thomas (1804-1875). Union Major General in U.S. Army. Was Chief of Staff to General Winfield Scott until 1861. Commissioned Brigadier General, May 1861; Adjutant General (August), while maintaining full rank of Brigadier General. In 1864-65 he organized and trained Negro troops in Southern states. When President Johnson removed Edwin M. Stanton from his post as Secretary of War, he appointed Thomas to that position on Feb. 21, 1868. But, since Stanton refused to vacate, Thomas never filled the office. He was commissioned Major General on March 13, 1865. He affiliated with Potomac Lodge No. 5, Washington, DC on Jan. 19, 1857.

Hugh S. Thompson (1836-1904). Graduate of South Carolina Military Academy in 1856. Confederate Captain of battalion of state cadets, 1861-65. Member of Richland Lodge No. 39, Columbia, SC.

Jacob Thompson (1810-1885). Served as aide-de-camp to General Beauregard in Confederate Army. In summer of 1864 went to Canada as Confederate commissioner. From there he planned (without success) to release Confederate prisoners of War from Camp Douglas near Chicago, then seize that city, and burn other surrounding cities. In 1849, received his degrees in Oxford Lodge No. 33, Oxford, MS.

George Thornburgh (1847-1923). Served in Confederate Army in 1865. Was Grand Master of Grand Lodge of Arkansas, Grand High Priest of the Grand Chapter, and Grand Commander of the Grand Commandery.

James W. Throckmorton (1825-1894). In Texas he served continuously in the state legislature from 1851 until the beginning of the Civil War. He entered the Confederate Army in 1861, serving as Captain, then Major. In 1864 was promoted to Brigadier General of state troops. After the war he returned to Texas politics and became Governor for four years. Member of St. Johns Lodge No. 51, McKinney, TX.

33° Robert Toombs (1810-1885). Brigadier General in Confederate Army. Was a Mason before the Civil War began. Member of Lafayette Lodge No. 23, Washington, GA. In Scottish Rite, after the Civil War, he received honorary 33° on May 7, 1872.

Alfred T. A. Torbert (1833-1880). Union Major General. April 1861 was sent to muster in New Jersey volunteers and commissioned Colonel of 1st New Jersey Regiment. Served in the Peninsula campaign, beginning with the Battle of Manassas, then the Maryland campaign. Wounded at Battle of Crampton's Gap in a bayonet charge. Was at Gettysburg and finally Rappahannock. Commissioned Brigadier General of volunteers, Nov. 1862.

Breveted Major General of volunteers, Sept. 9, 1864. Breveted Brigadier General, March 13, 1865. Mustered out of the War on Jan 15, 1866. Member of Temple Chapter No. 2, R.A.M., Milford, DE. In 1869 was first Grand Secretary of the Grand Chapter, R.A.M. of Delaware.

Benjamin F. Tracy (1830-1915). Union Brigadier General. He raised the 109th and 137th New York volunteers and was Colonel of the former in Aug. 1862. Received Congressional Medal for gallantry in the Battle of the Wilderness. Breveted Brigadier General, March 14, 1865. Member of Friendship Lodge No. 153, Owego, NY.

William T. Truxtun (1824-1887). Union Commodor, U.S. Navy. Served in North Atlantic squadron. Commanded steamers *Alabama, Chocura*, and *Tacony*. Fought many battles with these ships. Member of Owen's Lodge No. 164, Near Norfolk, VA.

Thomas J. Turner (1815-1874). In 1861 he was a delegate to the Peace Conference held in Washington, DC in an effort to prevent the impending Civil War. When war broke out, he served (1861-62) with the 15th Illinois Volunteer Infantry as a Colonel in the Union Army, but was forced to resign because of ill health. In 1854 was Master of Excelsior Lodge No. 97, Freeport; 1863-65 Grand Master of Grand Lodge of Illinois; 1864 received Royal Arch Degree in Freeport Chapter No. 23, R.A.M.; 1865 was Senior Warden of Freeport Commandery No. 7, Knights Templar.

Peter Turney (1827-1903). Colonel of Turney's 1st Tennessee Regiment in Confederate Army. Recommended for promotion, but failed to receive it because of mutual dislike between he and Jefferson Davis. Member of Cumberland Lodge No. 158, of Winchester, in which his father also held membership.

Richard S. Tuthill (1841-1920). Mason who served in Civil War as a scout under Gen. J. A. Logan, also a Mason.

Adin B. Underwood (1828-1888). Union Major General. Raised recruits at beginning of war. Appointed Captain in 2nd Massachusetts Infantry, April 1861. Advanced to Lieutenant Colonel same year. Participated in battles of Fredericksburg, Chancellorsville, and Gettysburg. Served under General Hooker at Lookout Mountain, where he was wounded. Appointed Brigadier General of Volunteers, Jan. 1863. Major General, Aug. 1865. Member of Bunker Hill Army Lodge No. 5 (Mass.) and later Montgomery Lodge, Milford, MA.

William H. Upham (1841-1924). Entered Union Army (1861) in the 2nd Wisconsin Infantry. Shot through lungs at Bull Run on July 21, 1861. Left on field as dead, but survived. Was prisoner of war six months. Lincoln appointed him to the U.S. Military Academy. Graduated at close of War. Resigned from Army in 1869. Was a Mason.

Zebulon B. Vance (1830-1894). Entered Confederate service in 1861 as Captain. Promoted to Colonel. His Masonic credentials are too lengthy to list them all. He received his first three degrees in Mt. Hermon Lodge No. 118, Asheville, NC, Feb. thru June, 1853. Member of Asheville Chapter No. 25, R.A.M., 1855. Named in his honor was Z. B. Vance Lodge No. 2, 40th Regiment Heavy Artillery of North Carolina, a Confederate military lodge.

TWO FACES OF FREEMASONRY

William Vandever (1817-1893). Union Major General. Before War began, served in the 36th and 37th Congresses (1859-61). Was a member of the peace convention held at Washington, DC in 1861 in an effort to prevent war. That failing, he resigned from Congress and mustered in to the Union Army as a Colonel of 9th Iowa Volunteer Infantry. Promoted to Brigadier General in 1862. Breveted Major General in 1865. In 1858 became a member of Dubuque Lodge No. 3, Dubuque, IA.

James C. Veatch (1819-1895). Union General. Began as Colonel of 25th Indiana Volunteers, 1861; Brigadier General, April 1862; Major General, Aug. 1865, after which he retired. Was at battles of Corinth and Vicksburg, the Atlanta Campaign, and the siege and capture of Mobile. Member of Rockport Lodge No. 112, Rockport, IN.

Egbert L. Viele (1825-1902). Union Brigadier General of Volunteers. Captain of 7th New York Engineers. Brigadier General of volunteers in Aug. 1861. Second in command of Port Royal expedition. Commander at the capture of Fort Pulaski. Planned and executed the march on Norfolk, Virginia. Was military governor of Norfolk. Member of Kane Lodge No. 545, NYC.

William M. Voorhies (?). Brigadier General in Confederate Army. Raised to Master Mason in Mississippi in 1863. Received York Rite Royal Arch in Columbia, TN in 1866. Member of DeMolay Commandery No. 3. Served as Senior Warden of the lodge, High Priest of the chapter and Generalissimo of the Commandery.

Louis Wagner (1838-1914). Brigadier General in Union Army, 1861. Rose through the grades to Colonel in 1863, and Brigadier General in 1865. Was badly wounded at Second Battle of Bull Run. Wound broke open anew at Chancellorsville. Received blue degrees in Harmony Lodge No. 52, Philadelphia on Jan. 4, Feb. 1, and March 1, 1865. Master of the Lodge in 1871.

Lewis Wallace (1827-1905). Union Major General. Beginning war he was appointed Adjutant General of Indiana. Soon became Colonel of 11th Indiana Volunteers. Commissioned Brigadier General, Sept. 1861 and Major General, March, 1862. Took part in capture of Fort Donelson. Saved Cincinnati from capture in 1863. Defeated by Early at Monocacy in July, 1864. Member of the court-martial that tried those accused in assassination of Lincoln. Received blue degrees in Fountain Lodge No. 60, Covington, IN on Dec. 15 & 30, 1850, and Jan. 15, 1851.

William H. L. Wallace (1821-1862). Union Brigadier General. In 1861 appointed Colonel of 11th Illinois volunteers. At Battle of Fort Donelson commanded a brigade with such ability that he was appointed Brigadier General of Volunteers. In Battle of Shiloh, commanded General C. F. Smith's brigade and fell mortally wounded. Received first two blue degrees in Occidental Lodge No. 50, Ottawa, IL on June 15, 16, 1846 and Master in 1848. Exalted in York Rite in Shabbona Chapter No. 37, Ottawa, on July 17, 1855. Was High Priest in 1858. Knighted in Blaney Commandery No. 5, Knights Templar, of Morris, IL. Charter member of Ottawa Commandery, Ottawa, and served a Generalissimo.

Edward C. Walthall (1831-1898). Confederate Major General. Entered Civil War as Lieutenant in the 15th Mississippi Regiment. Promoted to Brigadier General in 1862, and Major General in 1864. Member of Coffeeville Lodge No. 83.

Henry C. Ward (1843-1925). Enlisted in 15th Massachusetts Infantry (Union) in 1861 and mustered out as Captain in 1865. Served in following battles: Ball's Bluff; Yorktown; Fair Oaks; Richmond; Wilderness; Antietam; Fredericksburg; Spottsylvania, and many others. Wounded twice, taken prisoner and confined in Libby prison until rescued after capture of Richmond in March, 1865. Was a Mason.

Max Webber (1824-1901). Union Brigadier General. Served in U.S. Army as Colonel of 20th New York Volunteers, 1861-62, and Brigadier General, 1862-65. Lost his right arm at the Battle of Antietam. Had command of Harper's Ferry against General Early. Member of Trinity Lodge No. 12, NYC, from 1851 until his death.

Godfrey Weitzel (1835-1884). Major General in Union Army. After he captured New Orleans he became assistant military commander and mayor of the city. Was in Louisiana until 1864. Was Major General of volunteers same year (1864). Promoted to Brigadier General in regulars in 1865, and Major General in regulars same year. Was later in charge of all troops north of the Potomac River during final operations against General Lee's Army. Mason.

Joseph Wheeler (1836-1906). Confederate Lieutenant General. Resigned from U.S. Army (April 22, 1861) and was commissioned Colonel of 19th Alabama Infantry the following September. Promoted to Brigadier General, Oct. 1862; Major General, Jan. 1863; and Lieutenant General, Feb. 1865. At end of war he was senior cavalry General of the Confederate Armies. Raised (3°) in Courtland Lodge No. 37, Courtland, AL. Member of Courtland Chapter No. 25, R.A.M. and DeMolay Commandery No. 14, Knights Templar of Decatur, AL..

Julius White (1816-1890). Union General. Commissioned Colonel of 37th Illinois Volunteers, known as "Fremont Rifle Regiment." Commanded under General Fremont in expedition to Southwest Missouri, autumn 1861. Advanced to Brigadier General at Battle of Pea Ridge, June 9, 1862. Major General in 1865. Member of Oriental Lodge No. 33, Chicago.

Washington C. Whitthorne (1825-1891). In Confederate service as Adjutant General of Tennessee, 1861-65. Member of Columbia Lodge No. 31, Columbia, TN.

John Stuart Williams (1818-1898). Entered war as Confederate Colonel in 1861. Promoted to Brigadier General in 1862, and served until end of war. Member of Winchester Lodge No. 20, Winchester, KY and Louisville Chapter No. 5, Royal Arch Mason.

James A. Williamson (1829-1902). Union Major General of Volunteers. Lieutenant of 4th Iowa Infantry, 1861. Later became Colonel. At Vicksburg he commanded 2nd Brigade, 1st Division, 15th Corps. Following capture of Savannah, was promoted to Brigadier General of Volunteers. In 1865 he was breveted Major General. Member of Pioneer Lodge No. 22, Des Moines, IA.

Isaac J. Wistar (1827-1905). Brigadier General of Volunteers in Civil War. Mason.

33° Simon Wolf (1836-1923). President of National and International Order of B'nai B'rith (Jewish Freemasonry), 1904-05. Began law practice in Washington, DC in 1862. Wrote several books, the last of which is entitled *The Presidents I Have Known*. On page 461 he relates this story: "While I was delivering a wagon load of food supplies to Gen. Pope to feed his Confederate prisoners at Charleston, SC, I was captured by Confederate soldiers, and when I asked to be taken before their commanding officer they complied. Same proved to be none other than Gen. Stonewall Jackson, to whom I gave the Masonic Signal of Distress. The General answered and not only set me free, but saw that I was safely taken back to the Union Lines." Wolf was a member of Lafayette Lodge No. 19, Washington, DC, and a 33° AASR (SJ).

32° Urban A. Woodbury (1838-1915). Served in Civil War as enlisted man and officer, losing right arm and taken prisoner in first Battle of Bull Run. Affiliated with Mount Vernon Lodge No. 8, Morrisville, VT on July 5, 1865. Member of Burlington Lodge No. 100, Burlington, VT. Was 32° AASR (NJ) in Vermont Consistory and a Shriner.

Stewart L. Woodford (1835-1913). Union Brigadier General of Volunteers in Civil War. Served as Master (3°) of Continental Lodge No. 287, NYC.

William B. Woods (1824-1887). Civil War officer in Union Army. Entered war as Lieutenant Colonel of 76th Ohio Volunteers. From then to end of war, was continually on the front lines. Appointed Brigadier General of Volunteers in Jan. 1865; Major General and Brigadier General, May 1865. Participated in the battles of Shiloh, Chickasaw Bayou, Arkansas Post, Resaca, Dallas, Atlanta, Jonesboro, Lovejoy Station and Bentonville. Commanded a division in Sherman's march to the sea. Member of Newark Lodge No. 69 (now 97) of Newark, OH.

32° Thomas L. Young (1832-1888). Entered Union Army at beginning of Civil War. Became Brigadier General of Volunteers in 1865. Member of McMillan Lodge No. 141, McMillan Chapter No. 19, R.A.M., Cincinnati Commandery, K.T. (York Rite), and 32° Scottish Rite.

Felix K. Zollicoffer (1812-1862). Brigadier General in Confederate Army. Member of 1861 peace conference at Washington, DC to devise means to prevent impending Civil War. Commanded 10,000 troops in Civil War. Died of wounds received near Mill Springs, KY on Jan. 19, 1862. Member of Cumberland Lodge No. 8.

Figure 49: Not only did President Andrew Johnson pardon many Confederates soldiers and officers who were Masons, he also pardoned wealthy Masons who had funded the southern rebellion. To receive their pardons, Johnson required both the officers and the wealthy to present themselves at the White House. Before pardoning them, he shook their hand to confirm they were Masons.

HANDBOOK OF FREEMASONRY
"Masonic handshake"
1973, page 176

PARDONS FOR MASONIC SOUTHERNERS AT THE WHITE HOUSE

The "handshake" inset directly above is the Masonic "grip" of the Blue Lodge Mason, as recorded in *Handbook of Freemasonry*. The enlarged cutout above it is the handshake of Pres. Johnson (right) and a Southerner (left). Notice the passive palm down handshake of Johnson, enabling the Southerner's thumb to be in the aggressive position for a Masonic grip.

Before President Johnson pardoned a war criminal, he was confirming the person was truly a Mason. For such partiality, (as well as Johnson's dismissal of Edwin M. Stanton), he was impeached, but not convicted.

War criminal Albert Pike was one of the Masons pardoned. A few years after Pike's pardon, Freemasons erected a statue to Pike in Wash., DC.

Fig. 50 — Pres. Andrew Johnson, 32° Freemason, was impeached.
See *S&B*, Vol.1, ch.17; Vol.3, ch. 3.

32° Andrew Johnson (1808-1875)
17th President of the United States.

V.P. under Lincoln. When Lincoln was assassinated in 1865, Johnson succeeded to the presidency on death of Lincoln, serving until 1869. And he was the first president to be impeached.

Although a Southerner, Johnson was loyal to the Union during the Civil War. As military governor of Tenn., he held the rank of Brigadier General.

Johnson's Freemasonry was very important to him. He received his first 3 Masonic degrees May 5, 1851 at Greeneville TN Lodge No. 119, and remained a member of that lodge until his death. He was definitely a Knight Templar, since there is a picture of him in Commandery regalia owned by Nashville Commandery No. 1, K.T.

Why, then, was Johnson impeached by Congress. Was he not a Mason?

And, don't Masons protect each other from these things?

The primary reason behind Johnson's impeachment was his pardon of Confederate war criminals— most specifically, of 33° Freemason Albert Pike. Pike's crime? After war broke out, Pike was named Indian Agent and Brigadier General of the area, which included Indian Territory. Pike allowed his band of Indians to scalp Union soldiers while yet alive. After the war, Pike was trialed as a war criminal and convicted. Before Pike was sentenced, Freemasonry put pressure on President Johnson, who stepped in and pardoned Pike. (see *S&B* Vol. 1, 3rd ed., chap. 14)

Johnson' reward? "On June 20, 1867 the President received some Scottish Rite officials in his bedroom at the White House where he received the 4° through the 32° as an honorarium, administered by Benjamin B. French and A.T.C. Pierson.

"His close association with Freemasonry was one of the factors that led to his impeachment trial. Thaddeus Stevens, the anti-Mason, was ringleader in the impeachment proceedings against Johnson in 1868." *10,000 Famous Freemasons.*

The hidden power of Freemasonry won the day. By one vote Johnson was acquitted.

32° Pres. Johnson pardoned convicted war criminal 33° Albert Pike

Fig. 51 — Anti-Mason and Congressman Thaddeus Stevens was the principal leader in the impeachment of President Johnson for pardoning war criminals.

Thaddeus Stevens (1792-1868)

Anti-Mason. Born with a clubfoot in Danville, Vt. One of four sons of Sarah and Joshua Stevens. When he came of school age, he was constantly taunted by schoolmates about his limp. Because of this he grew up with empathy for society's poor and disenfranchised.

It was claimed by some and disclaimed by others that Stevens was rejected for membership in Good Samaritan Lodge No. 336 of Gettysburg, PA because of his deformity. For this reason alone, claim the Masons, he became an anti-Mason.

Stevens studied at Dartmouth, then practised law in Gettysburg, PA. He did much for the public schools and higher education in his state. Stevens served in the state's House of Representatives (1833-41).

Under the Whig Party, he went to the US House of Representatives (184953), but left in impatience over the Party's stand on slavery. After helping to form the new Republican Party in Pennsylvania, he returned to the House (1859-68).

Throughout his career he vigorously opposed slavery. After the Civil War, he advocated harsh policies against the Confederate states, emerging as the leader of the "Radical Republicans." He denounced President Andrew Johnson for readmitting some former Confederate states to the Union, arguing that they had committed treason and should be made territories until they wrote constitutions providing black suffrage.

Stevens was also a leader in the congressional reconstruction plan following our Civil War. However, his idea of treating the South as what he called "a conquered province" brought him into open conflict with President Andrew Johnson. Because of Johnson's pardon of war criminals, such as Albert Pike, Stevens was the principal leader in the proposed impeachment of President Johnson, and managed the trial himself. Stevens died soon after Johnson's acquittal.

Fig. 52 — Central Bank for U.S.A.

Salmon Portland Chase (1808-1873)

Jurist and statesman, born in Cornish, NH. In 1830 he settled as a lawyer in Cincinnati, where he acted as counsel for the defence of fugitive slaves. He was twice Governor of Ohio (1855-9), and became secretary of the Treasury (1861-4). In 1864 Lincoln appointed him Chief Justice of the United States of America. As such he presided at the impeachment trial of President Andrew Johnson (1868). Pres. Johnson was not convicted. See Fig. 50-51. Salmon Chase is most noted by his name attached to a bank; the Chase Manhattan Bank. The story below is told in more detail in *S&B*, V1 ch 14 & V3 ch. 4.

"In July 1862, an agent of the London bankers sent a letter to the leading financiers and bankers of America informing them that the greenback would put the American Masonic bankers out of business if they did not act fast. London wanted American bankers to pressure Congress to issue bonds that would be 'used as a banking basis.' The message said in part: 'It will not do to allow the greenback[s], as [they are] called, to circulate as money any length of time, for we cannot control them. But we can control the bonds and through them the bank issues.' The instructions were urgent. The American financiers were not to wait on Treasury Secretary Salmon P. Chase to make his recommendations to Congress. They were instead to meet with the congressmen and senators in lodge, where they could discuss the matter in private.

"Even President Lincoln, as resolute as he was in frustrating every move of the Masonic bankers of Europe to establish a central bank in America, could not hold at bay a greedy Congress. On February 25, 1863, Congress passed the National Banking Act, which created a federally chartered national bank that had the power to issue U.S. Bank Notes. The notes were, in fact, money created by private bankers to be loaned to the government at interest — paper money supported not by gold but by debt."

Figure 53 — Famous American Masons during our Civil War. Read about the "Knights of the Golden Circle" evolving into the "Knight of the Ku Klux Klan" in *Scarlet and Beast,* V1, 3rd ed., ch. 8 & V3, chps. 5&7.

1°Nathan Bedford Forrest, Sr. (1821-1877)

Grand Wizard of the KKK

Born in Bedford, Tenn. First farmed in Hernando, Miss., but moved to Memphis in 1852. There he became a real estate dealer & broker in slaves. Entering the war in 1861 as a Lieutenant Colonel of Cavalry in the Confederate Army, he distinguished himself with daring cavalry raids. After his attack on Murfreesboro in 1862, he was promoted to Brigadier General. Following the battle at Chickamauga, he was transferred to northern Miss. and made a Major General.

His harassment of the Union forces by cavalry raids and his capture of Fort Pillow in April, 1864 led to his promotion to Lieutenant General in Feb. 1865. He was an Entered Apprentice (1°) in Angerona Lodge No. 168 at Memphis, Tenn.

All the above comes from *10,000 Famous Freemasons,* by 33° Denslow. It is interesting to note that Freemasonry says nothing about Forrest's hatred of Blacks, nor his involvement in the massacre of Blacks during the war, nor his involvement in the Ku Klux Klan after the war.

We read in *The Cambridge Biographical Encyclopedia,* 2nd edition, 1998, that while Forrest was a General in the Confederate Army, "troops under his command carried out an infamous massacre of 300 black Union troops at Fort Pillow, TN."

Patsy Sims, in *The Klan,* 1978, writes that in 1871, "Bedford Forrest, Sr. was Grand Wizard of the Klan." His son, Nathan Bedford Forrest, Jr. was also a member of the Klan.

KU KLUX KLAN.

A secret terrorist organization following the Civil War, became the leading underground resistance group that fought the political power of the newly freed slaves during Reconstruction. Its goal was to reestablish the dominance of prewar plantation aristocracy.

Organized in 1866 as a social club in Pulaski, TN by Confederate veteran and Freemason Nathan Bedford Forrest, Sr., it was restructured at Nashville, TN a year later along political and racial lines. Called the "Invisible Empire of the South," it was presided over by grand wizard Forrest and a descending hierarchy of grand dragons, grand titans, and grand cyclopses. Dressed in white robes and sheets designed to frighten superstitious victims and to prevent identification by Federal troops, Klansmen whipped and killed innocent freed blacks in nighttime raids. With intimidation and threats, they drove blacks (and their white sympathizers) out of their communities, destroying their crops and burning their houses and barns.

Because of the increase in kidnappings and murders, Forrest ordered it disbanded in 1869. Local groups, however, remained active, resulting in the rest of the country reacting strongly to the increased violence in the South. This forced Congress to pass the Force Act in 1870 and the Ku Klux Klan Act in 1871, authorizing the president to suspend the writ of Habeas corpus, suppress disturbances by force, and impose heavy penalties on terrorist organizations. The resulting federal prosecutions of Klan members that followed created widespread Southern sympathy in the Klan's behalf. During the 1870s, as Southern political power gradually reverted to traditional white Democratic control, the need for anti-Republican, antiblack organizations to remain secret decreased.

20th-Century Revival. The Klan was reorganized near Atlanta, GA in 1915 by Freemason William Joseph Simmons, and peaked in the 1920s. To the old Klan's hostility toward blacks, the new Klan (strong in the Midwest as well as in the South) added bias against Roman Catholics, Jews, foreigners, and organized labor. Stressing white Protestant supremacy, the Klan enjoyed a last spurt of growth in 1928 when Roman Catholic Alfred E. Smith received the Democratic presidential nomination. During the Depression of the 1930s, the Klan's membership dropped drastically, but in the mid-1960s, as civil rights workers attempted to spur compliance with the Civil Rights Act of 1964, the Klan revived once again. In March 1965 President Lyndon Johnson denounced the Klan in a nationwide television address announcing the arrest of four Klansmen in connection with the slaying of a white civil rights worker in Alabama. The Klan then faded rapidly, only to revive with renewed vigor in the late 1970s. By the early 1980s it was estimated to have 10,000 members active in 24 states with another 100,000 people sufficiently interested to give personal and financial support.

Figure 54 — Royal Arch Freemason, Colonel William Joseph Simmons, resurrected the KKK in 1915.
Read *Scarlet and Beast*, Vol. 1, Chap. 8.

Figure 55 — Two of several politicians who belonged to the KKK.

◀ **33° Robert C. Byrd** (1918-) U.S. Senator from W.V. since 1959. 33° Scottish Rite Freemason. Member of Mountain Lodge No. 156, Coal City, WV. Member of Shrine in Charleston. One-time member of the KKK.

33° Hugo Black (1886-1971) ▶
U.S. Supreme Court Justice
(1937-1971)
33° AASR (SJ), Shriner, and
one-time member of the KKK.

SECTION 5
RECONSTRUCTION PERIOD TO WORLD WAR I

Fig. 1 — As Civil War started, first well drilled to obtain oil. Drake is standing right with top hat.

Edwin L. Drake (1819-1880) American Pioneer in the oil industry, he was the first to tap petroleum at its source by drilling at Titusville, PA, Aug. 27, 1859.

Drake was born on a farm near Greenville (Greene Co.), NY. Eight years later the family moved to Castleton, VT, where he lived until he was 19. He left for Michigan, worked for a year on an uncle's farm, and then worked for two years as a hotel clerk in the nearby town of Tecumseh. Returning to the East, he was a dry-goods clerk — a first in New Haven, CT.

About 1845 he moved to Springfield, MA, where he was an express agent for the Boston & Albany Railroad, then later returned to New Haven where he became a conductor on the upstart New York & New Haven train. Ill health required him to retire.

He owned stock in the Pennsylvania Rock Oil Co., and the company hired him to visit its property on Oil Creek near Titusville, PA. He secured a lease on the company's land and started drilling, hitting oil at 69 feet.

He perfected the use of pipe as a casing, but failed to patent it. The money he had saved (about $16,000) was soon lost in oil speculation.

He retired to Vermont in broken health and later lived destitute in Long Branch, NJ. The citizens of Titusville contributed to his support and the Pennsylvania state legislature gave him a $1,500 annual grant. His original lodge is not known, but on Oct. 6, 1859, Oil Creek Lodge No. 303 of Titusville elected him to affiliation. This is now Titusville Lodge No. 754. Drake died in Bethlehem, PA.

Fig. 2 — Famous American Masons following our Civil War.
See *Scarlet and the Beast*, Vol. 1, 3rd edition, chapter. 14; and Vol. 3, chapter 5.

33° Jesse James (1847-1882)

Wild West outlaw and 33° Freemason. Born in Centerville, Mo. Fought in a guerrilla group in the Civil War. Upset over loss of the war to the North, he and his brother Frank (1843-1915) planned to rekindle the War. To fund their operation, they began robbing numerous banks, trains, and stagecoaches in and around Missouri. In 1882, Robert Ford, a gang member, was paid a reward to murder Jesse. Read the entire plot in *Scarlet and the Beast*, Vol. III.

Richard J. Gatling (1818-1903)

Inventor of the "Gatling Gun," the world's first practical repeating gun, which changed the tactics of warfare worldwide.

He conceived the idea of his revolving battery gun in 1861. The first gun was made at Indianapolis in 1862. With further improvements in 1865, the gun was adopted by the U.S. Army. At first it fired 250 rounds per min. Later improvements of a motor drive raised the rounds to 3000 per minute. Gatling was a member of Center Lodge #23, Indianapolis, IN.

Fig. 3 — Inventor of revolving firearms. COLT 45.

Freemason Samuel Colt (1814-1862

Inventor of the Colt firearms. Born in Hartford, CT. Apprenticed in his father's factory, but ran away in 1827 for an East India voyage, returning to his father's factory to work in the fabrics dyeing department.

At age 17, Colt again left home to seek his fortune. He toured the continent under the name "Dr. Coult," giving lectures on chemistry, and making a considerable profit on his lectures.

Colt's first model of his pistol (1829) was made of wood. In 1835, he took out his first patent for revolving firearms. He established the Patent Arms Company and supplied the government with revolvers for the Seminole War, as well as for the Texas and Indian frontiers.

Samuel Colt was a member of St. John's Lodge No. 4; Pythagoras Chapter No. 17, and Washington Commandery No. 1, all of Hartford.

Fig. 4 — Famous American Masons following our Civil War.

3° **Leland Stanford** (1824-1893)

Stanford drove the golden spike at Promontory Point, Utah.

Founder of Leland Stanford, Jr. University, Palo Alto, CA in 1885 in memory of his son. Stanford was a capitalist; governor of California (1861-63), and U.S. Senator from California (1885-93).

Stanford studied law and was admitted to practice in 1848. He moved to Port Washington, WI that same year, and to California in 1852. There he opened a general store at Michigan Bluff. In 1855 he moved to Sacramento and engaged in mercantile pursuits on a large scale.

As a U.S. railroad developer, he was one of the "big four" who built Central Pacific Railroad, linking the Union Pacific and the Southern Pacific lines to form the first transcontinental road 1,776 miles long. He himself drove the golden spike at Promontory Point, UT, May 10, 1869.

He gave $22,500,000 to establish Leland Stanford, Jr. University. He is buried on the university grounds.

He was raised 3° in Prometheus Lodge No. 17, Port Washington, WI, in March 1850. He demitted (quit) from this lodge in 1852. On Jan. 11, 1854 he become charter member and first Senior Deacon of Michigan City Lodge No. 47, Michigan City, CA. A year later he withdrew from Freemasonry altogether. No explanation given.

Fig. 5 — John Bidwell, who went west armed with nothing more formidable than a pocket knife, eventually became one of California's richest men.

3° John Bidwell (1819-1900)
California pioneer and politician
Born in Chautaugua Co., NY

John Bidwell was just a 20-year-old schoolteacher in 1840, but he had already moved from New York to Pennsylvania to Ohio to Weston, MO — where a claim-jumper stole his land. Unwilling to return to Ohio in disgrace and with nothing much to lose, he heard a French-Canadian trader tell of the wonders he had seen in California and was spellbound.

A few weeks later, a widely published letter from an American resident of California, Dr. John Marsh, made it seem still more alluring. "The Agricultural capabilities of California as yet are but very imperfectly developed."

With only a pocket knife in his possession, he emigrated to California, being one of the first to make the hazardous journey overland, and became the state's first great agriculturist, owning an immense estate of several thousand acres.

Gov. Leland Stanford commissioned him Brigadier General of California Militia. Later he was made a regent of the Univ. of California. In 1849 he was a member of the state constitutional convention and the same year became state senator. From 1865 to 1867 he was state Representative to the U.S. Congress from California.

He was raised (3°) in San Jose Lodge No. 10 in 1851 and later was affiliated with Chico Lodge No. 111.

Fig. 6 — Buffalo Bill Cody furnished buffalo meat to the railroad crews.

3° William F. Cody "Buffalo Bill" (1846-1917)

Better known a "Buffalo Bill," the famous pony express rider, Indian fighter, scout, plainsman and showman.

His father was killed in the Kansas border war. He was a pony express rider from 1860-61. From 1861-65 he was a government scout and guide with the 7th Kansas Cavalry. He contracted to furnish the Kansas Pacific Railroad with all the buffalo meat required to feed the laborers engaged in road construction and in 18 months (1867-68) killed 4,280 buffalo, earning the name "Buffalo Bill" by which he is best known.

From 1868-72 he was again a government scout and guide, operating against the Sioux and Cheyenne. In 1872 he was a member of the Nebraska legislature. From 1883 he headed the famous "Wild West Show" that toured America and Europe. He served as a general in the Nebraska national guard during the Sioux outbreak in 1890-91. He was in the Battle of Wounded Knee, Dec. 29, 1890. He killed Yellow Hand, the Cheyenne chief, in a hand-to-hand fight. Cody was president of the Shoshone Irrigation Co. and coauthor of *The Great Salt Lake Trail*.

He was raised (3°) in Platte Valley Lodge No. 32, North Platte, Neb. on Jan. 10, 1871. Member of Euphrates Chapter No. 15 at North Platte, and when he received his Mark Master Degree, he appropriately selected a buffalo's head as his Mark. Cody was buried with Masonic honors on Lookout Mountain near Golden Colorado.

Fig. 7 — In 1887 Congress passed the "Dawes Act" alloting 160 acres each to individual Indian families to encourage Indians to assimilate.

Freemason Henry L. Dawes (1816-1903)

U.S.Senator from Massachusetts, 1875-93. Born in Cummington, MA. Graduate of Yale. He edited the *Greenfield Gazette* and later the *Adams Transcript.* He was admitted to the bar in 1842 and was a member of the state legislature from 1848-50 and state senate, 1850-52. From 1857-73 he served in the U.S. Congress. In 1893 he was chairman of the commission to the Five Civilized Tribes, Indian Territory.

Dawes was a member of Lafayette Lodge, North Adams, MA. He was Marshal of the Lodge in January 1853, and one of the stewards in December 1853.

Fig. 8 — Authorsship of Pledge of the Allegiance to the Flag of the United States is claimed by two people — both Freemasons.

3° James Bailey Upham (1827-1909)

Wrote original "Pledge of Allegiance" to the flag of the United States. Born in New Hampton, NH. He was a member of Perry Mason & Co., publishers of *The Youth's Companion.* The "pledge" was moulded into final form by his firm's editorial staff and was first printed in the issue of Sept. 8, 1892 in conjunction with the public school celebration of the 400th anniversary of the discovery of America. He was a member of Converse Lodge, Malden, MA. Received his 1° degree on Feb. 16, 2°on Mar. 15, and 3° on May 15, 1888.

3° Rev. Francis J. Bellamy (1855-1931)

Author of the American "Pledge of Allegiance" to the flag. Bellamy, a Northern Baptist, was a socialist who preached socialism from the pulpit. Sermon topics were "Jesus the Socialist" and "The Socialism of the Primitive Church." He also helped the socialist oriented NEA plan a massive celebration of public schools. He wrote in *The Youth's Companion*, "Our fathers in their wisdom knew that the foundations of liberty, fraternity and equality must be universal education controlled by government." He even argued that God opposed parochial (Christian) schools. The original pledge as written by Bellamy did not contain the words "of the United States of America," or "under God." In 1939 the United States

Flag Association ruled Bellamy was the author of the original pledge.

Bellamy was a member of Little Falls Lodge No. 181, Little Falls, NY. The Order of Eastern Star (lodge for Mason's wives) erected a memorial tablet to him in 1955 at the O.E.S. Home in Oriskany, NY.

Figure 9 — Freemason Bartholdi, here in his Paris, France studio, was already an established sculptor when he began his monumental work. For two decades the "lady of liberty" was little more than a grandiose notion, an improbable dream concocted at a dinner party. No one knows what was served at that dinner in 1865, although the cuisine was certainly French, since it took place at Glatigny, a country estate near Versailles.

Freemason Frederic A. Bartholdi (1834-1904)

French designer of *Statue of Liberty* in New York Harbor.

On Oct. 14, 1875 Bartholdi became a member of Lodge AlsaceLorraine, Paris. Membership consisted of prominent intellectuals, authors, and government officials.

When *Liberty Enlightening the World* was complete, and before it was shown to the United States delegation, Bartholdi convened his lodge on June 19, 1884. The entire body marched in procession to review this gift of the French people to the United States of America.

On Nov. 13, 1884, Bartholdi delivered a lecture to the lodge on the history and various methods used in the execution of building his statue.

Fig. 10 — August 5, 1884 33° William A. Brodie, Grand Master of Grand Lodge of New York, laid the foundation stone of the Statue of Liberty in New York harbor.

Fig. 11 — During three years in which he worked on other commissions, Bartholdi also made an untold number of drawings and models of Liberty Enlightening the World. The definitive 4-foot model of clay was finished in 1875. Construction was under way in the Parisian workshops of Gaget, Gauthier and Company. Workmen from the company displayed the statue's first finished part in 1876.
The torch took about ten months to complete.

Figure 12 Whose face is on the statue? The answer came from a French senator who had joined Bartholdi at the opera. "I noticed an aged woman sitting in a corner," he said. "When the light fell on her face, I turned to Bartholdi and said to him, 'Why that's your model for the Statue of Liberty!" 'Yes,' he answered calmly. 'It's my mother.'"

Fig. 13 — Ringling Brothers Circus

The Ringling Brothers Circus
32° Alfred T. Ringling (1861-1919)
32° John Nicholas Ringling (?-1936)
32° Albert Charles Ringling (1852-1916)
32° August George Ringling (1854-1907)
32° Charles Edward Ringling (1866-1926)
32° William Henry Otto Ringling (1858-1911)
32° Henry William George Ringling (1868-1918)

All branches of this family had early and strong connections with Masonry. This is most remarkable in view of the fact that these people were German in ancestry, members of a Lutheran Church in a synod in bitter opposition to Masonry. In fact, membership in Freemasonry terminated their church ties.

Initially, The Ringling Brothers played in small towns. John, who outlived his brothers, became the best known of the brothers. When Ringling merged with Barnum & Bailey, John became head of the American Circus Corp, which also included Sells-Floto Circus, Hagenbach Animal Show, and John Robinson, Sparks, and Al G. Barnes Shows.

John financially aided Tex Rickard in building Madison Square Garden in NYC, He also engaged in oil production in Oklahoma, and was noted for his philanthropies.

August Ringling, father of the seven brothers listed above, was raised (3°) in Baraboo Lodge No. 34, Baraboo, WI, on August 19, 1891, and held membership until his death in 1898.

The seven brothers were all members of the same lodges — Baraboo Lodge No. 34, Baraboo Valley Chapter No. 49, R.A.M. St. John Commandery No. 21, K.T., and 32° AASR at Milwaukee. The brothers actually preceded their father into Masonry. The treasurer of Ringling, Dan DeBaugh, was a 33° AASR (NJ) and Grand Master of IL Grand Lodge.

Fig. 14 — Famous American Masons following our Civil War.

William M. Stewart (1827-1909)

U.S. Senator from Nevada 186475 and 1887-1905. Born in Galen, N.Y. Moved with parents to Trumbull Co., Ohio. In 1850 moved to San Francisco and engaged in mining. Studied law, admitted to the bar in 1852. In 1854 was Attorney General of Calif. Moved to Virginia City, Nev. in 1860 and helped develop the Comstock lode. First U.S. Senator from Nevada. Member of Nevada Lodge No. 13, Nevada City.

Florida.

3° William Jennings Bryan (1860-1925)

Secretary of State, U.S. Congressman and presidential nominee three times. Lawyer. Was member of 52nd and 53rd Congresses (1891-95). Edited *Omaha World-Herald* 1894-96. As a delegate to the Democratic convention of 1896, he wrote the famous "silver plank," of its platform and was nominated for President, but defeated by Mckinley. In Spanish-American War he was Colonel of the 3rd Nebraska regiment. In 1900 was again defeated for President by Mckinley. Nominated for third time for President in 1908. Was defeated by Taft. As Secretary of State in Wilson's cabinet (1913-15) he negotiated 30 treaties. He was raised to Master Mason (3°) in Lincoln Lodge No. 19, Lincoln, NE on April 15, 1902 and later affiliated with Temple Lodge No. 247, Miami,

Fig. 15 — Famous American Masons following our Civil War.

3° Mark Twain (1835-1910)

Born **Samuel Langhorne Clemens**. American author and humorist. He was apprenticed to a printer at age 12 and was Mississippi River boat pilot for a short time. He went west as secretary to his brother who had been appointed Territorial Secretary of Nevada. Was city editor of the *Virginia City Enterprise* (Nev.) in 1862 and alternated between mining and newspaper work. From this experience he became a noted humorist and began lecturing and writing books.

Clemens founded the publishing house of C.L. Webster & Co. in 1884, and its failure nearly ruined him financially. Among his many famous books are *The Innocents Abroad, Roughing It, Adventures of Tom Sawyer, The Prince and the Pauper, The Adventures of Huckleberry Finn, A Yankee at the Court of King Arthur,* etc.

Clemens was a member of Polar Star Lodge No. 79, St. Louis, MO. He earned his first three degrees on May 22, June 12, and July 10, 1861. He was later suspended and reinstated on April 24, 1867. He is recorded as having visited Carson City Lodge in Feb. and March of 1862.

During his trip to the Holy Land, he sent his lodge a gavel with this note: "This mallet is a cedar, cut in the forest of Lebanon, whence Solomon obtained the timbers for the temple." Clemens cut the handle himself from a cedar just outside the walls of Jerusalem. He had it made in Alexandria, Egypt, and it was presented to the Lodge on April 8, 1868.

Clemens demitted (quit the lodge in writing) Oct. 8, 1869 and presumably never again affiliated with any lodge. Whether his demit was connected in any way with the Anti-Masonic Movement is not known.

Fig. 16 — Famous American Mason. Invented the railroad sleeper car.

George M. Pullman (1831-1897)

Former cabinet maker and shopkeeper who popularized the longdistance rail travel with his innovative sleeper and dining cars, which were called the Pullman Sleeper Cars.

At age 17 he joined an elder brother in the cabinet making business in Albion, NY. In 1859 he moved to Chicago, and there built entire blocks of brick and stone buildings. In 1858 his attention was first directed to the discomfort of long distance railway traveling, and the following year, he remodeled two old day coaches of the Chicago and Alton into sleeping cars. In 1863 he built the prototype of the Pullman car, at the cost of $18,000. It was named the *Pioneer*.

The Pullman Palace Car co. was organized in 1867. He improved his invention with dining cars in 1868; chair cars in 1875; and vestibule cars in 1887. In 1880 he founded the industrial town of Pullman, near Chicago, where he built the company's shops. See elegant Pullman car on next page. George M. Pullman was a member of Renovation Lodge No. 97. Albion, New York.

Fig.17 — George M. Pullman (1831-1897) Member of Renovation Lodge No. 97, Albion NY. Inventor and founder of the Pullman Palace Car Co., Mar. 3, 1831. An elegant dining car was a key feature of Pennsylvania Railroad's "Broadway Limited." The "Limited" began its New York City-to-Chicago run in 1902 and competed with the Pullman Company's "Twentieth Century."

Fig. 18 — John D. Rockefeller, Sr. (left) with son John, Jr.

John D. Rockefeller, Sr.
(1839-1937)
John D. Rockefeller, Jr.
(1874-1960)

John Sr.'s personal wealth amounted to 2% of our nation's wealth.

John Sr. was born in Richford, NY. After high school he went into business and showed a talent for organization. In 1875, with his brother William (1841-1922), he founded the Standard Oil Company, securing control of the US Oil trade. In the late 19th century his power came under strong public criticism. So, he withdrew from active business in 1897, and devoted the rest of his life to philanthropy. He gave over $500 million in aid of medical research, universities, and churches, and established in 1913 the Rockefeller Foundation, "to promote the wellbeing of mankind." John Jr. built the Rockefeller Center.

First and second generation of Rockefellers were not members of Freemasonry. The second and subsequent generations were and are involved in the Masonic *Round Table Groups* and their appendages, the *Council on Foreign Relations* and *Trilateral Commission*. See *Scarlet and the Beast*, vol.1; 3rd ed; chps 9, 10, 19, 24, 25, 27, 30; vol. 3, chps 3-5.

Fig. 19 — Crude gushes from Rockefeller Standard Oil well, Damman No. 7, the first of the Saudi wells to produce oil.

Rockefeller's Standard Oil Co. unearths Saudi Arabia's BLACK GOLD

The King of Saudi Arabia, Abdal-Aziz ibn Saud, had authorized a team of American engineers to explore the trackless desert bordering the Persian Gulf, an arid landscape marked only by the occasional palm-fringed oasis. He hoped they would find water. A tribal leader with precarious finances, Ibn Saud believed the Americans might discover places where he could refresh his warriors' horses and camels. But the team, from Standard Oil of California, had something else on its mind.

Oil had been discovered in other countries in the region, and the engineers thought they would find more in Saudi Arabia. Over several years, they drilled more than half a dozen holes without result. In desperation, they decided to dig deeper at well No. 7. They plumbed to a depth of 4,727 feet and finally hit what would turn out to be the largest supply of crude oil in the world.

The king did not appear to appreciate the news fully at first. It was an entire year after the discovery when he and his retinue arrived in a caravan of 400 automobiles at the pumping station of Ras Tanura to witness the first tanker hauling away its cargo of Saudi crude. Henceforth the king would no longer rely for income on the pilgrims arriving in Mecca, Islam's holiest city. And his kingdom's petroleum wealth would soon emerge as a crucial factor in Middle East politics and the bargaining over global energy supplies. — by Adam Zagorin, TIME, "80 Days that changed the world" 2003.

Fig. 20 — Socialist utopian and inventor of safety razors and blades.

King Camp Gillette (1855-1932)

Gillette was the inventor and first manufacturer of the safety razor.

Born in Fond du Lac, WI. Reared and educated in Chicago. At age 16 he was forced by his family's loss of possessions in the fire of 1871 to go to work as a travelling salesman of hardware.

An employer who noticed his predilection for mechanical tinkering, which sometimes resulted in commercially profitable inventions, advised Gillette to invent "something that would be used and thrown away, so that customers would keep coming back."

While honing a permanent, straightedge razor, Gillette had the idea of substituting a thin double-edged steel blade placed between two plates and held in place by a "T" handle. Though the proposal was received with skepticism because the blades could not be sharpened, the manufactured product was a success from the beginning. In 1903, the first sale consisted of a lot of 51 razors and 168 blades. By the end of 1904, Gillette's company had produced 90,000 razors and 12,400,000 blades.

While Gillette was a young man, socialism was sweeping western and eastern Europe. Intrigued with the idea, he wrote a book in 1894 entitled *The Human Drift,* in which he envisioned an ideal city he named "Metropolis." The city would house most of the country's population in 24,000 closepacked skyscrapers, contain vast public gardens, and run on the natural power of nearby Niagara Falls. Gillette reasoned that if mankind were perfectly organized in such a place, crime and strife would disappear.

After making his millions, he turned his intellectual energies to publicizing his utopian ideals. He wrote that he found competition wasteful and envisaged a planned society in which economic effort would be rationally organized by engineers. In 1910 he vainly offered former Pres. Theodore Roosevelt one million dollars to act as president of an experimental "World Corporation" in the Arizona Territory. Twenty-three years later this same utopian ideal was tried in Russia. It took the murder of 50 million Russians to accept the idea, and 70 years to bankrupt the Soviet Union's "worker's paradise." *10,000 Famous Freemasons* lists Gillette as "a Freemason."

Fig. 21 — The 2-year-long Boxer Rebellion in China was principally against foreigners, ending in a siege of foreign legations in Peking. The Rebellion was put down by an international expeditionary force. According to *Random House Dictionary of the English Language*, Boxer was "a member of a Chinese secret society that carried on an unsuccessful uprising, 1898-00."
Boxer" was a member of a Chinese secret society! Read details below.

The Boxer Rebellion

A Chinese secret society against Christians specifically and Westerners generally. Below is over a year of news clips & analysis of the rebellion compiled by *20th Century Almanac* — World Almanac Publications NY.

News report — January 1, 1900

"Two days ago an English Christian missionary was killed by members of a secret society whose name in Chinese means 'The Righteous and Harmonious Fists," and today an Imperial Edict is issued that is ambivalent in its criticism of the incident — only one of a growing number of attacks on foreigners and Christians by secret societies. At this point, awareness of the mounting tension is limited to the international diplomatic community in Peking, but behind it lies a history of Chinese sentiment that will soon explode on the world stage. "For some decades now, China has been increasingly exploited by foreigners; indeed, it has been invaded and divided up by commercial and governmental representatives of Britain, France, Germany, Italy, Russia, and Japan. Mining and railroad projects have forced large concessions from the Chinese; ports have been appropriated by foreigners for naval stations; hard-pressed for cash and credit, China has signed away much of its future income, and foreigners are gaining a stranglehold on the Chinese economy. Meanwhile, some 2000 Christian missionaries have not only gained the right to protect themselves and their families by laws of 'extraterritoriality,' they are also trying to get special privileges for their Chinese converts.

"During the 1890s, therefore, several secret societies grew up dedicated to getting rid of the foreigners, especially Europeans and Christians. The best known is The Righteous and Harmonious Fists, and because of this name and the fact that members engage in calisthenics, Westerners have taken to calling them 'The Boxers.'"

"The Boxers are a small group, but they can mobilize (at least in northern China) large numbers of Chinese who resent the foreign presence and power. And the Manchu Dynasty — ruled by the Dowager Empress Tzu Hsi as a figurehead — is itself viewed by many Chinese as a foreign element, so the Dowager Empress and her advisers are willing to exploit the resentment and let the Boxers do what the Imperial Government cannot: attack the Westerners.

"On 6 September 1899, John Hay, the US Secretary of State, sent a note to the foreign governments that were dividing China and proposed that they all support an open door' policy, guaranteeing 'no interference with the free commerce' between China and any Foreign state. One by one, these nations agreed to this policy in principle, but their verbal agreement does not change the situation."

News report — March 20, 1900

"**International.** US Secretary of State John Hay announces that all nations to whom he sent notes calling for an 'open door' policy in China have essentially accepted his stand, and that he considers their agreement 'final and definitive.' It comes too late to have much effect on Chinese relations with these foreign powers."

News report — May 17, 1900

"**China.** Disorder has been spreading throughout northern China as resentment against foreigners, fanned by Boxers, aggravates the age-old problems of flooding, plague, famine, and unemployment. On this day, three villages within 100 miles of Peking are burned by Boxers and 60 Chinese Christians killed. Christians begin to take refuge in Peking, Tientsin, and other treaty ports (among them a young American mining engineer, Herbert Hoover, & the son of an American missionary, Henry Luce. Most foreign powers still do not regard this as serious."

News report — May 28, 1900

"**China.** Attacks on and killings of foreigners and Chinese Christians have continued as the Boxers become more confident that the Imperial Court is tacitly approving. Today rioters provoked by Boxers burn the Fengtai Railway Station, junction of the Peking-Tientsin line; besiege the staff, many Belgians, in the compound; and cut the telegraph lines. The government will respond next day only by issuing another of its ambivalent edicts."

News report — May 31 June 4, 1900

"**China.** A contingent of what will eventually number 426 foreign officers and men has been moved from their nations' ships (US, British, German, Austrian, Japanese, Italian, Russian, and French) off Tientsin and been assigned to guard the legations in Peking. Reports of attacks on foreign missionaries and engineers continue."

News report — June 1900

"**China.** The governor of China's province of Manchuria, which borders on Russia and has long been coveted by her, declares war on Russia as part of the Chinese uprising against foreigners. Attacks on Russians across the Amur River will lead to retaliation and invasion by the Russians."

News report — June 6, 1900

"**China.** Boxers cut off all railroad links between Peking and Tientsin, main port city for Peking."

News report — June 9, 1900

"**China.** Boxers destroy the race course in Peking, a few miles from the legations and the center and symbol of diplomatic social life and Western privilege. Legation leaders refuse to evacuate women and children, but they have asked Admiral Edward Seymour of Great Britain, ranking officer of the foreign presence at Tientsin, to bring more troops to guard foreigners in Peking."

News report — June 10, 1900

"**China.** A relief column of some 2000 men — largely naval personnel from the several nations' ships and led by Admiral Seymour — sets out from Tientsin to relieve foreigners trapped in Peking. During the next two weeks, this international force will defeat Chinese insurgents at several points."

News report — June 13, 1900

"**China.** Baron von Ketteler, the German minister to China, beats two young Boxers with his walking stick; when word of this circulates, rioting and arson spread through Peking during the night. The Manchu Court has been wavering about how to deal with the Boxers, but the Empress decides to support them and their attacks on foreigners by issuing an edict that refers to Boxers as 'people's soldiers."

News report — June 16-17, 1900

"**China.** Foreign legations in Peking are now all but isolated by violence rampant in the streets. Legations send out patrols of guards who seek to confront the Boxers. On the 16th, a terrible fire set by the Boxers virtually destroys the Western Quarter, then spreads to engulf many Chinese landmarks. Meanwhile, the Taku forts guarding the port of Tientsin bombard foreign ships offshore, but the forts are captured by foreign forces."

News report — June 19, 1900

"**China.** After deliberations in the Imperial Palace, notes are delivered to the 11 major legations: since foreign troops are firing on Chinese. 'We break off all relations with your government.' Each legation is asked to leave for Tientsin with all its personnel, escorted by Imperial troops. A majority of foreigners wish to accept this offer, but are soon persuaded that this will mean abandoning Chinese servants and staffs to almost certain slaughter."

News report — June 20, 1900

"**China.** Most foreigners in the Peking legations now accept that they are under siege. But Baron von Ketteler, the German minister, decides he will go to Chinese authorities and demand more guards for those who wish to go to Tientsin. He is killed by Boxers en route, and by afternoon it is clear that no foreigners are going to get away."

News report — June 22, 1900

"**China.** Practically the whole foreign community in Peking, including many Chinese Christians, retreat to the British compound. In the afternoon, in an attempt to drive them out, Boxers set fire to the nearby Hanlin Yuan, the greatest library of Chinese scholarship; the flames serve only to destroy much of the library. At Tientsin the foreign community is now besieged and isolated."

News report — June 25, 1900

"**Russia.** Russia mobilizes its army in eastern Siberia preparatory to acting against the Chinese; the excuse is Boxer-instigated attacks on Russian territory across from Manchuria, but Russia has been seeking control of that province for some time so as to crowd out the Japanese on the Asian mainland."

News report — June 26, 1900

"**Japan.** Japan mobilizes 20,000 troops to help put down the Boxer uprising — but also to advance its long-term interest in gaining land and power in Mainland Asia."

News report — June 29, 1900

"**China.** The Imperial Court issues what is essentially a declaration of war against the foreigners in China and blames hostilities on them. This will become a license for the Boxers and their supporters to turn against foreigners and their Chinese converts with even greater ferocity. Most actions occur in northern China, particularly in Shantung Province, under the Manchu governor Yu Hsien, and in Manchuria, where the Roman

Catholic bishop and others are burned alive after taking refuge in the cathedral in Mukden."

News report — July 6-14, 1900

"**China.** International forces in and around Tientsin — now about 14,000 launch an assault on this key port. After taking at least 800 casualties, the allies control the forts and the city by the 14th; the foreign troops proceed to loot the city, stealing or destroying millions of dollars worth of goods."

News report — July 16, 1900

"**International.** A report appears in London, and spreads throughout the world, that all foreigners in Peking have been massacred. Although it is soon exposed as false, the story helps mobilize governmental support for relief of the foreigners under siege."

News report — July 19-21, 1900

"**China.** The Emperor appeals to France, Germany, Japan, and the USA to help 'mediate' the Boxer uprising. Foreign powers believe the Chinese should stop these attacks, which continue in parts of China."

News report — August 4, 1900

"**China.** The allied expeditionary force sets off from Tientsin for Peking, comprises of some 10,000 Japanese, 5,000 Russians, 3,000 British, 2,000 Americans, and 800 French (the Germans have not yet arrived)."

News report — August 14, 1900

"**China.** Several foreign units in the relief force have agreed to coordinate their movements into Peking, but at the last minute the Russian forces begin to move ahead, so all units race to be the first to relieve foreigners. (The British troops are first into the compound.) Before the afternoon is over, all legations are relieved, including at least 400 officers and enlisted men who had been serving as guards, many civilians, and many Chinese who had taken refuge. (In the weeks under siege, 67 were killed, 120 wounded, and five died from other causes.) In Manchuria, Russia declares it has annexed the right bank of the Amur River and is moving to seize the city of Harbin and the port of Newchang."

News report — August 15, 1900

"**China.** The Empress and some of her family, the court, and retainers flee (after executing some retainers considered disloyal, while others commit suicide) and make their way slowly to Sian, 700 miles southeast of Peking and capital of Shensi Province. (They will arrive on 26 October.) In Peking foreign troops begin to move through the city, not only inflicting losses on the Boxers, but destroying and pillaging the property of innocent Chinese. In subsequent weeks foreign civilians (including diplomats) join the troops in what becomes one of the most shameful looting on record: the famed Peking Observatory is virtually dismember-ed, and many artistic and cultural valuables stolen. By 28 August, the allies have taken over the Imperial City, but have been ordered to stay out of the innermost Forbidden City; now the allied leaders call on the Imperial Court to return. Elsewhere in China, Boxers continue their attacks on missionaries and their converts. The Russians advance in Manchuria."

News report — September 3, 1900

"**China.** The Russians have had their eye on Manchuria since the 16th century, and the Boxer Rebellion has given them the desired excuse to invade and conquer it. The Russians now control both sides of the Amur River, the Russo-Manchurian boundary, and at Blagovestchensk, a Russian town with a sizable Chinese population, Russian Cossack troops drive some 5000 Chinese residents into the Amur, where they are clubbed, stabbed, and drowned. Similar incidents are reported elsewhere along the Amur, and travelers on the river report that it is virtually blood-red and clogged with bodies."

News report — September 14, 1900

"**China.** There are now 62,000 foreign troops in Peking and nearby cities; they are still defeating the Boxers in confrontations, but attacks on isolated Chinese Christians continue, providing foreign troops with the excuse to continue attacks on Chinese."

News report — October 1, 1900

"**China.** During this month German troops sent to participate in the relief of Peking arrive, led by Count von Waldersee, who assumes the role of commander of the International Relief Force. Having come too late to take part in the true relief, the Germans send out 'punitive expeditions" against the Boxers and are soon engaged in looting the Chinese populace."

News report — October 10, 1900

"**China.** Foreign ministers in Peking begin their first serious negotiations over what conditions their nations will impose on the Chinese. Some nations demand more severe penalties than do others, but they will agree on a compromise proposal fostered by the French Government: punishment (including death for some) of those responsible for the Boxer uprising; indemnities for governments, organizations, and individuals; dismantling of forts, including the Taku forts at Tientsin; and other terms that will force the Chinese to accept occupation in some areas. In Manchuria, meanwhile, the Russians capture the major city of Mukden on this day, part of their own plan to take over the whole province."

News report — November 1, 1900

"**China.** Allied military units continue to fight Boxer-led resistance in cities and outposts, while anti-Christian outbreaks continue."

News report — November 6, 1900

"**USA.** In the national elections, President McKinley and his Vice-President, Theodore Roosevelt, defeat the Democrats' William Jennings Bryan."

News report — December 24, 1900

"**China.** The ministers accredited to Peking have been conferring since October and have now reached agreement, adopting terms proposed by the French. Today they meet for the first time with the Chinese representatives of the Empress and present their list of 'irrevocable conditions' before their nations withdraw troops. The Chinese, knowing the situation in Peking and elsewhere, realize they must agree to these terms and submit them to the Empress, now in Sian. (But it will be September 7, 1901 before the final agreement is signed.)"

News report — January 4-10, 1901

"**China.** The Dowager Empress and advisers, exiled at Sian, receive the note with the conditions from the foreign nations for withdrawing troops. At first the Empress will try to modify some of the more stringent terms, but when persuaded that the foreigners will not negotiate any further, she issues the acceptance order to her representative in Peking."

News report —February 1, 1901

"**China.** As negotiations proceed over final details of terms demanded by the foreigners, leaders of the Boxer uprising are named by the diplomats as 'deserving death'; many will be killed, others allowed to commit suicide, some banished, and some will flee."

News report — September 6, 1901

"**USA.** President McKinley, visiting the Pan-American Exposition in Buffalo, NY, is shot by Leon Czolgosz, regarded as a half-crazed anarchist. McKinley's wounds seem to be healing, but gangrene sets in."

News report — September 7, 1901

"**China.** Representatives of 11 foreign nations and of China sign what is variously known as the *Peace of Peking* or the *Boxer Protocol*. It established that China is to pay $333 million in indemnities (with the USA to get $25 million): permits the stationing of foreign troops in Peking; and leaves Russian troops in Manchuria. China remains hostage to foreign powers. (It is estimated that about 250 foreign missionaries, including 50 children, were killed by the Boxers; 32,000 Chinese converts to Christianity were also killed by the Boxers)."

Fig. 22 — The Boxer Rebellion
Chinese print: Boxers smite fleeing Westerners.

Fig. 23 — McKinley's photo is also in Section 4, Figure 37 as a Major in the Union Army during our Civil War.

13° R.A.M. William McKinley
(1843-1901)

25th President of the U.S.A. (1896-1901)

Although a Union Army major in our Civil War, he received his Masonic degrees in a southern lodge during the war.

While protecting and managing the army hospital at Winchester, Va., he was struck by the ties which he saw existing between the Union surgeons and Confederate prisoners. When he learned the reason for such a brotherly spirit in spite of war and hatred, he asked to be admitted to the Craft. His petition was presented to Hiram Lodge No. 21 of Winchester. He was initiated May 1, 1865, passed May 2, and raised May 3.

He was made an honorary member of the Illinois Masonic Veterans Association on Oct. 28, 1898. On Oct. 23, 1899 he tendered a reception to the Supreme Council, AASR (SJ) at the White House. On May 23, 1900, during an Imperial Council meeting of the Shrine in Washington, DC, he received members of the Mystic Shrine at a reception at the White House.

On Aug. 4, 1900, he sent 2000 American troops to China to protect American missionaries during the Boxer Rebellion.

On Sept. 6, 1901, he was shot by anarchist, Leon Czolgosz, at Buffalo, NY and died Sept. 14. At his viewing Sept. 17 in Washington, DC, five comanderies of Knights Templar escorted his remains from the White House to the Capitol. At the immense funeral on the 19th, two thousand Knights Templar in uniform formed the 4th division of the funeral escort.

Fig. 24 — **3° Theodore "Teddy" Roosevelt** (1858-1919)
26th President of the United States upon the death of McKinley.

Member of Matinecock Lodge No. 806 of Oyster Bay, N.Y. Received blue degrees shortly after he became Vice President under McKinley. Was made honorary member of many lodges. Delivered address at Masonic laying of cornerstone at Army War College, 1903; laid cornerstone at north gate to Yellowstone Park, under auspices of Grand Lodge of Montana, 1903; broke ground for Masonic Temple at Spokane, WA 1903; attended Masonic corner stone laying of House of Representatives' office building, 1906, and much more. Was a proud and active Freemason.

SECTION 6
FEDERAL RESERVE ACT WAS PASSED BY FREEMASONRY WHILE THE SAME FREEMASONRY WAS PLANNING WORLD WAR ONE !!!

Fig. 1 — Federal Reserve Act passed while our attention was diverted on impending World War.
Read *Scarlet and the Beast*, Vol. 3, Chaps. 4-5 about Masons who advised Pres. Wilson to sign this unconstitutional Act.

33° Carter Glass (1858-1946)
Secretary of the Treasury under Pres. Wilson, and U.S. Senator from Virginia.

Born in Lynchburg, VA. Educated in public and private schools at Lynchburg. He later received honorary doctorates from 13 colleges and universities. He was the owner of the *Daily News* and *Daily Advance* of Lynchburg. He was a member of the state legislature several terms before serving as U.S. Congressman to the 57th to 65th Congresses (1909-19). He resigned from Congress in 1918 to become Secretary of the Treasury in Wilson's cabinet, serving until 1920. That year he resigned to accept senatorship by appointment of Virginia's governor. He served in that capacity from 1920 until his death in 1946.

Glass was president pro-tem of the Senate from 1941 until his death in 1946. He was chairman of the important Appropriations Committee of the Senate and member of the Foreign Relations Committee.

Glass was a member of Hill City Lodge No. 183 of Lynchburg. He received the 32° AASR at Lynchburg, Aug. 16, 1929. He was later coronated 33°.

In 1940 he wrote his lodge as follows: "It seems to me I was taken in Hill Lodge considerably more than 50 years ago. I was lectured for entrance by the late Thomas N. Davis, one of the most brilliant Masons who ever wielded a gavel; and, before I entered public life 40 years ago, I could recite the ritual backward as well as forward, and took the most intense interest in Masonic work. I have never ceased to regard the Masonic fraternity in a little less reverential vein than my church. No good Mason could fail to be a good churchman, and no churchman should omit to become a good Mason." Senator Glass handed Pres. Woodrow Wilson the Federal Reserve Act.

Read about this traitorous Act in *Scarlet and the Beast*, Vol. 3, Chaps. 4-5.

Fig. 2 — Federal Reserve Act

32° William Gibbs McAdoo (1863-1941)

Secretary of Treasury (1913-18) under Woodrow Wilson. U.S. Senator from California (1933-39). Chairman of board of American President Lines (1939-41).

Born in Marietta, Ga. Educated at U. of Tennessee. His second marriage was to Eleanor Randolph Wilson, daughter of President Wilson. The wedding took place at the White House, May 7, 1914.

He was admitted to the bar in 1885, practiced at Chattanooga until 1892, moved to NYC to be partner in a law firm with William Mc Addo (no relation).

William G. was president and director of Hudson & Manhattan Railroad, which built and operated four tunnels under the Hudson River, the first being completed in 1904. He was also chairman of the Federal Reserve Board; chairman ex-officio of Federal Farm Loan Board and director general of U.S. railroads.

In 1920 and again in 1924, he was a leading contender for the Democratic nomination for president.

In New York he was a member of Chancellor Walworth Lodge No. 271, and in California of Henry S. Orme Lodge No. 456, Los Angeles. He was Exalted in Signet Chapter No. 57, R.A.M., Los Angeles on June 15, 1925. Became a Knight Templar and a 32° AASR (SJ).

Fig. 3 — The unconstitutional Federal Reserve Act was passed by Congress.
Freemason House advised President Wilson to sign this Act into law.

33° Edward M. House (1858-1938)

US diplomat. Born in Houston, TX. Awarded 33° in that city, according to Dr. John Coleman. During and after War he represented USA in many conferences, and was long a close associate of Wilson, helping him to draft terms for peace at end of WWI. Also supported the establishment of the League of Nations.

When WWI began, American Freemasonry immediately went into action. May 1917 issue of *The Freemason*, a British Masonic monthly, confirmed American Masonic activity: "Already during the first weeks of the war a great Masonic meeting held in the United States passed a resolution to give to Great Britain and her allies all possible support in the present war."

That support came by favorable propaganda created by Masonic journalists, including Col.

E.M. House. (See *S&B*, Vol 1, 3rd ed., Ch. 21, 22, 25)

Woodrow T. Wilson (1856-1924)
28th President (1913-21). Born in Stanton, VA. Studied at Princeton and Johns Hopkins. Became a lawyer and university professor. President of Princeton and Gov. of New Jersey (1911). Elected Democrat President 1912 and 1916. His administration brought us into WWI. He was not a Mason, but intentionally surrounded himself with Masonic advisors.

In 1917 he supposedly coined the name for postwar League of Nations when the League of Nations had already met under that name in 1913, one year before WWI began. Wilson is also credited with delivering the Federal Reserve System. See *S&B*, V1, 3rd ed., ch. 21, 22, 24, 25.

Figure 4 — Anti-Mason Archduke Franz Ferdinand and his wife Sophie. Their assassination by Serbian Freemasons triggered World War I. See *Scarlet and the Beast*, Vol. I, 3rd edition, chaps. 21, 22, 24, 25.

Count Czernin, in his book *Im Welt-Krieg (In the World War)* wrote that the Archduke was well aware of the Freemason's plot against his life: "The Archduke knew quite well that the risk of an attempt on his life was imminent. A year before the war, he informed me that the Freemasons had resolved his death. He also told me the town where that decision was said to have been taken, and mentioned the names of several Hungarian and Austrian politicians who probably knew something about it."

Fig. 5 — Assassin Gavrilo Princip (right) with co-conspirator Trifko Grabez (left) and friend on a bench in Belgrade's Kalmedgan Park. The assassins were members of Young Serbia, the youth corps of European Freemasonry.

"On the 28th of June 1914 the Archduke, heir to the crown of the Austrian monarchy, and his wife succumbed to the bullets of Serbian freemasons [sic]... Distributed among the crowd were eight assassins armed with bombs and revolvers, of whom the most resolute were Cabrinovic, Princip, and Grabez." All eight were members of Young Serbia, the youth corps of Serbian Freemasonry — equivalent to the DeMolays in America. Oct. 12, 1914, the assassins were tried. Freemason Cabrinovic unconcernedly told judges of the military court: "In Freemasonry it is allowed to kill." See excerpts of trial from *Pharos Shorthand Transcript,* pp. 425-426.

Fig. 6&7 — Masons plotting the assassination of Archduke Ferdinand.

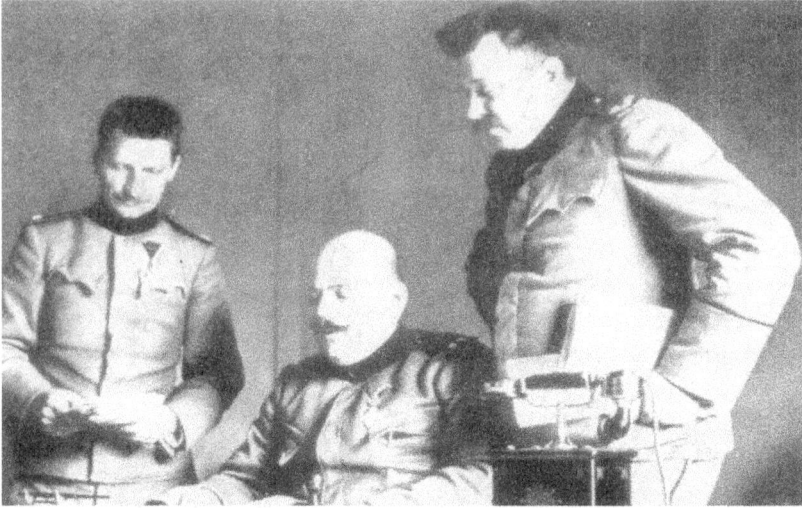

Chief of Serbia's Intelligence Bureau, Colonel Dragutin C. Dimitrijevic, flanked by aides. Dragutin was known to his intelligence officers as "Apis." As head of Serbian Freemasonry (The Black Hand), he was aware of and funded the assassins. In the automobile below is the Archduke and his wife. Within the hour both will be dead and within 5 weeks WWI will begin.

Fig. 8 — Arresting Freemason Princip, the Assassin (under the arrow).

Freemasonry's assassination of Archduke Ferdinand triggered World War One !!!

Read the story in *Scarlet and the Beast*, Vol. I, 3rd Edition, Chapters 20, 22, 24, 25!

Gavrilo Princip (1894-1918). Nationalist and revolutionary, born in Obljaj, Bosnia. He was a member of a secret Serbian terrorist organization known as the "Black Hand", dedicated to the achievement of independence for the South Slav peoples from the Austro-Hungarian empire. Princip died in a Austrian prison during World War One. *The Cambridge Biographical Encyclopedia* — Cambridge University Press.

All eight assassins were members of "Young Serbia" the youth corps of Muslim Serbian Freemasonry. Young Serbia is equivalent to the Demolays in America. While World War One was raging throughout Europe, the Young Serbian assassins were tried and convicted.

Before reading their arrogant confessions during their trial on the next two pages, American Freemasonry stated in 1950 that this trial never took place, but gives absolutely no evidence to that claim. Whereas, at least two authors (one Frenchman in 1928 and one English woman in 1933, who respectively wrote 19 years and 14 years after the fact, both confirm that the trial did take place (read above chapters in *S&B*).

Excerpts from the Pharos Shorthand Transcript of the trial

More detail found in Chap. 21 of *Scarlet and the Beast*, Vol. 1, 3rd edition

The President — Did you believe that Slavs of southern Austria-Hungary would gain any advantage from your act?

Princip — We were agreed upon the choice of means for helping the southern Slavs.

The President — What were those means?

Princip — Murder; the disappearance of all those who were opposed to the realization of Pan-Slavia and who are injust [sic] to the people.

Certain passages of the interrogations during the trial confirm the influence and involvement of International Freemasonry in the plan to kill the Archduke Franz Ferdinand:

Cabrinovic — He [Casimirovic] is a Freemason, even in some degree one of their chiefs. He travelled abroad immediately after the men had offered themselves to carry out the assassination. He went to Russia, France and Buda-Pesth. Every time when I asked Ciganovic how far our projects had advanced, he replied that I should know when Casimirovic should return. About this time Ciganovic also told me that the Freemasons had already condemned to death the heir to the throne two years ago, but that they had not found men to carry out their judgment.

Premusic — Have you read the books of Rosic?

Cabrinovic — I have read his treatise on Freemasonry.

Premusic — Were these books distributed in Belgrade?

Cabrinovic — I set them in type as a printer.

Premusic — Tell me, do you believe in God or anything?

Cabrinovic — No.

Premusic — Are you a Mason?

Cabrinovic — Why do you ask me that? I cannot answer you on that subject.

Premusic — Is Tankosic a Mason?

Cabrinovic — Yes, and Ciganovic also.

The President — From which it follows that you also are a Mason, for a Freemason never admits to anyone but another Mason that he belongs to that society.

Cabrinovic — Please do not ask me about that subject for I shall not reply.

The President — Tell me something more about the motives. Did you know before deciding to attempt the assassination that Tankosic and Ciganovic were Freemasons? Had the fact of you and they being Freemasons an influence on your resolve?

Cabrinovic — Yes.

The President — Did you receive from them the mission to carry out the assassination?

Cabrinovic — I received from no one the mission to carry out the assassination. Freemasonry had to do with it because it strengthened me in my intention. In Freemasonry it is permitted to kill. Ciganovic told me that the Freemasons had condemned to death the Archduke Franz Ferdinand more than a year before.

The President — Did he tell you that from the very beginning or only after you spoke to him of your wish to carry out the assassination?

Cabrinovic — We had already spoken about Freemasonry but he said nothing to me of the condemnation to death before we had quite decided to carry out the assassination.

The following passage is from the interrogation of Princip, who fired the fatal shots at the Archduke and who also confirms the origin of the assassination plot in the Lodge:

The President — Did you speak about Freemasonry with Ciganovic?

Princip (insolently) — Why ask me that?

The President — I ask because I must know. Did you speak to him about it or not?

Princip — Yes, Ciganovic told me that he was a Freemason.

The President — When did he tell you that?

Princip — He told me when I was asking about the means of carrying out the assassination. He added that he would speak with a certain person and that he would receive the necessary means. On another occasion, he told me that the heir to the throne had been condemned to death in a Masonic Lodge.

The President — And are you also a Freemason?

Princip — Why that question? I shall not reply. (After short silence): No.

The President — Is Cabrinovic a Mason?

Princip — I do not know. Perhaps he is. He told me once that he was going to join a lodge.

Leon de Poncins, writing 14 years after the trial, reports in his *Secret Powers Behind Revolution*, 1928, that "Twenty accused persons appeared on the 12th Oct. 1914 before the military court at Sarajevo. All were Masons. Eight were directly concerned in the murder. The four most active participants were Princip, Cabrinovic, Grabez and Illic. All were young men 18-20 yrs. old." Illic and two other accused were condemned to death and hanged on Feb. 2, 1915. Cabrinovic and Grabez were sentenced to 20 years imprisonment, but died before WWI ended.

Fig. 9 — Homeland for the Jews. For a list of Masonic players behind the Balfour Declaration, which declared a return of the Jews to Palestine after World War One. see *Scarlet and the Beast*, Vol. 1, 3rd ed., chaps. 17, 21, 22.

Theodore Herzl (1856-1941)
Founder of Zionism

33° Louis (Dembitz) Brandeis (1856-1941)
U.S. Supreme Court Justice
Brandeis was intimate with 33° Col. Edward House, who was constantly at Pres. Woodrow Wilson's side (see Fig. 3 this Section). Brandeis suggested to House that the White House back negotiations with the Zionists for a homeland.

Fig. 10 — Masonic players behind Balfour Declaration. Declaration was to return the Jews to their homeland (see S&B, Vol. 1, 3rd ed., ch. 17,21,22).

Arthur James Balfour (1848-1930)
Author of Balfour Declaration (1917)
Balfour was the British prime minister from 1902-1905 and foreign secretary from 1916-1919. In the latter post he wrote the Balfour Declaration (1917) that expressed

official British approval of Zionism and led indirectly to the establishment of Israel as an independent state in 1948.

33° Baron Edmond de Rothschild (1856-1941)
Jewish financier who sponsored the first Jewish colonies in Palestine.

SECTION 7
RUSSIAN COMMUNIST REVOLUTION OF 1917

To create the Communist Worker's Paradise seeds of rebellion were sown in Russia by Grand Orient Freemasonry a century before the 1917 Bolshevik Revolution.

Those seeds were watered by the blood of two million Russian soldiers killed during World War One. After the War, Grand Orient Freemasonry's Communist experiment was forced on Russia by the starvation of another two million. By 1935, Stalin had slaughtered an additional 46 million. Between 1915 and 1935 a total of 50 million Russians were killed to perfect Masonry's "Worker's Paradise."

Read about the carnage in *Scarlet and the Beast* Vol. I, 3rd ed., Chaps. 17, 22-23.

Fig. 1 — Born Levi Mordechai to Jewish parents. Was a 32° Grand Orient Freemason. Wrote under the pen name "Karl Marx." Became the socalled Father of Communism.

32° **Karl Marx** (1818-1883)

Following is generally accepted history of Marx.

Founder of international communism. Born in Trier, Germany. Studied law at Bonn and Berlin, but took up history, Hegelian philosophy, & Feuerbach's materialism. He edited a radical newspaper, and after it was suppressed, he moved to Paris (1843) and Brussels (1845). There, with Engels as his closest collaborator and disciple, he reorganized the Communist League, which met in London in 1847. In 1848 he finalized the Communist Manifesto, which attacked the state as the instrument of oppression, and religion and culture as ideologies of the capitalist class. He was expelled from Brussels, and in 1849 settled in London, where he studied economics, and wrote the first volume of his major work, *Das Kapital,* 1867, with two further volumes added in 1884 and 1894 after his death. He was a leading figure in the First International from 1864 until its demise in 1872. He held Communist meetings in Freemason's Hall in London, England. The last decade of his life was marked by increasing ill health. He is buried in Highgate Cemetery, London.

Karl Marx was a 32° German Grand Orient Mason. He is famous for having said, "Religion is the opiate of the People." In 1844 he remarked, "The criticism of religion is the beginning of all criticism." He hated his Jewish heritage, and wrote about his hatred in "A World Without Jews," and, "The Jewish Nigger." His books helped promote anti-Semitism. (Read more about Karl Marx in *Scarlet and the Beast,* Vol. 1, 3rd ed, Chps. 7, 9, 12, 22-23).

Fig. 2 — Karl Marx edited the radical paper, *Die Rheinische Aeitung*, until it was suppressed in 1843. Here he is shown as a Promethean figure, chained to his printing press. The Grand Orient "League of the Just," known in Germany as the "Bund," financed Karl Marx's communist activity in France and England. See *Scarlet and the Beast*; Vol. I, 3rd ed, Ch.22.

Fig. 3 — Jewish poet Heinrich Heine accurately predicted the Bolshivic Revolution some 74 years before it occurred.

Heinrich Heine (1797-1856)
Masonic poet and critic

In 1843, the celebrated Jewish poet Heinrich Heine organized into a book a selection of articles he had written for the *Augsburg Gazzette* between 1840 and 1843. The book, *Lutece*, prophesied (or did it expose a plan for) the future horrors of a communist revolution in Russia. Listen to Heine's uncanny prophecy:

"I have not described the storm itself. I have described the great storm-clouds which bore the approaching tempest, advancing dark and menacing across the sky. I have made frequent and exact descriptions of those sinister legions, those titans buried underground, who lay in wait in the lowest ranks of society; I have hinted that they would arise from their obscurity when their hour was come. These shadowy creatures, these nameless monsters, to whom the future belongs, were then usually only looked down on through lorgnettes; from this angle they resembled fleas gone mad. But I have shown them in their greatness, in their true light, and seen thus, they resemble if anything, the most fearsome crocodiles and gigantic dragons that have ever emerged from the foul abyss. "Communism is the secret name of this tremendous adversary which the rule of the proletariat, with all that that implies, opposes to the existing bourgeois regime. It will be an appalling duel. How will it end? That is known to the gods and goddesses in whose hands lies the future. For our part, all we know is that, however little talked-of at present, however miserable an existence it drags out in concealed attics on wretched beds of straw, Communism is nonetheless the dark hero, cast for an enormous if fleeting role in the modern tragedy, and awaiting only its cue to enter the stage. "There is an approaching rumble of hard times filled with upheavals.... Any prophet wishing to write a new Apocalypse will have to invent new monsters so frightful that the old symbolic beast in St. John would appear in comparison no more than cooing turtledoves and gracious Cupids.... The future smells of Russian knouts, of blood, of impiety and of violent blows. I advise our descendants to have good thick skins on them when they are born into this world."

Fig. 4 — Russian Freemasonry planned the Communist Revolution more than a century before the event. Tzars and Tzarinas alike fell into its snare, whether they joined,

protected, or persecuted the Craft.

Peter the Great (1672-1725)
Regent Sofia

Tzar of Russia (1682-1721) and Emperor of Russia (1721-1725). Born in Moscow, the son of Tsar Alexis and his second wife Natalia Naryshkin. Peter was joint Tzar with his mentally retarded half-brother, Ivan, under the regency of their sister, Sophia (1682-89). On Ivan's death (1696) Peter became sole tzar.

Peter fought major wars with the Ottoman empire, Persia, and in particular Sweden, which Russia defeated in the Great Northern War. This victory established Russia as a major European power, and gained a maritime exit on the Baltic, where in 1703 Peter founded his new capital, St. Petersburg. Peter traveled widely and became impressed with the western world and introduced western culture into Russia, raising it to a recognized place among European powers. However, when he embarked on a series of sweeping military, fiscal, administrative, educational, cultural, and ecclesiastical reforms, all based on western European models, all classes of society suffered from the impact and the brutality of their implementation. His own son, Alexis, died under torture (1718), suspected of leading a conspiracy against his father's reforms.

While in Europe, Peter was initiated into European Masonry, and upon his return established the first Masonic Lodge in St. Petersburg, then placed his favorite councillor, General Lefort, as first Master of the Lodge.

He failed to name a successor, and was succeeded by his wife, Catherine I.

Fig. 5 — Russian Freemasonry and the Communist Revolution

Empress Catherine I (1684-1727)
Tzarina of Russia (1725-1727)

Tzarina of Russia, who succeeded her husband, Peter the Great. She was of lowly birth, of Livonian peasant origin, taken prisoner in 1702 and made a serf of Prince Menshikov. She attracted the attention of Peter the Great. She first was his advisor, then mistress. She married him in 1712. In 1722 Tzar Peter passed a law allowing him to nominate a successor. He chose Catherine, having her crowned empress in 1724. After the Tzar's death, Prince Menshikov ensured her succession to the throne in 1725-27.

Shortly after their marriage in 1712, aware that Peter had established the first Masonic Lodge in Russia, Catherine asked permission to found the Order of St. Catherine, an order of Knighthood for only women, of which she would be Grand Mistress. It was a quasi-Masonic body, equivalent to the Eastern Star in America.

Fig. 6 — Russian Freemasonry and the Communist Revolution.

Catherine II Catherine the Great (1729-1796)

Empress of Russia (1762-1796). Through a conspiracy coordinated by her lover, Catherine gained the support of the army, and Peter III was dethroned. A few days afterwards, Peter III was murdered by her lover. In 1762 Catherine had herself crowned Empress, and began a reign that lasted 34 years.

The year Catherine was crowned, she issued an edict against all Masonic meetings in her dominions, but subsequently learned the "true character of the institution," and not only revoked her order, but invited the Freemasons to reestablish their lodges and constitute new ones. This began the undoing of Tzarist Russia.

Paul I (1754-1801)

Emperor of Russia, 1796-1801. Son of Emperor Peter III and Catherine the Great. Paul succeeded Catherine and ruled despotically, but inaugurated some reforms in the treatment of serfs.

He is said to have been a Freemason, and during the early part of his reign the Order received some impetus. But later in his reign he turned his protection away from Freemasonry and toward the Knights of Malta, which was influenced by the Jesuits. Freemasonry languished during his reign. He was assassinated by the Freemasons on March 12, 1801. His son, Alexander I, succeeded him and embraced Freemasonry.

Fig. 7 — Russian Freemasonry and the Communist Revolution.
See *Scarlet and the Beast,* Vol. 1, 3rd ed., chap. 11.

Alexander I (1777-1825)

In 1801 Alex I succeeded Paul 1 as Tzar of Russia and reigned to 1825. At first he prohibited secret societies, but rescinded the order in 1803. It is said that he was convinced by Johann Boeber of the benefits of Masonry and he not only lifted the ban, but joined the lodge himself. Boeber later became Grand Master of Russia.

Some sources claim Alex I was initiated in Canongate Kilwinning Lodge of Edinburgh, Scotland. In 1814 he acted as Master, conferring the degrees on William III, Emperor of Germany, in a military lodge in Paris.

He was likewise a member of the Polish Grand Lodge. In November 1815 the Polish Masons gave a banquet in his honor after which he left generous gifts. He has been accused of using Freemasonry for political purposes.

In 1822 he became suspicious of the political dangers inherent in some of the Russian Lodges, and on the advice of Grand Master Kushelev of the Grand Lodge "Astra," banned Freemasonry on August 1, 1822. Within three years he died under mysterious circumstances. His successor, Nicholas I, confirmed the ban on April 21, 1826.

It was only an outward ban, however. Revolutionary Grand Orient Freemasonry simply buried its intrigue under a new name — communism. The future Alexander II will lose his life to these communist bomb throwers. From *Peter the Great* we read, "This information was presented in a document to Emperor Alexander I by the last Grand Master of the Astera Grand Lodge in an effort to save Russian Freemasonry from being outlawed by that emperor."

Masons in the Court of Tzar Alexander I

Freemasonry came to Russia as a result of the Napoleonic Wars, (*see Scarlet and the Beast*, Vol 1, 3rd edition, "Introduction and Chaps.11&22). After Alexander I joined Freemasonry, he surrounded himself with "fellow travelers." In 1822 the European kings convinced him of the danger of Freemasonry, after which he banned the Order. A few of the powerful Masons in his court are listed by Denslow:

Alexander A. Gerebzov: Russian Major General was raised (3°) in a Paris lodge. On his return to Russia he opened the Grand Orient Lodge *Les Amis Reunis* at St. Petersburg on June 10, 1802. Gerebzov's lodge was a military lodge impregnated with French ideas. It represented the "liberal" branch of Russian Freemasonry, bent on abolishing religion, abolishing national and social differences, and forming a true brotherhood of man.

Count Alexander I: Ostermann Tolstoy (1770-1837). Russian infantry general who distinguished himself in the wars against Napoleon. Member of Les Amis Reunis Grand Orient Lodge at St. Petersburg.

Konstantin Pavlovich (1779-1831). Second son of Paul I and brother of Alexander I. Both he and Alexander were initiated into Freemasonry at the same time. Pavlovich became a member of Grand Orient Lodge *Les Amis Reunis.*

Mikhail M. Speransky (1772-1839). Initiated at a secret meeting of the Grand Lodge of the *Polar Star* at the request of Alexander I. He was later a member of a governmental committee to look into the political status of all Masonic lodges.

Count Pavel Andreevich Shuvalov (1773-1823). *aide-de-camp* to Emperor Alexander I, was elected ruler of the Russian Directorial Grand Lodge in 1814 to replace Boeber. The grand lodge was so split with dissension that Shuvalov declined the post, and Count Mussin-PushkinBruce was elected in his place.

Count Mussin-Pushkin-Bruce. Russian secret councillor and chamberlain of Emperor Alexander I, was head of *Directorial* Grand Lodge of Russia in 1814. Also Grand master of Grand Orient Lodge *Astrea* in 1815. He received the edict on Aug. 1, 1822 from Alexander I to close all his Grand Orient lodges.

Count Adam Rgevussky. Grand Master of the Russian Grand Orient Lodge *Astrea* in 1820, following Count Mussin-Pushkin-Bruce. His Deputy Grand Master was Prince Alexander Lobanov-Rostovsky, who was an honorary member of several Polish lodges in Warsaw and Cracow.

Sergei Stepanovich Lanskoy (1787-1862) was Deputy Grand Master of the Grand Lodge Provincial of Russia in 1817. Lanskoy also received the edict on Aug. 1, 1822 from Alexander I to close all his Grand Lodges.

Aleksander S. Pushkin (1799-1837). Russian poet and Freemason.

Fig. 8 — The 1825 Decembrist Revolt, organized and carried out by Freemasonry, was the first physical manifestation of what ended in the 1917 Bolshevic Revolution. See *Scarlet and Beast*, Vol. 1, 3rd ed., chp. 22.

The Decembrist Revolt, Dec. 14, 1825

From the beginning of 1814, Grand Orient Freemason Pavel Ivanovich Pestel had been persistent in his attempt to unite under one federal republic all of Russia, Poland, Bohemia, Moravia, Dalmatia, Hungary, Transylvania, Serbia, Moldavia, and Valachia. Conspiring with him were many princes initiated into Freemasonry and indoctrinated in subversion. When Pestel disclosed his plans to murder the whole Russian imperial family and proclaim a republic, Prince Jablonowski of Poland, a fellow Mason, recoiled in horror, and the Poles were allowed to form their own government.

The revolution was planned for 1829, but the sudden death of Alexander 1st in 1825 hastened the revolt. The uprising occurred on Monday, December 14, 1825, failed, and the leaders of the "Decembrists," as the rebels were called, were arrested and executed a few months later.

Under the new Tzar Nicholas I, Freemasonry was severely suppressed. The Scottish Rite *New Age Magazine*, Feb, 1945, reports: "After 1825, many Russian Masons exiled themselves to France where lodges operating in the Russian language were sponsored by atheistic Grand Orient Freemasonry. Some of the exiles later returned to Russia, and organized lodges in St. Petersburg and Moscow...and had 'an avowedly political aim and view; namely, that of the overthrow of the autocracy.'"

Fig. 9 — Famous Russian Masons used literature to incite revolution.
See *Scarlet and the Beast,* Vol. 1, 3rd edition, notes section for chap. 22.

Aleksander S. Pushkin (1799-1837)
Russian poet. His *Ode to Liberty*, written in 1820, caused his exile to South Russia. He was reinstated in good graces to write the life of Peter the Great.

Russian Freemason and author Telepneff, in his *Russian Freemasonry During the Reign of Alexander I*, credits Pushkin as being a Freemason.

In 1837 Pushkin was killed in a duel.

Leo Tolstoi (1828-1910)
Russian novelist, social and moral philosopher, who wrote the famous *War and Peace*. Many have thought him a Freemason, for in his War and Peace he describes a Masonic initiation with great accuracy, and several of his characters are Freemasons.

Fig. 10 — Russian Freemasonry and the Bolshevic Revolution.
See *Scarlet and the Beast*, Vol. I, 3rd ed., chapter 22.

Tzar Alexander II (1818-1881)

In 1861 Alexander II, emancipated the serfs and became known as "the Liberator. Liberation was not good enough for Freemasonry, which was bent on forcing Grand Orient Freemasonry's atheistic Communist experiment on all Russia, regardless of the Tzar's reforms.

Their plans were made in 1862, at the First Communist International held at Freemasons Hall in London, England. There Alexander II was condemned to death. Twenty years later, Freemason Mikhail Bakunin gave the order to assassinate the Tzar with a T.N.T. bomb. The assassin was a member of Young Russia, the youth lodge of Freemasonry. Read the story in *Scarlet and the Beast*, Vol. I, 3rd edition, chaps. 18 & 23.

Also read of Alexander II's military assistance to Abraham Lincoln during our Civil War in *Scarlet and the Beast*, Vol. 1, Chap. 14.

32° Alexander Fyodorovich Kerensky (1881-1970)

Russian revolutionary leader. After the Revolution of Feb. 1917, which was a Rite revolution, Kerensky was made Minister in the provisional government, and later of War. He succeeded Prince Lvov in July, Prime Minister, yet because of his moderate and indecision, he was overthrown by atheist Orient Freemasonry's ruthless Bolshevik Revolution of Nov. 1917. He fled to Paris where he edited the Social Revolutionary paper, *Dni.* He was a 32° Scottish Rite Mason. See *Scarlet and the Beast*, Vol. I, 3rd ed., ch.17, 22-25.

first Scottish of Justice Minister 1917 as policies Grand

Figure 11 — Rasputin's assignment — weaken Russian leadership.
See *Scarlet and the Beast*, VI, 3rd. ed., ch. 17.

Grigorii Rasputin (1871-1916)

General knowledge: Rasputin was a peasant — a self-styled religious elder, born in Pokrovskoye, Russia. A member of the Schismatic sect of Khlysty (flagellants), he was introduced into the royal household, where he quickly gained the confidence of the emperor (Nicholas II) and empress by his ability to control through hypnosis the bleeding of the Hemophiliac heir to the throne.

Rasputin was a notorious lecher and drunkard, and created a public scandal through the combination of his sexual and alcoholic excesses, and his political influence in securing the appointment of government ministers, who were incompetent.

Before Rasputin came upon the royal court of Russia, he was first prepared by French and English Freemasonry through Rosicrucian, Martinist and Mizraim Masonic Lodges. His controller was a man known as Papus, who sent Philippe de Lyon to Russia in 1899 to establish Martinist Lodges in that vast country. Rasputin was one of his first initiates.

In 1900 Papus followed Philippe to St. Petersburg, where Papus became confidant of the Tzar and Tzarina. Both Papus and Philippe introduced Rasputin to the Tzarina.

Rasputin's Masonic assignment was to weaken the leadership of Russia. And he did it admirably, under the guise of incompetence. Papus' last trip was in 1906. With him were the rituals of the Ordo Templi Orientis (O.T.O.), the homicidal lodge, whose initiates (following the revolution) became the K.G.B. The entire story of Rasputin and his French and English Masonic controllers is found in *Scarlet and the Beast*, Vol. 1, 3rd ed., chap. 22.

Figure 12 — The Bolshevic Revolution dethroned the last Tzar of Russia. See *Scarlet and the Beast,* Vol. I, 3rd edition, chapters. 22-23.

Tzar Nicholas II (1868-1918) and his beautiful family

In the midst of WWI the Communist Revolution began. The first act of the Revolution was the Masonic ritual murder of the Tzar and his entire royal family, including their dog. We know the murders were Masonic, because the assassins confirmed it in a cabalistic message on the wall above the blood-soaked bed where the crime occurred.

Bedroom in which imperial family was murdered. On the pillow is a sheet of paper placed by the emperial investigators, dating the crime "1917."

Within the circle on the wall above the bed is a Cabbalistic inscription, which documents this murder was ordered and carried out by Freemasonry. Read details in *Scarlet and the Beast* Vol.1, 3rd edition Chaps. 17, 22-23.

"In the first years of the Communist regime public buildings were occasionally decorated with the six-pointed Magen David, the Star of David. The fivepointed star or pentagram that the Red Army adopted in 1918 as its emblem was known to be a Masonic design, and for many Russians, Freemasonry was synonymous with Jewry." Consequently the Jews were blamed for the revolution. *Russia Under The Bolshevik Regime,* by Richard Pipes, 1993.

Fig. 13 — Because of the cabalistic message written on the wall above the murder scene, Jews, not Masons, were blamed for the murders. Covers to two *Protocols* books below (Spanish & French) reveal the anti-Semitism that pervaded Western Europe prior to WW2. Top picture reads, "The Program of the Jews." Bottom reads, "Jewish Peril."

Title page from a
French Protocols edition

Title page from a
Spanish Protocols edition

The *Protocols of the Learned Elders of Sion* was the most vicious attempt by Freemasonry to make Jews the scapegoats should the conspiracy of the Bolshevic Revolution be exposed as Masonic. But, Russian royalty knew better. Empress Alexandra noted in her diary, dated April 7, 1918: "Nicholas read to us the protocols of the free masons." (Read facts on the origin of the *Protocols* in *Scarlet and the Beast*, Vol.1, 3rd ed., chap. 17).

Figure 14 — Dictatorship of the Proletariat.
Gentile Freemasonry successfully fronted the Jews

These cartoons were circulated by Russians living in exile in Europe following the Bolshevik Revolution. Since most leaders in all the Revolutionary posts were Jews, Russians blamed Jews for Bolshevism. No one knew at that time that Jews were fronts for anti-Semitic Gentile Grand Orient Freemasonry, for every revolutionary Jew was first a Freemason.

THE DIKTATORSHIP OF THE PROLETARIAT. – DIE DIKTATUR DES PROLETARIATES.

Above is a drawing that had been widely distributed by Russians who were driven out of their country when the Reds came into power. Practically all Russians living in exile blamed the Jews for the plight of their native land, so successful was Grand Orient Freemasonry in fronting them.

Figure 15 — Famous Russian Masons.
See *Scarlet and the Beast*, Vol. 1, 3rd edition, chaps. 7, 12, 16, 22-23, 25, 27.

Leon Trotsky (Lev Davidovich Bronstein — Jewish) (1879-1940)
Grand Orient Freemason
When Trotsky accused Stalin of "betraying the Revolution," Stalin sought to kill him. Trotsky fled Russia and settled in Central America. He is credited with communizing the Grand Orient Lodges in Latin and South America. To this day the communist uprisings south of our borders, including Cuba, originated from these lodges.

Lenin was pragmatic

Stalin was ruthless

Vladimer Iyich Lenin
mother was Jewish
(1870-1924)
Grand Orient Freemason

33° Joseph Stalin (1879-1953)
was a bank robber, known as the
"Jesse James" of the Urals.
Rosicrucian Freemason

Figure 16 — Anti-Semetic "White" propaganda poster of "the Jew' Leon Trostsky. Belorussia, or White Russia, blamed the Bolshevik Revolution on the Jews.

"In the first years of the Communist regime public buildings were occasionally decorated with the six-pointed Magen David, the Star of David... The five-pointed star or pentagram that the Red Army adopted in 1918 as its emblem was known to be a Masonic design, and for many Russians Freemasonry was synonymous with Jewry." *Russia Under The Bolshevik Regime*, Alfred A. Knopf, New York, 1993, p. 102-103.

Figure 17 — Russian Grand Orient Freemason Bukharin defines "ethics."
See *Scarlet and the Beast*, Vol. 1, 3rd edition, Chapter 22.

Nikolay Ivanovich Bukharin (1888-1938)

"Bukharin, head of the Petrograd Committee of the Russian Communist Party, gloated over the bloodbath of the Bolshevik Revolution..., 'here, in our country [Russia], where we [Bolsheviks] are absolute masters, we fear no one at all. This country worn out by wars, sickness, death and famine (it is a dangerous but splendid means), no longer dares to make the slightest protest, finding itself under the perpetual menace of the CHEKA and the army. Often we are ourselves surprised by its patience which had become so wellknown...there is not, one can be certain in the whole of Russia, a single household in which we have killed in some manner or other the father, the mother, a brother, a daughter, a son, some near relative or friend.

"Bukharin dismissed ethics as useless baggage. What philosophers call ethics is merely 'fetishism' of class standards. As the carpenter performs whatever actions are necessary to make a bench, 'exactly so does the proletariat in its social struggle. If the proletariat wishes to attain communism, than it must do such and such, as does the carpenter in building a bench. And what ever is expedient from this point of view, this must be done. Ethics transforms itself for the proletariat, step by step, into simple and comprehensible rules of conduct necessary for communism, and, in point of fact, *ceases* to be *ethics*.'

"The obvious flaw in this ethical philosophy is that it assumes the abstraction called 'proletariat' to be capable of acting. In point of fact, a communist society, like any other, is directed by individuals — in this case, the leaders of the Communist Party — and these individuals, with every action they undertake, make decisions. There is no scientific way of predetermining what is 'necessary' for the cause of a class, since at every point there emerge choices: choices that are not only technical but also moral. Years later, Preobrazhenskii and Bukharin, having been subjected to torture and then executed for crimes they had not committed, by their own ethical standards had no grounds for complaint: 'Communism' in this instance, too, acted as it deemed necessary."

Richard Pipes. *Russia under the Bolshevik Regime*. New York: Dial Press, 1993, pp. 328-329.

Figure 18 — From where did America's "Women's Liberation" originate?

Alexandra Mikhaylovna Domontovitch Kollontai (1872-1952)

"Russian feminist and revolutionary, the world's first female ambassador, born in St. Petersburg into an upper-class family. She rejected her privileged upbringing and joined the Russian Social Democratic Party. She travelled widely in the USA, returning to Russia after the Revolution (1917), and becoming commissar for public welfare. In this post she agitated for domestic and social reforms, including collective child care and easier divorce proceedings..., her private liaisons sho*cked the Party.... Her...[book], The New Morality and the Working Class* (1918), aroused considerable controversy because of their open discussion of such subjects as sexuality and women's place in society." *The Cambridge Biographical Encyclopedia*, Cambridge University Press. 1998.

"In Soviet Russia, as in the rest of Europe, World War I led to a loosening of sexual mores, which here was justified on moral grounds. The apostle of free love in Soviet Russia was Alexandra Kollontai, the most prominent woman Bolshevik.... [E]vidence suggest that she had an uncontrollable sex drive coupled with an inability to form enduring relationships... To escape home, she married young, but left her husband after three years. In 1906 she joined the Mensheviks, then, in 1915, switched to Lenin [the Bolsheviks], whose antiwar stand she admired. Subsequently, she performed for him valuable services as agent and courier.

"In her writings, Kollontai argued that...women should be set free to choose their partners. In 1919 she published The *New Morality and the Working Class*,... In it she maintained that women had to be emancipated not only economically but also psychologically.... To be capable of it, individuals had to undergo an apprenticeship in the form of "love games" or "erotic friendships," which taught them to engage in sexual relations free of both emotional attachment and personal domination. Casual sex alone conditioned women to safeguard their individuality in a society dominated by men. Every form of sexual relationship was acceptable: Kollontai advocated what she called "successive monogamy." In the capacity of Commissar of Guardianship...she promoted communal kitchens as a way of 'separating the kitchen from marriage.' She, too, wanted the care of children to be assumed by the community. She predicted that in time the family would disappear, and women would learn to treat all children as their own. She popularized her theories in a novel, *Free Love: The Love of Drones* (1924)... Its heroine preached divorcing sex from morality as well as from politics. Generous with her body, she said she loved everybody, from Lenin down, and gave herself to any man who happened to attract her....

"Studies of the sexual mores of Soviet youth conducted in the 1920s revealed considerable discrepancy between what young people said they believed and what they actually practiced: usually, in this instance behavior was less promiscuous than theory. Russia's young people stated they considered love and marriage 'bourgeois' relics and thought Communists should enjoy a sexual life unhampered by any inhibitions: the less affection and commitment entered into male-female relations, the more, 'communist' they were. According to opinion surveys, students looked on marriage as confining and, for women, degrading: the largest number of respondents — 50.8 percent of the men and 67.3 percent of the women — expressed a preference for long-term relationships based on mutual affection but without the formality of marriage.

"Deeper probing of their attitudes, however, revealed that behind the facade of defiance of tradition, old attitudes survived intact. Relations based on love were the ideal of 82.6 percent of the men and 90.5 percent of the women: 'This is what they secretly long for and dream about," according to the author of the survey. Few approved of the kind of casual sex advocated by Kollontai and widely associated with early Communism: a mere 13.3 percent of the men and 10.6 percent of the women. Strong emotional and moral factors continued to inhibit casual sex: one Soviet survey revealed that over half of the female student respondents were virgins.

"The decisive influences on the sexual behavior of the postrevolutionary generation were economic: the unprecedented hardships of everyday life, especially the shortages of food and housing, and the stresses induced by relentless government demands. They forced the majority of soviet youth, particularly women, to follow traditional norms of sexual behavior: the evidence gives 'little support to the suggestion in the impressionistic literature of the time that promiscuity and an ideology of sexual liberation were widespread among women students.' "Asked how the revolution had affected their sexual desires, 53.0 percent of the men reported these desires to have weakened; 41.0 percent of the men blamed hunger and other deprivations and pressures for complete or partial impotence; 59.0 percent of the female respondents saw no change in their desire for sex...

"Unrestrained sexual license did not prevail, because it was not acceptable to most young people, nor in the end, to the authorities..."

Pipes. pp. 331-334.

Fig. 19 — 33° Armand Hammer in 1987. Son of Jewish parents who migrated from Russia to America. Father was member of American Communist Party. Armand was not, but was a personal friend of Grand Orient Mason and communist leader Vladimir Lenin. See *Scarlet & Beast*, VI, 3rd ed, ch 22.

33° Armand Hammer (1899-1990)

Businessman, born in NYC of Reform Jewish parents who had migrated from Russia to America before the Bolshevik Revolution. He trained as a physician at Columbia University, and served with the US Army Medical Corps (1918-19). In 1921, he went to Russia to help with a typhus epidemic, and turned it into a business deal. In his own words, Hammer wrote: "As a newly qualified young doctor, I went to Russia in 1921 to work in the Urals among the victims of famine and an epidemic of typhus. For supplying much-needed grain to the starving Russians, I was personally thanked by Lenin, who took me under the wing of his patronage." The famine was created by the Bolshevik government following a misconceived venture of the Soviets in what they called "the reorganization of agriculture." As a result, 12 million peasants starved to death. Hammer made his first million dollars by shipping desperately needed food from America to Russia.

In appreciation to Hammer, the Soviets gave him free access to Soviet air space. In fact, up to the time of his death Hammer was the only man in the world who could fly his private jet to Soviet borders, make a phone call to the Kremlin, and be escorted by MIG jets to Moscow.

Scuttle butt has it that Armand Hammer owned Arm & Hammer Baking Soda. He did not. However, he did own stock in that company (S1.F71). Hammer founded the A. Hammer Pencil Co. in 1925, operating in NYC, London, and Moscow. He bought the Occidental Petroleum Corporation of California in 1957. He maintained strong connections with the USSR, acting as US intermediary on a number of occasions, including the Soviet troop withdrawal from Afghanistan in 1987.

SECTION 8
BETWEEN TWO WORLD WARS

"The Good Old Times" when the World was at Peace, Industry boomed, Labor Unions began and Fun and Pleasure reigned !!!
If you had talent and/or money, and were a Mason, it appears you also had the "edge" over others who were as capable.

Fig. 1 — Famous American Masons of the 20th Century.

33° Charles H. Mayo (1865-1939)
William J. Mayo (1861-1939)

Mayo Clinic & Freemasonry

Charles, with his brother William (not a Mason) was cofounder of the Mayo Foundation for Medical Education and Research at Rochester, MN, in affiliation with the University of Minnesota.

Charles received his M.D. degree from Northwestern University in 1888 and M.A. in 1904. He did postgraduate work at N.Y. Polyclinic, and received honorary degrees from numerous universities throughout the world. With his brother, he donated $2,800,000 for the present Mayo Clinic at Rochester, which first opened in the Masonic Temple building. Charles served as surgeon and associate chief of staff of the clinic; surgeon to St. Mary's and Worrall hospitals; and professor of surgery, Medical School, University of Minnesota, 1919-36.

Charles served in WWI as Colonel of Medical Corps. He was later chief consultant for Office of Surgeon General and was Brigadier General in the Medical Reserve.

Charles was a member of Rochester Lodge No. 21, Rochester, MN, receiving 1° on Jan. 27, 2o Feb. 24, and 3° May 12, 1890. He was also a member of Halcyon Chapter No. 8, R.A.M. and Home Commandery No. 5, K.T., both of Rochester. He became a 32° AASR (SJ) at Winona, MN, and 33° in Oct., 1935.

Fig. 2 — Publicity shot of 1950s Hoover model alongside a 1907 model.

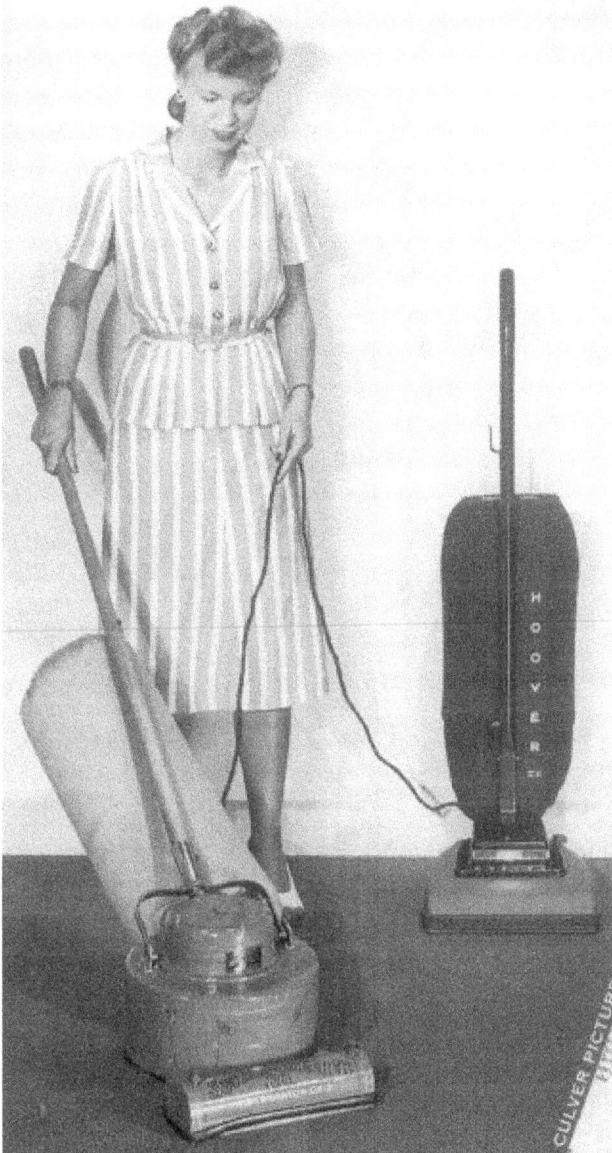

33° Frank G. Hoover (1883-1954) — President of the Hoover Co. (vacuum cleaners) from 1948. Born in New Berlin, Ohio. Educated at Oberlin College and Ohio State U. He was with the Hoover company from 1904. Member of William McKinley Lodge No. 431, Canton, OH. Awarded 33° AASR (NJ).

Figure 3 — Freemasons Walter P. Chrysler & Ransom E. Olds.

Walter P. Chrysler (1875-1940)
Motor car manufacturer.

Born at Wamego, KN. He was a descendant of Tuenis Van Dolsen, the first male child born in Manhattan NY. He began work as a machinist's apprentice on the railroad. In 1910 he was assistant manager of the Pittsburgh works of the American Locomotive Co., and was manager in 1911. From 1912-16 he was works manager of Buick Motor Co. and president and general manager from 1916-19. He was vice president in charge of operations of General Motors Corp. from 1919-20 and executive vice president of Willys-Overland Co. 1920-22. He was later chairman of the board of

Chrysler Corp. He was a Mason.

1903 curved dash Oldsmobile

33° Ransom E. Olds (1864 -1950)

Pioneer in automobile field, who in 1886, built the first three-wheeled horseless carriage, and brought out a practical four-wheeled automobile in 1893. The Oldsmobile is named for Mr. Olds. He was president of the REO Motor Car Co. from 1904-24 and chairman of the board from 1924-36. He was the donor of Science Hall to Kalamazoo Coll., the engineering Building to Michigan State Coll., and the clubhouse to the affiliated women's clubs, and social welfare house to city of Lansing.

Olds became a member of Capitol Lodge of S.O., No. 66, Lansing, MI on May 20, 1908; exalted in Capitol Chapter No. 9, R.A.M. on April 23, 1909; knighted in Lansing Commandery No. 25, K.T. on May 28, 1909; 32° AASR (NJ) in DeWitt Clinton Consistory, Grand Rapids in May, 1913, and crowned 33° on Sept. 15, 1925. He was also a Shriner. (See Shriners' oath to Allah, Section 1, page 29).

Figure 4 — Founder of J. C. Penney Co.

33° James Cash Penney (1875-1971)

Born in 1875 in Hamilton, MO. Graduate of Hamilton High School. In 1949 he attended the Masonic cornerstone laying of the new high school building at Hamilton. Both he and his sister donated $250,000 toward the cost of building the high school.

Penney holds honorary doctorates from eleven colleges and universities. He founded the J. C. Penney Co. in 1902. Known as "the Golden Rule merchant," he quit using the word "employee," and called each of his 90,000 workers "associates," giving each a share in the profits in addition to a salary. After the 1929 stock market crash, Penney, at age 56, lost his fortune, and wound up in a sanitarium, beaten and despondent. When he was released he borrowed money and staged a comeback in which he recouped his fortune.

J. C. Penney has influenced great numbers of young people through his business operations, by speeches, articles, and letters. His own comeback from the depths of financial and mental depression was made possible by a sudden and dramatic rekindling of Christian faith within him.

He received his three blue degrees in Wasatch Lodge No. 1, Salt Lake City, Utah, April 28, May 19, and June 2, 1911. In 1955 he became a dual member of United Services Lodge No. 1118, NYC. He was a member of Utah Chapter No. 1, R.A.M., Utah Council No. 1, R. & S.M., and Utah Commandery No. 1, K.T., all of Salt Lake City. He has contributed generously to the retirement of the bond on the Masonic Temple in Salt Lake City.

Penney received the 32° AASR (SJ) in Utah Consistory No. 1, April 23, 1936, KCCH, Oct. 24, 1941, and 33° Oct. 16, 1945. He has addressed many Masonic groups. In April, 1958 he was presented the gold distinguished service award by the General Grand Chapter, Royal Arch Masons, at Kansas City, MO.

Fig. 5 — Labor Unions and Freemasonry.

32° Samuel Gompers (1850-1924)
Born in London, England
One of the founders and first president of the American Federation of Labor, serving from 1886-1924.

A cigarmaker by trade, he was an advocate of the rights of labor from the time he was 14 years old. He helped develop the Cigarmakers International Union, and was one of the founders of the Federation of Trades and Labor Unions in 1881, being president of the same for three years. He probably did more for American labor than any other man.

Gompers fought socialism relentlessly. In his autobiography, he states that his Masonic affiliation frequently protected him. For example, he said, "In my Masonic life I have visited lodges in many lands, and I have learned that Freemasonry in many countries, particularly in Latin countries, is the principal means whereby freedom of conscience, of thought, and expression is preserved."

Gompers was a member of Dawson Lodge No. 16, Washington, DC. He received his degrees on Feb. 8, March 28 and May 9, 1904, and the 32° AASR (SJ) in Albert Pike Consistory of Washington, DC on Feb. 10, 1906. Samuel Gompers Lodge No. 45, Washington, DC is named after him.

Fig. 6 — Famous American Masons of the 20th Century.

3° Grant Wood (1892-1942)
Born in Anamosa, Iowa. Most famous American Gothic painter — the above painting, his most recognizable. He was a student at the Minneapolis Handicraft Guild, 1910-12; Art Institute of Chicago, 1912-14; and Academy Julian, Paris, France, 1923. Received many honorary degrees from American universities.

He began his art in 1912 as a craftsman in metal and handmade jewelry. He became a teacher of art in the public schools of Cedar Rapids, Iowa, 1919-24. He won the Harris Bronze Medal on "American Gothic" at the American Exhibit, Art Institute of Chicago in 1930.

The Iowa Masonic Library possesses a three-panel painting by Wood entitled, "Freemasonry." Wood was a member of Mount Hermon Lodge No. 263, Cedar Rapids,

Iowa, receiving 1-3 degrees on April 14, May 6 and 19, 1921. Was suspended on March 6, 1924 for not paying dues.

Fig. 7 —List of Masons credited with founding the Boy Scouts of America.

32° Griffith O. Ellis (1869-1948)
Editor and publisher. Founder of the **Boy Scouts of America**. Born in Urbana, Ohio. Graduate of U. of Michigan. Became connected with the Sprague Publishing Co., Detroit MI, in 1891. President of the company from 1908-40.

Editor of the *American Boy*, published by Sprague. Also was president of the William A. Scripps Co. Ellis participated in the organization of the Boy Scouts of America in 1910 and served on the national council till his death. He received the award of Silver Buffalo from the Boy Scouts in 1931. Was an officer of two banks and president of the Detroit Street Railway Commission from 1920-30, which municipalized Detroit's rail system. Ellis was raised (3°) April 11, 1911 in Oriental Lodge No. 240. Later he became 32° AASR (NJ).

3° Benjamin L. Dulaney (1857-1930)
Financier who developed the Black Mountain Coal Field in Virginia and Kentucky (1890-1914). **He is also credited as "a founder of the Boy Scouts of America**, and was its vice president for 14 years from its origin in America. Dulaney taught school for two years. He built Bristol, Tenn. Iron Furnace and Bristol, Elizabethton & Carolina Rail Road (1880-90). He organized Va.&

S.W. Railroad and Virginia Iron, Coal and Coke Co. He succeeded in making Charleston, SC a coal loading port for all southeastern coal mines. He was a Master Mason.

3° Daniel Carter Beard (1850-1941) — American painter, illustrator and **organizer of the Boy Scout movement in the United States**. Mt. Beard, the peak adjoining Mt. McKinley, is named for him. Started as book and magazine illustrator and teacher of drawing. Originator and founder of the first boy scout society from which others were modeled. Was National Scout Commissioner and honorary vice-president of Boy Scouts of America, the only one ever given. Was Chief Scout, Dept. of Woodcraft at Culver, IN Military Academy (1911-15). Beard wrote many books on scouting and wilderness lore including: *Moonlight and Six Feet of Romance* (1890); *American Boys' Handy Book* (1882); *Boy Pioneers and Daniel Boone* (1909); *Shelters, Shacks and Shanties* (1914); *Bugs, Butterflies and Beetles* (1915); *Signs, Signals and Symbols* (1918); *American Boy's Book of Wild Animals* (1921), and at least a dozen others. Was Associate editor of *Boy's Life*. He was also Chief of School of Woodcraft. Raised (3°) on November 30, 1917 in Mariners' Lodge No. 67, New York City and later became a member of Cornucopia Lodge No. 563, Flushing, NY just before he passed on to the Grand Lodge on High.

3° Arthur A. Schuck (1895-?) — **Chief Scout Executive, Boy Scouts of America from 1948 until his death**. Began in 1917 as a scout executive in Lancaster, PA. Became supervisor of region 3, which included four states and Washington, DC, 1919-22. From 1931-44 he was with the National Council of Boy Scouts. From 1944-48 was scout executive of Los Angeles. Contributor and member of editorial board of several youth magazines. Raised (3°) in West Chester, PA Lodge No. 332, Dec. 1929. Affiliated with Century Lodge No. 100, South Orange, NJ.

3° E. Urner Goodman (1891-?) — **Boy Scout executive and founder of Order of the Arrow** in 1915. He became a scout field executive at Philadelphia in 1915, and was scout executive at Philadelphia from 191727, and at Chicago 1927-31. Was national program director from 193151 and national field scout commissioner. He wrote *Leaders Handbook for the Boy Scouts of America*. Raised (3°) Mason in Lamberton Lodge No. 487, Philadelphia, PA in 1917.

32° Charles W. Froessel (1892-?) — Justice, Supreme Court of New York, 1937-39. A member of the executive board, National Council, Boy Scouts of America. Member of Tadmor Lodge No. 923, Ridgewood, NY.

Fig. 8 — Another man is given credit for founding the Boy Scouts.
This British General "had an intense interest in teenage boys and their bodies."

TIME Magazine, April 29, 2002, p.49, reports on this founder. Article is entitled: *The Thin Line Between Love and Lust*, subtitled, "Men who serve boys and men who abuse them have some things in common."

Robert Stephenson Baden-Powell (1857-1941)

"Robert Baden-Powell, the British military hero who founded the Boy Scouts, had an intense interest in teenage boys and their bodies. This interest expressed itself with a forthright innocence that to our postFreudian sensibilities seems to have pretty clear sexual overtones. There is no evidence that Baden-Powell ever acted on this aspect of his enthusiasm for youth, and scouting enthusiasts both deny and resent the implication. "Sure, there is a pretty obvious distinction between thinking illicit thoughts and acting on them. But it is not so easy to purge the actual predators without punishing those heroes of sublimation or losing their valuable contributions to society. Why? Because the line is hard to draw in practice... Even this obvious distinction between thinking and acting is being swept away in the nation's current frenzy over predatory priests.

The correct response to all this may well be, 'To bad! Protecting children is more important.'" TIME Magazine, April 29, 2002, p.49.

Fig. 9 — Famous American Masons of the 20th Century.

3° Robert E. Peary (1856-1920)

Discoverer of the North Pole. Born in Cresson PA. Graduate of Bowdoin College in 1877 and 1894. He entered the U.S. Navy in 1881 as a civil engineer. From 1887-88 he was engineer in charge of the Nicaragua Canal surveys. While there he invented the rolling lock gates for the canal.

He started his Arctic explorations with a voyage to the interior of Greenland in 1886. In 1891-92 he made a voyage to northern Greenland. In 1893-95, a third voyage (intended to reach the North Pole) failed in its objective.

In 1897 he was granted five years' leave of absence from the Navy and was presented with a ship, the *Windward*, by Lord Northcliffe, which had been used by a British expedition. On his fourth voyage of 18981902, he reached 84o 17' N., the farthest north in the American Arctic. Granted another three years' leave in 1903, he sailed in the specially equipped *Roosevelt* in 1905-1906, and reached within 174 miles of the pole before being forced back. His final and successful expedition in 1908-09 reached the pole on April 6, 1909. When announcing the success of the expedition, he learned that Dr. Frederick A. Cook, who had been a surgeon on the 1891 expedition, had claimed he reached the pole on April 21, 1908 — a year before Peary. Cook's claim and Cook himself, were later discredited, and Peary's attainment recognized.

Captain Peary was a member of the explorer's lodge, Kane No. 454 of NYC. He received his degrees (1-3) Feb. 4, 18, and March 3, 1896. To this lodge he presented the Masonic flag that was displayed at Independence Bay, Greenland on May 20 and 25, 1895. To the Grand Lodge of New York, Peary presented two specimens of the great meteorite weighing 90 tons, which he discovered in North Greenland. On March 30, 1920 the lodge presented his widow with a special medal in honor of her distinguished husband.

Fig. 10 — Famous American Masons of the 20th Century.

32° Dr. Hiram Bingham (1875-1956)

Governor of Ct. (1924) Senator from CT (1925-33)

Explorer/aviator. Grandfather and father were missionaries in Hawaii. Grandfather reduced Hawaiian language to writing. Father did same for Gilbert Islands. Bingham held A.B., M.A., Ph.D. and Litt.D degrees. Taught at Harvard, Yale, Princeton and Johns Hopkins.

From 1906-7, Bingham explored Bolivar's route across Venezuela and Colombia; 1908-9, Spanish trade route from Buenos Aires to Lima; 1911-15, Inca ruins in Peru. A member of both

Scottish and York Rite bodies, and a Shriner. Wrote on Masonic subjects and on Lost City of the Incas (below).

MACHU PICCHU — LOST INCA CITY: Indian masons & engineers of Inca Empire built this mountaintop city before Spanish conquest. It was abandoned and hidden under forests growth until discovered in 1911 by Bingham.

Fig. 11 — Famous French Mason of the 19th Century.

French archeologist Augustus le Plongeon (?)

Wearing full Masonic regalia, French Archeologist Augustus le Plongeon strikes a somber pose. His excavations of Mayan ruins in the 1880s convinced him that refugees from Mu, a lost continent resembling Atlantis, had founded the Mayan civilization.

Fig. 12 — Famous American Masons of the 20th Century.

32° Gutzon Borglum (1871-1941). Sculptor and painter, best known for the gigantic Mt. Rushmore national memorial in the Black Hills of S.D. Born in Idaho and educated in public schools of Nebraska. Studied art in San Francisco and Paris. M.A. from Princeton, and L.L.D., Oglethorpe University. Painted, studied and traveled in Spain, Europe, England until 1901 when he settled in New York. Among his many marbles and bronzes are Sheridan Equestrian, Washington, DC. and Chicago, IL. Colossal marble head of Lincoln in rotunda of Capitol in Washington, etc., etc. His greatest work is pictured above — the Black Hills carving of four presidents, which he designed and officially started on August 10, 1927. He lived to see the fourth head unveiled in 1939. The work was completed by his son, Lincoln.

Borglum, Sr. was an active Mason. Raised (3°) in Howard Lodge No. 35, NYC, June 10, 1904. Served as Master 1910-1911. Was appointed Grand Representative of Grand Lodge of Denmark near the Grand Lodge of New York, 1915. Received Scottish Rite Degrees in NYC Consistory, Oct. 25, 1907. The cornerstone of his studio on the hills above Stamford, CT was laid with Masonic ceremonies by the grand master of New York.

3° Lincoln Borglum (1912-?). Son of Gutzon Borglum. Worked with his father for 12 years at the National Memorial, Black Hills, SD. Following the death of his father, he was assigned to complete the memorial. Lincoln was raised (3°) in Battle River Lodge No. 92 of Hermosa, SD.

Fig. 13 Famous American Masons of the 20th Century.

3° Rear Admiral Richard E. Byrd (1888-1957). Polar explorer, naval officer, pioneer aviator. Graduated from U.S. Naval Academy, 1912. Advanced to Lt. Commander, 1916. Following flight over North Pole in 1926, was promoted to Commander. Made Rear Admiral in 1930. During WWI he entered the Aviation Service and commanded US Air Forces until Armistice. In WWII he served with Admiral King in Washington and Nimitz in Pacific, going overseas four times. Byrd was highly decorated including the Congressional Medal of Honor in 1926. Made plane flight over North Pole on May 9, 1926 with Floyd Bennett. Byrd became a member of Federal Lodge No. 1, Washington, D.C. on March 19, 1921 and affiliated with Kane Lodge No. 454, NYC Sept. 18, 1928. He was a member of National Sojourner Chapter No. 3 at Washington. He and his pilot, 32° Bernt Balchen, dropped Masonic flags on the two poles. Balchen also added his Shrine fez (See Shriners' oath to Allah, Section 1, page 29). In the Antarctic expedition of 1933-35, 60 of the 82 members were Freemasons and on Feb. 5, 1935 the expedition established the First Antarctic Lodge No. 777 with a New Zealand constitution.

Fig. 14 — Famous American Masons.

32° David Sarnoff (1891-1971)

Born in Minsk, Russia. As a boy in Russia he spent several years in preparing for a career as a Jewish scholar of the Talmud. At age 9, he emigrated with his family in 1900 and settled first in Albany, NY, and then in New York City. Brought to the U.S.A. when 9-years-old, he immediately took over the support of his family. While going to school, he helped support his family by selling newspapers and singing the liturgy in a synagogue.

In 1906 he left school to become a messenger boy for a telegraph company, and with his first paycheck bought a telegraph instrument. He soon became proficient in Morse Code and found work as a radio operator for the Marconi Wireless Telegraph Company.

After service on shore and at sea over the next few years, Sarnoff became operator of the most powerful radio station in the world, established by John Wanamaker atop his Manhattan department store. There, on April 14, 1912, Sarnoff picked up the distress signal from the sinking Titanic. He remained at his instrument for 72 hours, receiving and passing on the news. Rewarded by the Marconi company with rapid promotion, he became an important official of the company and in 1916 first proposed the "radio music box," or commercially marketed radio receiver. In 1919 Radio Corporation of America (RCA) absorbed Marconi. In 1921 Sarnoff became general manager of RCA.

He demonstrated his marketing potential in broadcasting the DempseyCarpenter boxing match, which created a sensation. Within three years RCA sold more than $80,000,000 worth of receiving sets. In 1926 he formed the National Broadcasting Company (NBC). By that time Sarnoff had perceived the potential of television, which the contributions of several inventors were making technically feasible. In 1928 he launched an experimental NBC television station for research purposes. By 1939 he was able to give a successful demonstration of the new medium at the New York World's Fair. Development was delayed by World War II, during which he served under Gen. Dwight D. Eisenhower as a communication consultant.

Sarnoff became a Mason in Lodge of Strict Observance No. 94, NYC, June 14, 1921. In June, 1955 he received the coveted award for distinguished achievement from the Grand Lodge of New York.

Fig. 15 — William Harrison "Jack" Dempsey (1895-1983).

"Jack" Dempsey (1895-1983).

Former world's heavyweight boxing champion.

Born in Manassa, CO. He won the heavyweight championship by defeating Jess Willard at Toledo, OH on July 4, 1919. He lost the title to Gene Tunney at Philadelphia Sept. 23, 1926.

Member Kenwood Lodge No. 800, Chicago, IL..

Fig. 16 — Famous magician Mason.

32° Harry Houdini (1874-1926)

Magician and escape artist. Born in Appleton, WI. Houdini's original name was Ehrich Weiss, son of Rabbi Mayer S. Weiss, who emigrated to the United States from Hungary.

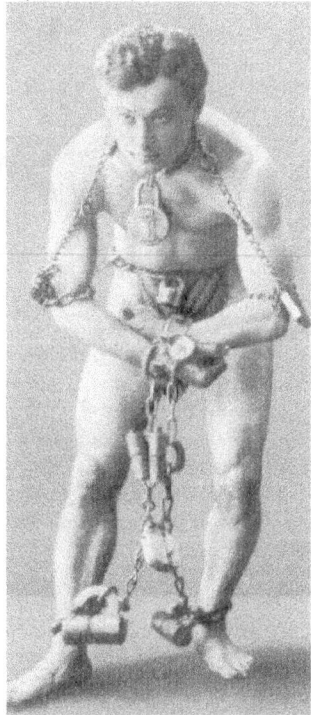

Houdini took his stage name from the great French prestidigitator, Robert Houdini. Later he legalized the name by trademark.

Houdini achieved his fame with tricks which permitted him to escape from any box, bag, or handcuffs into which he was put.

He began performing in 1882 at age 8 as a trapeze performer. With this act he made several tours of the world, performing before rulers and notables.

In 1894 he married Wihelmina Rahner, who thereafter, as Beatrice Houdini, served as his stage assistant.

Houdini campaigned against mind readers, mediums, and others who claimed supernatural powers.

In 1910 he was awarded a prize by the Australian Aeronautic League for being the first successful flier in Australia.

Houdini is the author of The Right Way to Do Wrong; Unmasking of Robert Houdini; Miracle Mongers; Paper Prestidigitation; Rope Ties and Escapes; A Magician Among the Spirits.

Houdini was a member of St. Cecil Lodge No. 568, New York City. He received his blue lodge degrees July 17, 31, and Aug. 21, 1923. He became a life member of the lodge Oct. 30, 1923. He was also a member of Mecca Shrine Temple of New York City.

Fig. 17 — Famous baseball player and Mason.

32° Tyrus "Ty" Cobb (1886-1961)

Member of Baseball Hall of Fame. Born in Narrows, GA. Played with the Detroit American League team from 1905 to 1926, then with Philadelphia from 1927-28.

He held the American League in batting 12 times and created or equalled more major league records that any other ball player. He retired with 419 major league hits. His all-time high batting average for lifetime was .369. Ty was one of the first four players elected to Baseball's Hall of Fame.

He was a member of Royston Lodge No. 426 (now No. 52), joining in 1907 at the age of 21. He received his 32° AASR (NJ) in Detroit on Jan. 25, 1912. He was elected honorary life member of City of Straights Lodge No. 452, Detroit on May 7, 1921. He joined the Moslem Shrine Temple, Detroit in 1912. A Shrine class was named for him in Newark, NJ in Dec. 1955. His father, William H. Cobb, was Master of Royston Lodge No. 426 from 1899 to 1903, and organized a fine fellowcraft team that traveled over Georgia.

Fig. 18 — Famous Shriners. See Shriners' oath to Allah, Sect 1, pg. 29.

33° Roy Rogers (1911-1998). Actorsinger in movies, radio, and television. In 1932-38 he organized and appeared with the band, "Sons of the Pioneers." In 1938 he appeared in his first movie, *Under Western Stars*, after which he starred in 89 Westerns. Was a radio singer beginning in 1937, and in 1952 was an actor and producer of TV films. Was member of Hollywood Lodge No. 355, receiving all three degrees. Received 33° AASR (SJ) at Los Angeles and member of Al Malaikah Shrine Temple. Honorary member DeMolay Legion of Honor.

32° Will Rogers (1879-1935)

American humorist. His great grandmother on his fathers side was a Cherokee. His father Clem served as a Captain in the Confederate Army under the Cherokee General Standwaite. He went to Africa, where he joined Texas Jack's Wild West Circus. Next he joined Wirth Brothers Circus in Australia, and returned to America to join the Cummins Wild West Show. In St. Louis he turned to burlesque, and made his first appearance on the New York Stage, June 11, 1905.

Received his blue degrees 19051906. Became 32° in 1908. He was twice suspended from the Scottish Rite (1918 and 1921), but each time reinstated. Joined Akdar Shrine Temple at Tulsa in 1914. Killed in plane crash near Point Barrow, Alaska. Plane was piloted by his friend Wiley Post.

32° Red Skelton (1913-1997). Comedian. Beginning in 1951, he starred on television in The Red Skelton Show. Was raised to 3° Vincennes Lodge No. 1, Ind. In 1939. Unknown when he received 32o. Member of Al Malaikah Shrine Temple, L.A.

32° Bud Abbott (1896-1974). Radio, stage, and *Abbott and Costello* comedy film partners. Born at Asbury Park, NJ. Began as a cashier in theatres in 1916. In a 31-day tour during WW2, sold $78 million in war bonds. Also entertained 300 Army and Navy camps. Mason and a Shriner.

32° Alfred C. Fuller (1885-?). President of Fuller Brush Co. in Welsford, Nova Scotia, Canada. He became a U.S. citizen in 1918. He established the Fuller Brush Co. at Somerville, MA in 1906, and was president and chairman of the board. He was a 32° Mason AASR, Knight Templar & Shriner.

Fig. 19 — Famous Hollywood character actor.

Royal Arch Mason Charles D. Coburn (1877-?)

Stage and Screen Actor

Born in Savannah, GA. Became manager of Savannah Theatre at age 18 and took up stage acting at age 22. He served in stock companies throughout the South and Middle West and became a leading man.

In 1906 he organized the Coburn Players. From then until 1917 he and Mrs. Coburn played the principal parts in many plays, including 16 Shakespearean plays.

He moved to the legitimate stage in New York, and for the next 20 years was one of the most famous actors of that period. He was closely associated with the greatest writers and producers of the time, and for a while was under the management of George M. Cohan, a Freemason.

In 1935, with Mrs. Coburn and Dixon Ryan Fox, he founded at Union College the Mohawk Drama Festival Institute of Theatre. He made his first appearance in moving pictures in 1937, appearing in over 50 movies.

On Feb. 6, 1913, Coburn was raised (3°) in Prince of Orange Lodge No. 16, New York City. That same year he was exalted in Constitution Chapter No. 230, R.A.M. and knighted in Palestine Commandery No. 18, K.T. He was created a noble in the Mecca Shrine Temple in Jan. 1914. He is a life member of lodge, chapter, commandery and Shrine. On May 19, 1957 he received the gold medal for distinguished service from the General Grand Chapter, Royal Arch Mason.

Fig. 20 — Famous "Singing Cowboy" actor and Freemason.

32° Gene Autry (?)

Singer, actor, producer, writer of Screen, stage, radio and TV. Born in Tioga, Texas. Graduated from Tioga High School in 1925. That same year his first job was a railroad telegraph operator in Sapulpa, OK. In 1929, Autry made the first phonograph record of cowboy songs. From 1930-34 he was a radio artist on WLS, Chicago. From that time he was an actor, as well as a motion picture director. His first picture was *In Old Santa Fe*. Since then he starred in 55 musical Western feature films.

During World War Two he joined the Army Air Force (1942) as technical sergeant. Discharged in 1945 as flight officer. After World War Two, with the advent of TV, he produced and starred in many productions. He has written over 250 songs, including "Tears on My Pillow (1941).

Gene Autry was raised (3°) in Catoosa Lodge No. 185, Catoosa, OK in 199927. He was a life member of Long Beach, CA AASR (32o) and life member of Al Malaika Shrine Temple, Los Angeles, CA.

Fig. 21 — Famous Holywood Actors

32° Cecil B. de Mille (1881-1959)
Motion picture producer. Educated in Pennsylvania Military College and American Academy of Dramatic Art, NYC. Was organizer and president of the Mercury Aviation Co., Hollywood, CA (1918-23), which was the first commercial aviation company to carry passengers on regular flights.

He has been identified with the motion picture industry since 1913 as a playwright, actor and producer. He produced the Lux Theater radio programs from 1936-45. As president of Cecil B. De Mille Productions, Inc., he gave the world the greatest spectacular movies ever produced, including Ten Commandments (1923; remade in Cinema-Scope (1957) The Volga Boatman; The King of Kings; The Sign of the Cross; Cleopatra; The Crusades; The Plainsman; The Buccaneer; Union Pacific; North West Mounted Police; Reap the Wild Wind; Unconquered; Samson and Delilah, etc.

He was a member of Prince of Orange Lodge No. 16, N.Y.C. and Al Malaikah Shrine Temple, Los Angeles.

Joseph M. Schenck (?)
Motion picture executive. He started in the moving picture industry as manager for Norma Talmage and Roscoe "Fatty" Arbuckle. He married Miss Talmage in 1917. In 1924 he became president of Motion Picture Producers, Inc. Became chairman of the board of United Artists in 1925. Founded Twentieth Century Pictures Corp. in 1933. Merged with Fox Film and became vice president and chairman of the board. He became executive director of productions of Twentieth Century-Fox.

Was a member of both the Pacific Lodge No. 233, NYC, and the old "233: Club" in Hollywood, CA.

Fig. 22 — Famous Holywood Actors

3° Douglas Fairbanks (1883-1939)
Movie Star of the silent film era. Born in Denver, CO. He attended Jarvis Military Academy at Denver, East Denver High School and the Colorado School of Mines. Three marriages.

Fairbanks made his first stage appearance in New York City in 1901. There he appeared in Hawthorne of the U.S.A.; Frenzied Finance; All for a Girl; A Gentleman from Mississippi; The Cub; Gentleman of Leisure; Comes Up Smiling; Henrietta; Show Shop.

He entered motion pictures and was head of his own production company in 1916. His productions were: His Majesty the American; When the Clouds Roll By; The Mollycoddle; The Mark of Zorro; The Nut; The Three Musketeers; Robin Hood; The Thief of Bagdad; Don Q, Son of Zorro; The Black Pirate; The Gauch; The Iron Mask; and The Taming of the Shrew. Fairbanks was raised (3°) in Beverly Hills Lodge No. 528 on Aug. 11, 1925, and was a member of the "233 Club" — whose members were all Freemasons of the movie colony.

Fig. 23 — Famous Holywood Masons

W.C. Fields (1880-1946)
Comedian on Stage, motion picture, and radio. Born in Philadelphia, PA. Was in vaudeville for several years and appeared in musical productions on Broadway, including the Ziegfield Follies and Earl Carroll's Vanities. Among his motion pictures were: *So's Your Old Man; It's the Old Army Game; The Potters; Six of a Kind; One in a Million; It's a Gift; David Copperfield; Mississippi; The Man on a Flying Trapeze; Poppy; The Big Broadcast of 1938; The Bank Dick; Never Give a Sucker an Even Break;* and *My Little Chickadee*. In 1937 he starred on the *Chase and Sanborn Radio Hour*. He was famous for his bulbous nose and his Fieldisms, such as "my little chickadee" and "imagine that — a check for a short beer." He was a member of E. Coppee Mitchell Lodge No. 605, Philadelphia, PA.

Leon Errol (1881-1951)
Movie comedian, often second man with W.C. Fields. Member of Pacific Lodge No. 233, New York City.

Fig. 24 — Famous American Masons of the 20th Century.

32° Irving Berlin originally **Israel Baline** (1888-1989)

Composer who helped to launch 20th century American popular music. Born in Temun, Russia. Parents were Moses and Leah Baline, who brought him to the U.S.A. in 1893 to escape Jewish persecution. His only education was two years in the public schools of N.Y.C. He worked for a time as a singing waiter in a Bowery beer hall, introducing some of his own songs, such as *Alexander's Ragtime Band*. The 1940s saw him at the peak of his career with songs like *God Bless America* (1939), *White Christmas* (1942), *Annie Get You Gun* (1946), and *Call Me Madam* (1950). These hits gave him worldwide popularity. In 1954 he received a special presidential citation as a composer of patriotic songs. In all, he wrote the words and music for over 900 songs. He retired in 1962, and lived as a recluse in Manhattan. On several songs he had turned over all royalties to a foundation to assist youth in "less chance" areas.

He received the first three degrees of Freemasonry in Munn Lodge No. 190, N.Y.C. on May 12, May 26, and June. 3, 1910, becoming a life member of the lodge on December 12, 1935. Berlin also received the 32° AASR (NJ) on December 23, 1910. This Jewish man was initiated into Muslim Mecca Shrine Temple on January 30, 1911, becoming a life member of the Shrine in Dec. 1936. (See Shriners' oath to Allah, Section 1, page 29).

Fig. 25 — Famous American Masons of the 20th Century.

3° Al Jolson (1888-1950)

Actor and singer. Born in St. Petersburg, Russia. He first appeared on stage as a member of the mob. Later he traveled with circuses, vaudeville, and Dockstader's Minstrels. He was particularly noted for his blackface minstrel songs. He starred in the first talking pictures *The Jazz Singer; The Singing Fool* and *Say it with Songs*. In 1940-41 he starred in his own production *Hold On to Your Hat*. Jolson was a member of St. Cecile Lodge No. 568, NYC. Jolson was raised (3°) July 1, 1913. He died in San Francisco after entertaining troops.

Jolson starred in the first "talkie" movie produced by Warner Brothers. **32° Jack Warner** was raised (3°) in Mt. Olive Lodge No. 506, Los Angeles, CA on Nov. 30, 1938. Jack Warner was also a Shriner.

Fig. 26 — Famous Holywood Masons

3° Clark Gable (1901-1960)
Actor born in Cadiz, OH. Attended Akron U. (Ohio). He had various industrial jobs before joining a small theatrical stock company. His first leading film role was in *The Painted Desert* (1931). Growing popularity in tough but sympathetic parts soon labelled him "the King of Hollywood," with the film *Mutiny on the Bounty,* reaching its peak with his portrayal of Rhett Butler in *Gone With the Wind* (1939). He received an Oscar in 1934 for his role in *It Happened One Night.*

In 1942, after the death of his third wife (Carole Lombard) in a plane crash, he joined the US 8th Air Force, and was decorated for bomber combat missions. His final film was *The Misfits* (1961).

Clark Gable was raised to (3°) Master Mason in Beverly Hills Lodge No. 528, Oct. 31, 1933, having already received his 1st and 2nd degrees on Sept. 19 and Oct. 17 of the same year.

Fig. 27 — Famous Holywood Masons.

Laurel & Hardy
Comedians who formed first Hollywood film comedy team. The "thin one," Stan Laurel (1890-1965), was born in Ulverston, Lancashire, NW England, UK. He began in a British Touring company. Went to the USA in 1910, and worked in silent films. The "fat one," **3° Oliver Hardy** (1892-1957), born near Atlanta, GA, left college to join a troupe of minstrels before drifting into the film industry. Laurel and Hardy came together in 1926 and made many full-length feature films. Their best efforts were their early (1927-31) shorts. Their contrasting personalities, general clumsiness, and disaster-packed predicaments made them a universally popular comedy duo.

Of the duo, only Oliver Hardy was a Mason. He was a member of Solomon Lodge No. 20 in Jacksonville, FL. He also was a frequent visitor at Hollywood and Mount Olive Lodges in California.

Fig. 28 — Famous American Masons of the 20th Century.

33° Will H. Hays (1879-1954)

Postmaster General of the U.S. under Harding (1921-22) and "czar" of the motion picture industry 1922-45. Graduate of Wabash College, Indiana in 1900 and 1904. Admitted to bar in 1900.

Active in Republican politics, he was chairman of the National Committee in 1918-21. As president of the Motion Picture Producers and Distributors of America, Inc. he accepted the job at a time when the film industry was beset with public criticism which threatened its independence.

Hays ruled the "Hays Office" with firmness and fairness, and was credited with having saved the industry from government regulation. He retired in 1945, but acted as advisor until 1950.

Hays was raised in Sulivan Lodge No. 263; he was a member of both York and Scottish Rites. He received the 33° AASR (NJ) in Sept. 1945. He received his 50-year service emblem from the Grand Lodge in 1950.

32° Jack M. (Eichelbaum) Warner (1916-?)

Motion Picture producer. Worked in home office of Warner Brothers. Raised (3°) in Mt. Olive Lodge No. 506, Los Angeles, CA on November 30, 1938. 32° Scottish Rite Mason and Shriner.

Fig. 29 — Famous American Masons of the 20th Century.

13° Clyde Beatty (1903-1965)

Animal trainer. Member of Craftsman Lodge No. 521, Detroit, MI. Received chapter degrees in Monroe Chapter No. 1, R.A.M., Nov. 22, 1958; commandery orders in Damascus Commandery No. 42, K.T., Nov. 24, 1958, and became a member of Moslem Shrine Temple on the same date, all in Detroit. (See Shriners' oath to Allah, Section 1, page 29).

Fig. 30 — Famous American Masons of the 20th Century.

3° Carl Ben Eielson (1897-1929)

Born in Hatton, ND. Early Arctic aviator who taught others about Arctic flying and flew Sir Hubert Wilkins over the North Pole. The plane in which they made the trip is in the North Dakota state historical building at Bismarck, where it was deposited as a memorial to Eielson.

He was lost while on a rescue mission in Siberian Arctic on Nov. 9, 1929.

A member of Garfield Lodge No. 105 at Hatton, ND. His Masonic degrees were conferred March 31, June, 3, and Sept. 16, 1921.

Robert S. Kerr (1896-1963) Admitted to the bar in 1922. Practiced law in Ada, OK. Beginning in 1926 was drilling contractor, oil producer, and President of KerrMcGee Oil Industries, Inc.

Governor of Okla. 1943-47; U.S. Senator from Okla. 1949-63.

In 1944 was chairman of the Oklahoma Baptist General Convention. Member of Ada, OK Lodge No. 118.

Fig. 31 — Famous American Masons of the 20th Century.

32° George W. Norris (1861-1944)

U.S. Senator from Nebraska, 1913-43. He taught school while studying law, and graduated from Valparaiso U. (Ind.) in 1883. In 1899 he moved to McCook, Neb. Was elected as a Republican to 58th through 62nd Congresses, becoming U.S. Senator the next election. Received Masonic degrees in Beaver City Lodge No. 93 on May 3 and June 28, 1890. Member of Sesostris Shrine Temple, Lincoln, NE. (See Shriners' oath to Allah, Section 1, page 29).

33° Roscoe Pound (1870-1964)

Former dean of Harvard Law School, internationally known for the vastness of his learning, and probably the greatest authority on Masonic jurisprudence.

Graduate of U. of Neb. in 1888 and Ph.D. in 1897. Admitted to the bar in 1890, he practiced at Lincoln from 18901901, and 1902-07.

He was Professor of Law at Harvard from 1910-47 and Dean of same from 1916-36. He retired in 1947.

Beginning in 1950 he was President of the International Academy of Comparative Law, and an advisor to ministry of justice, Republic of China from 1946. He was raised to 3° in Lancaster Lodge No. 54, Lincoln, in 1901. Was Master of the lodge in 1905. In 1907 he was Grand Orator of the Grand Lodge of Neb. He was honorary Past Grand Master of the Grand Lodge of Neb.; recipient of the Gourgas Medal of the Scottish Rite (NJ) in 1940; Deputy Grand Master of the Grand Lodge of Mass. in 1916.

"Masonry" said Pound, "has more to offer the twentieth century than the twentieth century has to offer Masonry."

Figure 32 — Famous American Masons of the 20th Century.

33° Luther Burbank (1849-1926)
Horticulturist & naturalist

Farmboy who became interested in plant life. Moved to Calif. where he established Burbank's Experimental Farms. Created Burbank potato; edible cactus; 11 types of plums; 4 types of prunes; the new fruit "Plumcot; various new apples, peaches, nuts, berries, trees, fruits, flowers, grasses, grains and vegetables.

Burbank was raised (3°) in Santa Rosa Lodge No. 57, 8-13-21; coronetted 33° AASR (SJ), 10-20-25.

33°William Randolph Hearst (1863-

1951)
Newspaper barron

Born in San Francisco, CA. Studied at Harvard. Took over *San Francisco Examiner* from his father, 1887. Acquired *New York Morning Journal*, 1895; launched *Evening Journal*, 1896. Other newspapers included *Chicago Examiner, Boston American, Cosmopolitan*, and *Harper's*.

He advocated political assassinations in an editorial just months before Pres. McKinley was assassinated.

Member of U.S. House of Rep. His life inspired the Orson Welles film *Citizen Kane* (1941).

Figure 33 — Famous American Masons of the 20th Century.

32° George M. Cohan (1878-1942)

Actor, Playwright, Comedian, Shriner & 32° AASR (NJ) 1906.

Both a Roman Catholic and a Mason. First professional role played as Daniel Boone. Played in vaudeville shows; authored many plays; wrote many popular songs. He was a life member of Pacific Lodge No. 233, NYC. Raised (3°) on Nov. 16, 1905.

Received 32° Feb. 3, 1906. Although he took an oath to Allah as a member of Moslem Mecca Shrine Temple, NYC, at his death he was buried with Catholic services.

1° Sam Rayburn (1882-1961)

Speaker of the House

Born in Roane Co., TN. Graduate of East Texas Coll. Studied law at U. of Texas. Began law practice in Bonham, TX. Member of Texas lower house for 6 years. Speaker of the House for two years.

Received Entered Apprentice degree Aug. 7, 1922 in Constantine Lodge No. 13, Bonham, TX.

Figure 34 — After WWI, industry boomed and adventuresome men and women strutted their achievements. Below is Freemason Charles Lindbergh, first solo flight across the Atlantic.

3° **Charles Lindbergh** (1902-1974)

Lindbergh received his degrees in Keystone Lodge No. 243, St. Louis, Mo., June 9, Oct. 20, and Dec. 15, 1926, and was a life member of that lodge. He was also a member of St. Louis Chapter No. 33, National Sojourners, and of the Scots at San Diego, Ca. On his history-making flight from New York to Paris, he wore the square and compass on his jacket as a luck charm. The plane also bore a Masonic tag from his lodge. He received many medals and citations from grand lodges throughout the world and they are now on display at the Jefferson Memorial in St. Louis.

SECTION 9
FREEMASONRY "TRIGGERS" WORLD WAR
TWO TO HALT THE ANTI-MASONIC MOVEMENT
IN EUROPE & JAPAN !!!

Fig. 1 — Cover page to the Minutes of the International Masonic Congress of Allied and Neutral nations to create League of Nations.

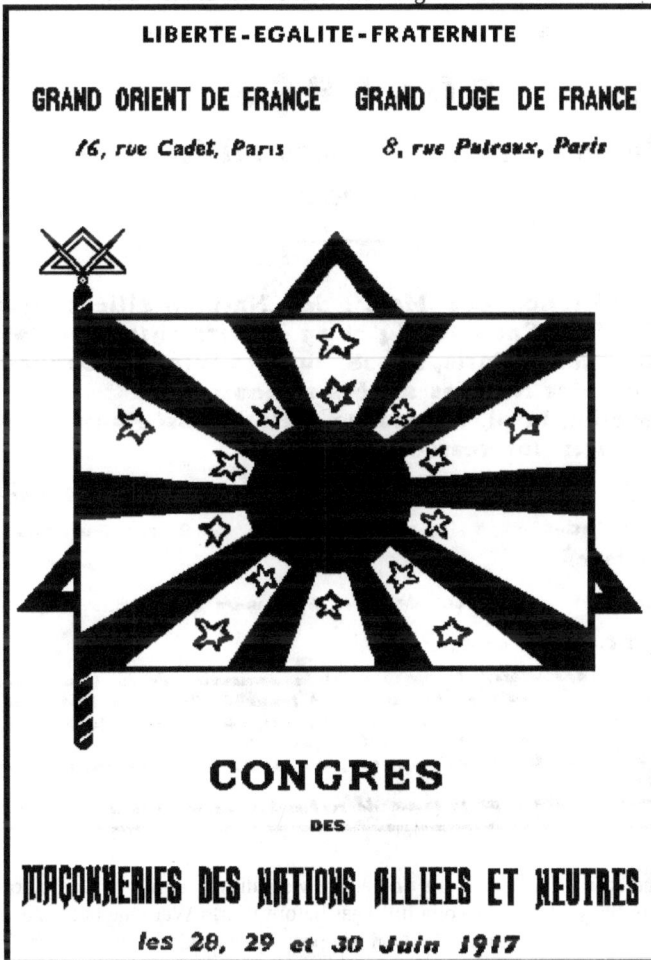

LIBERTE - EGALITE - FRATERNITE

GRAND ORIENT DE FRANCE   GRAND LOGE DE FRANCE

16, rue Cadet, Paris   *8, rue Puteaux, Paris*

CONGRES

DES

MAÇONNERIES DES NATIONS ALLIEES ET NEUTRES

les 28, 29 et 30 Juin 1917

Copy of cover and title page to Minutes of International Masonic Congress of Allied and Neutral Nations, held to discuss formation of League of Nations at headquarters of Grand Orient, Paris, France on June 2830, 1917. For an analysis and detailed extracts from this document see *Scarlet and the Beast*, Vol. I, 3rd edition, chap. 24.

Fig. 2 — Opening page to the minutes of the Masonic congress held in Paris in June 1917 to create the League of Nations.

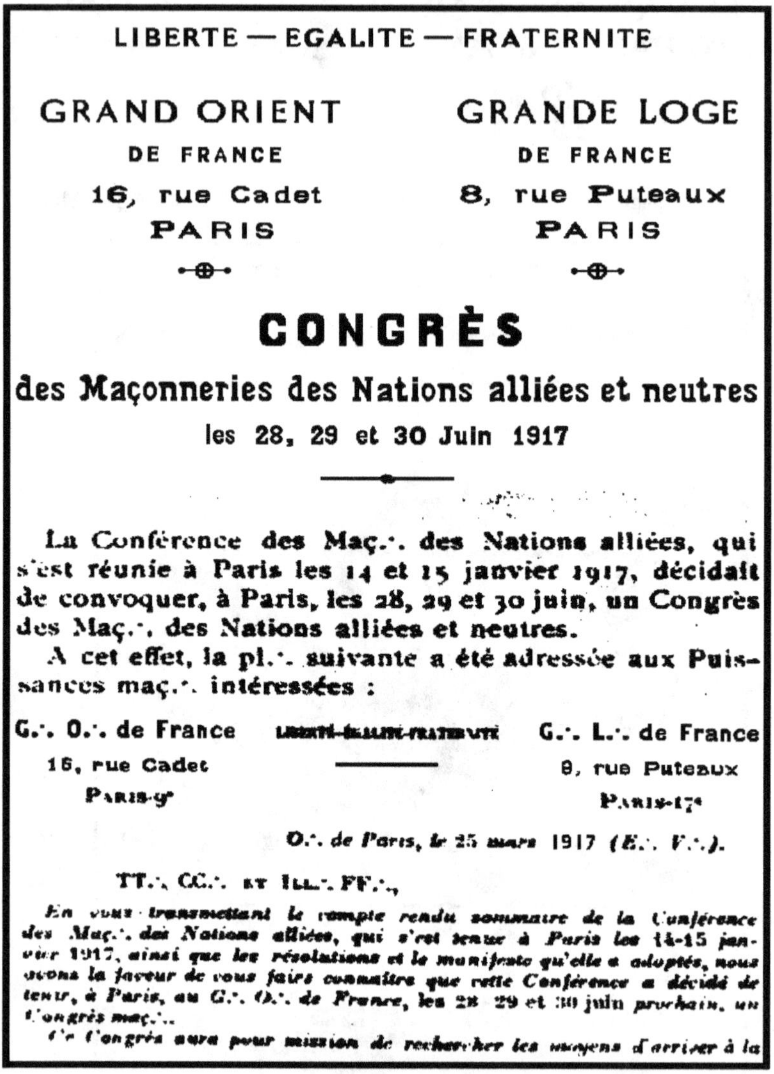

LIBERTE — EGALITE — FRATERNITE

GRAND ORIENT
DE FRANCE
16, rue Cadet
PARIS

GRANDE LOGE
DE FRANCE
8, rue Puteaux
PARIS

CONGRÈS
des Maçonneries des Nations alliées et neutres
les 28, 29 et 30 Juin 1917

La Conférence des Maç∴ des Nations alliées, qui s'est réunie à Paris les 14 et 15 janvier 1917, décidait de convoquer, à Paris, les 28, 29 et 30 juin, un Congrès des Maç∴ des Nations alliées et neutres.

A cet effet, la pl∴ suivante a été adressée aux Puissances maç∴ intéressées :

G∴ O∴ de France   LIBERTÉ-ÉGALITÉ-FRATERNITÉ   G∴ L∴ de France
16, rue Cadet   ————   8, rue Puteaux
Paris-9°   Paris-17°

O∴ de Paris, le 25 mars 1917 (E∴ V∴).

TT∴ CC∴ et Ill∴ FF∴,

En vous transmettant le compte rendu sommaire de la Conférence des Maç∴ des Nations alliées, qui s'est tenue à Paris les 14-15 janvier 1917, ainsi que les résolutions et le manifesto qu'elle a adoptés, nous avons la faveur de vous faire connaître que cette Conférence a décidé de tenir, à Paris, au G∴ O∴ de France, les 28 29 et 30 juin prochain, un Congrès maç∴.

Ce Congrès aura pour mission de rechercher les moyens d'arriver à la

Name of and plans for the League of Nations were drawn up in a Masonic Lodge in Paris, France in the year 1913 — one full year before World War One began, and four years before President Woodrow Wilson supposedly coined the name "League of Nations." In *Scarlet and the Beast*, Vol. I, 3rd edition, chap. 12 & 24, read excerpts from the 1913 minutes of that meeting.

Figure 3 — Paris Peace Conference.

Paris Peace Conference following World War One
Peace Conference was planned & organized by French Grand Orient Freemasonry.
See *Scarlet and the Beast*, Vol. 1, 3rd edition, chps. 12&24

Figure 4 — Founding meeting of the League of Nation in 1920.

League of Nations founding meeting in Paris France (1920). Plans for the League of Nations were discussed in a Masonic Lodge one full year before World War One began. See transcript of meeting *S&B*. V1, 3rd ed, ch 24.

BIRTH AND DEATH OF THE LEAGUE OF NATIONS

Quoting from *Mackey's Encyclopedia of Freemasonry* we read, "The paramount social purpose of French Masonry was to help establish a permanent peace in Europe. Long before Woodrow Wilson's presidency it held conferences for discussing a League of Nations.... It is true that a Masonic Congress held in Paris in 1913 by representatives of the Allied or neutral countries advocated a League of Nations." See *Scarlet and the Beast*, Vol. 1, 3rd edition, chap. 24.

Following are excerpts taken from minutes of the French Masonic Lodge:

After the League of Nations is constituted, the Orator of the 1922 French Grand Lodge convention lauds its founding with this comment: "My brother Masons, my hope is that Freemasonry, which has done so much for the emancipation of men, and to which history owes the national revolutions, will also know how to make that greatest revolution, which will be the International Revolution." See *S&B*, V. 1, 3rd ed. ch. 9.

Quoting from the 1922 convention minutes of the Grand Lodge of France we read: "The principal tasks of the League of Nations consist in the organization of peace, the abolition of secret diplomacy, the application of the right of peoples to self-determination, the establishment of commercial relations inspired by the principle of Free Trade...; the creation of a European spirit, of a League of Nations patriotism — in brief, the formation of the United States of Europe, or rather World Federation." See *Scarlet and the Beast*, Vol. 1, chap. 12.

Quoting from the 1923 convention minutes of Grand Orient Freemasonry of France we read: "It is the duty of universal Freemasonry to give its absolute support to the League of Nations, so that Freemasonry no longer has to be subject to the partisan influences of Governments." See *Scarlet and the Beast*, Vol. 1, chap. 12.

In 1939, when World War Two began, the failed League of Nations ceased operations.

Figure 5 — Military aides of the Allied peacemakers peering through windows of the Paris Peace Conference. At the moment this picture was taken, the humiliating Treaty of Versailles peace terms of which the Allies had agreed were being handed to a stunned, deeply angry German Delegation. Many delegates who had read the terms predicted it guaranteed a Second World War. And they were right!

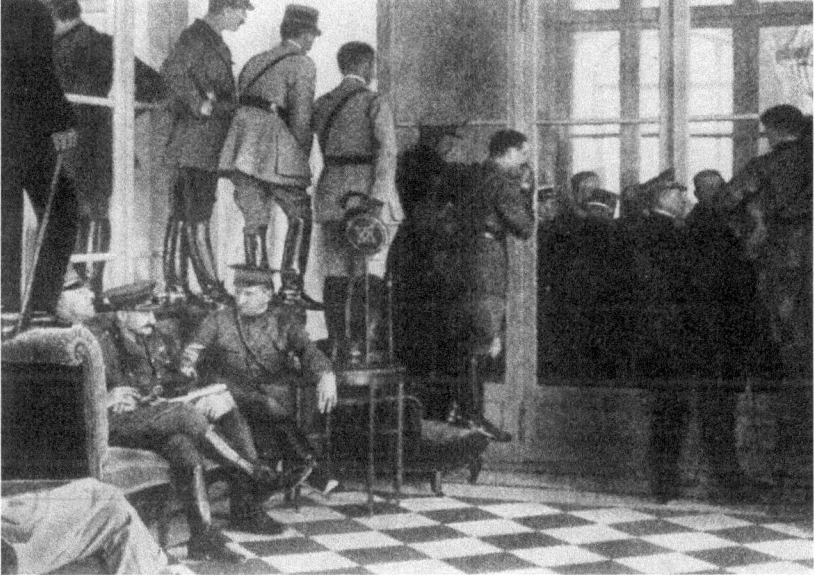

Figure 6 — Freemason Henry Ford. Read of his anti-Semitism in *Scarlet and the Beast*, Vol. I, 3rd ed., chaps. 18 & 25.

33° Henry Ford (1863-1947)

Henry Ford was raised to 3° in Palestine Lodge No. 357, Detroit, Mi. on Nov. 28, 1894. He continued a staunch member of this lodge for almost 53 years. When he received the 33° AASR (NJ) in Sept., 1940, he stated: "Masonry is the best balance wheel the United States has, for Masons know what to teach their children."

Fig. 7 —33° Freemason Henry Ford receiving Hitler's "Great Cross of the German Order of the Eagle" in July 1938.

THE NEW YORK TIMES, WED., OCT. 6, 1999, p A13

"Henry Ford was a Nazi sympathizer whose notorious anti-Semitic tract, The International Jew, a Worldwide Problem, was published in both the U.S. and Germany. A great admirer and personal friend of Adolf Hitler, Ford gave Hitler annual birthday gifts of tens of thousands of dollars. In turn, Hitler awarded Ford 'The Great Cross of the German Order of the Eagle.'

"From 1940 (even before the U.S. entered the war) to 1945, Ford Werke AG profited greatly from the forced labor of thousands of captive people from occupied countries... Ford Werke AG also leased inmates from the Buchenwald concentration camp for slave labor. By the end of the war, these laborers accounted for over half of the work force at the Ford plant in Cologne. "The workers were subjected to horrific treatment. They were expendable. Workers who disobeyed or tried to escape were either shot on the spot or sent to the Gestapo for execution. Many who failed to meet production quotas were beaten with rubber truncheons." See *Scarlet and the Beast*, Vol. 1, 3rd ed., chapter 25-26.

Figure 8 — "We had no names, only numbers. The Nazis demanded total obedience. We were treated like animals," said Elsa Iwanova, age 17, who was forced to labor at a Ford plant in Germany during WWII. *THE NEW YORK TIMES* , Oct. 6, 1999, p. A13.

Figure 9 — Henry Ford enjoyed upsetting the apple cart more than anyone else. In 1914 he announced that he would pay $5 a day to his workers, double the going rate. With the extra cash, Ford reasoned, they could purchase his Model Ts. The workers were becoming a bulwark of the middle class.

Fig. 10 — Prominent Jews were mentioned in Henry Ford's newspaper called the *Dearborn Independent*, and his notorious anti-Semitic tract, *The International Jew*.
See *Scarlet and the Beast*, V1, 3rd ed., chs.18 and 25-26.

33° **Bernard M. Baruch** (1870-1965)

Financier and US statesman, born in Camden, SC. Educated in New York City, he began life as an office boy, but made a fortune by speculation. He became a powerful political influence — "the adviser of presidents" and of Churchill during World War Two.

He came under attack by Henry Ford in the *Dearborn Independent*, which charged that several well known Jews in America were the instigators of World War I. One of them was Bernard Baruch, known as the "proconsul of Judah in America," a "Jew of Super-Power." When requested by news reporters to comment on Ford's charges, Baruch replied, tongue-in-cheek, "Now boys, you wouldn't expect me to deny them would you?"

Entering the fray was 33° Jewish Mason "Colonel" Edward House, who urged President Woodrow Wilson to act against Ford. When Wilson called upon Ford to stop his "vicious propaganda," Ford refused.

In 1922 Ford's articles were compiled in a book entitled, *The International Jew*. Translated into German, the book was renamed *The Eternal Jew*. This book led many Germans to become Nazis.

Finally, Ford struck at the Jews where they would later prove to be most vulnerable. He financed Hitler. In September 1940, Ford received the 33° in a New Jersey lodge in the Northern Jurisdiction of Scottish Rite Freemasonry, which is under the English Masonic obedience.

Why should the British-controlled Northern Jurisdiction of Freemasonry honor Ford with the 33° after he financed the Nazis, unless it was to reward him for furthering the Masonic conspiracy against the Jews? You will find the answer in *Scarlet and the Beast*, *Vol. 1*, 3rd edition.

Fig. 11 — Masons on Roosevelt's 1933 Cabinet.

32° Roosevelt, 3° Homer Cummings, Attorney General, 13° Claude A. Swanson, Sec. Navy, 32° Henry C. Wallace Sec. Agriculture, 32° Daniel C. Roper, Sec. Commerce 33° George H. Dern, Sec. War.

Fig. 12 — Masons on Roosevelt's Cabinet at the start of WW2.

32° Claude Wickard, Sec. Agriculture, 32° Henry C. Wallace, VP Attorney General, 3° Jesse H. Jones Sec. Commerce, 32° Roosevelt, 33° Henry Morganthou Sec. Treasure, 32° W. Frank Knox Sec. Navy.

One page from Chapter 24, *Scarlet and the Beast*, Vol. 1, 3rd edition.

British World Governance and the United Nations

After World War I, French Grand Orient Freemasonry considered itself mistress of the future. Grand Orient Masons were in charge of the new European politics from 1918 to 1930. They promised the world an era of peace, happiness and prosperity through Grand Orient-created socialism and communism. Instead Europe was plunged into revolution followed by counterrevolution, fought between proponents of English and French Freemasonry. Traditional monarchies, under the aegis of English Freemasonry, were destroyed in favor of French Freemasonry's socialist and communist republics. Left-wing dictators — more despotic than former sovereigns had ever been — ruled the new republics.

Grant Orient republics, whether communist or socialist, became instruments for terror and disruption of order. French Freemasonry showed that when in power it was incapable of governing and maintaining order. General chaos and financial breakdown followed — ending in the Great Depression of the 1930s.

In Germany, Austria, Hungary and Italy, communism was eventually strangled at great cost and much bloodshed. In place of communism, authoritarian regimes sprang up by popular consent.

Such were the dictatorships of Admiral Horthy in Hungary, Mussolini and fascism in Italy, Chancellor Dollfuss in Austria, Hitler and National Socialism in Germany.

By 1939, the French Grand Orient, previously thinking itself mistress of the future, found it had fallen on difficult times. DePoncins wrote: "The results were disastrous. The Treaty of Versailles quickly led to widespread breakdown of order, to revolutionary unrest, to the opposing reactions of the Fascist and Hitler regimes, the Spanish Civil War, and finally to the Second World War."

The Whore of Babylon Mounts the Beast

English Freemasonry, which had been patiently implementing its policy of "gradualism" through the Round Table Groups, saw its opportunity to regain dominance, not by reinstating her kings throughout Europe, but by funding the extreme right-wing dictators who had wrested government from the hands of the extreme left-wing despots.

In 1939, when World War II began and the League of Nations ceased operations, London's Round Table Groups in America made their move to take over world governance.

Figure 13 — Benito Mussolini — anti-Mason.
See *Scarlet and the Beast*, Vol. I, 3rd edition, chaps. 9, 10, 16, 24-27.

Benito Mussolini (1883-1945)
Anti-Mason
Italian dictator and anti-Mason. Revolutionary from youth. Was many times jailed or under constant police surveillance. In 1912 became editor of *Avanti*, the official Socialist paper of Italy, and resigned in 1914 to establish his own *Il Popolo d'Italia*. He appealed for Italy to enter WWI with the allies and served as a private in that war. After the war he engaged in a campaign against Communism and organized the *Fascio di Combattimento* at Milan on March 23, 1919. This was the beginning of Fascism in Italy.

Fascism officially took the form of a political party in 1921. In 1922 he led the Fascists in a march on Rome against Freemasonry (see next page). When the cabinet resigned, Mussolini was summoned by the king to form a ministry. By gaining control over a number of ministries, changing the electoral law, and suppressing all opposition, he gained control of the government. In 1929 he signed a treaty with the Roman Church, ending a 59-year-old dispute. He conquered Ethiopia in 1936; withdrew from the League of Nations in 1937; did away with the chamber of deputies in 1938; conquered Albania in 1939; aided Franco in Spanish Civil War against Freemasonry and entered WWII on side of Hitler in May 1940. At the time of Mussolini's rise to power, there were two Grand Lodges in Italy. He played one against the other, and finally played the Roman Church against what remained. He banned Freemasonry in Italy in 1923.

Torrigiani, the Grand Master of Grand Orient Freemasonry in Italy, died in prison on the island of Lipari, a martyr to the Masonic cause.

Other Grand Officers of Freemasonry suffered various punishments.

Fig. 14 — Rome 1922 anti-Mason Benito Mussolini and his Fascist March on Rome against Freemasonry.

Fig. 15 — 1937 anti-Mason Franco inspects trenches on Madrid front in Spanish Civil War (1936-1937). Spanish Civil War was against Masonry. See *Scarlet and the Beast*, Vol. 1, 3rd edition, chapter 26.

Figure 16 — Francisco Franco — anti-Mason.
See *Scarlet and the Beast*, Vol. I, 3rd edition, chapter 26, entitled "Spanish Masonic Civil War."

Francisco Franco (1892-1975)
Spanish Generalissimo and dictator of Spain, beginning in 1939. Anti-Mason.

He served in the army in Morocco and was appointed chief of staff of Spanish army in 1935. At outbreak of the revolution, he organized the transport of foreign legionnaires and Moorish troops in Spain and became commander of the insurgents.

He received aid from Nazi Germany and Fascist Italy..., enabling him to buy war supplies.

In 1941 he signed a concordat with the Vatican which empowered him to designate Spanish bishops, subject to ratification by the Holy See.

33° Freemason William Denslow states in *10,000 Famous Freemasons*, "This unholy alliance was the beginning of a modern inquisition, and since that date Freemasons have been persecuted, imprisoned, and executed in Spain."

Franco held that Freemasonry is as subversive as Communism — if not more so. After winning the war, one of his first acts was to set up a special tribunal for the "Repression of Masonry and Communism." It was a secret court and no reports of its activities appear in print.

Freemasonry was behind the "Spanish Masonic Civil War" that raged in Spain a decade before World War Two began. You can read about it in *Scarlet and the Beast* , Vol. 1, 3rd edition, chapter 26.

Fig. 17 — Famous German Masons. See *Scarlet and the Beast*, Vol. 1, 3rd ed., chaps, 19 and 25.

Richard Wagner (1813-1883)

German composer. Some say Wagner was a Mason, because Masonry played a large part in much of his music. Freemasonry says he was not a Mason, but wanted to be.

Wagner had many Masonic influences in his life, including his family and friends. His brother-in-law, Prof. Oswald Marbach, was one of the most important personalities in Freemasonry during Wagner's time, and in view of the Masonic aspect of his *Parsifal*, it is speculated that he learned much of Masonic ritual and ideas from Marbach, who held the chair of the chapter *Balduin, Zur Lindi* of Leipzig for more than 30 years, and was an honorary member of more than 50 lodges.

Another great friend of Wagner was the banker, Feustel in Bayreuth, who from 1863-69 was master of the lodge *Zur Sonne* in Bayreuth. In 1847 Feustel proposed that the lodge abolish the restrictions on nonChristians becoming members, apparently at the request of Wagner, since Wagner informed Feustel of his desire to become a member of the lodge *Eleusis zur Verschuregenheit* in Bayreuth. But, Feustel was advised not to submit a formal petition, since there were members who reproached Wagner for his personal life.

Wagner was selfish and vain. He was unkind to his friends and made those near him unhappy. For example, when Wagner's first wife died in 1866, he married his best friend's wife in 1870, who deserted her husband for Wagner.

Wagner took part in the German political revolt in 1848-49, when all Europe exploded with Masonic revolutions. He was forced to flee to Switzerland, where he stayed for the next ten years.

Wagner's opera "Rienzi" was successfully produced at Dresden in 1842 and resulted in his appointment as musical director of the Saxon court. Seventy years later this work would influence a man named Adolph Hitler, who considered himself Rienzi, destined to throw off the yoke of the Judao/Masonic conspiracy.

Fig. 18 — Lytton's novels greatly influenced Adolf Hitler.
See *Scarlet and the Beast*, Vol. 1, 3rd ed., chapter 25.

Edward George Earl Bulwer-Lytton
(1803-1873)
Rosicrucian Freemason
Born in London, England. Politician, poet, and critic. He is chiefly remembered as a prolific novelist.

He was influenced by the Romanticism of Freemason Goethe. His plots are elaborate and involved. His characterization is exaggerated and unreal. His style is grandiose and ornate. His books, though dated, remain immensely readable to this day. And his personal experience of society and politics gives his work an unusual historical interest.

Bulwer-Lytton was the youngest son of Gen. William Bulwer and Elizabeth Lytton. After university at Cambridge, he went to France and visited Paris and Versailles. It was in France that he was influenced by the occult. From this experience he produced *Zanoni* (1842) and *A Strange Story* (1862).

A long line of Masons implemented Lytton's teachings, both founding and controlling secret societies based upon them. These societies can be directly linked to Hitler and his Nazi Party.

Lytton's novels were the favorite reading of German composer and Freemason, Richard Wagner (1813-1883), who put them to music in theater. Later, Wagner's wife helped fund Hitler's rise to power.

Lytton presented his utopia in *Vril: The Power of the Coming Race* (1871), which in 1912 heavily influenced Adolf Hitler. *Vril* was the story of a superman race of white Aryans that would take over the world. Hitler was so inspired that he planned to implement the program.

Hitler was also inspired by another of Lytton's novels, *Rienzi: The Last of the Roman Tribunes*. In fact, the future Nazi Fuehrer returned to the theater in Vienna a hundred times to see the opera. Hence, Bulwer-Lytton is recognized by conspiracy researchers as the Godfather of the Nazi movement, for Hitler considered himself a reincarnation of Rienzi.

Another example of how Lytton influenced Hitler came in 1887, fourteen years after Lytton's death, when the first mystic society based on Lytton's *Vril* was founded. At the behest of the Quatuor Coronati Lodge, the Hermetic Order of the Golden Dawn was founded on the doctrine of Lytton's Rosicrucian Society. The swastika was a key symbol of the Golden Dawn.

Fig. 19 — The man who changed Hitler by introducing him to black magic. Excerpt below from *Scarlet and the Beast*, Vol. 1, 3rd ed., chap. 25.

Dietrich Eckart (1868-1923)
Rosicrucian Freemason

The man who changed Hitler by introducing him to black magic.

Eckart broke from Freemasonry because he could not embrace its internationalism. Finding his spiritual home in the Thule Society, Eckart, a dedicated Satanist, was a master of magic and practiced rituals that were anything but harmless.

Eckart, with Alfred Rosenberg, was a top officer in the Thule Society. He participated in a series of seances with Rosenberg and the infamous Russian occultist G.I. Gurdjieff. During these seances, Eckart was "told of the imminent appearance of the German messiah, a Lord Maitreya." Eckart was further instructed about his own destiny. He was "to prepare the vessel of the Anti-Christ, the man inspired by Lucifer to conquer the world and lead the Aryan race to glory."

Eckart was a heavy drinker who used "drugs, including peyote, the South American hallucinogen, which Aleister Crowley introduced into Europe's artistic and occultist circles. In his younger years in Berlin, Eckart spent some time in a psychiatric clinic because of morphine addiction. This man was destine to become Hitler's mentor. Later he became one of the most powerful members of the Thule Society's hierarchy.

Eckart composed a bardic verse in which the coming of a national redeemer was prophesied. Obviously, his so-called "prophecy" was prompted by the seance with Gurdjieff where Eckart received his "annunciation" that he was destined to prepare a messiah for the German people. A few weeks after the circulation of "prophecy," Eckart brought to the Thule Society's supreme council the idea that the hour for a great charismatic leader had come: "We need a leader familiar and foreign at the same time, a nameless one.... We must have a fellow as a leader who won't wince at the rattle of a machine gun. The rabble must be given a damned good fright. An officer wouldn't do; the people don't respect them any more. Best of all would be a worker, a former soldier who could speak...." The Thule Society was well on its way to accepting Hitler.

Fig. 20 — Deathbed photo of Nietzsche. *Nazi* is a derivative of *Nietzsche*.
Portions of excerpt below from *S&B*, V.1, 3rd ed., chap. 25.

Friedrich Wilhelm Nietzsche (1844-1900)

Philosopher and critic, born in Röcken, Germany. Strongly religious as a child. Brilliant undergraduate, accepting chair of classical philology at Basel (1869-79) before graduating. Dedicated his first book, *The Birth of Tragedy*, to his friend Richard Wagner, whose operas he regarded as the true successors to Greek tragedy. Much of his esoteric doctrine appealed to the Nazis, and he was a major influence on existentialism. In 1889 he had a mental breakdown, from which he never recovered.

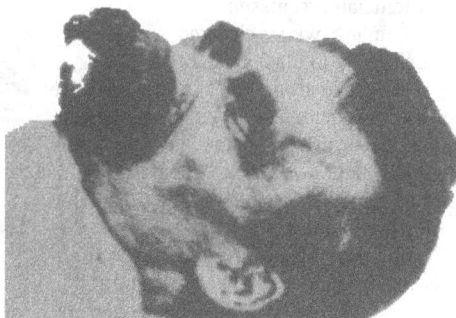

Edith Starr Miller, in *Occult Theocrasy*, lists Nietzsche as one of the many Masons who was involved in the 19th Century revival of witchcraft, which led to founding the O.T.O. In fact, the name *Nazi* is a derivative of *Nietzsche*. That Hitler's last birthday gift to Mussolini in 1943 was *The Collected Works of Nietzsche* testifies to the enduring influence of this philosopher upon Aldolf Hitler.

Adolf Hitler's Nietzsche Memorial opened in 1938.

Figure 21 — Horatio Herbert Kitchener. *Scarlet and the Beast,* Vol. 1, 3rd ed., chap.25.

33° Viscount Horatio Herbert Kitchener (1850-1916)

British field marshal, born near Ballylongford, Co., Kerry, Ireland. He joined the Royal Engineers in 1871, and served in Palestine (1874), Cyprus (1878), and the Sudan (1883). By the final rout of the Khalifa at Omdurman (1898), he won back the Sudan for Egypt, and was made a peer. He was chief-of-staff and commander-in-chief in South Africa (1900-2), and brought the Boer War to an end. He then became commander-in-chief in India (1902-9). He was lost with *HMS Hampshire,* which was mined off the Orkney Is.

Mackey's Encyclopedia of Freemasonry states that Lord Kitchener was accomplished in oriental languages, which enabled him to advance Freemasonry in the Orient. As a famous English soldier serving seven years in India, he was responsible for founding three Lodges there, becoming Grand Master at Punjab. While serving in Egypt he was Grand Master of both Egypt and Sudan. He also visited Japan, Australia and New Zealand.[33] *10,000 Famous Freemasons* states he became a Mason in Egypt. In 1885 he was one of the founders of Drury Lane Lodge No. 2127 of London. He was made Past Grand Warden of the Grand Lodge of England in 1897; district Grand Master of Egypt and the Sudan in 1899; and Past Grand Warden of District Grand Lodge of Punjab, India (1902).

Four English lodges have been named in his honor.

During his sojourn in India, Kitchener made many trips to Tibet where he was introduced to the German general Karl Ernst Haushofer, who was a Freemason and member of the Berlin Golden Dawn. Before World War I, Haushofer had spent many years as military attaché in Japan and traveled extensively in Asia. Kitchener, and the Russian occultist G.I. Gurdjieff, also an expert on Tibetan mysticism, initiated Haushofer into the secret cult of the Tibetan lamas (who claimed to possess the secret of the "superman") and introduced Haushofer to the meaning of the swastika. Then in 1910 Kitchener went to Vienna where a series of secret assignations occurred in connection with the "Hitler Project." Read the full story in *Scarlet and the Beast,* Vol. 1, 3rd edition, chap. 26.

Fig. 22

Benedictine
Monastery
at
Lambach
where Hitler
attended
school
in the
1890s

Closeup photo of
Coat of Arms,
showing Swastika
above abbé doorway
at Benedictine
Monastery
above

Scarlet and the Beast
Vol. 1, 3rd ed.
Chapter 25

Fig. 23 — The legendary **Spear of Destiny**, also known as the Spear of Longinus, reputed to have pierced the side of Jesus. See *Scarlet and the Beast*, Vol. 1, 3rd ed., ch. 1, 3, 4, 25, 26, 28.

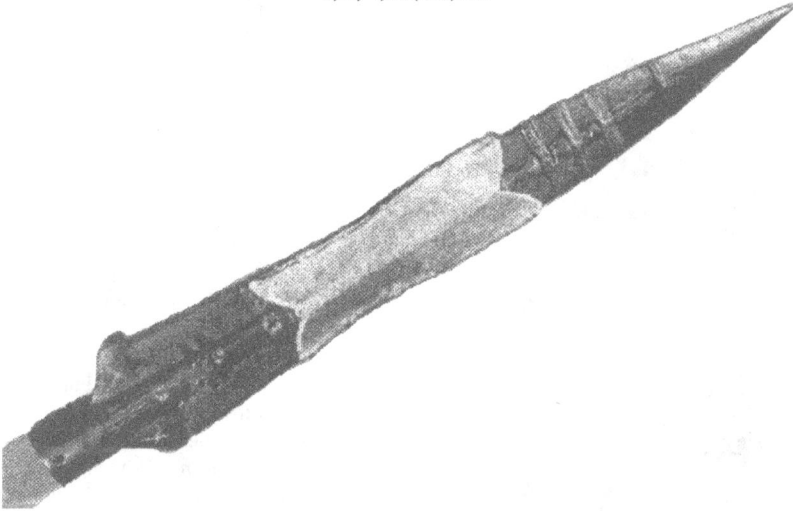

According to legend, the one who possesses the Spear of Destiny rules the world.
For centuries it was in possession of the Hapsburg dynasty, until Hitler conquered Austria. Hitler took the spear back to Berlin.
During the final weeks of WWII, when the Allies were controlling West Germany, the spear was found in a church. General Eisenhower bluntly said, "Return the Habsburg Regalia to Austria."
It remains there to this day.

Fig. 24 —See *Scarlet and the Beast*, Vol. 1, 3rd ed., chapter 25.

Anton Drexler (1881-?)
Founder of German Workers' Party
The Thule Society recruited Anton Drexler and his German Workers' Party (GWP), financing and promoting it as its own political Party. The GWP adopted the anti-Semitic and promonarchist Thule agenda.

In the fall of 1919, Hitler joined Drexler's Thule-backed GWP, which was still meeting in the beer halls. Hitler's charismatic speeches increased membership in the fledgling Party, Within a short time, Hitler dominated the Party, pushing Drexler to the sidelines and putting his new friends from the Thule Society in key positions. Under Hitler's direction, an obscure workers' party left the beer halls to become a mass movement.

Figure 25 — Adolf Hitler — anti-Mason. See *Scarlet and the Beast,* Vol. I, 3rd edition, chapter 25-26.

Adolf Hitler (1889-1945)

Anti-Mason. German Chancellor & Fuhrer. Dorothy Thompson, writing about Hitler for the *Ladies Home Journal* in Oct. 1955, stated that Hitler was suffering from paranoia and a persecution complex: "Those whom he imagines to be conspiring against him (are) Priests, Freemasons, Jews, & the crowned heads of Europe."

Hitler forbade meetings of, and membership in Freemasonry. He even established a museum which depicted the foolishness of the fraternity. The following is part of Hitler's official decree against the lodge, which was presented as evidence at the Nuremberg Trials: "Freemasons and the ideological enemies of National Socialism who are allied with them are the originators of the present war against the Reich. Spiritual struggle according to plan against these powers is a measure necessitated by war. I have, therefore, ordered Reichsleiter Alfred Rosenberg to accomplish this task in cooperation with the Chief of the High Command of the armed forces. He has the right to explore libraries, archives, lodges, and other ideological and cultural establishments of all kinds for suitable material and to confiscate such material for the ideological tasks of the N.S.D.A.P. for scientific research. The regulations for the execution of this task will be issued by the Chief of the High Command of the armed forces in agreement with Reichsleiter Rosenberg." Read *Scarlet and the Beast,* Vol. 1, 3rd edition, chapter 27 how closet Masons, who also were Nazis, received protection at the Nuremberg Trials (German spelling *Nurnberg*).

Treason trial put Hitler on the map by Bruce Kauffmann
Longview News-Journal, **March 30, 2005**

On April 1, 1924 in Germany, Adolf Hitler was sentenced to five years in Germany's Landsberg Prison for leading the Beer Hall "Putsch" (coup) of 1923, in which he and a cluster of followers had tried to overthrow the German government. Yet the joke was that instead of destroying his political career, the trial and his subsequent conviction for treason gave his political aspirations a tremendous boost.

For one thing, the trial attracted nationwide press coverage, which made the little known Hitler a household name in Germany. For another, Nazi sympathizers in the government made sure the trial's appointed judges were sympathetic to Hitler's politics. As a result, the judges allowed Hitler to use the trial — and the media coverage it generated — as a soapbox to espouse his political, racial and social beliefs.

Hitler took full advantage of the opportunity. Rather than deny the charges against him, he reveled in them, boasting that he purposely tried to overthrow the government in 1923, but he explained that his motivation was to take back Germany from the "traitors" who had "betrayed" the country by prematurely suing for peace at the end of World War I. Hitler's long-held contention that Germany had not lost World War I, but had been "stabbed in the back" by Jews, Communists and spineless bureaucrats, resonated with many Germans, and his trial afforded him the perfect opportunity to communicate that message on a national scale.

By the time the trial ended, Hitler had morphed from defendant into political superstar, and he used his closing statement to send a clear message of his future intentions. "The man who is born to be dictator is not compelled," Hitler exclaimed. "He wills it! He is not driven forward but drives himself!"

Hitler concluded by telling the judges that, "It is not you, gentlemen, who pass judgment on us. That judgment is spoken by the eternal court of history — (and) she acquits us."

The judges agreed, and only found him guilty on the assurance that he would be treated well in prison and granted early parole.

They got their wish. Hitler got a private cell with a view of the grounds and was allowed gifts and visitors. His longtime assistant and fellow Landsberg inmate, Rudolph Hess, even became his private secretary, and in the scant nine months that Hitler was incarcerated he dictated to Hess his autobiography, *Mein Kampf* (My Fight), which was a blueprint of how he planned to take power in Germany and what he intended to do with that power. World War II and the Holocaust were the ultimate results.

Figure 26 — Pagan symbols below are said to "represent the good and evil forces of nature." This explanation, while true in only one of its occult meanings, is simply a santitized phrase to describe fertility worship. Each symbol below represent both good and evil, as well as male and female. The "female" aspect is always represented as evil.

Swastika rotating clockwise represents male & good

Swastika rotating counter clockwise represents female & evil

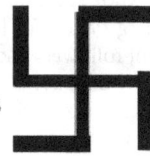

Nazis used version to the right

Yin & Yang

White represents male & good

Black represents female & evil

Yin & Yang is also the phalic 69 symbol of homosexuals.

Although Nazis hated Jews and Freemasons, the Zionist symbol to the right and Masonic symbol to the left carry same meaning as the Swastika.

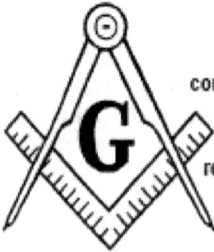

Upright compass represents male & good. Square represents female & evil.

Upright triangle represents male & good. Upside-down triangle represents female & evil.

Figure 27 — **Edward VIII** (1894-1972) King of England (Jan-Dec 1936). Eldest son of George V. He succeeded his father in 1936, but abdicated Dec. 11 in the face of opposition to his proposed marriage to Wallis Simpson, a commoner who had been twice divorced.
He was then given the title of Duke of Windson. They lived in Paris when not in Bahamas.

Edward VIII was crowned both king and Grand Master of English Freemasonry on January 20, 1936. Edward, however, married a divorced commoner from the United States and was forced to abdicate eleven months later on December 10th. His younger brother ascended the throne the next day and downgraded Edward's title to the Duke of Windsor.

In July 1940 the Duke assumed the governorship of the Bahamas. Edward VIII not only supported Hitler, he did so loudly. From the time of Hitler's rise to power, the Windsors were fascinated by the Fuehrer and his New Order in Europe. Speaking in Masonic terms, the King expressed the views of the Brotherhood concerning Hitler: "Whatever happens," he said, "whatever the outcome, a New Order is going to come into the world.... It will be buttressed with police power... When peace comes this time, there is going to be a New Order of Social Justice. It cannot be another Versailles." During his short reign, King Edward VIII made every effort to promote Nazism. As a result some of the most prominent aristocrats in England joined the Nazi Party. (See *Scarlet and the Beast*, Vol. 1, chapter 25).

Figure 28 — Advertizing poster to join Nazi military.
See *Scarlet and the Beast*, Vol. 1, 3rd. edition, chapter 25.

SAMME SLAGS B
(JEMPER I FELLES
MOT SAMME FIE

The most secret order in the Nazi regime was the SS

Like Hitler, the SS had deep roots in occult mysticism. But its organizational success owed much to Hitler's study of Freemasonry.

Duplicating the pyramid structure in the lodge, the SS was a secret society within another secret society, called the Vril. Moreover, the coldblooded SS were Satan worshippers. Their insignia (SS), shaped like two lightning bolts, is an ancient symbol of Satan. In Eastern mysticism the lightning bolts signify the speed and power by which the Adversary of God was cast out of heaven. Jesus Christ Himself said in Luke 10:18, "I beheld Satan as lightning fall from heaven."

The Nazi hierarchy established the SS as a secret society, developing its character from a mixture of Tibetan, Masonic, and Jesuit mysticism. SS Reichsfuehrer Heinrich Himmler was a necromancer, frequently conducting seances for the SS hierarchy at his castle in Wewelsburg.

Each SS officer took a secret blood oath to obey Hitler without question. Collectively, they were the ears and eyes of the Fuehrer — present at every meeting of political or social significance, yet never taking part in discussions. Instead, they just sat or stood in the background, observing and taking notes. See *Scarlet and the Beast*, Vol. 1, 3rd. ed., chap. 25-26.

Fig. 29 — Leopold Bernhardt — Prince of The Netherlands.

33° Prince Leopold Bernhardt (1911-2004)

Founder of the "Bilderbergers"

What history books say about the Prince

Prince of The Netherlands. Born in Jena, Germany. Son of Prince Bernhardt Casimir of Lippe. In 1937 he married Juliana, the only daughter of Wilhelmina, Queen of The Netherlands. The royal family owns Royal Dutch Shell Oil Corp.

During World War 2, the Prince commanded the Netherlands Forces of the Interior (1944-1945).

In 1976 he was involved in a bribery scandal, in which he was found to have received money for promoting the Dutch purchase of aircraft from the Lockheed Aircraft Corporation.

What history books do not say about the Prince

After Hitler conquered Holland, Bernhardt renounced Freemasonry and became an SS officer. (See *Scarlet and the Beast*, Vol. 1, 3rd edition, chapter 25). After the war he returned to the Brotherhood, and rose to the top as a 33° Mason in The Hague Grand Lodge.

In 1954 Prince Bernhardt hosted for the members of the British Round Table a supersecret meeting at the Bilderberg Hotel in Oosterbeek, Holland. When Journalists heard of the gathering, but could not discover the name of the hush-hush group, they labeled the attendees the "Bilderbergers." The Bilderbergers have since met at least once a year. Members of the Bilderbergers founded the Council on Foreign Relations and the Trilateral Commission, which together control the politics and economy of the world. In 1992 the Bilderbergers met at the Royal Hotel and the Ermitage Hotel in Evian, France. Both hotels are owned by the Grand Orient Masonic Lodge of France. (*Spotlight Magazine*, June 8, 1992, p.2.)

Read *Scarlet and the Beast* to learn of Prince Bernhardt's activity during the 1980s as Freemasonry's Supreme Council Inspector General, who frequented many neo-Nazi New Age Movement gatherings. See *Scarlet and the Beast*, Vol. 1, 3rd ed. chaps. 19 & 25.

Fig. 30 — As Hitler entered every country in Europe, his troops arrest- ed Jews and Masons, then entered every Masonic Lodge to confiscate their books. He brought the books to Berlin and burned them in great bonfires. The major Masonic-controlled news media of the day reported the following" "Party members and students burning 'anti-German' books in Berlin."
(Photo from *U.S. News & World Report*, 4/28/03).

Fig. 31 — Occultist. See *Scarlet and Beast*, Vol. 1, 3rd. ed., ch. 25, 27.

Heinrich Himmler (1900-1945)

Born in Munich, Germany. German Nazi leader and chief of police. He joined the Nazi Party in 1925, and in 1929 was made head of the SS, which he developed from Hitler's personal body guard into a powerful Party weapon. Himmler was a necromancer, frequently conducting seances for the SS hierarchy at his castle in Wewelsburg. Each SS officer took a secret blood oath to obey Hitler without question. Collectively, they were the ears and eyes of the Fuehrer.

Himmler also directed the secret police (*Gestapo*), and initiated the systematic liquidation of Jews. In 1943 he became minister of the interior, and in 1944 commander-in-chief of the home forces. He was captured by the allies, and committed suicide in Lüneburg.

Figure 32 — Anti-Mason Vidkun Quisling — Nazi war criminal.
See *Scarlet and the Beast*, VI, 3rd ed. ch 26. Below is two versions of same story.

Vidkun Quisling (1887-1945)
Encyclopaedia Britannica **version of his war crimes**

Norwegian army officer whose collaboration with the Germans during WWII established his name as a synonym for "traitor" (*Random House Dictionary*).

Quisling entered the army in 1911 and served as military attache in Petrograd (Leningrad) 1918-19, and in Helsinki, 1919-21. Assisted in relief work in Russia and later for the League of Nations. In the absence of diplomatic relations between Britain and Soviet Russia, he represented

British interests at the Norwegian legation in Moscow (1927-29). As minister of defense in an agrarian government (1931-33), he gained notoriety for repressing a strike by hydroelectric workers. He resigned from the government in 1933 to form the fascist Nasjonal Samling (National Union) Party, which stood for suppression of Communism and unionism.

At a meeting with Adolf Hitler in Dec. 1939, Quisling urged German occupation of Norway. After the German invasion of April 1940, Quisling proclaimed himself head of the government. As of Feb. 1942, he continued to serve in the Nazi occupation government as "minister president."

Quisling was held responsible for sending nearly 1,000 Jews to die in concentration camps. After the liberation of Norway in May 1945, he was arrested, found guilty of treason and other crimes, and executed.

10,000 Famous Freemasons' **version of his war crimes**

Norwegian Anti-Mason whose name has become a synonym for *traitor*. During WWI he was in the diplomatic and intelligence service, mainly in Russia. From 1931-32 he was the Norwegian minister of defense, resigning to found his own political party, the National Union, with a platform calling for the suppression of Communism and the freeing of Norwegian labor from unionism. He was chief collaborator in the German Conquest of Norway in 1940. The Nazis proclaimed him sole political head of Norway and head of the state council of 13 Nazi-dominated commissioners. In this capacity he took over the beautiful Masonic Temple in Oslo and converted it into an officers quarters, ruining it for Masonic use. He ordered all the library and belongings shipped to Germany to be burnt in great bonfires. He was tried by the Norwegian courts following the war. Ironically, the trial was held in a former Masonic lodge room, in order to seat more spectators. He was convicted and shot in 1945.

Figure 33 — Alfred Rosenberg — Nazi war criminal and anti-Mason.
See *Scarlet and the Beast*, VI, 3rd ed., chaps. 22, 25-27.

Alfred Rosenberg (1893-1946)

Born the son of a cobbler in Reval, in what was at the time a part of Russia. Studied architecture in Moscow until the Bolshevic Revolution of 1917. In 1919 he went to Munich, where he joined Adolf Hitler, Ernst Rohm, and Rudolf Hess in the nascent Nazi Party. When Hitler was imprisoned after the Munich *Putsch* (November 1923), he made Rosenberg leader of the party, knowing him to be incompetent as an organizer and thus unlikely to establish a position of power.

In his 1927 book, *The Future direction of the German Foreign Policy*, Rosenberg urged the conquest of Poland and Russia. His 1934 book, *The Myth of the 20th Century*, was a tedious exposition of German racial purity. According to Rosenberg, the Germans descended from a Nordic race that derived its character from its environment; a pure, cold, semi Arctic continent, now disappeared. The Germans, as representatives of this race, were entitled to dominate Europe.

Rosenberg entered the Reichstag in 1930, and in 1933 was the director of the newly established foreign policy office of the Nazi Party.

As editor of the party newspaper, *Volkischer Beobachter*, he drew on the ideas of the *Protocols of the Learned Elders of Zion*. According to the Nazis, Jews and Masons were synonymous. Hence, Hitler chose Rosenberg to lead in the persecution of both.

On March 1, 1942, Hitler ordered Rosenberg to seize all libraries and materials found in Masonic lodges in occupied countries and bring them to Berlin and burn them. In 1930 Rosenberg wrote, "The idea of honor, national honor, will be for us the beginning and end of all our thoughts and deeds. It does not permit besides itself any other equivalent center of power, be it of whatever kind, neither Christian love, nor the humanity of the Freemasons, nor the Roman philosophy."

Among his writings was the book, *The World Policy of Freemasonry*. At the Nuremberg Trials, he was closely questioned concerning his attacks on Freemasonry and Jews, and his confiscation of Masonic Libraries and records, which he had burned in great bonfires in Berlin.

In 1946 Rosenberg was hanged as a war criminal.

Fig. 34 — Nuremberg Trials. U.S. prosecutor Robert H. Jackson, a 32° Freemason, said in court, "Civilization itself is the real complaining party."

In the crowded courtroom at Nuremberg, U.S. prosecutor, 32° Robert H. Jackson (standing center), examines a witness (top) while 21 Nazis sit in the dock at far left. See (Fig. 27), Hermann Goring, one of 21 leading Nazis on trial, arriving in court on Nov. 26, 1945 in a uniform stripped of all but buttons. See *S&B*, V1, 3rd ed., Chapters 10 & 27.

32° Robert H. Jackson (1892-1954)

U.S. Attorney General; U.S. Supreme Court Justice; and American prosecutor at Nuremburg war crimes trials in Germany. See *Scarlet and the Beast*, Vol. 1, 3rd ed., chapters 10 and 27.

Born at Spring Creek, PA. Educated in Albany, NY Law School. Received honorary degrees from many universities. Admitted to New York bar in 1913; began practice at Jamestown; assistant attorney general of U.S., 1936-38; solicitor general of U.S., 1938-39; U.S. attorney general, 1940-41. Associate justice U.S. Supreme Court, 1941-45. In 1945 he was appointed by President Truman to represent the U.S. in negotiating with Russia, England, and France on agreement for international trials of European Axis war criminals. Was named chief of counsel for U.S., to conduct prosecution of Goering, Ribbentrop and others.

Jackson was a member of Mt. Moriah Lodge No. 145, Jamestown, NY. He received his degrees Sept. 17, Oct. 1, & 22, 1929; 32° AASR (NJ) in Nov. 1930 at Jamestown. Member of Ismailia Shrine Temple, Buffalo, NY.

33° **Edward F. Carter** (1897-?)

Served as judge on 5th Military Tribunal, Nuremburg, Germany, to try German war criminals in 1947-48. Justice Supreme Court of Nebraska since 1935. Admitted to bar, 1919. Practiced in Bayard, NE until 1917, when he became judge of the 17th district. Raised (3°) in Scotts Bluff Lodge No. 201, Gering, NE, Feb. 22, 1929. Past Master of same lodge. Grand Master of Grand Lodge of Nebraska, 1941. Member of Oregon Trail Chapter No. 65, Royal Arch Mason; Mt. Moriah Commandery No. 4, Knights Templar of Lincoln; consistory membership at Alliance; 33° AASR (SJ); member of Shrine, Red Cross of Constantine (Muslim Masonry), High Twelve and Eastern Star.

Fig. 35

Rudolf Hess (1894-1987)

Hitler's deputy as Nazi Party leader, born in Alexandria, Egypt. Educated at Godesberg, he fought in World War I, then studied at Munich. He joined the Nazi Party in 1920, and became Hitler's close friend and (in 1934) deputy. In 1941, on the eve of Germany's attack on Russia, Hess flew alone to Scotland to plead the cause of a negotiated anglo-German peace. He was temporarily imprisoned in the Tower of London, then placed under psychiatric care near Aldershot.

During his trial at Nuremburg, his anti-Masonic speech that he delivered Aug. 28, 1939 was read at trial. "Jews and Freemasons want a war against this hated Germany, against the Germany in which they have lost their power."

He was sentenced to life imprisonment, and remained in Spandau prison, Berlin as the only prisoner until his death. See S&B, V1, 3rd ed, chs. 26-27.

Fig. 36 — Hermann Goering arrives in court Nov. 26, 1945.
He committed suicide in jail, while awaiting trial for war crimes.

Hermann Goering (1893-1946)

On April 7, 1933, in an interview with Von Heeringen, Germany's Grand Master of Freemasonry, Goering informed him, "In a National Socialist state... there is no place for Freemasons." Later, German Masonic leaders suggested "if the intention of Minister Goering should find general approval in the Reich cabinet, there need be no question of the continuance of grand lodge of Freemasons." Heeringen proposed the following rules under which Freemasonry might carry on; discontinuation of the use of words "Freemason" and "Lodge"; breaking off all international relations; require all members be of German descent; removal of requirement of secrecy; and elimination of those parts of

ritual which have Old Test. origin. Result? National Grand Lodge changed its name to "The National Christian Order of Frederick the Great."

3° Ralph G. Albrecht (1896-?)

Specialist in international law. Prosecuted Herman Goering before International Military Tribunal, 1945-46. Albrecht was raised (3°) 11-16-1921 in Dalhousie Lodge, Newtonville, MA.

Fig. 37 — Nuremberg Trials: Nazis are listening to the verdicts.
See *Scarlet and the Beast*, Vol. 1, 3rd edition, chapter 27.

Alfred Rosenberg: Closely questioned concerning his attacks on Freemasonry and Jews, as well as his confiscation of Masonic libraries and records and burning them in great bon fires. Hanged as a war criminal.

Joachim von Ribbentrop: offered the following defence — "I have been a patriot all my life. I have placed myself at the disposal of Adolf Hitler in the desire to help him save our country from ruin in 1933 and to build up a strong and united Germany in Europe... I have always opposed the policy against the Jews, churches, and Freemasons... which I considered in principal a fault and which has caused considerable difficulties in foreign politics." — Hanged as a war criminal.

Wilhelm Frick: In 1935 called for the immediate disbandment of all Masonic Lodges in Germany and ordered a confiscation of their property to be burned in great bon fires. Hanged as a war criminal.

See next page for more details.

Bernard Fay: French professor in Vichy government, who published documents and lists of French Freemasons, resulting in their deportation or death. Life imprisonment at hard labor.

Rudolph Hess: Anti-Masonic speech Aug. 28, 1939 was read at trial. "Jews and Freemasons want a war against this hated Germany, against the Germany in which they have lost their power." Life in solitary confinement.

Two versions of the "Frick" account

Encyclopaedia Britannica version

Wilhelm Frick (1877-1946)
Frick was a longtime parliamentary leader of the German National Socialist Party, and Adolf Hitler's minister of the interior, who played a major role in drafting and carrying out the Nazis' anti-Semitic measures. As an official in the police administration at Munich, Frick was convicted of high treason for participating in Hitler's Munich (Beer Hall) Putsch of Nov., 1923, but managed to avoid imprisonment. He was elected to the Reichstag in May 1924 and began to lead the Nazis in the Reichstag in 1928, serving in that position until the fall of the Third Reich.

As minister of the interior in the state government of Thuringia (193031), Frick was the first Nazi to hold any German ministerial post. Thereafter he became the recognized party expert in German domestic Politics. As Hitler's national minister of interior (1933-43), he played a significant role in devising and obtaining passage of legislation providing for government by decree (March 1933), and in drafting subsequent measures against the Jews, especially the notorious Nürnberg (German spelling) laws of Sept. 1935.

With the growth of the SS as the state's principal internal security force, Frick's importance in the government declined. In 1943 he was replaced at the interior ministry by SS chief Heinrich Himmler. Thereafter Frick served as Reich protector for Bohemia and Moravia until the end of World War II.

Note above: there is no mention of Freemasonry! Now, read the whole truth below, meant strictly for Masonic consumption.

10,000 Famous Freemasons version of Frick

German politician who was minister of interior from 1933-43 under Hitler. Frick was hanged as a war criminal in 1946.

Hitler's newspaper *Voelkischer Beobachter* announced the final dissolution of all Masonic lodges in Germany on Aug. 8, 1935. The paper blamed Masonry for the incidents leading to WWI, saying that Freemasonry believed the time had come for a "bloody war between nations and the erection of a world republic." The national Socialist press gave the lodges a final obituary in which they were accused of all imaginable historic crimes, including the undermining of the German empire and the assassination of Ferdinand at Sarajevo which precipitated WWI. Acting under a decree that had been issued by Hindenburg, which charged that the Masonic lodges had engaged in "subversive activities," Dr. Frick, then minister of interior, called for the immediate disbandment of all lodges throughout Germany and ordered the confiscation of their property. This was a step the German Freemasons had expected for some time.

Fig. 38 — Hjalmar Schacht, (far left in picture below), was a Banker and a Freemason — and the only Nazi acquitted at Nuremberg.

Hjalmar Schacht (1877-1870)

Censored historic version of Schacht's position as Financier of the Nazi Party and his acquittal at Nuremberg.

Born in Tinglev, Germany. In 1923 he became president of the Reichsbank and founded a new currency which ended the inflation of the mark. He was Minister of Economics (1934-37), but in 1939 was dismissed from his bank office for disagreeing with Hitler over rearmament expenditure. Interned by the Nazis, he was acquitted at Nuremberg. In 1953 he set up his own bank in Dusseldorf.

Masonic apologetic version of Schacht's position as Financier of the Nazi Party and the real reason for his acquittal at Nuremberg.

German financier Hjlmar Schacht was probably one of the greatest financial wizards of his time. From 1908-15 he was director of the Duetsche Bank and later a partner of the Darmstaedter and National Bank. During the [preNazi] Weimar Republic in 1923, he was appointed commissioner of currency. As president of the Reichsbank, he stopped the German inflation. He was president of the Reichsbank until 1930 and again appointed by Hitler tothe same position in 1933-40. It is certainly true that at this time he helped Germany to arm, but in 1940 he was put under house arrest by the Nazis. At the end of the war he was brought into court as a war criminal at the Nuremberg Trials, but acquitted in 1946. His only defense in this trial is remarkable, "I belong to the Lodge *Zur Freundschaft* under the Grand Lodge of Prussia."

This was the grand lodge which hoped to continue under Hitler by virtue of its strong national feeling. As late as January of 1960, Schacht wrote an article concerning some Masonic subjects which came up during the time of Hitler. *10,000 Famous Freemasons*, 1962, by 33° W.R. Denslow.

Read *Scarlet and the Beast*, Vol. 1, 3rd edition, chapters 25-27 for more details of British Freemasonry's protection of Schacht at Nuremberg.

Fig. 39 — Famous Czechoslovakian Mason. See *Scarlet and the Beast*, Vol. 1, 3rd ed., chaps, 26 & 27 for full details of where the gold went.

Edvard Benes (1885-1948)

President of Czechoslovakia during WWII. Educated in universities of Prague, Paris, and Dujon. A disciple of Masaryk, he worked in Paris with him from 1915-19 in the Czech nationalist movement. He was Czech delegate at peace conference in 1919-20 and first foreign minister of Czechoslovakia from 1918-35 and prime minister from 1921-22. He was cofounder of the Little Entente. Elected president of Czechoslovakia in 1935, and resigned in October, 1938 on German occupation of Sudetenland. Was appointed professor of sociology at the University of Chicago in 1939. During WWII President of the Czechoslovak government in exile from 1939-45, with headquarters in England. Returned to Czechoslovakia in March, 1945. Was reelected president in 1946.

When elected President of Czechoslovakia, he withdrew from Masonic activities, but remained interested in the fraternity and rendered his full moral and financial support in London where the National Grand Lodge of Czechoslovakia in Exile was established, as well the Comenius in Exile Lodge.

In 1924 or 25 Benes was initiated in the Jan Amos Komensky Lodge No. 1 of Prague, the oldest Czech lodge in modern times. Later he became a member of Pravda Vitezi (Truth Shall Prevail) Lodge of Prague, being passed (2o) and raised (3°) in the latter about 1927-28.

"The Nazis, after assimilating Austria in 1938, marched on Czechoslovakia. Grand Orient Mason Dr. Edvard Benes...naively welcomed Hitler as preferable to the Merovingian Habsburgs, the former rulers. On March 15, 1939, Hitler followed his storm troops into Prague, arrested the directors of the Czech National Bank and held them at gunpoint, demanding their $48 million in gold reserves — gold that could not be found in the bank's vaults. Nervous bankers told Hitler that days earlier the BIS had instructed the Czech bank to forward the gold to the Bank of England. Montgue Norman, a rabid supporter of Hitler, had already made a paper transfer of the gold to Berlin."

Fig. 40 — Chest of gold wedding rings SS took from gassed victims. Such valuables went to secret SS accounts in Reichsbank. After WW2 the gold was shipped in Nazi U-Boats to Argentina.
See *S&B*, Vol. 1, 3rd ed., ch. 26-27

Juan Perón (1895-1974)

Argentinian soldier and president (1946-55 and 1973-74)

Born in Lobos, Buenos Aires. Took leading part in army coup of 1943 and gained widespread support through his social reforms. Became president in 1946. In 1955, having antagonized the Church, the armed forces, and many of his former labor supporters, he was deposed. Returned in triumph in 1973, winning an overwhelming electoral victory, but died a year later.

While Perón served as military attaché in Italy during the late 1930s, he observed the successes of the Fascists and Nazis. He planned to put those techniques into effect when he became president of Argentina. The attempted assassination of Hitler in 1944 solidified the resolve of the SS to escape to Argentina. Awaiting them was Juan Perón.

In *S&B*, vol. 1, 3rd ed., ch. 27 and vol. 3, read of Perón's involvement in assisting the Nazis in transporting their stolen gold and jewels to Argentina by U-boat. Also read of Licio Gelli's involvement in setting up the South American drug cartel using both Perón and his ex-Nazis.

Fig. 41 — Post World War II Neo-Nazis and Freemasonry both resurrected the Nazis myth of an all white Aryan nation. See *S&B*, Vol. 3, Epilogue.

Richard Butler (1918-2004)

Time Magazine, September 20, 2004, writes: "White Supremacist Richard Butler founded in the early 1970s a 20-acre compound in Hayden, Idaho called the Aryan Nations, spawning chapters in a dozen states and contacts with neo-Nazis around the globe. Dubbed "the elder statesman of hate" by civil rights advocates, the former aerospace engineer housed a spectrum of right-wing extremists, some of whom would later be convicted of racially motivated crimes."

Scottish Rite Freemasonry in America published the following in its *New Age* Magazine, Sept. 1950, by Freemason C. William Smith:

"God's plan is dedicated to the unification of all races, religions and creeds. This plan, dedicated to the new order of things, is to make all things new — a new nation, a new race, a new civilization and a new religion, a nonsectarian religion that has already been recognized and called the religion of "The Great Light."

"Looking back into history, we can easily see that the Guiding Hand of Providence has chosen the Nordic people to bring in and unfold a new order of the world. Records clearly show that 95 percent of the colonists were Nordics — Anglo-Saxons.

"Providence has chosen the Nordics because the Nordics have prepared themselves and have chosen God. The Nordics are God's chosen people always looking for more light on the mission of life...

"Just as Providence has chosen the Jewish race — the Children of Israel — to bring into the world righteousness by carrying the 'Ten Commandments' which emphasize "Remember the Sabbath Day and keep it holy, " so also Providence has chosen the Nordic race to unfold the "New Age" of the world — a Novus Ordo Seclorum (New Secular Order). "One of the first of the Nordics to reach the New World was the Viking, Leif Ericsson... It is easy to sense that Leif Ericsson was sent by the Guiding Hand of Providence to bring the Norse spirit of the "All Father" to the shores of the New World. The Nordics are the highest branch of the fifth Aryan Civilization. The Latins are the fourth Aryan Civilization, and the American race will be the Sixth Aryan Civilization...

"George Washington, Thomas Jefferson, Benjamin Franklin, John Adams, Thomas Paine and many others of the founders of the new nations in the New World were Nordics.

Fig. 42 — Italian P-2 Freemasonry, after World War II, assisted ex-Nazi SS to escape Europe to South America, where their descendants today are the drug cartels south of our border. Founder of P-2 was Licio Gelli. Read the entire story in *Scarlet and Beast,* Vol. 3, ch. 27. Excerpts below.

Licio Gelli (?)

Ency. Britannica (1989-90) reports: "Supremely diabolic Italian who created the maverick Masonic lodge, called the P2 (Propaganda 2, patterned after P1 Lodge founded in 1830 by Italian Mason and MAFIA founder Joseph Mazzini), solely to manipulate politicians, bankers, generals and admirals, and ultimately the entire country... When the Italian public first heard of the nefarious P2 lodge, Gelli was already out of the country, probably in South America."

Resurrection of Propaganda Lodges

Stephen Knight, a British investigative journalist, informs us in *The Brotherhood: The Secret World of the Freemasons* (1984), of how P-2 Freemasonry got its start:

> *P-2 was formed in 1966 at the behest of the then Grand Master of the Grand Orient of Italy, Giordano Gamberini. The Grand Master's plan was to establish a group of eminent men who would be sympathetic and useful to Freemasonry. The man chosen to create this elite band was a rich textile manufacturer from the town of Arezzo in Tuscany. He had entered Masonry two years before and had risen to the Italian equivalent of Master Mason. His name was Licio Gelli.*

Licio Gelli had joined a conventional Grand Orient lodge in November 1963. He rapidly rose to the position of Master Mason, which made him eligible to lead a lodge. His competence came to the attention of Gamberini, who assigned Gelli the task of resurrecting Propaganda lodges. Gelli, however, had ambitions for P-2 which Gamberini had never so much as imagined.

Gelli's ex-Nazis and his South American Drug Cartels

The origins of Gelli's plans for Propaganda-Duo (P-2) reach all the way back to the beginnings of the Spanish Civil War. In 1930 the Spanish Communist Revolution began, but not being well-organized, it faltered. Russian dictator Joseph Stalin sent "technicians" to Spain to assist in the revolution. All were bloodthirsty Grand Orient Masons who had participated in the indiscriminate slaughter of Russians during the Bolshevik Revolution. Upon arriving in Spain, they made contact with brother Masons, who offered them haven within the protected walls of the Spanish Grand Orient Lodges to plan their strategy. The Spanish Revolution proceeded in the same way as the Bolshevik Revolution, by the mass slaughter of Spanish citizens. Through these brutal means, the faltering Spanish Grand Orient revolution was strengthened.

The Spanish Civil War, 1937 to 1939, began as General Francisco Franco retaliated against the communists for the bloody revolution. Fighting alongside of Franco was the young Licio Gelli. Gelli had witnessed the brutality of the Masons, and he developed an inveterate hatred of all things Masonic. Later he became a passionate supporter of Mussolini in the Duce's drive to annihilate Freemasonry from Italy and her colonies.

During World War II, Gelli became a Nazi SS-liaison officer in Italy. In 1943, when Nazi Germany SS officers realized that the Third Reich would fall, they planned their escape to a new homeland in South America, Gelli was there to assist them. Argentinian Juan Perón, an ambitious army colonel who took power there before the war ended, was a Nazi sympathizer. Martin Bormann, Hitler's secretary, began shipping millions of dollars from the Berlin Reichsbank in armored trucks to ports in southern Spain, where German U-boats transported it to Argentina. Despite the official neutrality of his country, Perón made certain that Bormann's treasure was kept in a safe place. In 1946, after Perón was elected president, the Nazis in Argentina were guaranteed protection. A United States report stated in 1945: "Nazi leaders, groups, and organizations have combined with Argentine totalitarian groups to create a Nazi-Fascist state."

In 1947 the CIA paid Licio Gelli to spirit away to South America the remaining members of the SS who were not useful for intelligence gathering against the USSR. Later, Gelli himself fled to Argentina, where he planned to turn that nation into a Western Hong Kong in competition with British bankers. Gelli held dual citizenship in Argentina and Italy, and was appointed an economic adviser in Italy. In 1963, Gelli returned to Italy to join Italian Freemasonry, the same Freemasonry that his beloved Mussolini so hated.

A paradox? Not at all. Gelli had developed his own strategy for the destruction of Freemasonry. Where he differed with Mussolini was in how to do the job. Mussolini ruthlessly persecuted Masons. Gelli would take over from within. Yallop notes that, "ever anxious to increase his circle of power and influence, Gelli saw the [postwar] rehabilitated Masonic movement as the perfect vehicle." Gelli had long played the doubleagent. Under Mussolini, he naturally hated communism as much as he did Freemasonry, since the former had developed from the latter. But, to destroy communism, one had to join the movement in order to learn its secrets. Gelli allowed himself to be recruited as a KGB agent, and during and after the war, he spied for the Communists. He logged everything he discovered about their movement and plans to be used against them at a later date. He planned to succeed where his friend Mussolini had failed. In 1963, Gelli employed the same tactic by joining Grand Orient Freemasonry. He would use this cover to hide his plans from the British Masonic bankers. In 1966, he founded P-2, which while operating under the auspices of the Grand Orient, was directly controlled by Gelli. Gelli was able to recruit the top men of the world to his P-2 Lodge. In America, he initiated into P-2 two high officials, Henry Kissinger and Alexander Haig, both 32nd degree Scottish Rite Masons. Through their assistance, Gelli dined with Presidents Nixon, Carter, and Reagan, and many less important decision-makers in America. In Italy, "Gelli had his Freemasons in every decision-making centre in Italian politics, and was able to exert significant influence over those decisions.... [N]othing of vital importance had occurred in Italy in recent years which Gelli had not known about in advance or shortly after."

Gelli organized P2 according to a similar structure employed by Weishaupt's Illuminati. The 953 men on P2's membership list, which was published by the Italian government in the late spring of 1982, "were divided into seventeen groupings, or cells, each having its own leader. P2 was so secret and so expertly run by Gelli that even its own members did not know who belonged to it. Those who knew most were the seventeen cell leaders and they knew only their own grouping. Not even Spartaco Mennini, the then Grand Secretary of the Grand Orient of Italy, knew the entire membership of the Lodge. Only Licio Gelli knew that."

Gelli made sure that the Italian Communist party had no links with P2. He had long since gathered all the information he needed to use against those involved in the Communist party. To assure his success, he used blackmail as a trump card, and he used this unashamedly against all, even those in his own P2 Lodge. Yallop wrote that "in Gelli's blackmail file he had information on this banker, a secret dossier on that politician

— his network spread from Argentina into Paraguay, into Brazil, Bolivia, Colombia, Venezuela, and Nicaragua."

At Licio Gelli's right hand was the sinister, yet brilliant banker, Roberto Calvi. Gelli found in Calvi a greedy little man through whom he could capture the banking business and drug trade from the British — at least in Italy and South America. Calvi was destined to became the "paymaster" of P-2.

Figure 43 — World War II Anti-Masonic Stamps.

On April 6, 1941, the German Army breached the Yugoslavian frontier, subjecting yet another country to Nazi occupation. The military divided Yugoslavia into the three constituent states of Croatia (including Bosnia and Herzegovina), Montenegro, and Serbia. Of these states, only Croatia enjoyed a certain semblance of independence. Montenegro and Serbia both remained occupied by German forces for the duration of the war.[1]

Although the Nazis controlled Serbia, a puppet government, under the leadership of former Yugoslav general Milan Nedich, was instituted to create the impression of continuing sovereignty.

The idea of an independent Serbia partially was perpetuated with the issuance of stamps that featured the Serbian coat of arms, including a group of four semipostals issued on January 1, 1942, to commemorate Belgrade's Anti-Masonic Exposition of October 22, 1941.[2] These stamps wove together anti-Masonic, anti-Semitic, and anti-Communist symbolism and funded further anti-Masonic propaganda with their surtax.

These semipostals — listed in the Michel Germany Specialized Catalogue under Serbia 58-61 and the Scott Stamp Catalogue under Serbia 2NB15-18 — were printed by photogravure. The 0.50+0.50-dinar stamp was printed in a light brown color; the 1+1-dinar stamp, in dark green; the 2+2-dinar stamp, in light red; and the 4+4-dinar stamp, in a dark blue. Many color shade variations resulted from successive printings; darker to lighter color shades appeared as time went on and as the printing inks were used up.

Engraved by S. Grujic, the stamps were printed on unwatermarked paper with a wax-like shiny coating in sheets of twenty-five stamps (5 x 5) for each denomination. They were comb perforated 11½. The gum on the stamps ranges from a shiny bright yellow to a flat dull white color.

Only 303,074 sets of these semipostals were printed; therefore, collectors may have some difficulty acquir-

Figure 44 — World War II Anti-Masonic Stamps.

ing the stamps. Postmarks indicate that most used stamps were canceled to order at Belgrade after March 31, 1942. These stamps were valid for postal use only from January 1 to March 31, 1942. Thus, postally used covers with single stamps are extremely scarce. Since forged cancels exist, covers should be expertized to determine legitimate postal use.

Two special Anti-Masonic Exposition commemorative cancellations — Belgrade "A" and Belgrade "B" — were used on first day covers for a period of about a week. Belgrade A was used on January 1, 1942, for canceling special gold-numbered first day covers, which sold for 100 dinars. About 1,000 covers with the gold-colored writing and gold-colored cancellations were issued. Belgrade B was used on January 1, 1942, for regular first day covers with blue writing and black (regular) cancellations.

Some regular first day covers received the Belgrade A and/or B cancels in black during the period from January 2 to January 6, 1942.

aximum cards, which are very scarce, were made in a very small quantity and they were canceled on January 1, 1942, with Belgrade A and/or Belgrade B cancellations in black.

Engraver S. Grujic's initials appear as "c." or "c.r." — the Cyrillic equivalent of "S." or "S.G." on the middle, or thirteenth, stamp position in a sheet. On the 0.50+0.50-dinar stamp, the letter "c." is found to the right of the denomination table on the stamp and on the 1+1-dinar stamp, "c." appears above the denomination table on the stamp. The 2+2-dinar stamp features the letters "c.r." in the upper left-hand corner of the stamp under the inscription. On the 4+4-dinar stamp, "c.r." is found above the

Due to their short period of postal validity, used sets of these stamps are more valuable than mint sets.

denomination table on the stamp. Due to printing variations, these small letters in some instances are difficult to notice. Regardless, mint single stamps with the engraver's initials are unusual and valuable; a complete mint set of the four values is worth approximately $200.

Regular first day covers with engraver's initial stamps are very difficult to find. The special gold first day covers with or postally used covers with engraver's initial stamps are extremely scarce. Stamps do exist with forged engraver's initials added; consequently, these stamps and covers should be expertized to determine their legitimacy. The initials' position can be more easily checked when purchasing intact sheets.

I found the stamp designs, with their propaganda-inspired symbols, most interesting. They are the only Nazi propaganda stamps to illustrate that group's belief in an international conspiracy among Masons, Jews, and Communists to rule the world.

The 0.50+0.50-dinar stamp features a man in Masonic dress — cloak, hood, apron, and sword — wearing the six-pointed Star of David and shielding his eyes from rays of bright sunlight. This stamp attempted to portray Masons and Jews as being cloaked in secrecy, preferring darkness or lies over light or truth, and trying to hide from or reject the light or truth that is exposing and overwhelming them. Perhaps this stamp best serves as a reminder of the Nazi persecution of Masons and Jews.

A snake, patterned with Stars of David, is being choked by a hand on the 1+1-dinar value. Under the snake lies a Masonic compass and ruler. and a world globe. This stamp depicts the Jews and Masons as an evil, cunning creature that is intent on spreading poisonous lies and ideas in order to control or rule the world. The stamp portrays the snake's destruction — the killing of Jews and Masons.

Figure 45 — World War II Anti-Masonic Stamps.

This gold first day cover received the Belgrade "A" cancel on January 1, 1942.

Blue ink printing and the black Belgrade "B" cancel identify this regular first day cover, which was canceled on January 4, 1942.

Austria issued four out of its eight anti-fascist semipostals in response to the Serbian issues.

The 2+2-dinar stamp illustrates a Communist five-pointed star, along with a hammer and sickle on a world globe, being broken apart by the Serbian national coat of arms symbol. In this stamp design, the threat of Communism spreading and ruling the world is crushed by the prosperous nationalism of the fascists (the bushel of wheat). The stamp glorifies fascist attacks on Communism and the battles against Communist partisans.

The two Biblical pillars of "Jachin" and "Boaz" from Solomon's Temple have Jewish and Masonic significance.[3] The 4+4-dinar stamp pictures a man breaking down these pillars as he steps on a Star of David on a globe. This figurative destruction of Jewish and Masonic beliefs was representative of the physical destruction of Jewish synagogues and Masonic temples.

Such harsh propaganda and actions did not go unnoticed or unanswered postally. On September 16, 1946, Austria issued a set of eight semipostals (Scott B171–78) to raise funds for anti-fascist counter propaganda. Four of the Austrian stamps closely mirrored the imagery of the Serbian issues, but inverted the messages to attack the fascists of the former Reich. The Austrian semipostal designs demonstrate the manipulable nature of propaganda and philatelically suggest that what goes around, comes around.

Endnotes

1. The German Army launched an invasion of Yugoslavia on April 6, 1941. Eleven days later Yugoslavia surrendered. Germany subsequently divided her territory into smaller countries — one of those was the former independent state of Serbia. During the occupation, two groups struggled for power: the Partisans, led by Josip Broz Tito, wanted to establish a Communist government. The Chetniks, led by Draza Mihailovich, were nationalists and monarchists who supported the existing government. For more on this subject, see *2194 Days of War — An Illustrated Chronology of the Second World War* compiled by Cesare Salmaggi and Alfredo Pallavisini (Milan, Italy: Arnoldo Mondadori Editore, S.P.A., 1977).

2. The information presented in this article is based on the Michel Germany Specialized Stamp Catalogue, Scott Postage Stamp Catalogue, the Bible, and my own philatelic collection and research.

3. *The Holy Bible*, I Kings 7:21 and II Chronicles 3:17.

The Author

Julian Goldberg, an optical technician from Toronto, Ontario, has collected stamps for more than twenty years, including those of Canada, Israel, Italian States, Palestine, Russian Republics, and Yugoslavia.

Fig. 46 — Gen. MacArthur masonically outranks his Camander-in-Chief.
See *Scarlet and the Beast*, Vol. I, 3rd edition, chapter 27.
32° President Roosevelt went to the Pacific to observe the war's progress.
Here he confers on the strategy problems with 33°General Douglas MacArthur.

33° Gen. Douglas MacArthur (1880-1964) was made a Mason "at sight" by Samuel
Hawthorne, Grand Master of the Philippines. He affiliated with Manila Lodge No. 1 and
received the 32° AASR (SJ) at Manila the same year; made KCCH in 1937 and honorary
33° on Dec. 8, 1947 at the American Embassy, Tokyo, Japan. He was a life member of
the Nile Shrine Temple, Seattle, WA. (see Shriners' oath to Allah, Section 1, page 12).

MacArthur has praised Freemasonry on many occasions, saying, "It embraces the
highest moral laws and will bear the test of any system of ethics or philosophy ever
promulgated for the uplift of Man... Its requirements are the things that are right, and its
restraints are from the things that are wrong...inculcating doctrines of patriotism and
brotherly love, enjoying sentiments of exalted benevolence, encouraging all that is good,
kind and charitable, reprobating all that is cruel and oppressive, its observance will uplift
everyone under its influence...to do good to others, to restrain passions, to honor parents,
to respect authority, to return good for evil, not to cause anger, not to bear false witness,
not to lie, not to steal — these are the essential elements of the moral law."

Figure 47

33° Henry C. Clausen (1905-1993)

Sovereign Grand Commander of The Supreme Council of Freemasonry, 33° (Mother Supreme Council of the World) 1969-1993. Lawyer in charge of investigating Pearl Harbor disaster of World War Two. Member of Lucifer Trust.

See Section 1, Figs. 44, 83-88. Read more about Clausen in *Scarlet and the Beast*, Vol. 1, 3rd ed. chaps. 15 & 19 (PB.S1. F32-45 Baphomet & F44 & 88)

Figure 48 — 33° Freemason General Douglas MacArthur discussing logistics with 33° Freemason, Attorney Henry C. Clausen. Read more about it in *Scarlet and the Beast*, Vol. 1, 3rd edition, ch. 27.

33° Henry C. Clausen's Masonic Credentials: Member of Ingleside Lodge No. 630, San Francisco. Grand Master of Grand Lodge of CA. 33° AASR (SJ) 1954-55. Sovereign Grand Inspector General of CA. Member of Islam Shrine Temple. Sovereign Grand Commander of Supreme Council, 33°, Mother Supreme Council of the World. Admitted to California bar in 1927. Practiced in San Francisco. During WW2 served in Judge Advocate General's dept. Lawyer in charge of investigating Pearl Harbor disaster of WW2. In 1992, Henry C. Clausen is writing about 33O MacArthur's plan to revive Freemasonry in the Far East. (see next page)

33° Henry C. Clausen writing about MacArthur's post war plan to revive Freemasonry in the Far East

"After I had typed up these affidavits, I went back to get them signed. MacArthur signed his even though I had misspelled his name. As I was putting the papers in my briefcase, MacArthur asked me some personal questions. I told him that when the war began, I had been the Grand Orator of the Masonic Grand Lodge of California, and I congratulated him, as I later did President Truman, on being made a 33° Scottish Rite Mason.

"He kept me in his office for nearly another hour, talking about how to expand in the Far East the moral principles of Freemasonry. Every dictator in history has tried to put the Masons out of business because they believe in freedom. MacArthur was positive that Hitler had poisoned the minds of the Japanese against the Masonic Order for this very reason, and that was why even the Constitution of Japan forbade anyone from joining the order. MacArthur promised me that if and when he got to Japan, he was going to make sure that provision was eliminated from any future Constitution. He did, too.

"'Since we're talking in this fashion," I said, "may I tell you about the plight of some Masonic people in Manila? We have a lodge not far from here. I drove there the other day, and they don't have any pencils. They don't have paper. The Japanese confiscated everything. I went to the PX and got a load of groceries and gave it to one of the heads, and he gave me a ring to give to my wife. Would there be any objection, General, to my using the military mail to send over some implements that are used to start up the Masonic Lodge, items such as rods, Bibles and so forth?'

"'Absolutely not,'" MacArthur said. "'I'm a Mason, My G-2, Willoughby, is a Mason. We'll make the arrangement for you.'"

"Well, Willoughby went overboard. He told me to send anything I wanted. So, when I got back to Washington, I thought that the first thing I should send was a master's hat, because the master of the Masonic Lodge wears a tall silk hat, plus the rods and other implements of the Order. The Masons in Washington thought I was nuts, but I managed to get everything that was needed to start the lodge going again, and shipped it to Manila. In later years, whenever Willoughby came through San Francisco from Japan, where he was stationed in MacArthur's occupation headquarters, he'd stop by and tell me about the Masons in Manila. MacArthur was also instrumental in getting the confiscated property in Manila and Japan returned to the Masons, and the Order has had the basis to flourish in both places and inculcate the spiritual values MacArthur recommended."

Pearl Harbor, Final Judgement, pp. 148-149 by Henry C. Clausen, 1992

Fig. 49 — On Corregidor Gen. MacArthur confers with Pres. Manuel Quezon of the Philippines as Philippine campaign approaches climax. Shortly before his nation was occupied, Quezon left by submarine for Australia; later went to U.S.A. to set up government in exile. MacArthur departed by PT boat for Mindanao, then flew to Australia, where he established new HQs.

32° Manuel Luis Quezon (1878-1944)
"Father of the Philippines"

Prepared the predominant Catholic Philippine Islands to accept post-WWII Freemasonry.

President of the Philippines from Sept. 17, 1935 until his death in 1944. During his entire term as president he fought for separation of church and state. He was leading figure in the movement which led to the gradual independence of the islands.

Grand Master of the Grand Lodge of the Philippines, 1918-19.

Fig. 50 — Oct, 20, 1944, 33° Freemason Gen. Douglas MacArthur returns to liberate the Philippine Islands, as he had promised. Credentials for the first president of post-World War Two Philippines had MacArthur's fingerprints. He would be a national, a Brigadier General and former aid to MacArthur. And most important, a Mason. In mid-March 1942, MacArthur was ordered by his commander-in-chief to leave the Philippines. He promised the Filipinos — "I shall return," and he did!

Fig. 51 — On July 4, 1946, the Philippine Islands achieved independence from the United States of America. Manuel Roxas becomes first president of the newly formed Republic of the Philippines.

32° Manuel A. Roxas (1892-1948). First President of the Philippine Republic, 1946-48. Graduate of U. of Manila in 1913. Admitted to the bar that year. Was municipal councilor of Capiz in 1918 — provincial governor of same, 1920. Head of Philippine independence missions to Washington four times after 1923. In Philippine house of representatives, 1924-36. Member of constitutional convention of 1934. Secretary of finance, 1938-41. Senator, 1941-45, and president of senate. Entered Philippine Army as a Colonel Dec. 1941. Was Brigadier General and aide to General MacArthur. Although a Roman Catholic, he was also a Freemason — Past Master of Makawiwili Lodge No. 55 in his native town of Capiz. Received 32° AASR in Rizal Consistory on Nov. 13, 1923.

Fig. 52 — Navy Secretary James Forrestal (standing right), accompanied by 33° General Mark Clark, reviewing an honor guard of JapaneseAmerican troops in Leghorn, Italy, who were with the highly decorated 442nd Regimental Combat Team, which saw action in Italy and France.

33° **Mark Wayne Clark** (1896-1984)

Standing tall on left. US General, born in Maddison Barracks, NY, of a military family. He trained at West Point, and served abroad in World War 1. Designated as Commander II Corps under Eisenhower for the invasion of North Africa during World War 2. Clark subsequently became Eisenhower's deputy.

Clark commanded the 5th Army at the Salerno landing (1943) and the capture of Rome (1944), and was much criticized for choosing the latter instead of encircling the German forces. He commanded the US 6th Army in the Far East (1947-49), and relieved Ridgway in command of UN Forces in Korea (1952-53). See "Ridgway" next page.

Clark was raised (3°) in Mystic Tie Lodge No. 398 at Indianapolis on Dec. 30, 1929. He was later affiliated with Hancock Lodge No. 11 at Ft. Leavenworth, KN. He received his 32° and 33° AASR at Indianapolis in 1930 and 1946. In 1954 the Supreme Council AASR (NJ) presented him the Gourgas Medal, their highest decoration, "in recognition of notably distinguished service in the cause of Freemasonry, humanity, or country."

Fig. 53 — Famous American Military Masons of the 20th Century.

33° Lt. General James H. Doolittle (1896-1993)

Born in Alameda, CA. Graduate of Univ. of Calif. and Mass. Institute of Technology. As a speed pilot he won the Schneider, Mackay, Harmon, Bendix and Thompson trophies. Was U.S. Army aviator from 1917-30, when he resigned to manage aviation department of Shell Petroleum Corp. until 1940. That year he entered the U.S. Army Air Force (AAF), and advanced to Lt. General by 1944.

He commanded the first bombing force over Tokyo in 1942 with sixteen B-25 bombers, decisively effecting Japanese naval strategy. He later commanded the 12th AAF in North Africa, the 15th AAF in Italy (1943), and the 8th AAF in Britain for operations in Northwest Europe (1944). After the war he returned to Shell Oil as vicepresident and director (1945-59).

Doolittle received all three Masonic degrees in Hollenbeck Lodge No. 319, Los Angeles, CA on Aug. 16, 1918; 32° AASR (SJ) in San Diego Consistory on Dec. 14, 1918; and 33° on Oct. 19, 1945.

As the lead plane, (piloted by Doolittle), dissolves into a speck in the distance, the 2nd Japan-bound B-25 lifts off the sprayswept deck of the U.S.S. Hornet.

Fig. 54 — Famous American Military Masons of the 20th Century.

33° John J. Pershing (1860-1948)

General of the Armies. Graduate of U.S. Military Academy in 1886, and L.L.B. from U. of Neb. in 1893. His wife and three daughters lost their lives in the burning of The Presidio (Calif.) on Aug. 27, 1915.

He became Brigadier General in 1906, Major General in 1916, General in 1917, and General of the Armies on Sept. 3, 1919. Retired in 1924.

He served in the Apache and Sioux campaigns; taught at West Point and U. of Neb.; in Cuba campaign of Spanish-American War; in Philippines and in charge of operations against the Moros. He was military attache in Japan; with Kuroki's army in Manchuria; on general staff; pursued Villa into Mexico in 1916; commander-in-chief of American forces in WWI and chief of staff, U.S. Army from 1921-24.

General Pershing was a member of Lincoln Lodge No. 19, Lincoln, NE, receiving first through third degrees on Dec. 4, 11, and 22, 1888. Was Exalted to Royal Arch in Lincoln Chapter No. 6, R.A.M. March 28, 1894 and knighted in Mt. Moriah Commandery No. 4, K.T., Dec. 3, 1894, both lodges in Lincoln, NE. In 1919 he was made an honorary member of Stansbury Lodge No. 24, Washington, DC. Received 32° AASR (SJ) at Wheeling, WV on April 9, 1920. Received 33° in Washington, DC on Jan. 6, 1930. Member of Sesostris Shrine Temple, Lincoln and New York Court No. 30, Royal Order of Jesters (See Shriners Oath, Sect. 1. p. 29).

Received 50-year award on Jan. 5, 1939. On Sept. 30, 1941 he was made an honorary member of the Grand Lodge of Missouri and the certificate was presented to him at Walter Reed Hospital, Feb. 24, 1942 by 33° Harry S. Truman, who was then a senator. In 1943 he laid a wreath on the tomb of the Unknown Soldier during a Knight Templar rite.

Fig. 55 — Famous American Military Masons of the 20th Century.

33° Henry H. "Hap" Arnold (1886-1950)

Commanding general of the U.S. Air Force. Graduated from West Point in 1907 and a pioneer in military aviation, who in 1912 was awarded a trophy for "a 30-mile flight." From a 2nd lieutenant in 1907 he advanced to the highest American rank in 1944 (5-star general).

Was flight commander of the U.S. Alaska Flight, 1934; assistant chief Air Corps, 1936-38; chief of Army Air Corps, 1938; commanding general Army Air Forces, 1942.

He was raised (3°) in Union Lodge No. 7, Junction City, Kansas on Nov. 3, 1927, received the 32° AASR on April 11, 1929 at Ft. Leavenworth, Kansas and 33° on Oct. 19, 1945.

On Nov. 21, 1958 the lodge at Edwards A.F.B. in California was constituted as General Henry H. Arnold Lodge No. 791.

Gen. Arnold standing center to right hand of Gen. Marshall, seated.

Fig. 56 — Famous American Military Masons of the 20th Century.

32° Jonathan M. Wainwright (1883-1953)

American general. Hero of Bataan in the Philippine fight, for which he was awarded the Congressional Medal of Honor in 1945. Born in Walla Walla, WA. Graduate of U.S. Military Academy, 1906. Advanced through grades to Brigadier General, 1938; Lieutenant General in 1942. General, 1945. Retired from service on Aug. 31, 1947.

In WWI he was on General Staff of the 82nd Division at Toul, St. Mihiel and MeuseArgonne. On general staff of 3rd Army in Germany.

In preparation for WWII he was assigned to Philippine duty in Oct., 1940 and commanded the Philippine Div. He served throughout the Bataan campaign, and assumed command of all troops when MacArthur went to Australia. He was a prisoner of war for three years and three months. Rescued in Manchuria, Aug. 1945.

In 1946 he became Commander of the 4th Army. At that time he was stationed at Fort Sam Houston, Texas, but he lived in Kansas.

It was in Kansas that he belatedly joined Freemasonry. He made application to the Grand Master of Kansas for a special dispensation to confer the degrees in less than required time. Many of his military comrades were present. The degrees were given in full on the day of May 16, 1946 in Union Lodge No. 7, Junction City, KN. The Entered Apprentice (1°) was given in the morning; Fellow Craft (2o) and first section of the Master Mason (3°) in the afternoon, with second section completed in the evening. The proficiency only was waived, the work being conferred in full form throughout.

The following day (May 17) he received the Scottish Rite degrees (SJ) at Salina, KS, and on the same day took the Shrine degrees in Isis Temple, Salina. (See Shriners' oath to Allah, Section 1, page 12).

Wainwright thus holds what is probably a record — from nonmember to Shriner in two days! Later he received the KCCH, and in 1948 was awarded the medal of the Grand Lodge of New York for distinguished achievement.

He died Sept. 2, 1953 and was buried on Sept. 8 in Arlington Cemetery with Masonic services.

Fig. 57 — 32° and Shriner, Lt. General Jonathan
M. Wainwright (1883-1953) broadcasts at a Manila radio station, reluctantly or- dering his troops in the Philippines to lay down their arms. As he speaks, a Japanese guard listens attentively. Guer- rilla resistance by Filipino patriots and American survivors continued to harass the victors until the long-awaited return of American troops took place.

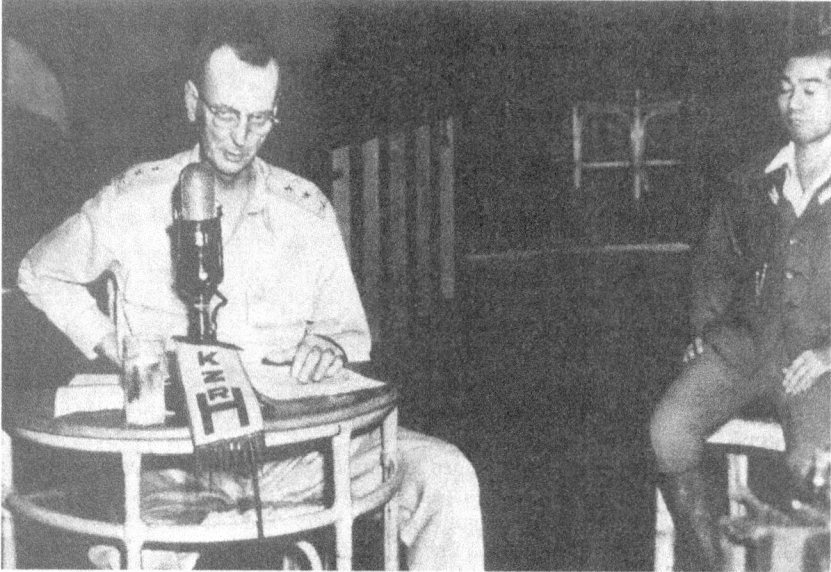

32° Wainwright in captivity.

Fig. 58 — Famous American Military Masons of the 20th Century.

The tiger-shark design on the Curtiss P-40s of the Flying Tigers accurately depict the unit's fighting ability.

32° Claire L. Chennault (1890-1958)

Air Force Major General famous for his "Flying Tigers" in WW2. Born in Commerce, Texas. Commissioned 1st Lieutenant of Infantry in 1917 and transferred to aviation section of Signal Corps. Retired from Army in 1937 to become advisor to 32° Freemasonry Chiang Kai-shek.

In 1941 he was recalled to active duty. In 1942 he was promoted to Brigadier General. From 1943-45 he activated and commanded the 14th Air Force. Was made Major General in 1943 and again retired in 1945 to organize the CNRRA Air Transport, of which he became president.

Brother Chennault writes "You will note my Masonic affiliations are widely scattered — Texas to China to California. This is particularly unfortunate since I now divide my time between Louisiana and Formosa."

Chennault was a member of League City Lodge No. 1053, League City, Texas. He was a 32° AASR Orient of China at Shanghi (in exile) and member of Islam Shrine Temple, San Francisco, CA.

Fig. 59 — Famous American Military Masons of the 20th Century.

32° Matthew B. Ridgeway (1895-1993)

US Soldier, born in Fort Monroe, VA. Graduate of West Point Military Academy in 1917. He advanced through the grades to full general in 1951. Became full General and Chief of Staff, U.S. Army, 1953-55.

Between the two World Wars he served as technical adviser to the governor general of the Philippines, 1932-33; Assistant Chief of Staff of 6th Corps Area, 1935-36; same for 2nd Army, 1936; assistant chief of staff Fourth Army, (1937-39); on War Dept. general staff, 1939-42; assistant division commander of 82nd Infantry Division, 1942; commanding general of the 82nd Airborne Division in Sicily, Italy, Normandy, 194244; commander of 18th Airborne Corps in Belgium, France, Germany, 1944-45; senior U.S. Army member of military staff, United Nations, 194648; chairman of Inter-American Defense Board, 1946-48; commander in chief of Caribbean Command, 1948-49; deputy army chief of

staff and commanding general of the 8th Army in Korea, succeeding Douglas MacArthur, 1950-51; commander in chief of Far East Command; Commander in chief of United Nations Command and Supreme Commander of Allied Powers in Europe in succession to Eisenhower (1952-53), and chief of US Army Staff (1953).

Masonic credentials: Became a member of West Point Lodge No. 877 (New York), receiving first three degrees on April 3, 17, and May 1, 1924. Received 32° AASR (SJ) at Tokyo, Japan in October, 1951.

Figure 60 — Audie Murphy, most decorated hero of World War II.

32° Audie Murphy (1924-1971)

Born near Kingston, TX. Most decorated soldier of WWII. Afterwards was a movie actor, making about 40 movies, including his autobiography. Received the 32° AASR (SJ) at Dallas, Texas in 1957.

Fig. 61 — Famous American Military Masons of the 20th Century.

3° George C. Marshall (1880-1959)

General of the Army; U.S. Secretary of State; U.S. Secretary of Defense; Ambassador to China; author of the "Marshall Plan" for European economic recovery. Born in Uniontown, PA.

Marshall was a student at Virginia Military Institute, 1897-1901. He held honorary degrees from many universities and colleges. He was commissioned in 1901 as an Infantry Lieutenant, advancing to Major General in 1939, and to General of the Army (5-star) in 1944. He served in the Philippines in 190102, and again in 1913-16.

In WWI (1917-19) he was with the A.E.F.; 1st Infantry Division; Chief of Operations 1st Army; Chief of Staff 8th Army Corps, participating in the Battles of Cantigny, Aisne-Marne, St. Mihiel, and Meuse-Argone. From 191924 he was aide-de-camp to General Pershing. From 1924-27 he was in China, followed by Stateside commands.

He was deputy chief of Staff, U.S. Army from 1938-39, and Chief of Staff with rank of General, 1939-45. In 1945 he was appointed special representative of the President to China, with rank of Ambassador. He served as U.S. Secretary of State from 1947-49; and U.S. Secretary of Defense, 1950-51. He was President of the American Red Cross, 1949-50. Marshall received many decorations and high honors, including the Nobel Peace Prize in 1953.

Marshall was made a Mason "at sight" on December 16, 1941, by Ara M. Daniels, Grand Master of the Grand Lodge of District of Columbia, in the Scottish Rite Cathedral of the District.

Distinguished leaders from many states were present. Freemason Carl H. Claudy, who had served as Senior Warden, gave the candidates a general briefing on Freemasonry.

Marshall's father had been an active Freemason at Uniontown, PA. He was High Priest of Union Chapter No. 165, R.A.M. in 1889, and Commander of Uniontown Commandery No. 49, K.T. in 1883.

Figure 62 — World War II Generals.

3° Gen. Omar N. Bradley (1893 1981)
Five-star General of Army
Born at Clark, MO. Graduated West Point in 1915; Infantry School, 1925; Command and General Staff School, 1929; and Army War College, 1934.

Between 1915 and 1941 he advanced from 2nd Lieut. to Brigadier General; Major General, 1942; Lieut. General, 1943; General, 1945; and General of the Army, 1950. Gen. Bradley received honorary LL.B. and other degrees from 20 institutions of higher learning.

In WWII he commanded the 2nd Corps in the Northern Tunisian and Sicilian Campaigns; the 1st U.S. Army in the Normandy Campaign and the 12th Army Group in France, Belgium, Holland, Luxembourg and Germany.

In 1945-47 he was administrator of Veterans Affairs. In 1948-49 he was Chief of Staff, U.S. Army. And in 1949-53 he was chairman of U.S. Joint Chiefs of Staff. In 1953 he became chairman of the board of Bulova Research and Development Labs, Inc.

In 1923 he was raised (3°) in West Point Lodge No. 877, Highland Falls, NY.

Fig. 63 — Famous American Military Masons of the 20th Century.

3° Gen. Joseph W. Stillwell (1883-1946)

"Vinegar Joe" Stillwell"

Graduate of U.S. Military Academy in 1904. Rose through the ranks to Major General by 1940; Lieutenant General in 1942; full General in 1944. Nicknamed "Vinegar Joe."

After a tour of duty in the Philippines, he was an instructor at West Point (1906-10 and 1913-17). It was during this last tour of duty ending WWI that he became a member of West Point Lodge No. 877, June 1, 1916. In WWII he was appointed by 32° Freemason, Gen. Chiang Kai-Shek to Commander of the 5th and 6th Chinese Armies in Burma. In 1942-44, Stillwell was Commanding General of U.S. forces in China-Burma-India theater. In 1945 he was appointed Commander of the U.S. ground forces. And that same year, Commander of the 10th Army in the Pacific Theater.

Fig. 64 — Famous American Military Masons of the 20th Century.

3° Gen. Lemuel C. Shepherd, Jr.
USMC (1896-?)

General and Commandant of U.S. Marine Corps. Graduate of Virginia Institute in 1917 and commissioned 2nd Lieutenant in Marine Corps that year. Full General in 1952.

In WWI he participated in battles of Aisne, St. Mihiel, Meuse-Argonne, and defensive sectors of Toulon-Troyons and Chateau Thierry. He was the Army of Occupation in Germany in 1919.

In WWII he was regimental commander of 9th Marines, 3rd Marine Division; assistant Division Commander in 1st Division; participated in landing at Cape Gloucester, New Britain; Commanding General 1st Prov. Marine Brigade; participated in landing and seizure of Guam; Commanding General of 6th Marine Division; participated in Okinawa campaign; received surrender of Japanese forces in China; Commandant of Marine Corps Schools; Commanding General of Fleet Marine Force, Pacific; participated in Inchon landing; and was Commandant of the U.S. Marine Corps from 1952 until retirement in 1955.

Member of American Overseas Lodge No. 40, Providence, RI.

Figure 65 — Famous British Masons. See Churchill's involvement in *Scarlet and the Beast*, Vol.I, 3rd edition, chapters 16, 17, 22 and 25-2.

3° Sir Winston (Leonard Spencer) Churchill (1874-1965)

British statesman and author. Eldest son of Lord Randolph Churchill, a Conservative statesman, and Jennie Jerome, daughter of a New York financier. The often lonely young Churchill was brought up by his affectionate nurse, Mrs. Everest.

Churchill's early army career was punctuated by well-received journalistic writings and a self-inflicted course of reading, launching him on a literary career which he pursued throughout his life. He was one of the most outstanding leaders of the 20th Century at both national and international levels. The most famed photograph of Winston is on the next page.

Sir Sidney White, grand secretary of the Grand Lodge of England states that "Sir Winston Churchill was initiated into Freemasonry as a young man, but he never progressed in the Order, and has taken no part for many years." He was initiated in Studholme Lodge No. 1591, London and raised to 3° March 25, 1902 in Rosemary Lodge No. 2851.

Figure 66 — Yalta Agreement conference following World War II.

Winston Churchill 3° Master Mason, Franklin Roosevelt 32° Scottish Rite, Joseph Stalin 33° R.FM

THE YALTA CONFERENCE - FEBRUARY 1945

At Yalta in the Crimea, President Roosevelt and Churchill (having spent a few days conferring on Malta) join Stalin to discuss the final phase of the war. Anxious to gain Soviet participation against Japan, Roosevelt and Churchill promise territorial concession in the Sakhalin and Kurile Islands. The three leaders agree on the post-war borders of such Eastern European countries as Poland, in return for which Stalin concurs on fair elections within these countries. Finally, they agree to call a meeting of the United Nations in San Francisco on 25 April to establish a permanent international organization, which is the UNITED NATIONS. See *Scarlet and the Beast*, Vol. 1, 3rd edition, chapters 22, 26-27.

Fig. 67 — Big Three Conference continues after death of 32O Scottish Rite Mason, Pres. Franklin D. Roosevelt. Taking his place is 33O Scottish Rite Mason, Pres. Harry S. Truman (lower center looking right with arrow above his head). Two other Big Three" are 33O Rosicrucian Mason Joseph Stalin (to right holding cigarette with arrow behind his head), and 3O English Freemason, Winston Churchill (upper left with arrow over his head). Churchill suggested Truman lead the opening session — Truman's first as member of the Big Three.

Fig. 68 — Yalta Agreement. See *Scarlet and Beast*, V1, 3rd. ed. chs. 21, 26 & 27.

Big 3 at Yalta Conference : 33° Stalin (1879-1953) 33° Truman (1884-1972) 3° Churchill (1874-1965)

Before the demise of 32° Pres. Franklin D. Roosevelt in 1945, the following is a summary of what he handed over to the Russians at Yalta:

1. The Baltic countries — Latvia, Estonia, Lithuania.
2. All the eastern part of Poland, which the Russians had occupied in 1939, following the Molotov-Ribbentrop agreement.
3. All eastern and central Europe, including Berlin and Prague.
4. Access to the Mediterranean through the recognition of Grand Orient Freemason Tito (Josip Broz 1892-1980) as ruler of Yugoslavia and the abandonment of his rival, the monarchist Mihailovich.
5. Manchuria ceded to Russia without the knowledge of Chian Kai-shek (1887-1975), the Chinese republican leader, and in flat contradiction of the undertakings which had been given to the latter at Cairo.
6. Inner Mongolia, North Korea, the Kuril Islands, and the part of Sakhalin (French Indo-China, also known as Vietnam).
7. Return to Soviet Russia all freedom-loving anti-Communist Russians in Europe who had fled the Soviet Union.

Fig. 69 — Communism begins to spread over Eastern Europe.
See *Scarlet and the Beast,* V1, 3rd. ed. chs. 25 & 27.

Joseph Broz — alias Tito (1892-1980)
Jewish Grand Orient Freemason and dictator of Yugoslavia

Yugoslav statesman and president (1953-80), born in Kumrovec, Croatia. In World War One he served with the Austro-Hungarian Army, was taken prisoner by the Russians, and became a Communist. He was imprisoned for conspiring against the regime in Yugoslavia (1928-29). When released from prison he became secretary of the Communist Party in 1937. In 1941 he organized partisan forces against the Axis conquerors, and after the war became the country's first Communist prime minister (1945). He then consolidated his position with the presidency in 1953. He broke with Stalin and the Cominform in 1948, developing Yugoslavia's independent style of Communism (Titoism), and played a leading role in the association of nonaligned countries.

Fig. 70 — Aldolph Hitler's legacy below and pages following !!!

Nazi Prison Camp Records Unsealed — AP 11-19-06.

HISTORY'S HARSH LIGHT

Opening of archives likely to spur new generation of Holocaust scholarships

Associated Press — Nov. 19, 2006 by Arthur Max

The 21-year-old Russian sat before a clerk of the U.S. Army Judge Advocates's office, describing the furnaces at Auschwitz, the Nazi death camp where he had been a prisoner until a few weeks previously.

"I saw with my own eyes how thousands of Jews were gassed daily and thrown by the hundreds into pits where Jews were burning," he said.

"I saw how little children were killed with sticks and thrown into the fire," he continued. Blood flowed in gutters, and "Jews were thrown in and died there. More were taken off trucks and cast alive into the flames." Today the Holocaust is known in dense and painful detail. Yet the young Russian's words leap off the faded, onionskin page with a rawness that transports the reader back to April 1945, when World War II was still raging and the world still knew little about gas chambers, genocide and the Final Solution.

The two pages of testimony, in a file randomly plucked off a shelf, are among millions of documents held in Bad Arolsen, Germany, by the International Tracing Service, of ITS, an arm of the International Committee of the Red Cross.

Unsealed files

This vast archive — 16 miles of files in six nondescript buildings in a German spa town — contains the fullest records of Nazi persecutions in existence. But because of concerns about the victims' privacy, the ITS has kept the files closed to the public for half a century, doling out information in minimal amounts to survivors or their descendants on a strict need-to-know basis.

This policy, which has generated much ill-feeling among Holocaust survivors and researchers, is about to change.

In May, after years of pressure from the United States and survivors' groups, the 11 countries overseeing the archive agreed to unseal the files for scholars as well as victims and their families. In recent weeks, the ITS' interim director, Jean-Luc Blondel, has been to Washington,

The Hague and to the Buchenwald memorial with a new message of cooperation with other Holocaust institutions and governments.

ITS has allowed Paul Shapiro, of the U.S. Holocaust Memorial Museum in Washington, to look at the files.

"This is powerful stuff," said Shapiro, leafing through the file containing the Russian's statement and about 200 other testimonies that take the reader into the belly of Hitler's death machine — its camps, inmates, commandants, executioners and trusted inmates used as lowlevel guards and known as kapos.

"If you sat here for a day and read these files, you'd get a picture of what it was really like in the camps," he said.

New Perspective

Moved to the town in central Germany after the war, the files occupy a former barracks of the Waffen-SS, the Nazi Party's elite force. They are stored in long corridors of drab cabinets and neatly stenciled binders packed into floor-to-ceiling metal shelves. Their index cards alone fill three large rooms.

Mandated to trace missing persons and help families reunite, ITS has allowed few people through its doors, and has responded to requests for information on wartime victims with minimal data, even when its files could have told more.

It may take a year or more for the files to open fully. Until then, access remains tightly restricted. "We will be ready any time. We would open them today, if we had the go-ahead," Blondel said.

When the archive is finally available, researchers will have their first chance to see a unique collection of documents on concentration camps, slave labor camps and displaced persons. From toneless lists and heartrending testimony, a skilled historian may be able to stitch together a new perspective on the 20th century's darkest years from the viewpoint of its millions of victims.

"The overall story is pretty well established, but many details will be filled in," said Yehuda Bauer, professor of Holocaust Studies at the Hebrew University of Jerusalem. "(The archive) has material that nobody's ever seen."

A visitor to the archive comes into direct contact with the bureaucracy of mass murder.

In a bound ledger with frayed binding, a copy of a list of names appears of Jews rounded up in Holland and transported to the death camps.

Among the names is "Frank, Annelise M," her date of birth (June 12, 1929, Amsterdam address before she went into hiding (Merwereeplein 37) and the date she was sent to a camp (Sept. 3, 1944. Frank, Annelise M. is Anne Frank.

Anonymous death

She was on one of the last trains to Germany before the Nazi occupation of Holland crumbled. Six months later, age 15, she died an anonymous death, one of about 35,000 casualties of typhus that ravaged the Bergen-Belsen camp. After the war, "The Diary of Anne Frank," written during her 25 months hiding in a tiny apartment with seven others, would become the most widely read book ever written on the Holocaust.

Most of the lives recorded in Bad Arolsen are known to none but their families.

To critics who accuse them of being tightfisted with their information, the Red Cross and ITS counter they have to abide by German privacy laws and protect the reputations of victims whether alive or dead. They say the files may contain unsubstantiated allegations against victims, and that opening up to researchers would distract ITS from its main task of providing documentation to survivors or victims' relatives. One area of study that will benefit from the ITS files is the "Lebensborn" program, in which children deemed to have the "proper genes" were adopted or even kidnapped to propagate the Aryan master race.

Another subject is the sheer scope of the Holocaust system. The files will support new research from other sources showing the network of concentration camps, ghettos and labor camps was nearly three times more extensive that thought.

Postwar historians estimated about 5,000 to 7,000 detention sites. But after the Cold War ended, records began pouring out of the former communist nations of East Europe. More sites were disclosed in the last six years in claims by 1.6 million people for slave labor reparations from a $6.6 billion fund financed by the German government and some 3,000 industries.

"We have identified somewhere in the neighborhood of 20,000 camps and ghettos of various categories," said Geoffrey Megargee of the Holocaust Museum in Washington.

The archive has about 3.4 million files of DPs — Displaced Persons. Between 1933 to 1945, the Nazi persecution grew to assembly-line proportions, slaughtering 6 million Jews and an equal number of Gypsies, homosexuals, mental patients, political prisoners and other "undesirables."

Detailed recordings

To operate history's greatest slaughter, the Nazis created a bureaucracy that meticulously recorded the arrest, movement and death of each victim. Sometimes even the lice plucked from their heads in concentration camps were counted.

But as the pace of genocide stepped up, unknown numbers were marched directly from trains to gas chambers without being registered. What documents survived Nazi attempts to destroy them were collected by the Allies to help people find missing relatives.

About 50 million pages — scraps of paper, transport lists, registration books, labor documents, medical and death registers — make reference to 17.5 million people caught up in the machinery of persecution, displacement and death.

Over the years, the International Tracing Service has answered 11 million requests to locate family members or provide certificates supporting pension claims or reparations.

Two years ago, it had a backlog of nearly half a million unanswered queries. Director Blondel says it was whittled down to 155,000 this summer and will disappear by the spring of 3008.

One of ITS' critics is Sabine Stein, archivist at the Buchenwald concentration camp 150 miles from Bad Arolsen. She says the archive's refusal to share its files has caused heartbreak to countless survivors and their descendants.

In 1989, Emilia Janikowska asked ITS to trace her father, Ludwig Kaminski of Poland who was never heard from again after his arrent in 1939. It took more that three years to send her a standard form reporting Kaminski had died in Buchenwald on Dec. 1, 1939.

But there was more she could have been told.

Documents copied by the U.S. Army before they went to Bad Arolsen, which were seen by AP at Buchenwald, include mention of Kaminski. They say he was prisoner No. 8578, that he had arrived in Buchenwald six weeks earlier with 600 other Poles and had been placed in Camp 2. The known history of Buchenwald says Camp 2 was a wooden barracks and four big tents, jammed with 1,000 Poles and Vienna Jews. Dozens of inmates died from the cold that winter. The cause of Kaminski's death was pneumonia. No one ever told his daughter any of this.

"We had no news from my father since the moment he was arrested," Janikowska said when contacted at her home in Krakow, Poland. She now wants more information for a compensation request.

Disappearing names

Earlier this month. ITS went some way to make amends, delivering a full inventory of its records on Buchenwald and promising to give priority in searching for 1,000 names Stein had requested.

Compounding the delay in releasing the files is the cumbrous makeup of the governing committee. Any decision on their future requires the assent of all 11 member nations — Belgium, Britain, France, Germany, Greece, Israel, Italy, Luxembourg, the Netherlands, Poland and the United States.

Last May's agreement to open the archive stipulates that it will remain off-limits until formal ratification by the 11 governments. After that, each of the 11 countries can have a digital copy of the files and decide who has access to it.

But some delegations are worried the process will take too long, at a time when aged survivors are dying every day.

"What victims of these crimes fear the most is that when they disappear — no one will remember the names of the families they lost," said Shapiro of the Washington museum, who was a delegate to the talks.

"It's not a diplomatic timetable, and not an archivist's timetable, but the actuarial table. If we don't succeed in having this material public while there are still survivors, then we have failed, he said.

SECTION 10
POST WORLD WAR II FREEMASONRY, MASONIC SPACE TRAVELERS & MISCELLANEOUS

Figure 1 — After WWII, Grand Orient Mason Mao Zedong saw his opportunity to bless China with Communism. The Western Masonic Powers made no attempt to stop this Masonic brother. Instead, they pulled their support from Scottish Rite Freemason Chiang Kai-Shek. The reason? Vietnam drug war! For explanation read *Scarlet and the Beast*, Vol. 3, chap.8.

Oct. 1, 1949 ►
Grand Orient Freemason
Mao Zedong said in a
speech proclaiming the
People's Republic of China...

"Today, our China enters
into the family of
nations who love
peace and freedom..."

Compton's, vol. 4, p.305

◄ Scottish Rite Freemason
Gen. Chiang Kai-shek
(member of Pagoda Lodge)
and his wife, Meiling,
when he was the
"strong man of China."

In 1949 his democratic
government fell to Grand
Orient Freemasonry's
Chinese Communists

Fig. 2 — The credential prerequisite of all male Secret Service, F.B.I., and C.I.A. agents that protect the President of the U.S.A. is that they be Freemasons.

3° Leslie Coffelt (-1950)

"Secret Service man was killed on Nov. 1, 1950 by a Puerto Rican who was attempting to force his way into the Blair House and kill President Truman. Truman was at the time living at the Blair House while the White House was being remodeled. Coffelt was a member of Potomac Lodge No. 5, Washington, DC. He was raised 3° on Sept. 28, 1945. The Lodge gave him a Masonic burial in Arlington Cemetery with President and Mrs. Truman present. Seven Freemasons of the White House Police were active pallbearers, while six other Masonic White House guards were honorary pallbearers." The only time the Masonic Secret Service did not protect a President was during the Masonic murder of President John F. Kennedy. Figs. 12-18 confirm his assassination was Masonic.

33°
Harry S.
Truman
(1884-1972)

The Cornerstone of the White House removed

"THIS STONE, bearing the Masonic "signature" of an unknown Master Mason, forever linking his preferment in Freemasonry with the construction of the first 'Home of the Presidents,' nearly one hundred sixty years ago, was removed with others of similar marking, from the foundation walls of the original White House, Washington, district of Columbia, in the year 1950.

"Through official action by the President of the United States, Most Worshipful Harry S. Truman 33°, charter member and first Worshipful Master of Grand View Lodge No. 618, Grand View, Missouri, in 1911, and Grand Master of the Grand Lodge, Ancient Free and Accepted Masons, State of Missouri, 1940-1941, these stones are preserved for all time.

"The President, recognizing this historic association of the Ancient Craft of Freemasonry with the founding days of the American Republic, directed his Military Aide, Major General Harry H. Vaughn, 32°, to place these stones in the custody of the Grand Master of Masons, District of Columbia, with instructions to distribute one to each Grand Lodge in the United States. This trust was fulfilled during the Masonic Year 1952.

"On this day, Thursday, May 7, 1964, City of Washington, at a gathering honoring Most Worshipful Harry S. Truman, 33°, and the Grand Master of Masons of the District of Columbia, Most worshipful Harry B. Savage, joins with his predecessor of 1952, Most Worshipful Renah F. Camalier, 33°, Grand Cross, in presenting this stone to the Grand Master of Masons of the State of Missouri in 1940, that it might be forever enshrined in the Harry S. Truman Library, Independence, Missouri, there to remind future generations of Americans, and citizens of all countries, of the participation of brethren of the Craft of Freemasonry in the forming and building of the American System of Government.

"These precious ashlars intimately link Freemasonry with the Government of the United States. — Harry S. Truman."

Figure 3 — Conant's "dumbing down" of American Schools.

33° James B. Conant (1893-1978)

Harvard University president beginning in 1933. U.S. high commissioner for West Germany following World War II. Member of National Education Association's Educational Policies Commission. Member of Council on Foreign Relations (CFR).

Read of his involvement in secularizing our schools, and the "dumbing down" of America's educational curriculum. *Scarlet and the Beast*, Vol. 1, Chap. 9.

33° Sam Walton (1918-1992)

A Shrewd merchandising maverick who, as founder in 1962 of Wal-Mart Stores Inc., wrought a revolution with a retailing strategy that included everyday low prices, and homespun personal service to attract customers to his discount store chain. In 1991 Wal-Mart surpassed Sears, to become the largest retailer in the U.S. Walton was a 33° Freemason.

Figure 4 — TIME Magazine, March 31, 2003, p.A30 — (1952) THE BLOODY MAU MAU REVOLT 10-20-1952. "The gunmen were Mau Mau rebels, members of a secret society who had vowed to drive the white man from the British colony of Kenya."

Mau Mau Rebellion

"Kenya (Africa) had no minerals or marketable established skills. All it had, in its vast, overheated, infertile area, was a small zone, plumb on the Equator, which was high enough to be cool and to attract rain. Here the early (British) settlers, by dint of many a massacre, subjugated the natives. The young Winston Churchill in 1908, when Under-Secretary of the Colonies, wrote of one punitive expedition, 'It looks like butchery, and if the House of Commons gets hold of it all our plans in the East African Protectorate will be under a cloud. Surely it cannot be necessary to go on killing these defenseless people on such an enormous scale.' From start to finish the Colonial Office tried to restrain the excesses of the settlers, but with little success.

"So in the end, the Africans rose in a revolt which the panic and anger of the settlers made famous. They called it Mau Mau and put about the idea that it was the most brutal, bloodthirsty, murderous rising of black men against the white in the history of mankind. Never can a Minister have reacted with greater horror than Colonial Secretary Oliver Lyttelton when he wrote about Mau Mau. In Britain it was widely believed that Mau Mau fighters had slaughtered white people in their thousands. But it was not so. The actual number of white civilians killed was thirty-two."

Kenya was a settlers' dream: the last white dominion, 1890-1948. It was also the large game hunter's dream. During the next half century the white man subjugated the black population. By the 1940's the Kenyans demanded independence. Following the white man's style of secret intrigue through their secret society of Freemasonry, the blacks formed their own secret society to retaliate against the whites. A Mau Mau tells the story:

"Mau Mau started in a small way in 1946-47. Then in 1949-50 the Nairobi branch formed their own group, training them with arms. This group had grown very fast. By 1951 we had trained people, we had managed to get guns..."

Following Freemasonry's style, "they used an...initiation oath as a way to secure loyalty to their secret political army... The early violence of Mau Mau was of the press-gang variety, directed against those of their fellowAfricans who refused to swear the initiation oath...

"Something about Mau Mau oaths and activities created feelings beyond even the normal hatred, fear and misrepresentation inspired by an enemy at war. The British came to believe that Mau Mau was black African witchcraft... The Kenyan Government employed a psychiatrist...to write a report entitled *The Psychology of Mau Mau*, published in 1954." In part it reads, "...a meal was taken which sometimes included human blood and urine and the flesh of infants who had been exhumed or murdered, and the meetings ended in a sexual orgy..." *End of Empire*, 1985.
Brian Lapping.

Figures 5 — Arrest of two Mau Mau's.

Fig. 6 — One of the camps in which suspected Mau Mau were held.

Fig. 7 — Sugar Ray Robinson (1920-89). Onetime middle weight and light heavyweight boxing champion of the world. Member of Prince Hall Freemasonry, Joppa No. 55, New York City. In the photo below, Sugar Ray jolts Randy Turpin (1925-1966) of England with a right in their bout for the 160-pound title in 1951.

Figure 8 — Desegregation in Public Schools — Little Rock, Arkansas.

32° Orval E. Faubus (1910-1994)

Born at Combs, AR. Governor of Arkansas for six 2-year terms (1955 67). Was educated in the public schools, and ultimately became a schoolteacher in his home state for ten years (1928-38). In 1939 he became circuit clerk and county recorder at Huntsville. In 1946-47 he was acting postmaster of Huntsville, and from 1953-54, postmaster.

Beginning in 1947, Faubus was editor, owner, and publisher of *Madison County Record* at Huntsville. He served as rural scout commissioner for Northwest, AR for 14 years, and was an infantry Major in WWII.

In Sept., 1957 he became the most controversial figure in the United States when he refused to allow integration in the Little Rock high schools. Integration was soon enforced by Federal troops.

Faubus was a member of Huntsville Lodge No. 367, receiving his blue degrees April, May, June of 1947. He became a 32° AASR (SJ) on Oct. 28, 1953 at Ft. Smith. As a Shriner, he took an oath to Allah, god of Muslims. He also was a member of the Northwest Arkansas Scottish Rite Club.

Figure 9 — Dr. Martin Luther King often attended Prince Hall Masonic Lodges. But never was he permitted in a white lodge.

KING SPEAKS A crowd of 200,000 people joined the Washington gathering

Martin Luther King Jr. (1929-1968)

In one of his speeches, Dr. King is telling of his membership in a fraternity, but is discreet in not naming Freemasonry. He said, "Snobbish exclusivism is the danger of social clubs, and fraternities. I'm in a fraternity... I'm saying its dangerous... because it's the best fraternity in the world and everybody can't get in this fraternity." *A Testament of Hope*, 1986, p. 262.

USA Today (10-6-88) quoted M.L.K. preaching a Masonic phrase to a Hartford crowd of 300 that they must rededicate themselves to a nation "united in justice, equality and brotherhood."

It is still debated who actually killed Dr. King. Was it a lone gunman, FBI or CIA? It is a known fact that Hoover loathed Dr. King, trailing him with secret agents, photographing him at compromising events, such as meetings with known communists.

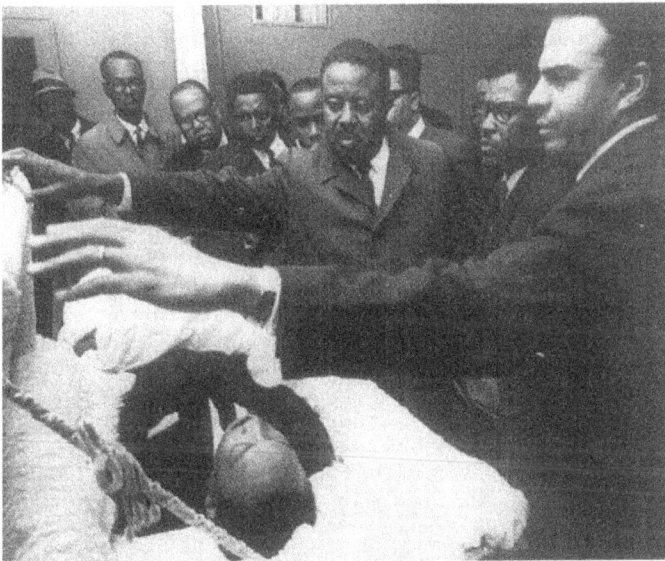

Figure 10 — Famous African-Americans speak out on Freemasonry.

Louis Farrakhan (1933)
Black Muslim leader speaking at Morgan State University on the snobbishness of Freemasonry

"You have robbed your own people of correct knowledge that would have allowed young white students to have a genuine appreciation for blacks. You would not teach your own the value of these black people, and you learn about us behind the closed doors. You talk about you want integration, you want to integrate Morgan into the University of Maryland, but you will not integrate the Black Masons and Shriners into your white shrines and your white masonry. You won't integrate that, and the reason you won't integrate that is because you know that... they (the Blacks) are Hiraim, the master architect that got hit in the head, carried away and buried in the North corner in a shallow grave where no light shines (description of 3° Masonic initiation). But someone came to raise him up and didn't have the proper grip. It took a master's grip to pull him up because he's a master mason..." from *Black Where We Belong:* Selected speeches by Minister Louis Farrakhan, 1989.

33° Thurgood Marshall (1908-1993)
Supreme Court Justice
Lawyer and Prince Hall Freemason. Born in Baltimore, MD. Graduate of Lincoln U. 1930 and 1947. Admitted to bar in 1933 and practiced at Baltimore (1933-37) and afterwards in New York City. Beginning in 1938, he was special counsel for the National Association for Advancement of Colored People. He won a number of important decisions before the U.S. Supreme Court. In 1951 he visited Korea to make investigation of court-martial cases involving Negro soldiers. He was nominated to the US Court of Appeals (1961), named solicitor general (1965), and became the first African-American member of the Supreme Court (1967-91). He was director and counselor of Prince Hall Grand Master's Conference and was a 33° AASR (Prince Hall). See *Scarlet and the Beast*, Vol.I, Introduction.

Black Masons. From book written in 1988 "to bring about a better understanding between Muslims and Masons."

Black Masons. From book written in 1988 "to bring about a better understanding between Muslims and Masons."

Freemasonry, Ancient Egypt and the Islamic Destiny
by Mustafa El-Amin, 1988
lists the following Blacks as Prince Hall Masons

Rev. Jesse Jackson
Rainbow - Push

Andrew Young
former Mayor Atlanta Ga.

Harold Washington
former Mayor Chicago

Thomas Bradley
former Mayor Los Angeles

Marion Barry
former Mayor District of Columbia

Coleman Young
former Mayor Detroit

Kenneth Gibson
former Mayor Newark NJ

Benjamin Hooks
former NAACP Executive Director

Louis Stokes
former Congressman

Julian Bond
former State Senator

John A. Johnson
Publisher of Ebony & Jet Magazines

Figure 11 — A debate about Freemasonry vs. Blacks on the Senate floor!

33° Robert C. Byrd (1918)

U.S. Senator from W.V. since 1959. Served in W.V. House of Delegates, 1946-50; State Senate, 195052; U.S. Congressman to 83rd-85th Congress. 33° Scottish Rite Mason. Member of Mountain Lodge No. 156, Coal City, WV. As member of Shrine in Charleston, he to an oath to Allah, god of Muslims. Member of Ku Klux Klan.

An interesting exchange of words occurred in the Senate, recorded in the *Congressional Record Senate*, Sept. 9, 1987. The nomination of a judge to the federal judiciary was questioned by the Senate Judiciary Committee on the basis of his Masonic membership. Some asked, "Could this Judge, while on a federal bench, make an unbiased decision when he belongs to a Lodge that forbids membership to a certain race of people?"

Masons in the Senate were strangely silent until debate seemed to move in their favor. They then came out of the woodwork, defending Masonry on the basis of philanthropy. Sen. Simpson of Wyoming said, "It is my pleasure to hold the 33° in Masonry.... [Sen.] Byrd holds that distinction.... Forty-one members of the Federal judiciary are presently Masons... I just say that Masonry in this country is the bedrock."

Sen. Byrd of West Virginia spoke. "I am proud to be a Mason. I have been a Mason since 1958 or 1959... I am a 33° Mason.... I hope that this ugly head of prejudice against Masons will not rear itself again."

Sen. Thurmond of South Carolina spoke, "I guess about half of the members of the Judiciary Committee are members of the Masonic order. I have been a member since 1924 and as was stated by the able assistant leader here, Senator Simpson, it simply means people who believe in God and love their fellow man. In short that is what it stands for."

Thurmond continued, "I commend the majority leader, who is a 33° Mason and Bob Dole, who is a 33° Mason.... I think the Masons have done a lot of good in the world. You have to be a Mason before you become a Shriner and the Shriners are maintaining hospitals throughout the nation to treat little cripple children and to cure burns, a most worthy cause. So I hope the question about Masonry being raised to try to keep one from becoming a judge is now finally settled. That will be the end of it and we will not hear any more on it." (see Shriner's oath to the Muslim god Allah, Sect. 1, page 29). The benevolent strategy worked. Stunned non-Mason Senators dropped their objections. The question of Masonic race bias was dropped. And Judge Sentelle was unanimously appointed to the federal judiciary. See *Scarlet and the Beast*, Vol. I, Introduction.

Fig. 12 — Freemason Kim Philby (1912-1988), British spymaster toppled the Soviet Union. "Many in the KGB still suspected he was a triple agent." writes *U.S. News & World Report*, Special Issue, May 26, 2003, "Spy Stories," pp. 61-62. Read his incredible story in *Scarlet and the Beast*, Vol. 1, Chap. 22, how he single-handedly brought down the Soviet Union.

Before Freemason Kim Philby (1912-1988) defected to the USSR in 1963, he trained our C.I.A. in pre-war Vietnam, from 1949-51. Read a portion of the story on the next few pages, which is recorded in its entirety in... *Scarlet and the Beast* Volume 3, Chapter 8.

Fig. 13

SCARLET AND THE BEAST VOLUME 3 — CHAP. 8
VIETNAM AND THE DRUG WARS

> *In 1950 the CIA had started to regroup remnants of the defeated Chinese Kuomintang army (KMT) in the Burmese Shan States, where they rapidly became the area's opium barons.... The CIA's other allies in the Golden Triangle, the Meo, were opium farmers.*
>
> Christopher Robbins, *Air America*

During the 1950s and 1960s, while British Masonic operatives in the academy, music business, and intelligence field were preparing our American youth psychologically and emotionally to enter the rock-drugsex counterculture, CIA agents were in southeast Asia to guarantee that the increased demand for drugs would be met. In his book *Air America* (1979), Christopher Robbins presents the thesis that the Vietnam War was a CIA-war largely fought over who would control the opium trade in the Golden Triangle: the communists or the Mafia.

The Golden Triangle is bounded by the rugged Shan hills of northeastern Burma, the mountain ridges of northern Thailand, and the Meo highlands of northern Laos — the world's largest source of opium, morphine, and heroin. "Opium was a fact of economic existence," says Robbins, "as vital as rice, and in Laos it was legal to grow it, transport, and smoke it."

In 1950, as the Chinese Communists moved south and divided Chiang Kai Shek's tattered Chinese Kuomintang (KMT) army east and west, Chiang and his eastern forces fled to the island of Taiwan and founded the new Republic of China. The western forces of the KMT, isolated and abandoned by both the United States and Chiang Kai Shek, fled south into Burma. Digging themselves into the heart of the opium area to hide from the communists, the KMT expatriates began developing their own defense lines, airstrips, and helicopter landing pads.

One year earlier in 1949 the U.S. government had contracted British intelligence (SIS) to train its newly recruited CIA agents on how to fight the communists. The man sent to Washington to work in liaison with the CIA and the FBI was Kim Philby, the highly specialized triple agent, who defected to Russia in 1963 to single-handedly topple the Soviet Union. Subsequent events suggest that Philby instructed the Agency in how to fund its covert operations against communism in Southeast Asia with drug money. The CIA held that whatever it took to fund a war against communism was patriotic.

After Philby's tenure with the CIA, many CIA agents were deployed to Burma, Laos, and South Vietnam to assist the ousted KMT Chinese Army in its fight against the Communists. The CIA started to regroup remnants of the KMT in the Burmese Shan States, where they had rapidly become the area's opium barons. The CIA's other ally against the Communists in the Golden Triangle was a local tribe called the Meo, also opium farmers. While the KMT and the Meo fought the war against communism for the CIA, the agency turned a blind eye to the their profitable sideline business in opium. Transporting the dope for the dope generals were a number of chartered airlines known collectively as "Air Opium," which were owned and operated by the Corsican Mafia. The receiver and distributor of most of the dope was the American Mafia. Almost all the KMT opium was flown south in unmarked C-47s to Thailand. From there it was smuggled into South Vietnam where it was sold in opium dens; the proceeds were used to finance Saigon's secret police. Eventually the Corsican Mafia was eliminated by a more ruthless warlord in northwestern Laos, General Ouane Rattikone, who himself was a bigtime opium merchant. Without the Corsicans to fly his opium, the general turned to the only air transport available in northern Laos (Air America) owned and operated by the CIA. The CIA had little choice in the matter, for if the Meo's opium was not flown to market, the whole financial apparatus of opium warlords would collapse and their fight against communism would crumble as well. From 1965 to 1971, Air America flew opium from mountain villages north and east of the Plain of Jars in Burma to the headquarters of General Vang Pao at Long Tienge in northern Laos. Paul Withers, a 22-year-old sergeant in the Green Berets, explained the procedure for buying opium when he testified at the 1971 Winter Soldier Hearings in Boston: "An Air America plane would arrive at Pak Seng twice a week with supplies and kilo bags of gold dust [from Hong Kong banks] which were given to the Meo in return for their opium. The opium was then loaded onto the planes, each bag marked with the symbol of a particular tribe."

The Kennedys' War Against the Mafia

When President John F. Kennedy assumed office in 1961, he planned to eliminate the drug apparatus of America. He appointed as attorney general his brother Robert, who had personally made a commitment to destroy the crime syndicates. The Kennedy brothers also planned to replace both J. Edgar Hoover as head of the FBI, and Allen Dulles as head of the CIA and then splinter the CIA into a thousand pieces, replacing it with an alternative intelligence agency. The establishment of this new agency was to be undertaken upon the replacement of Dulles.

From the 1950s, the Kennedy brothers' entire political career had been a war against the Mafia, the CIA, and the FBI. They knew that Mafia-controlled Cuba was the hub for South American drugs distributed to North America. When Robert Kennedy conducted a sustained drive against labor racketeering, Hoover opposed him at every turn. Then, in 1956, as counsel to a Senate committee investigating military procurement, Robert Kennedy learned of the machinations of America's directorate of crime in assisting the Mafia in its attempt to take over the labor unions. He discovered that a deal had been struck in the early 1940s between New York Mob boss Frank Costello and 33° Freemason J. Edgar Hoover, to allow the Mafia to take over the labor unions in order to keep the communists out of labor. In 1959, Castro's communist revolution in Cuba ousted the Mafia in that island nation. Immediately the CIA planned what is known as the Bay of Pigs operation to topple Castro and return Cuba to the Mafia. In 1961, when John F. Kennedy moved into the White House and reappointed Dulles as the CIA director, he put a stop to the CIA's LSD experiment, and pulled the plug on Dulles's CIA-backed Bay of Pigs operation, which had been set for April, 1961. Allen Dulles resigned as director of the CIA that autumn. President Kennedy also knew that the American Mafia was involved in the southeast Asian heroin trade. He was fully aware that the CIA-backed Vietnam War was being fought over the control of drugs. He understood that to offer the South Vietnamese our CIA and military assistance against the communists was also to assist the Mafia in their drug business. For these reasons, in the spring of 1963, Kennedy planned the withdrawal of one thousand troops from Vietnam, beginning December, 1963. He said to his aide, Kenneth O'Donnell, "I'll be damned everywhere as a communist appeaser, but I don't care." Six months after his decision to pull the troops out of Vietnam, Kennedy was assassinated, and three days after the assassination, Freemason President Lyndon B. Johnson reversed Kennedy's movement toward a military disengagement, permitting American troops to stay in South Vietnam.

Narcotics and the Vietnam War

In 1967, another opium war was being waged in northwestern Laos between the Communists and the CIA-backed army of opium farmers under the control of General Ouane Rattikone. At stake was Burma's opium exports (five hundred tons annually), a third of the world's total illicit supply. General Ouane and the CIA won the war against the communists' attempted takeover of their drug business, but their victory precipitated an escalation of the Vietnam War. Only the British Masonic bankers benefited. For example, not only did the Vietnam War in the south distract from the growth of the drug traffic to the north in the Golden Triangle, the increased production of opium in the north (which was used to fuel the new drug market developing in America by the British rock groups) also added billions of dollars to the bottom line at the British-controlled Hong Kong banks, which funded the entire southeast Asia drug business. As the war in Vietnam intensified, the CIA recruited more and more farmers to grow opium. When rice production declined as a result of the farmers growing the more lucrative opium, the CIA's Air America flew in regular supplies of rice, and flew out the farmers' opium. In exchange for this service, the opium farmers were expected to furnish young men to fight the communists in Vietnam. Air America helicopters would fly the young men off to battle. Opium farmers who refused to send their young men to war were warned that unless recruits were forthcoming, Air America's rice drops would stop.

In 1971, the CIA reported that the narcotics output in the largest of seven factories just north of Ban Houei Sai in northern Laos was "capable of processing some one hundred kilos of raw opium per day." The output from this factory alone produced 3.6 tons of heroin a year, one-third the supply consumed by heroin addicts in America.

During the Vietnam War "the U.S. Bureau of Narcotics was growing increasingly alarmed by the thousands of GIs who had become addicted to Laotian heroin." "The first large influx of heroin to be introduced directly into American military units in Vietnam was in 1968 when a detachment of soldiers, coming from Thailand to South Vietnam to assist American combat forces, brought a supply with them."

One of the soldiers said, "'I just wanted to get out of Nam, and "scag" [heroin] just took me out for a while at least.'" Another soldier, returning home, told army doctors: "'My first tour there in '67, a few of our guys smoked grass. Now the guys walk right in the hootch with a jar of heroin or cocaine. Almost pure stuff. Getting "smack" is like getting a bottle of beer. Everybody sells it. Half my company is on the stuff.'"

When U.S. servicemen began to be pulled out of Vietnam in 1971, the local dealers, all ethnic Chinese tied to the Triads, found their market vanishing. It was only natural that they should turn to the two areas where the servicemen were sent — the United States and Western Europe.

In 1972, President Nixon ended the Vietnam War and began his war on Drugs in America, which included sending the Drug Enforcement Agency back to southeast Asia to track down the dope dealers and destroy their factories. For his efforts, Nixon was Watergated.

Figure 14 — **33° J. Edgar Hoover's** (1895-1972) Masonic credentials.

Hoover testifying before the Senate Internal Security Subcommittee

Hoover kept massive files on J.F.K., his brother Atty. Gen. R.F.K., and their father, Joseph Kennedy. J.F.K. planned: (1) to replace Hoover because of his Mafia/ drug connections; (2) de-escalate the Vietnam War to curtail drugs from the Orient; and (3) keep Castro in power, who had kicked out the drug mob from Cuba. J.F.K.'s plans, however, were aborted by his assassination.

J. Edgar Hoover became a member of Federal Lodge No. 1, Washington, DC., Nov. 9, 1920, and was a charter member of Justice Lodge No. 46. He was exalted in Lafayette Chapter No. 5, R.A.M., and knighted in Washington Commandery No. 1, K.T., both of the district of Columbia. He received the Scottish Rit e degrees (SJ), and became a 33° honorary. He belonged to Almas Shrine Temple of the district, and was an active member of the Grand Council, Order of DeMolay. On May 2, 1950, he received the Grand Lodge of New York's Achievement Award, and in 1954 was awarded the gold medal of the General Grand Chapter, Royal Arch Masons. d. May 2, 1972. Hoover's preference was to first hire Masons and Mormons as F.B.I. agents, "Because," he said, "the binding oaths taken in each institution, they know how to keep secrets." Hoover founded Fidelity Lodge #1 inside FBI HQs. Anyone desiring advancement joined. See *Scarlet and the Beast*, Vol. I, 3rd edition, chapter. 8, Vol. III, chapters. 6-8.

Fig. 15 — J. Edgar Hoover's control through blackmail — *AP* 12/12/83.

Documents show Hoover gathered sex life gossip

WASHINGTON (AP) — More than 7,000 pages of documents from the confidential files of J. Edgar Hoover confirm that the late FBI director collected gossip on the sex lives of some of the nation's top political figures, according to U.S. News & World Report.

The magazine's Dec. 19 issue says Hoover kept the documents in his office during the nearly half a century in which he headed the FBI. The files contain many unsubstantiated allegations about the private lives of former President Kennedy, Eleanor Roosevelt, former Undersecretary of State, Sumner Welles, and others.

The material also details how Hoover drew on the defamatory information to curry favor with presidents and other officials.

The documents were released under a Freedom of Information Act request by historian Athan Theoharis of Marquette University in Milwaukee.

Some of the information is heavily censored and more than 10,000 other pages have been withheld altogether. The FBI cited national security, personal privacy or other grounds for keeping the material under wraps.

Fig. 16 — J.F.K. was planning to fire 33° Freemason J. Edgar Hover, but did not live to accomplish the task. You can read of Masonry's involvement in the assassination and cover-up in *Scarlet and the Beast*, Vols. 1 & 3.

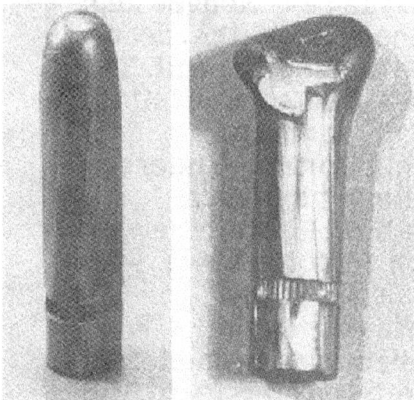

Photo 19 (left). Bullet 399—found on Dallas stretcher
Photo 20 (right) Bullet 856—fired through wrist of a cadaver

To prove the bullet that killed Kennedy came from Oswald's rifle, they found this unspent bullet on a stretcher that carried Kennedy. A spent bullet that hits its bony target, looks like the bullet to the right.

The large slash in Kennedy's throat was made after he arrived dead at the hospital. Supposedly it was made by the tracheotomy. But, Dr. Perry's incision was only 2-3 cm. This wound is 6.5 cm.

Consider the Masonic oath of a 1° Mason: "All this I most solemnly and sincerely promise and swear... binding myself under a no less penalty than that of having my throat cut across..."

Could Kennedy's slashed throat be the signature of a Masonic murder?

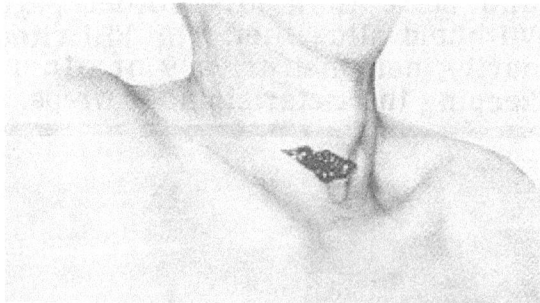

Fig. 17 — Everything having to do with the Kennedy assassination smacks of Freemasonry, including Dealey Plaza, named after a father and son, both of whom were 33° and 32° Masons. A Masonic Lodge once stood on Dealey Plaza, nearly equidistance between the 33° and 32° parallels.

33° George B. Dealey (1859-1946)

Publisher in Manchester, England, coming to the U.S. in 1870. In 1874 he became office boy at *Galveston News*. He became vice president and general manager of the paper in 1906. In 1926 he purchased controlling interest of the firm and reorganized it. He served as president from 1926-1940, at which time he turned the reins over to his son, Edward M. Dealey. Dealey, Sr. became Chairman of the Board.

Other newspapers and periodicals he owned included the *Texas Almanac; State Industrial Guide,* as well as several radio stations (WFAA & KGKO). Dealey, Sr. was a 33° Ancient and Accepted Scottish Rite Mason (SJ), a Knight Templar and a Shriner. He also was a director of the Dallas Scottish Rite Temple Association.

32° Edward M. (Ted) Dealey (1892-?)

Publisher. Graduate of University of Texas and Harvard. Began as a reporter on the *Dallas News* in 1915. Became President of the paper in 1940. Was also president of the A.H. Belco Corp, which published the *Dallas Morning News* and *Texas Almanac.* Member of the editorial board of *This Week Magazine.* 32° AASR Mason (SJ).

Figure 18 — The Warren Commission — a Masonic cover-up?

33° Earl Warren (1891-1974)

Supreme Court Justice during the Kennedy Assassination

U.S. Politician and judge, born in Los Angeles, CA. He studied at the University of California, practiced law, and served successively in California as State Attorney General and Governor (1943-53). In 1948 he was the Republican candidate for the Vice President of the United States. In September, 1953 he was Special Ambassador of the United States to the coronation of Queen Elizabeth II.

In the 1920s, Warren was Grand Master of Grand Lodge in California. In his 1936 annual message to the Masonic Brethren in that state, he spoke on the necessity of "destroying Prejudice [Christianity] in our schools and replacing it with reason." See his success in *Scarlet and the Beast*, Vol. I, chap. 9. He was appointed Chief Justice of the US Supreme Court (1953-69). He led a number of notable liberal decisions, such as ending segregation in schools (1954), outlawing prayer and Bible reading in our public schools (1962-64), guaranteeing the right to counsel in criminal cases, and protecting accused persons from police abuses.

Earl Warren joined the Scottish Rite in Oakland in December 1919 and became a member of Sequoia Lodge No. 349. He was Past Potentate of Ashmes Shrine Temple of Oakland, 1933, and took an oath to Allah; was a member of St. Phillip Conclave No. 23, Red Cross of Constantine; Grand Master of the Grand Lodge of California from 1935-36; member of Oakland Chapter No. 36, R.A.M. and Oakland Commandery No. 11, Knights Templar; Wise Master of Rose Croix in 1938; received honorary 33° AASR (SJ) on Dec. 23, 1941; and was Venerable Master of Lodge of Perfection in 1945.

In 1963-64, Earl Warren headed the Commission which investigated the assassination of President John F. Kennedy. Warren's Commission members were exclusively made up of 33° Masons and/or members of the Council on Foreign Relations (CFR), a think tank founded by English Freemasonry to secretly control our economy and politics. The Commission concluded that the killing was not part of any domestic or foreign conspiracy. Dr. John Coleman, former British intelligence agent, in *Secrets of the Kennedy Assassination Revealed* (1990), bluntly said, "The Warren Commission was a Masonic cover-up." See *Scarlet and Beast*, Vol. 1, 3rd ed. Ch. 27.

Fig. 19 — FDR stacked the Supreme Court with "Fellow Travelers." Photo below taken in 1970. Six Masonic justices were on the bench when they outlawed prayer and Bible reading in public schools, under the misleading metaphor — "Separation of Church and State" — based on bad history. And at least three were on the bench when "Roe vs. Wade" was passed. See *Scarlet and the Beast*, Volume I, chapter 9 to learn how these laws were worded so as not to be considered treasonous.

1. Thurgood Marshall (1967-91) 33° AASR Prince Hall Freemason
2. Potter Steward (1958-81) Freemason 3. Bryan R. White (1962-2003)
3. Harry A. Blackmun (1970-94)
4. John M. Harlan (1955-71) Freemason
5. Hugo Black (1937-71) 33° Freemason appointed by FDR
6. Warren E. Burger (1969-70) Chief Justice
7. William O. Douglas (1939-75) Freemason appointed by FDR
8. William J. Brennan Jr. (1956-90)

"The record shows that from the inception of the Supreme Court in 1789 through 1940, there never were more than three Masonic Justices during any term, except on two occasions. During the period of 18821887, four Masonic...Justices sat on a nine-man bench, and a similar situation prevailed during the 1921-1922 term.

"However, suddenly, beginning with appointments to the Court by President Franklin D. Roosevelt — himself an ardent Mason — and continuing through the first three years of President Richard M. Nixon's first term..., members of the international secret society dominated the high bench in ratios ranging from five to four (beginning in 1941) to seven to two (beginning in 1946).

"During the 1949-1956 terms, seven members of the Craft served on the Court with a former Mason, Justice Sherman Minton, who resigned from the Fraternity in 1946." *Behind the Lodge Door*, by Paul Fisher, 1988.

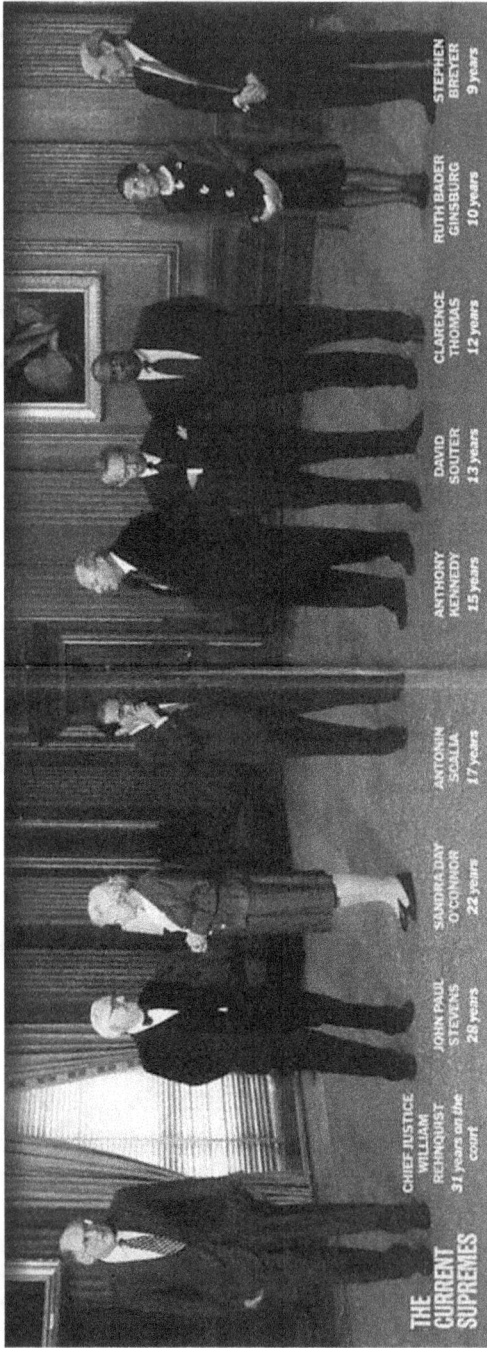

Fig. 20 — Supreme Court Justices as of 2003. *Time* magazine, June 30, 2003.

Chief Justice William Rehnquist has spent more than 31 years on the high court, 17 of them as chief. That has been time enough to see the court, and much of the nation, come around to the conservative views that once made Rehnquist so isolated that he kept a Lone Ranger doll on his mantelpiece, symbolic of his many solitary dissents. He gained two strong allies after Antonin Scalia and Clarence Thomas joined the court. Rehnquist spearheaded a determined effort to stem (and roll back) the liberal advances made by the Masonic Warren and Burger courts. For example, the Barrier between church and state is more porous. **Rehnquist once wrote that the separation of church and state "was a misleading metaphor based on bad history."** To his way of thinking, the framers of the Constitution intended merely to forbid the establishment of an official state religion, as exists in England. Rehnquist has had a mixed record in getting a majority of the court to sign on to this view. In 1995 he was in the majority that ruled 5 to 4 that a school could not deny student-activity funds to a Christian student newspaper when it provided such funds to other student publications. In the important 2002 schoolvouchers decision (a 5-4 ruling written by Rehnquist), the court allowed needy families to use vouchers for religious as well as secular schools.

Figure 21 — Among many subjects, Vatican II was to address the Catholic Church's stand on Freemasonry, which the Church identified as the "Synagogue of Satan." Will the Church continue to forbid Catholic affiliation with this age-old enemy? Or, will she soften her stand?
Read the story in *Scarlet and the Beast* Vol.1, chap. 8

CONVENING:
In St. Peter's,
big room, big
expectations

Figure 22 — Freemason Mikhail Gorbachev dissolves the Soviet Union and reinstates Freemasonry. Read of this British Masonic coup d'etat of the Soviet Union in *S&B*, Vol. 1, 3rd ed., chap. 22.

32° Mikhail S. Gorbachev (1931) Soviet statesman, General Secretary of the Communist Party of the Soviet Union (1985-91), and President of the Supreme Soviet (Council) of the USSR (1985-91). Born in Privolnoye, Russia. He studied at Moscow State University and Stavropos Agricultural Institute. Began work as a machine operator (1946), and joined the Communist Party in 1952. He held a variety of senior posts in the Stavropol city and district Party organization (1956-70), and was elected a Deputy to the USSR Supreme Soviet (Council) in 1970 and a member of the Party Central Committee (1971). He became Secretary for Agriculture (1979-85) and beginning in 1980 a member of the Politburo. On the death of Chernenko, he became General Secretary of the Central Committee (198591). In 1988 he also became Chairman of the Presidium of the Supreme Soviet, and in 1990, the first (and last) Executive President of the USSR. He was also awarded the Nobel Peace Prize in 1990.

On becoming party General Secretary, he launched a radical program of reform and restructuring (perestroika) of the Soviet economic and political system. A greater degree of civil liberty, public debate, journalistic and cultural freedom, and reappraisal of Soviet history was allowed under the policy of *Glasnost* (openness of information). Following the abolition of the Communist Party and the dissolution of the Soviet Union in Dec. 1991, Gorbachev was forced to resign. Since 1992 he has been president of the International Foundation for Socio-Economic and Political Studies, headquartered in California.

In 1984, a year before Gorbachev took office, he travelled to the two Masonic headquarters (London and Paris) to make a "report." Subsequent events suggest that while on that trip he was initiated into French Freemasonry. The next year (1985), Gorbachev was at the helm of the Soviet Union. A major Paris daily newspaper, *Le Figaro*, reported on Gorbachev's intense interest in Freemasonry. By 1989 reports were coming out of France that Gorbachev was planning to reopen Masonic lodges inside the Soviet Union and its satellite states. According to *Flashpoint* (Sept. 1990), a monthly publication from Austin, TX, "Both of the top Masonic organizations in France, the Grand Orient...and the Grand Lodge...are now working on this high priority project." On December 26, 1991, when Gorbachev voluntarily stepped down from power, he said in true Masonic terminology. "I hereby discontinue my activities at the post of President of the Soviet Socialist Republics. We're now living in a New World." For more details on the British Masonic coup d'etat of the Soviet Union, read *Scarlet and Beast*, Vol. 1, 3rd ed, ch 22.

Figure 23 — Grand Orient Freemason Eduard Shevardnadze, Reform Movement leader following the fall of the Soviet Union.

Eduard Amvrosiyevich Shevardnadze (1928) Born in Mamati, Georgia (former province of the Soviet Union). Georgian head of state (1992-2004), and former Soviet statesman. He studied at the Kutaisi Pedagogical Institute, joined the Communist Party of the former Soviet Union in 1948, and worked in the Komsomol Youth League during the 1950s and the Georgian interior ministry during the 1960s, where he gained a reputation as an opponent of corruption. He became Party Chief in 1972, and introduced agricultural experiments. In 1978 he was inducted into the Politburo as a candidate member, and in 1985 was promoted by the New Soviet leader, Mikhail Gorbachev, to full Politburo status and appointed Foreign Minister. He resigned in 1990, expressing concern over some of Gorbachev's decisions and warning of dictatorship. He helped defeat the attempted coup in August 1991, and was briefly Foreign Minister again at the end of that year. He then returned to Georgia, which had become an independent republic following the breakup of the Soviet Union (1991), and was elected Chairman of the State Council in December 1992, but was unable to prevent the country's slide into civil war.

To assist in preventing both a civil war and a total collapse of the former U.S.S.R., our CIA bankrolled Grand Orient Masonic operatives within Russia. Following are three of those Masons: Ahmed Ben Bella, Chadli Bendjedid, and Eduard Shevardnadze. (*Spotlight*, Feb. 3, 1992).

Figure 24 — Masonic Square and Compass displayed on wrist sweatbands of Boris Yeltsin (1931-?). Russian President 1991-1999.

French Freemasonry created the Soviet Union. English Freemasonry toppled the Soviet Union. See *Scarlet and Beast*, Vol. I, 3rd ed., ch. 22.

Geoffrey F. Fisher (1887-1972) Archbishop of Canterbury. Ordained a deacon in the Church of England in 1912; priested in 1913; consecrated bishop of Chester in 1932; bishop of London in 1939; and archbishop of Canterbury in 1945. Initiated in Old Reptonian Lodge No. 3725 in 1916. Later became a member of Tyrian Lodge No. 253 in Derby. As Bishop of Chester, he joined St. Anselms Lodge No. 5166 in 1936. He has twice been grand chaplain of the Grand Lodge of England (1937 & 1939) and served as provincial grand master for Norfolk. No photo available.

Figure 25 — Rowan Williams Archbishop of Canterbury (r. 2003), Initiated a Druid.
See *Scarlet and the Beast*, Vol. 1, Chapter 28. Dr. Rowan Williams becomes a Eisteddfod Druid.

What "bonds" in Christianity "unite us" with sin?

On the controversial election of a homosexual priest in the USA, Aug. 2003, Williams snarled: "I hope we will find that there are ways forward in this situation which can preserve our respect for one another and for the bonds that unite us."

Figure 26 — KGB infiltrated British Intelligence. *AP*, January 26, 1984. The original KGB were members of the O.T.O., which was founded in England by Freemasons, See *Scarlet and the Beast*, Vol.1, 3rd edition.

Book says Freemasonry us[ed]

LONDON (AP) — A book published today says the Soviet KGB used Freemasonry to get spies into top British intelligence jobs, and that its biggest success was the naming of the late Sir Roger Hollis as head of MI5 counter-intelligence in 1956.

The book says the KGB instructed spies to become Freemasons, then exploited what author Stephen Knight calls Freemasonry's "jobs for the brethren" network to place spies in senior positions in MI5 and the MI6 Secret Intelligence Service.

Knight says in the book, "The Brotherhood: The Secret World of the Freemasons," that he believes Hollis be-

come a member of the secret when he worked for a tobacco c in Shanghai in China in the 193[

Knight's book says Hollis was ly rejected by MI5 on grounds o and talent, but then was accepte service by a fellow Freemas[

Hollis was director-general from 1956-65. Chapman Pincl fense specialist of the Londor paper, the Daily Mail, created a March 1981 when he charged book, "Their Trade Is Treacher Hollis was a Soviet agent.

Knight says he has a copy of memorandum warning of the of KGB infiltration of Freem[

Figure 27 — *Cleveland Plain Dealer*, June 13, 1985

Methodist tract finds 'danger' in Freemasonry

LONDON (AP) — A report from a Methodist Church committee has called the international fraternity of Freemasonry a competitor to Christianity and counseled church members not to join the centuries-old society whose members have included 13 U.S. presidents.

"There is a great danger that the Christian who becomes a Freemason will find himself compromising his Christian beliefs or his allegiance to Christ, perhaps without realizing what he is doing," the church's faith and order committee on instructions said in a report released today.

The Methodist report will be presented to the British church's conference later this month and is expected to win approval as church policy. It comes at a time when Freemasonry is under growing attack in Britain.

"I most sincerely hope the Methodist Conference will recognize the illogicalities contained in the report and the lack of evidence to support the committee's conclusions," said Michael Higham, grand secretary of the United Grand Lodge of England.

Freemasons, who number more than 6 million worldwide, trace their society's roots to English and Scottish fraternities of stonemasons and cathedral builders in the Middle Ages.

The order practices charity, but has been regarded with suspicion by some because of its secret rituals.

The Roman Catholic Church has long frowned on Freemasonry, and both the Church of England and the Baptist Church in Britain have questioned whether their members should be Freemasons.

Prominent U.S. Masons have included Benjamin Franklin and 13 presidents, among them George Washington. Membership in the two main Masonic councils in the United States reportedly totals more than 1 million.

In Britain, the number of Freemasons is estimated at 500,000 to 1.5 million.

The church's report acknowledges assistance from the United Grand Lodge of England, the controlling body of British Freemasonry, whose Grand Master is the Duke of Kent, cousin of Queen Elizabeth II.

The report says Freemasons practice "syncretism, an attempt to unite different religions in one, which Christians cannot accept."

Higham said the committee misunderstood Masonic terms for God that are "convenient descriptions to enable men of different faiths to meet together without differences on matters of religion marring their meetings."

Figure 28 — The F.O.P. (Fraternal Order of Police) is the Masonic Lodge for law enforcement in the United States of America.

Williamson County Sheriff's
Police Lodge #197

Is Sponsoring A Gospel Music Show
Sunday April 19, 1998, 3:00 P.M.
At The Marion High School Auditorium
featuring

FIRM FOUNDATION

Representatives of the F.O.P. #197
will be contacting businesses and
residents by telephone seeking funds
for local community projects
supported by the organization.
Our F.O.P. Annual Yearbook will
also be distributed at the show.

For inquiries call 998-8222

*YOUR PAST AND PRESENT
SUPPORT IS GREATLY
APPRECIATED*

Fig. 29 — B'nai B'rith is the Masonic Lodge for Jews, founded in America in 1843, encouraged by American Freemasonry and backed by 33° Albert Pike. See *Scarlet and the Beast*, Vol. 1, 3rd edition, chapters 7 & 26.

B'nai B'rith turns 150

Greer Fay Cashman

Marina Dolnikov remembers the days when she was tongue-tied and got help from a 150-year-old source.

B'nai B'rith "saved us in many situations, because we didn't know Hebrew," said Dolnikov, a retired English teacher who moved here from St. Petersburg in December 1990.

B'nai B'rith also helped solve some more immediate problems, lending Dolnikov and her son Mikhail a gas stove and a refrigerator.

Now, Mikhail gives free performances on the organ and piano at B'nai B'rith functions; his mother plans to help children improve their knowledge of English.

They are trying to give back some of what they got from the world's oldest, largest and most broadly based Jewish service organization. B'nai B'rith celebrated its 150th anniversary on October 13.

Like Dolnikov, some 40 Haifa-based immigrants last April decided to give to the organization that helped them as newcomers. They formed their own lodge, Ken.

"I wanted to get the 'mortgage grannies' out of the house and into the social mainstream," said Ken co-ordinator Shoshana Stroh.

She was referring to new immigrant households of three generations crowded into a small apartment acquired with the help of the grandparents' mortgage rights.

LOCALLY, B'nai B'rith has also adopted the network of Miftanim vocational schools, set up about 40 years ago by the Labor Ministry. The 33 Miftanim schools are the educational institution of last resort for youngsters who have been rejected by or expelled from all other schools.

The Rehovot Lodge, which was founded around that time, was looking for an educational project.

"We settled on Miftan Alonim in Rehovot because it would give us personal contact with the students. We wanted to be personally involved," said founding president Mordechai Barak.

Alonim principal Ruth Gantz blesses the relationship.

"We were encumbered by so much red tape whenever we needed new books or equipment," Gantz said. "Now we get what we need almost immediately."

Barak showed off the library, to which B'nai B'rith has made a considerable contribution, in addition to purchasing a computer and distributing gifts to each student at Hanukka.

One of the tasks which the Rehovot Lodge has set itself is to remove the stigma from the nearly 60 students who attend Alonim.

Most of the youngsters, when asked why they were at Alonim, replied sheepishly, "I was a little bit crazy." They declined to elaborate beyond admitting to having thrown something at a teacher.

Gantz said they had been totally disruptive and impudent, overturning and damaging furniture and other items and picking fights at their previous schools.

The turnaround in their behavior has been nothing short of dramatic.

It began with $60 for orphans and widows

Twelve New York Jews who could not get into American clubs and organizations because of antisemitism met in 1843 in a cafe on the Lower East Side of Manhattan.

They formed the nucleus of B'nai B'rith by collecting $60 for a fund to support widows and orphans.

Now, a century-and-a-half later, B'nai B'rith operates on a budget of around $20 million and has more than half a million members in 51 countries.

B'nai B'rith has sponsored orphanages, old-age homes, hospitals, trade schools and agricultural villages.

In response to antisemitism in the US, B'nai B'rith in 1913 founded its Anti-Defamation League which, while monitoring religious and racial intolerance, seeks to strengthen interreligious cooperation and to pro-

tect the status and rights of Jews.

Ten years later, alert to the assimilationist trends of Jews studying at American universities, B'nai B'rith established the Hillel Foundation at the University of Illinois. Hillel now operates on approximately 300 campuses on six continents.

As early as 1865, B'nai B'rith sent money to the Holy Land to alleviate the plight of cholera victims.

Jerusalem, which is the home of the B'nai B'rith World Center, the bridge between Israel and the Diaspora, is also the home of the Jerusalem Lodge, which in 1888 was inaugurated as the first B'nai B'rith lodge in the Land of Israel.

There are now 133 lodges with about 6,000 members. B'nai B'rith for many years had separate units for men and women.

In more recent years, in response to requests from married couples

who wanted to work together on the same projects, the lodges opened up to include women.

According to the chairman of the B'nai B'rith World Center, Shalom Doron, "The Jerusalem Lodge represented the first time that Ashkenazi and Sephardi young people joined together in a civic venture."

Hebrew-language revivalist Eliezer Ben-Yehuda was the first secretary of the Jerusalem Lodge. Not surprisingly, it became the first organization in the Yishuv to conduct and record its meetings in Hebrew.

Under Ben-Yehuda's influence, it introduced Hebrew courses. In 1903, Jerusalem's first Hebrew-speaking kindergarten was established under its auspices.

The country's first lending library, which it initiated in 1892, still stands in the capital's B'nai B'rith Street. 8-23-93 *G.F.C.*

B'NAI B'RITH IS THE MASONIC LODGE FOR JEWS

Excerpt below from *Scarlet and the Beast*, Vol. 1, chap. 7.

In 1843, New York Reform Jews founded the exclusively Jewish Masonic Lodge, B'nai B'rith. Their institutions and influence grew. At the turn of the 20th century, the B'nai B'rith founded the Anti-Defamation League (ADL), the American Jewish Congress (AJC) and the Federations of Jewish Charities (FJC). According to Rabbi Antelman, Reform Jews who became lawyers were, and still are active in the subversively oriented National Lawyers Guild (NLG).30 In addition these lawyers were instrumental in founding the American Civil Liberties Union (ACLU).

Once the Frankist-Reform Jews were established in the illuminated Masonic Lodges, they pushed for civil rights for the downtrodden, primarily Blacks, according to Antelman, "to exploit them for their own ends." He further remarks on their influence on the events of the 1960s:

> *I have found their descendants in the United States to be very active in Marxist-Leninist and Third World activities. They have attempted to convert the Civil Rights movement into a Black revolution, and are attempting to further polarize this country by promoting women's liberation. Their children who are prominent in the SDS [Students for a Democratic Society] organize and recruit for the El Fatah, and have succeeded in destroying synagogues and Jewish institutions by instigating Black radicals mostly concentrated in nine urban centers in the U.S.*

Excerpt below from *10,000 Famous Freemasons*, Vol.2.

32° Frank Goldman (1890-?) — A member of B'nai B'rith since 1920. He served as President of the Lowell Lodge of B'nai B'rith, 1947-53, and honorary president since that date. Graduate of Boston University. He was editor of *The National Jewish Monthly* beginning in 1947. Active in civic and Jewish charity organizations. 32° AASR (NJ).

Excerpt below from *Grocers' Spotlight*, November, 1983, p.27

Ira Waldbaum is Honored in NYC — Ira Waldbaum, pres. Waldbaum, Inc., was honored last month by the Food Industry division of the AntiDefamation League Appeal (ADL) and the Harvest Lodge of B'nai B'rith. For many years he chaired the Food Industry division of ADL and was an active member of the Harvest Lodge. Also present were Bernard Paroly, president of Pathmark, Inc., and Irving Mendelson, president of Good-O-Beverage Co., both members of Harvest Lodge.

Figure 30 — Two Masonic Brothers — one Gentile, one Jewish. Read the part each played in the Masonic conspiracy. *Scarlet and the Beast*, Vol. I, 3rd edition, chapters 22, 24.

33° Harry Truman 1884-1992

33° Chaim Weizman 1874-1952

Truman is holding a Torah, a hand-written scroll of the five books of Moses in Hebrew, that Weizmann has given him.

Gentile Freemasonry claims to be Jewish. In the Book of Revelation, where the Apostle John is writing on the seven churches, we read Christ's words in chapter 2, verse 9, "I know the blasphemy of them which say they are Jew, and are not, but are the synagogue of Satan." (see Section 1, Figs. 29-30).

Figure 31 — Since the founding of the State of Israel in 1948, every Israeli Prime Minister has been a high-level Freemason. And in Freemasonry, enemies can unite in fellowship.

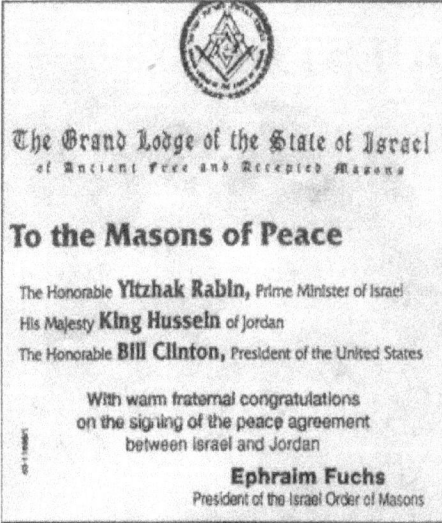

The Grand Lodge of the State of Israel
of Ancient Free and Accepted Masons

To the Masons of Peace

The Honorable **Yitzhak Rabin**, Prime Minister of Israel

His Majesty **King Hussein** of Jordan

The Honorable **Bill Clinton**, President of the United States

With warm fraternal congratulations
on the signing of the peace agreement
between Israel and Jordan

Ephraim Fuchs
President of the Israel Order of Masons

Notice below the "MASTER MASON" masonic handshake between JORDAN'S KING ABDULLAH II and ISRAELI PRIME MINISTER EHUD BARAK at their meeting in Amman, Jordan in August, 2000.

HANDBOOK OF FREEMASONRY 1973 (page 176)
Worshipful Master: What is this? (pressing hard with his thumb)."
Senior Deacon: "The pass grip of a Master Mason"

Figure 32 — From *U.S. News & World Report*, September 9, 2002, p.46, For full story on the Masonic connection to Skull & Bones, see *Scarlet and the Beast*, Vol. 1, 3rd edition, chap. 30.

THE ONE QUESTION

GEORGE W. BUSH
(S&B 1968)
CANNOT ANSWER...

His Membership in a German Secret Society

"(Averell) Harriman regularly went back to the tomb (Bones Temple) on High Street, once even lamenting that his duties as chief negotiator at the Paris Peace Talks prevented him from attending a reunion. So complete was his trust in Bone's code of secrecy that in conversations at annual dinners he spoke openly about national security affairs. He refused, however, to tell his family anything about Bones. Soon after she became Harriman's third wife in 1971, Pamela Churchill Harriman received an odd letter addressing her by a name spelled in hieroglyphics. 'Oh, that's Bones,' Harriman said. 'I must tell you about that sometime. Uh, I mean I can't tell you about that.'"–Walter Isaacson and Evan Thomas, *The Wise Men* 82 (1986).

"Think about this: Skull and Bones is not American at all. It is a branch of a **FOREIGN** secret society."–Antony C. Sutton, *America's Secret Establishment* 188 (1986).

Now, for the first time, you can find out the real details on Skull and Bones. The entire membership list from (1833 to 1983) is now exclusively posted on the worldwide web at http://www.biblebelievers.org.au/weekdx.htm

You will also find the latest list of the Trilateral Commission membership, 16 years of Bilderbergers, a booklist, monthly "hot" titles, weeks with elites in the news identified, years and links to help you do further research on the web. There will soon also be a series of introductions to various secret societies, beginning with the Yale-based Skull and Bones!

Figure 33 — From *U.S. News & World Report,* Sept. 9, 2002, p.46. For full story on Skull & Bones, see *Scarlet and the Beast,* Vol. 1, 3rd ed., chap. 30.

A tomb raider's revelations about Yale's bare Bones

The truth about Skull and Bones is shocking: In just a few days, Yale's most exclusive secret senior society will convene at nightfall in its mysterious tomb headquarters for the year's first meeting. Its 15 new members, students deemed destined for glory and power, will engage in a ritual performed by their forebears for more than a century—they'll discuss what they did on their summer vacations.

Forget the tales of young men running a covert government and owning all the real estate in Connecticut. Or rumors of lurid initiation rites like masturbating in coffins. They didn't even fund Hitler. As journalist Alexandra Robbins reveals in her new book, *Secrets of the Tomb: Skull and Bones, the Ivy League, and the Hidden Paths of Power* (Little, Brown), the Bonesmen are all talk. But their soul-searching discussions are far from idle chitchat. The year's rigid schedule of biweekly meetings starts with the summer roundup, then several weeks of "Connubial Bliss" (a chronicling of their sexual pasts), followed by lengthy "Life Histories," in which each member delivers a roughly three-hour oral autobiography. Se-

lecting each year's class of Bonespeople (the club went coed in 1991) consumes the rest of the year.

Fight club. Conspiracy theorists are bound to be disappointed, but Robbins, who interviewed more than members, argues that the 170-year-old traditions are more meaningful tha sound. "They want th roster to be prestigio they make it a traini ground to succeed in throat world," she sa Bones "knights" can i rupt each other's pre tions to pose questio request elaboration, the speeches are coupl with "criticisms"—a and sometimes bruta analysis of the speak count of himself."

Tomb life also inch homework, intoning thems, and playing b ball, a soccer-hockey

Yale's Skull and Bones society isn't as creepy as it appears.

that uses a half-deflated ball. (But no drinking alcoh it's a dry tomb.) And yet the mystique lingers, drawi power from what members, such as George W. Bush after leaving college—mainly, a lot of networking wi low Bones members. Or maybe, it's something more Robbins puts it, "Fifteen people per year. Three presidents. That's weird." *–Vicky Hallett*

Figure 34 — Written of the first George Bush, who also was a Bonesman.

Skull & Bones *May 19, 1991*

It's time to immediately leave the room

By Russell Baker

The Eastern Establishment press. also known as the press for people who think they're better than everybody else, has been filled lately with news about Skull and Bones. This is a secret society at Yale. It is composed of men who are expected to do very well in life and sometimes do. A typical member is George Bush, of whom it is often said, "He is Skull and Bones to the marrow."

This is one of the highest compliments a member of Skull and Bones can pay another. If, however, the compliment is paid by anyone not a member of Skull and Bones, the complimented member must immediately leave the room. In the highly unlikely event that President Bush, for example, had started reading this column over breakfast at the White House, he would already have dropped his toast and jam without a word to Barbara and marched out of the room, since I am not a member of Skull and Bones.

THIS IS BUT one of the many Spartan rules Bonesmen must live by. Note, for instance, that they are always called "Bonesmen." Never "Skull-and-Bonesman." Never "Skullmen."

When a Bonesman hears either of these proscribed terms applied to members of the society, he must immediately form his lips into an "O" and rap the top of his skull five times with the knuckle of the middle finger on his right hand. This produces a hollow-drum sound known in Bonestalk as a "Bonescram alert," since it alerts all Bonesmen within range of its lugubrious echo to "scram," which is Bonestalk meaning, "Stop whatever you are doing and walk out of the room in which you are doing it."

WHAT HAS MADE Skull and Bones newsworthy in the Eastern Establishment press is the attempt by Yale's undergraduate members ("Boneskids") to admit women. This has so flustered old-timer members ("Bonesfogeys") that they locked the doors of their historic old windowless meeting hall (the "Bonestomb"), thus shutting off access to their astonishing museum of relics.

These include Dink Stover's skull fitted into his high-school football helmet and the secret pornographic letters of Frank Merriwell, for which the late Nizam of Hyderabad is said to have offered his own considerable weight in rubies and pearls.

CONTRARY TO RUMOR, the Bonestomb contains neither the calcified body of John Wilkes Booth nor the Scroll of Thoth with its terrifying power to recall Boris Karloff to life every 3,000 years if slipped under an Egyptian pyramid with a few tanner leaves.

Why the opposition to admitting women? No, it is not because tradition dies hard. In America nothing dies easier than tradition. The problem is with language. Bonesmen capable of thinking things through have asked, "After we admit women, what will they want next?"

They fear the answer is that women will balk at being called Bonesmen. At best, they suspect that women would insist on being called "Boneswomen," but they suspect the worst; to wit, that women would denounce both "Bonesmen" and Boneswomen" as oppressively sexist words and demand that everyone — even Bonesmen! — be called "Bonespersons."

IT TAKES LITTLE imagination to grasp how somebody long accustomed to thinking of himself as a "Bonesmen" might feel life had lost a lot of ginger once he became a "Bonesperson." He might even feel foolish giving a Bonescram alert when he hears somebody refer to members as "Skull-and-Bonespersons" or "Skullpersons."

When secret-society members start feeling foolish about doing what's necessary, they stop doing it, and soon it's no fun at all being a member. Pretty soon Skull and Bones might start letting down its standards, and before long nobody at all, anywhere in the world, would be leaving the room immediately just because somebody had asked a perfectly boring question.

SPEAKING OF WHICH, I am unable to confirm a rumor that nothing matters more to Bonesmen than having their shirts starched perfectly.

"You can always tell a Bonesmen," they say in the laundry trades. "Put too much starch in his shirt, and he'll whip you within an inch of your life. Put in too little, and he'll immediately leave the room."

I HAVE TALKED constantly of starch in rooms infested with great men and everyone has always left the room almost immediately. This proves nothing, of course, except what everybody has always known: While Bonesmen leave rooms for no reason, the whole world hates a starch bore.

Russell Baker is a columnist for The New York Times.

Figure 35 — Astronauts and Freemasons John Glenn and Buzz Aldrin

33° Edwin "Buzz" Aldrin (1930-)

Aldrin (above right) presents to Masonic Grand Commander Luther A. Smith the Scottish Rite flag carried to the moon on Apollo 11 in 1969. *Lodge of the Doubleheaded Eagle*, by William L. Fox, *University of Arkansas Press*, 1997.

33° John Glenn (1921)

Astronaut. First American to orbit the earth. Senator since 1975.

John Daniel, author of *Scarlet and the Beast*, was on a Navy ship sailing through the Straits of Gibraltar when John Glenn (orbiting the earth) was picked up overhead on the ship's radio.

Fig. 36 Freemason and Satanist Jack Parsons, inventor of solid fuels for rockets, was head of Aleister Crowley's O.T.O. in Pasaena CA.

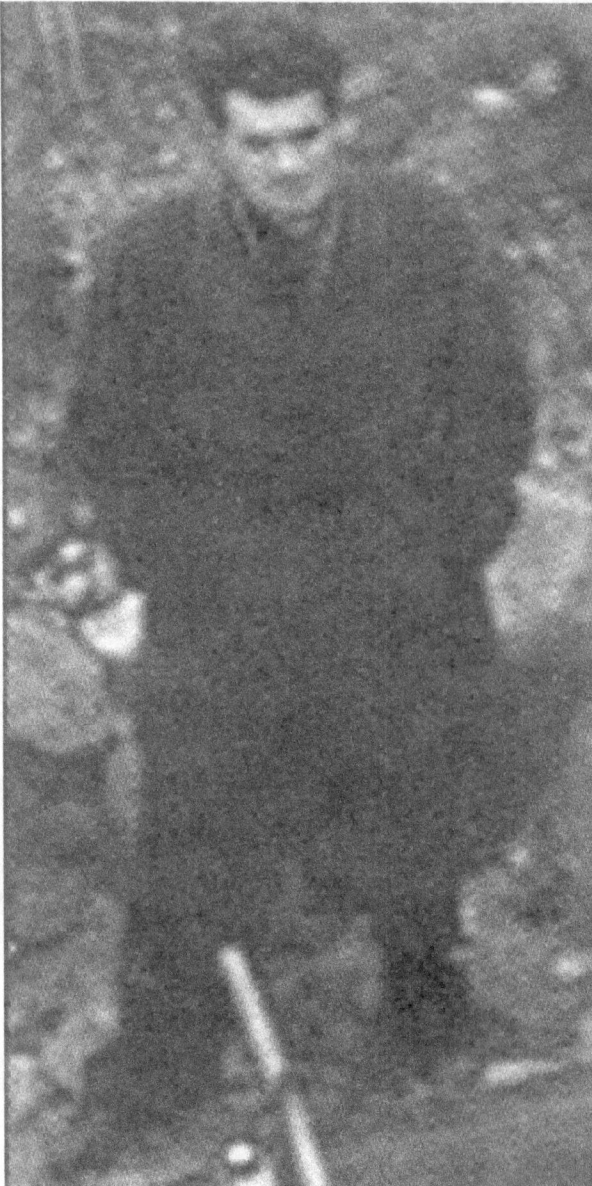

NASA's occult origins is seen in the life of Jack Parsons, the scientist who helped found JPL Labs, Pasadena, CA.

Parsons was the genius who invented solid fuel technology that made space shots possible.

NASA honored Parsons by naming a crater after him on the dark side of the moon.

In the book *Sex and Rockets: The Occult World of Jack Parsons*, Parsons is revealed as a sexual pervert who headed the American branch of Satanist Aleister Crowley's notorious secret society, the O.T.O. In S&B, Vol. 1, 3rd ed., read the Satanic ritual murders in America by the O.T.O. during the 1980s. Also see more on the O.T.O. in Sect. 2, Figures 10-15.

Fig. 37 — Masons were the first on the moon? Jim Erwin on the moon!

During the summer of 1989, John Daniel, author of *Scarlet and the Beast* had the privilege of being Jim Erwin's chauffeur to and from a Christian conference where Erwin was the guest speaker. In John Daniel's possession was a Masonic brochure that listed astronauts as Masons. Of course Erwin's name was on the list. After the conference, as John Daniel was taking Erwin back to the airport, he asked the moon walker if he had renounced Freemasonry?" Erwin asked, "How did you know I was a Mason?" Daniel told him of the brochure. Erwin replied:

John Daniel at Christian conference with Jim Erwin

"I was unaware they were still using my name. I renounced Masonry years ago." Mr. Daniel then asked, "Isittrue that a prerequisite to becoming an astronaut is to join the Lodge?" Erwin remained silent.

When Mr. Daniel informed Erwin of his book *Scarlet and the Beast*, the moon walker agreed to write the Foreword, but died two days before the manuscript was ready to mail.

Figure 38 — Masons were the first to reach the North Pole!

3° **Robert E. Peary** (1856-1920)

Discoverer of the North Pole. A member of the explorers' lodge, Kane No. 454 of N.Y.C. He received his blue degrees, Feb. 4, 18, and Mar. 3, 1896. To this lodge he presented the Masonic flag that was displayed at Independence Bay, Greenland, on May 20 and 25, 1895. His final and successful expedition in 1908-09 reached the North Pole on Apr. 6, 1909.

Matthew A. Henson (1866-1955)

Negro explorer with Admiral Peary, when he reached the North Pole in 1909. Member of Celestial Lodge No. 3, of Prince Hall jurisdiction in New York City. He is the author of *A Negro Explorer to the North Pole*.

Figure 39

Freemason Robert F. Scott (1868-1912)

British Antarctic explorer. In Nov., 1911, with four companions, he began a sledge journey and reached the South Pole on Jan. 18, 1912. He perished with his companions on the return trip. He was a member of Drury Lane Lodge No. 2127, London. Also member of St. Alban's Lodge No. 2597, Christ Church, New Zealand, and Navy Lodge No. 2613 of England.

Figure 40 — Masons were the first to reach the South Pole!

Roald Amundsen (1872-1928)

Norwegian polar explorer, who in 19031906 navigated the northwest passage and fixed the position of the North magnetic pole. In 1910 he set sail in the Fram in an attempt to reach the North Pole, but hearing that Peary had beaten him to it, he switched to the Antarctic, and on Dec. 1911 discovered the So. Pole. In 1926 he, with Lincoln Ellsworth, flew the airship *Norge* across the North Pole. He disappeared in June, 1928 on a flight to rescue aviator Umberto Nobile (1885-1978), who was lost in the airship *Italia*, which had gone missing in another flight to the North Pole. Amundsen was born in Borge, Norway Several sources claim he was a Freemason, but no lodge was specified.

Figure 41

33° Richard E. Byrd (1888-1957)

Polar explorer, naval officer, pioneer aviator; born Oct. 25 at Winchester VA. Brother of governor and senator, 33° Mason Harry F. Byrd (1887-1966). Richard graduated from U.S. Naval Academy in 1912 and at retirement in 1916 had advanced to Lt. Commander. Later, after his flight over the North Pole in 1926, he was promoted to Commander. In 1930 he was commissioned Rear Admiral. During WWI he entered Aviation Service and commanded the U.S. forces until armistice. In WWII he served with Admiral King in Washington, then with Nimitz in the Pacific. During the war he went overseas four times. He was highly decorated with the Congressional Medal of Honor in 1926 and special Congressional Medals in 1930, 37, and 46. He, with Floyd Bennett, flew over the North Pole on May 9, 1926. In 1927, with three companions, he made a trans-Atlantic flight of 4,200 miles from New York to France.

His made two Antarctic expeditions, 1928-30 and 1933-35. While spending five months alone near the South Pole, he discovered then named Edsel Ford Mountains and Marie Byrd Land. In 1939 he was made Commander of the U.S. Antarctic Service and again went to the south Polar region, discovering five new mountain ranges, five islands, and more than 100,000 square miles of area. In 1946 he was named commanding officer of the U.S. Navy Antarctic Expedition and again in 1956 headed the U.S. expedition in Antarctic exploration.

Richard E. Byrd became a member of Federal Lodge No. 1, Washington DC on March 19, 1921. He was affiliated with Kane Lodge No. 454, New York City, Sept. 18, 1928. He was a member of National Sojourner Chapter No. 3 at Washington. He and his pilot, 32° Freemason Bernt Balchen, dropped Masonic flags on the two Poles. Balchen, a Shriner, who took an oath to Allah, the god of Muslims, dropped his Shrine fez. In their 1933-35 Antarctic expedition, 60 of the 82 members were Masons. On Feb. 5, 1935 they established the First Antarctic Lodge No. 777 with a New Zealand constitution.

Figure 42

32° Lloyd Bentsen (1921-2006)
Courtly, influential former Senator from Texas and Democratic candidate for Vice President in 1988. As chairman of the Senate Finance Committee from 1987-92 and Bill Clinton's first Treasury Secretary, the pro-choice, pro-business Democrat was widely admired as a bipartisan coalition builder. Yet Bentsen will be forever remembered for a singularly potent moment during a 1988 debate. The vice presidential candidate on Michael Dukakis' ticket, Bentsen bridled at 41-year-old Dan Quayle, a Senator from Indiana, who was defending his youth and experience by comparing himself to John F. Kennedy. "Senator," Bentsen said, seething, "I served with Jack Kennedy. I knew Jack Kennedy. Jack Kennedy was a friend of mine. Senator, you're no Jack Kennedy."

Bentsen was born in Mission TX. Rcvd. LL.B at Univ. of Texas, 1942. Practiced law at McAllen, TX (1945-46); judge of Hidalgo Co. TX (194648). Elected member of 80th Congress (1948) to fill unexpired term. Member of 81st Congress from 15th Texas district (1949-51). Entered WW2 as private and rose to major in 1945. Served in European theater as squadron commander of bombers. 32° Mason and Shriner, who took an oath to Allah, god of Moslems.

Figure 43

33° Dan Rather (1931)
Television news presenter and writer, born in Wharton TX. Educated at Sam Houston State Teachers College. Became a television journalist for CBS in Dallas, then White House correspondent and London bureau chief (1963-74). Became nationally known for his reports on such major events as the Kennedy assassination (see Masonic connection to assassination, F12-19), Vietnam, and the Watergate scandal. His national profile grew when he became co-editor of *60 Minutes* (197581). Later he became anchor of *CBS Evening News* (from 1981-2003). He has been involved in many other TV specials, two of which were Masonic in nature. First were the Cubans exiled by Castro. In this *60 Minutes* episode (March 20, 1983), several Masonic Square and Compasses were displayed on the prisoners and on the wall behind Rather as he interviewed the exiles on TV, obviously signaling American Masons to accept them. Second, the 2004 false report on George W. Bush's National Guard service. When the hypothesis of the report was exposed as bogus, Rather was forced to step down. The Masonic connection in this report is below. Following Dan Rather's Sept. 2004 discredited report on President George W. Bush's National Guard Service, he was questioned by *The Dallas Morning News* about his loyalty to CBS. Rather replied, "I probably have the CBS *eye* tattooed someplace on my anatomy, and still proudly so." See the Masonic all-seeing eye logo in all news networks and Hollywood companies in *Scarlet and the Beast*, Chapter 4, p. 136.

Fig. 44 — Twenty-Sixth President of the United States.

3° Theodore Roosevelt (1858-1919)

Born in N.Y.C. Oct. 27, 1858. Graduate of Harvard in 1880; held honorary degrees from 13 universities. Member of the N.Y. State legislature, 1882-84, and in the latter year purchased a large ranch in N. Dak., where he resided for his health until 1886. Was U.S. Civil service commissioner, 1889-95; president of N.Y. Police Board, 1895-97; Assistant Secretary of Navy, 1897-98; resigned to organize with 32° Mason, Major General Leonard Wood, the 1st U.S. Cavalry, known as Roosevelt's Rough Riders, and fought in SpanishAmerican War in Cuba. Gov. of New York, 1899-1900. Elected Vice President of U.S. 1901-05; succeeded to presidency on death of William McKinley, 9-14-1901.

Elected to presidency 1905-09. Awarded the Nobel Peace Prize ($40,000) in 1906. Big game hunter in West and in Africa. Wrote many books, one of which was *The Rough Riders.*

Member of Matinecock Lodge No. 806 of Oyster Bay, N.Y. Shortly after his election to the Vice Presidency, he received his blue degrees Jan. 2, Mar. 27, Apr. 24, 1901. Honorary member of many Masonic Lodges; received the annual inspection and review of Knights Templar on the ellipse of the White House, May 26, 1902; delivered an address at the Masonic laying of the cornerstone of the Army War College, Feb. 21, 1903; attended the Masonic cornerstone laying of the House of Representatives' office building in Wash. DC on April 14, 1906 and delivered the address; was present at the memorial service by the Grand Lodge of Pennsylvania on April 19, 1906 at Christ Church, Philadelphia, in honor of the 200th anniversary of the birth of Benjamin Franklin; attended the Masonic cornerstone laying of the House of Representatives' office building in Washington, DC on April 14, 1906. Theodore Roosevelt was involved in a host of Masonic activities, and received many Masonic awards, too numerous to mention here.

T. Roosevelt visited lodges in many parts of the world, including Africa, Europe, and South America. His correspondence contains many letters to Masonic groups. See Spanish-American War in S&B, App. 1, pp.795-806.

Fig. 45 — Commander of the "Rough Riders" in Spanish-American War.

32° Leonard C. Wood (1860-1927)

Born Oct. 9 in Winchester, NH. Received medical degree from Harvard, 1884. Entered the Army as an assistant surgeon in 1886. That same year he was awarded the Congressional Medal of Honor for distinguished conduct in the campaign against the Apache Indians. In the SpanishAmerican War (1898) Cuban Campaign, he commanded the 1st U.S. Vol. Cavalry called Rough Riders. In 1899 he became Governor of Cuba and the same year received his law degree from Harvard.

Wresting the Philippines from Spain was an arm of The SpanishAmerican War. From 1906-08 he commanded the Philippine Division, then the Department of East, 1908-09. From 1910-14 he was Chief of Staff of the U.S. Army. He was again Commander of the Department of the East from 1914-17. In 1920 he was the Republican candidate for the presidency of the U.S.A. From 1921-27 he was Gov. of Philippine Islands. After being made Brigadier and Major General of Volunteers in the Spanish-American War, he became Brigadier General in regular U.S. Army in 1901 and Major General in 1903, retiring in 1921 after 30 years of service. Fort Leonard C. Wood, in Missouri is named in his honor.

Wood was raised 3° in Anglo Saxon Lodge No. 137 of Brooklyn, NY on April 3, 1916; exalted in Normal Park Chapter No. 210, R.A.M. of Chicago, IL on July 26, 1919; knighted in Englewood Commandery No. 50, Knights Templar, Chicago on Aug. 23, 1919 and same year became a member of the Medinah Muslim Shrine Temple, Chicago. He received the 32° AASR (NJ) in 1927 and was elected to receive the 33°, but died before it could be conferred. Read about all the Masonic players in the Spanish-American War in *Scarlet and the Beast*, App. 1, pp. 795-806.

Fig. 46 — Franklin Delano Roosevelt (1882-1945)
Thirty-first President of the United States of America.

32° F.D.R.

Born in Hyde Park, NY. Graduate of Harvard, 1904. Attended Columbia U. Law School, 1904-07. Practiced law in NYC, 1907-33. Member of New York State Senate, 1910-13, when he resigned to become Assistant Secretary of the Navy, 1913-20. Elected to governorship of New York two terms, 1929-33. Democratic nominee for V.P. in 1920. Became President in 1933, serving until his death in 1945, being elected four terms. He is the only President to have served more than two terms,

Member of Holland Lodge No. 8, N.Y.C. Received Blue Degrees (1-3) Oct. 10, Nov. 14, and Nov. 28, 1911. While Governor of NY, received the 32° AASR (NJ) at Albany on Feb. 28, 1929. Member of Cypress Shrine Temple, Albany NY, and took a oath to Allah, god of Muslims. Joined Tri-Po-Bed Grotto, Poughkeepsie NY; Greenwood Forest Tall Cedars of Lebanon at Warwick, NY. In 1930 he was appointed representative of the Grand Lodge of Georgia near the Grand Lodge of New York. He had three sons, all of whom were raised to 3° in Freemasonry. During his years as President, he received many delegations of Freemasons at the White House. On April 13, 1934 he became the first honorary Grand Master of the Order of DeMolay, the lodge for teenage sons of Masons.

Fig. 47

Wallace confers with Sidney Hillman (1887-1946) about labor's part in the 1944 campaign.

32° Henry A. Wallace (1888-1965)
VP of USA 1941-45 under F.D.R.
Wallace was Secretary of Agriculture, 1933-40; Vice President of the U.S.A., 1941-45; Secretary of Commerce, 1945-46.

Born Oct. 7 in Adair Co., IA. Son of Henry C. Wallace. His father was a Mason and a Shriner, who took an oath to Allah, god of the Muslims.

Henry A. Wallace was raised to 3° Mason on Oct. 4, 1927 in Capital Lodge No. 110, Des Moines, IA. He received the 32° AASR (SJ) on Nov. 23, 1928 at Des Moines. He was affiliated with the District of Columbia Masonic bodies (AASR) on Jan. 15, 1935, and dimitted from Capital Lodge No. 110 of Des Moines on Jan. 13, 1948. It is not known if his membership was transferred elsewhere. VP Wallace wrote many books on agriculture and politics.

Fig. 48

33° Douglas MacArthur (1880-1964)

Made a Mason "at sight" on Jan. 17, 1936 by Samuel Hawthorne, Grand Master of Philippines. Affiliated with Manila Lodge No. 1. Rcvd 32° AASR (SJ) at Manila same year. Made KCCH in 1937 & honorary 33° Dec. 8, 1947 at American Embassy, Tokyo, Japan. Made a life member of Nile Shrine Temple, Seattle WA. and took an oath to Allah, god of Moslems. MacArthur praised Masonry with these words, "It embraces the highest moral laws and will bear the test of any system of ethics or philosophy..."

33° Harry Truman (1884-1972)

Truman, at age 24, petitioned Belton Lodge No. 450, Grandview, MO on Dec. 21, 1908. Rcvd. 1st degree on Feb. 9, 1909; 2nd degree on Mar. 9; and 3rd degree Mar. 18. In 1911, Truman was honored by being made the first Master Grandview Lodge No. 618. He was Master and Secretary over other Lodges as well. After WWI he was given many other Masonic honors. His wife, Bess Wallace, was the daughter of David W. Wallace, grand commander of the Grand Commandery K.T. of Missouri. Truman's sister was an Eastern Star.

Fig.49 — The inauguration of Dwight D. Eisenhower as the 34th president ended 20 years of Democratic rule. He was sworn in by Royal Arch Mason Frederick M. Vinson, Chief Justice of the United States, standing left.

R.A.M. Frederick Moore Vinson (1890-1953)

U.S. Secretary of the Treasury, 1945-46; Chief Justice, Supreme Court of U.S., 1946-53. Born in Louisa KY. Graduate of Centre College, KY, 1909 and 1911. Began law practice at Louisa KY. Member of 68th-70th and 72nd-75th Congresses. Resigned from Congress in 1938 to become Associate Justice of U.S. Court of Appeals for Dist. of Col., and served until 1942 when appointed Chief Judge of U.S. Emergency Court of Appeals. Resigned in 1943 to become director of Office of Economic Stabilization, serving until 1945 when he was appointed federal loan administrator. April 1945 was appointed Dir. of Office War Mobilization and Reconversion. July of same year appointed Sec. of Treasury. Member of Apperson Lodge No. 195 and Louisa Chapter No. 95, Royal Arch Mason (R.A.M.), both of Louisa KY.

Fig. 50 — Dwight D. Eisenhower, as the 34th president of the U.S.A., gives his opinion of Freemasonry.

Dwight D. Eisenhower (1890-1969)

Born in Denison, Texas, Eisenhower, nicknamed "Ike," was a U.S. Army General and the 34th President of the United States of America (1953-61). He trained at West Point, and by 1939 had become chief military assistant to 33° Mason, Gen. Douglas MacArthur in the Philippines. His greatest contribution to the war effort was his talent for the smooth co-ordination of Allied staff. In 1952, the popularity he had gained in Europe, swept him to victory in his Presidential election. Eisenhower was not a Mason, but held the fraternity in high regard.

On February 24, 1955 he addressed 1,100 Masons at a breakfast in the Statler Hotel in Washington, DC, hosted by 33° Mason and Shriner, Frank S. Land, founder of the Order of DeMolay. In his speech, Eisenhower stated:

> *I feel a distinct sense of pride in appearing before this group which takes on its own shoulders the care and welfare of the unfortunate. This group, by action, recognizes the responsibilities of brotherhood by helping one another...you are setting an example to all of us that we must do our duty if we are to prove the Communist to be in error — to be liars.*

Fig. 51 — Lyndon Baines Johnson (1908-1973)

1° Mason Lyndon B. Johnson (1908-1973)

36th Pres. of U.S.A. (1963-1969)

Born in Stonewall, TX. Studied at Southwest Texas State Teachers College, and became a teacher and congressman's secretary before being elected a Democrat representative in 1937. He became Senator in 1948, and an effective leader of the Democratic majority. He was Vice Pres. under John F. Kennedy in 1960, and was made President after Kennedy's assassination, and was returned to the post in the 1964 election with a huge majority. His administration passed the Civil Rights Act in 1964 and the Voting Rights Act in 1965, which helped the position of AfricanAmericans in U.S. society. However, the escalation of the war in Vietnam led to active protest and growing unpopularity, and after 1969 he retired from active politics. On Oct. 30, 1937 he received the Entered Apprentice (1°) in Johnson City Lodge No. 561, Johnson City, TX.

Fig. 52

33° Barry Goldwater (1909-1998) 1964 Republican nominee for presidency, but was defeated by L.B.J.

Attended Staunton Military Academy and U. of Arizona. Was with Goldwater's Inc, 1929. Received the U.S. Junior Chamber of Commerce award in 1937. Became president of Goldwater's Inc, 1937-53, then chairman of the board. Served in WWII from 1941-45 as a pilot in the Air Force, then chief of staff of the Arizona national guard, 1945-52. Member of the advisory committee on Indian Affairs, Department of Interior, 1948-50. U.S. Senator from Arizona 1952. Resigned seat in 1964 to become the Republican nominee for presidency, but was defeated by L.B. Johnson. Returned to U.S. Senate (1969-87), and was one of the architects of the conservative revival within the Republican Party. His most notable book was *The Conscience of a Conservative* (1960).

Raised 3° in Arizona Lodge No. 2, Phoenix, April, 1930; 32° AASR (SJ) at Tucson; given honorary 33° in Oct., 1959. Member of the Muslim Shrine Temple and took an oath to Allah, god of Muslims. His wife joined the Eastern Star, a lodge for wives and daughters of Masons. He likewise joined, because Masonic law requires male spouses to be present at female Eastern Star meetings. Barry's uncle, 33° Morris Goldwater (1852-1939) was 8th Grand Master of the Grand Lodge of Arizona; Grand High Priest of the Grand Chapter of Arizona and Grand Master of the Grand Council of AZ.

Fig. 53 — 33° Robert Dole (1923) & 33° Gerald Ford (1913-2006)

33° Freemason Gerald R. Ford (1913-2006) chose **33° Freemason Robert Dole** (1923), a senator from Kansas, as his vice-presidential running mate. With their wives, they acknowledge the applause of party officials and delegates at the close of the Republican convention in Kansas City, MO, August 1976. Vice-President Nelson A. Rockefeller (left with glasses) joins in the applause for the candidates.

Robert (Bob) Dole was born in Russell, KN. A senator for Kansas, and for several years the minority leader in the Senate, he sought the Republican nomination for the presidency in 1980 and 1988. He became majority leader in the Senate in 1994, following Republican gains in the 1994 elections, resigning in 1996 to campaign for the presidency. He was defeated by Bill Clinton in the presidential election. He is married to Elizabeth Dole (1936), born in Salisbury, NC, who became Secretary of Transportation in the Reagan administration in 1983, and Secretary of Labor under the first George Bush (1989-90) Elizabeth Dole was a member of the Eastern Star, the female appendage of Freemasonry.

Fig. 54

33° Gerald R. Ford (1913-2006)

US Statesman. 38th President (1974 76). Born in Omaha NE. Studied at Michigan and Yale Universities. Served in US Navy during WW2. Became Republican member of US House of Rep. (1949-73). On resignation of Spiro Agnew in 1973 was appointed Vice-President. In 1974 became the only nonelected President in America's history when Nixon resigned because of the Watergate scandal. The full pardon he granted Nixon in 1974 made him unpopular, and this, along with economic recession, led to his defeat by 33° Jimmy Carter in the 1976 presidential election. Ford was the nation's oldest living President. In 1999 he received from Pres. Clinton the Presidential Medal of Freedom, our nation's highest civilian honor. Notice Masonic 6-pointed star in center of pentagram.

According to *TIME Mag*, 1/15/07, pp 40-41, Ford had accepted Christ as his Savior, but there was no mention of him renouncing Freemasonry.

Fig. 55 — Oliver Goldsmith, James Boswell & Samuel Johnson.

3° James Boswell (1740-1795) Scottish lawyer acquainted with the literary greats of his age, such as Voltaire, Rousseau and Wilkes. He was Biographer of Dr. Samuel Johnson, a Scottish lawyer who likewise was acquainted with the literary greats. Boswell met Dr. Johnson in London in 1763, then visiting him between 1772 & 1784 and taking voluminous notes of Johnson's conversations. Boswell was raised to the 3° in CanongateKilwinning Lodge, Edinburgh, on Oct. 14, 1759; He became Master of Lodge 1773-75; and Deputy Grand Master of Grand Lodge Scotland, 1776-78. He was honorary member of Edinburgh Lodge.

Dr. Samuel Johnson (1709-1784) Great English lexicographer, critic, and conversationalist whose life was immortalized by his biographer James Boswell in *Life of Samuel Johnson*. Johnson's greatest accomplishment was the 1755 compilation of the world's first dictionary of the language. This brought him doctorates from Oxford and Dublin U. He opened a school in Lichfield. He contributed heavily to literary magazines of the day. He wrote many books. He first met Boswell in May, 1763. There is no definite proof Johnson was a Mason, but as Mackey says, "the probabilities in favor are weightier than the probability against."

Fig. 56 — Ball carrier for
Notre Dame plunges through
the Stanford line during the
Rose Bowl game, Jan. 1, 1925.

Knute Rockne (1888-
1931) of Notre Dame achieved
a celebrity that surpassed that of
any other coach in history, with
the possible exception of Stagg.
Rockne created little, but he
was the most magnetic of all
coaches, one of the smartest and
wittiest. Becoming head coach
at Notre Dame in 1918, he saw his team win every game in 1919 and again in 1920. His
fame became nationwide when his team of 1924 won the national championship.
Sportswriter Grantland Rice began his account of that years's Notre Dame-Army game
with these words:

> Outlined against the blue-gray October sky, the Four Horsemen rode again. In
> dramatic lore they were known as family, pestilence, destruction and death. These
> are only aliases. Their real names are Stuhldreher, Miller, Crowley and Layden.

Knute Kenneth Rockne was born at Voss, Norway, and came to the U.S.A. in 1893,
settling in Chicago. He graduated from Notre Dame in 1914. He was captain of the
football team in 1913; assistant coach from 1914-18, and head coach from 1918-31. He
was killed in an airplane crash on March 31, 1931. He was not a Mason, although the
Masonic press had carried many references to his membership. Freemason Carl L.
Hibbard, Past Grand Master of Indiana, who was a good friend of Rockne's, had discussed
Freemasonry with him several times.

Fig. 57 — Twenty-ninth President of the United States.

32° Warren G. Harding (1877-1934)

Born Nov. 2 at Corsica OH. Newspaper publisher of *Marion Star* from 1884. Member of the Ohio senate, 1900-04; Lieutenant Gov. of Ohio, 1904-06. U.S. Senator from Ohio, 1915-21. Resigned in 1920. Same year nominated for President by Republicans. Elected for term 192125, but died Aug. 2, 1923.

Harding was initiated (1°) on June 28, 1901 in Marion Lodge No. 70, Marion OH. Nineteen years later he was passed (2o) on Aug. 13, 1920, and raised (3°) on Aug. 27, 1920. On May 4, 1921 he was made an honorary member of Albert Pike Lodge No. 36 of Washington; made honorary member of Washington Centennial Lodge No. 14, Wash. DC, Feb. 16, 1922, and same year, honorary member of America Lodge No. 3368, London, England. Member of Marion Chapter No. 62, R.A.M., receiving his degrees on Jan 11 and 13, 1921. Was knighted in Marion Commandery No. 36, K.T. on March 1, 1921, and made honorary member of Columbia Commandery No. 2, K.T. in Washington, March 4, 1921. He was elected to receive his R. & S.M. degrees in Marion Council No. 22, but died before they could be conferred. He received the 32° Scottish Rite (NJ) at Columbus OH, Jan. 5, 1921.

He was elected to receive the 33° on Sept. 22, 1921, but died.

He joined Aladdin Shrine Temple of Columbus, Ohio, and on Jan. 7, 1921 took a oath to Allah, god of Muslims. He was made honorary member of Almas Temple of Washington on March 21, 1921. Was associate honorary member of the Imperial Council of the Shrine, June 1923. Kallipolis Grotto MOVPER conferred the degrees on him at the White House on May 11, 1921, and made him a life member.

Harding visited many Masonic groups from Alaska to the Canal Zone. On July 8, 1923 he laid the cornerstone of Ketchikan Lodge No. 159. Other Masonic events are too numerous to mention. He died Aug. 2, 1923. His body was conducted from the White house to the Capitol on 8 Aug, with six commanderies of Knights Templar of Washington DC. The asphalt container in which his body was placed was the gift of Boumi Muslim Shrine Temple of Baltimore MD.

Fig. 58 — Thirtieth President.

Calvin Coolidge (1872-1933)
Thirtieth President of the United States of America. Non-Mason. His wife was a member of the Order of the Eastern Star, and his son, John, became a member of Wyllys Lodge No. 99, West Hartford, CT on Oct. 18, 1944. While governor of Mass., Coolidge addressed the Grand Lodge of Massachusetts, having this to say: "It has not been my fortune to know very much of Freemasonry, but I have had the great fortune to know many Freemasons, and I have been able in that way to judge the tree by its fruits. I know of your high ideals. I have seen that you hold your meetings in the presence of the open Bible, and I know that men who observe that formality have high sentiments of citizenship, of worth, and of character. That is the strength of our Commonwealth and Nation."

Fig. 59 — Masonic Kings of England.

3° George V (1865-1936)
His father was Edward VII (1841-1910), who was initiated into Freemasonry in 1868 in Stockholm, Sweden by King Adolphus Frederick, Grand Master of Swedish Freemasonry. In 1852, George V was proclaimed protector of Freemasonry, and initiated (1°) on Jan. 14, 1957 in Black Bear Lodge. 300 Masonic brethren assembled to assist in his initiation. He was initiated at 7:15, retired, returned, and passed (2o) at 8:00; retired again, and introduced at 8:15 for the Master Mason (3°) degree. At the conclusion, he said, "I am now one of you..."

33° George VI (1895-1952)
Royal Arch & 33° Scottish Rite Mason
Son of George V. From Dec. 11, 1936, he was king of Great Britain and Northern Ireland, and emperor of India until Aug. 15, 1947. Although he was an important symbolic leader of the British people during WWII, his reign was important for the accelerating evolution of the British Empire into the Commonwealth of Nations. He was initiated (1°) in Naval Lodge No. 2612 Dec. 1919. In 1922 he was appointed Senior Grand Warden of the Grand Lodge

of England; made Provincial Grand Master for Middlesex. When he ascended the throne in 1938, he accepted the rank of Past Grand Master of the Grand Lodge of England before an audience of Masons from all parts of the World.

The New York Times Tuesday June 3, 1952

Fig. 60 — The legendary Sen. Everett M. Dirksen, in the forefront pointing, is holding forth with the press in May 1967. Dirksen Minority leader of most of the 1960s, regularly switched positions on issues. They called him the "Grand Old Chameleon."

33° **Everett McKinley Dirksen** (1901-1966)

US Representative and Senator. Born in Pekin, IL. After serving in the Army, he worked in family businesses before entering local politics in 1926. As a Republican member of the US House of Representatives (193351), he supported the "New Deal" domestic programme while championing isolationist foreign policy. A Political pragmatist, he drafted the Legislative Reorganization Act of 1946. In the US Senate (1951-69) he was a conservative McCarthyite until 1956, when he became an Eisenhower loyalist and moderate, chosen as Republican whip in 1957 and Republican leader in 1959. Ironically the high point of his career came during the Republican support for the Test Ban Treaty of 1963 and the Civil Rights acts of 1964, 1965, and 1968.

Member of Pekin Lodge No. 29. Pekin, IL. He was Grand Orator of the Grand Lodge of Illinois in 1954. Received 33° AASR (NJ) at Boston on Sept. 29, 1954.

The nature of the House and Senate has given rise to some larger than-life characters. 33° Mason, Sen. Robert Byrd, a staunch guardian of Senate tradition, regularly takes to the floor to declaim the body's proper operations.

33° Francois Mitterrand 1916-1996
President of France 1981-1995

French statesman and president. Born in Jarnac, France. He studied law and politics at the University of Paris. During World War II he served with the French forces, was wounded and captured, but escaped and joined the French resistance. He was a deputy in the French National Assembly almost continuously from 1946, representing the constituency of Nievre (near Dijon), and held ministerial posts in 11 centrist governments (1947-58). He opposed de Gaulle's creation of the Fifth Republic, and lost his assembly seat in the 1958 election. For many years he remained a stubborn opponent of de Gaulle. He worked for unification of the French Left, and became secretary of the Socialist Party in 1971. Following his victory in 1981, he embarked on a programme of nationalization and job creation in an attempt to combat stagnation and unemployment. He was re-elected president in 1988, but defeated by Jacques Chirac in 1995.

SECTION 11
THE CRUSADES 1099 1314 THE MUSLIM EXCUSE FOR THE "SECRET SOCIETY" BEHIND OSAMA BIN LADEN AND HIS AL-QAEDA

To understand why this Muslim secret society was founded at the dawn of the 20th Century, we must return to the 11th Century thru the dawn of the 14th Century, when Freemasonry was born during The Crusades.

FIRST CRUSADE

Fig. 1 — Pope Urban II

Salvation through violence was a revolutionary idea when in 1095 Pope Urban II preached it to call up the Crusaders to take the Promised Land from the Muslims by force.

The First Crusade in 1099 A.D — The birth of Freemasonry See *Scarlet and the Beast*, Vol. 1, Introduction and Chapter 1.

Fig. 2 — Peter the Hermit

Charismatic itinerant preacher, promised peasants a better life in the Holy Land. But few made it.

Fig. 3 — First View of Jerusalem by the Crusaders from the Hill of Emmaus, June 10, 1099. "Jerusalem!! Jerusalem!! It is the Will of God!!! It is the Will of God!!!

Fig. 4 — **First Crusaders** entered Jerusalem with Peter the Hermit and Godfrey de Bouillon. Godfrey organized the Priory of Sion in 1099. Notice Christian cross on the breast of Peter the Hermit (standing), and Templar cross on breastplate of Godfrey de Bouillon (mounted). A few years later the Priory of Sion founded the Knights Templar as its protector. Knights Templar founded Freemasonry.
See *Scarlet and the Beast*, Vol. 1, chap. 1.

Fig. 5 — After the Muslims captured the stronghold of Edessa (modern Urfa) in 1144, Pope Eugene III asked the great French monk Bernard to preach the Second Crusade. Here knights in chain mail thrust their swords up toward the cross held by Bernard. Others flourish their personal standards. Merchants and clergy lift their arms in response to Bernard's fervent plea.

Bernard of Clairvaux preaches the Second Crusade.

THIRD CRUSADE

Fig. 6 — **Saladin** (1137-1193) His chivalry and generosity stood in sharp contrast to many of the Christians he fought at Jerusalem.

Fig. 7 — **Richard the Lion-Hearted** (1157-1199) Fighting Saladin in the Holy Land, this ruthless English king became one of the Crusaders' best-known figures. In photo to left, Richard and his Knights Templar prepare to attack Joppa on Palestine's coast in the **Third Crusade**. Notice the splayed Templar cross on Richard's tunic.

Fig. 8 — Defeat of the Crusaders at Acre in 1187. See *Scarlet and the Beast* Vol. 1, chap. 1.

Fig. 9 — Supsequent Crusaders looted Moslim wealth in the Holy Land.

Crusaders were the founders of what is today English and French Freemasonry
(edited excerpt below taken from "Introduction" of *Scarlet & Beast*, Vol. 1)

There are two streams of Freemasonry. First, the Rosicrucians, the secret society behind the Crusaders in 1099 A.D. In 1717 the Rosicrucians founded English Freemasonry. The second stream of Freemasonry are the Knights Templar, loosely formed by the Rosicrucians immediately following the First Crusade. Hugh de Payens formally organized the Templars in 1118 and became their first Grand Master. The name "Templar" is derived from the Temple of Jerusalem. In 1725 the Templars founded French Freemasonry.

Templars were the first religious community to yoke cross and sword. Their initial stated purpose was to guard and guide pilgrims to the Holy City of Jerusalem. Gradually Templar duties expanded to defend the Holy Land against all infidels, or any force menacing Jerusalem of their religion.

The nucleus of Templars consisted of nine men. As the order grew, de Payens created 13 degrees within the order.57 Why he chose to stop at "thirteen" is not known. Perhaps it represented the tribes of Israel (eleven full tribes and the two half tribes of Joseph — Ephraim and Manasseh). Maybe it stood for the twelve disciples and Jesus Christ. What is significant about the number "13" is that it identifies the Templar headquarters of our day, which nation continues to defend the Holy Land against the Muslims.

Another symbol that identifies the Templars is the emblem of their order. They adopted the famous splayed red cross of the Merovingian kings of France, placing it on their mantles, swords, buildings, and gravestones. This symbol is also important in tracing Templar movements to their present-day headquarters in the "extreme west" (region of the setting sun) according to Scripture, discussed in detail in Scarlet and the Beast, Volume 1, 3rd edition, chap. 30, entitled "Headquarters of the Beast Empire."

After founding their order in Jerusalem in 1118, the Templars headquartered themselves in a fortified abbey above the ruins of Solomon's Temple on the Temple Mount in Jerusalem — hence the name "Templar." Their domicile is of great significance, for somewhere beneath it was allegedly buried the unfathomable wealth of King Solomon.

As Templar fame increased, so did their wealth. According to standard histories, one source of their wealth was gifts from kings and princes grateful for their services.

As their influence grew, so too did their power and wealth. Eventually the Templars "developed into an efficient military organization that adopted absolute secrecy to cover all internal activities...."

Templars also made powerful enemies, among them King Philip IV (the Fair), who ascended the throne of France in 1268, his country near bankruptcy. The Templars possessed both money and land in abundance, which King Philip needed.

Failure of the Knights Templar to defend Jerusalem against the Muslims in 1187, their extensive banking and financial interests in both London and Paris, their rich establishments, and rumors of heretical practices within the order, gave Philip the ammunition needed to launch a successful campaign to destroy the order throughout Europe. On Friday, October 13, 1307, Philip ordered the arrest of all Knights Templar in France. Seven years later Philip ordered then Grand Master Jacques de Molay and other dignitaries of the Templars be burned at the stake. (See Section 11, Figure10).

Three centuries later, during the reign of James Stuart I, the embryos of both Scottish and York Rites of Masonry developed in England. At that time it was called Jacobite Masonry, in memory of martyred Templar Grand Master Jacques de Molay. Later these rituals became known to Masons in England and America as York Rite, and in France and America as Scottish Rite. Both are Templar rites. Today, under the flags of the U.S.A. and England, Templar Crusaders continue to defend the Holy Land against the Muslim.

Fig. 10 — Jacques de Molay, Grand Master of the Knights Templar, burned at the stake in Paris, France on March 18, 1314.

3rd degree initiation in Blue Lodge Masonry is a reenactment of the interrogation and execution of Templar Jacques de Molay. It is a brutal initiation, from which comes the common saying by someone questioned about his dubious activity, "He gave me the 'third degree.'" (See Sect.1, Fig. 18).

EUROPEAN FREEMASONRY FOUNDS TERRORIST YOUTH CORPS

(edited excerpt below taken from Chapter 12 of *Scarlet & Beast*, Vol. 1)

33O Freemason Giuseppe Mazzini, after three years of intense revolutionary training (1827-1830), concentrated on recruiting rebellious youth to further his conspiracy of revolution. In 1831 he was exiled to France. In 1832 he founded for his young revolutionaries their own form of Freemasonry prefixed by the word Young. By 1833 Young Italy had grown to 60,000 members.

In 1835, with help from Freemason Henry Palmerston, Mazzini founded Young Europe in Switzerland. Young societies continued to organize in new territories long after Mazzini's death. In the new world they were called Young America; in England, Young England; in Italy, Young Italy; in Turkey, Young Turks. On the Continent they were generally called Young Europe.

Young societies consisted of radical and riotous youth, many of whom were later initiated into Templar Grand Orient lodges in their respective countries. The Scottish Rite hierarchy directed their activity, while the Masonic press described them as students expressing their grievances.

All Young society members throughout Europe were taught the art of subversion by Grand Orient Freemasonry. They were ready when called upon to agitate, demonstrate, instigate worker strikes, hold rallies, or spy, bomb, and assassinate. Also known as Anarchists and Nihilists, they were reckless of every consequence, using dynamite, the knife, or the revolver for the benevolent cause of Grand Orient Freemasonry. Msgr. Dillon specifically mentions that these hoodlums (whose protection had been written into the French Constitution), would go to Paris where they were taught the use and manufacture of dynamite.

Although Young society members in Mazzini's day were described as loose-knit with no direction, they were in fact highly organized. A few were wealthy. Some were laborers and students, others, paid rioters. The majority had no jobs at all, yet spent money freely — an enigma to those who had no knowledge of their Masonic backers. After their grievances were aired by the Masonic press, public opinion turned in the direction favorable to Grand Orient Freemasonry.

In short, Young society members were hoodlums trained to do the bidding of the Templar Scottish Rite hierarchy. Their duty was to spread the secular Templar revolution throughout Europe. Mazzini was their leader.

With this rabble, Mazzini brought Italy her Masonic Revolution. Throughout these insurrections, Young Italy hoodlums, with no skills or aims other than causing havoc, supported themselves by kidnapping for ransom, robbing banks, looting or burning businesses if protection money was not paid. This rabble became known as Mazzini's Association For Insurrection and Assassination. For short the acronym M.A.F.I.A. was used.

Organized crime was born!

Fig. 11 — Colonel T.E. Lawrence, mystery man of the desert, made use of secular "**Young Societies**" to assist winning freedom for Arabs from their Muslim fundamentalist leaders. In retaliation against the secular **Young Societies**, Muslim fundamentalist founded their own secret society for youth, the **Muslim Brotherhood**. See *Scarlet and the Beast*, Vol. I, 3rd ed., chaps. 9, 12, 17, 20-22, 28.

T.E. Lawrence (1888-1935)

Thomas E. Lawrence, the mystery man of the desert, better known as Lawrence of Arabia, was a soldier, Arabist, and writer. Born in Tremadoc, Gwynedd, N. Wales, UK, he studied at Oxford, and became a junior member of the British Museum archaeological team at Carchemish, on the Euphrates (1911-14). In WWI he worked for Army Intelligence in North Africa.

Lawrence was a Freemason, yet no record of his credentials are forthcoming. He was deeply involved with the **secular youth corps of Freemasonry known as Young Societies**, founded 1830 in Italy by 33O Freemason Guiseppe Mazzini. Wherever Lawrence journeyed in Muslim or Arab countries, he founded many secular **Young Societies**. For example, when he was assigned to Intelligence at Cairo to investigate the Arab revolt against the Turks, he set up secular **Young Egypt**, and initiated Arab male youth and trained them in subversion against Egypt.

When the West was preparing to return the Jews to Palestine at the close of World War One, the Arabs were unhappy. So, Lawrence immediately went to work through that group of Arabs who were members of **Young Egypt** and **Young Turkey** to quell the revolt.

In 1916 T.E. Lawrence joined the Arab revolt against the Turks, entering Damascus in October 1918. He was a delegate to the Peace Conference, and later became adviser on Arab affairs to Great Britain's Colonial Office (1921-1922). He withdrew from his legendary fame in 1922.

More details on T.E. Lawrence's Masonic involvement can be found in *Scarlet and the Beast*, vol. 1, 3rd edition, chapter 22. (see next pages for a continuation of the Masonic Young Turks struggle).

Excerpts from the book *What Went Wrong? The Clash Between Islam and Modernity in the Middle East.* By Bernard Lewis, 2002, Perennial.

"In the mid-1860s a new movement was launched — the **Young Ottomans**... It is interesting that both the **Young Ottomans** and their later successors, the **Young Turks**, avoided using the normal Turkish word for 'young' in their nomenclature. The **Young Ottomans** called themselves Yeni, which literally means 'new.' The **Young Turks** called themselves Yonturk, simply transliterating their French designation...

"The **Young Ottomans** were obviously formed on the analogy of the Italian liberal patriot [33O Freemason] Giuseppe Mazzini's **Young Italy** and **Young Europe**; they agitated for a constitution and parliament, with the inevitable result that in 1867 their leaders went into exile, mostly to London and Paris [where both English and French Freemasonry reside]. They returned in 1870, and in 1876, with the help of some pressure from the European powers, they were able to persuade the sultan to proclaim a brand new constitution, providing for a parliament, with a nominated senate and popularly elected chamber.

"This constitution, which owed much to the example of the Belgian constitution and more to that of the Prussian constitutional enactment of 1850, was far from libertarian. Even so, it was too much. Two elections were held, the first in March 1877, the second, after a forced dissolution, in December of the same year. The first Ottoman parliament sat for two sessions, of about five months in all. Nevertheless, the elected members showed considerable vigor, and no doubt for that reason on February 14, 1878 the sultan, exercising the imperial prerogative, summarily dismissed parliament. It did not meet again for 30 years."

20th Century Almanac, World Almanac Publ. NY. Report on Young Turks, June 23, 1900

Turkey. "The **Young Turks**, a group that includes many students, exiles in Western Europe, and members of the Turkish military who are determined to get rid of the ineffectual Sultan Abdel Hamid, present a manifesto to the major foreign embassies in Constaninople [Turkey] demanding that these foreign powers end the Ottoman Sultan's rule. The Ottoman Empire has been coming apart since the early 19th century, as subject peoples began to demand freedom. Such minorities as the Kurds and Armenians demanded at least tolerance, and foreign powers tried to gain territory or access at the expense of the Empire. It will take a world war to demolish the Ottoman Empire, after which the **Young Turks** will bring Turkey into the concert of modern nations."

Hijackers of Freemasonry

By **33° Henry C. Clausen** (1905-1993) Past Sovereign Grand Commander of The 33O Supreme Council of the Ancient and Accepted Scottish Rite of Freemasonry, Southern Jurisdiction (SJ), U.S.A.

Clausen writes in the above booklet the following account of the Young Turk revolution "Masons historically have been in the forefront of movements that fired the imagination of freedom-loving people throughout the world. Goethe, Mozart, LaFayette were enthusiastic Masons as was the great Hungarian hero of democracy Kossuth, who found temporary refuge in America. Garibaldi was a 33O Scottish Rite Mason and a Grand Master. Leaders of the Young Turkish Committee [teenage youth corps of Turkish Freemasonry, comparable to the DeMolays in America] that in 1908 forced Sultan Hamid "the Damned" to give their nation a parliamentary form of government, were Masons."

Following is a photo history of that Turkish revolution, which was the catalyst that turned fundamentalist Muslims into haters of the West's freedom-loving Masonic democracy and secularism, culminating in al-Qaeda's 9/11 terrorist attack on America. This attack led to our war in Afganistan, and (as an aside) our war ill-fated with Iraq. Pres. Bush has said, "The world will be a secular democracy, like it or not." (Read more on Clausen in Scarlet and the Beast, Vol. 1, 3rd ed., chaps. 15&19).

Fig. 12 — Beginnings of Masonic secularization of Turkish government.

Abdulmecid I (1823-1861)
Ottoman sultan (1839-61), who issued two major social and political reform edicts known as the Hatt-i Serif of Gulhane (Noble Rescript of the Rose Chamber) in 1839 and the Hatt-i Humayun (Imperial Rescript) in 1856, heralding the new era of Tenzimat (Reorganization) that won the respect of European Masons.

Well educated, liberal minded, and the first sultan to speak French, Abdulmecid continued the reform program of his father, Mahmud II, and was strongly assisted by his ministers Mustafa Resid Pasa, Mehmed Emin Ali Pasa, and Fuad Pasa. The reform edicts were in part directed toward winning the support of European powers. The edicts proclaimed the equality of all citizens under the law and granted civil and political rights to the Christian subjects. The main purpose of the reforms, however, remained the preservation of the Ottoman state.

The army was reorganized (1842) and conscription introduced; new penal, commercial, and maritime codes were promulgated; and mixed civil and criminal courts with European and Ottoman judges were established. In 1858 a new land law confirming the rights of ownership was introduced, and an attempt was made to establish a new system of centralized provincial administration. The Sultan's educational reforms included the formation of a Ministry of Education, military preparatory schools, and secondary schools and the establishment of an Ottoman school in Paris (1855).

In 1849, Abdulmecid's refusal to surrender Freemason Lajos (Joseph) Kossuth and other Hungarian masonic revolutionary refugees to Austria, won him the respect of the European Masons. (See Section 4, Fig. 24).

In 1853 the Ottomans were assisted by France, Great Britain, and Sardinia in the Crimean War against Russia and were admitted as participants in the Treaty of Paris (1856).

The European powers, however, while insisting on reforms aimed toward the Christians and minorities in the Ottoman Empire, obstructed the Sultan's efforts at centralization, or at recovering power in Bosnia and Montenegro in the Balkans. (See S&B, V1, 3rd ed., chaper 20).

Fig. 13 — Continuing the secularization of Turkish government.

Abdulaziz (1830-1876)
Ottoman sultan — 1861-1876

Abdulaziz was a member of the Mawlawiyah (Mevlevi) order of dervishes (Muslim mystics), yet he was an ardent admirer of the material progress in western Europe, as had been his brother, Abdulmecid I, who had continued the Westernizing reforms initiated by his predecessor.

Of strong physique, Abdulaziz loved wrestling and hunting. He was also interested in music and painting.

Between 1861 and 1871, reforms were continued under the leadership of Abdulaziz' able chief ministers, Fuad Pasa and Ali Pasa. New administrative districts were set up in 1864. On French advise, a council of state was established in 1868. Public education was organized on the French model and a new university founded. And the first Ottoman civil code was promulgated.

Abdulaziz cultivated good relations with France and Great Britain and was the first Ottoman sultan to visit western Europe. However, educated in the Ottoman tradition, he could not always accept the adoption of Western institutions and customs. Consequently, in 1871 his reign took an anti-Western absolutist turn.

That same year Abdulaziz' ministers, Ali and Fuad, died. France, the Sultan's Western model and backer, had been defeated by Germany. Willful and headstrong, without powerful ministers to limit his authority, Abdulaziz became the sole ruler and placed greater emphasis on the Islamic character of the empire.

As turmoil in the Balkan provinces continued, he turned to Russia for friendship. When insurrection in Bosnia and Herzegovina spread to Bulgaria (1876), ill feeling mounted against Russia for its encouragement of those rebellions. (See S&B, V1, 3rd ed., chapter 20).

The crop failure of 1873, the Sultan's lavish expenditures, and the mounting public debt had also heightened public discontent. Consequently, Abdulaziz was deposed by his ministers on May 30, 1876. His death a few days later was attributed to suicide.

Fig. 14 — Continuing the secularization of Turkish government.

Abdulhamid II (1842-1918)
Ottoman sultan —1876-1909

A son of Sultan Abdulmecid I, he came to the throne at the deposition of his mentally deranged brother, Murad.

Under his autocratic rule the reform movement of Reorganization reached its climax. Abdulhamid's reform adopted a policy of pan-Islamism in opposition to Western intervention in Ottoman affairs.

He was brought to power by a group of liberal ministers led by Midhat Pasa. The Sultan had pledged to Midhat the position of Grand Vizier if he would assist his rise to power. Abdulhamid fulfilled his pledge to Midhat, who then promulgated the first Ottoman constitution on Dec. 23, 1876. This liberal charter was, to a large extent, adopted to ward off foreign intervention at a time when the Turks' savage suppression of the Bulgarian uprising in May 1876, and Ottoman successes in Serbia and Montenegro had aroused the indignation of Western powers and Russia.

After a disastrous war with Russia in 1877, and humiliating terms for an armistice, Abdulhamid was convinced that little help could be expected from the Western Powers without their intrusion into Ottoman affairs. He then dismissed the Parliament, which had met in March 1877, and suspended the constitution in February 1878. For the next forty years he ruled from his seclusion at Yildiz Palace in Istanbul [modern Turkey], assisted by a system of secret police, an expanded telegraph network, and severe censorship.

Discontent with Abdulhamid's despotic rule and resentment against European intervention in the Balkans, however, led to the military revolution of the **Young Turks** in 1908. After a short-lived reactionary uprising in April 1909, Abdulhamid was deposed, and his brother was proclaimed sultan Mehmed V. (See S&B, V1, 3rd ed., chaper 20).

Fig. 15 — Continuing the secularization of Turkish government. (See *S&B*, V1, 3rd ed., chaper 20).

Mehmed V (1844-1918)
Ottoman sultan — 1909-1918
His reign was marked by the absolute rule of the Committee of Union and Progress, and by Turkey's defeat in World War I.

After having lived in seclusion most of his life, Mehmed Resad became sultan after his brother Abdulhamid II was forced to abdicate. A kind and gentle man, educated in traditional Islamic subjects and Persian literature, he showed a keen interest in Ottoman and Islamic history. Nevertheless, he lacked the ability to govern.

Attempting to rule as a constitutional monarch, he surrendered all authority to the Committee of Union and Progress, the liberal-nationalist organization of the **Young Turk** movement.

On the advice of the committee, the Sultan went on a goodwill tour of Thrace and Albania in 1911. In the two Balkan Wars during 1912-13, however, the Ottomans lost almost all their European possessions, and in the war with Italy in 1911-1912, Tripoli was lost.

Although Mehmed was opposed, the Ottoman Empire entered World War One on the side of Germany and Austria-Hungary, and as caliph, he declared holy war and invited all Muslims, especially those under the rule of the Allies, to rally to the support of Ottomans.

By the time of Mehed's death, most of the empire had fallen to the Allies, and six months later Istanbul [Turkey] was under military occupation.

Fig. 16 — Continuing the secularization of Turkish government. (See *S&B*, V1, 3rd ed., chaper 20).

Mehmed VI (1861-1926)
Ottoman sultan — 1918-1922

The last sultan of the Ottoman Empire, whose forced abdication and exile to San Remo, Italy in 1922 prepared the way for the emergence within a year of the Turkish Republic under the leadership of Mustafa Kemal Ataturk.

Clever and perceptive, Mehmed VI became sultan July 4, 1918, and attempted to follow the example of his elder brother Abdulhamid II by taking over personal control of the government.

After the Armistice of Mudros on Oct. 30, 1918, and the establishment of the Allied military administration in Istanbul on Dec. 8, 1918, the nationalist-liberal Committee of Union and Progress had collapsed, and its leaders had fled abroad. The Sultan, opposed to all nationalist ideologies and anxious to perpetuate the Ottoman dynasty, acceded to the demands of the Allies. On December 21 he dissolved parliament and undertook to crush the nationalists.

The nationalists, however, who were organizing in Anatolia under the leadership of Mustafa Kemal, sought the Sultan's support in their struggle for territorial integrity and national independence. After negotiations, the Sultan agreed to elections, which were held late in 1919. The nationalists won a majority in the new parliament. The Allies, alarmed at the prospect of Turkish unity, extended the occupied area in Istanbul and arrested and exiled the nationalists. The Sultan dissolved the parliament on April 11, 1920. The nationalists set up a provisional government in Ankara. Mehmed's signing of the Treaty of Sevres on Aug. 10, 1920, however, reduced the empire to little but Turkey itself and served to strengthen the nationalist cause. After the defeat of the Greeks, the nationalists were in solid control of Turkey. The Grand National Assembly on Nov. 1, 1922, abolished the sultanate. Sixteen days later Mehmed VI boarded a British warship and fled to Malta. His later attempts to install himself as caliph in the Hejaz failed.

Fig. 17A — Kemal Ataturk used "Young Turks," Freemasonry's secular youth organization, to depose the Sultan and win freedom for the Turks. On March 24, 1923, TIME magazine wrote, "Mustapha Kemal Pasha...has lifted the people out of the slough of servile submission to alien authority, brought them to...independence of thought and action." (See S&B, V1, 3rd ed., ch. 20).

Kemal Ataturk (1881-1938)

Emergence of Turkey as a modern nation in this century was due in large part to the implacable energy and vision of one man, born Mustafa Kemal, who as leader of his country took the not unwarranted name Ataturk, meaning "Father of the Turks." He was instrumental in the liberal **Young Turk** (earlier called **Young Ottoman**) revolution of 1908, which deposed the sultan. **Young Societies** in Europe were founded in 1830-1860 by 33O Freemason Giuseppe Mazzini, head of Italian Freemasonry.

Lawrence of Arabia followed by planting **Young Societies** throughout the Near East, using young secular Mulims to topple the Ottoman Empire.

Despite quarrels with the new government about its German allegiance, Ataturk led the Turkish forces to victory over the Allies at Gallipoli during World War I. After the war, when the Allies reinstated the sultanate, Ataturk (with his **Young Turks**), mounted a resistance movement that expelled the Greek invasion in 1920 and abolished the sultanate again in 1922. Ataturk, when becoming President of the New Turkish Republic in 1923, changed Turkey into a modern secular country in the Western mold by ruthless force of will. As violent and vindictive as his reforms often were (particularly those directed at Islam), his nation mourned his passing in 1938.

Howard Chua-Eoan writes in TIME's 80 Days That Changed The World, "Ataturk Commands His People: Westward, Ho!" (2003):

> *General Mustafa Kemal, who had repelled the British at Gallipoli in 1915 and had just recently done the same to invading Greeks, now planned a civil takeover of his own country. Just hours before he did it, Kemal was telling a journalist that popular Islam had become a morass of superstitions that would destroy those who professed it. He declared, "We will save them," according to biographer Andrew Mango. A 101-gun salute greeted the announcement: Turkey had ceased to be an Islamic empire. It was a republic, and its leader, Kemal, became President — not Sultan, not Caliph, the titles that Ottoman monarchs paraded for 600 years — the first as despots who once made Europe cower, the second as "Commanders of the Faithful," leaders of Sunni Muslims everywhere. Soon Western clothing was enforced and Roman letters replaced Arabic-based script. The man who would adopt the name Ataturk ("father of the Turks") inaugurated an era in which nationalism, not Islam, would be seen as the solution to the trouble of Muslim peoples. But by the 1980s, a reaction would set in, and the cause of the caliphate eventually would be taken up by, among others, Osama bin Laden.*

Eighty years after Mustafa Kemal Ataturk revolutionized his nation and turned its face toward Europe, Turkey remains an outsider in two worlds, held at arm's length by both its European and Arab neighbors. Long a member of NATO, Ataturk's nation smarted as the European Union accepted a gaggle of former Warsaw Pact nations but put Turkey on hold. On Istanbul's streets, conservative Muslims pass artsy young women with their hair uncovered. In its governing councils, democracy and its freedoms are hailed as shining ideals, but open debate is discouraged. In some ways, the nation is not so far removed from the days of Ataturk, dictator-ofdemocracy who issued fiats banning Arab garb — in the name of freedom.

Turkey's ruling elites followed Ataturk's resolute secularism for decades, but lately some Turks have called for a society more in tune with the nation's Islamic heritage. In the November 2002 elections, voters threw out the longtime ruling party in favor of a pro-Islamic party headed by former Istanbul Mayor Recep Tayyip Erdogan. Turkey soon found itself caught between its twin beacons: U.S. President George W. Bush wanted Turkey to allow U.S. troops to invade Iraq from Turkish soil, but in a major blow to U.S. plans, the new Parliament vetoed the plan. With the U.S. looking forward to a post-Saddam Middle East, its diplomats will confront a Turkey in evolution, as the most democratic nation in the Islamic world turns its face toward Mecca again.

32O Mehmet Talaat Pasha (1872-1921)

Turkish political leader. After Turkish revolu-tion of 1908, he became leader of **Young Turks**. He later became minister of interior, postmaster general and eventually succeeded Said Halim Pasha as grand vizier of Turkey (1917). Was forced into retirement Oct. 1918. Served as Grand Master of the Grand Orient Masonic Lodge of Turkey. Left Turkey in 1919. Two years later was assassinated in Berlin by an Armenian student.

33O Selim Sarper (1899-?)

Permanent representative of Turkey to UN beginning in 1947 with rank of ambassador. Educated at U. of Ankara. Officer of foreign service of Turkey since 1927. Served in Odessa, Moscow, Berlin, Bucharest. Press officer to prime minister, 1940-44. Ambassador to Moscow, 1941-46, and Rome, 1946-47. 33O AASR Mason. Appeared at numerous Masonic functions in NYC.

33O Khedive Ismail Pasha (1830-1895)
First Grand Master of the Grand Lodge of Egypt and khedive of Egypt (1863-1879), who, in 1879 presented the famous "Cleopatra's Needle" to the United States. It was originally erected in Heliopolis, Egypt, about 1500 B.C. Weighing 200 tons, its removal and re-erection was quite a problem. It was shipped under the direction of Comdr. H. H. Gorrige, a Mason, and on Oct. 9, 1880 the foundation stone of the monument's base was laid with Masonic ceremonies.

Muslim Brotherhood — An organization founded in Egypt in 1928 by Hasan al-Banna (1906-1949), calling for a return to rigid orthodoxy, the overthrow of secular governments, and a restoration of the theocratic state — Random House Dictionary; — see Fig. 17B

"Turkey"
Mackey's Revised Encyclopedia of Freemasonry Vol. 2, p. 1061 — 5th printing, 1950

"A writer in the Freemasons Quarterly Review (1844, page 21), says that there was a Masonic meeting in Constantinople, at which some Turks were initiated, but that the government prohibited...future meetings....

"Many and various authorities have founded Lodges in Turkey. Mention of Lodges at Smyrna and Aleppo occurred in a London newspaper as early as 1738. Oriental Lodge under the Grand Lodge of England has been active since 1856 at Constantinople.

"A Grand Lodge of Turkey formed by Ionic, Anatolia, and Benzenzia Lodges was declared illegal in 1859 by the Grand Lodge of England.

"A District Grand Lodge was establish in 1861 with Sir Henry Bulwer, British Ambassador, as District Grand Master. A Supreme Council was opened in 1869 and a Grand Orient of Turkey in 1908.

"Since 1894 the Grand Lodge of Hamburg has had a Lodge working in German, Die Leuchte am goldenen Horn, meaning Light at the Golden Horn, these last two words referring to the crescent-shaped strait, the Bosporus, on which Constantinople is situated. The Grand Orient of Italy has three, the Grand Orient of France one, all at Constantinople.

"The Grand Orient of France has two Lodges at Smyrna, Homere from 1909 and Meles from 1913; Bakai from 1905 at Jaffa, and Moriah Lodge at Jerusalem since 1913. The Grand Orient has also had a Lodge at Beyrouth in Syria, Le Liban from 1868; and at Zahle, also in Syria, Etoele du Liban, meaning in French Star of the Liban, since 1913. The Grand Orient of Italy has Lodges at Adana and Angora, two at Smyrna, one at Syrian Tripoli, and another at Rodi.

"In these Lodges many native Mohammedans have been initiated. The Turks, however, have always had secret societies of their own, which has led some writers to suppose, erroneously, that Freemasonry existed long before the date of its actual introduction. Thus, the Begtaschi form a secret society in Turkey, numbering many thousands of Mussulmans in its ranks, and none but a true Moslem can be admitted to the Brotherhood. It is a religious Order, and was founded in the year 1328 by the Hadji Begtasch, a famous dervish, from whom it derives its name. The Begtaschi have certain signs and passwords by which they are enabled to recognize the "true Brethren," and by which they are protected from vagabond impostors. A writer in Notes and Queries says, in summer of 1855, and English merchant captain, while walking through the streets of a Turkish quarter of Constantinople, encountered a Turk, who made use of various signs of Freemasonry, some of which (the captain being a Mason), he understood and others he did not. It is, however, probable in this instance, considering the date, that the Turk was really a Freemason, and possessed some higher Degrees, which had not been attained by the English Captain. There is also another equally celebrated Order in Turkey, the Melwi, who have secret modes of recognition."

"Young Turks and Masonry"
Mackey's Revised Encyclopedia of Freemasonry Vol. 3, p. 1393 — 1950

"Bro. Ernest Jackh, a member of the faculty of Columbia University, New York, began in 1908 his extraordinary career as political and diplomatic expert on Turkey and the Balkans. He saw the fall of the Ottoman Empire, was in continuous relationship with Enver Pasha, Mustapha Kemal [Ataturk], etc., during the ten years of the Young Turks movement, and had a part in the founding of the Turkish Republic under Kemal. Regularly constituted Masonic Lodges take no part in political and military enterprises, but oftentimes for that reason are in the center of them because within their tiled doors men from every side and opinion can meet and become acquainted without embarrassment or political commitments. On page 92 of...The Rising Crescent (Farrar & Rinehart; New York; 1944) Bro. Jackh writes:

> Besides vatan (fatherland) there was another word in everybody's mouth and in every newspaper: hurriet, Liberty. At that time (1908) I frequently attended Masonic Lodge meetings of the Young Turks. Among my Brother Masons I would meet Moslems and Christians, Turks, Arabs, Armenians, Greeks, Bulgarians, Jews, and Doenmés (Jewish Moslems) — all with the common headdress, the fez, the mark of citizenship in the Ottoman Empire. When liberty was discussed it would be applied to all the national groups within the supranational empire, all now liberated from the Hamidian regime of absolutism and palace intrigue. Under the constitution renewed by the Young Turks the non-Moslem nationalities had their full share of "liberty, equality, and fraternity." In the Bill of Rights included in the Constitution of the Republic of Turkey, Freemasonry is explicitly provided for, not by name, but by means of the words italicized in the sentence: "No one shall be molested on account of his religion, sect, his ritual or his philosophic convictions.

This was written in 1944. Today Turkish attitudes toward secular freedom and the Freemasonry that brought it about, is despised by the Muslim world, as evidenced by the news clipping on the next page.

Payback time. Muslims know that western Freemasonry is behind democratizing their world. Prior to World War I, when Turkey was in the throws of revolution, Muslims lost the Ottoman Empire to a Masonic Turkish democracy. In retaliation Muslim terrorists infiltrated Young Serbia, the youth order of European Freemasonry, and assassinated Archduke Ferdinand in 1913, triggering World War One. Western democracies have not learned their lesson, for once again the West is forcing democracy on Muslim nations, with democrats hidden within Masonic Lodges in their lands. Beginning with Afganistan, then Iraq, Muslims know that following a democracy comes secularization. And behind both is Western Freemasonry. Hence, we see increased attacks on Masonic Lodges by Muslims. But the press will report few of them. Below is one back page report in Istanbul.

10A · WEDNESDAY, MARCH 10, 2004 · USA TODAY

Blast at Masonic lodge kills two in Istanbul

Gunmen stormed a Masonic lodge in Istanbul on Tuesday and detonated two bombs, authorities said. At least two people were killed, including one assailant, and five were wounded. Police suspected a suicide bomb attack. It was not clear how many people were inside at the time of the attack.

Four suicide attacks against two synagogues, the British Consulate and a British bank killed 62 people in Istanbul in November. Prosecutors have indicted 69 people suspected of belonging to a local al-Qaeda cell.

The Masons are a secretive society that traces its roots to medieval craft associations. Radical Islamic groups say the Masons support the policies of Israel and the United States.

FREEMASONRY'S YOUNG SOCIETIES VIS-À-VIS MUSLIM BROTHERHOOD'S AL-QAEDA

As are the Scottish and York Rites of Freemasonry both secret societies, al-Qaeda is likewise a secret society. Like Freemasonry, al-Qaeda denies its own existence in order to remain in the shadows. In this regard al-Qaeda is set up identically to Adam Weishaupt's Illuminati.

In 1830 Illuminated Freemasonry, under the leadership of 33O Freemason Giuseppe (Joseph) Mazzini, organized Freemasonry's terrorist arm (**Young Societies**), consisting of 16 to 21-year-old male youth. Their assignment? Secularize both Christian and Muslim countries through terror and revolution.

Within their respective host nations, Young Societies became known as Young Italy, Young Germany, Young Serbia, Young Russia, Young America, Young Egypt, Young Turks, etc.

In 1908 the Young Turks compelled the unwilling sultan of the Ottoman Empire to restore the constitution of 1876. These early constitutional reforms were obviously the result of European Masonic influence and example, along with the desire to compete with Europe on equal terms. They were also gestures of propitiation — to qualify for loans and other benefits, while at the same time ward off intervention and occupation by European powers.

At that same time the Armenian leadership cooperated with the Young Turk committees in overthrowing the despotic rule of Sultan Abdulhamid II, and in accomplishing the Young Turk revolution of 1908. In 1912, Young Serbia was behind the terrorist attacks that triggered a series of Balkan Wars. Balkan allies, Bulgaria, Serbia and Greece, made substantial territorial gains at Ottoman expense, and Albania was added to the roster of independent states. The final attack, which triggered World War I, was by Young Serbian Freemasons, who assassinated Archduke Ferdinand, heir to the Austria-Hungarian throne. (see Section 6, Figs. 4-8, and S&B, Vol. 1, 3rd ed., Chaps. 19-20). The Young Turks blundered into World War One on the side of the Central Powers and found themselves involved in a death struggle, in which their traditional Masonic friends of Western Europe became their enemies.

Eleven years following World War One the Muslim Brotherhood was founded in Egypt as an Islamic fundamentalist counteraction to western Freemasonry's secular youth corps of Young Societies. The Muslim Brotherhood called for a return to rigid Muslim orthodoxy, the overthrow of secular governments, and a restoration of the theocratic Muslim state.

In 1954 the Muslim Brotherhood made an attempt on the life of Prime Minister Gamal Abdel Nasser of Egypt. Nasser shut down the Brotherhood by driving it into exile in Syria.

June 25, 1980, the Muslim Brotherhood tried to assassinate Hafiz al-Asad of Syria — an Alawite Muslim. An angered Asad made a decision to destroy the Brotherhood. The next morning two of Asad's elite guard units (the Defense Companies) loaded into choppers, then flew east to Palmyra's notorious military prison where Muslim Brothers were being held. Waiting guards threw open the doors. The Defense Companies stormed in, moving from cell to cell, executing prisoners. The Brothers had only time enough to yell, "God [Allah] is great!"

Although 500 Brothers died that day, the Muslim Brotherhood was not intimidated. February 1982 the Brotherhood seized the city of Hama on the Orontes River, Syria's fourth largest city, with roots going back to the Bronze Age. When they started cutting throats of Alawite Muslim officials and their families, Asad acted. He called in the Defense Companies again and ordered, "Level the city." Two days of continuous shelling left Hama a smoldering pile of rubble. An estimated 20,000 were killed, including most of the Muslim Brotherhood. Hafiz al-Asad was not happy to go down in history as the butcher of Hama, or the man who destroyed a world-class historic city, but it was either that or run for it, along with a million other Alawites. The Muslim Brotherhood would never again pose a serious threat to Asad. Instead, it came to terms with Syria, formed "Hamas" (named after the city of Hama), and based out of Syria, directed its terror against Israel.

On October 6, 1981, the world first witnessed the bloody consequences of the Muslim Brotherhood when it assassinated Anwar Sadat. Again in 1993 the Brotherhood tried to kill the interior minister and later the prime minister of Egypt. In 1995 they tried to kill Hosni Mubarak while he was visiting Ethiopia. Two years later, the Brotherhood attacked the temple at Luxor, killing fifty-eight foreign tourists and four Egyptians.

Muslim Brotherhood attacked once more on 9/11/01, in New York City and suburban Washington, DC. The press, however, kept calling the attackers "al-Qaeda," thanks to Osama's relentless publicity machine.

Fig. 17 B — **Hasan al-Banna** (1906-1949) founder of
The Muslim Brotherhood in 1928

Founder of al-Qaeda

Dr. Abdullah Azzam, born in 1941 to a Muslim family in northern Palestine, was the Palestinian-Jordanian ideologue who conceptualized al-Qaeda in 1987. As a young man, Azzam joined the Egyptian Muslim Brotherhood and later became a stalwart of its Jordanian chapter. Like Freemasonry, the Muslim Brotherhood's multinational members are designated as "brothers," operating in groups called cells, as did illuminated Freemasonry from its beginning, and continues the same today. Each cell is self-contained. Hence, any cell plucked would not affect the whole.

Osama bin Ladan

Osama was taught Islamic studies by Muhammad Qutb, whose brother was Sayyid Qutb, the ideologue of the Muslim Brotherhood. When Osama arrived in Afghanistan, he fell under the influence of Dr. Abdullah Azzam, who mentored him. Both men together ran the Afghan Service Bureau through a network of offices, including thirty in United States cities, which disseminated their propaganda, raised funds, and recruited new members.

On November 24, 1989, in Peshawar, Dr. Azzam was driving to a local mosque with his two sons and one of their friends when his car evaporated in a giant explosion. No one was ever charged with Azzam's death. Early reports said he had had the misfortune of running into one of the region's many land mines. However, the ISI, whose file on Azzam was the largest of any intelligence agency, concluded that al-Zawahiri's Islamic Jihad carried out the murder as a favor to Osama bin Laden.

The hierarchy in al-Qaeda is formed identical to Freemasonry's Illuminati capstone atop the pyramid. And as Freemasonry's pyramid base consists of student "cells," so too does the Al Qaeda al-Sulbah, which means "The Solid Base" of the pyramid. And like Freemasonry, al-Qaeda's cellular network makes it resistant to intelligence service penetration.

The Taliban, which means students, is identical in structure to the original student membership of the Illuminati, and later to Freemasonry's Young Societies. And like cells of students within the Illuminati, represented by the bricks on the base of the Illuminati pyramid (as seen on the back of the U.S.A. $1 bill), al Qaeda likewise set up student cells for its base of operation. And as did the Illuminati build a worldwide network of secret societies, so too did al Qaeda's leadership build a secret organization that now covers the entire world, including many cells in Mosques in the U.S.A.

Al-Qaeda membership was and continues to be recruited from the Muslim Brotherhood, which made certain Islamists receptive to Osama's message. Muhammad Atta, the al-Qaeda team leader of September 11, for example, was first a member of the Egyptian Muslim Brotherhood. And while the bloodthirsty Brotherhood only spoke of martyrdom, al-Qaeda actually practiced it on a worldwide scale.

Sources: *The Middle East*, subtitled *A Brief History of the Last 2000 Years*, by Bernard Lewis, Simon & Schuster; A Touchstone Book, 1997. *Inside Al Qaeda*, by Rohan Gunaratna, Berkley Books, NY, 2003.

Sleeping with the Devil, subtitled *How Washington Sold Our Soul for Saudi Crude*, by Robert Baer, Crown Publishers, NY, 2003.

Why America Slept, subtitled *The Failure to prevent 9/11*, by Gerald Posner, Random House, NY, 2003. For full details read *Scarlet and the Beast*, Vol.1, 3rd ed., Chap. 19.

Fig. 18 — TIME Magazine — December 19, 2005 — The Muslim Brotherhood becomes political through the ballot box.

STRATEGIST El-Erian led the Brotherhood's surge

Posters on the wall herald the march of Islam, but tonight the Cairo headquarters of the Muslim Brotherhood is a different kind of war room. Essam El-Erian, chief political strategist for the banned but officially tolerated fundamentalist group in Egypt, performs evening prayers with a dozen other officials and then starts working the phones...checking on the results of the final round of the parliamentary elections held last week in Egypt. Early returns look promising.

HITLER, MUSLIMS, AND WORLD WAR II'S ANTI-SEMITISM

From *Scarlet and the Beast*, Vol. 1, 3rd ed. Chapter 26

Thule Society: Its Founder and Membership

"Although the Thule Society was an offshoot of the Golden Dawn, its official founder and head was Baron Rudolf von Sebottendorff (1875-1945), a Knight of the Masonic Order of Constantine (Turkish Freemasonry). Sebottendorff was the leader of the 'Turkish Crescent,' which fought in the Balkan War of 1912-1913 against the Grand Orient revolutionists backed by Serbia. In the ranks of the revolutionists were Jews, and consequently during the conflict Sebottendorff [a Moslem] became violently anti-Semitic. In 1913 he returned to Germany fortified with a vast knowledge of the occult and substantial funds from an unknown source. During the next four years he made extensive contacts with the leading members of numerous international occult groups that were rapidly proliferating in Germany at that time, focussing his Contacts on the Order of the Golden Dawn. Late in 1917 Sebottendorff was in Munich to begin organizing the Thule Society. With assistance from Golden Dawn members, on August 17, 1918, the Thule Society was officially founded. Sebottendorff elevated himself to Grand Master, then recruited from among the German noble families and aristocracy to use the Society as their counterrevolutionary headquarters. To his later discredit and ultimate downfall, Sebottendorff published a list of the Thule Society's membership.

"Sebottendorff claimed he had been sent to Germany by the Ascended Masters of Islam, who 'had entrusted him with the mission of illuminating Germany through the revelation of the secrets of advanced magic and initiation into ancient oriental mysteries.' One of the mysteries Sebottendorff imparted to the Thule membership was the so-called revelation that the Jews were behind world revolution and therefore must be annihilated."

Anti-Semitism and the Thule Society

Another Thule Society member who added strength to Sebottendorff's anti-Semitic accusations was Alfred Rosenberg (1893-1946). Rosenberg grew up as a Baltic German in Revel, Estonia, and spoke perfect German and Russian. He studied architecture at Moscow University and graduated there in 1917. He witnessed Kerensky's revolution in February and saw it destroyed in October by Lenin, a half-Jew, and Trotsky, a full-blooded Jew. In the spring of 1918, he read the newspaper headlines which announced the assassination of the Czar and his royal household at the hands of a Jew. Then he watched as 82 percent of the new Communist bureaucracy was staffed by Jews. (see following pages of Nazi Muslims).

Fig. 19 — Mufti of Jerusalem. Mufti: Muslim official who interprets law of Koran & tradition. He was a Muslim fundamentalist opposed to secular societies.

Mufti of Jerusalem inspects Muslim unit of German army — January 1944.

Haj Amin al-Husseini, the Mufti of Jerusalem, had been blackened as a suave Muslim religious leader who encouraged terrorism and fascism. He was particularly influential in the fundamentalist **Muslim Brotherhood** headquartered in Egypt. Murder of political opponents and intimidation of the uncommitted became the normal tools of his trade in the 1930s.

Following Hitler's coming to power in Germany in 1933, a brutal and systematic persecution of Jews spread across central Europe. Thousands fled and sought sanctuary in Palestine. In 1935 alone some 60,000 Jewish immigrants arrived. Arabs saw this influx as confirmation of their fear that the British and the Zionists were conspiring to reduce them to a minority in their own land.

Much as the Colonial service officers on the spot tried to be fair to the Arabs, the pull of Zionist influence in London and Washington constantly overrode them.

Finally, in 1939 the white paper offered the Arabs practically all they asked. Had the Mufti and **Muslim Brotherhood** around him been politically skilful they would have seized the moment. But the Mufti insisted on all or nothing — and got nothing.

Britain, in its role as patron of Arab interests, had encouraged the creation in 1944-45 of the Arab League, to coordinate the policies of the independent Arab states. After WWII the Mufti was living in Cairo, Egypt. However, the Mufti found the Arab League less helpful than he had hoped. End of Empire, by Brian Lapping, St. Martin's Press, NY., 1985, pp. 113, 140, 246.

Fig. 20 — Bosnia and Herzegovina Muslim volunteers in the Nazi Army.
(See *S&B*, V1, 3rd ed., chaper 20).

Fig. 21 — Croatian Muslim volunteers in the Nazi Army.

Fig. 22 — Egyptian Freemasonry used to throw off the yoke of colonialism.

Pasha Saad Zaghlul (1860-1927)
Premier of Egypt in 1924. A lawyer and statesman, he was minister of public instruction in 1906, and later, minister of justice.

After the close of WWI, he became head of the Nationalist Party, which advocated and demanded the breaking of ties binding Egypt to Great Britain. He failed in his attempt to conclude the negotiation with British Prime Minister MacDonald. He was deported to Malta in 1919 and then to Ceylon, returning to Egypt in 1921. One of the two Egyptian **Grand Lodges** to which he belonged ordered 7 weeks of mourning after his death.

Fig. 23 — King Farouk I Last reigning king of Egypt (1936-1952) and a Freemason, lost his secular throne to a fundamentalist secret society, the **Muslim Brotherhood**, counterpart to Masonry's secular **Young Societies**.

King Farouk I (1920-1965)
Last reigning king of Egypt (1936-52), born in Cairo, the son of Faud I. He was educated in England and studied at the Royal Military Academy, Woolwich. After WWII he turned increasingly to a life of pleasure. At this time the Allies handed the Jews Palestine. Although Britain did not support the partition of Palestine, nor openly back the Jews in 1947, Egyptians were familiar with British deception, and heaped blame on them.

The Mufti of Jerusalem was living in Cairo at that time and helped to persuade Egyptians that the handing of Palestine to the Jews was an act of British perfidy. The Mufti was particularly influential in the fundamentalist **Muslim Brotherhood**, a counterpart secret society to secular **Young Egypt**. The growth of the **Muslim Brotherhood** had been a problem to secular Farouk for many years. Its members wanted Egypt to be an austere Islamic state. The Partition of Palestine boosted the popularity of the **Muslim Brotherhood** to new heights. Muslim countries united to take back Palestine, but were soundly defeated. The defeat of Egypt by Israel and continuing British occupation led to increasing unrest, and General Neguib's coup (1952) forced Farouk's abdication and exile.

Fig. 24 — Nasser used Freemasony's secular youth organization to win freedom for the Egyptians.

Gamal Abdel Nasser (1918-1970)

Egyptian statesman, prime minister (1954-1956), and president (1956-1970), born in Alexandria.

Nasser was only a babe when Freemason Lawrence of Arabia was using **Young Societies** (youth corps of Freemasonry founded in the Middle East a century earlier by 33O Freemason Joseph Mazzini) to throw off the yoke of Muslim fundamentalist mid-Eastern tyranny.

As a young man in Egypt, Nasser joined **Young Egypt**, which organized demonstrations against British control of Egypt.

As an army officer, he became dissatisfied with the corruption of the Farouk regime and was involved in the military coup of 1952. He assumed the premiership in 1954, and then presidential powers.

Thereafter, he developed the Nation's military strength and the economy, began building the Aswan Dam, and nationalized the Suez Canal (which led to an abortive invasion by Britain, France, and Israel).

The respect he commanded among Arabs helped Nasser promote pan-Arab movements, including the United Arab Republic formed by Syria in 1958 with Nasser as president. (Syria withdrew in 1961).

A fervent anti-Zionist, Nasser attacked Israel in 1967. After the resulting quick defeat by Israel, he resigned, but was immediately returned to office by popular acclaim.

His last years were spent rebuilding his military forces with Soviet support, and seeking inroads to negotiations with Israel. He died in 1970, having brought increased respect and dignity to the Arab world.

Fig. 25 — Cover of *TIME Magazine*, 11/25/02

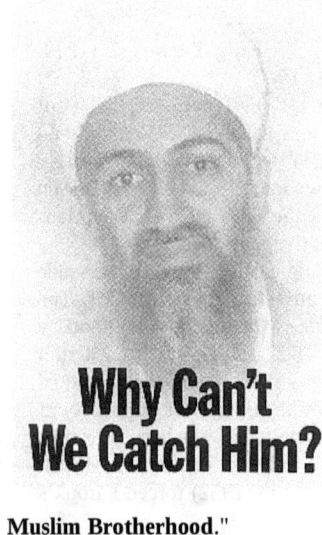

Why Can't We Catch Him?

Because the Muslim Brotherhood is alive & well today!

It should come as no surprise that al-Qaeda members are recruited from this fundamentalist Muslim youth order. TIME Magazine, "Architect of Terror" 3/10/03, p. 24, confirms that the recently captured Khalid Shaikh Mohammed, the architect of 9/11, who became the "third man" upon the death of Mohammed Atef, "was committed to Islam from an early age. The son of a devout Pakistani living in Kuwait, he joined the Egypt-based **Muslim Brotherhood** as a young man."

On March 20, 2003, as our military was advancing on Baghdad, FOX NEWS reported: "The riots against the war by young Muslims in Yemen were sponsored and promoted by the **Muslim Brotherhood**."

The Muslim Brotherhood founded and organized the Islamic fundamentalist secret society (**al-Qaeda**) in the same format as Western Freemasonry's **Young Societies**. Visit website www.scarletandthebeast.com.

Click on **9/11 Terrorist Attacks, Freemasonry & Bible Prophecy.** (See S&B, V1, 3rd ed., chapter 20).

Fig. 26 — Bagdad's sorcery and witchcraft. Saddam's wizard tells of a leader obsessed with sorcery. Twenty-four million people in Iraq use some sort of magic. AP Photo, August 15, 2003.

Sayed Sadoun Hamid el-Moussaoui al-Refai, 56, meditates in his magic room recently in Baghdad, Iraq. Al-Refai uses his 7-year-old son as a medium to find things, or people that are lost.

The wrinkled old man sprays perfume around the sparse, dingy room, then holds out his hands and feet and instructs one of his visitors to tie him up, knot the cloth three times and blow on it. The lights die and small red flashes go off beneath the black cloak that covers a bowl of magic powders and water. In the darkness, visitors feel pokes and jabs and things fluttering over their heads.

"Birds," the wizard says. Water splashes from the bowl. The genies arrive, and the questions begin.

"Will Saddam be found?"

A genie answers in the old man's voice: "Yes."

"Dead or alive?"

"Dead."

"Where is he?"

"In Dhuluaiyah," a village 55 miles north of Baghdad.

Thousands of magicians, fortune-tellers and faith healers make up a huge world of Iraqi spirituality that thrives despite being considered by many Muslims as sinful. But this man is different. He was Saddam's own sorcerer, and, therefore, his visions of the dictator's demise carry special weight for Iraquis. According to the magician and several others interviewed in Baghdad, Saddam was a firm believer in magic.

Figure 27 — So much for the accuracy of Saddam's wizard.
The "Butcher of Bagdad" was captured alive Dec., 2003.

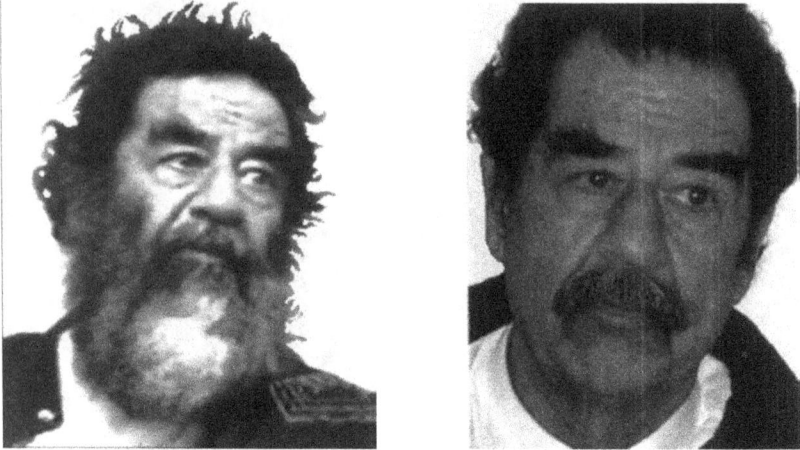

CAPTURED ALIVE

These soldiers had been scouring the area for months in the belief that he would stay close to home, where loyalty among those who most benefited from his rule still ran deep. U.S. intelligence sources tell Time Magazine that over the past month they were getting better leads.

Saddam's sorcerer had predicted he would be found dead!

It was a team of 600 soldiers from the 4th Infantry Division and U.S. special forces that acted on the tip that Saddam was hiding in a little town called al-Dawr, (15 miles from his hometown of Tikrit), not in Dhuluaiyah, 55 miles north of Baghdad, as Saddam's sorcerer had predicted.

Fig. 28 —Saddam Hussein's first day in court — frightened, yet defiant.

New York Times News Service (July 2, 2004)

BAGHDAD, Iraq — With the image of Saddam Hussein in the dock flickering on the television screen before him, Sami Hassan shook his head in disbelief, struggling against the tears that came down his cheeks.

"This is a theater," said Hassan, a 47-year-old ex-member of the Baath Party, mimicking the words of his former boss on the day that he appeared in court.

Hassan's reaction was part of the outpouring of emotion that coursed through the Iraqi capital Thursday. The images of a once-omnipotent dictator charged with mass murder seemed to open up a conversation on every street and in every home.

Across Baghdad, Iraqis sat spellbound, leaving their television sets only to test the feelings of neighbor and friend.

Dhafar Muhammad, a small grocery operator in central Baghdad, closed shop, dashed home and flicked on the electrical generator he had rigged to power his television just for the occasion. "The happiest day in my life was when they found him in that dirty hole, but this was very exciting," said Muhammad, a Shiite.

Jesus said, "Every kingdom divided against itself is brought to desolation..." MT 12:25.

Fig. 29 — Leader of Hamas assassinated by Iaraeli military — 3-22-04.

Sheik Ahmed Yassin (1937-2004)
USA TODAY — March 23, 2004
JERUSALEM — Yassin, 67, was blown up, along with seven Hamas leaders, in an Israeli missile strike.

Israel said it eliminated a man who sought to destroy it. Hamas has killed nearly 400 Israelis in three years. Israel warned Palestinian authority head Yasser Arafat that he, too, could be targeted if terrorism does not stop.

Israeli Prime Minister Ariel Sharon said after the strike that Yassin was a "mastermind of Palestinian terror, a mass murderer who is among Israel's greatest enemies. It is the natural right of the Jewish nation, as it is the right of any peoples, to hunt down those who wish to exterminate them."

Yassin, a quadriplegic from a childhood accident, has long been a symbol of the Palestinian uprising against Israel. He spread his message from pulpits and in TV interviews, denouncing Israel's right to exist and pushing for it [the nation of Israel] to be taken over by an Islamic state. His supporters said he was a spiritual leader and did not take part in the planning of attacks. Israel disagreed, saying he had a direct role.

Yassin's death was not expected to disrupt Hamas' immediate ability to carry out terrorist attacks, and Israel was bracing for a wave of bombing attempts. The group is tightly organized and takes its cues from leaders being sheltered in Syria and Lebanon. (USA Today, March 23, 2004).

Origin of the name — Assassin
Compton's Encyclopedia, Vol.2, p.703, 1984

"The adoption of assassination as a political weapon derives from the Islamic world of the 11th century. A secret order of Muslims was founded in Persia about 1090 by a man named Hasan ibn al-Sabbah. After gaining control of a mountain fortress near the Caspian Sea, Hasan founded a sect to fight his political enemies by means of murder. For two centuries this secret organization terrorized the Middle East." See S&B Vol. 1, chap. 19.

"Hasan, who gained the nickname 'Old Man of the Mountain' from his fortress hideaway, is said to have given his followers a vision-inducing drug called hashish, made from Indian Hemp. The visions of Islamic Paradise (or Heaven) brought on by the drug persuaded his disciples they would have a glorious afterlife if they followed Hasan's orders and killed his enemies. The killers were called Hashishins, from hashish. This name was eventually corrupted into its present form, Assassins.

"The Hashishins were a threat to the stability of the Middle East until 1256, when the Mongol khan Hulagu stormed their fortress and massacred 12,000 of them. A branch of their organization in Syria was destroyed by the Egyptian sultan Baybars a few years later.

"From then on, the sect of Hashishins became little more than another Muslim faction, with no political influence. But assassination did not disappear."

Assassination as a means to a political end continues in Islam today, including the use of mind-altering drugs to induce the euphoric "hope" of Paradise following the act. A modern "hope" has been added: "Awaiting you in Paradise are 72 virgins." In the hopeless squalor in which the modern "hashishin" recruits live, death appears to be better than life.

Fig. 30 — In the 1979 photo below, the Ayatollah Khomeini had just arrived in Tehran, Iran after having been flown from Paris in an Air France 747.

"Terrorism" is not modern, nor does it apply only to the Muslims. The word was coined in 1795 in France following French Freemasonry's 1793 "Reign of Terror." During nine months 8 million French men and women were either beheaded, thrown over cliffs, or drowned. In 1795, to protect the terrorists from like death, France passed a law which to this day permits their government to harbor terrorists, whom they call "political activists."

In the 1979 photo on the facing page, Khomeini has just arrived in Iran from France, where he had met in lodge with Grand Orient Masons to negotiate the supply of funds following the collapse of the pro-Western regime of the Shah of Iran. Khomeini was to replace the Shah with fundamentalist rule of the Muslim Brotherhood, Islam's counterpart to France's terrorist Freemasonry. You can read the whole story in Scarlet and the Beast, Vol. 3, chapter 6 entitled "A Freemasonry of Terrorists." Following is an excerpt:

> *Beginning in the mid-1970s and continuing through the mid-1980s, the assassinations of European politicians, judges, and bankers by so-called terrorists, the mysterious death of one pope, and the attempted assassination of another put Europeans in a quandary. It was not surprising to learn that the 'terrorists' were traced to organized crime. The links between the terrorist Red Brigades and the Mafia are well-documented. What was shocking to hear was that European "terrorists" did not take orders from the Mafia, but from a Masonic Lodge called Propaganda Duo, or P-2 Freemasonry. P-2 was heavily involved in a multi-billion dollar drugs-for-weapons deal with the Ayatollah Khomeini's Iran (Yallop, In God's Name, 1984).*

When and How will this Conflict end?

Rev. 16, beginning with verse 12, gives the answer, which is prophesied to take place at the end of the seven-year Tribulation:

"And the sixth angel poured out his vial upon the great river Euphrates [Iraq]; and the water thereof was dried up [Strong's, Gr. #3584, 'through the idea of scorching'], that the way of the kings of the east [possibly Arab nations] might be prepared. And I saw three unclean spirits like frogs come out of the mouth of the dragon..., the beast, and..., the false prophet. For they are the spirits of devils, working miracles, which go forth unto the kings of the earth and of the whole world, to gather them to the battle of that great day of God Almighty... And he (the Lord Jesus Christ] gathered them [the Kings of the east] together into a place called in the Hebrew tongue Armageddon. And the seventh angel poured out his vial into the air; and there came a great voice out of the temple of heaven, from the throne, saying, 'It is done.' And there were voices and thunders, and lightnings; and there was a great earthquake, such as was not since men were upon the earth, so mighty an earthquake, and so great. And the great city [Jerusalem] was divided into three parts, and the cities of the nations fell; and great Babylon [Iraq] came in remembrance before God, to give unto her the cup of the wine of the fierceness of his wrath.

"And every island fled away, and the mountains were not found. And there fell upon men a great hail out of heaven, every [hail] stone about the weight of a talent [100 pounds]: and men blasphemed God because of the plague of the hail; for the plague thereof was exceeding great."

Fig. 31 — U.S. troops are in Armageddon territory! See Fig. 33

Freemasonry establishes military lodges in Iraq, as it did in post WW2 Germany and Japan. Pictured from left to right are Bro. Tyrone Goolsby, Junior Warden; Bro. Bobbie Brown, Jr., Worshipful Master, and Bro. Jayson Sims, Senior Warden. On March 22, 2006, the reactivated charter for Cyrus Forbes Miliary Lodge #640 was delivered to Master Masons, beholding to the Most Worshipful Prince Hall Grand Lodge of Texas that are stationed in Bagdad, Iraq. This was indeed an historical and significant event in the history of our Grand Lodge. Not only will our worthy Brethren serving in the Armed Forces of our nation have the opportunity to continue practicing the art that they love so dearly; in addition the jurisdiction of our Grand Lodge now extends from Texas to the Tigris River!

Early Dec., 2005, First Sergeant Bobbie Brown Jr., a proven and well qualified Past Master Masonic leader, made known to me the need for a military lodge on Camp Victory, located in the "Green Zone" of Baghdad, where there exists a very large community of Prince Hall Master Masons desiring to work and make masons. After close coordination and assurances that the Green Zone was conducive to the safe operation of a Masonic Lodge, command authority approval and infrastructure support was sought. Past Master Brown's formal request was submitted to Grand Master Wilbert M. Curtis for his approval. After careful consideration, Grand Master Curtis granted permission on Jan. 2, 2006 (with stipulation) to reactivate the charter of Cyrus Forbes Military Lodge #640 to operate on Camp Victory in Baghdad. This historic event empowers our beloved Brethren of the 14th Masonic District, and Prince Hall Masons of the Texas Jurisdiction, to continue to work and make Masons in the "cradle of civilization."

Vernon J. James, Special Dist. Deputy Grand Master, 14th Masonic Dist. (Germany; Iraq. MWPHGL of Texas & Jurisdiction.

Fig. 32 — After WWII, following the defeat of Germany and Japan, the first act of the U.S. Military occupation forces was to establish Masonic Lodges throughout both nations. We see the same action taking place in Iraq. Of course it begins with military lodges for the service men, but will expand to civilian lodges for the Iraqi people. Freemasonry states, "If all men were Masons we would have peace on earth." But, alas, Scripture prophesies the final battle will be southeast of Iraq. See Figs. 33-34.

Military Masonic Lodge in Iraq at Airport AL ASAD AB on the 33O parallel.

Fig. 33 — **MAP OF ARMAGEDDON TERRITORY**
Random House Dictionary: "Armageddon: the battlefield of Megiddo, where the final battle will be fought between the forces of good and evil."

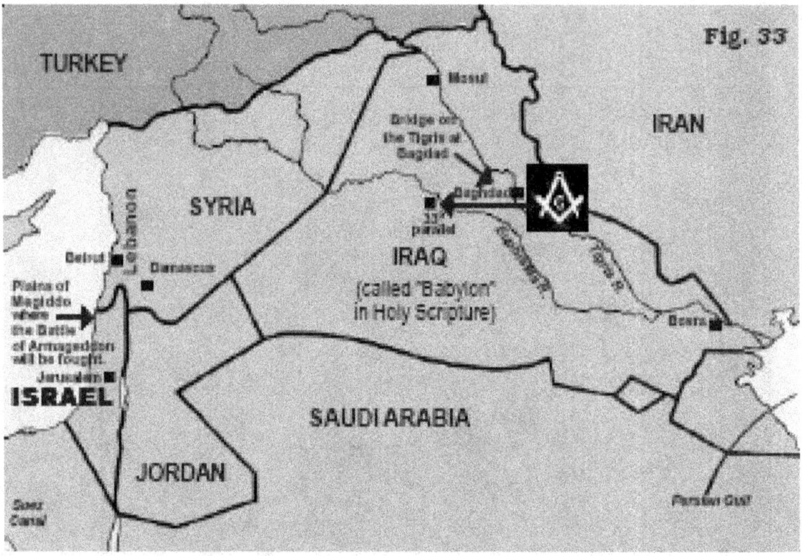

"And he gathered them together into a place called in the Hebrew tongue Armageddon" (using this map as reference, now read Revelation 16:10-21)

Plains of Megiddo are in northern Israel, where the final battle will be fought. Holy Scripture prophesies that the Euphrates River will dry up before the battle begins, allowing kings of the east (Syria, Iraq, and Iran) to cross over a do battle. Strong's Concordance confirms that the phrase "dry up" (Gr. #3584) carries "the idea of scorching." A drought strong enough to "scorch" the Euphrates would also "scorch" the Tigris. Scripture is specific to the Euphrates "scorching," thus isolating the location."

A bridge crosses the Tigris at Bagdad where Iran's army would have passage into Iraq. The Euphrates has no bridge, but does have a dam. For armies to cross the Euphrates, the dam's spillway must be cut off. After the runoff deep mud would remain on the river bottom. Iran could drop a nuclear bomb on any portion of the muddy riverbed, which would instantly "dry up through the idea of scorching," allowing kings of the east to cross over (Rev. 16:12). Fear of nuclear radiation would have no affect on suicidal Moslems.

Passive Jordan and Saudi Arabia would most likely remain neutral, forcing Syria, Iraq, and Iran to conquer Israel from the north, which are the Plains of Megiddo. Such a war against Israel would activate treaties with western nations, ending in nuclear world war — the affects of which are prophesied in Holy Scripture, and explained scientifically on the next page.

Turn your head sideways to view explosion

Moments In Time
PP. 28-29, 1984

ARMAGEDDON
Revelation
16:10-21

Fig. 34 — Bikini Islands atomic blast caused 100 pound chunks of ice to fall to Earth

The Bikini atoll, a ring of 27 small islands around a lagoon in the Pacific, was the site of an atomic bomb experiment by US Military following WW II. 70 decommissioned U.S. Ships were strategically placed to assess damage. Ships you see on the horizon had huge dents in them. It was determined the dents were caused by ocean water forced into the upper atmosphere by the explosion, quickfreezing into chunks of ice, then falling back to earth. Each chunk of ice was estimated to have weighed at least 100 pounds. Scripture suggests such a nuclear war in Rev. 16:20-21! "And he gathered them together into a place called in the Hebrew tongue Armageddon... And there fell upon men a great hail out of heaven, every [hail] stone about the weight of a talent [100 lbs.]: and men blasphemed God because the plague of...hail...was exceeding great."

OTHER PUBLICATIONS

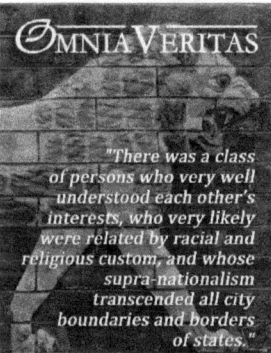

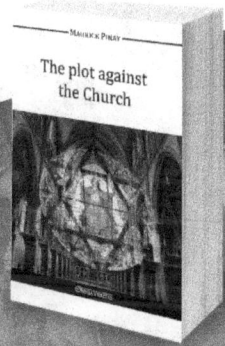

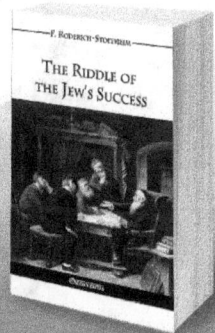